Your Introduction to Education:

Explorations in Teaching

Fourth Edition

Sara Davis Powell
Belmont Abbey College

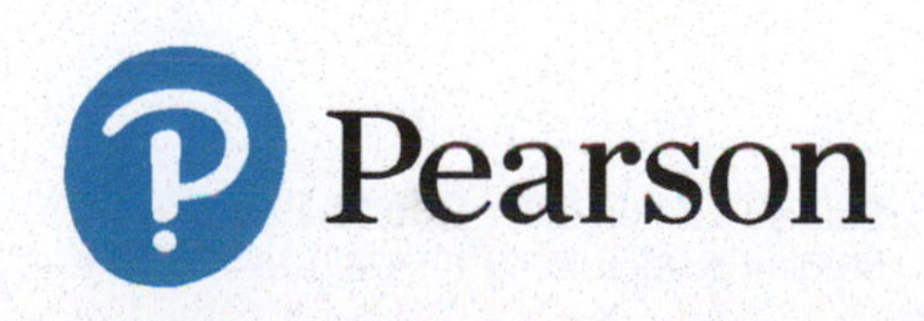

330 Hudson Street, NY NY 10013

Editorial Director: Kevin Davis
Portfolio Manager: Rebecca Fox-Gieg
Managing Content Producer: Megan Moffo
Content Producer: Yagnesh Jani
Portfolio Management Assistant: Maria Feliberty
Development Editor: Christina Robb
Executive Product Marketing Manager: Christopher Barry
Executive Field Marketing Manager: Krista Clark
Procurement Specialist: Deidra Smith
Cover Design: Studio Montage
Cover Art: Shutterstock Rawpixel; Gettyimages FatCamera; Gettyimages Steve Debenport; Gettyimages Hero Images
Editorial Production and Composition Services: SPI Global
Full-Service Project Manager: Heather Winter
Printer/Binder: LSC Communications
Cover Printer: LSC Communications
Text Font: Palatino LT Pro 9.5/13

Acknowledgments of third party content appear on the approriate page within the text

11 2022

www.pearsonhighered.com

Student Edition ISBN 10: 0-13-473692-3
Student Edition ISBN 13: 978-0-13-473692-1

Dedication

Jesse White teaches in an innovative charter school where students learn through experimentation and real-life problem solving. He represents dedicated teachers everywhere who use their creativity and energy to engage students in the teaching and learning process—teachers who make critical differences in the lives of their students. To these teachers, and to Jesse, my son, I dedicate this fourth edition.

Brief Contents

Contents

12 Professionalism in Relationships, Reality, and Reform 352

Preface

Using an approach that is unique among introduction to education college texts, the fourth edition of *Your Introduction to Education: Explorations in Teaching* takes you on a journey into authentic classrooms. It guides you through issues and dilemmas as they affect real teachers and students in real schools to help you determine whether teaching is for you and, if so, what your teaching identity may be.

The most distinctive feature of this text is how it weaves the real-life experiences of 8 teachers and 8 students from 4 schools across the country into its content. These people and places are drawn from urban, suburban, and rural settings, allowing you to examine teaching and learning from a variety of perspectives.

The teachers and students are from Summit Station, Ohio; Spanish Fork, Utah; Mt. Pleasant, South Carolina; and Fresno, California. Classroom scenarios, person-to-person features, and nearly every photo in this book—along with hours of video—are the direct result of time the author spent at each school with every one of the teachers, principals, students, and family members we met.

Current and relevant issues in education are discussed in engaging ways through two features: The Opinion Page and SocialMEdia. **The Opinion Page** feature presents real opinion editorials published in recent newspapers from across the country to explore today's dilemmas and controversies. You are asked to think about your own opinions and respond to prompts that require reflection and critical thinking. In each **SocialMEdia** feature, a social media tool is presented through a teaching and learning lens to ignite your imagination and sense of innovation concerning possibilities for your own future classrooms.

The **art** and **service** of teaching are emphasized right alongside the **science** of teaching. Just as we know that effective teachers teach the *whole* child, we also know that teachers are most effective when they use their minds and hearts, as well as their gifts and talents, to interact with students in growth-promoting ways.

Each chapter begins with a **Dear Reader** letter that introduces in personal and engaging ways the topics to come. This book, built entirely on authentic classroom experience, will empower future teachers to *explore* content and classrooms, *reflect* on their learning, and *develop* an image of the teacher they aspire to be.

New to this Edition

REVEL: A New Interactive Format

One of the many enhancements in this new edition of *Your Introduction to Education: Explorations in Teaching* is the new format of the digital version, REVEL. Fully digital and highly engaging, REVEL can completely replace the print textbook and give you everything you need to efficiently master course concepts. This new version is an interactive learning environment that seamlessly blends this book's narrative, media, assessments, and grading, enabling you to read, practice, and study in one continuous experience. Informed by extensive research on how people read, think, and learn, REVEL is designed to measurably boost your understanding, retention, and preparedness.

The REVEL version of this fourth edition presents content in manageable pieces that makes it easier for you to locate, process, and remember key material. Videos and interactive exercises are interspersed regularly within the text to foster your active engagement with the content, helping you to remember it better—and more important—to use and apply it. The unique presentation of media as an intrinsic part of course content brings the hallmark features of Pearson's best-selling titles to life. The media interactives in REVEL have been designed to be completed quickly, and its videos are brief, so you remain focused and on task.

Dynamic content designed for the way today's students read, think, and learn brings concepts to life:

- Self-exploration inventories called **Where Do I Stand?** occur at the beginning of each major section of the book. These inventories activate your prior knowledge and opinions—a teaching strategy that promotes interest and effectively sets the stage for leaning.
- Integrated within the narrative, **videos** empower you to engage with concepts and view a variety of teachers and classrooms that otherwise wouldn't be available to you at this stage in your education.
- Interactive **Application Exercises** are interspersed frequently and foster a more active role in learning. These take a variety of forms. At times, you will be presented with a video and an open-ended question that requires you to examine the video critically and respond using evidence from the video and your understanding of

chapter concepts. Feedback is provided for support. At other times, you will be asked to provide correct labels for an image. Other opportunities quiz you on your understanding of text concepts by asking you to align examples with their concepts in a table. At the end of every chapter the **Developing Professional Competence** exercises ask you to read a scenario, reflect on it, and respond to short-answer and multiple-choice items.

- **Check Your Understanding** quizzes, located at the end of each major section of text present you with opportunities to check your understanding of text concepts at regular intervals via a four-item multiple-choice quiz before moving on.
- A chapter-ending **Shared Writing** assignment allows all the students in your class to read and respond to the same prompt. You and your classmates have the opportunity to see each other's postings, creating a space for asynchronous discussion of the text.
- **Flash Cards,** also located at the end of each chapter, allow you to ensure your mastery of key terms.
- Detailed **Standards Mapping** document that shows how each REVEL activity aligns with the subcategories of the 10 InTASC Standards and the edTPA content addressing planning, instruction, and assessment.
- The REVEL **mobile app** lets you read, practice, and study—anywhere, anytime, on any device. Content is available both online and offline, and the app syncs automatically to work across all registered devices, giving you great flexibility to toggle between phone, tablet, and laptop as you move through your day. The app also lets you set assignment notifications to stay on top of all due dates.
- **Highlighting, note taking,** and a **glossary** let you read and study however you like. Educators can add notes for you, too, including reminders or study tips.

Superior assignability and tracking tools help educators make sure students are completing their reading and understanding core concepts:

- The **assignment calendar** allows educators to indicate precisely which readings must be completed on which dates. This clear, detailed schedule helps students stay on task by eliminating any ambiguity as to which material will be covered during each class. When they understand exactly what is expected of them, students are better motivated to keep up.
- The **performance dashboard** empowers educators to monitor class assignment completion as well as individual student achievement. Actionable information, such as points earned on quizzes and tests and time on task, helps educators intersect with their students in meaningful ways. For example, the trending column reveals whether students' grades are improving or declining, helping educators to identify students who might need help to stay on track.
- **Blackboard Learn™ integration** provides institutions, instructors, and students easy access to their REVEL courses. With single sign-on, students can be ready to access an interactive blend of authors' narrative, media, and assessment on their first day. Flexible, on-demand grade synchronization capabilities allow educators to control exactly which REVEL grades should be transferred to the Blackboard Gradebook.

Important Content Changes in the New Edition

NUMEROUS NEW TABLES AND FIGURES DEPICTING THE SOCIETAL CONTEXT OF CHILDREN AND ADOLESCENTS Future teachers envision realistic portrayals of dilemmas and life circumstances of the children and adolescents who will fill their classrooms.

INCREASED EMPHASIS ON BULLYING PREVENTION Future teachers learn to recognize signs and symptoms of bullying in its many forms—including cyberbullying, along with productive ways to approach the bully, the bullied, and the bystander.

TABLES DETAILING LAWS AND THEIR IMPLICATIONS FOR TEACHERS Future teachers need to have a basic understanding of how laws affect them, their students, and their profession. The tables help you comprehend implications of multiple case law rulings through commonsense explanations, written in easy-to-understand language.

COMMENTARY ON CURRENT ATTACKS ON PUBLIC EDUCATION Because public education is just that—public—it will always be the topic of discussion, often disparagingly, of all who attended or didn't attend public schools. Some find public education to be the hope of the future and some blame much of what they view as wrong in our country on public schools. This pretty much describes everyone. Read and reflect on the commentary in Chapter 12 concerning what appears to be attacks on public teaching and learning.

COMPARING AND CONTRASTING U.S. PUBLIC SCHOOLS AND FINISH SCHOOLS An examination of the context and practices of U.S. public schools and those of other countries helps us better understand possible reasons for international test score disparities, as well as innovations to improve teaching and learning in the 21st century. In recent years, U.S. educators searching for possible solutions to dilemmas have looked to Finland, an international leader when countries are compared. In a special section, public education in Finland is explored.

NEW VIDEOS This new edition includes some video segments from the previous edition, involving focus teachers and students. There are also exciting new opportunities to vividly engage with additional real teachers and students as they tackle relevant and important issues and classroom practice:

- **Principal's advice to new teachers:** A dynamic principal of a Title I middle school discusses the challenges and joys of working with teachers and students, and offers commonsense advice to new teachers.
- **Teacher's view of being black in a classroom of primarily black students:** A relatively new teacher says being black allows him to serve as a positive role model for nonwhite students. His primary message, however, is that race doesn't matter as much as forming close and caring relationships with all students.
- **Teacher's philosophy of family involvement in students' school experiences:** Although it's natural for new teachers to be timid when it comes to inviting families to be partners in the education of their students, this teacher says the effort is worthwhile and pays big dividends in terms of student interest and success in school.
- **Unique approach to teaching acceptance of LGBTQ students:** A middle school language arts teacher uses young adolescent literature to help her students explore issues that affect LGBTQ students. She encourages acceptance of all people, regardless of differences.
- **Joys of teaching at-risk students:** A teacher discusses the joys of teaching the students who need him most. His obvious love of the children in his classroom inspires others to look for their special calling.
- **Variety of teaching strategies:** Engaging classroom strategies are exemplified through videos of a high school math teacher forming small groups to learn about angles, and a third-grade teacher using unique practices to address vocabulary acquisition.
- **Discussion of Bloom's taxonomy:** A high school biology teacher explains how he works through the levels of Bloom's taxonomy in lectures and labs.
- **Emphasis on reflection** A group of new teachers is led by their principal through an experience of watching videos of classroom teachers and then reflecting on what they see and how they might better respond to management issues.

This text will help you EXPLORE Teaching and Classrooms

Authentic Classrooms

The teachers and students you will meet and revisit throughout the text are *real* teachers and students who teach and learn in authentic classrooms. You'll have many specific opportunities to meet and get to know these important people. Look for the **Teaching in Focus** headings to alert you to opportunities to get acquainted.

Teaching in Focus

We visit classrooms of the teachers you come to know as they talk about specific topics that affect their classroom teaching in **Teaching in Focus** features throughout each chapter. Each of these features is accompanied by a picture of the teacher speaking to us in his or her own words. Watch the interviews, room tours, and lessons as you read about these outstanding teachers.

Where Do I Stand?

These five fascinating inventories ask you to think about concepts before reading more about them. Not only does this engage you in what's to come but it also helps you personalize information you are asked to examine and reexamine as each chapter progresses.

This text will help you REFLECT On Your Evolving Understanding of Yourself as an Educator

POINT OF REFLECTION These features ask you to pause and think through what you've read and apply the ideas to your own notions of teaching and learning. You will find **Points of Reflection** throughout each chapter.

SHARED WRITING These experiences ask you to reflect on what you learn and then share your responses with others to expand your thinking and perspective.

THE OPINION PAGE This feature in each chapter explores issues in education through opinion editorials published in newspapers, asking you to consider the expressed opinions, the issues, and your own opinions, and then to respond to items related to **The Opinion Page** piece. The context is set by the chapter content, along with background information about the specific topic or issue involved.

DEVELOPING PROFESSIONAL COMPETENCE This end-of-chapter feature probes the issues of classroom teaching and helps prepare you for licensure exams by posing a case, again featuring the focus teachers you have come to know. Following the case are multiple-choice and essay questions that connect classroom issues with pertinent standards, providing an excellent study tool.

CHAPTER	EARLY CHILDHOOD	ELEMENTARY	MIDDLE SCHOOL	HIGH SCHOOL
Chapter 1: Teachers and the Teaching Profession	08: *Teaching in Focus* 09–11: Traditional Paths to Teacher Preparation	09–11: Traditional Paths to Teacher Preparation	24: *Teaching in Focus* 09–11: Traditional Paths to Teacher Preparation 11–14: Focus Teachers	04–05: Interest in Subject Matter 09–11: Traditional Paths to Teacher Preparation
Chapter 2: Student Similarities and Differences	39: Developmental Characteristics by Level 43–52: Language Diversity	33–34: *Focus Students* 39: Developmental Characteristics by Level	39: Developmental Characteristics by Level	34–35: *Teaching in Focus* 39: Developmental Characteristics by Level 43–52: Language Diversity 50: Bilingual Education 63–64: *Getting to Know Trista*
Chapter 3: School Similarities and Differences	87: *Focus School* 85–86: Structure and Organization	89 Focus School 88–90: Structure and Organization	90–91: Structure and Organization	93: *Focus School* 92: Structure and Organization
Chapter 4: Curriculum, Assessment, and Accountability	123: *Teaching in Focus* 121–123: Assessment of Dylan	115: *Teaching in Focus*		
Chapter 5: The Science, Art, and Service of Teaching	148: Instruction	155: *Teaching in Focus* 149: Instruction	150: Instruction	150–151: Instruction
Chapter 6: Creating and Maintaining a Positive and Productive Learning Environment	178–179: Routines 183–185: Extrinsic Incentives 190–196: Developing a Classroom Management Plan	179: Routines 183–185: Extrinsic Incentives 190–196: Developing a Classroom Management Plan	179–180: Routines 190–196: Developing a Classroom Management Plan	180–181: Routines 190–196: Developing a Classroom Management Plan
Chapter 7: History of Education in the United States	212: Kindergarten 219: Montessori Method	211–212: Common Schools	219: Junior High and Middle School	215: *Teaching in Focus* 204–205: Latin grammar school 208–209: Academies 212: Secondary schools 229: *Teaching in Focus*
Chapter 8: Philosophical Foundations of Education in the United States		236: *Teaching in Focus* 245: *Teaching in Focus* 251: Brenda's Philosophy Tree	247: *Teaching in Focus*	
Chapter 9: The Societal Context of Schooling in the United States	258: Child abuse statistics 272–274: Childhood obesity study	261: *Teaching in Focus* 268–270: Substance abuse statistics 272–274: Childhood obesity study	268–270: Substance abuse statistics 270–272: Sexuality-Related Concerns 275–276: Suicide	268–270: Substance abuse statistics 270–272: Sexuality-Related Concerns 275–276: Suicide 278–280: Immigration 280–281: Bullying and Columbine 285–289: Dropping Out
Chapter 10: Ethical and Legal Issues in U.S. Schools	296: Recognizing Ethical Dilemmas	296: Recognizing Ethical Dilemmas	296: Recognizing Ethical Dilemmas 305–306, 308–309: Legal cases	296: Recognizing Ethical Dilemmas 305–306, 308–309: Legal cases
Chapter 11: Governing and Financing Public Schools	338: Characteristics of Principals	338: Characteristics of Principals	338: Characteristics of Principals	338: Characteristics of Principals
Chapter 12: Professionalism in Relationships, Reality, and Reform	358: *Teaching in Focus*	364: *Teaching in Focus*	364: *Teaching in Focus* 380: *Teaching in Focus*	

DEVELOP GRADE LEVEL AND CONTENT UNDERSTANDING Throughout this text, your attention is drawn to the basic levels of early childhood, elementary, middle school, and high school. Regardless of the school grade configuration, student growth and learning generally move along a continuum that we address within these four broad levels. We approach teaching and learning differently based largely on the developmental level of the students. A first-grade teacher in a primary school and a first-grade teacher in an elementary school both teach children in the phase of early childhood. Similarly, sixth-grade students in an elementary school and sixth-grade students in a middle school are all young adolescents in the middle-level phase of development. The following table indicates where you can find grade-level specific information about a range of content in the text.

Ancillaries

The following supplements to the textbook are available for download. Visit www.pearsonhighered.com; enter the author, title, or ISBN; and then select this textbook, *Your Introduction to Education: Explorations in Teaching*, 4th edition. Click on the "Resources" button to view and download the supplements detailed below.

Online Instructor's Manual with Test Items

An expanded and improved online Instructor's Resource Manual (0-13-356337-5) includes numerous recommendations for presenting and extending text content. The manual consists of chapter overviews, focus questions, outlines, suggested teaching strategies, and Web resources that cover the essential concepts addressed in each chapter. You'll also find a complete chapter-by-chapter bank of test items.

This new edition Instructors' Manual also includes a detailed mapping of 162 text features to the subcategories of the 10 InTASC Standards and the edTPA content addressing planning, instruction, and assessment, all in one comprehensive table.

Digital Test Generator

The computerized test bank software, Test Gen (0-13-356339-1), allows instructors to create and customize exams for classroom testing and for other specialized delivery options, such as over a local area network or on the Web. A test bank typically contains a large set of test items, organized by chapter, and ready for your use in creating a test based on the associated textbook material. The tests can be downloaded in the following formats:

- **TestGen** Testbank file—PC
- **TestGen** Testbank file—MAC
- **TestGen** Testbank—**Blackboard 9**
- **TestGen** Testbank—**Blackboard CE/Vista (WebCT)**
- **Angel** Test Bank
- **D2L** Test Bank
- **Moodle** Test Bank
- **Sakai** Test Bank

Powerpoint Slides

These lecture slides (0-13-356335-9) highlight key concepts and summarize key content from each chapter of the text.

Acknowledgments

As a teacher and teacher educator for more than four decades, I found the writing of this text to be a labor of love. I have experienced extraordinary professional development opportunities through this project as I have probed deeply the many and varied issues involved in teaching PreK–12 children and adolescents.

Numerous people have been instrumental in the revision of this text. Here are some to whom I owe special thanks:

- Kevin Davis, Pearson Vice President and Editorial Director, for his consistent professionalism.
- Julie Peters, Executive Editor, for her insight, wisdom, and faith in me.
- Christie Robb, Development Editor, for her expertise, professional guidance during the revision process, and her kind, thoughtful spirit throughout.
- Heather Winter, Project Manager, for prompt and efficient attention to the details of production.
- Lynda Griffiths, copyeditor, for her keen eye for detail and thoughtful suggestions throughout the text.
- Krista Clark, Executive Marketing Manager, for her expert sense of what professors and students need and want, in addition to her generous spirit.
- Principals Laura Hill, Mike Larsen, Carol Bartlett, and Maria Romero, for opening their schools to me.
- Brandi Wade, Renee Ayers, Chris Roberts, Brenda Beyal, Traci Peters, Deirdre Huger-McGrew, Craig Cleveland, and Angelica Reynosa, the text's focus teachers, for opening their classrooms to me and sharing their wisdom with teacher candidates.
- Dylan Todd, Sherlonda Francis, Amanda Wiley, Hector Mancia, Patrick Sutton, Trista Kutcher, Hugo Martinez, and Khammany Douangsavanh, the text's focus students, for teaching me so much.
- Rus, my husband, for his unwavering support throughout, as well as the many hours of brainstorming and editing.
- The professors who contributed time and thought in their feedback:
- Maria Balderrama, California State University, San Bernardino
- Stephan Ellenwood, School of Education, Boston University
- Jerry Ann Harris, Northeast Texas Community College
- Laura Lamper, Central Texas College
- Denise Patmon, University of Massachusetts, Boston
- Elyse C. Pinkie, Liberty University

Chapter 1

Teachers and the Teaching Profession

Learning Objectives

After studying this chapter, you will have knowledge and skills to:

1.1 Explain who teaches in the United States and why.

1.2 Summarize ways to prepare to teach.

1.3 Determine if teaching is a profession.

1.4 Identify characteristics of teacher professionalism.

1.5 Describe the characteristics of effective teachers.

Dear Reader

No African tribe is considered to have warriors more fearsome than the Masai. Even with this reputation, the traditional greeting between Masai warriors is *Kasserian ingera,* which means "And how are the children?"

This traditional tribal greeting acknowledges the high value the Masai place on their children's well-being. Even warriors with no children of their own give the traditional answer, "All the children are well," meaning that peace and safety prevail; that the priority of protecting the young, the powerless, is in place; and that Masai society has not forgotten its proper function and responsibility, its reason for being. "All the children are well" means that life is good.

When teachers hear the word *multitasking,* most teachers just grin, knowing that they are, and always have been, expert multitaskers. It's nothing new, it's not something they have to practice—it is simply how teachers do their work day in and day out. The hundreds of decisions that teachers make each day; the ever-changing scenarios that confront them hour to hour, minute to minute; and the faces of the students they serve, 20 to 120 at a time, create multiple roles that teachers fill simultaneously—all for the well-being of the children and adolescents in their care.

If we greeted each other with the Masai's daily question, "And how are the children?" how might it affect our awareness of children's welfare in the United States? If we asked this question of each other a dozen times a day, would it begin to make a difference in the reality of how children are thought of and cared for in the United States?

If everyone among us, teacher and nonteacher, parent and nonparent, comes to feel a shared sense of responsibility for the daily care and protection of all the children in our community, in our town, in our state, and in our country, we might truly be able to answer without hesitation, "The children are well. Yes, all the children are well."

Where **Do I Stand?**

 **Click here to complete the inventory online**

This is the first of the self-exploration inventories you will also complete at the beginning of Chapters 4, 6, 7, and 9. The purpose of the inventories is to activate your prior knowledge and opinions, a teaching strategy that promotes interest and effectively sets the stage for learning. As you explore the content of your course and this text, some of your initial responses will likely change. This is how we grow. We consider what we know and what we think. Then we explore and learn more and more, leading to inevitable changes of opinions and broadening of perspectives. Exciting prospect, don't you think?

This first inventory helps you explore your personal reasons for considering teaching as a career. Read each item and decide how meaningful it is to you. If an item resonates very strongly within you, then choose "4: I strongly agree." Reserve a choice of "4" for those items you genuinely care most about. If you agree with a statement, but are not overly enthusiastic about it, then choose "3: I agree." If you really don't care one way or the other about a statement, choose "2: I don't have an opinion." If you simply disagree with a statement, choose "1: I disagree." If you feel adamantly opposed to a statement, choose "0: I strongly disagree." In this inventory, **there are no right or wrong answers, just differing experiences and viewpoints**. *Following the inventory are directions for how to organize your responses and what they may indicate in terms of where you stand.*

4 I strongly agree

3 I agree

2 I don't have an opinion

1 I disagree

0 I strongly disagree

____ 1. Some of my fondest memories involve experiences working with children/teens.

____ 2. The health insurance and retirement benefits of teaching mean a lot to me.

____ 3. In K–12 school I excelled in a particular subject.

____ 4. As a teacher, I look forward to growing professionally.

____ 5. At least one member of my family is an educator.

____ 6. I am considering teaching because I believe education has necessary societal value.

____ 7. Teaching is most worthwhile because of the opportunity to influence students.

____ 8. Although I may be interested in other professions, the stability of a career in the public school system draws me to teaching.

____ 9. Both the daily work hours and the yearly schedule of a teacher appeal to me.

____ 10. Doing the same thing in the same way repeatedly does not appeal to me.

____ 11. My desire to teach is based on my love of a particular subject.

____ 12. There was a teacher in my K–12 experiences who had a profound impact on my life.

____ 13. Change is invigorating to me.

____ 14. A teacher's primary task is to help students become productive citizens.

____ 15. Being with children/adolescents is something I enjoy and look forward to.

____ 16. I am anxious to read whatever I can about the teaching profession.

____ 17. A major reason for choosing the teaching profession is the appeal of having holidays and spring break time off.

____ 18. Being a teacher means always having a job.

____ 19. Education is necessary for the continued success of our country.

____ 20. I have very fond memories of my relationship with one or more teachers in K–12 school.

____ 21. Having a long summer vacation means a lot to me.

____ 22. I have been drawn to topics in a particular subject area for years.

____ 23. Professional self-growth motivates me.

____ 24. I am interested in teaching because I want to work with children and/or adolescents.

____ 25. Variety in terms of challenges keeps me interested and motivated.

____ 26. I want to teach because of the promise of job security.

____ 27. Being a camp counselor appeals to me.

____ 28. I want to teach to positively benefit society.

____ 29. Content knowledge is the primary goal of education.

____ 30. I can "think on my feet."

____ 31. Predictability is not particularly important to me.

____ 32. I like the idea of having days off when my own children will also have time off.

____ 33. I have a passion for a content area.

____ 34. Even in difficult economic times, the fact that teachers will always be needed appeals to me.

____ 35. My family values education and emphasizes the worth of teachers.

____ 36. I often get bored with routine.

____ 37. Without quality public education our society suffers.

____ 38. I am comfortable with improvisation.

____ 39. Being home by about 4 p.m. is important to me.

____ 40. Teaching appeals to me most because I love to learn new things.

In the table, record the number, 0 to 4, that you responded for each indicated item. Then find the sum for each column's responses.

ITEM #	*MY #*	*ITEM #*	*MY #*	*ITEM #*	*MY #*	*ITEM #*	*MY #*	*ITEM #*	*MY #*	*ITEM #*	*MY #*	*ITEM #*	*MY #*	*ITEM #*	*MY #*
1		*6*		*13*		*5*		*3*		*9*		*2*		*4*	
7		*14*		*25*		*12*		*11*		*17*		*8*		*10*	
15		*19*		*31*		*20*		*22*		*21*		*18*		*16*	
24		*28*		*36*		*30*		*29*		*32*		*26*		*23*	
27		*37*		*38*		*35*		*33*		*39*		*34*		*40*	
Sum A		*Sum B*		*Sum C*		*Sum D*		*Sum E*		*Sum F*		*Sum G*		*Sum H*	

Now it's time to graph your responses. Mark then shade your sums on the Choosing to Teach *bar graph. The results show how much you value, relatively speaking, eight reasons for becoming a teacher that we discuss in this chapter. Your instructor may ask you to share your graph with others as part of the exploration of teachers and the teaching profession.*

Ultimately, by the end of this book you will have explored many aspects of the teaching profession in very personal ways. As teachers, the better we know ourselves, the closer we come to understanding our students and finding ways to address their needs to help them grow.

Choosing to Teach

Sum A: Desire to work with children and/or adolescents	
Sum B: Importance of education to society	
Sum C: Motivated by variety	
Sum D: Impact of teachers and family	
Sum E: Interest in a particular subject	
Sum F: Schedule of teachers	
Sum G: Job security	
Sum H: Opportunity for self-growth	

0 4 8 12 16 20

1.1 Who Teaches in the United States and Why?

1.1 Explain who teaches in the United States and why.

Teaching is the largest profession in the United States, with about 3.5 million teachers in both public and private schools (National Center for Education Statistics [NCES], 2016). Examine Figure 1.1 to see gender, race, and age statistics of these teachers. Most teachers are white and female. It is interesting to note, although probably not surprising, that 58% of high school teachers, 72% of middle school teachers, and 89% of elementary teachers are women (Ingersoll, Merrill, and Stuckey, 2014). There is considerable need for more diversity and gender balance in the teaching force. Do we want to discourage white women from becoming teachers? Absolutely not. Is there a need for more male teachers and teachers from minority population groups? Absolutely yes.

Deciding to Teach

You are considering the most challenging and exhilarating career—one that is absolutely necessary for the preservation and enhancement of our way of life in the United States. Think about this: Teachers make every other profession possible. Most people join the teaching profession purposefully; some consider it a "calling." Entering the teaching profession requires a commitment beyond that required by many other careers. Brenda Beyal discovered her calling to teach while preparing for a different career. Watch Video Example 1.1: Brenda's Interview, and listen as Brenda expresses her reason for deciding to teach.

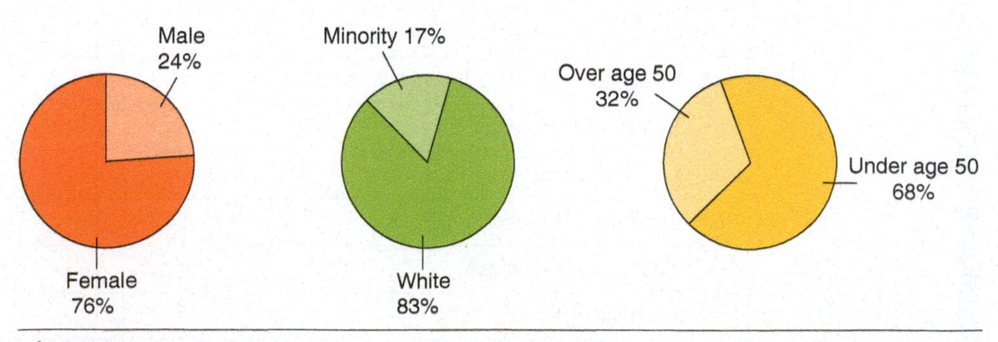

Figure 1.1 U.S. teachers

Based on: Ingersoll, R., Merrill, L., & Stuckey, D. (2014). Seven trends: The transformation of the teaching force, updated April 2014. CPRE Report (#RR-80). Philadelphia: Consortium for Policy Research in Education, University of Pennsylvania.

Currently, the United States is in the midst of a teacher shortage, not necessarily at all levels and in all fields, but the shortage is real for math, science, special education, and teachers equipped to teach children for whom English is not their first language. Schools of education report far fewer teacher candidates enrolling in programs (Gardner, 2016). You are needed!

Helping you first make the decision to teach and then find your teaching identity is at the heart of this text. Exploring why other people choose to teach may help you clarify your own thoughts and desires. Although there are, of course, many personal reasons, let's consider some that are widely stated in research studies. As you read, reflect on your own reasons for thinking about teaching as a career.

DESIRE TO WORK WITH CHILDREN AND/OR ADOLESCENTS. Because 6 to 7 hours of a teacher's day are spent in direct contact with students, enjoying their company is a must. Getting to know the students we teach allows us to become familiar with their emotional and social needs as well as their cognitive needs. You may hear teachers talk about teaching the **whole child**. This simply means attending to all of a child's developmental stages and needs, along with teaching the child's grade-level and subject-area content. When we view the whole child, we realize the depth of our responsibilities as classroom teachers.

BELIEF IN IMPORTANCE OF EDUCATION TO SOCIETY. Education is widely viewed as the great equalizer. This means that differences in opportunity and privilege diminish as children reach their potential through quality education. In other words, the achievement gap narrows with the increased educational success of the students who historically underachieve. An **achievement gap** is a disparity among students, as some excel while others languish with respect to learning and academic success. Through teaching, you will make a difference in the lives of individuals and thereby benefit society as a whole.

MOTIVATED BY VARIETY. No two days as a classroom teacher are the same. Teaching is a service profession involving human beings, so surprises abound! Even the same basic lesson plan used years in a row is never the same because children and adolescents in a classroom setting vary by the year, semester, week, day, and, yes, within the same school day. If you enjoy ever-changing challenges and delights, you may be motivated by variety to join the teaching profession.

IMPACT OF TEACHERS AND/OR FAMILY. Can you name the last five vice presidents of the United States? How about the current Miss America? Who represents your home district in the state legislature? Who was your fifth-grade teacher? Who taught your favorite class when you were a freshman in high school? The last two questions are the easiest, aren't they? That's because teachers influence us. They are uniquely positioned to shape students' thoughts and interests during the formative years of childhood and adolescence.

Most of us who consider being teachers grew up in families that valued education and respected teachers. If there are teachers in your family who are energetic and enthusiastic about their careers, they may influence you to follow in their footsteps. Many teachers cite the influence of family as a factor in the decision to teach.

INTEREST IN A PARTICULAR SUBJECT. An intense interest in a subject area is important if you are going to teach that subject all day. Middle school is a happy compromise for people who have both a strong desire to work with students and a passion for a specific subject. Most middle school teachers teach one or possibly two subjects all day to students whose development is challenging and intriguing.

OTHER FREQUENTLY CHOSEN REASONS. A joke that's been around for a long time goes like this: "What are the three best things about teaching?" Answer: "June, July, August." Here's another: "What's the best time to be a teacher?" Answer: "Friday at 4."

Within our ranks we smile at these harmless jokes. But the *schedule and hours of teachers* attract some to the field. Those who have not taught, or don't understand the pressure of having 15 or 25 or even 100 students dependent on them for at least part of each day, may view the schedule of a teacher as excessively punctuated with days off. However, time away from school is well deserved, even if it is used to catch up on teaching-related tasks. The change of pace is refreshing, allowing opportunities for revitalization.

Aside from summer vacation and days off, other aspects of scheduling make teaching a desirable choice for many. During the school year, most teachers do not have students after about 3:30 or 4:00 in the afternoon. To people who work 8-to-5 jobs, 4:00 seems like a luxury. However, most teachers spend additional time either at school or at home planning for the next day and completing necessary administrative tasks. The teaching schedule allows for this kind of flexibility. A teacher's schedule is also ideal for families with school-age children. Having a daily routine similar to that of other family members has definite benefits.

The world will always need teachers. The prospect of *job security* is attractive to many who choose to teach. Those who are competent are generally assured positions, even in difficult economic times. It's unlikely that a career in teaching is chosen because of salary, although some districts and states are making progress in raising teachers' pay to be competitive with other fields that require a bachelor's degree. Table 1.1 ranks states based on mean average salary. Keep in mind that salary amounts alone do not reflect many of the financial benefits that accompany a teaching position. In addition to an annual salary, you will also likely receive healthcare benefits at a reduced rate, along with a pension or retirement plan and possibly more. These "extras" often amount to an additional 30 to 40% of your salary. This aspect of job security is important.

Teaching offers many *opportunities for self-growth.* Teachers experience growth, both personally and professionally, in many ways: through relationships, reading, attending conferences, and the wide variety of professional development opportunities available. Few careers are as exciting or as rewarding on a daily basis, including the satisfaction of having a positive impact on the future of children. Teaching is not a stagnant career; rather, it continually presents new experiences, all of which offer opportunities for self-growth.

In almost all states and school districts, teachers are paid for both longevity in the profession and levels of education completed. A beginning teacher with a master's degree will likely receive a higher salary than a beginning teacher with a bachelor's degree. Two teachers with bachelor's degrees will be paid differently if one has 3 years of teaching experience and the other has 15 years in the classroom. In many cases, a teacher with 3 years of experience may contribute to outstanding verifiable improvement in student achievement, whereas a more experienced teacher may have little to show with regard to influencing measurable student learning, makes no difference in compensation. Is this fair? No. Have we found ways to measure student growth and pay teachers accordingly? Some ideas exist. School systems have tried for decades to pay teachers based on performance, or merit, but without the kind of success that perpetuates merit pay to the satisfaction of those affected, the teachers themselves. Merit, or performance, pay is a hot topic in education, with education leaders at district, state, and federal levels proposing plans for paying teachers based on a variety of variables, including student success on standardized tests. However, most systems go back to teacher level of education and longevity as the determiners of pay because of the lack of measures that take inevitable student variability into account when considering test scores. We take a closer look at the pros and cons of merit pay in Chapter 12.

When considering salary, investigate the cost of living where you want to live. For example, teachers who teach in suburbs outside New York City may make more than $100,000 a year. An examination of the cost of living in such places as Westchester County, New York, shows that $100,000 there is equivalent to a much lower salary in

Table 1.1 Teacher mean average salaries by state (2015-16)

Rank Based on Mean Average Salary	State	Mean Average Salary
1	New York	$79,152
2	California	$77,179
3	Massachusetts	$76,981
4	District of Columbia	$75,810
5	Connecticut	$72,013
6	New Jersey	$69,330
7	Alaska	$67,443
8	Maryland	$66,456
9	Rhode Island	$66,197
10	New Hampshire	$65,616
11	Pennsylvania	$65,151
12	Michigan	$62,028
13	Illinois	$61,342
14	Oregon	$60,359
15	Delaware	$59,960
16	Vermont	$58,901
	U.S Average	**$58,353**
17	Wyoming	$58,140
18	Hawaii	$57,431
19	Nevada	$56,943
20	Minnesota	$56,913
21	Ohio	$56,441
22	Iowa	$54,416
23	Georgia	$54,190
24	Wisconsin	$54,115
25	Washington	$53,378
26	Kentucky	$52,134
27	Texas	$51,890
28	Virginia	$51,834
29	Nebraska	$51,386
30	Montana	$51,034
31	Indiana	$50,715
32	Maine	$50,498
33	North Dakota	$50,472
34	Louisiana	$49,745
35	Florida	$49,199
36	South Carolina	$48,796
37	Alabama	$48,518
38	Arkansas	$48,218
39	Tennessee	$48,217
40	Missouri	$47,957
41	North Carolina	$47,941
42	Kansas	$47,755
43	Arizona	$47,218
44	New Mexico	$47,163
45	Utah	$46,887
46	Colorado	$46,155
47	Idaho	$46,122
48	West Virginia	$45,622
49	Oklahoma	$45,276
50	Mississippi	$42,744
51	South Dakota	$42,025

Based on: National Education Association. (2017). Rankings and Estimates. Copyright 2017 by the National Education Association. All Rights Reserved. Retrieved May 26, 2017, from http://www.nea.org/assets/docs/2017_Rankings_and_Estimates_Report-FINAL-SECURED.pdf

most of small-town America. Also consider both the beginning salaries and the average salaries when thinking about a state in which you might want to teach. Some states may lure teachers with higher beginning salaries that tend to not grow as rapidly as in other states.

Teacher salaries tend to change often. For the most up-to-date numbers, check state department of education websites in addition to individual district websites. Often, salaries within a state can vary widely. For instance, in North Carolina the state sets the minimum salary with districts adding to the amount. Illustrating the advantage of finding the most recent data, North Carolina has increased beginning teacher salary from about $31,000 in 2013 to over $36,000 for the 2016–2017 school year, with individual districts adding from $1,000 to $8,000 to the amount. In Florida in 2016, average teacher salaries varied between $39,044 in Union County, the smallest in the state, and $58,389 in Monroe County, the county seat of Key West— almost a $20,000 difference. When cost of living is considered, the difference is not as extreme.

Brandi Wade, one of our focus teachers at Summit Primary School in Summit Station, Ohio, tells us that perhaps we don't choose teaching, but rather teaching *chooses us*. Read about her philosophy in *Teaching in Focus.*

Teaching in Focus

Throughout this text, you will read **Teaching in Focus** segments. These real-teacher scenarios help illustrate concepts you are learning. Some scenarios will include brief videos and follow-up questions, while others are stand-alone features. Read them carefully to better understand teachers' work in today's classrooms.

Brandi Wade, kindergarten, Summit Primary, Ohio. *In her own words. . . .*

Sara Davis Powell

It may not so much be that you choose teaching, but that teaching chooses you. It will be in your heart and on your mind constantly. Although it's never easy for more than 5 minutes at a time, teaching is the most important profession you can pursue. I am truly blessed to be a kindergarten teacher. I get to teach a different lesson, meet a different challenge, and see life from different perspectives every day in my classroom.

Laugh with the children, laugh at yourself, and never hold a grudge. Don't be afraid to say "I'm sorry" to a child when you have done something unprofessional or hurtful. If children do hurtful things, just hug them a little more tightly and make them feel safe. Children learn best when they feel safe and loved no matter what.

I don't teach to be remembered, although it's nice to think that you'll never be completely forgotten. I teach so that I can remember. I remember their personalities and how they grow. I remember the times we struggled with learning and succeeded, as well as those times when we fell short of our goals. I remember the laughter and the tears we shared.

Some people say, "Leave school at school." The best teachers I know often lose sleep thinking about and worrying about their students. It's worth every toss and turn!

Reprinted by permission from Brandi Wade

Point of Reflection 1.1

You discovered your top reasons for considering the teaching profession through *Where Do I Stand?* Are there other reasons we haven't discussed that perhaps resonate with you? If so, what are they?

Check Your Understanding 1.1

1.2 How Do We Prepare to Teach?

1.2 Summarize ways to prepare to teach.

You may have heard it said of someone, "He's just a natural-born teacher." There's some truth in this statement. Teaching comes more naturally to some than to others. With varying degrees of natural talent and inclination for teaching, we all have much to do to prepare to effectively make the teaching and learning connection. Our nature-given attributes must be enhanced by the knowledge and skills gained through studying content, learning about theory and methods of teaching, being mentored, reading, observing, practicing, and reflecting.

Each state has its own preparation requirements for those who teach in public school classrooms. Most states require a prospective teacher to pass a test before they grant certification or licensure. The most widely used tests are part of the **Praxis Series** published by the Educational Testing Service (ETS). The state issues a teaching certificate or license when a teacher candidate is determined to be sufficiently qualified. Let's examine two broad paths to initial teacher preparation: traditional and alternative.

Traditional Paths to Teacher Preparation

The traditional paths to initial teacher preparation come through a university department of education. National and state organizations carefully scrutinize university programs and evaluate how teacher candidates are prepared. About two thirds of states require university teacher education programs to be accredited (authorized to prepare teachers) through the **Council for the Accreditation of Educator Preparation (CAEP).**

All three initial teacher preparation paths—bachelor's degree, fifth-year program, and master's degree—include one or two semesters of **student teaching,** also called **clinical internship.** During this extended fieldwork, teacher candidates teach lessons and, for a designated time frame, take over all classroom duties. A classroom teacher serves as the **cooperating teacher** (host and mentor) while a university instructor supervises the experience.

BACHELOR'S DEGREE. A 4-year undergraduate teacher preparation program consists of a combination of general education courses, education major courses, and field experiences. Most early childhood and elementary teacher preparation programs result in a degree with a major in education. Many programs in middle-level education result in a degree with a major in education and two subject-area concentrations (15 to 24 hours each). To teach in high school, most programs require a major in a content area and a minor, or the equivalent of a minor, in education coursework.

FIFTH-YEAR PROGRAM. Some universities offer a fifth-year teacher preparation program. Teacher candidates complete a major other than education and stay for a fifth year for more education coursework plus student teaching. For instance, a teacher candidate interested in science may major in biology and then stay a fifth year to become a certified, or licensed, teacher. Some of these programs include a master of arts in teaching degree rather than an extended bachelor's degree.

MASTER OF ARTS IN TEACHING. People who have a bachelor's degree in an area other than teacher education may pursue teacher preparation through a Master of Arts in Teaching (MAT) degree. Most early childhood and elementary MAT programs consist of all teacher education courses and fieldwork, whereas middle-level MAT programs typically require 18 to 24 hours of subject-area coursework in addition to education courses. High school MAT programs generally require a degree in a content area or the accumulation of enough content hours to be considered a concentration.

Alternative Paths to Teacher Preparation

In the 1980s, alternative certification began as a way to address projected teacher shortages. Since those first efforts, various models evolved for recruiting, training, and certifying people who already had at least a bachelor's degree and wanted to become teachers.

Since 1983, the number of teachers entering the classroom through alternative means rapidly increased. Today, all 50 states offer one or more of over a hundred different programs offering alternative certification/licensure, with some estimates stating that as many as a third of new teachers are using alternative routes to the classroom. Adults who decide that teaching is for them after having other careers are likely to enter the profession through alternative paths. In fact, 70% of those seeking certification through alternative routes are over 30 years old, most with noneducation-related careers. Alternative routes attract more men and minorities to the profession than the national averages (as shown in Figure 1.1). Men account for 30% and minorities account for 30% of the teachers who prepare in alternative ways (Teacher-Certification.com, 2016).

Many alternative programs grow out of specific needs and are developed and coordinated through partnerships among state departments of education, school districts, and university teacher education programs. Their structures vary widely, and they tend to be controversial. Some people doubt that teacher preparation is as effective outside the realm of university-based programs.

Perhaps the most widely known alternative path to the classroom is through the nonprofit organization **Teach for America (TFA).** Teach for America began in 1990 to help the United States through a period of teacher shortages in schools primarily populated by children living in poverty. The organization has grown rapidly, with or without a teacher shortage, and recruits individuals who are college seniors, recent graduates, and professionals who agree to teach in high-needs rural or urban schools for at least 2 years and become life-long leaders in the effort to end educational inequity. Teach for America teachers may receive student loan forbearance. Over the past 25 years, TFA has prepared about 50,000 college graduates to enter classrooms across the country. In the 2015–2016 school year, almost 9,000 TFA corps members taught in public schools, both traditional public schools and public charter schools (Teach for America, 2016).

In recent years, Teach for America has become quite controversial. Among the issues are charges that the organization does not adequately prepare new teachers and that districts can hire TFA teachers and replace them on a regular basis with new recruits, ultimately saving money. Some fear that TFA teachers are not only filling hard-to-staff schools but are also in many cases displacing veteran teachers. As with most education initiatives, Teach for America has both advocates and critics.

Getting to Know Schools, Teachers, and Students

Regardless of the route you take to become a teacher, the more experiences you have in schools with teachers and students, the better prepared you will be to have a classroom of your own. The more experiences you have, the more certain your decision will be concerning whether teaching is for you. Experience in classrooms will also lead to more informed decision making about your teaching identity.

Most preparation programs require field experiences throughout. Perhaps you will begin with observations in one course and then work with individual students and small groups in another, and then teach whole-group lessons before and during student teaching/clinical practice. These experiences may hold many surprises for you. Having a 5-year-old nephew you enjoy seeing several times a year is very different from working all day with 20 5 year olds in a kindergarten classroom. Your memories of senior advanced placement literature that inspired you to want to teach high school English may be a romantic picture of students paying rapt attention as the sonnets of Elizabeth Barrett Browning are discussed. However, this may be a far cry from an actual freshman English class. If you fit the profile of most teachers and are a white female from suburbia, chances are that classrooms in urban America will expand your view of what it's like to be a teacher. Although you can read about differences in settings and students in this and other books and be somewhat informed, seeing for yourself brings reality into view.

There are other ways to gain insights into the classroom. Finding opportunities to have conversations with teachers is an excellent way to learn more about the realities of the classroom. Volunteering at schools, places of worship, and community organizations will present opportunities both to get to know kids and to observe adults interacting with them. Being a summer camp counselor, tutoring in an after-school program, and coaching in community recreation leagues all provide valuable experiences. This text provides opportunities to get to know eight real teachers in four real schools teaching nine real students.

Meet the Focus Teachers

"You just had to be there!" we often exclaim when words aren't enough. Learning about teachers, students, and schools is one of those situations when photos or video clips can help convey what a thousand words cannot. Is it as good as being there? No, but it helps.

Our eight focus teachers are introduced here, our eight focus students are introduced in Chapter 2, and their four schools are introduced in Chapter 3. Let's meet the eight teachers now.

Focus Teachers

Brandi Wade

Kindergarten teacher

Summit Primary School, Summit Station, Ohio

Teaching experience: Grades 5–6 (2 years)

Preschool and K (14 years)

Brandi says she has found her place in life. From her family to her friends to her teaching career, everything fits for this exuberant kindergarten teacher. One look around her classroom and one brief conversation are enough to know that 5- and 6-year-olds who spend time in Brandi's care are fortunate children.

Brandi believes in active involvement of children. She finds ways to teach the Ohio kindergarten curriculum standards through a wealth of movement, music, hands-on experiences, and play. Each year she spends whatever time is necessary to help her 15 to 25 kindergarten students per class form positive habits so the necessary routines of the classroom take care of themselves. She knows that classroom management and learning go hand in hand.

Sara Davis Powell

"My heart is where the children are" is a phrase Brandi says and lives. She believes that children must feel comfortable and loved in their environment before they can learn and thrive. She laughs and cries with her students, allows herself to be vulnerable to their needs, and provides a warm, developmentally appropriate setting in which children learn and grow.

Brandi and her husband have two sons, a Jack Russell terrier, and two turtles. Brandi enjoys swimming, camping, reading mysteries, and going to movies.

Renee Ayers

Second-grade teacher

Summit Primary School, Summit Station, Ohio

Teaching experience: Reading teacher (2 years)

First grade (3 years)

Second grade (4 years)

Renee exudes enthusiasm for life. From the soccer field to the energy she puts into teaching second grade, Renee's personality shines through. She says summers as a camp counselor influenced her teaching philosophy of infusing active learning and fun into instruction.

Renee is a reflective teacher who spends time in her classroom diagnosing student needs. She states that her biggest challenge is to design learning experiences for each child that take into account what the child already knows and is able to do. Renee believes strongly in individualizing assignments even when her instruction is geared toward the whole class. The children in her classroom are learning to be reflective, too. She saves samples of work from the beginning of the school year and periodically shows the samples to the students so they can compare and recognize their own progress. This is a simple process that is gratifying for the children.

Sara Davis Powell

At the end of the school year a very shy little boy said, "Mrs. Ayers, can you go to third grade with us?" The children pull at her heartstrings. All the effort is worth it.

(*continued*)

Renee and her husband have a baby daughter, the delight of their lives. In addition to her adult women's soccer league, Renee enjoys skiing, snowboarding, mountain biking, and taking evening walks with her family.

Chris Roberts

Third-, fourth-, and fifth-grade teacher

Rees Elementary School, Spanish Fork, Utah

Teaching experience: Special education (14 years)

Multiage third, fourth, and fifth grade (13 years)

Chris's adventurous spirit and active lifestyle permeate both his personal and his professional life. He has climbed Mount Kilimanjaro, rafted his way through the rapids of the Grand Canyon, and explored the shores of remote islands.

Chris brings his treasures to the classroom and shares his adventures with his students. Listening to real-life stories of scuba-diving encounters with giant sea rays and six-foot eels makes learning about ocean life and geography pure joy! Imagine spending three straight years in Mr. Roberts's class!

A fan of all kinds of art, Chris has posters of some of his favorite paintings on the walls of his classroom, along with inspirational poems, essays, and even cartoons. Chris infuses lessons in math, science, social studies, and language arts with a sense of curiosity and elements of critical thinking. One of his goals is for his students to see beyond the classroom walls, beyond Spanish Fork, and beyond Utah and the United States, to learn there's a whole world to experience.

Sara Davis Powell

Chris's family shares his love of adventure. He and his wife raised their children without television. He says there's nothing inherently wrong with television, but it distracts people from doing more worthwhile things such as reading and experiencing life rather than just watching other people experience it.

Brenda Beyal

Third-, fourth-, and fifth-grade teacher

Rees Elementary School, Spanish Fork, Utah

Teaching experience: Third grade (8 years)

Multiage third, fourth, and fifth grade (13 years)

The teaching profession is very personal to Brenda, and she approaches it with a sense of calling. The classroom environment she creates is warm and inviting.

Brenda's favorite subject to teach is language arts. She views literature as a child's window on the world, and reading as a way of experiencing both events and points of view. When her class of third-, fourth-, and fifth-graders read a book together, they explore meanings, not just words. They enjoy finding out about the author and rereading the story for deeper meaning. They write in their journals about story themes and act out sequences.

The fact that Brenda is Native American brings extra richness to her classroom. The wisdom of generations of her ancestors influences her. She has meaningful Native American objects and posters in her classroom and believes it's important for her to share parts of her heritage with her students. As they grow and encounter other Native Americans, Brenda wants her students to recall, "I know a Native American. I like the kind of person Ms. Beyal is. I'd like to get to know this person I have just met."

Sara Davis Powell

Brenda's family time with her husband, son, and daughter is very meaningful to her. She also enjoys drawing, sculpting, and collecting Native American artifacts.

Traci Peters

Seventh-grade math teacher

Cario Middle School, Mt. Pleasant, South Carolina

Teaching experience: Seventh-grade math/science (6 years)

Seventh-grade math (2 years)

Traci's classroom is filled with math—the shelves, the walls, the tables—math is everywhere! The seventh-graders in her classes know they'll be actively involved in tasks that help them understand concepts. From using geoboards to examine perimeter and area, to paper triangles they tear apart to prove the angles add up to 180 degrees, problem solving becomes something these students do, rather than something they just read about. One of Traci's primary goals is to show students that learning math can be lots of fun.

Sara Davis Powell

She offers her students before-school tutoring to help with concepts that may be difficult. The sessions also help students who have been absent to get caught up. The tutoring not

(*continued*)

only gives an academic boost, but it also gives Traci and her students time to get to know one another better.

Traci believes it's important for teachers to reveal some of their personal selves to students. She freely talks about her son and proudly shows students pictures of him as she encourages students to talk about their families and what they like to do in school and out of school.

Traci is married and has a 2-year-old son. She says she loves the fact that she is his first teacher. Walking on the beach, traveling to see family and friends, and spending everyday time with her husband and son make life a real joy for Traci.

Deirdre Huger-McGrew

Sixth-, Seventh-, and eighth-grade language arts, social studies teacher

Cario Middle School, Mt. Pleasant, South Carolina

Teaching experience: First, fourth, and fifth grades (7 years)

Sixth-, seventh-, and eighth-grade language arts, social studies (4 years)

Deirdre has taught a variety of grade levels and subjects. She says each one is interesting and challenging, but none so much as her current assignment on a two-person team charged with implementing a new program at Cario Middle School called CARE: Cario Academic Recovery and Enrichment. The program is designed to assist children in grades 6, 7, and 8 who are low achievers in working toward grade-level competency.

This unique opportunity has been given to Deirdre and her teaching partner, Billy, to begin a program and design it in ways that are responsive to their students. Principal Carol Bartlett has given the two teachers a good deal of professional autonomy. Deirdre says she is thriving in this situation, even though her students are among the most challenging at Cario.

Sara Davis Powell

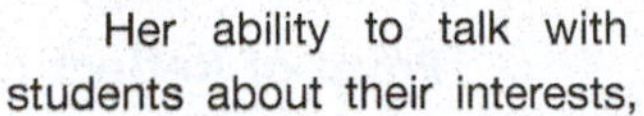

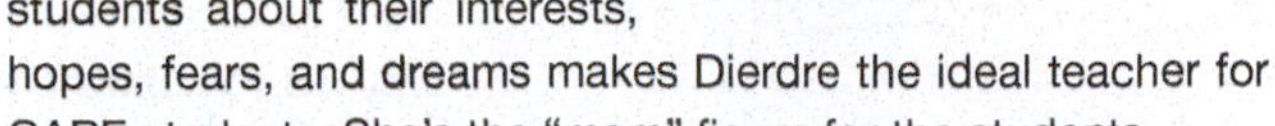

Her ability to talk with students about their interests, hopes, fears, and dreams makes Dierdre the ideal teacher for CARE students. She's the "mom" figure for the students.

Deirdre not only has students at Cario to care for, but her own home is brimming over with children. She and her husband have six children, all under 19 years old. Deirdre's attitude is "the more, the merrier." She says she's a teacher 24 hours a day! In her little free time, she enjoys writing and pursuing art activities.

Craig Cleveland

History, government, economics teacher

Roosevelt High School, Fresno, California

Teaching experience: History, government, economics (18 years)

Every day, during lunch as well as in the 5-minute passing periods between classes, students gather in Mr. Cleveland's classroom to play a tune on his piano or strum a chord or two on his guitar. Several other students sit at desks and listen or participate. This doesn't happen by accident. It happens because Craig welcomes students to express themselves, to be comfortable finding their own voice in his classroom and in his presence.

Craig's philosophical stance concerning teaching and learning involves his belief that students learn best when they are interested and involved through authentic reading, writing, speaking, and listening activities. The lessons he plans in his history, government, and economics classes include reading materials that push students to think and to interact with the text and one another. Students form opinions and write about them. Students speak to both question and persuade, to communicate in order to learn. The first rule of thumb in Craig's planning is "Give the students something worth thinking about."

Sara Davis Powell

Craig is an avid observer of human nature and the learning process both at school and in his home. He considers the home a fascinating lab for learning as he and his wife delight in watching their five daughters read, draw, create skits, and solve problems. Craig enjoys playing tennis and writing songs.

Angelica Reynosa

Modern world history teacher

Roosevelt High School, Fresno, California

Teaching experience: World history (3 years)

Angelica's tenth-grade bilingual modern world history class is filled with enthusiasm. There are 34 students in the class, all of whom have been in the United States for less than 2 years. Angelica is a young Latina whose fluency in both Spanish and English makes her an ideal teacher at Roosevelt High School.

The students' enthusiasm for the class is enhanced by the fact that Angelica teaches

Sara Davis Powell

(*continued*)

(*continued*)

in both Spanish and English. But language is not the only reason students are engaged. Angelica says her goal is to make every day enjoyable, memorable, and meaningful for all her students. She admits that it can be difficult to continually search for interactive, hands-on activities for teaching history, but the effort is worth it.

With a master's degree in school counseling, Angelica sees herself teaching several more years and then becoming a guidance counselor. She has aspirations to pursue a doctoral degree and plans to be part of the education profession for a long time.

Something that is particularly enjoyable for Angelica is the fact that she married a high school history teacher who teaches at a nearby school. Angelica remarks that their conversations are filled with empathy because they each understand the other's dilemmas and can listen attentively and make helpful suggestions when challenges arise.

We follow these 8 teachers through interviews, room tours, and lesson clips in **Teaching in Focus** features throughout the text.

Point of Reflection 1.2

Why did you choose the path to teaching that will prepare you for the classroom? Did you consider other options?

Check Your Understanding 1.2

1.3 Is Teaching a Profession?

1.3 Determine if teaching is a profession.

This text repeatedly refers to teaching as the *teaching profession.* Whether a particular job or career qualifies as a **profession** depends, in large measure, on who is making the determination. We hear references to the plumbing profession, the culinary profession, and the cosmetology profession, but there are established guidelines for determining if a career or job is universally considered a profession. These characteristics of a profession will likely not affect common usage of the word, but examining teaching with regard to them helps spotlight aspects of what we do that may need to be strengthened.

Characteristics of a Profession

For decades authors have delineated the characteristics of a "full" profession. For equally as long, educators and others have debated whether teaching is indeed a profession. This debate is healthy because, as we consider the characteristics of a profession and measure teaching by them, we see what teaching is and is not, what teachers have evolved into, and what teachers may still need to become. A summary of a full profession's characteristics, from both a historical perspective and a modern one, is presented in Figure 1.2. Let's look briefly at these 10 characteristics and think about whether each applies to teaching. (The next few paragraphs show these 10 numbered characteristics in parentheses.)

Considering that in the United States children ages 5 through 16 are required to receive a formal education, and that most do this through public schools, a dedicated teaching workforce can collectively deliver this *essential service* (1). Members of this teaching workforce agree that teaching requires *unique knowledge and skills* (2), whether acquired through traditional or alternative paths. On-the-job *training, ongoing study, and development* (2) are encouraged, but not necessarily required, although most teachers

Figure 1.2 Characteristics of a full profession

1. Provides an essential service no other group can provide.
2. Requires unique knowledge and skills acquired through extensive initial and ongoing study/training.
3. Involves intellectual work in the performance of duties.
4. Individual practitioners committed to service and continual competence.
5. Identifies performance standards that guide practice.
6. Self-governance in admitting, policing, and excluding members.
7. Members allow for a considerable amount of autonomy and decision-making authority.
8. Accepts individual responsibility for actions and decisions.
9. Enjoys prestige, public trust.
10. Grants higher-than-average financial rewards.

Based on: *Foundations of American Education 8e* by L. D. Webb, A. Metha, and K. F. Jordan (2017). New York, NY: Pearson.

must renew their teaching certification/license every 5 years or so by completing graduate coursework or by participating in other forms of professional development.

Teaching definitely *involves intellectual work* (3). Teachers pass along intellectual concepts and skills, which is the very heart of what teachers do. To enter and remain in a teaching career requires a *commitment to service* (4) and, hopefully, *continual competence* (4) as guided and measured by *performance standards* (5). The word "hopefully" is included because teachers rarely *police their own ranks* (6) to the point of excluding someone who does not live up to accepted teacher standards. If policing occurs, it is generally accomplished by administrators.

When the classroom door closes, teachers have considerable *autonomy* (7), sometimes approaching isolation. However, public school teachers must accept any student placed in their classrooms and must teach a set curriculum over which they have little or no control. Even with certain constraints, we teachers are *decision makers* (7), and we must *accept individual responsibility* (8) for the decisions we make.

A great level of *trust* (9) is placed in teachers. After all, for 7 to 10 hours a day, families allow teachers to have almost exclusive control over their children. In most communities, teachers enjoy a degree of positional *prestige* (9), but they are rarely *granted higher-than-average financial rewards* (10).

As you can see, not all 10 characteristics of a full profession apply to teaching. We still have few mechanisms for policing our own ranks (6), and the financial rewards of teaching are not higher than average (10). Teachers should continue to work together to perpetuate each of the eight characteristics we exemplify while exploring ways to incorporate the other two. Many associations and organizations are helping teaching to be a profession by allowing teachers through collaborative efforts to set common goals, speak with a collective voice, and build research-based foundations to support what we do and how we do it.

Professional Associations

National and regional professional associations provide leadership and support for teachers. Some serve the general teacher population; others are specific to a grade span or subject area. Most associations solicit members, hold annual conferences, publish materials, provide information, and advocate for those who teach and those who learn. Participating in professional organizations is a positive step toward growing as a professional.

The **National Education Association (NEA)** and the **American Federation of Teachers (AFT)** are the largest professional education associations in the United States, with a total of more than 5 million members, including teachers, administrators, professors, counselors, and other educators. Both organizations are unions and represent their members in **collective bargaining,** or negotiating with employers and states to gain additional benefits for their members. Large nonunion professional organizations such as **ASCD Learn Teach Lead, Kappa Delta Pi (KDP)**, and the **Council for Exceptional Children (CEC)** serve a wide spectrum of educators. Most national organizations have regional and state affiliate associations. These more local groups provide easily accessible face-to-face opportunities for interaction among members.

Interstate Teacher Assessment and Support Consortium (InTASC) standards address what teachers should know and be able to do and provide the framework for teacher performance standards. The original standards were written in 1992 specifically for beginning teachers. In 2011 the Consortium revised the standards to apply to all teachers.

Each subject area has a professional organization that provides guidelines for what to teach, sponsors annual conferences, publishes relevant books and journals, represents subject areas in educational and political arenas, and both encourages and disseminates research on teaching and learning. Table 1.2 lists some of the professional associations available to teachers to assist with their professionalism. Visiting their websites will give you valuable insight into just how important these and other professional organizations are and can be.

Table 1.2 Professional organizations

Teacher Unions	
AFT	American Federation of Teachers
NEA	National Education Association
Subject-area organizations	
AAHPERD	American Alliance for Health, Physical Education, Recreation and Dance
ACTFL	American Council on the Teaching of Foreign Languages
IRA	International Reading Association
MTNA	Music Teachers National Association
NAEA	National Art Education Association
NBEA	National Business Education Association
NCSS	National Council for the Social Studies
NCTE	National Council of Teachers of English
NCTM	National Council of Teachers of Mathematics
NSTA	National Science Teachers Association
RIF	Reading Is Fundamental
Level-specific organizations	
ACEI	Association for Childhood Education International
AMLE	Association for Middle Level Education
NAEYC	National Association for the Education of Young Children
Need-specific organizations	
CEC	Council for Exceptional Children
InTASC	Interstate Teacher Assessment and Support Consortium
NABE	National Association for Bilingual Education
NAGC	National Association for Gifted Children
NAME	National Association for Multicultural Education
SCA	Speech Communication Association
TESOL	Teachers of English to Speakers of Other Languages
General associations	
ASCD	ASCD Learn Teach Lead
KDP	Kappa Delta Pi
PDK	Phi Delta Kappa

Point of Reflection 1.3

Do you think teaching is a profession now that you know more about what qualifies as a profession? What is one idea that might help elevate teaching even more in terms of professionalism?

Check Your Understanding 1.3

1.4 What Is Teacher Professionalism?

1.4 Identify characteristics of teacher professionalism.

Professionalism is a way of being. It involves attitudes and actions that convey respect, uphold high standards, demonstrate commitment to those we serve, and fulfill responsibilities. Teacher professionalism demands that we put students first, strive for excellence, and commit to growth.

Put Students First

Student welfare and learning must be paramount. Ask yourself, as a Masai might, "And how are the children? Are they all well?" Putting students first requires that we become advocates for their welfare.

ADVOCATE FOR STUDENTS. To **advocate for students** is to support and defend them, always putting their needs first. Advocacy guides our efforts and decisions directly toward our goal—improving students' learning, which, ultimately, improves students' lives. How do we become advocates for our students? Here are some components of advocacy to consider:

- Understand that advocacy takes multiple forms with individuals, groups, or causes, in both large endeavors and small actions.
- In all conversations, with educators and noneducators alike, keep the focus on what is best for students.
- Take an informed stance on issues that affect children. Actively promote that stance to have widespread impact.
- Support families in every way possible.

MAKE WISE DECISIONS. Teachers continually make decisions. Some of the decisions are made on autopilot, especially those that have to do with routines in the classroom. The quality of other decisions often rests on common sense and maturity—characteristics that are enhanced by preparation and experience. It's important to remember that our decisions have consequences and require thoughtful consideration to make sure we are advocating for your students and maintaining a classroom climate that is conducive to learning.

DETERMINE CLASSROOM CLIMATE. Our classrooms can be respectful environments that promote learning, or not. The sobering words of Haim Ginott (1993, p. 15), a respected teacher and psychologist, should occupy a prominent position in both your classroom and your consciousness.

> I've come to a frightening conclusion. I am the decisive element in the classroom. It's my personal approach that creates the climate. It's my daily mood that makes the weather. As a teacher, I possess a tremendous power to make a child's life miserable or joyous. I can be a tool of torture or an instrument of inspiration. I can humiliate or humor, hurt or heal. In all situations, it is my response that decides whether a crisis will be escalated or de-escalated, a child humanized or de-humanized.

Strive for Excellence

In everything involved with teaching—knowledge of content, teaching skills, and relationships and interactions with students, colleagues, administrators, and families—we must strive for excellence. Will we always achieve it? Of course not. But in our striving, we will achieve as much excellence as we can in all we do.

FACILITATE LEARNING. Making the teaching and learning connection is the primary role of a teacher. Learning is why students are in school, and teaching is how we guide and facilitate learning. We should measure our effectiveness as teachers in large measure by how much and how thoroughly students learn.

The responsibilities involved in facilitating learning may be categorized in a number of valid ways. Perhaps none is more important than evaluating each of our actions in terms of its contribution to academic rigor and developmental appropriateness. **Academic rigor** refers both to teaching meaningful content and to having high expectations for student learning. **Developmental appropriateness** means that our teaching addresses students' physical, cognitive, social, emotional, and character development. Academic rigor without developmental appropriateness will result in frustration for teachers and foster discouragement and defeatism in students. Developmental appropriateness without academic rigor will accomplish little in terms of student learning. Neither concept is mutually exclusive. In fact, they shouldn't be exclusive at all, but rather should interact in supportive ways and balance one another as they guide our decision making.

DEVELOP POSITIVE DISPOSITIONS. **Dispositions** are composed of your attitudes, values, and beliefs. They powerfully influence our teaching approaches and actions. Dispositions that are favorable to effective teaching include, among many others:

- I believe all students can learn.
- I value student diversity.
- I respect individual students and their families.
- I am enthusiastic about the subjects I teach.
- I value other teachers as colleagues and partners in teaching and learning.
- I believe families are important in making the teaching and learning connection.

Commit to Growth

Teacher effectiveness is enhanced when a lifelong learning orientation is in place. A commitment to continual growth provides a powerful model for students.

BE A REFLECTIVE PRACTITIONER. We grow when we reflect on our teaching practices. As discussed earlier in this chapter, **reflection** with regard to teaching is thinking about what we do, how we do it, and the consequences of our actions or inactions, all with the goal of being better teachers. To be **reflective practitioners** means that we deliberately think about our practice—that is, what we do as teachers. We do this with the purpose of analysis and improvement. Sounds pretty automatic and unavoidable, doesn't it? But it's not. A teacher can repeatedly go through the motions of planning, teaching, and assessing throughout a career yet seldom engage in reflection that results in improved practice.

John Dewey (1933), one of the great American educators, described reflection using words such as *active, persistent*, and *careful.* So how do we become reflective practitioners who actively, persistently, and carefully think about how we teach? Here are some concepts to consider:

- Reflective practice requires conscious effort.
- Self-knowledge is vital and can be aided by thoughtfully completing the *Points of Reflection* throughout this text.

- Reading about and researching aspects of teaching will ground our practice and provide subject matter on which to reflect.
- Talking with other educators will both inform and strengthen what we do and how we do it.
- Being deliberate—doing what we do for a reason—will result in better decisions based on reflection.

Video Example 1.2 shows a brief portion of a new teacher "boot camp" with teachers watching clips of classrooms, recording what they observe, and then reflecting on student and teacher actions and reactions. The new teachers, with the help of veteran educators, share and learn together in very purposeful ways.

BUILD 21ST-CENTURY KNOWLEDGE AND SKILLS. Teachers committed to continual growth are determined to increase their knowledge and skills to keep up with current research and thought concerning teaching practices. During the first decade of this century some major forces both inside of, and external to, the education community recognized and espoused the need for knowledge and skills that reflect the realities of the 21st-century world. Perhaps the most influential source of information about teacher and learner characteristics for the new century is the **Partnership for 21st Century Skills (P21).**

In 2016, 20 states officially and voluntarily aligned with the Partnership for 21st Century Skills: Arizona, California, Illinois, Iowa, Kansas, Kentucky, Louisiana, Maine, Massachusetts, Mississippi, Nevada, New Jersey, North Carolina, Ohio, Oklahoma, South Carolina, South Dakota, Vermont, West Virginia, and Wisconsin. The Partnership for 21st-Century Skills is a national organization that advocates for student acquisition of 21st-century knowledge and skills. To help the United States compete in a global economy, P21 and its member states provide tools and resources that stress critical thinking and problem solving, communication, collaboration, creativity, and innovation. In doing so, P21 has emerged as the leading advocacy organization for infusing 21st-century skills into education. To strengthen its focus, P21 brings business and education leaders together with policymakers to define and implement a vision for 21st-century education (Partnership for 21st Century Skills, 2016).

The Partnership for 21st Century Skills outlines characteristics of teachers that help them teach students in ways that lead to success, including:

- Critical thinker
- Problem solver
- Innovator

- Effective communicator
- Effective collaborator
- Self-directed learner
- Information and media literate
- Globally aware
- Civically engaged
- Health conscious
- Financially and economically literate

These characteristics are developed and improved throughout the career of a professional teacher. A commitment to continual growth requires it.

SocialMEdia

Yes, you read it correctly . . . the ME is emphasized because your use of social media both inside and outside the classroom is, in large measure, up to you. Few schools dictate the use of social media as an instructional tool, yet many schools discourage, or even prohibit, the use of some "tech" devices if they are in the hands of students. So this is a personal issue, largely within your control. What will you do with your decision-making power?

In the not-too-distant past, textbooks contained pages of instructions on how to utilize computers, word processing, and the Internet in the classroom. Most of today's teachers, and practically all of today's students, take these features of technology for granted and assume their use. So let's move on.

The astonishing and rapidly growing quantity and quality of technology-enabled devices make comment on them almost obsolete before a book can be published. However, widespread use of technology-enabled devices such as *instructional tools* occurs at a much slower pace. Sharing innovations in teaching and learning tools has value, even if the particular piece of technology is several years old.

Social media is part of everyday life for most of us, so why not employ it in the classroom? Throughout this text you will read teaching strategies that include iPods, iPads, wikis, digital photography, blogs, Twitter, Skype, and handheld devices in features titled *SocialMEdia.* In addition, these features will offer suggestions on how you can teach students to use social media wisely and safely.

In this chapter we look at **webinars**, the name given to web-based seminars. The effectiveness of a webinar is in its interactivity possibilities, with participants receiving and giving information in a discussion format. Many school districts and state departments of education offer professional development through webinars. Is this kind of conferencing as effective as face-to-face interactions? Probably not, but webinars are both cost- and time-efficient.

- One of the most inclusive sites for webinars, both for a schedule of what's ahead and an amazing archive of recorded webinars, is provided by ASCD Learn Teach Lead. The site is completely free and available to anyone. Take a few minutes to explore it.
- Edtechteacher offers free webinars to help teachers incorporate technology in the classroom. Anyone can register for these informative, interactive sessions by simply going to the site and participating.

Try a webinar! Occasionally there are glitches in getting everyone on board, but webinar technology is constantly improving. The learning is well worth the effort.

This text will continue to refer to a career in teaching as the *teaching profession* and to teachers as *professionals.* Our commitment to continual growth includes consistent reflection and building of 21st-century knowledge and skills. Keep this growth mindset front and center as we next examine what it means to be an effective teacher.

Point of Reflection 1.4

Does the commitment to continual growth overwhelm you or excite you? Explain the reason(s) for your answer.

Check Your Understanding 1.4

1.5 What Are the Characteristics of Effective Teachers?

1.5 Describe the characteristics of effective teachers.

The search for a neatly packaged description of an effective teacher dates back for centuries, even millennia. The best we can come up with are lists of characteristics based on observation and available data, along with narrative anecdotal descriptions. There's a lot to be learned from considering a number of perspectives. But the bottom line is that effective teachers contribute to student learning.

Standards for teachers describe expectations for what they should know and be able to do to ensure learners reach their learning goals. All teacher education standards address teacher effectiveness. School-level organizations such as the **Association for Middle Level Education (AMLE)** and the **Association for Childhood Education International (ACEI)** prescribe standards for new teachers. The 10 standards of the Interstate Teacher Assessment and Support Consortium (InTASC) describe what effective teachers should know and be able to do regardless of the level they teach. An overview of these standards is seen in Figure 1.3. The InTASC Standards are divided into four general categories to help us understand them. The full document detailing the standards is a valuable tool for conceptualizing the effective teacher.

An important factor to understand when it comes to the characteristics of effective teachers and teaching is that much of what makes teachers effective comes through experience in the classroom. This is not to say that new teachers can't be effective. Of course they can! But think about this: Teaching is a profession that expects a brand-new teacher to do the same job as an experienced veteran. Don't count on someone saying, "Hey, it's okay if only half your kids learn about half of what you attempt to teach. After all, you're new." Some of the characteristics of effectiveness take time to develop. In other words, it takes time to be able to automatically make the wisest decisions and to draw on experience to supplement formal training.

Teachers can be effective using very different approaches. You can probably name two teachers in your own experience who were effective but who had different traits. Effective teachers, regardless of whom or what they teach, share many common characteristics. Teacher professionalism is a thread that binds them all. Teachers of students with special needs; teachers who specialize in art, music, or physical education; teachers who teach all or most subjects to one group of students; and teachers who teach the same content area each day to several groups of students—all have specific preparation requirements and position responsibilities.

The federal government, through the Department of Education, the president, and the legislature, helps shape this nation's concept of teacher and school quality. In 2016, the **Elementary and Secondary Education Act (ESEA)**, originating in 1964, was reauthorized as the **Every Student Succeeds Act (ESSA)**. This was the first official update since 2001, when ESEA was reauthorized as the **No Child Left Behind Act (NCLB)**, an update that included accountability measures that were well-intentioned but ultimately proved unwieldy and, in the opinion of many educators, unfair. The more recent Every Student Succeeds Act is addressed in more detail in Chapter 12.

The people who are with teachers at least 7 hours a day, 180 days a year are students. The following list of attributes is used by many students to gauge teaching and learning effectiveness. They want teachers who:

1. Care about them as a group and as individuals.
2. Teach in interesting and varied ways.
3. Do their best to help everyone learn.

4. Act in fair and consistent ways in terms of classroom management.
5. Display passion about what they teach.
6. Listen to them and help them express their voices.
7. Show interest in their activities and relevant social trends.
8. Demonstrate respect for everyone.
9. Develop relationships with them.
10. Enjoy teaching and have a sense of humor.

Figure 1.3 InTASC standards

The Learner and Learning

Standard #1: Learner Development.
The teacher understands how learners grow and develop, recognizing that patterns of learning and development vary individually within and across the cognitive, linguistic, social, emotional, and physical areas, and designs and implements developmentally appropriate and challenging learning experiences.

Standard #2: Learning Differences.
The teacher uses understanding of individual differences and diverse cultures and communities to ensure inclusive learning environments that enable each learner to meet high standards.

Standard #3: Learning Environments.
The teacher works with others to create environments that support individual and collaborative learning, and that encourage positive social interaction, active engagement in learning, and self motivation.

Content

Standard #4: Content Knowledge.
The teacher understands the central concepts, tools of inquiry, and structures of the discipline(s) he or she teaches and creates learning experiences that make the discipline accessible and meaningful for learners to assure mastery of the content.

Standard #5: Application of Content.
The teacher understands how to connect concepts and use differing perspectives to engage learners in critical thinking, creativity, and collaborative problem solving related to authentic local and global issues.

Instructional Practice

Standard #6: Assessment.
The teacher understands and uses multiple methods of assessment to engage learners in their own growth, to monitor learner progress, and to guide the teacher's and learner's decision making.

Standard #7: Planning for Instruction.
The teacher plans instruction that supports every student in meeting rigorous learning goals by drawing upon knowledge of content areas, curriculum, cross-disciplinary skills, and pedagogy, as well as knowledge of learners and the community context.

Standard #8: Instructional Strategies.
The teacher understands and uses a variety of instructional strategies to encourage learners to dev elop deep understanding of content areas and their connections, and to build skills to apply knowledge in meaningful ways.

Professional Responsibility

Standard #9: Professional Learning and Ethical Practice.
The teacher engages in ongoing professional learning and uses evidence to continually evaluate his/her practice, particularly the effects of his/her choices and actions on others (learners, families, other professionals, and the community), and adapts practice to meet the needs of each learner.

Standard #10: Leadership and Collaboration.
The teacher seeks appropriate leadership roles and opportunities to take responsibility for student learning, to collaborate with learners, families, colleagues, other school professionals, and community members to ensure learner growth, and to advance the profession.

Based on: Council of Chief State School Officers. (2011, April). Interstate Teacher Assessment and Support Consortium (InTASC) Model Core Teaching Standards: A Resource for State Dialogue. Washington, DC: Author.

Throughout this text you will read editorial opinions that have been published in newspapers, both print and online, that express opinions of people who may be staff writers for the papers or guest columnists. In most cases these pieces are logically constructed and easy to understand. They are written by people who feel strongly, even passionately, about an issue. At the end of each *The Opinion Page* feature are prompts or questions to help you think through your own opinions. As you respond, you are doing what good teachers do—reflecting on issues and ideas and then recording your own thoughts with the purpose of professional growth.

When a lone gunman broke into the school and murdered 26 students and staff at Sandy Hook Elementary School, the people of the United States were stunned. Discussions of school safety, gun control, and how to approach mental health were renewed that day in December 2012. In the midst of national debate, one incontrovertible truth was evident—teachers and administrators care for students. Read this chapter's *The Opinion Page* feature and respond to the items that follow it.

The Opinion Page

This Opinion Editorial appeared in the *CantonRep*, the online newspaper of Canton, Ohio, on December 26, 2012.

What Is a Teacher Really Worth?

by Charita Goshay, staff writer and regular opinion contributor for the *CantonRep.*

In recent months, teachers, first responders and other public employees have been whipping boys for people who think they enjoy too much compensation for their services. So what, exactly, is the dollar value of a teacher who saves the lives of 15 first-graders? How about one who sacrifices her life in an effort to save them? Which part of the faculty handbook advises a teacher on how to deal properly with unmitigated madness?

For those people who actually know a teacher, the heroism and sacrifice demonstrated by the educators in Newtown, Conn., are the least surprising aspects of the tragedy. Teachers don't just teach. The good ones inspire, challenge and change the lives of their students every day. They open up worlds of knowledge and introduce children to possibilities they otherwise wouldn't know existed. They go into their own pockets to level the playing field. They worry about "their kids," particularly those who they know have turbulent lives, even years after they move on.

Our culture has become such that we don't even blink or flinch at the news that someone will earn $10 million a year for throwing a ball or running a corporation into the ground. But a teacher gets flayed for falling test scores, even when the reasons are multifaceted and complicated.

These days, a lesson plan isn't enough. Teachers frequently must also be psychiatrists, substitute parents and bouncers. They're caught between uncooperative and irresponsible parents, ever more complicated school policies, a cynical taxpaying public that demands to know why schools aren't doing better, and kids who are expected to miraculously rise above the chaos and instability in which they live. Even children from affluent and stable, supportive homes can have struggles that they bring with them to school. Because of all of this, no one in his or her right mind would become a teacher simply for a paycheck and a pension.

Being a public servant is a calling, one as compelling and clear as entering the clergy or becoming a physician. If teachers were compensated based on what they contribute to society, we couldn't afford them. The annual minimum salary for a National Hockey League rookie is $525,000. For baseball, it's $390,000. In the NBA it's $473,604. The average elementary-school teacher makes $40,283 a year, what many major-sport athletes make in a month.

Despite this bargain, we still find reasons to complain about teachers, ignoring the irony that if it were not for teachers, we'd be unable to express ourselves very well. Who has time to decipher someone else's cave-drawing rant? Not me. As we saw in Connecticut and as is demonstrated virtually every day, a teacher's dedication is immeasurable.

This Opinion Page piece covers a lot of ground with respect to teachers' dedication to the well-being of students. She also writes about the relative absurdity of salary discrepancies between teachers and professional athletes. Write a well-developed paragraph in response to each of the following questions.

1. Why, in Ms. Goshay's opinion, would our country not be able to pay teachers enough for what they do? Do you agree? Explain.
2. What is your response to the multiple roles teachers have in the lives of students? Have you considered how all-encompassing teaching can be? Does this knowledge overwhelm you? Excite you?

Effective Teachers are 100 % Present

Emily Dickinson wrote, "Forever is composed of nows." Each moment with your students is important. The productivity of both the "nows," and the sum of the "nows" that comprise forever, depends on focus and the will to capture every opportunity for teaching and learning with our presence. Education doesn't just occur within our lesson plans. Spontaneity in our ability to use everyday happenings, as well as spectacular events and tragic misfortunes, presents teachable moments we will recognize only if our mind and heart are focused on our students as whole people.

The classroom can be a very distracting place simply because it's filled with human beings. Not only will students become distracted at times, but so will teachers. In addition, our lives outside the classroom are sometimes complex, in both positive and negative ways. Leaving personal concerns and plans at the schoolhouse door will help us be 100% present for students.

This certainly doesn't mean teachers must sacrifice their personal lives for the profession. The key to longevity and success in teaching is finding balance. Happy, thriving adults make the best teachers. In this *Teaching in Focus* segment, we learn more about how Traci Peters finds and maintains balance. In her video, she discusses how she plans for instruction.

Teaching in Focus

Traci Peters teaches seventh-grade math at Cario Middle School in Mt. Pleasant, South Carolina. By all accounts she's an excellent teacher—just ask her principal, her colleagues, and, most importantly, her students. Outside school, Traci enjoys a very happy home life with husband Dwayne and young son Robert. The seventh-graders in Traci's classes know all about these two very important people in her life, and that's the way Traci wants it. Although math is the subject she has chosen to teach, she is conscious of the fact that her responsibilities go well beyond fractions and equations. She views each student as an individual with relationships and often complex growing-up issues. Traci reveals herself to them, and they, in turn, feel comfortable enough to share with her.

Sara Davis Powell

In a prominent place in the classroom Traci has a "Mrs. Peters" bulletin board on which she displays, among other things, family photos (from her childhood to the present), her favorite poems and book titles, her own seventh-grade report card, and her 5 × 7 middle school picture. Traci says her students spend lots of time examining the board's contents, laughing and asking questions.

Traci sees herself as a role model of a healthy, positive adult who makes good choices and tries to make a difference in other people's lives. When asked if she would just as freely share with students the not-so-positive aspects of her life, she replies, "Yes." When she's not feeling well, she lets her students know. If her son Robert is sick and she needs to stay home to care for him, she tells her students.

Traci attends her students' basketball games, concerts, spelling bees, Odyssey of the Mind competitions—the typical year-long parade of events. She views this as a tangible way to show her students she is interested in them, their growth, and their lives. Watch Traci's interview to get to know her better.

Application Exercise 1.1: Traci's Interview

Effective Teachers make a Difference

"From the moment students enter a school, the most important factor in their success is not the color of the skin or the income of their parents, it's the person standing at the front of the classroom." This powerful statement was made in a speech to the Hispanic Chamber of Commerce in 2009 by President Barack Obama. Sobering, isn't it? Our former president of the United States is stating what recent research corroborates. Teachers make the most difference when it comes to student learning. Our effectiveness, or lack of it, matters.

The most important person in the teaching and learning cycle when it comes to both student academic and personal growth is the classroom teacher. Although other factors discussed in the text significantly influence student learning, none do so as much as the teacher. An effective teacher can help students overcome some of the negative circumstances in their lives and positively impact student learning. When the outside influences on student learning result in achievement gaps, student learning can dramatically improve when provided quality teachers.

Teaching is Hard Work

We've considered who teaches and why, teacher preparation, whether teaching is a profession, teacher professionalism, and characteristics of effective teachers. Most of the information is positive and encouraging. However, leaving the initial picture of teaching as a rosy, always exhilarating career, is not honest. Teaching is hard work—but not *just* hard work.

Teachers face circumstances daily that are beyond their control and affect what they can and cannot accomplish. This is true in many professions, but few have the ability to tug at our heart-strings and keep us awake at night as we plan and worry, try new approaches and worry, build relationships and, you guessed it, worry. Our concern for the welfare of our students can be overwhelming unless we find ways to balance our personal lives and our professional lives. Much of this text is designed to help you learn to do this. The more you know, the greater your ability will be to put aspects of your life into perspective.

Carol Ann Tomlinson (2016) believes that societal, political, economic, and structural pressures on teachers have rarely been greater. Over the years she has observed teachers who are effective year after year and through the ever-changing landscape of teaching. One primary characteristic of these consistently resilient teachers is what she calls *energy renewal,* resulting from the ability to keep life in perspective. Tomlinson says that energy renewal comes from working hard, becoming involved with students on multiple levels, and bringing joy to the classrooms, while also understanding the need to separate periodically from the profession to define ourselves in fun and personal ways. Doing so will keep us from being consumed by the challenges of teaching and keep the inevitable satisfactions and pleasures in the foreground.

Sara Davis Powell

Effective teachers purposefully and collaboratively plan for instruction.

Point of Reflection 1.5

How do you typically face adversity? When some of the initial excitement of teaching is met with realities of student hardships or frustrating circumstances beyond your control, will you be resilient?

Check Your Understanding 1.5

Concluding Thoughts

Throughout this text you are urged to ask repeatedly, as the Masai do, "And how are the children? Are they all well?" However, when you are a novice teacher, your primary question may often be "How am I doing?" With time, your focus will increasingly shift to the growth and progress of the children and adolescents you serve.

Learning to be a teacher . . . teaching so others learn . . . learning to be a better teacher—this life-affirming cycle can be yours. Think of the cycle as a wheel that gathers momentum and takes you on a profound journey. You have begun to grow toward the profession. As a teacher, you'll grow within the profession. After reading the Chapter in Review, interact with Traci Peters and her middle school team as they face a dilemma in this chapter's Developing Professional Competence.

Chapter in Review

Who teaches in the United States and why?

- Teaching is the largest profession in the United States.
- Most teachers are white women, leading to a need for more men and people of color in teaching.
- The most common reasons for choosing to teach include the desire to work with children and/or adolescents, the importance of education to society, the trait of being motivated by variety, interest in a particular subject, and the impact of teachers and/or family.
- Teachers' beginning salaries and mean average salaries vary by district, by state, and by specialty area based on many variables.

How do we prepare to teach?

- States issue a certificate or license to teach in public schools based on their own criteria.
- The traditional path to becoming a teacher is through a university-based teacher preparation program.
- Alternative paths to teacher preparation provide timely, but somewhat controversial, routes to teacher certification.
- There are many ways to get to know teachers, students, and schools, including field experiences through teacher preparation programs, volunteer opportunities, watching movies about teachers, and participating online through this and other texts.

Is teaching a profession?

- A profession is an occupation that includes extensive training before entering, a code of ethics, and service as the primary product.
- Teaching meets most of the criteria generally agreed on for a full profession.
- Numerous professional organizations support teachers and teaching.
- Teachers can and should make contributions to the knowledge base of the teaching profession.

What is teacher professionalism?

- Teacher professionalism entails putting students first and striving for excellence.
- Teacher professionalism requires a commitment to continual growth.
- Teacher professionalism requires purposeful reflection.
- Teacher professionalism requires building of 21st century knowledge and skills.
- The Partnership for 21st Century Skills challenges states, communities, schools, and teachers to prepare students for the future.

What are the characteristics of effective teachers?

- Effective teachers may have very different styles of teaching.
- The one consistent characteristic of effective teachers is student learning.
- There are established guidelines for teacher effectiveness through the Interstate Teacher Assessment and Support Consortium and other professional organizations.
- Both individuals and organizations have opinions about what makes a teacher effective. There is much to learn from the differing viewpoints.
- Teaching is hard work and requires balance and perspective to be effective over time.

Developing Professional Competence

Sara Davis Powell

Thoughtfully reading this scenario and responding to the items that follow it will help you prepare for licensure exams.

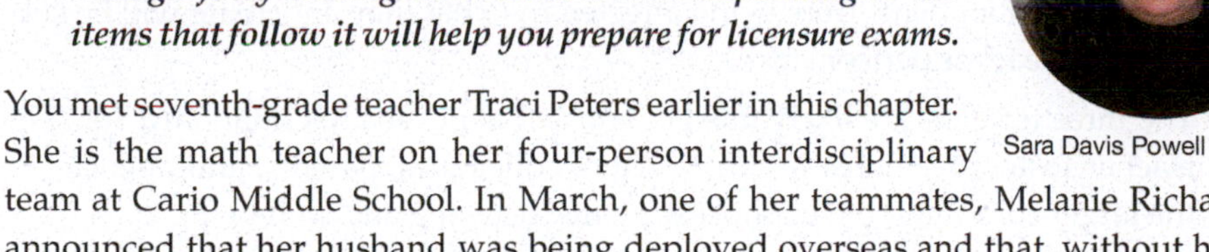

You met seventh-grade teacher Traci Peters earlier in this chapter. She is the math teacher on her four-person interdisciplinary team at Cario Middle School. In March, one of her teammates, Melanie Richardson, announced that her husband was being deployed overseas and that, without his help with their five children, she was going to have to move to another state where her parents live. Melanie teaches English-language arts and has been on Traci's team, the Dolphins, for 3 years. This is a big blow to Traci and her two other teammates. Melanie will leave Cario in mid-April. The Dolphin team teachers are very easy to work with and have enjoyed a collegial relationship with Melanie.

Carol Bartlett, principal of Cario, understands the importance of finding the right person to fill the position, but she is told by the superintendent that a teacher from another school will be placed in Melanie's classroom for the remainder of the school year. Carol knows the teacher the district personnel office plans to place on the Dolphin team. Leo Merchant's reputation is that of a veteran teacher who does not collaborate, sits behind his desk during class, and consistently finds ways to undermine administrators. The principal suspects Leo's position was purposefully eliminated at the other school and the district just needs to find a place for him. Carol is certain the Dolphin teachers will not be pleased with the district's choice.

Now it's time for you to respond to two short essay items involving the scenario. In your responses, be sure to address all the dilemmas and questions posed in each item. These items are followed by three multiple-choice questions.

1. Traci and her teammates understand that Leo will be a temporary member of their team, or at least that's their hope. They have been assured by the school district that they will be able to interview candidates for the English-language arts position and that a new teacher can be in place by August. This helps them get through the remainder of the school year. As they look to the future, what are three qualities you would recommend they look for as they, along with the principal, choose a new teacher for their team?
2. Teacher evaluation is problematic for a variety of reasons. The seventh-grade team at Cario is about to experience some of the consequences of a system that not only fails to discriminate between effective and ineffective teachers but also allows ineffective teachers to remain in the classroom. How would meaningful ongoing teacher evaluation help fix the system? How would you recommend the results of the evaluation be used?

Application Exercise 1.2 Developing Professional Competence

3. Which of the following attributes of a full profession does this scenario directly violate?
   a. A full profession enjoys prestige and public trust.
   b. A full profession admits, polices, and excludes members.
   c. A full profession provides an essential service no other group can provide.
   d. A full profession involves intellectual work in the performance of duties.
4. Which of the following statements applies *least* to this situation?
   a. The three teachers on the Dolphin team will likely have to expend extra effort to keep their students from being affected by what they anticipate will be substandard teacher performance.
   b. The three teachers are likely most concerned about InTASC Standard 10: "The teacher fosters relationships with school colleagues, parents, and agencies in the larger community to support students' learning and well-being."
   c. The three teachers will continue to instill academic rigor while making their classrooms developmentally appropriate.
   d. Leo has a master's degree in education, so the rumors about him are very likely exaggerated.
5. As they have always done, the Dolphin teachers take individual responsibility for the success of their team of students. Which of the following would *not* be evidence of this?
   a. They use opportunities to say positive things about their students in the community.

b. They don't get involved in decisions that affect their students because they believe that designated experts know best.

c. They invite families to come to school to discuss areas of concern for their children.

d. They consistently talk about and act on what they believe to be best for their students.

Application Exercise 1.3: Developing Professional Competence

Flash Cards 1.1

Shared Writing 1.1: Challenges

Chapter 2

Student Similarities and Differences

Learning Objectives

After studying this chapter, you will have knowledge and skills to:

2.1 Articulate how students are similar.

2.2 Express how gender differences are manifested in schools.

2.3 Explain how cultural diversity and language diversity are manifested in schools.

2.4 Identify the impact on students of family structure, religion, and socioeconomic status.

2.5 Summarize how learning differences are manifested in schools.

2.6 Define students with exceptionalities and how we serve them in schools.

Dear Reader

It's all about the kids . . . schools, teacher preparation, lesson plans, activities, professional development, and so on. Our focus must always be on learners—those children and adolescents who enter our classrooms and live within our care at least 180 days a year. A teacher's entire career is an adventure in observing and interacting with whole—yet still developing—people. Their needs and gifts and challenges keep the classroom fresh and vibrant so long as we positively approach our responsibilities as teachers. What a wonderful profession!

This chapter looks at how students are both similar and different. A quick look tells you that we give differences much more attention than we do similarities. The primary similarity is that kids are kids—regardless of how they may differ from one another, they are first and foremost kids. Once that's established, we need to understand that each learner is a complex composite of multiple factors, many of which we'll explore in this chapter. Every child has learning preferences, life circumstances, a personality, potential, and gifts, and each deserves our best efforts. This is in no way a comprehensive look at student diversity, but it's a good way to begin. Our responses to "And how are the children? Are they all well?" will be more meaningful when we see them as whole people, developing every day.

2.1 How Are Students Similar?

2.1 Articulate how students are similar.

In the time it takes you to read a few pages in this chapter, a whole classroom of students will be born. That's right—statistically, 30 babies are born in the United States every 8 minutes. Your entire future kindergarten class, third-grade class, middle school social studies class, or high school algebra class may be coming into the world right now. Statistically, we can predict that of these 30 future students, 14 will be considered a racial minority, 8 will be born into poverty, and 9 will be born out of wedlock. Of these 30 children, 17 will have parents who divorce before the students graduate from high school, 5 will serve jail sentences, 5 will be victims of violence, 4 will commit a violent crime before age 16, and almost half will drop out before finishing high school (National Center for Education Statistics [NCES], 2011; U.S. Census Bureau, 2012). "And how are the children?"

Chances are your classroom won't mirror the statistics you just read. Classroom populations vary from little cultural or socioeconomic diversity to a challenging and invigorating mix. You might teach in a school with students whose families are financially well off, or one with families that move when the rent comes due. Perhaps you will teach in a stable rural community with conservative values and lifestyles, or in a suburban area that affords a great variety of opportunities and educational options, but where students tend to move often.

The 30 new lives that have begun in this 8-minute time frame may appear to be diverse, but they are actually more similar than they are dissimilar. They are individual beings with unique attributes and a variety of needs. But the most important thing to remember is that they are children, all worthy of our best efforts. Mark Twain said that children are born every day who could change the world. We just don't know who they are yet.

We begin our look at similarities with a brief discussion of nature and nurture, the two sources of influence that make us who we are. Then, through the views of Abraham Maslow, we look at the needs shared by every human being. We follow with an exploration of physical, cognitive, emotional, social, and character development.

Nature and Nurture

Debate continues on the question of what has the greater influence in determining who we are—nature or nurture. These two concepts are generally presented as oppositional: nature *versus* nurture. **Nature** refers to genetically inherited influences. Not only are certain physical characteristics, such as eye color, skin tone, and adult height, determined by nature, but some aspects of our intelligence and personalities are established genetically as well. **Nurture** refers to the influences of our environment, encompassing everything that cannot be accounted for genetically. For instance, how we are raised, the people we meet, the schools we attend, and our economic status are all part of nurture.

Each child arrives in the world with predispositions, or tendencies, accounted for by nature and over which we have little control. However, teachers do have some influence over nurture that can positively impact what students receive through nature. That's why we create classroom environments that stimulate growth—physical, cognitive (intellectual), emotional, social, and character. To more fully realize why we need to create these environments, let's examine the importance and relative priority of human needs that we all share.

Maslow's Hierarchy of Needs

Psychologist Abraham Maslow (1908–1970) proposed that all human beings experience the same needs. Figure 2.1 shows his classic **hierarchy of needs**, which is widely accepted as an accurate depiction of the order, from bottom to top, in which needs have to be met for healthy and full human development.

Maslow proposed that basic needs for survival and safety must be met first. Once these needs are satisfied, humans are motivated to move up the pyramid toward higher-order needs. Makes sense, doesn't it? If students don't have food and shelter, or if they feel physically threatened, it's unlikely they will be concerned about understanding the Pythagorean theorem. Providing opportunities and support for needs fulfillment and promoting positive student development will help them ascend Maslow's pyramid and develop in positive ways.

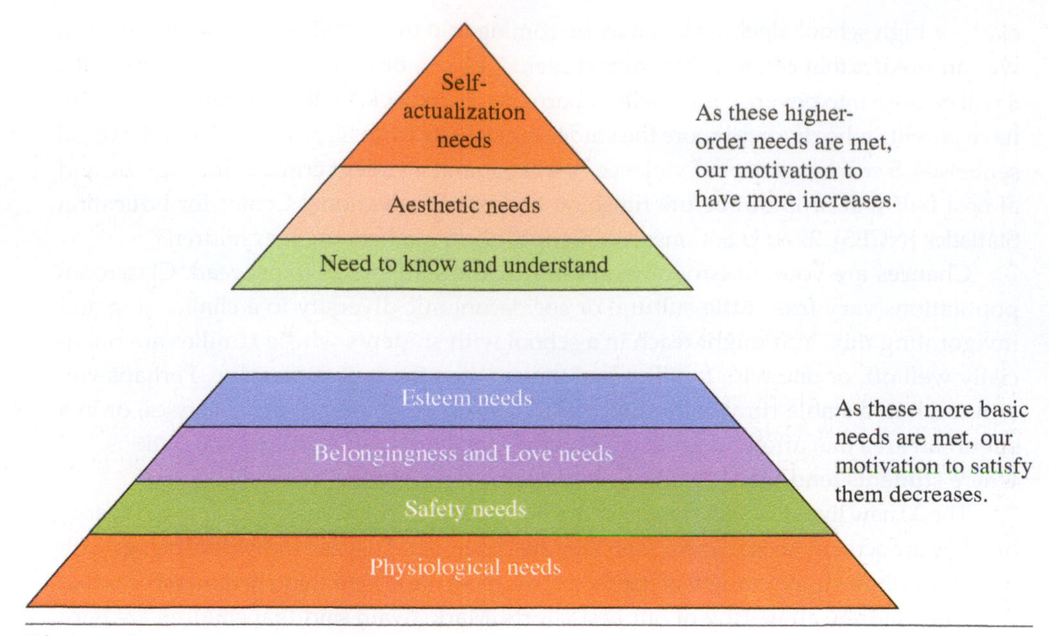

Figure 2.1 Maslow's hierarchy of needs

Student Development

Most children progress through predictable age-related stages of development. The more we know about these developmental stages, the more empathy and support we can offer. In this section you will meet eight children and adolescents at various stages of development who are students of the eight focus teachers we met in Chapter 1 at four focus schools. Take the time necessary not only to read the brief descriptions of the students but also to look carefully at the photos of these real learners. Consider them as you read about five developmental areas: physical, cognitive (intellectual), emotional, social, and character.

Focus Students: Early Childhood

Dylan Todd

Kindergarten

Summit Primary School, Summit Station, Ohio (student of Brandi Wade)

Dylan is the only child of Brandon and Lisa Todd. Their pride is obvious as they talk about what a delightful little boy he is. When Dylan smiles, everyone smiles. When he giggles, his pure expression of joy is contagious.

We meet Dylan in the middle of his second year of kindergarten. During his first year, Dylan made progress and perhaps could have gone on to first grade. However, in consultation with the school staff, Mom and Dad decided it would benefit Dylan to experience another year of kindergarten, giving him time to mature a bit more socially.

Dylan's teacher, Brandi Wade, says that he has made wonderful progress in learning to read. In terms of the reasoning ability needed for progress in math, Brandi says Dylan is continually growing and learning.

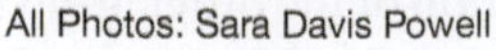
All Photos: Sara Davis Powell

Sherlonda Francis

Second grade

Summit Primary School, Summit Station, Ohio (student of Renee Ayers)

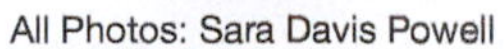
All Photos: Sara Davis Powell

Sherlonda's personality shines. The challenge is to help her develop academically and find success in school so that high school graduation will be in her future. Renee Ayers, her teacher, is afraid that if Sherlonda doesn't experience grade-level-appropriate academic success soon, her penchant for socializing may actually get in the way of her success.

Sherlonda is doing better in second grade. However, in first grade she had some difficulty paying attention and staying on task. Although this isn't unusual for early childhood students, it was chronic enough to concern the Summit Primary staff. Renee talked extensively with Sherlonda's first-grade teacher, and they worked together to plan Sherlonda's second-grade experience so she would experience success.

Sherlonda's mom is the sponsor of her church dance group, and her dad is very active in Sherlonda's life, saying his daughter loves to learn new things and figure out how things work. Both parents say they have always read to Sherlonda, and now she is reading to them.

Focus Students: Elementary

Amanda Wiley

Third grade

Rees Elementary School, Spanish Fork, Utah (student of Chris Roberts and Brenda Beyal)

Amanda's mom, president of the Rees Elementary PTA, describes Amanda as "just plain fun." All it takes is 5 minutes of classroom observation to know the description fits. Amanda loves school now, but reading did not come easily for her, and first grade proved to be very challenging. Toward the end of second grade, things began to click for Amanda. Now in third grade, she is an avid reader.

Amanda is crazy about math. Her mom says Amanda doesn't behave like a stereotypical girl. She would rather be involved in rough-and-tumble play than do what most girls want to do. Amanda is the middle of three sisters and doesn't seem to have time for relationships with other girls.

The summer before going to third grade, when Amanda would be in Tim Mendenhall's homeroom, she talked her family into letting her be the caretaker of Rosie, the class pet. As it turns out, the class pet is not a cuddly guinea pig or a cute little rabbit, but a large hairy tarantula.

All Photos: Sara Davis Powell

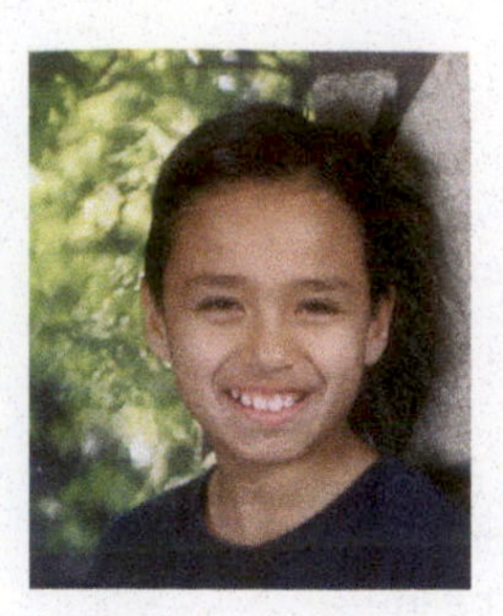

All Photos: Sara Davis Powell

Hector Mancia

Fourth grade

Rees Elementary School, Spanish Fork, Utah (student of Chris Roberts and Brenda Beyal)

Hector's smile would warm the heart of any teacher. As a fourth-grader, he is a fluent English speaker, vibrant, curious, and determined to succeed. Hector's family came to Utah from Mexico. One of his biggest challenges is to help his family learn English. His mom understands and speaks some English, but his dad and older brother do not.

Hector enjoys school. He fits right in with other third-, fourth-, and fifth-graders in Chris Roberts's multiage class at Rees Elementary. Hector tells us he really likes reading, sports, recess, and lunch—pretty typical of fourth-graders. His mom says he takes delight in basketball, school, and cleaning his room. This last may seem surprising, but Hector likes to please those around him.

Hector is happy with Mr. Roberts's lessons and tells us his teacher's travels add a lot to the classroom. Chris Roberts's teaching style draws Hector in and keeps him excited about school.

Focus Students: Middle School

Patrick Sutton

Seventh grade

Cario Middle School, Mt. Pleasant, South Carolina (student of Traci Peters)

Patrick is a very self-assured 13-year-old seventh-grader who likes school. He enjoys being with friends the most and doing homework the least (no surprise here!). He tells us that he likes teachers who challenge him and dislikes teachers who are mean and yell at kids. Patrick thinks he would like to join the NFL. But if that's not in his future, he would like to be an architect.

Patrick's mom tells us he is a delight at home. She says he is independent, easy to be around, loves his family, and enjoys attention. The main challenge he has faced is that the family has moved often. Patrick has had to make new friends and start over several times in his eight years of schooling. Mom thinks this has actually made him stronger and a better student. Her hope for him is that he will retain his love of learning and be true to himself.

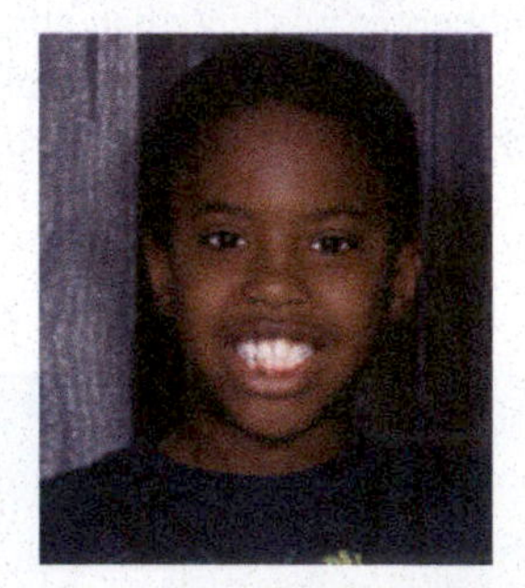
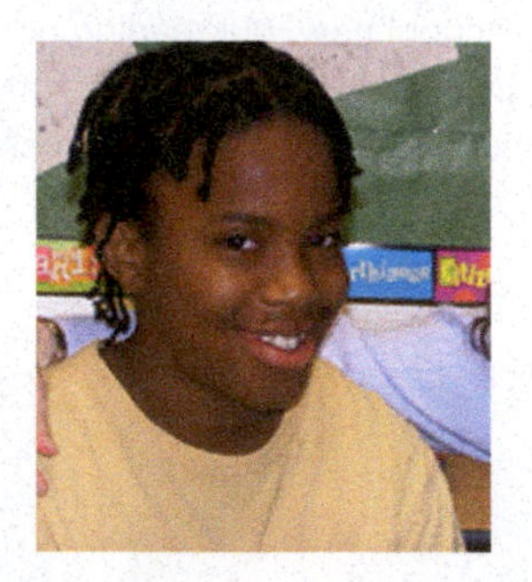

All Photos: Sara Davis Powell

Focus Students: High School

Trista Kutcher

Ninth grade

Wando High School, Mt. Pleasant, South Carolina (former student of Deidre Huger-McGrew)

Trista is as friendly as any high school freshman could be. She thrived at Cario Middle School. Wando High School students pass her and smile when they say hello. Trista is a cheerleader and an athlete—and she has Down syndrome.

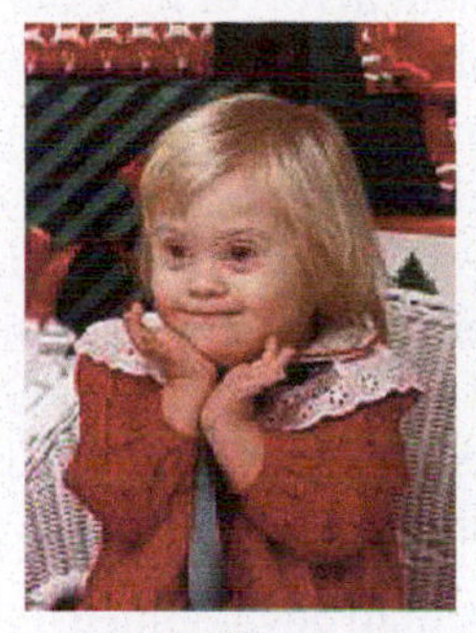
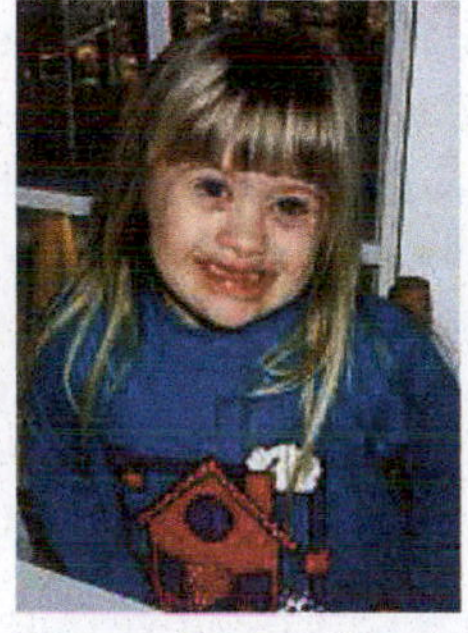

All Photos: Sara Davis Powell

Trista's coach and fellow cheerleaders tell us they anticipated problems because of Trista's disability. They soon discovered that their fears were not justified. Trista has proven to have both the skill and the attitude to be an asset to the squad.

Trista, her parents ReBecca and Joe, and her two sisters form a loving, supportive family. ReBecca and Joe are both teachers. When Trista was at Cario Middle School, ReBecca was there to make sure she had every advantage possible in a public school setting. At Wando High School, Joe is her homeroom teacher. Their interest and involvement have played a major role in Trista's success.

Hugo Martinez

Eleventh grade

Roosevelt High School, Fresno, California (student of Angelica Reynosa)

All Photos: Sara Davis Powell

Hugo is a 17-year-old junior with a very outgoing personality. Are you wondering why there's only one school picture of him? When Hugo, his mom and dad, and three brothers crossed the Mexican border into California 18 months ago, they brought only the clothes they were wearing.

Angelica Reynosa, Hugo's bilingual teacher, interprets the question about what he would like to do in the future. He responds in English, "I have a dream in my life." Then in Spanish he says he wants to graduate from high school, go to college, and be a doctor or a teacher. Hugo's mom and dad, with Angelica interpreting, express their pride in Hugo and say he is responsible, does his chores and homework, and is well rounded. Their hope is that Hugo's teachers will be positive and continue to motivate him.

Perhaps the biggest roadblock for Hugo is his lack of U.S. citizenship. This likely precludes him from receiving many grants and government loans. Without financial assistance, Hugo will probably not go to college.

Khammany Douangsavanh

Twelfth grade

Roosevelt High School, Fresno, California (student of Craig Cleveland)

Khammany speaks fluent English at school but only Laotian at home. She participates in class consistently and demonstrates an appreciation for the value of education. As a learner, Khammany says interest in a subject is the key to motivating her to succeed. She comments that she likes history in Craig Cleveland's class because there's so much in the past to think about and so much in the future to predict.

Khammany's mom, who speaks no English and relies on Khammany to interpret, is very emotional when she says she wants her daughter to receive a good education to help her succeed. This is especially important since the death of Khammany's dad about a year ago. Mom views her daughter as the hope of their family. She's bright and determined, and her mother is obviously proud of her.

Khammany will be the first in her family to graduate from high school and would be the first to enter college. However, she will likely feel compelled to help support her mom and extended family, making four years of college fairly elusive.

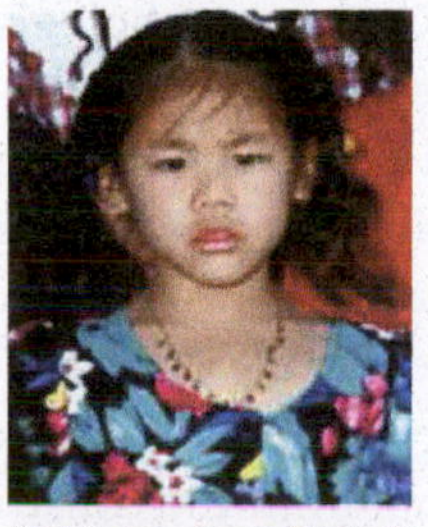
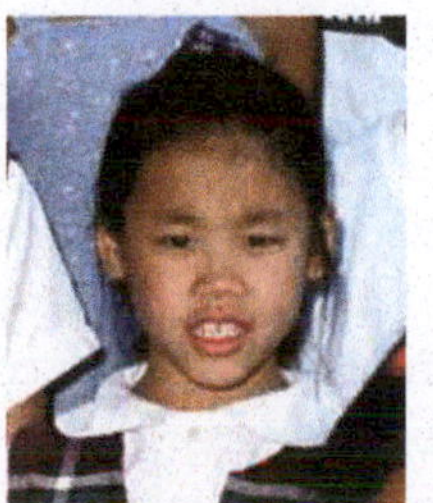

All Photos: Sara Davis Powell

PHYSICAL DEVELOPMENT. Physical development involves how our bodies appear and how they function. Patterns of physical development are orderly in that the progression is generally predictable. Body parts mature at rates that make physical development the most obvious of the five areas of development.

Although each child follows a distinct growth curve, the most rapid growth occurs in early childhood, with steady growth through elementary school. In early adolescence there may be an explosive growth rate, leveling off in late adolescence. Girls often experience puberty as much as 2 years earlier than boys, but boys generally grow taller and heavier than girls by late adolescence (McDevitt and Ormrod, 2016).

COGNITIVE DEVELOPMENT. Cognitive (intellectual) development is considered the primary focus of school. Changes in cognition are just as profound—but often much more subtle—than outward physical changes. Yet, the brain grows faster than any other part of the body. By age 5, the brain has reached approximately 90% of its full size, but the body is only 30% developed (Feldman, 2014).

Jean Piaget (1896–1980) was one of the most renowned cognitive development theorists. Piaget recognized distinct differences in children's and adolescents' responses to questions that directly correlated to their chronological ages. This was the beginning of his research into the four **stages of cognitive development**, encapsulated in Figure 2.2.

Figure 2.2 Piaget's model of cognitive development

Sensorimotor intelligence (birth to 2 years of age)

Children primarily learn through their senses as their motor capabilities develop. Children in this stage don't actually "think" conceptually.

Preoperational thought (2–7 years of age)

Children begin to use symbols and their grasp of concepts develops rapidly. They begin to think about things and people outside their observable environment. Their viewpoint is generally limited because they have little ability to see things from different perspectives.

Concrete operations (7–11 years of age)

Children begin to think logically. They understand the concept of conservation, that quantities don't change because they are moved. Through manipulation of concrete objects they understand concepts such as number, space, and causality. They begin to see things from varied perspectives and draw conclusions.

Formal operations (11 years of age and on)

Adolescents progress from concrete thinking to the capability of thinking abstractly. They are able to make predictions, experience metacognition (thinking about thinking), and appreciate and use the structure and subtleties of language.

Based on: McDevitt, T. M., & Ormrod, J. E. (2016). *Child development and education.* Upper Saddle River, NJ: Merrill/Pearson Education.

Although Piaget's work is still held in high esteem, researchers have concluded that he based much of his theory on children's deficits rather than on their strengths. Children may be more capable at younger ages than Piaget believed. Teachers may benefit from knowing about Piaget's stages, but should never use them to limit how and when the intellectual capabilities of students are stretched.

Rather than looking at their deficiencies, noted Russian psychologist Lev Vygotsky (1896–1934) advocated determining children's intellectual abilities and then providing opportunities for intellectual growth. He proposed that a child's cognitive development increases through exposure to new information and that learning takes place within the individual's **zone of proximal development**. This zone is the level at which a child can almost, but not completely, grasp a concept or perform a task successfully. As learning takes place, the zone widens. This theory is akin to **scaffolding**, a concept widely accepted within education that takes its name from the construction term for temporary supports placed around a structure to allow work to be completed. Vygotsky viewed learning scaffolding as the support given to children to help them move through progressive levels of learning.

Additionally, Vygotsky believed that children's learning is shaped by the culture and society around them. The more interactions, the greater the learning, as a child moves forward within an ever-expanding zone of proximal development (Feldman, 2014).

Focus student Dylan Todd repeated kindergarten, a situation his teachers and parents decided was best. Dylan's cognitive development was not the reason for repeating the grade level, but rather his social development.

Video Example 2.2 shows Dylan's progress as a kindergarten student and what his parents have to say.

Video Example 2.1: Dylan's Interview

EMOTIONAL DEVELOPMENT. Human experiences are given meaning through emotions. Both our emotions and our responses to them become more complicated with time. Children and adolescents experience a wide array of emotions, including happiness, anxiety, anger, fear, sadness, shame, and pride. For young adolescents, all these emotions—and more—may be experienced in one class period. Teachers need to be able to identify emotions as well as know how and when to respond to them.

Daniel Goleman (2011) proposes that a person's **emotional intelligence quotient (EQ)** may be the best indicator of future success in life. An emotional intelligence quotient involves a set of skills that accompany the expression, evaluation, and regulation of emotions. A high-level emotional intelligence quotient indicates an ability to understand others' as well as one's own feelings, respond appropriately to them, and, in general, get along.

SOCIAL DEVELOPMENT. Learning to get along with others is a process that begins when young children sit next to each other in **parallel play**, agreeably sharing the same space but not communicating. When children begin to share toys and verbally communicate, they are engaged in **associative play**. Progressing to **cooperative play**, children actively coordinate ways to keep the interaction going. When you think about it, these stages of socialization describe how people relate to others regardless of age. Relating to others and thinking about them (and ourselves) is called **social cognition**. Whether we are simply coexisting (parallel play), communicating when necessary (associative play), or actively engaging with others (cooperative play), we are social creatures.

Relationships matter to us; adolescents are, at times, consumed with them. Relationships are part of America's youth culture, much of which revolves around groups that inevitably form as adolescents search for their identities. It's quite easy to see which youth subcultures appear to fit most easily into the traditional school setting—generally it's the "cool kids," the "jocks," and the "preppies." Other students may exhibit different developmental patterns and be labeled "nerds," "stoners," "loners," "goths," "indies," and so on. The names may change, but the subgroups live on. As teachers, our challenge is to connect with all our students and let them know we care about them, regardless of their social affiliations. Helping students develop positive and productive relationships within society is a major aspect of what teachers do.

Application Exercise 2.1: Sherlonda and Her Parents' Interviews

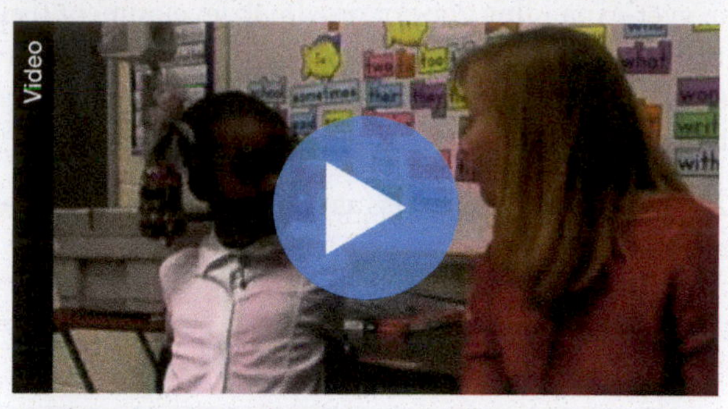

CHARACTER DEVELOPMENT. A discussion of character, or moral, development can easily become value laden, depending on particular religious or ethical beliefs. Even so, certain character traits are considered positive by almost everyone, including honesty, trustworthiness, fairness, caring, and citizenship.

Many packaged programs are available for schools and teachers to use to help students think through moral issues. School districts will often purchase programs with glossy posters and prepared lessons in hopes teachers will use the materials since they don't have to use their time to actually create anything. These programs are seldom effective or long-term (Weissbourd, 2012). However, when a school faculty determines to make an impact on student character development through modeling and emphasis throughout the curriculum, students often benefit.

Character education is one of the nonacademic pieces that are often the key to success in school and in life. To talk about character education in ambiguous ways will likely have no effect on students. However, when we attach traits with definitions and examples, character education may take on a practical slant that will actually be good for students. The Knowledge Is Power Program (KIPP) charter school network of public schools emphasizes seven character strengths: grit, zest, optimism, self-control, gratitude, social intelligence, and curiosity (Kamenetz, 2015). These strengths and others can be talked about each day, in any classroom, and by every teacher.

The phrase **moral compass** refers to a person's ability to judge what is right and wrong and act accordingly. Building a secure, honest, positive, and empathetic moral compass is what character education is about. Helping students develop a moral compass appears to be nonexistent in many school environments (Barnwell, 2016). With increasing pressure to concentrate on content knowledge and skills, some teachers feel that they don't have time to emphasize character development. However, please understand that it's *unavoidable*. We teach who we are; students learn *us*. Every day we impact students' character development by the way we treat others and handle dilemmas. With awareness of our powerful influence and responsibility, we will infuse our curriculum with elements of a moral compass through our example and purposeful discussions of life-affirming philosophy.

Noted developmental psychologist Lawrence Kohlberg contends that people pass through **stages of moral reasoning**, as illustrated in Figure 2.3. Kohlberg's stages are based primarily on observations of males in Western culture and have been criticized for not being more universal or sensitive to gender differences. Even so, carefully considering the stages and thinking about the overall developmental stages of our students will help us understand some of their attitudes and actions.

Information about how people develop in all five of the major areas abounds. A brief summary of generalizations of development within early childhood, elementary, middle, and high school levels is shown in Table 2.1.

Figure 2.3 Kohlberg's stages of moral reasoning

Stage 1: A rule is a rule, and people obey rules to avoid punishment.

Stage 2: Rules are followed or disobeyed based on rewards.

Stage 3: People obey rules because it's what others expect of them.

Stage 4: Society's rules are what's right, and people conform to expectations.

Stage 5: People follow rules out of obligation to what is agreed-upon behavior in their society. Laws and rules can be changed if society sees a compelling need.

Stage 6: People follow rules that agree with universal ethics. If a law doesn't, they feel free to disobey it.

Based on: Adapted from Kohlberg, L. (1984). *The psychology of moral development: Essays on moral development*. San Francisco: Harper & Row.

Table 2.1 Developmental characteristics by level

	Early Childhood	Elementary	Middle	High
PHYSICAL	• Dramatic changes in appearance and abilities • Boundless energy • Rapid brain growth • Healthiest time of life	• Coordination increases • Dexterity improves • Steady growth • Significant differences in size among children	• Onset of puberty • Sudden growth spurts may change appearance • Specialized gross and fine motor skills develop • Some risk-taking behaviors exhibited	• Sexual/reproductive maturity reached • Girls complete growth spurt; boys continue to grow • High level of physical risk-taking activities exhibited
COGNITIVE	• Piaget's preoperational stage • Very intense brain activity • Increased ability to speak with coherence, understand organization and patterns, and learn prerequisites for reading	• Piaget's concrete operational stage • Increased ability to think logically, apply learning strategies, view multiple perspectives, decode phonetically, and read aloud	• Beginning of Piaget's formal operational stage • Often self-absorbed • Increased ability to reason, solve complex problems, and use varied learning strategies	• Capacity for adultlike thought • Increased ability to reason abstractly, make decisions with more realism, and discern which learning strategies are effective
EMOTIONAL	• Self-concept develops and is influenced by family and society • Self-conscious emotions such as guilt and pride develop	• Self-concept becomes more complex and differentiated • Coping skills develop • Emotional ties beyond family develop	• May be emotionally volatile • Drop in self-esteem • Strong emotional ties with friends develop • Frequent mood changes • Begins to establish a sense of identity	• Sense of being invulnerable • May be prone to depression • Seeks independence and a sense of control • Sense of identity develops
SOCIAL	• Relationships with adults centered on direction, care, and protection • First friendships are developed • Types of play change from individual to cooperative • Becomes aware of other people's feelings	• Increasingly concerned with making and keeping friends • Becoming more assertive • Groups are generally same-gender • Capable of empathy • Awareness of social conventions and rules	• Conflicts with parents and other adults likely • Peers become more influential than adults • Popularity, or lack of it, becomes very important • Awareness develops of sexuality and gender-related relationships	• Identity crisis may lead to social dysfunction • Mixed-gender groups • Conformity with others decreases • Desire for self-reliance • Often overwhelmed with demands of relationships
CHARACTER	• Rules are rigid • Begins to understand intentionality • Aggression declines as language develops • Beginning awareness that actions may cause others harm	• Rules come from shared knowledge • Increased awareness of others' problems • Experiences guilt and shame over moral wrongdoing	• Strong sense of fairness • Desire to help those less fortunate • May value social approval over moral conviction	• Understands the need for rules to promote society • Increased concern about fulfilling duty to benefit others

Based on: Feldman (2014); Gallahue and Ozmun (2012); Goleman (2011); McDevitt and Ormrod (2016); Powell (2015).

Check Your Understanding 2.1

2.2 How Are Gender Differences Manifested in Schools?

2.2 Express how gender differences are manifested in schools.

It's common in U.S. households for girls to be encouraged to engage in what are considered gender-appropriate activities, such as playing with dolls and cooking on make-believe stoves; boys are encouraged to play with cars and throw balls. Household chores are often assigned by gender, with girls asked to wash dishes and boys asked to cut the grass. Boys and girls sense very quickly that there are expectations based on gender. **Gender stereotyping** occurs when perceived gender differences are assumed for all people, as in assuming that the play and chores just described are always appropriate for one gender or the other. **Generalizations** about gender differences appropriately begin with phrases such as *tend to.* These two words indicate generalizing, as opposed to stereotyping. **Gender bias** is the favoring of one gender over the other in specific circumstances.

The federal government recognized gender bias in schools in 1972 when Congress passed **Title IX of the Education Amendments Act**, which states, "No person in the United States shall, on the basis of sex, be excluded from participation in, be denied the benefits of, or be subjected to **discrimination** under, any education program or activity receiving Federal financial assistance." Title IX has helped correct inequitable treatment of males and females in schools, most notably in athletic programs involving teams.

Social Aspects of Gender

During early childhood, children are friends with whoever is convenient at day care, in preschool, or in the neighborhood. During the elementary school years, children begin choosing friends of the same gender who have similar interests. With the advent of puberty, friends of the opposite gender begin to be included, and this trend continues through high school.

Boys tend to base their play on activities, whereas girls tend to base their play on talking. In group play, boys tend to play in more adventurous ways, such as acting out battles and physically challenging each other, whereas girls tend to take on roles that are calm, such as playing house or school. Research shows that boys tend to be more aggressive than girls, at least in physical ways. Boys most often show what researchers call **instrumental aggression**, or aggression based on attempting to meet a specific goal, such as grabbing a toy or establishing dominance in an activity. Girls may be as aggressive, but usually in more subtle ways—ways that are more emotional than physical. This type of aggression is known as **relational aggression** and may include name-calling, gossiping, or saying mean things just to be hurtful.

Achievement and Gender

In general, researchers have found that boys tend to set higher goals than girls and attribute their achievement to ability. When they fail, they tend to attribute their failure to lack of effort. In contrast, when girls meet their goals, they tend to attribute their success to effort. When they fail, they tend to attribute their failure to lack of ability (Vermeer, Boekaerts, and Seegers, 2000). This generalization, illustrated in Table 2.2, is significant for teachers to understand. It indicates that one gender may view failure as the result of lack of effort, which is easily corrected. The other gender may view failure as the result of a lack of ability, which is not easily corrected.

Until recently, it was generally held that boys scored higher than girls in almost every area tested. In the last 20 years, however, the academic gender gap has been closing. Society's expectations have also changed. With girls excelling in sports and boys in the arts, for example, it is evident that gender doesn't predict talent or aptitude, physical or cognitive (American Academy of Pediatrics, 2015).

Despite the closing of the gender gap in classrooms, some teachers, consciously or subconsciously, call on boys more often than girls, allow boys to call out answers while scolding girls for doing so, give boys more encouragement to attempt difficult tasks, or generally have higher expectations for boys than for girls. This subtle discrimination is almost always unintentional, but it nevertheless has an effect on classroom participation.

Table 2.2 Boys' and girls' perceived reasons for success and failure

Perceived Reason for	Boys	Girls
Success	High ability	High effort
Failure	Low effort	Low ability

Based on: Vermeer, H. J., Boekaerts, M., & Seegers, G. (2000). Motivational and gender differences: Sixth-grade students' mathematical problem-solving behavior. *Journal of Educational Psychology, 92*, 308–315.

Sexual Diversity

It's important to understand the terminology used to describe variations of sexual diversity. **Sexual orientation** is the sex to which a person is romantically attracted. People who are **heterosexual** are attracted to people of the opposite sex. They are commonly referred to as **straight**. People who are **homosexual** are attracted to people of the same sex. They are commonly referred to as **gay**. Females who are gay are often referred to as **lesbian**. People who are **bisexual** have romantic attractions to both males and females. Most estimates of the percentage of Americans who are gay or lesbian hover around 10%. It is reasonable to assume that these estimates apply to the U.S. student population as well. In the recent past, these seven definitions were enough to describe people's sexual preferences. Enough, that is, when the topic was taboo in polite conversation. Today, however, we know so much more about the complex topic of sexuality, a topic that is part of our everyday lives (American Psychological Association, 2016b [APA]).

Before continuing our discussion, consider that most major medical organizations agree that homosexuality is not a disorder or an illness, and not a choice. These organizations include the American Psychiatric Association, the American Psychological Association, and the American Academy of Pediatrics.

Children and adolescents who are **gender nonconforming** are those who identify with a gender different from their physically evident sex at birth. They may have interests that are more common with the other gender: Boys, for instance, may play with dolls, want to grow their hair long, and wear typically more feminine clothes; girls may play with trucks, ask to have very short hair, and insist on boylike clothes. These statements admittedly contain stereotypes; just because a girl wants to play with trucks and have very short hair does not necessarily imply gender nonconformity. However, when these preferences persist throughout childhood, accompanied by insistence on not "feeling like a boy" or not "feeling like a girl," the child may go through adolescence and then, in adulthood, live as a **transgender** person—a person who lives as his or her self-identified gender rather than the gender that conforms to his or her anatomy at birth. Research also shows that many nonconforming gender children grow up to be gay, lesbian, or bisexual (APA, 2016b).

HEALTH AND SAFETY CONCERNS. **LGBTQ** (lesbian, gay, bisexual, transgender, questioning) individuals are more likely to experience anxiety and depression so severe that 30% of homosexual youth and 50% of transgender youth attempt suicide before the age of 20 (Youth Suicide Prevention Program, 2011). In fact, LGBTQ students in grades 7 through 12 are twice as likely to attempt suicide as their heterosexual peers. Violence, including bullying, physical assault, and victimization, is more likely to be directed at LGBTQ students than heterosexual youth. A national study found that 60% of LGBTQ students are more likely than non-LGBTQ students to feel unsafe, primarily because of their sexual diversity. They are also more likely to experience substance abuse (Centers for Disease Control and Prevention, 2014).

DISCRIMINATION. Discrimination toward those who identify as LGBTQ has become more public in recent years. Only about one third of the states have anti-discrimination laws to protect people based on sexual orientation. Even fewer have laws that protect transgender teens and adults who face discrimination is most aspects of their lives (GLAD, 2016). A 2011 report titled *Injustice at Every Turn* (Grant, Mottet, and Tanis, 2011) surveyed over 6,000 transgender people and found that they regularly experience discrimination in employment, housing, healthcare, and more. People in the LGBTQ community who have lower socioeconomic status and who belong to minority racial groups suffer even more discrimination that white people with secure socioeconomic status. Because of widespread and very vocal discrimination, in May 2016, the U.S Departments of Education and Justice officially advised public schools to permit transgender students to use the bathrooms and locker rooms that align with their gender identity (APA, 2016b).

A person's sexual orientation usually becomes evident in late childhood or early adolescence, whereas gender identity differences may be evident in early childhood. Both are often the subject of moral debate and scientific exploration. Regardless of a teacher's belief system, sexual orientation and gender identity must have nothing to do with how we care for and teach children and adolescents.

The two places that we like to think of as safe and supportive—home and school—are often the very places where the most hurtful slurs and overt rejection of LGBTQ students occur. Although acceptance of sexuality differences remains elusive in some communities, others are stepping up and openly expressing support for students who are gay, lesbian, bisexual, or transgender, or who are questioning their sexuality. One such community is Springfield, Illinois, as we see in this chapter's *The Opinion Page* feature.

GENDER DIVERSITY: IMPLICATIONS FOR TEACHERS. It is undeniable that girls and boys are different in some ways, whether the differences stem from nature, from nurture, or from the inevitable combination. With awareness, we can diminish gender-biased behaviors and attitudes in our schools. The most important contribution we can make toward alleviating gender bias in our classrooms is to treat our students as individuals, realizing that each is unique. In modeling this behavior, we will help promote it among our students.

For all students to thrive in school, they need to feel safe and supported. Our goal in creating **gender equity**, the fair and balanced treatment of boys and girls, including those with sexual diversity, is to provide learning environments where all students are free from limitations that might accompany gender stereotyping of what they can or should accomplish. Addressing the following questions will help foster gender equity in the classroom:

- Do I use examples of males and females in all roles and occupations?
- Do I encourage girls as well as boys to explore science and math?
- Do I encourage boys as well as girls to read for pleasure and to participate in poetry writing and drama?
- Am I careful to include historical contributions of both males and females?
- Do I have a way of assuring that I call on boys and girls in equal numbers during class discussions?
- Do I encourage respect for all students and prohibit bullying, harassment, and homophobic behavior?
- Do I use the gender-specific pronoun that aligns with the gender identity of the student?

The Opinion Page

This Opinion Editorial appeared in the State Journal-Register, *Springfield, Illinois, on August 9, 2012.*

New SHS Student Alliance a Great Idea

by staff writer

For a lot of men, hurling gay epithets or having them tossed at you was an unfortunate rite of passage in junior high and high school. As our culture becomes more sensitive to sexual orientation and bullying in general, such incidents hopefully will be fewer and further between regardless of your gender.

But adults telling teenagers how they ought to treat each other can only go so far toward solving the problem. They are far more likely to respond to their peers' attitudes and behaviors. That's why it was heartening to hear about the effort to form a gay–straight student alliance at Springfield High School.

Madisen Morhet, a 15-year-old SHS student, was surprised at the vitriol of the name-calling when she arrived there as a freshman, particularly the kind directed at openly gay teens or those perceived to be. Morhet decided, along with her friend Emily Abate, to circulate petitions to start a club aimed at providing a support system for those being bullied because of their sexual orientation. "I don't think it's fair for students to come to learn and have to be treated that way," Morhet said.

She got 342 signatures from students and teachers, and principal Mike Grossen will review the petition once he receives it. He should seriously consider the idea. We also commend the Springfield School Board for adding *sexual orientation* to language in its policy manual to protect gay students and staff from discrimination. Board president Susan White said the lack of protection for people based on their sexual orientation was not intentional and had "just been left out." Board vice president Bill Looby asked that it be included. "Clearly, it's something that at least should be addressed in terms of discrimination language and in sending a message that we are tolerant," he said.

Regardless of your moral views regarding someone's sexual orientation, the time has long passed in our country where it is acceptable to pick on, make fun of, or discriminate against someone because of the gender they are attracted to. The change in policy at the district is long overdue and should be made in other school districts' policy manuals if it already hasn't.

This Opinion Page piece approves the formation of a student support group for those whose sexual orientation differs and commends the school board's recognition and condemnation of bullying aimed at students who are questioning or expressing their sexual orientation. Write a well-developed paragraph in response to each of the following questions:

1. Do you agree with the writer's statement that teenagers are more likely to respond to their peers than to adults? If so, what might adults do in schools to provide support for student efforts to right wrongs?
2. Madisen Morhet's reason for circulating the petition lets us know that there's a real problem at SHS. With 342 signatures of those who agree with the formation of a gay–straight alliance, how might these "bystanders," who hear the cruelty but have not stepped up to try to stop it, now express their disapproval of bullying?
3. What statement will the principal make if he approves the formation of this alliance? If he does not approve, how might Morhet and other students proceed to change the culture of Springfield High with regard to acceptance of different sexual orientations?

Point of Reflection 2.1

When you consider generalizations for how boys and girls respond to success and failure, which of the four cells in Table 2.2 ring true for you and why?

Check Your Understanding 2.2

2.3 How Are Cultural and Language Diversity Manifested in Schools?

2.3 Explain how cultural diversity and language diversity are manifested in schools.

Classrooms that were once populated with white students, black students, and perhaps a few students with other cultural identities are now filled with students of many races and

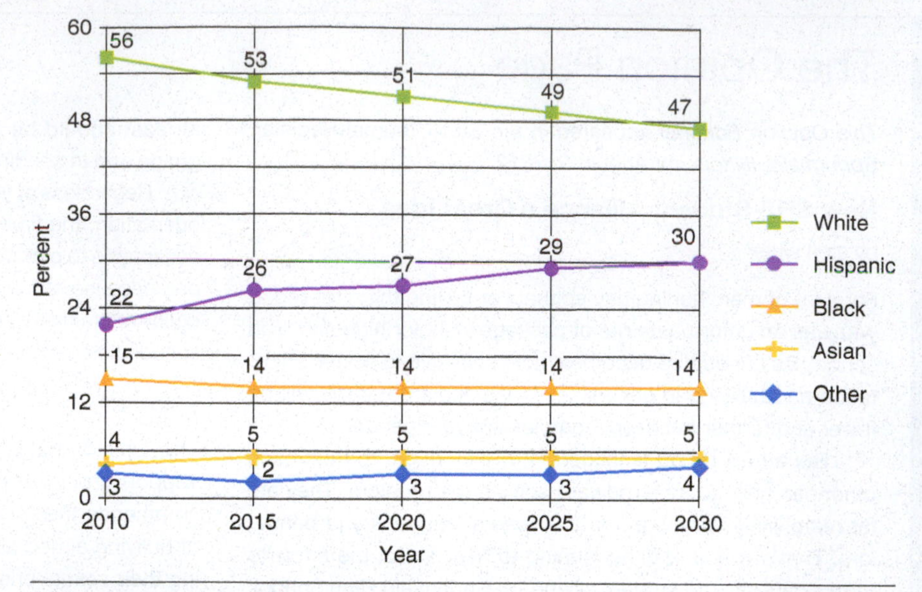

Figure 2.4 Projections of U.S. population, ages 5–19

Based on: US Census Bureau Data

ethnicities. Along with this diversity come more and more students whose first language is not English. Figure 2.4, representing more than 63 million children and adolescents in 2010, shows projections for the changing student population ages 5 to 19. Note the trend of white students comprising diminishing percentages while the black student percentage remains relatively stable and the Hispanic percentage steadily increases. Also increasing are Asian students, found in the 2010 census to have the most rapidly increasing percentage of growth, although still relatively small in total population.

Teachers in the United States are overwhelmingly white; only about 5% are black, and only 5% are Hispanic, Asian, and other races combined. Add this information to the fact that by 2025 less than half of children and adolescents in the United States will be white, and you can see that appreciating, acknowledging, and altering our curriculum and instruction to be responsive to the students in our classrooms will be increasingly challenging. Knowing our students well is imperative.

Cultural Diversity

A widely accepted definition states that **culture** is a "dynamic system of social values, cognitive codes, behavioral standards, world views, and beliefs used to give order and meaning to our own lives as well as the lives of others" (Delgado-Gaitan and Trueba, 1991, p. 3). Culture, and the complex combination of elements that compose it, should have a prominent place in any discussion of American education. (Geneva Gay 2000) tells us that "culture is at the heart of all we do in the name of education" (p. 8).

Gollnick and Chinn (2013) contend that culture has three primary characteristics. First, culture is *learned*. The language, the ways we behave, the social rules, the expectations, the roles—all these aspects of a culture are learned from family and others who influence our daily lives. The second primary characteristic of culture is that it is sustained and strengthened because it is *shared*. To learn how to "be" in a culture requires mentors, those who share the culture and, in doing so, perpetuate the culture. Third, a culture is *adaptive* to its environment. The culture of a large group of people changes, or adapts, over time in response to many variables.

The characteristics that apply to cultures of groups also apply to cultures of individuals. Each individual has a cultural identity.

CULTURAL IDENTITY. The interactions of many factors—including language, religion, gender, socioeconomic status, age, values, beliefs, race, and ethnicity—form a person's **cultural identity**. This identity is adapted throughout a person's life in response to his or her experiences.

The words *race, ethnicity,* and *culture* are often used interchangeably, but they do not have the same meaning. As teachers, we need to understand the meanings of the terms to better navigate the complexities of our students' lives. Although the color of our skin (race) and the country of our origin (ethnicity) may contribute strongly to our cultural identity, neither encompasses the total concept of culture. Let's consider race and ethnicity separately.

RACIAL COMPONENT OF CULTURE. The word **race**, when applied to a group of people, simply categorizes them according to the physical characteristics they have at birth, such as skin color and facial features. Characterization by race is a social, political, economic, and psychological reality (Henze, Mukhopadhyay, and Moses, 2014). Some researchers say there are actually as few as three races, whereas others claim there are more than 300. Not a very precise way to categorize people, is it?

The federal government uses race to categorize people in the United States. For census taking, five races are designated: White, Hispanic, Black, Asian/Pacific Islander, and American Indian/Alaskan native. Most Americans still refer to races other than White as **minorities**. Because race is based solely on physical characteristics, what box would a person check whose mother is Chinese and father is Cuban? According to the 2010 census, over 8 million people indicated they were multiracial by marking more than one of the five races listed.

In Figure 2.4 we saw graphically how children and adolescents ages 5 to 19 comprise the U.S. population, and may in the future. Now, in Table 2.3, you can see the relative percentages of students of specific races in our public schools by region, along with predictions for U.S. K–12 students in 2020 and 2025.

It's interesting to note that the West has the smallest percentage of white people and black people, yet the largest percentage of Hispanics and Asians. The Midwest has the largest population of white people, whereas the South has the largest percentage of black people. No region has as much as 10% Asian/Pacific Islander and no region has more than 2% Native American/Alaskan. When it comes to predictions, notice that the black, Asian, and Native American populations tend to stay stable, while the white population shows a downward trend and the Hispanic population shows a definite

TABLE 2.3 Enrollment and percentage distribution of enrollment in public elementary and secondary schools, by race/ethnicity and region: 2013 and U.S. predictions for 2020, 2025

Region	Enrollment in Thousands													
	Total		White		Black		Hispanic		Asian/Pacific Islander		American Indian/Alaskan Native		Two or More Races	
	#	%	#	%	#	%	#	%	#	%	#	%	#	%
U.S.	**50,045**	**100**	**25,160**	**50**	**7,805**	**16**	**12,452**	**25**	**2,593**	**5**	**523**	**1**	**1,511**	**3**
U.S. Prediction for 2020	**50,477**	**100**	**23,882**	**47**	**7,756**	**15**	**14,142**	**28**	**2,892**	**6**	**463**	**1**	**1,638**	**3**
U.S. Prediction for 2025	**51,420**	**100**	**23,465**	**46**	**7,863**	**15**	**14,677**	**29**	**3,139**	**6**	**439**	**1**	**1,863**	**4**
Northeast	7,961	100	4,593	58	1,158	15	1,492	19	533	0.7	28	.3	1,582	2
Midwest	10,573	100	7,111	67	1,464	14	1,212	12	341	3	87	0.8	358	3
South	19,299	100	8,722	45	4,561	24	4,671	24	614	3	185	1	546	3
West	12,212	100	4,733	39	623	5	5,077	42	1,105	9	224	2	49	4

Based on: U.S. Department of Education, National Center for Education Statistics, Common Core of Data (CCD), "State Nonfiscal Survey of Public Elementary and Secondary Education," 1995-96 through 2013-14; and National Elementary and Secondary Enrollment by Race/Ethnicity Projection Model, 1972 through 2025.

increasing trend. In 2013, about half the students in public K–12 schools were white, and half were minority. In 2025, 46% of the students are predicted to be white, with the rest minority. Although no one race will have as many students as the white race, if the pattern continues, by 2040 the Hispanic population may be about the same or more than the white population in U.S. public schools.

ETHNIC COMPONENT OF CULTURE. This text will use the word **ethnicity** to mean simply an individual's country of origin (Gollnick and Chinn, 2013). Even if families are two, three, or more generations removed from their ancestral country, they may still strongly identify with both the country and the people who share their ethnicity. The category of ethnicity often reveals much more about your students than race. Knowing that a student is Hispanic (race) doesn't necessarily tell you much, but knowing that the child is of Cuban, Chilean, or Mexican heritage may be much more revealing and much more personalized.

CULTURAL PLURALISM. Often the United States is referred to as a *melting pot*, a metaphor that conjures up visions of a big caldron into which all Americans jump, are warmed to the melting point, and stirred with a big spoon that blends us together until we lose unique and characteristic traits. This pretty much describes **assimilation**, the process of bringing persons of all races and ethnicities into the mainstream by having them behave in ways that align with the dominant culture. Some assimilation is inevitable, and even productive, but the notion that to be successful we all must look, think, and act in similar ways is unhealthy in a nation that values individualism and human rights.

Cultural pluralism involves the recognition that the United States is populated by a rich variety of people of varying races and ethnicities—and thus cultures—all with the potential to positively contribute to our common goal of a productive, free society. So what would a school that purposefully promotes cultural pluralism look like? Such a school would teach a curriculum that includes the history and contributions of a variety of cultures; would encourage the expression of cultural traditions in the school setting; would work toward closing achievement gaps that exist among racial, ethnic, and cultural groups; and would assure that no student is excluded from participation in school activities based on race, ethnicity, or any other aspect of culture.

The teachers at Roosevelt High School try to create an environment that promotes cultural pluralism by working to close the achievement gap by getting to know their students and how they learn best. Craig Cleveland talks personally with his students as we see in his conversation with Khammany.

Application Exercise 2.2: Khammany's Interview with Craig Cleveland

CULTURAL DIVERSITY: IMPLICATIONS FOR TEACHERS. Three broad concepts have implications for effective teaching and learning with regard to cultural diversity.

Global Awareness and 21St-Century Skills. One of the themes of the Partnership for 21st Century Skills (P21) is global awareness, not just for inclusion in what we teach students but as a vital component for teachers themselves. **Global awareness** involves understanding the environmental, societal, cultural, political, and economic concepts and issues that affect our world. We must know what's happening on our planet and understand—as well as respect—the fact that there are many worldviews and perspectives among people (Partnership for 21st Century Skills, 2014). Not being globally aware is a disservice to our students.

Multicultural Education. The response of many U.S. educators to the fast-paced growth of diversity is **multicultural education**, an approach that celebrates diversity and promotes equitable educational opportunities. James Banks (2004), an expert in the field, states that multicultural education has several goals, including

- The creation of equal opportunities for students of all cultures
- The development of knowledge, attitudes, and skills needed to function successfully in a diverse society
- The promotion of communication and interaction among groups that work for the common good

Unfortunately, many teachers make inadequate attempts to include multicultural education simply by observing February as Black History Month or including a social studies unit on Native Americans. Chances are these lessons have little impact on the day-to-day lives of students.

Some people actually oppose any attempt to address cultural diversity, fearing that multicultural education will divert attention from more important curriculum or weaken the sense of continuity and tradition in a school. According to Banks (2004), those who promote the inclusion of multicultural education neither approve of shallow inclusion of concepts nor intend for it to in any way weaken U.S. schools.

Cultural Responsiveness. To make multicultural education a reality in the classroom requires culturally responsive teaching. A **culturally responsive** teacher is sensitive to diversity and regularly asks questions such as these:

- Do I know the culture of each of my students beyond his or her obvious race and ethnicity?
- In what ways might I help my students see their similarities as clearly as their differences?
- How can I help validate the cultures represented in my classroom?
- How can I promote communication among all students?
- How can I assure equal opportunities for learning for all students?

Language Diversity

We have looked at race and ethnicity as major contributors to our cultural identity. These two factors are largely based on nature and can't be changed. Our language, however, is rooted in nurture and can be changed. **Language** is our primary means of communication; through it, we transmit knowledge. Assimilation in terms of language, with all students becoming proficient in English, has benefits because most public school classrooms are conducted in English. Few would argue with the notion that communicating proficiently in English is a major factor for academic success in the United States. Lack of English proficiency may be a major barrier to accessing the benefits or services available and understanding and exercising rights and responsibilities. Title VI Prohibition Against National Origin Discrimination Affecting Limited English Proficient Persons was added in 2004 to the Civil Rights Act of 1964 to prevent discrimination and to encourage resource development to help students and others become proficient in English. The dilemma, however, is how to ensure this for all students.

Some immigrants are already English proficient, but for most, English is not their first language. Some immigrant students arrive in the United States with strong records of academic achievement in their native languages, but many do not. Some students may have mastered conversational English in that they can speak and understand it, but they lack the ability to use English to keep up with grade-level coursework. School settings require **Standard English**, a composite of the language spoken by educated middle-class people in the United States. There are two forms of Standard English: one that's spoken in our everyday lives, and a more formal version that is written and considered grammatically correct.

But even within the English language there are variations. In the United States there are at least 11 regional **dialects**, or deviations from standard language rules used by identifiable groups of people. You may have been the brunt of jokes when you traveled outside your region, or you may have poked fun at someone in your college dorm who spoke with a regional dialect unlike your own. Black English, sometimes referred to as **Ebonics**, is one of the best known and most controversial dialects in the United States. In most school settings, Black English, along with Hawaiian Pidgin and Appalachian English, are associated with lower levels of both intelligence and social class (Gollnick and Chinn, 2013).

ENGLISH LEARNERS. Students with limited English proficiency may speak and understand some English but not enough to be successful without additional assistance in classes taught in English. Students who are not proficient English speakers are referred to as **English learners (ELs)** or **English language learners (ELLs)**. The five most frequently spoken non-English languages in the United States are Spanish, French, Chinese, Vietnamese, and Tagalog, a language spoken by many Filipinos (U.S. Census Bureau, 2012).

We serve English learners through TESOL, ESOL, ESL, ENL, SEI, and any number of bilingual education program configurations whose acronyms seem to multiply on a regular basis. Confused? If your answer is "yes," you are more than justified. The dilemma faced by students who do not speak English well enough to learn at adequate levels in a timely fashion in U.S. schools is both recent and rapidly growing. While organizations such as Teachers of English to Speakers of Other Languages (TESOL) and the National Association for Bilingual Education (NABE) continue to research effective ways to best serve this population, most teachers are not specifically prepared to do so. In addition, the vocabulary pertaining to this situation hasn't solidified, often with overlapping and indistinct definitions.

Whether in the mall or filling out a job application, the value of fluency in English is obvious to students who are learning English. Children in immigrant families often believe that continuing to speak their native language will hurt them in school settings, where often language is the most obvious characteristic that sets them apart. Another phrase used to refer to students whose native language is other than English, regardless of their current level of English proficiency, is **language minority students**. Hector, an EL student in Chris Roberts's class, has the responsibility to help family members learn English.

Video Example 2.2 shows you more about Hector and his family.

Video Example 2.2: Hector's and His Mom's Interview

As Craig Cleveland looks around his classroom at Roosevelt High School in Fresno, California, while his second-period U.S. History students are making their way to their seats, he sees 32 adolescents—7 sophomores, 21 juniors, and 4 seniors. The class includes 6 native English speakers, 15 native Spanish speakers, and 11 students who are Hmong and speak various dialects of Chinese, mirroring the ethnic mix at Roosevelt High School. Although Craig is fluent in Spanish and that's very helpful, many of his students designated as ELs are Asian. Besides their cultural and ethnicity diversity, all 32 students qualify for free or reduced-price meals. Craig knows that students from low-income families struggle more to achieve academically. When measured by standardized tests with "basic" as average, over half are considered "below basic" or "far below basic" in both English language arts and math. In addition, 19 of the 32 have impairments of some kind that are recognized by the school and require special accommodations by teachers. Craig's challenge today is to pique every student's interest in the question, "Is separate ever really equal?" To do this, Craig must find ways to define the issues, present background information, make it relevant to his heterogeneous class, and then facilitate an activity that engages every student.

The students in Craig's class are alike in many ways: They are all adolescents, most are from low-income homes in the same geographic area, and they have all gone through similar developmental stages to become 15-, 16-, 17-, and 18-year-olds. They also have many differences: Some are male, and some are female; some were born in the United States, whereas others are recent immigrants; some are Catholic, some are Protestant, and some are Buddhist. When viewed as a group, Craig's students are a wonderful but challenging example of diversity in many American classrooms. To meet this challenge head on, Craig involves all his students by

- Giving them as many curricular and instructional choices as possible
- Having them talk to each other in their native languages about class content
- Using role-play to reinforce concepts
- Reading picture books that make concepts more transparent
- Using written materials in students' native languages when available

Video Example 2.3 shows Craig using instructional methods specifically designed for English learners.

Video Example 2.3: Craig's Diverse Classes

You don't have to be in an urban area to have English learners in your classroom. One of our focus schools, Summit Primary, in Summit Station, Ohio, has gone from a mostly white, all English-speaking school to one with the 17 languages listed in Figure 2.5. Summit Station, considered rural just a decade or so ago, is now more like a suburb of the urban city of Columbus.

SERVICES ADDRESSING ENGLISH LEARNERS. Regardless of the method used to address the needs of English learners, teachers can't limit services to language alone. The National Board for Professional Teaching Standards (2013) states that the services should include:

- Teaching students about their new school, community, and country
- Teaching students to inquire about ways to contribute to their new school, community, and country
- Helping students collaborate with people from a variety of backgrounds and perspectives
- Encouraging students to advocate for themselves and their families

The acronyms mentioned earlier indicate the variety of ways we attempt to meet the needs of English language learners. Let's look briefly at three approaches to delivering EL services to students: bilingual education, English as a second language (ESL), and structured English immersion (SEI).

BILINGUAL EDUCATION. One of the primary responses of public education to the needs of English language learners is **bilingual education**, the delivery of instruction in two languages. Attempts are made to preserve native language abilities as students acquire skills in English. Perhaps the greatest barrier to bilingual education programs is the lack of teachers who speak both English and another language fluently. In addition

Figure 2.5 Native languages at Summit Primary School, Ohio

English	Russian	French
Somali	Macedonian	Creole
Ohomo	Serbo-Croatian	Korean
Bosnian/Albanian	Spanish	Japanese
Sierra Leone/Creole	German	Tagalog/Filipino
Chinese/Cantonese	Croatian	

to speaking two languages fluently, however, teachers in bilingual programs must also be qualified to teach math, science, social studies, reading, writing, and other subjects. Our focus teacher Angelica Reynosa at Roosevelt High School fits this description.

Application Exercise 2.3: Angelica's lesson

ENGLISH AS A SECOND LANGUAGE. **English as a second language (ESL)** programs may also be called **English as a new language (ENL)** programs. Students receive individualized assistance once or twice a week for about an hour or so each session. Unlike bilingual education, ESL/ENL services are delivered only in English. With ESL/ENL, little or no emphasis is placed on preserving native language or culture, and ESL/ENL teachers do not need to speak another language. ESL/ENL programs are far less expensive than bilingual programs for school districts to implement if they have limited numbers of students to serve.

STRUCTURED ENGLISH IMMERSION. In response to observations that teachers may be teaching *in* English, but possibly not *teaching* English itself, **structured English immersion (SEI)** was developed. This approach includes significant amounts of the school day dedicated to the explicit teaching of the English language, including other content to support instruction, but not as the primary focus. In SEI, students and teachers speak, read, and write in English. Teachers treat English as a foreign language and apply instructional methods used by teachers of foreign languages. Students are expected to transition out of SEI programs on a specified timetable with the skills necessary to be successful in English-only classes. Structured English immersion may be the logical solution, or partial solution, to helping groups of students who speak many different languages become proficient in English.

Some states, such as California, Arizona, and Massachusetts, have laws requiring the development of SEI programs to replace many of the existing bilingual programs.

Figure 2.6 Structured English immersion sample schedule

Emphasis/Activity	Time Allotted
Pronunciation and listening skills	20 minutes
Vocabulary	30 minutes
Verb tense instruction	20 minutes
Sentence structure	20 minutes
Integrated grammar skills application	20 minutes
English reading and writing	60 minutes
Math (specially designed academic instruction in English)	40 minutes
Science, social science, P.E.	40 minutes

Based on: Clark, C. (2009). The case for structured English immersion. *Educational Leadership, 66*(7), 45.

Sara Davis Powell

Khammany from Laos and Guillermo from Mexico are part of the rich fabric of diversity at Roosevelt High School in Fresno, California.

States and districts are creating SEI programs, given their student populations and resources available. Figure 2.6 is a sample schedule for students in an elementary SEI program. Notice that 40 minutes is allotted to math, with all other subjects taught in a total of 40 minutes.

LANGUAGE DIVERSITY: IMPLICATIONS FOR TEACHERS. Language diversity presents a major challenge for educators in the United States. As we welcome increasing numbers of English language learners to U.S. schools, both teaching and learning are affected. Here are some questions to keep in mind as you consider teaching in a language-diverse classroom:

- How can I make my classroom an academically, emotionally, and socially safe place for students who are English learners?
- How can I include the cultures of the English learners who are in my classroom?
- What resources will I need to communicate subject-area concepts to all students?
- How will I communicate with families who are English learners?
- What community services might benefit my English learners and their families?

The influx of diverse cultures with varied languages can be a source of richness for the United States rather than a phenomenon that is feared or avoided. Striking a balance between preserving native cultures and helping students adjust to life in a basically English-speaking environment is a worthy goal. Focus student Hugo Martinez struggles to master English.

Video Example 2.4 focuses on teacher Angelica Reynosa and is followed by an interview with Hugo's parents.

Video Example 2.4: Hugo's Interview

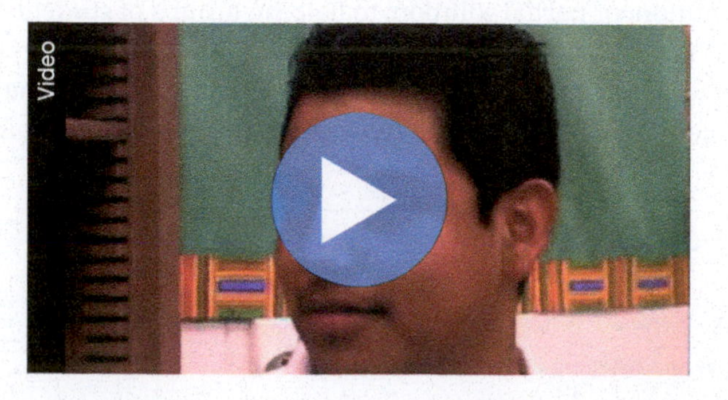

Check Your Understanding 2.3

2.4 What Is the Impact on Students of Family Structure, Religion, and Socioeconomic Status?

2.4 Identify the impact on students of family structure, religion, and socioeconomic status.

Students come to school wrapped in influences of family, religion, and socioeconomic status. They are whole people with complex factors that impact their attitudes toward, and achievement in, school. The more we understand about these influences, the better able we are to meet student needs.

Family Diversity

The 1970s, *The Brady Bunch* television situation comedy introduced many Americans to the concept of the blended family. Today, blended families come in a variety of configurations. Many students live with people other than their biological parents. With the divorce rate over 50%, single-parent homes have increased more than 300% since 1980. In 2014, 34% of K–12 students lived in single-parent homes, with Mississippi at 45% and Utah at 19% representing the range of state percentages. Children living in single-parent homes have a poverty rate of 36% compared to children in two-parent homes that have a poverty rate of 8%, making the children of single parents more than four times as likely to struggle economically (National Kids Count Program, 2015).

The increasing mobility of U.S. families also adds to the instability of students' home lives. Consider, for example, the influx of both documented (legal) immigrant families and undocumented (illegal) immigrant families. These families may move two to four times a year, with children changing schools, enrolling and withdrawing from the same school multiple times, or simply not going to school. Not only is all this mobility potentially harmful for students, but it can also wreak havoc on classroom teaching and learning.

FAMILY DIVERSITY: IMPLICATIONS FOR TEACHERS. Knowing with whom our students live can give teachers insight into behavior and achievement patterns. Ideally, families are our partners in educating children and adolescents. If this is going to be a reality in classrooms, our tactics for gaining and maintaining family support must be sensitive and flexible. Here are some questions to consider for your classroom:

- How can I restructure volunteer opportunities to include evenings and weekends?
- Are options available for child care that might lead to greater parental participation?
- Can the school provide easily accessible transportation to boost family involvement?
- Can I be more inclusive by practicing simple tactics such as addressing correspondence with "Dear family" rather than "Dear parents"?

Religious Diversity

Religion and faith have considerable daily influence on many of our lives. Over 230 million people, or about 77% of people in the United States, affiliate with a religious group. The rest say they have no affiliation, including atheists (3%) and agnostics (4%). Of those who say they have a religious affiliation, over 92% align with Christianity (Protestants, Catholics, Mormons, and more). About 2% are Jewish and about 1% align with each of Islam, Hinduism, and Buddhism, with the remaining aligned with lesser-known religious faiths and belief systems (Pew Forum, 2016). Freedom to practice a religion, or not, is central to our common political, social, and cultural heritage of the United States.

Private schools are often established to cater to and promote a particular religion. Public schools are open to all, and are obligated to serve all. Although separation of church and state is the official stance, religion has considerable influence on what we do in schools. Most of the issues teachers face in terms of religious diversity can be dealt with positively simply through awareness.

RELIGIOUS DIVERSITY: IMPLICATIONS FOR TEACHERS. Our responses to religious diversity must be within legal bounds and delivered with sensitivity. Here are some questions classroom teachers should consider concerning religious diversity:

- How do I make sure tolerance is modeled in my classroom?
- How can I guard against being offensive to students of varying faiths?
- How should holidays be observed?
- How can I best respond to the community in which I live and teach?

The last question will be very important to you. Although singing "Jesus Loves Me" at nap time in a kindergarten in the South might be not only tolerated, but encouraged, singing the same song in a kindergarten in suburban Denver might be seen as offensive and grounds for dismissal.

Socioeconomic Diversity

One in five U.S. school-age children lived in poverty in 2016 (National Kids Count Program, 2015). This means almost 16 million students are part of an area of diversity that not only transcends differences in gender, culture, language, family, and religion but also has widespread impact on success in school. Although **socioeconomic status (SES)** involves more than income level, the major determinant of SES is how much money a family makes. The gap between the haves and the have-nots is wider in the United States than in most other industrialized nations. We might call this a **privilege gap**. The government has determined the maximum pretax income a family may have to be considered living in poverty. Table 2.4 provides an overview of the poverty threshold levels for single- and two-parent incomes with one to five children.

Using the table, notice that a family of four—two parents and two children—that earns less than $24,036 a year is considered to be in poverty. A commonly used measure of a school's socioeconomic status is the percentage of students who qualify for free meals. A student is entitled to free meals if the family's income is below 130 percent of the annual income poverty-level guideline. So the two children in our example family of four would still qualify if the family makes less than 130% of $24,036, or $31,246. Students with family incomes below 185 percent of the annual income poverty level guideline are eligible for a reduced-price lunch. Again using our example family, that's $42,200. The National School Lunch Program provided over 31 million students with free or reduced-price lunches at a cost of over $11 billion in the 2011–12 school year (U.S. Department of Agriculture, 2013).

Table 2.4 Maximum income to be designated in poverty, 2015

	Children in Home				
Adults	**1**	**2**	**3**	**4**	**5**
1	$16,337	$19,096	$24,120	$27,853	$31,078
2	$19,078	$24,036	$28,286	$31,670	$35,473

Based on: U.S. Census Bureau, Poverty Thresholds for 2016.

CHALLENGES OF LOW SOCIOECONOMIC STATUS. The federal government acknowledges there are unique challenges in teaching students living in low-income settings. Title I funding, which is additional money given to public schools when more than 40% of the students qualify for free or reduced-price meals, is the government's attempt to make school experiences more equitable (U.S. Department of Education, 2015). These funds are intended to help educators better meet the needs of students in low-income settings who often are students with histories of low achievement.

Following are some important findings published by the Annie E. Casey Foundation as part of the *Kids Count Data Book (2016)*. We will delve more deeply into the concept of socioeconomic status in Chapter 9.

- Nationally, 21 percent of children (15 million) lived in families with incomes below the poverty line in 2015.
- The rate of child poverty for 2015 ranged from a low of 11 percent in New Hampshire, to a high of 31 percent in Mississippi.
- The child poverty rate among African Americans was 36 percent, among Hispanics was 31 percent, and among non-Hispanic whites was 12 percent in 2015.

SOCIOECONOMIC STATUS DIVERSITY: IMPLICATIONS FOR TEACHERS. The devastation of living in poverty is deeper than most teachers will ever completely understand. Even so, we have the privilege of interacting with children and adolescents who desperately need our care and support. We are ideally positioned to make meaningful differences in their lives. Can we solve their issue of poverty? Of course not. Can we impact their day-to-day lives in school and their futures? Absolutely yes.

Here are some questions to ask yourself. They are applicable to all children and adolescents, but answering them in positive ways will have a more profound effect on students living in poverty. The questions all begin with "Do I" because taking care of vulnerable children and students is a very personal responsibility.

- Do I expose my students to the wider world outside the school, including community resources and activities, local and regional attractions, and the many wonders of our country and the world through actual experiences and virtual means?
- Do I listen carefully to my students and guide them to available resources and services for assistance when needed?
- Do I provide books, magazines, and technology opportunities during the school day so everyone has access?
- Do I understand that students may behave in class according to the "rules" they live during nonschool hours and do my best to help them develop acceptable behavior to keep them in school, able to function within school norms?
- Do I have a supply of basic materials for my students to use without embarrassment?

Point of Reflection 2.2

How has your own socioeconomic status affected your school experiences? Were you aware of socioeconomic differences among your classmates? Did this affect how you viewed your own circumstances or the circumstances of other students?

Check Your Understanding 2.4

2.5 How Are Learning Differences Manifested in Schools?

2.5 Summarize how learning differences are manifested in schools.

The revered **intelligence quotient (IQ)** affixes a number to intelligence that—in one single freeze-frame—labels us for life. Scores on IQ tests may provide useful information, but they are no longer considered the final answer in determining a child's intellectual capacity. Most educators have moved beyond the notion that intelligence is a fixed attribute. Researchers now believe that **intelligence**—a capacity for knowing and learning—can change and is manifested in various ways, as illustrated in Figure 2.7. Too often, however, a single number or a single test determines a student's class placement and learning expectations.

Multiple Intelligences Theory

Decades ago, Harvard psychologist Howard Gardner added an *s* to the word *intelligence* and revolutionized how we view the concept. Gardner theorized that intelligence is multidimensional and that our individual brains work in ways that give each of us our own personal intelligences. He called this **multiple intelligences (MI) theory**. The nine designated intelligences proposed by Gardner are not meant as a complete list and there is little research to validate them. Their value lies in the implication that we learn differently. Intelligences can be activated and connected in very individual ways. Figure 2.8 illustrates the nine intelligences.

Learning Preferences

We each have preferences for how we like to learn, or how we perceive we learn best. Until recently, theories persisted that we each have something labeled as a "learning style," or a way in which we naturally learn best. The most recent research tells us that

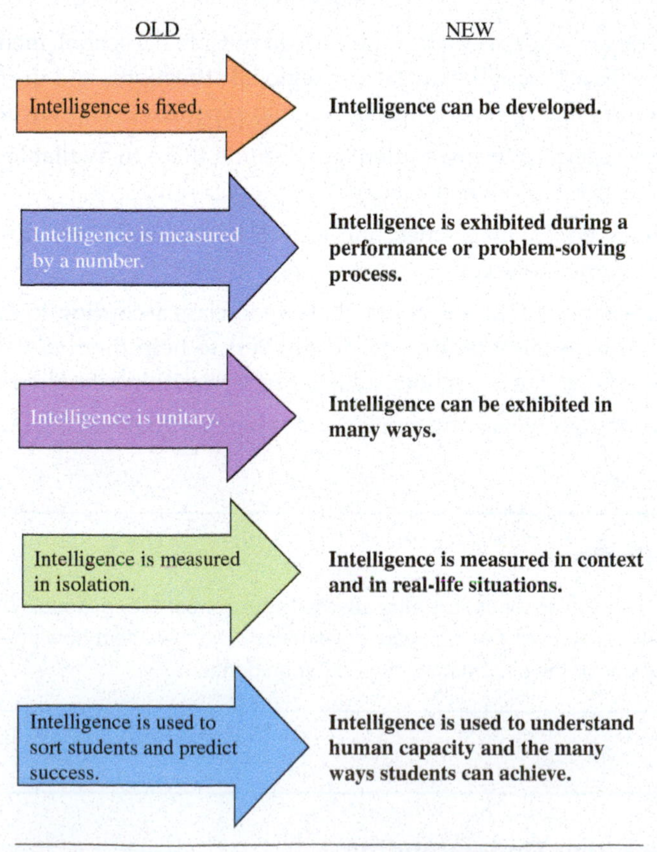

Figure 2.7 How our views of intelligence have changed

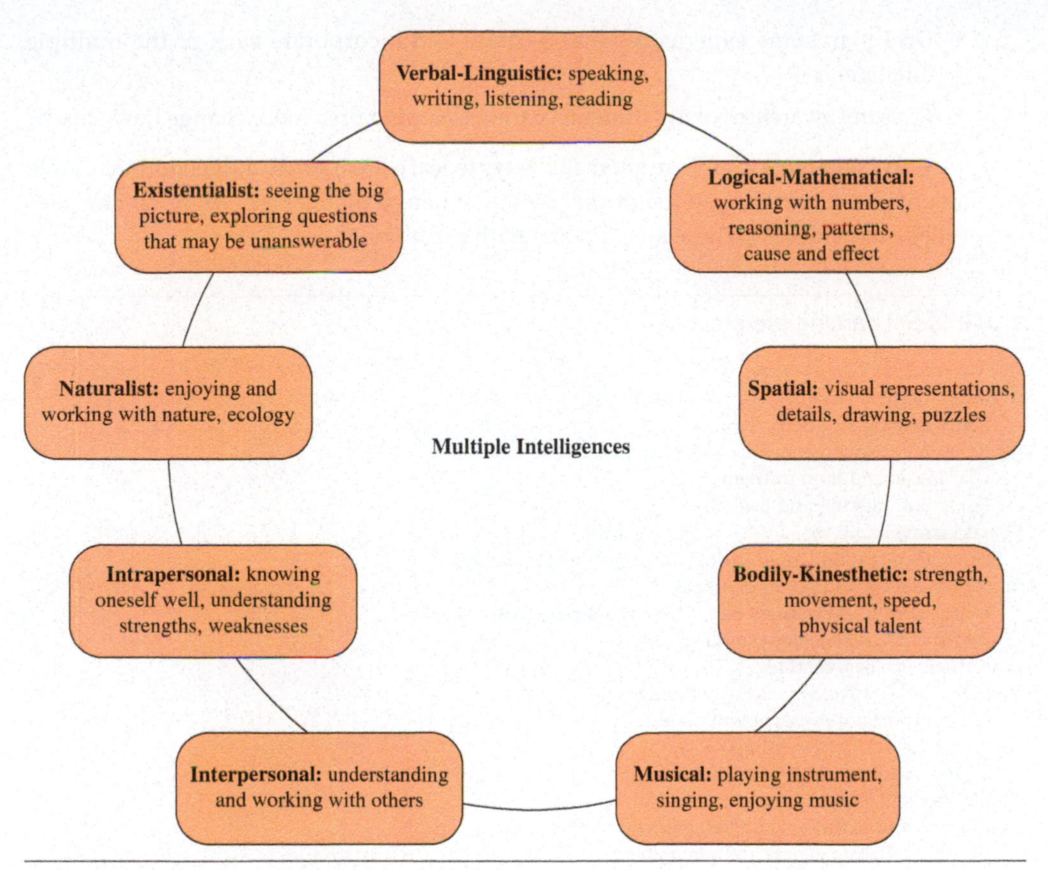

Figure 2.8 Multiple intelligences

even though we might have preferences, learning styles are more a "neuromyth" than fact (Noonoo, 2017). Researchers now believe that there is no credible evidence that teaching to learning styles has merit (Reiner and Willingham, 2014).

This doesn't mean we ignore what the theory of learning styles was based on, what some refer to as **learning modalities**, or learning preferences. We use all four learning modalities in the process of learning, but each individual may tend to favor one or two over the others. The four modalities are: auditory (hearing), visual (seeing), tactile (touching), and kinesthetic (moving). Traditional classrooms rely most heavily on auditory and visual modalities, such as lectures and demonstrations, especially in the upper grades, whereas active learning techniques such as hands-on manipulatives and group work activate tactile and kinesthetic modalities and may engage some students more effectively. The primary message of the most recent research is that we should include all four modalities regularly in our classroom instruction without the obligation to determine individual learning preferences and tailoring instruction to specific students based on the determination. By varying instructional strategies, we are aligning with **Universal Design for Learning (UDL)**, an approach that helps all students learn. The UDL approach promotes the expansion of how students learn, rather than concentrating on their preferences, by including visual, auditory, tactile, and kinesthetic experiences in our lessons. Figure 2.9 helps us understand what hearing, seeing, touching, and moving preferences may look like in classrooms.

DIFFERENCES IN HOW WE LEARN: IMPLICATIONS FOR TEACHERS. Incorporating what we know about multiple intelligences and learning styles into our plans for instruction helps meet the learning needs of more students. Here are some questions to keep in mind when considering these challenges:

- Do I view the students in my classroom as a collection of individuals, each with unique ways of being smart?
- Do I continually seek to understand the ways in which my students learn best?

- Do I plan some experiences that address and incorporate each of the multiple intelligences?
- Does my awareness of my students' various learning preference change how I teach?

Acknowledging that there are many ways to learn leads us to understand that some students have particular difficulties learning, whereas others learn more quickly and perhaps more deeply. These are students with exceptionalities.

Figure 2.9 Learning preferences

Auditory learners tend to. . .
 Enjoy reading and being read to.
 Be able to explain concepts and scenarios verbally.
 Like music and hum to themselves.
 Enjoy both talking and listening.
Visual learners tend to. . .
 Have good spelling, note-taking, and organizational skills.
 Notice details and prefer neatness.
 Learn more if illustrations and charts accompany reading.
 Prefer quiet, serene surroundings.
Kinesthetic learners tend to. . .
 Be demonstrative, animated, and outgoing.
 Enjoy physical movement and manipulatives.
 Be willing to try new things.
 Be messy in habits and surroundings.
Tactile learners tend to. . .
 Prefer manipulatives when being introduced to a topic.
 Literally translate events and phenomena.
 Tolerate clutter.
 Be artistic in nature.

Based on: *Introduction to Middle School* (3rd ed., p. 62), by S. D. Powell, 2015. Boston: Allyn & Bacon. Copyright 2015.

Point of Reflection 2.3

With which of Gardner's intelligences do you most closely align? Did your teachers accommodate your particular ways of being smart? Describe how the learning modalities affect how you learn best. How do you think you might strengthen the modality you use least?

Check Your Understanding 2.5

2.6 Who Are Students with Exceptionalities and How Do We Serve Them?

2.6 Define students with exceptionalities and how we serve them in schools.

Learners with abilities or disabilities that set them apart from other learners are often referred to as **students with exceptionalities**. Heward (2013) tells us that exceptional children

> differ from the norm (either below or above) to such an extent that they require an individualized program of special education and related services to fully benefit from education . . . . Thus, *exceptional children* . . . refers to children with learning and/or behavior problems, children with physical disabilities or sensory

impairments, and children with superior intellectual abilities and/or special talents. (p. 7)

Some exceptionalities are the result of nature; others may be the result of injury or illness, aspects of nurture. Two factors are especially important when we consider the education of students with exceptionalities:

- Identification: Deciding who has what exceptionality and to what degree
- Intervention: Determining how best to meet his or her educational needs

Students with Disabilities

The categories of student exceptionalities considered to be disabilities, along with the percentage of all disabilities that they represent, are shown in Table 2.5. Considering all the categories, about 12% of American students, or almost 6,000,000, receive **special education services**, which are services provided by schools to help students function and learn in ways optimal to the individual.

Many disabilities, especially those that impair daily functioning such as orthopedic disabilities and hearing, sight, and disease-related impairments, are diagnosed before children enter school. However, disabilities that are more subtle, perhaps intellectual or emotional, are often officially identified through a team of educators equipped with expertise and diagnostic tools.

A designation of **learning disabled (LD)**—accounting for almost 40% the students receiving special education services—includes a general category of students with disorders involving problems understanding or using language that results in significant differences between learning potential and achievement (Turnbull, Turnbull, Wehmeyer, and Shogren, 2016). Misdiagnosis or the absence of a diagnosis is problematic. Many students develop coping strategies that mask their learning problems for years, and very possibly for life. Students with learning disabilities may

- Have difficulties with word recognition and text comprehension
- Feel overwhelmed by the idea of getting started
- Struggle to organize and use the mechanics of writing
- Have difficulty differentiating numbers or copying shapes
- Have difficulty identifying, using, and monitoring problem-solving strategies (Turnbull et al., 2016)

Table 2.5 Categories of disabilities and percentages of students served, 2013

Disability	Percentage of Total Students Receiving Special Services
Learning disabilities	38.6
Speech or language impairments	19.1
Other health impairments	16.9
Intellectual disability	7.3
Emotional disturbance	6.2
Autism	8.4
Multiple disabilities	2.5
Developmental delay	2.4
Hearing impairments	1.2
Orthopedic impairments	0.9
Visual impairments	0.4
Traumatic brain injury	0.4
Deaf, blindness	< 0.1

Based on: University of New Hampshire. (2015). Annual disability statistics compendium. Retrieved July 22, 2016, from http://disabilitycompendium.org/statistics/special-education

Intervention for students with learning disabilities may include time each day with a special education teacher, often referred to as a **resource teacher**, who will help them develop strategies for school success.

Identification of **attention deficit hyperactivity disorder (ADHD)** may be as problematic as identification of learning disabilities. The American Psychological Association (APA) (2016) defines ADHD as a "behavioral condition that makes focusing on everyday requests and routines challenging. People with ADHD typically have trouble getting organized, staying focused, making realistic plans and thinking before acting. They may be fidgety, noisy and unable to adapt to changing situations. Children with ADHD can be defiant, socially inept or aggressive."

Students with ADHD demonstrate three defining characteristics: inattention, hyperactivity, and impulsivity. The APA estimates that 3 to 7% of students in an average class have ADHD, which falls within the "Other health impairments" category of Table 2.5. The intervention for students with ADHD may include specific strategies to help modify behavior or medication. These students receive services through special education only if they qualify through impairments other than ADHD (Turnbull et al., 2016).

In 2016, the U.S. Department of Education set new guidelines for services for students diagnosed with ADHD (Resmovits, 2016). They state that students with ADHD and those they suspect may have the ADHD are entitled to a diagnosis and a **504 plan**. This plan is developed by a school to ensure that a child who has a disability identified under the law and is attending an elementary or secondary educational institution receives accommodations that will ensure her or his academic success and access to the learning environment. A 504 plan is not as elaborate or complex as an individualized educational program that you will read about later, but it is a safeguard for students with disabilities that do not qualify them for special education services.

Autism, or **autism spectrum disorder (ASD)**, is a disability that is increasing at an alarming rate. According to the National Institutes of Health (2013), ASD is "a complex developmental disorder that affects how a person behaves, interacts with others, communicates, and learns." **Asperger syndrome**, once a stand-alone diagnosis, is now one of several subtypes of the single diagnosis of autism. People with autism often have medical problems such as allergies, chronic digestive disorders, limited gross and fine motor skills, seizures, sleep problems, and low pain threshold (Autism Society, 2016).

There are no medical tests for diagnosis of ASD, only observation by parents, educators, psychologists, and doctors. Specially trained individuals perform autism-specific evaluations. Autism spectrum disorder is often diagnosed between the ages of 18 and 24 months, using a series of "red flags" to determine the likelihood of the disorder, including:

- No big smiles or other warm, joyful expressions by age 6 months or thereafter
- No back-and-forth sharing of sounds, smiles, or other facial expressions by age 9 months
- No babbling by age 12 months
- No back-and-forth gestures such as pointing, showing, reaching or waving by age 12 months
- No words by age 16 months
- No meaningful, two-word phrases (not including imitating or repeating) by age 24 months
- Any loss of speech, babbling, or social skills at any age (Autism Speaks, 2016)

If an early diagnosis isn't made, students begin school where some of the symptoms begin to surface because they are rooted in social issues involving interactions and communication. A school evaluation should be conducted by a multidisciplinary team, including a classroom teacher and a specialist in the area of the suspected disability. If ASD is suspected, the child will also be screened for health issues, including vision, hearing, communication abilities, motor skills, and social/emotional issues. Diagnosis of autism spectrum disorder should become the basis for an individualized educational program (IEP) for the child.

Legal Support for Students with Disabilities

Until recently, students with disabilities were often isolated in a room at the end of a hallway—out of sight, out of mind—unless they happened to be seen walking as a group or boarding one of those short buses designed to hold that "special" group of kids. Prior to 1975, most students with disabilities, designated as *special education students,* weren't even in the same facilities as other students; there were no provisions for them to attend public schools. In 1975, the landmark legislation **Public Law 94-142 (PL 94-142)** changed all that.

Today, special education is viewed as a service rather than a place to send children. The **Education for All Handicapped Children Act (PL 94-142)** opened all public schools to students with disabilities and mandated that students with disabilities be given the opportunity to benefit from special education services at no cost to their families. The law established six governing principles, listed in Figure 2.10, that apply to the education of students with disabilities.

In 1990, PL 94-142 was amended and renamed the **Individuals with Disabilities Education Act (IDEA)**. Students with autism and traumatic brain injury were added to those entitled to services under PL 94-142. A change in attitude and philosophy became evident in the law when the language changed from "disabled individuals" to "individuals with disabilities." The person comes first, with the disability secondary. In 2004, IDEA was reauthorized as the **Individuals with Disabilities Education Improvement Act**. This latest reauthorization is the most comprehensive yet, including all U.S. laws affecting children with disabilities in one statute.

Assistive Technology

The Technology-Related Assistance to Individuals with Disabilities Act of 1988 authorized funding for **assistive technology** devices and services. These devices and services reduce the impact of disabilities by helping them communicate, increasing their mobility, and aiding in multiple ways that enhance their capacity to learn. The range of assistive technology includes wheelchairs, voice-activated and touch-screen word

Figure 2.10 Six principles governing the education of students with disabilities

1. **Zero reject**: A rule against excluding any student.
2. **Nondiscriminatory evaluation**: Requires schools to evaluate students fairly to determine if they have a disability and, if so, what kind and how extensive.
3. **Appropriate education**: Requires schools to provide individualized education programs for each student based on evaluation and augmented by related services and supplementary aids and services.
4. **Least restrictive environment**: Requires schools to educate students with disabilities alongside students without disabilities to the maximum extent appropriate for the students with disabilities.
5. **Procedural due process**: Provides safeguards for students against schools' actions, including a right to sue in court.
6. **Parental and student participation**: Requires schools to collaborate with parents and adolescent students in designing and carrying out special education programs.

Based on: Turnbull, R., Turnbull, A., Wehmeyer, M., & Shogren, K. A. (2016). *Exceptional lives: Special education in today's schools* (7th ed.). Upper Saddle River, NJ: Merrill/Prentice Hall.

processors, sound-augmenting devices, and closed-captioned television (Turnbull et al., 2016). Technology is making it possible for students with disabilities to function and learn at levels unimaginable only a decade ago.

Individualized Educational Programs

Serving students with disabilities (ages 3 to 21), regardless of the setting or combination of settings, requires an **individualized educational program (IEP)** as prescribed by Principle 3 of PL 94-142. An IEP is developed by educators, the family, and others as appropriate and involves a detailed plan to reach specific goals. A student's IEP must be revisited annually and the student's progress evaluated. Although IEP formats may vary, the required elements are listed in Figure 2.11.

An important part of an IEP is the designation of where and with whom students with disabilities will spend their school time. Principle 4 of PL 94–142 explicitly states that students with disabilities will be in the **least restrictive environment (LRE)** possible. The LRE is generally a setting with students who do not have disabilities that also meets the educational needs of the students with disabilities. This is often the regular education classroom.

Inclusion

Whether or not you are interested in teaching students with disabilities, you may be doing exactly that in a regular inclusive classroom setting if a student's IEP designates it as the LRE. **Inclusion** means that students with disabilities participate in academic, extracurricular, and other school activities alongside their nondisabled peers (Turnbull et al., 2016). If inclusion is not appropriate, chances are that a student with disabilities is served in a self-contained setting with other students with disabilities for much of the day, served by teachers with specific training to work with students with disabilities.

Simply placing students with disabilities in a regular classroom does not mean inclusive practices are in place or that a rigorous learning environment will be maintained. Teachers still must effectively focus on individualized objectives for every student, facilitate interactions and cooperative learning among students at every learning level, and maintain collaborative relationships with students, parents, and special educators. Given this approach, inclusion can be a healthy and positive experience for students without disabilities as well (Heward, 2013). There is a growing trend toward co-teaching, involving a regular classroom teacher and a special educator in a single classroom.

Inclusion is not embraced by all. Some parents believe their students with disabilities are better served in smaller, special education classrooms where they are more likely to receive one-on-one attention from teachers specifically trained to work with them. Some regular education teachers are wary of having a student with disabilities placed

Figure 2.11 Components of an IEP

An IEP must include a statement of:

1. student's present level of academic achievement and functional level
2. measurable academic and functional annual goals
3. how the student's progress toward meeting the annual goals will be measured
4. special education and related services to be provided to the student
5. extent to which the student will not participate with nondisabled students and the regular classroom
6. accommodations necessary to measure the student's achievement on state assessments
7. date of beginning services
8. postsecondary goals and transition services at age 16

Based on: Turnbull, R., Turnbull, A., Wehmeyer, M., & Shogren, K. A. (2016). *Exceptional lives: Special education in today's schools* (7e). Upper Saddle River, NJ: Merrill/Prentice Hall.

in their classrooms, an understandable hesitation if they receive little or no training in meeting the emotional, social, and cognitive needs of the student. Although the **Council for Exceptional Children (CEC)**, which is the professional organization of special education, endorses inclusion, the official stance is support for a continuum of services with inclusion as a desirable goal, but not the only appropriate option for all students with disabilities. Focus student Trista Kutcher benefits from an inclusive environment. Read *Getting to Know Trista* carefully to see all the possibilities she embodies.

Getting to Know Trista

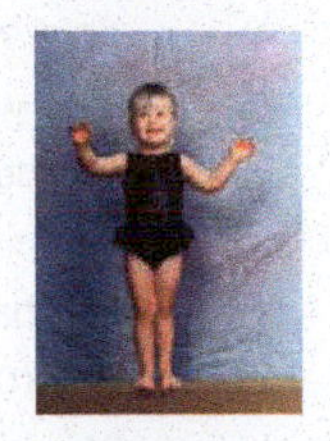

Sara Davis Powell

Trista Kutcher is one of our focus students. She is a very special young lady. Her happy life and remarkable accomplishments are evidence of what dedicated parents and sensitive, knowledgeable education professionals can do to help children, even those with disabilities, realize their potential. Trista has Down syndrome.

Trista's mom, ReBecca, teaches eighth-grade English language arts at Cario Middle School in Mount Pleasant, South Carolina, and Trista's dad, Joe, teaches math at Wando High School, where Trista is a freshman. Trista has two younger sisters, Suzanna, age 12, and Samantha, age 4. As a member of the 2003 USA Special Olympics gymnastics team, Trista won five medals at the Dublin, Ireland, games. She is a cheerleader at Wando High and is included in many regular education classes. Read this poignant story written by ReBecca, Trista's mom.

We Danced

by ReBecca Kutcher

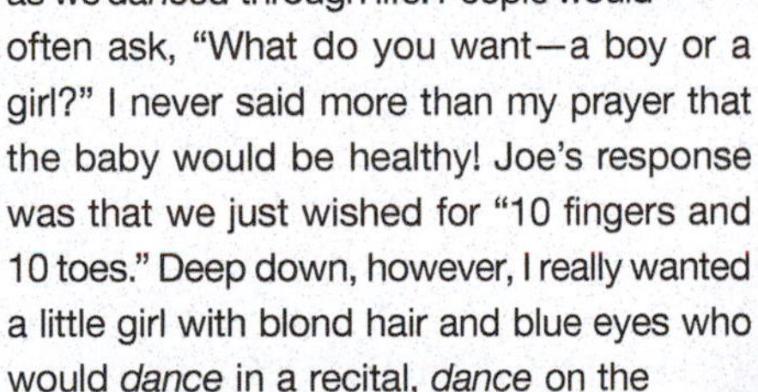

All Photos: Sara Davis Powell

Joe and I had the perfect life. . . . We dated in high school and married right out of college. Life was grand! We got pregnant and things were sailing along as we *danced* through life. People would often ask, "What do you want—a boy or a girl?" I never said more than my prayer that the baby would be healthy! Joe's response was that we just wished for "10 fingers and 10 toes." Deep down, however, I really wanted a little girl with blond hair and blue eyes who would *dance* in a recital, *dance* on the beach, and *dance* into everyone's heart!

The pregnancy was perfect, as was the delivery. Joe and I held Trista Sue and cooed over her late into the night.

A few hours later the music stopped. The doctors told us our little blond-haired, blue-eyed Trista Sue had Down syndrome. Joe and I no longer felt like *dancing*.

Knowing breastfeeding was important for her in many ways, I wanted to continue her feeding schedule, even though she was still in the hospital. I would wake up during the night at 1:00 and 5:00 and travel to the hospital to nurse her. I would waltz around the room with her in my arms. How wonderful those *dances* were . . . just us, loving each other.

I decided I was going to get Trista involved in activities that every "normal" girl does. At age two I took her to Tapios School of Dance and Gymnastics. I asked the owner if Trista could enroll in her tap and ballet classes. She welcomed her with open arms and taught her to dance with grace and poise.

Around this time Trista's sister, Suzanna, was born. How proud she was to be a big sister! Oh, the mischief they could get into together. Eventually, Trista and Suzanna were in a dance recital together, Trista 6 and Suzanna 3. Suzanna was amazed at the lights and people in the audience. She completely forgot her dance. Big sister to the rescue! Trista decided this was unacceptable and took matters into her own hands. Trista marched across the stage, positioned herself behind Suzanna, and proceeded to move her arms and legs for her. The audience roared with laughter while Trista made Suzanna *dance*.

When Trista started school, we decided she should be included in the regular classroom. Speech was definitely a concern and having her with the other kids would be great modeling. Each of her accomplishments was celebrated by kids in the class and by teachers who were initially worried about how they would teach her.

Through elementary and middle school Trista thrived, making friends and showing all of us what she could do, rather than what she couldn't do. In high school she eats, drinks, and sleeps cheering during the fall and, like her gymnastics, loves it dearly. The other girls could not be more accepting and supportive of her.

Along with regular gymnastics competitions, Trista competed in Special Olympics gymnastics. She was the state champion from the age of 8. Being involved provided many opportunities for independence and pride. During the summer of 2002, she received another very important letter. It asked her to be a part of the Special Olympics Team USA for the 2003 World Games. As she opened that letter she beamed from ear to ear. This adventure was one of meeting the governor and the mayor, being featured in a commercial, being on the news and in the newspaper regularly, and having an official day in Mt. Pleasant proclaimed by the mayor as Trista Kutcher Day! Everywhere we went people knew her. Suzanna began to make a joke about all of us being her entourage! Never did we think we would be *dancing in her shadow!* She was leading us on the adventure of a lifetime!

The competition in Ireland was tough but she was ready! She won five medals, two of which were gold! As she stood on the podium, she cried and told me later that she was so proud because "She did it!" After the awards ceremony, the audience flooded the gym floor, joined hands, and *danced the Irish jig.* What a celebration!

The *dance* has been wonderful. The music has played non-stop for 15 years! Our dance began with three people on the floor . . . and ended witha *whole community kicking up its heels!*

Poem Written by Trista's Sister

Trista—
Famous, idol,
Likes to run, jump, and play,
Annoys me when she says she is right when she is wrong.
She can do cartwheels—I wish I could.
She wishes she could play basketball like me.
I do not like to go to the same parties as she does
Because then I feel like I have to look after her
and I cannot have fun.
It amazes me when she does flips and is not scared.
It makes me sad when she says hi to someone
and they do not respond back to her.
I am proud to tell my friends about all the gold medals she has.
I like when she smiles and her nose crunches up . . . it is so cute.
She has Down syndrome.
She is my sister!

By Suzanna Kutcher

12 years old

All Photos: Sara Davis Powell

Video Example 2.5 presents more stories about Trista, her talents, and her challenges.

Video Example 2.5: Trista

Students Designated as Gifted and Talented

Characteristics of students who are **gifted and talented** include phrases such as

- Evidence of high-performance capabilities
- Intellectual, creative, artistic, or leadership ability well beyond average
- Excelling in specific academic fields

Identification of students who are gifted and talented can be objective or quite subjective, depending on the criteria accepted by a particular school district. When IQ is used for identification, the threshold number is 125 to 130, achieved by only about 2 to 3% of the general student population. However, evaluating creativity along with IQ testing allows more students to benefit from gifted and talented services.

Services for students who are gifted and talented vary significantly and include pull-out programs with students working on projects or an accelerated curriculum. In-school options such as grade skipping, concurrent enrollment in two levels of schooling, curriculum compacting (faster pace), and advanced placement courses (rigorous high school courses with possible college credit for completion) enhance the opportunities of students designated as gifted and talented. There are also specifically designed magnet schools for them.

When students who are gifted and talented are in regular classrooms—and most are—we can better meet their needs by

- Being flexible
- Accepting unusual ideas and encouraging alternative solutions to problems
- Not being intimidated by the intellectual and creative capabilities of students who have IQs that exceed our own
- Differentiating instruction often

STUDENTS WITH EXCEPTIONALITIES: IMPLICATIONS FOR TEACHERS. The most important aspect of teaching students with exceptionalities is to recognize that each student is an individual with learning potential, strengths, and limitations. Seeing and seeking a student's strengths before, or concurrently with, acknowledging limitations helps us embrace possibilities for each individual child, whether in an inclusive classroom or in a special education setting.

Including students with exceptionalities in the classroom is beneficial to all students because instruction is delivered in a variety of ways to engage diverse learners. To do so successfully, teachers need support and time for planning, as well as an appropriate curriculum, materials, and resources. Ongoing professional development is essential. During your field experiences, look closely for evidence of inclusion. Ask teachers to help you understand more about students with exceptionalities.

Here are some questions teachers of inclusive classrooms need to ask themselves:

- Do I take the time to get to know each student as an individual?
- Do I look for the strengths and abilities of all my students?
- Is cooperative learning used frequently in my classroom?
- Do I continually diagnose the progress of my students and adjust my instruction appropriately?

All students, those with exceptionalities and those without a diagnosis or designation, need to understand the inherent dangers of the exponentially increasing array of social media tools. When thinking about using social media in the classroom, we, as teachers, must recognize our responsibility to help students become wise consumers of technology, understanding the need for vigilance to stay safe in cyberspace. This chapter's *SocialMEdia* feature addresses safety concerns.

Social MEdia

Cybercitizenship is a recently coined term referring to the responsibilities of those who use social media. A recent survey by the National Cyber Security Alliance (2016) showed that over 90% of the adults in K–12 schools believe educators should teach students how to be safe and ethical cybercitizens. In 2012, the federal government passed the Children's Online Privacy Protection Act (COPPA), a bill designed to make more transparent the operations of websites that cater to children. But, as with so many societal issues, legislating safety must be accompanied by both common sense and vigilance. Immature self-regulation and vulnerability to peer pressure may put children and adolescents at risk when using social media.

The immediacy and instant gratification of social media, coupled with the vulnerability of children and adolescents, make safety hazards likely and teacher involvement absolutely necessary. Many lists of safety/ethics rules have been written by private organizations, nonprofit groups, school districts, and even the FBI. When examined side-by-side, they all include basically the same advice. Here is a summary of the most common tips for helping students stay safe as they use the Internet.

1. Always abide by school and home guidelines for when and how to use the Internet.
2. Treat people that you don't know on the Internet as strangers. Get to know your "online friends" just as you get to know all your other friends.
3. Do not give out any personal information related to your family, friends, or yourself such as passwords, addresses, and phone numbers.
4. Always tell an adult if you see something online that you know is wrong or that makes you feel uncomfortable. Never respond to such messages.
5. Never send out your picture without your parents' permission.
6. Don't respond when offered something such as gifts or money.
7. Don't ever accept a gift or an offer that involves having someone visit your house.
8. Never agree to meet someone you've met online in person unless you discuss it with your parents and an adult goes with you.
9. Never respond to provocative, rude, obscene, or threatening messages.
10. Always check with parents before downloading or installing software or doing anything that may jeopardize anyone's privacy.

Check Your Understanding 2.6

Concluding Thoughts

Now that we have looked at how students are similar and how they are different, perhaps the concept that all students can learn seems elusive to you. How, indeed, do we make "all children can learn" a reality given the circumstances that pervade some children's lives?

Understanding the uniqueness of each human being calls for an absolute commitment to individuality. Thomas Jefferson expressed the thought that there is nothing so unequal as the equal treatment of unequals. All children are equal in terms of their right to fulfill their own promise, but certainly children are unequal in the many ways we have discussed. The spirit of inclusion draws them all in; the unwavering determination to meet their needs requires attention and action based on each individual.

Yes, all children can learn. This statement is logically followed by these complex questions:

What can they learn?
When can they learn it?
In what ways will they learn it best?
As always, "And how are the children?" should be the center of our focus.

After reading the Chapter in Review, consider Craig Cleveland's concerns about his new student teacher's lack of experience with diverse student populations in this chapter's Developing Professional Competence.

Chapter in Review

How are students similar?

- As human beings, we are more similar than dissimilar.
- Nature (genetics) influences the human traits with which we are born.
- Nurture (environment) influences who we are through every aspect of our lives that nature does not determine.
- Human beings share the same basic hierarchy of needs.
- We all experience physical, cognitive, emotional, social, and character development.

How are gender differences manifested?

- Anatomical differences between males and females determine sex, whereas gender is the sense of being male or female.
- Gender determines many of the choices we make and the expectations others have for us.
- Perceived reasons for success and failure differ for males and females.
- Sexual diversity includes heterosexuality, homosexuality, bisexuality, gender nonconformity, and transgender status, as well as those who are questioning.
- Homosexuality is often the basis of discrimination.

How are cultural and language diversity manifested in schools?

- Race, although a social, political, economic, and psychological reality, is based solely on physical characteristics.
- Racism is a form of prejudice stemming from a belief that one race is superior to another.
- Ethnicity refers to a person's country of origin.
- Culture has many components and is learned, shared, and adaptive.
- Cultural identity relies on many factors such as race, ethnicity, language, gender, religion, income level, values, and beliefs.
- Multiculturalism involves beliefs concerning the value of looking at the world through the eyes of people who are different from us.
- To be most effective, multicultural education needs to permeate all areas of schooling.
- Language is an aspect of cultural identity that can be augmented and enhanced.
- Bilingual education involves instruction delivered in two languages.
- English as a second language (ESL), also known as English as a new language (ENL), is a pull-out program assisting English learners in English only.
- Structured English immersion (SEI) includes significant amounts of the school day dedicated to the explicit teaching of the English language, with other content secondary.

What is the impact on students of family structure, religion, and socioeconomic status?

- Blended families and family structures other than two biological parents and children are becoming more prevalent.
- The increasing mobility of American families potentially harms students and wreaks havoc on classrooms.

- Religion and faith have considerable influence on lifestyles and choices.
- The religious beliefs of families and communities influence decisions that relate to school issues.
- The gap between the haves and have-nots is wider in the United States than in most other nations.
- Low-income settings often contribute to lower achievement.

How are learning differences manifested in schools?

- There are many different ways to be smart and to exhibit intelligence.
- We all have learning preferences and modality predisposition.

Who are students with exceptionalities and how do we serve them?

- Students with exceptionalities include those with disabilities and those considered gifted and talented.
- A designation of learning disabled accounts for almost 40% of students receiving special services.
- Attention deficit hyperactivity disorder and autism spectrum disorder are both diagnoses that are rapidly increasing and in need of continuing research.
- Autism, or autism spectrum disorder, is a complex developmental disorder that affects how a person behaves, interacts with others, communicates, and learns.
- The concept of least restrictive environment means that students with disabilities are to be placed in the highest-functioning setting possible, usually the regular education classroom.
- An individualized educational program (IEP) is a plan for a student's journey through public education based on needs and services to meet those needs.
- Inclusion in schools means that students with disabilities participate in academic, extracurricular, and other school activities alongside their nondisabled peers.
- Students considered gifted and talented are most likely to be included in the regular education classroom and pulled out for special classes for brief periods of time.

Developing Professional Competence

Sara Davis Powell

Thoughtfully reading this scenario and responding to the items that follow it will help you prepare for licensure exams.

In this chapter we learned about one of Craig Cleveland's classes. Craig's student teacher this semester, Jenny Langley, grew up in the suburbs of Fresno, California, and attends Fresno State. Jenny never attended a Title I school and her PreK–12 school experiences were ideal by most standards, complete with advanced placement classes, a stable group of friends, and extracurricular activities that rounded out her high school years. In a conversation several weeks before her student teaching semester began, Craig discovered that Jenny's peer group had little diversity—although Jenny told him she had lots of experience with diversity because she was in the International Baccalaureate program and she knew two exchange students, one from Japan and one from Russia. Craig smiled to himself as she talked about her open-minded approach with those who are different from herself, knowing she was about to begin one of the most turbulent experiences of her young life.

Now it's time for you to respond to three short essay items involving the scenario. In your responses, be sure to address all the dilemmas and questions posed in each item. These items are followed by five multiple-choice questions. As you consider your responses, think about how these standards may apply.

National Board of Professional Teaching Standards, Proposition 1: Accomplished teachers recognize that in a multicultural nation students bring to schools a plethora of abilities and attitudes and aptitudes that are valued differently by the community, the school, and the family.

InTASC Standard #1: Learner Development

The teacher understands how learners grow and develop, recognizing that patterns of learning and development vary individually within and across the cognitive, linguistic, social, emotional, and physical areas, and designs and implements developmentally appropriate and challenging learning experiences.

This standard emphasizes the importance of providing challenging learning experiences that match individual learner needs from a variety of developmental perspectives, including physical, cognitive, social, emotional, and linguistic considerations.

InTASC Standard #2: Learning Differences

The teacher uses understanding of individual differences and diverse cultures and communities to ensure inclusive learning environments that enable each learner to meet high standards.

This standard emphasizes the need to create inclusive environments, recognizing students as individuals with learning and cultural differences and maintaining appropriately high standards for each.

1. Jenny is walking into a world that is foreign to her. Explain two reasons why she may be apprehensive or even fearful.
2. As a suburbanite from a middle-income family, Jenny is now experiencing adolescents who live in poverty. What characteristics might the students display that will require Jenny to adjust her attitudes and expectations to meet their needs effectively?
3. Given what we know about the students at Roosevelt High School, which of the three methods for serving their language needs (bilingual education, ESL, SEI) would you recommend, and why?

Application Exercise 2.4: Developing Professional Competence

4. Guillermo is a really good-hearted young man with acceptable English skills and a desire to help other people. Before and after class, Jenny might be able to best learn more about students with limited English proficiency if she:
   a. Asks Guillermo to help her talk more easily with students whose primary language is Spanish.
   b. Stays close to Guillermo and listen to his casual conversations in both English and Spanish.
   c. Talks with Guillermo about what he knows about students who are English language learners.
   d. Watches Guillermo's easy demeanor with other students and tries to develop the same persona.

5. Craig Cleveland explains Khammany's situation to Jenny by telling her about Khammany, her mom, and her younger brother moving into a project apartment with only two rooms and the difficulties they face since her dad died last year. Khammany, one of our focus students, has to work at least 30 hours a week to help support the family. Which of the following benefits of longer blocks of class time will Craig probably say is most important to Khammany?
   a. During the 100-minute class, Khammany has more time to concentrate on history.
   b. The longer blocks afford more time for a variety of participation activities.
   c. The block allows for time to begin homework assignments with Craig available to assist.
   d. Khammany can earn eight credits per year.
6. Remember Craig's diverse group of students? Which is the *least* important reason that longer blocks of class time benefit English language learners?
   a. They get to spend more concentrated time on one subject with one teacher.
   b. There is more time to fully develop a concept, using a variety of communication methods.
   c. There are fewer subjects to learn at a time.
   d. Fewer passing periods limit opportunities to be involved in turf issues among diverse groups of students.
7. What do you think will be the best way for Jenny to begin to acclimate to her student teaching situation?
   a. Study the culture of the students she will encounter at Roosevelt High School.
   b. Spend at least 5 days simply shadowing Craig.
   c. Jump in and begin working with students.
   d. Spend the month before student teaching brushing up on her Spanish language skills from taking 2 years of Spanish in high school.
8. Jenny has started her 16-week student teaching experience with enthusiasm based on the fact that she had 2 years of Spanish in high school. Which reason most likely causes her enthusiasm to quickly dim?
   a. She can read and write in Spanish to a moderate degree, but conversational Spanish is another story.
   b. There aren't many written resources in Craig's classroom that are in Spanish.
   c. Most of the students with limited English proficiency are Hmong.
   d. Craig's class is not designated as a bilingual class.

Application Exercise 2.5: Developing Professional Competence

Flash Cards 2.1

Shared Writing 2.1: Diversity Challenges

Chapter 3

School Similarities and Differences

Learning Objectives

After studying this chapter, you will have knowledge and skills to:

3.1 Describe the purposes of public schools in the United States.

3.2 Articulate the meaning of school culture.

3.3 Compare and contrast school venues.

3.4 Distinguish among different levels of school.

3.5 Elaborate differences among the three principal settings of U.S. schools.

3.6 Determine characteristics of an effective school.

Dear Reader

We live in a country where formal schooling of some sort is mandatory for children and adolescents. We have all participated. Whether in a public or private facility, or in a home, our experiences with schooling have a real impact on our viewpoint of what it means to be a student. This chapter considers a range of purposes of schooling. But first, we'll look at the differences between schooling and education. Mark Twain once said, "I have never let my schooling interfere with my education." This scathing view of formal schooling should drive us to be teachers who enhance, rather than impede, learning.

Schools are centers of our communities, foundations of our citizenry, targets of political and ethical debate, mirrors and shapers of our society, and keepers of the hopes and dreams of parents and children. Without exception, the greeting "And how are the children?" should be on the lips and in the hearts of every adult in every U.S. school. Mandatory attendance makes some form of schooling a common factor in our society. As such, we have all experienced schools.

As we examine public and private K–12 schools in a variety of settings, think about whether teaching is a career you want to pursue and, if so, what your teaching identity might be. Take your time considering the information about schools and, in particular, our four focus schools introduced in this chapter. Can you envision yourself in a suburban elementary school? How about a middle school in a rural area or an inner-city high school? Perhaps early childhood education is your choice. The world of teaching is wide open for you!

3.1 What Are the Purposes of Public Schools in the United States?

3.1 Describe the purposes of public schools in the United States.

We begin our discussion of the similarities and differences among schools by considering distinctions between education and schooling. We then consider the purposes of

public schools in the United States, those funded *by* the public, and accountable *to* the public, through local, state, and federal governments.

Distinctions between Education and Schooling

Remember in geometry class when the teacher told you that a straight line on the chalkboard wasn't a line but rather a line segment? You may have rolled your eyes and mumbled, "What difference does it make?" Well, for the content of the geometry class (and the inevitable test), it certainly mattered. But did your English teacher ever ask you to draw a *line segment* under a prepositional phrase in a sentence? Probably not. Outside the context of geometry class, most of us find it unnecessary to make a distinction between a line and a line segment.

So it is with the words *education* and *schooling*. As teachers, we need to understand the differences. Once we do, although we may use the words interchangeably in some contexts, we are always aware that distinctions do exist.

EDUCATION. Although it may not seem obvious, there is a distinct difference between education and schooling. **Education** is the lifelong process of learning. Every day of our lives, in every possible setting, we learn. When we see, hear, feel, or sense, we are learning. This is education—our lifelong formal and informal process of learning.

SCHOOLING. One specific, formalized element of education is **schooling**. Schools are institutions specifically designed to educate in formal ways. They involve organization and structure, both of which should be determined primarily by the needs of those who learn, as well as those who teach.

A discussion of American schools is often called a discussion of American education. That's fine. It's understood that we are talking about what goes on in school settings. The hope is that the education occurring in school is productive and accurate in nature, but regardless, learning of some kind is taking place just like it does continually in every walk of life. As teachers we are called educators. As long as we recognize and acknowledge that the whole world educates children, we may continue to interchange the words *education* and *schooling* as well as *educator* and *teacher*.

Complementary Purposes of Public Schools

There's no need to settle on—or settle for—narrowly defined purposes for public schooling. Although there are many, we will consider eight. These purposes may be best understood and put into perspective using the concept of balance. Each pair of purposes discussed is more complementary than oppositional. They balance each other.

TRANSMITTING SOCIETY AND RECONSTRUCTING SOCIETY. Both of these purposes deal with societal knowledge and values. On the more conservative side, *transmitting society* involves public schools both reflecting and supporting our American society. This process, called **socialization**, occurs through a variety of influences, including home, family, place of worship, print and electronic media, peers, and, of course, school. Students are influenced through the subjects we offer and the content of those subjects, as well as through our instruction, both actions and words. Transmitting society means promoting the concepts that preserve our democratic way of life and discouraging concepts that oppose it. Transmitting society is unifying, emphasizing what we have in common rather than our differences.

Teachers walk a fine line when it comes to achieving the purpose of transmitting society while continuing to respect the students and their families who bring differing societal views with them into the classroom. What many of us take for granted may be new and unusual to a growing number of our students. A democratic way of life involves acceptance of differences; in U.S. schools, acceptance should escalate to the embracing of differences. This in itself is transmitting a society that preserves democracy.

The complement of transmitting society is *reconstructing society*, challenging knowledge and values with an eye toward improvement. The concept of social reconstruction involves teaching students to recognize what needs to change, identifying the means of change, and encouraging students to work proactively for a common goal. Rather than only passing down knowledge and values to preserve society's status quo, students are urged to examine different aspects of our society, keep what is worthwhile, and seek to change or discard what isn't.

As you can see, transmitting society and reconstructing society do not have to be opposing purposes. When they are balanced, it is possible to pass on the best of society while questioning and changing other aspects of society for the better.

PARTICIPATING IN SOCIETY AND ACADEMIC LEARNING. Preparing students to *participate in society* involves socialization plus the teaching of survival skills that will help them to get along with others; obtain and keep employment; be politically, morally, and socially proactive; and be productive members of a community, with a sense of responsibility. Public schools, along with other institutions and groups, certainly help prepare students for participation in society.

At the same time as we prepare students to participate in society, we facilitate *academic learning*. Every subject area includes a body of knowledge that is, by and large, "society free," or independent from what's going on at the time within society. For instance, mathematical formulas, classic literature, history, and geography all have academic aspects that change little with time. Plato maintained that this kind of academic knowledge is the foundation for seeking truth that is not dependent on, or influenced by, current society, and that seeking truth is a necessary purpose of education. He encouraged students to look at possibilities through the lens of formal academic learning and to question the world around them.

In a classic study, *A Place Called School*, John Goodlad (1984) looked at many documents that have addressed the question "What is the purpose of schooling?" He concluded there are four broad goals:

1. ***Academic:*** Imparting knowledge and intellectual skills
2. ***Vocational:*** Preparing for the world of work
3. ***Social and civic:*** Participating in a democratic society
4. ***Personal:*** Developing self-expression and talent

Goal #1 obviously fits into the academic learning purpose, whereas the other three prepare students to participate in society.

MEETING INDIVIDUAL NEEDS AND COLLECTIVE NEEDS. These two purposes most certainly go hand in hand. A citizenry of formally educated individuals serves the collective good. American public schools provide opportunities for children to reach their learning potential. Some schools make this opportunity more feasible and more readily attainable than others.

Meeting the *individual needs* of students is sometimes referred to as the development of *human capital*. These words seem mechanistic and cold until we consider them separately. The word *human* describes us. The word *capital* in this sense is a noun meaning the knowledge and skills derived from education, training, and experience. The development of human capital is directly related to the well-being of individuals. It takes groups of people—the collective—to preserve our democratic way of life.

To serve *collective needs*, then, is to view the purpose of U.S. schools as ensuring strong, free communities by teaching knowledge as well as values such as honesty, hard work, civility, respect, compassion, and patriotism. The goals for the collective include economic prosperity, maintenance of our national security, and the development of a sense of both humanity and democratic ideals.

In American public schools we teach individual students who, together, form the collective of our country. The stronger the collective, the more opportunities there are for the individual. These two purposes of public education are complementary and interdependent.

SUSTAINING FOR TODAY AND PREPARING FOR TOMORROW. Schools *sustain for today* by providing a set of experiences for students. Yes, many of them will be successful in school. Some will go on to college and most will have productive careers. But some will not. Not because the nation's public schools want it to be so, but because the reality is that not all students will make the transition from school to adulthood and become citizens who contribute in positive ways. Some will drop out of school and lack the knowledge, skills, and/or credibility to fulfill their potential in adult life. Some will experience debilitating life circumstances or even death before they complete high school. What we need to remember in terms of schools serving to sustain for today is that children—regardless of what their futures hold—deserve a warm, caring, nurturing environment where they have opportunities to learn and grow. Ideally, home and family provide this environment. Whether that's the case or not, U.S. public schools should provide this environment day after day, year after year, as we ask one another, "And how are the children?"

Elliot Eisner (2004), one of our most influential educators, wrote, "Preparation for tomorrow is best served by meaningful education today" (p. 10). American public education that sustains for today, *prepares for tomorrow.* It's a building process, a self-perpetuating cycle.

Preserving our democratic way of life is accomplished through the fulfillment of these eight purposes and other related goals. Both education and schooling, as defined earlier, lead to learning for our students and for future teachers.

Point of Reflection 3.1

With which pair of the eight complementary purposes of public schools do you identify most? Explain your choice.

Check Your Understanding 3.1

3.2 What Is the Culture of a School?

3.2 Articulate the meaning of school culture.

School culture is the context of learning experiences; it's the prevailing atmosphere of the school. As places where people work together and learn together, schools function according to their cultures. Noted educator Roland Barth (2001) tells us, "A school's culture dictates, in no uncertain terms, 'the way we do things around here.' Ultimately, a school's culture has far more influence on life and learning in the schoolhouse than the state department of education, the superintendent, the school board, or even the principal can ever have" (p. 7).

A school's culture can be a positive force for learning or a negative influence that interferes with learning. It is important to recognize elements of a school's culture, both the forces that created it and those that perpetuate it. If the culture is positive, acknowledging the influential forces and then reinforcing them keeps the culture vibrant and growing. If the culture is negative or apathetic, altering it begins with looking closely at the influential forces and finding ways to begin the change process.

From a new teacher's standpoint, a positive school culture may be evident when experienced teachers consistently ask how things are going and offer to help with lessons, materials, managing student behavior, paperwork, and so on. Hearing teachers talking and laughing together, sharing what works in their classrooms, and speaking of students with caring and concerned attitudes demonstrate positive culture. On the other hand, when a school seems to have a territorial atmosphere with cliques of teachers criticizing other teachers and the principal, when offers of assistance are few, when students are spoken of primarily in critical terms, a new teacher will likely sense a negative culture. Because teachers comprise most of the adults in a school, their influence on school culture is immense.

Teachers and School Culture

Teachers' instructional skills and professionalism either improve a school's culture or keep it stagnant or negative. The level of respect teachers engender among their colleagues and in the community either builds a positive culture or serves to drag it down. This level of respect has much to do with the relationships that exist among a school's adults, which, in turn, influence the ways teachers relate to students. Because all teachers, experienced and new, have considerable influence on school culture, they must be instrumental in maintaining a positive culture or helping to change a negative culture into a more positive one. Alex Kajitani, California's 2009 Teacher of the Year, travels the country as he works with schools to improve their cultures. He says, "When it comes to success of an individual classroom, nothing is more important than the relationship between the teacher and the students. When it comes to the success of an *entire school,* nothing is more important than the relationship of the adults in the building" (Kajitani, 2016).

Changing School Culture

A school's culture can change. Can it change quickly or easily? Definitely not when improvement is the goal. Positive culture shifts require strong leadership, ownership of the problems and potential solutions by the adults in the school, and a steady, conscious influx of both attitudes and actions that produce the desired results. In contrast, changing a school culture from positive to negative may require only apathy and neglect.

All components of American education discussed in this text influence a school's culture. For instance, what is taught in a school can be dynamic and challenging, or mediocre and boring. Not only *what* is taught, but also *how* it is taught, influences culture. The level of respect teachers and students have for one another influences school culture as does the level of teacher expectations for student success. Remember that the context of schools is complex; schools are living systems. Because students, teachers, parents, communities, policies, and politics all potentially influence school culture, many variances exist among schools, even those with the same basic structure.

Check Your Understanding 3.2

3.3 How Do School Venues Differ?

3.3 Compare and contrast school venues.

Schools in the United States vary greatly, from the traditional neighborhood public school to the ultimate private school: the home. This section looks at **school venues,**— in other words, the variety of ways American students are educated in the more than 130,000 public and private schools in the United States (National Center for Education Statistics [NCES], 2016).

Public School Venues

The vast majority of educational settings in the United States are **public schools**, with most of the funding to support them coming from some form of taxation. Public schools are accountable to the community through elected or governmental officials who have policy and oversight responsibilities.

Public schools come in all shapes and sizes. Not only are they open to every student regardless of socioeconomic status, disability, race, or religion, but in fact they also provide a school setting for every child—that's part of being "public." The number of public school students hovers right around 50 million, with private school enrollment at about 5 million students.

TRADITIONAL PUBLIC SCHOOLS. The traditional school, also known as the **neighborhood school,** is still the predominant form of public schooling in the United States. **Traditional public schools** have no admission criteria, other than perhaps residency in a particular attendance zone. Their educational programs are designed to meet the needs of almost all students, with the possible exception of some with severe physical or mental disabilities. Most public school students attend traditional public schools.

A traditional public school that provides a comprehensive program of education and includes student and community services, such as after-school and family- education programs, may be considered a **full-service school**. Many of the components of a full-service school are made possible through community partnerships with businesses, healthcare providers, foundations, and government agencies. These services help students and their families cope with a variety of dilemmas. The goals of a full-service school may include the following:

- Meeting students' needs, both academic and nonacademic, through extended-day programs, counseling groups, homework assistance, and the like
- Increasing family stability through parent education
- Creating a safe haven for the community
- Providing role models for all family members
- Responding to physical and psychological needs
- Providing easy access to government services
- Involving community members from all walks of life in public education

Three particular venues of public schools draw specific groups of students: magnet schools, charter schools, and alternative schools. Each has a structure that uniquely matches the needs and interests of its student population.

MAGNET SCHOOLS. A school with a specific emphasis or theme may be known as a **magnet school**. The curriculum and/or instructional program of a magnet school are tailored with unique opportunities that attract certain students. A magnet school's focus may be math or science (or both), performing arts, technology, or high academic expectations requiring specific student qualifications. For example, a magnet school with an emphasis on preparation for a career in the trade arts, sometimes called a *vocational magnet,* would attract students interested in careers in construction, mechanics, cosmetology, culinary arts, and so on.

Magnet schools are more expensive to operate than traditional neighborhood schools. Their special programs may require funds for career-related equipment, performance studios, staff with specific expertise, smaller teacher-to-student ratios, and transportation beyond immediate neighborhoods. As parents and students seek more specialized environments, more and more magnet schools are opening and drawing specific groups of students out of the traditional neighborhood schools.

In 2012 about 3,000 public schools were magnets. Their population accounted for about 4% of students enrolled in public schools (NCES, 2013), serving about 2.3 million students.

CHARTER SCHOOLS. A **charter school** is a public school that is freed in specific ways from the typical regulations required of other public schools. Charter schools are publicly funded, but independently operated and have been around for over 25 years. Teachers and administrators in charter schools usually have more control than their counterparts in traditional public schools over how they spend their funds and the kinds of classes they offer. In most cases, charter schools must be approved by a state department of education and are open to all students within a specific school district. Attendance is often determined through a random lottery process involving students who want to attend. Charter school students take all state-mandated standardized tests and the schools are accountable for the quality of teaching and learning through test results.

Individuals or groups who see a need or an opportunity to fix a problem create charter schools. Themes may revolve around a particular content focus, specific teaching methods, a social problem, limited grade levels, or social issues the creators view as important. To attract students, leaders of charter schools must get the word out to the public and convince parents that the charter can better meet the learning needs of their children. Then, to keep students coming back year after year, they must follow through with their plans and goals.

Charter schools may be started from scratch or converted from preexisting schools. After they are approved and in operation, charter schools are usually governed through **site-based management**, meaning that the school is in the hands of those closest to it, generally teachers, administrators, and parents.

Government funding follows students to charter schools, which operate financially based primarily on per-student allocations, along with fund-raising. States and districts do not provide facilities, meal services, or transportation for charter schools. They must purchase or lease their own buildings and pay for utilities and upkeep of them, provide facilities and options for feeding students, and provide ways of getting students to and home from school. This means starting a charter school requires money. The founder and school supporters must raise funds to even get started.

Responding to the public's desire for school choices, the number of charter schools has increased exponentially in the last decade. In 2010 there were almost 5,000 charter schools in 41 states. In 2015, there were almost 7,000 educating about 6% of public school students (over 3,000,000 students) (National Alliance for Public Charter Schools [NAPCS], 2016).

Although most charter schools are independent, stand-alone schools, others are part of a larger system. Perhaps the best known of all charter school systems is the **Knowledge Is Power Program (KIPP)**, founded in 1994. A national network of 200 free, open-enrollment charter schools in 20 states, KIPP serves almost 80,000 K–12 students. About 88% of KIPP students are eligible for free or reduced meals and about 96% are African American or Hispanic. KIPP's successes include a high school graduation rate of 90%, with 80% of KIPP graduates attending college (Knowledge Is Power Program, 2016). Quite a success story!

STRIVE Preparatory Schools is a smaller, locally administered charter system in Denver, Colorado. STRIVE serves a population of 3200 students on 11 campuses, most with disadvantages similar to those of the KIPP schools' population, and was originally established to primarily meet the needs of Hispanic children in the Denver area. The system is growing and establishing new schools each year, focusing on students who need additional attention to succeed, regardless of race or ethnicity. In 2016, at least 87% of the system's student population were eligible for free or reduced price lunch, 97% were students of color, 42% were English language learners, and 12% receive special education services. Since the inception of STRIVE Prep in 2006, STRIVE middle schools have achieved top academic honors for the state of Colorado—an amazing feat, considering their students are primarily poor and are from homes where English is not the first language (STRIVE Preparatory Schools, 2016). Acquiring a teaching position in both KIPP and STRIVE is quite competitive. Both systems require longer working hours and considerably more ongoing professional development, but generally compensate teachers for the more demanding schedule.

Sara Davis Powell

STRIVE Prep World Studies teacher Jesse White enjoys a positive relationship with his 7th grade students.

Even with what may be considered success stories, charter schools remain controversial because of perceptions of lax accountability, absence of diversity, and funding dilemmas. Just as some regular public schools are effective and others are not, many charter schools are effectively educating students, but some are not. Because states have the right to support or close charter schools, some people are calling for closer supervision of the charters and more heavily monitored accountability, so that students and parents aren't lured in by promises that aren't fulfilled. Since charter schools receive state funding just like regular public schools, every time a student chooses a charter, the local noncharter public school loses funding. Many long-time vocal advocates for strengthening public schools oppose charter schools and maintain that they drain resources from traditional public schools. Regardless of the controversy, charter schools will likely play an even larger role in public education for years to come.

Some groups representing minority students, including the National Association for the Advancement of Colored People (NAACP), are vocal in their opposition of the increasing number of charter schools, maintaining that they are instruments of segregation. In 2016, black and Hispanic students dominated charter school enrollments and, in some cases, schools were exclusively minority. A major concern of the NAACP and others is that charter schools are usually established by individuals and groups that are not integral parts of the community and have appointed governing boards, as opposed to noncharter public schools that employ all local teachers and are governed by elected school boards. The controversy centers on the diminishment of local parent and community involvement and control (Prothero, 2016).

ALTERNATIVE SCHOOLS. Magnet and charter schools are both alternative forms of school organization. However, in public education, the term *alternative school* takes on a unique meaning. If a school is called an **alternative school**, more than likely it is a school designed for students who are not successful in a traditional school setting. Because school districts can't exclude students and attendance is compulsory until age 16, alternative settings have emerged that may be categorized in two ways: *remedial* and *last chance*.

Students who require more focused attention to be successful than what the traditional school can provide are in need of remediation: academic, social, emotional, or some combination of the three. When remediation is completed, a student may return to a more traditional setting. Often those who are characterized as being **students at risk**—those in serious danger of not completing school and who may be heading toward nonproductive or counterproductive lifestyles—are strongly urged to attend remedial alternative schools. Students who are not successful in a remedial setting may attend public alternative schools that are considered last-chance schools. In most cases the students have gotten into significant trouble in a traditional or remedial school; have been suspended multiple times; have consistently been disruptive in the classroom; or generally have not benefited from other, less intrusive programs.

To address the needs of students who require extreme measures to be successful, two schools in Washington, DC, have taken advantage of a special policy there saying schools that provide housing for students may receive additional funding. The **SEED Public Charter School** in Washington, DC, founded in 1998 (with newer campuses in Maryland and Miami) and **Monument Academy Public Charter School**, founded in

2015, qualify both as charter schools because of their vision and unique structure, and as alternative schools because they were developed to meet the needs of students at risk of not succeeding in traditional public schools. Both schools provide room and board 5 days a week and are referred to as urban **boarding schools** (Einhorn, 2015). Urban boarding schools are expensive and not without controversy. However, Harvard economist Roland Fryer compared students who were admitted to the schools through its annual lottery to those who applied but didn't get in. Fryer found that SEED students acquired significantly higher math and reading scores, a decrease in the probability that they will commit a crime, and a decrease in the likelihood of the child developing a health disability (Einhorn, 2015). In addition to SEED and Monument, San Diego County, California, opened the first residential education campus for adolescents in foster care in 2001. The San Pasqual Academy is part school and part foster-care group home.

The wide variety of public schools provides opportunities and choices. Table 3.1 summarizes the commonly available public school options.

Private School Venues

The two elements that make schools public—public funding and public accountability— are both absent in **private schools**. Over 5 million students in the United States attend private schools (Council for American Private Education [CAPE], 2016). Families choose private education for a variety of reasons. Some choose private schools for potential benefits such as smaller class size, specific instruction to meet the needs of students with learning disabilities, or travel and extracurricular opportunities. Still others may choose private education because of family history. In some cases, generations of family members have attended a particular private school.

Another reason some families choose private schools is their negative perceptions about local public schools. They may consider public schools inferior or inadequate. Still others want their children to have religious instruction or believe that their children's specific mental or physical needs require a private setting. Then there are other families who perceive that a private school may be more prestigious than the available public schools.

In most instances, public and private schools exist side by side in a community with little rancor. Yet there may be differences in underlying philosophy that cause friction. Unlike their public school counterparts, private schools are not obligated to educate all students, but are able to both selectively admit and dismiss students. Thus, their classrooms typically have fewer behavior problems, a smaller teacher-to-student ratio, and

Table 3.1 Public school venues

Venue	Definition	Admission Criteria	Advantages	Disadvantages
Traditional	Neighborhood school	None	Close to home; sense of ownership	May not have programs of interest or that meet specific student needs
Full-service traditional school	School offers student and community services that go beyond academics	None	Draws families in; provides services such as health promotion and community education	None
Magnet	School with specific emphasis or theme	Interest; talent; academic achievement	Specialized curriculum or instruction	May exclude some students; requires more funding
Charter	School freed from some district or state regulatory control	None; generally first come, first admitted	Site-based decision making; specialized curriculum or instruction	May lack sufficient oversight; danger of "ends justify means" mentality
Alternative	Usually a school for students who are not successful in other public school settings	Behavioral or academic problems	Can provide specialized assistance for students who need it most	May neglect some aspects of school while targeting specific needs; may stereotype or stigmatize students

stronger parental support. Some private school teachers see this as a trade-off because most of them are paid less than teachers in public schools.

PAROCHIAL SCHOOLS. Most private schools are affiliated with a particular religious sect (denomination) and are often called **parochial schools**. Most religion-affiliated schools are aligned with the Catholic faith.

Private schools that are not aligned with a religious group exist in many forms and cater to a wide spectrum of student and family needs and wants. They may resemble charter schools with themes and areas of emphasis, but they are free from all government regulation because they are privately funded.

SINGLE-GENDER SCHOOLS. Some private schools are **single gender**, enrolling either all boys or all girls. Although some public schools have opted for some single-gender classes and campuses, most single-gender opportunities come through private schools. When the National Association for Single-Sex Public Education (NASSPE) was founded in 2002, there were fewer than 20 public school single-sex education opportunities (NASSPE, 2013). In 2012, 116 of the 506 public schools offering single-sex education opportunities were completely either all-boy or all-girl settings. You can see that this is a growing trend. Note that when schools and classes are discussed by the National Association for Single-Sex Public Education, the label goes from *gender* to *sex*. The word *sex* is used rather than *gender* because it is a more readily definable attribute.

HOMESCHOOLING. Students who receive most of their academic instruction in their homes are considered to be **homeschooled**—the ultimate in private schooling. Although it's hard to pinpoint an exact number, there were about 2 million homeschooled students in the United States in 2013. This figure represents about 3.4% of the total U.S. student population, with the 2 million students including 68% white, 15% Hispanic, 8% black, and 4% Asian or Pacific Islander (Home School Legal Defense Association, 2016). The reasons for parents choosing homeschooling vary but are similar to parental reasons for choosing private over public school venues.

Over time, homeschooling has become a social movement, with parents involved as political activists, organizers of national networks, and developers of curriculum and instructional materials. As you can imagine, the quality of the education received in the home varies widely. However, on standardized academic achievement tests homeschoolers tend to score higher than students in public schools. How students fare socially has not been measured, only openly speculated about. A concern is that children who are homeschooled may miss out on the civic perspective and experiences gained only through going to school with students who are not like themselves in religious beliefs, racial or cultural background, socioeconomic status, or academic aptitude.

Homeschooling has always been part of the human experience. Some notable homeschooled students include Florence Nightingale, Thomas Edison, Margaret Mead, Charles Dickens, Benjamin Franklin, Orville and Wilbur Wright, Woodrow Wilson, and former U.S. Supreme Court Justice Sandra Day O'Connor.

FOR-PROFIT SCHOOLS. Nonreligious private schools are often **for-profit schools**. These schools are managed by some entity that receives a percentage of the money generated. Even some public schools may be for-profit. For years, public schools have contracted with private companies to provide some aspects of schooling such as transportation, custodial work, and food services. However, when companies contract with states or districts to take over all aspects of schooling and make money by doing so, then it's capitalism in the schoolhouse. These for-profit schools are given the federal, state, and local money per pupil that a public school receives and are referred to as **education maintenance organizations (EMOs)** (the educational equivalent of HMOs in healthcare). Public schools run by private companies are controversial. When they may make claims of increased student learning, some of their data calculations are often questioned by those who oppose privatization. Another controversial claim made by opponents of privatization is that when profit is the bottom line, services to the students with special needs may be neglected. More research is needed to determine the efficacy of for-profit companies managing public schools.

As you consider the variety of schools in both Table 3.1 and Table 3.2, keep in mind that what some may view as advantages may be considered disadvantages by others, and vice versa.

School Choice

School choice—letting parents and students decide which schools meet their needs—has a very democratic feel, doesn't it? Reasons for choice among schools include increasing parental involvement, providing learning environments more suited to individual students, attempting broader integration, accommodating particular interests and talents, and affording more desirable settings to students who are at risk or underprivileged.

Let's consider school choice in the context of competition. Marketplace theory says that competition leads to improvement. But does this apply to schools competing for student enrollment, when more students mean more money? If all schools were high performing and differed only in theme or focus, then competition would simply mean appealing to student interests or learning preferences. But when certain schools gain enrollment while others lose because of real or perceived failures to meet the needs of students, the failing schools are left in an even more untenable situation. If we close them down, we may be eliminating the possibility of improving the predominant public school setting (the neighborhood school). However, no child should be in a school that is not making progress toward improved levels of learning. Answering the question, "And how are the children?" becomes even more complex and important.

Table 3.2 Private and for-profit school venue

Venue	Definition	Admission Criteria	Advantages	Disadvantages
Religious	School with a religious affiliation	Agreement to either uphold or not interfere with the principles of the affiliation	Allows parents and religious groups to include their traditions and beliefs	Not accountable to any government agency
Nonreligious	School without a religious affiliation	Interest; can afford tuition; students may be rejected for any reason	Specialized curriculum or instruction	Not accountable to any government agency
Single gender	School for boys only or girls only	Must be gender of school; generally first come, first admitted	May better meet specific learning styles of either boys or girls	Not accountable to any government agency; may not mirror reality of the coed world
Homeschooling	Students are taught at home or in a home environment	Family member	Provides very specific one-on-one instruction in a manner desired by parents	Not accountable to any government agency; may isolate student from other cultures and viewpoints; may neglect some aspects of what is commonly agreed on as necessary curriculum
For-profit	Schools run by individuals or corporations that make and keep monetary gain	Any criteria set by school managers	Can be very specialized	If private, not accountable to any government agency

For any choice plan, there are two key ingredients for success: information and transportation. Without provisions for both, a choice plan only gives choices to families who seek out information and have the capability to provide transportation out of their neighborhoods. Figure 3.1 illustrates three ways that public school choice may be manifested.

PUBLIC-TO-PUBLIC SCHOOL CHOICE. Allowing for choice among public schools occurs in a variety of ways. The option of attending magnet, charter, and alternative schools versus a traditional neighborhood school within a district is by far the most common manifestation of school choice. Taking this option a step further, **open enrollment** allows students to choose from among all the schools in a school district with a few exceptions, such as magnet schools with specific student qualifications and alternative schools with student enrollment controlled by the district. Open enrollment may extend across district lines as well.

ELEMENTARY AND SECONDARY EDUCATION ACT. In 1965, President Lyndon B. Johnson proposed, and Congress passed, the **Elementary and Secondary Education Act (ESEA)** as a part of the "War on Poverty." The ESEA emphasized equal access to education and established high standards and accountability. In 2001, the ESEA was reauthorized as the **No Child Left Behind Act (NCLB)**. One provision of the act is that parents and students have school choice under certain conditions. Although the ESEA was reauthorized in 2016 as the **Every Student Succeeds Act (ESSA)**, school choice under NCLB is still relevant. If a Title I school is deemed unsatisfactory for 2 years, students may transfer to schools that are not deemed as failing. The school district has the responsibility to provide at least two designated recipient schools for each student and to make transportation available for students.

Are parents and students likely to take advantage of the choices? Maybe, maybe not. More will if they are informed of the options in a timely fashion, if they are comfortable that long bus rides won't be necessary, and if the students are not socially committed to staying with their neighborhood friends who opt not to move. These are powerful "ifs." Here's another to consider: *If* their parents do not explore options, students will likely remain in schools designated as failing.

VOUCHERS. Perhaps the most controversial of current efforts to provide school choice is the **voucher**, a government-issued form that represents part of the state's financial contribution for the education of a student. Parents choose a school and present the voucher, and the government allocates funding accordingly to the school.

Some vouchers are only for students living in poverty, allowing them to choose a school that perhaps better meets their needs than their neighborhood school or another

Figure 3.1 School choice options supported by government funding

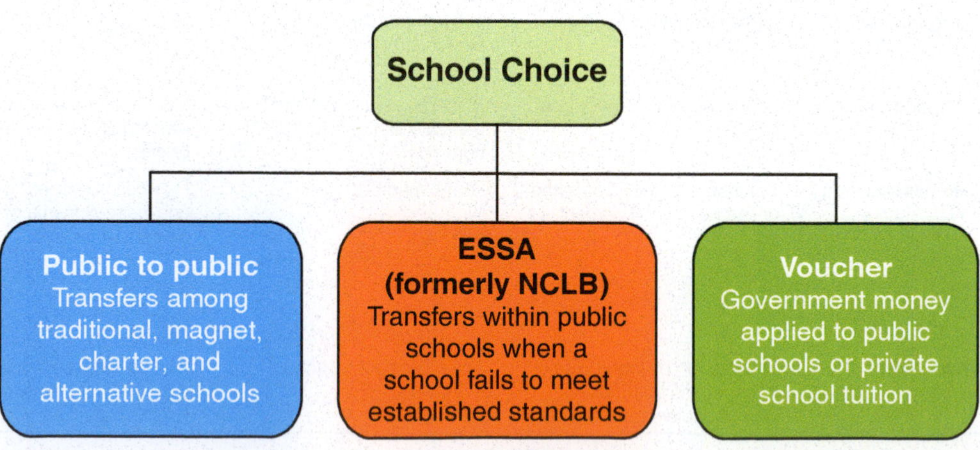

Sara Powell, Your Introduction to Education: Explorations in Teaching,4e © 2019, Pearson Education, Inc., New York, NY

public school. Other vouchers are awarded to any student within a designated area to use within a school district, or even across district lines. Some vouchers may be used only in public schools, whereas others may be applied to private school tuition or even to schools with a religious affiliation. The viability of voucher plans often sparks debates in state legislatures.

Consider this. Private schools are free to admit or refuse any student. They can decide not to take vouchers from students who don't fit in for any reason, including gender, race, past or potential achievement, or disability. Likewise, they can recruit and admit the most motivated, highest-achieving students. Public money in the form of vouchers thus has the potential to become a tool of discrimination.

The use of vouchers to attend schools with religious affiliation is perhaps the most controversial aspect of the program. Many people consider it a violation of the separation of church and state, and this obstacle may lead to the demise of vouchers as school choice alternatives. However, in 2002 the Supreme Court upheld a statewide voucher program in Ohio with Chief Justice William H. Rehnquist saying in the 5–4 decision that vouchers are neutral with respect to religion because parents choose the school where voucher money is used. With so many educators opposed to vouchers, the question will likely emerge again.

Do vouchers help more students succeed? In cities such as Milwaukee, Cleveland, New Orleans, and Washington, DC, there is little evidence that children who use vouchers to leave their home schools even keep up with their peers who opted to stay where they were, much less surpass them. Questions remain as reports emerge of entire schools made up completely of students with vouchers becoming private schools created just to take state money (Simon, 2013). In every state with vouchers we hear parental testimonials about how the voucher took their children out of failing schools. But until there are research findings that the vouchers have a positive effect on the larger body of children they serve, questioning their validity will continue.

ADVOCATES AND CRITICS OF SCHOOL CHOICE. School choice, regardless of the format, has its advocates and its critics. If we simply pose the question, "Should parents have the right to choose a school that best meets the needs of their children?" (Jenlink, Stewart, Stewart, 2012) most Americans would say yes. Table 3.3 lists several opposing views of school choice.

Table 3.3 Advocates' and critics' views of school choice

Advocates	Critics
Competition raises the standards, and consequently the performance, of all schools.	Competition destroys cooperation among teachers, schools, and communities.
Competition gives parents decision-making power to choose for their children.	Only parents who are vocal advocates for their children will take advantage of options.
Competition forces low-performing schools to go out of business.	Students remaining in low-performing schools suffer.
Choice better accommodates diversity.	Choice leads to the possibility of further segregation.
Choice provides equal opportunities.	Choice exacerbates inequities.

Application Exercise 3.1: Table 3.3 Advocates' and critics' views of school choice

Even with all the variety of schools and choice options, the needs of some learners are still not being met. This reality deserves urgent attention and our best efforts. In this chapter's *The Opinion Page* feature we find praise for vouchers that appear to have benefitted children in New York City, with implications for other communities.

The Opinion Page

This Opinion Editorial appeared in the *Florida Times-Union* on September 4, 2012.

Low-Income Parents Deserve a School Choice, and Other Opinions

by the Times-Union editorial staff

What is a low-income family to do with failing schools and the inability to move to a better school system? Too often, a stifling bureaucracy means that change won't happen soon enough for the students trapped in the system.

One alternative has been to create vouchers that allow students to take their funding to private schools. Much controversy surrounds them for understandable reasons.

Just fix the public schools, critics say. Easier said than done, and usually of no use to students who don't have many years to waste. Now a study shows that vouchers can provide better education, especially in low-income neighborhoods. A study from the liberal Brookings Institution and the conservative Hoover Institution has documented the benefits in New York City.

The study included groups of students from kindergarten in 1997 to college enrollment in 2011. The researchers followed students who won a voucher lottery with a group who did not, the control group. This is the gold standard of research. The result: An African-American student who used a voucher to attend a private school was 24 percent more likely to enroll in college than one who did not.

"We know of no other voucher study that has been as successful at tracking students over such a long period of time," wrote Mathew Chingos of the Brookings Institution and Paul Peterson of the Hoover Institution in *The Wall Street Journal*.

Vouchers can provide an escape from a failing school system as well as pressure [by] the public schools to improve. The largest provider of private schools in the New York study was the Catholic archdiocese, which has a history of educating low-income students without regard to race and creed. But this is no panacea, either, since Catholic schools often are under their own pressures.

Vouchers can help point out that there are options for educating low-income students that the public schools should be emulating. In the final analysis, there is no replacement for a good public school system. However, vouchers can help show the way and provide an outlet for families.

This Opinion Page piece makes the point that choices are necessary for the success of students who don't have time to wait for us to "fix" public schools that are not meeting their needs. Write a well-developed paragraph in response to each of the following questions:

1. Some U.S. public schools are failing to meet the needs of many children. Does this fact justify the use of public money to fund vouchers used for private school education? What dilemmas might this involve?
2. Now that you know more about school choice, what other solution besides vouchers may meet the needs of low-income families and their children who are "trapped" in low-performing schools? Explain.
3. The writer states, "Vouchers can help point out that there are options for educating low-income students that the public schools should be emulating." Do you believe that school choice can lead to improvement for all schools? If so, what do we need to do to make this a reality?

Point of Reflection 3.2

Did you attend public schools or private schools, or perhaps both at different times during your K–12 experience? Were the public schools traditional neighborhood schools, magnet schools, charter schools, or alternative schools? If you attended private school(s), write a brief description.

Check Your Understanding 3.3

3.4 What Is School Like at Different Levels?

3.4 Distinguish among different levels of school.

Schools in the United States are organized and structured in four basic levels: early childhood, elementary, middle, and high school. Grades included vary within the levels; it is not unusual for schools to combine levels. Perhaps the most common combination is early childhood and elementary in a K–5 configuration, with many public schools including 4-year-olds and sometimes 3-year-olds. Schools serving children in K–8 have recently become more prevalent. In smaller communities, middle and high school adolescents may be in one building. In very small communities, K–12 schools may serve all the students. Regardless of the grade configuration, developmental considerations are vital.

Structure and Organization of Early Childhood Education

Early childhood education is commonly divided into three basic age spans: preschool, kindergarten, and primary grades. Educators tend to agree that early childhood settings should be characterized by warmth, sensitivity, and nurture. Learning through play, with healthy doses of experimentation and discovery, describes a commonly held and balanced early childhood education philosophy. Let's briefly explore some of the structural and organizational components of early childhood educational settings.

PRESCHOOL. Experiences of 3- and 4-year-olds in the United States vary enormously. Some children stay home with a parent; some are provided simple child care. Others have a more structured **preschool** environment housed within a primary or elementary school. In this setting, often designated as a *prekindergarten* for 4-year-olds, care is enhanced by exposure to basic educational concepts. Preschool education may follow many different models.

The **Montessori** approach to early childhood education, with mixed-age grouping and self-pacing, is growing in popularity and has the reputation of being high quality when faithfully implemented (Morrison, 2014). Teachers in a Montessori setting are primarily guides, with children acting independently to choose learning activities. The **HighScope** approach, widely used in preschool through early elementary settings, is built on consistency and few transitions during the day as children construct meaning for themselves in problem-solving situations within learning centers. The **Reggio Emilia** approach to early childhood education for ages 3 months to 6 years is based on relationships among children, families, and teachers. Close long-term relationships are built because the teachers in each classroom stay with the same children for up to 3 years (Kostelnik, Soderman, and Whiren, 2015). **Head Start** is the largest provider of government-funded preschool education, serving over one million students each year across the United States in 1,700 agencies in local communities in every state. Most students are served in heavily regulated centers. Children attend for half or whole days (U.S. Department of Health and Human Services, 2016).

KINDERGARTEN. Once considered an optional bridge between preschool, or no school at all, and the beginning of formal education in first grade, **kindergarten** (meaning "child's garden") has become part of almost every 5- to 6-year-old child's educational experience, some for half a day and others for the entire day. However, full-day kindergarten is mandatory in only 15 states, plus Washington, DC, with 34 states requiring that full-day kindergarten be offered in every school district. Some districts offer half-day kindergarten free of charge and will extend to full-day for a fee (National Association for the Education of Young Children [NAEYC], 2015).

Figure 3.2 Sample half-day kindergarten schedule

8:50–9:10	Arrival, daily business, opening activities
9:10–9:30	Whole-group instruction in literacy
9:30–10:30	Small-groups rotate through reading and writing centers
10:30–10:45	Recess
10:45–11:45	Math instruction
11:45–12:15	Lunch
12:15–12:30	Read aloud
12:30–1:15	Science (physical education on Tuesday and Thursday)
1:15–1:30	Silent reading
1:30–2:15	Social studies (art on Monday; music on Wednesday)
2:15–2:45	Center time
2:45–3:10	Whole-group review of day, cleanup, dismissal

What occurs in both whole-day and half-day kindergarten classrooms across the country varies. In some kindergarten classrooms, children are involved in literacy-building activities; in others, there's little evidence of any emphasis on literacy. Some kindergartens are housed in K–5 or K–6 elementary schools, whereas others are in primary school settings that may include prekindergarten or kindergarten through grades 2 or 3. Figure 3.2 displays a possible schedule for half-day kindergarten, with teachers following a similar schedule twice a day. The step from kindergarten to first grade is a giant one, so it is crucial that the term *readiness* has become a major part of the vocabulary of early childhood education.

PRIMARY GRADES. Teachers in **primary classrooms**, grades 1 through 3, are faced with the challenge of meeting the needs of children with widely varying levels of both readiness for learning and acquired knowledge and skills. Imagine a first-grade classroom with 5 children who have received very little home encouragement for learning and did not attend kindergarten, 10 children who attended three different kindergartens that varied widely in their approaches, and 4 students who are reading independently. The challenge is to engage them all in learning based on where they are today, with a view of their unlimited potential. Figure 3.3 shows a general schedule for a primary classroom.

Summit Primary, one of our focus schools, doesn't have a preschool program. Children must be 5 years old to enter one of Summit's three levels of kindergarten. The *Boost* class is for children who need more basic guidance and instruction. The *Average* class is for most of the children. The *Enrichment* class is for children who have already mastered some of the typical kindergarten skills, such as recognizing and writing the alphabet, reading one-syllable and often-used sight words, recalling a story orally in correct sequence, counting to 100, and making and explaining simple graphs. Some children go directly from one level of kindergarten to first grade, and others have the

Figure 3.3 Sample primary grade schedule

9:25–9:40	Arrival, morning exercises
9:40–10:40	Learning centers
10:40–10:50	Cleanup
10:50–11:10	Outdoor or gym play/snack
11:10–11:30	Whole-group instruction
11:30–11:45	Small-group time, cooperative activity
11:45–12:00	Art projects
12:00–12:15	Closing exercises/dismissal

Repeat with another group of children 1:20–4:05

Focus School

Summit Primary School

Summit Station, Ohio

Kindergarten–second grade

Principal: Laura Hill

Summit Primary is the only K–2 school in the Licking Heights School District. This is a purposeful configuration. Principal Laura Hill says she likes the format because she has every kindergarten, first-grade, and second-grade teacher in the district in her building. This lends a great deal of consistency to how children are taught and what and when they learn as Summit Primary retains its specialty of early childhood education. The grade-level teachers work together as teams to provide instruction that is developmentally appropriate for young children.

To learn more about the structure and organization of Summit Primary School, where focus teachers Brandi Wade and Renee Ayers teach, take a school tour and watch Principal Laura Hill's school tour and interview.

Sara Davis Powell

Summit Primary School, Summit Station, Ohio

Application Exercise 3.2: Principal Laura Hill's School Tour and Interview

opportunity to stay in kindergarten for another year to build a stronger foundation for first grade.

We learned in Chapter 2 that Summit Primary student population has gone from almost all English-speaking to a rich mixture of 17 different languages as the town of Summit Station has grown from a small community to a suburbanlike area. This change has proven to be challenging as the faculty continues to provide effective education for all students.

Figure 3.4 Sample third-grade schedule (self-contained)

8:50–9:15	Whole-class morning meeting
9:15–9:35	Small-group reading
9:35–9:55	Whole-class instruction in writing/spelling
9:55–10:20	Reading and writing activities
10:20–10:40	Recess and snack
10:40–11:15	Whole-group math instruction/activities
11:15–12:00	Alternating physical education (M), art (T), physical education (W), music (Th), physical education (F)
12:00–12:35	Lunch, recess
12:35–1:15	Alternating social studies and science
1:15–1:45	Alternating computer and library time
1:45–2:00	Read aloud
2:00–2:30	Free choice centers
2:30–2:50	Reading and writing activities
2:50–3:10	Whole-group class meeting
3:15	Dismissal

Structure and Organization of Elementary Education

Elementary classrooms may be **self-contained**, meaning that one teacher has responsibility for one group of children most of the school day. In some schools, teachers may share responsibility for a group of children, each specializing in one or two subject areas. A sample schedule for a self-contained third-grade classroom is provided in Figure 3.4. A sample schedule for a fourth-grade classroom with a team of three teachers, each teaching a core subject area, is provided in Figure 3.5. A team of three teachers would accommodate three classes of fourth-graders.

The two focus teachers at Rees Elementary School in Spanish Fork, Utah, have multigrade, or **multiage classrooms**, where children in three grade levels learn together. Chris Roberts and Brenda Beyal, along with teammate Tim Mendenhall, each have homeroom classes made up of third-, fourth-, and fifth-graders. They teach all four **core subjects**—language arts, math, science, and social studies—to their own classes, but each specializes in a fine arts area. Chris teaches movement

Figure 3.5 Sample fourth grade schedule (three-teacher team)

8:50–9:05	Whole-class meetings in homerooms
9:05–10:10	Block time: Group 1: Math Group 2: English language arts Group 3: Science/social studies
10:10–10:30	DEAR (Drop everything and read) in homeroom
10:30–10:50	Journal writing in homerooms
10:50–11:10	Recess and snack
11:10–12:15	Block time: Group 1: English language arts Group 2: Science/social studies Group 3: Math
12:15–12:35	Lunch
12:35–1:00	Computer or library time
1:00–2:05	Block time: Group 1: Science/social studies Group 2: Math Group 3: English language arts
2:05–2:40	Physical education
2:40–3:00	Alternating art and music
3:00–3:10	Whole-class meetings in homerooms
3:15	Dismissal

Focus School

Rees Elementary School

Spanish Fork, Utah

Kindergarten–fifth grade

Principal: Mike Larsen

Rees Elementary is a school for kindergarten through fifth-grade students in Spanish Fork, Utah, just south of Salt Lake City. Located in a suburban area at the base of the Wasatch Mountains, Rees incorporates an emphasis on the arts supported by an experienced and enthusiastic faculty. Although each grade level provides traditional classrooms, Rees also has a dynamic team of three teachers who spend their days in multiage classrooms of third-, fourth-, and fifth-grade students, all learning together.

To learn more about the structure and organization of Rees Elementary, where focus teachers Chris Roberts and Brenda Beyal teach, watch Principal Mike Larsen's school tour and interview.

Sara Davis Powell

Rees Elementary School, Spanish Fork, Utah

Application Exercise 3.3: Principal Mike Larsen's School Tour and Interview

and dance, Brenda teaches visual arts, and Tim teaches theater arts to all three classes.

Let's consider Brenda's class as an example of a multiage classroom. In the beginning of the school year, she has third-graders who are new to her class, fourth-graders who have already been in her class for 1 year, and fifth-graders who have already been in her class for 2 years. At the end of the school year, the fifth-graders move on to middle school after having been in Brenda's class for 3 years, and a new group of children who have finished second grade will be assigned to their first year with Brenda. One third of her class will be new each school year.

Another possible elementary school teacher–student configuration with benefits similar to those of multiage grouping is **looping**, which occurs when a teacher stays with a particular group of students for more than 1 year. As the students go, for instance, from first to second grade, the teacher moves with them. Among the many positive reasons to loop are the following (Roberts, Kellough, and Moore, 2011):

- A consistent relationship develops between teacher and students and lasts for 2 or 3 years.
- Student learning preferences, strengths, weaknesses, interests, behavior patterns, potential, family circumstances, and the like, are well known to the teacher.
- The last few weeks of the school year are often used more productively, with summer reading and project assignments more meaningful.
- The beginning of the school year requires fewer getting-acquainted and routine-practicing experiences.

Structure and Organization of Middle-Level Education

Some schools that serve sixth-, seventh-, and eighth-graders are **departmentalized**, with teachers teaching their own subjects and meeting occasionally with other teachers who teach the same subject. For instance, with departmentalization, a teacher has Jamal in math but does not collaborate with Jamal's social studies or science teacher. The math teacher may not even know who Jamal has for social studies or science. According to the **Association for Middle Level Education (AMLE)** (formerly National Middle School Association), the preferred organizational structure for middle-level education is the student–teacher team, known as an **interdisciplinary team**. A team generally includes four core subject-area teachers and the 80 to 100 or so students they share. If Jamal is on a team, all his teachers know exactly who teaches him each core subject. The team of teachers meets at least three times a week to plan together and discuss student progress and concerns. This kind of teaming is developmentally appropriate for **young adolescents** (National Middle School Association, 2010).

Figure 3.6 Middle school student schedules

Traditional schedule (5 minutes to change classes)

8:00–8:10	Homeroom
8:15–9:10	Math
9:15–10:10	English language arts
10:15–11:10	Band/art/foreign language/drama (9 weeks each)
11:15–11:45	Lunch
11:50–12:45	Science
12:50–1:45	Computer education/physical education (one semester each)
1:50–2:45	Social studies
2:50–3:00	Homeroom
3:00	Dismissal

Block Schedule

8:00–8:15	Homeroom
8:20–10:00	English language arts block
10:05–10:55	Related arts rotation
11:00–11:30	Lunch
11:35–1:15	Math block
1:20–2:10	Science and social studies (rotating days)
2:15–3:05	Related arts rotation
3:05	Dismissal

In some **middle-level schools**, students attend six or seven classes a day, each 50 to 60 minutes long. These classes include the core subjects, as well as other subjects that are considered **exploratory courses** or **related arts courses**. These may include art, music, physical education, industrial arts, languages, drama, and computer education, among others. Figure 3.6 shows both a traditional six-period student schedule and a schedule allowing for longer class periods, commonly called a **block schedule**.

Focus School

Cario Middle School

Mt. Pleasant, South Carolina

Sixth–eighth grade

Principal: Carol Bartlett

Cario Middle School serves sixth-, seventh-, and eighth-grade students and is located in Mt. Pleasant, South Carolina, a medium-sized city just across the Wando River from historic Charleston. Cario provides young adolescents with the foundational components of a true middle school, including teams of teachers who teach specific groups of students, close teacher–student relationships, high expectations, and a support network that boosts both academic and personal growth.

At Cario, each core class is taught for 70 minutes. The students also have one class period for a variety of special classes that are rotated every 9 weeks. They have a 30-minute lunch period and 5 minutes to go from class to class. Cario teachers provide a rich array of clubs and after-school activities from which students may choose.

Sara Davis Powell

Cario Middle School, Mt. Pleasant, South Carolina

To learn more about the structure and organization of Cario Middle School, where focus teachers Traci Peters and Deirdre Huger-McGrew teach, watch Principal Carol Bartlett's school tour and interview.

Application Exercise 3.4: Principal Carol Bartlett's School Tour and Interview

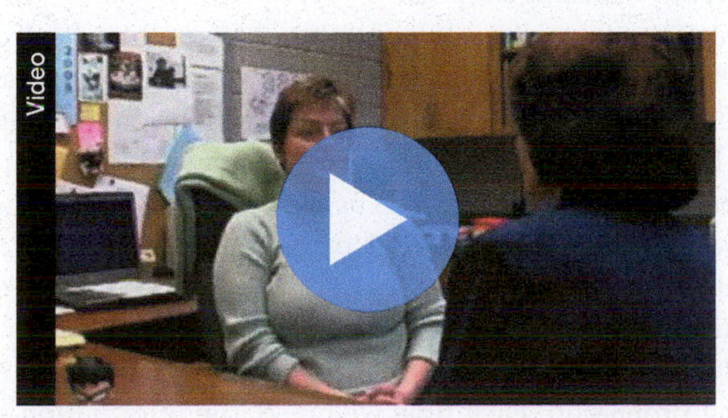

Structure and Organization of High School Education

High school may be a very recent experience for you, or it may have occurred decades ago. Virtually everyone agrees that high school represents a unique time of life. The four years of ninth, tenth, eleventh, and twelfth grades provide vivid memories. These memories are so revered that many graduates choose to relive them every 10 years or so as they make their way back to reunions to reminisce, to see what and how our classmates are doing, or perhaps to show off or embellish personal accomplishments. Then there are those who would rather forget that time and ambivalent or even painful memories. Regardless of personal feelings or memories from both an academic and a social perspective, high school experiences have a significant and long-lasting impact on most people.

High school teachers typically specialize in one major subject and teach different areas or levels of that subject. All teachers of a subject form a department and meet periodically to discuss issues such as course materials, innovations and dilemmas in the subject field, and professional development opportunities. Departmentalization is the primary organizational structure of high schools.

Some high schools adhere to a traditional schedule of six or seven classes a day, each about an hour long. Students attend these classes for two semesters to earn a credit in each. However, alternative schedules are gaining popularity. Some schools are choosing to use blocks of 90 to 100 minutes per class that allow for more complete cycles of learning, such as completion of labs, reading and reflecting on literature, and proving as well as applying math theories.

Block schedules may take one of two forms. Each has benefits. One form is composed of four classes per day of 90 to 100 minutes, every day, thus allowing four courses to be completed in a semester. One of the major benefits of this type of schedule is that students have only four subjects to study at a time, rather than six or seven. With four courses per semester, students have the opportunity to earn 32 credits in 4 years of high school. The other basic form of block scheduling is the alternating-day model. With this schedule, students also receive credit for eight courses a year, but each course meets for 90 to 100 minutes every other day for two semesters.

Our focus high school, Roosevelt High School in Fresno, California, is actually two high schools in one. Most students (about 2,100) attend the comprehensive program, and about 500 students attend the arts magnet school, Roosevelt School of the Arts. The student population of Roosevelt High School, primarily Hispanic and Asian, is not typical of most high schools in the United States but is more common in California, Texas, and Florida. Most of you did not attend high schools that mirror Roosevelt. Most of you will not teach in high schools like Roosevelt, but some of you will. The majority of Roosevelt's students are from low-income homes. The majority of you are not. So why is Roosevelt our focus high school?

There are several reasons. First, you need to see that effective teachers engage students in interesting and relevant lessons in all schools, regardless of the student profile or school setting. Second, because the high school that is so fresh in many of your memories is most likely a rural or suburban high school with families in middle-to upper-income brackets, you need to be exposed to a high school that is outside your zones of awareness and comfort. And, perhaps most important, adolescents are adolescents. Similarities outweigh elements of diversity. Focus teachers Craig Cleveland and Angelica Reynosa teach at Roosevelt High.

We often return to discussions of school levels as we address various aspects of the teaching profession. Each time we do so, the information will build on previous topics so that you will have a view of the big picture of what teaching is like in each level. Regardless of the level you decide to teach, your school will be in one of three principal settings.

Focus School

Roosevelt High School

Fresno, California

Ninth–twelfth grade

Principal: Maria Romero

Roosevelt High School in Fresno, California, is a large urban school for ninth- through twelfth-graders. The student population of Roosevelt is predominantly Hispanic and Asian. Many of the Roosevelt students are children of migrant farm workers, and a significant number have only recently moved to the United States. The dedicated and creative faculty at Roosevelt High provide rich learning opportunities for all students, regardless of race, ethnicity, primary language, or socioeconomic status.

To learn more about the structure and organization of Roosevelt High School, where Craig Cleveland and Angelica Reynosa teach, take a school tour with Assistant Principal John Lael and watch Principal Maria Romero's interview.

Sara Davis Powell

Roosevelt High School, Fresno, California

Application Exercise 3.5: Principal Maria Romero's Interview and John Lael's Tour

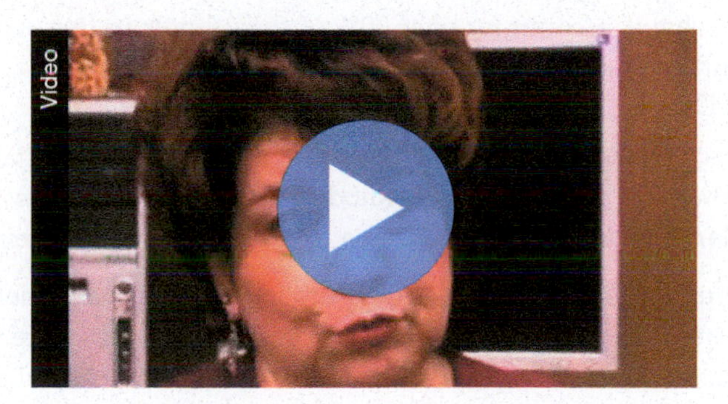

Point of Reflection 3.3

Which level of school appeals to you most as a future teacher? What experiences have you had with the school level and children/adolescents at this level?

Check Your Understanding 3.4

3.5 What Are the Three Principal Settings of U.S. Schools?

3.5 Elaborate differences among the three principal settings of U.S. schools.

When it comes to schooling, geography has a major impact. Sometimes a mile or two is significant with regard to educational experiences. Although the federal government has a new, more complicated system of classifying schools, the commonly accepted categories of schools—rural, suburban, and urban—exist in all 50 states and probably conjure up certain images in your mind that are generalized impressions of what each embodies. This section refines those images.

A focused view will reveal some generalities about the context of schooling in rural, suburban, and urban areas. The day-to-day realities of children within these three settings, both in and out of school, may be vastly different in terms of home, socioeconomic circumstances, and school opportunities. These differences may reflect the expectations held by parents, the community, and educators of what children can do and can be. Most teachers can do little to alter the out-of-school realities faced by their schools and schoolchildren. However, what teachers *can* alter are the ways they view students and their potential. It's a matter of values—both teachers' and students'.

Rural Schools

About a third of U.S. students attend **rural schools**, or schools in communities characterized by geographic isolation, sparse populations per square mile, and few retail stores. Here are some interesting facts about rural schools in the United States:

- Twenty percent of Alaska's schools employ three or fewer teachers each, indicating how rural they are.
- Rural schools account for over 70% of the schools in five states: Maine (highest percentage of students in rural schools), Vermont, Montana, North Dakota, and South Dakota.
- Rural schools account for fewer than 20% of schools in eight states—Massachusetts (the lowest percentage at 4%), Rhode Island, New York, New Jersey, Maryland, Florida, Connecticut, and California (Johnson, Showalter, Klein, and Lester, 2014).

Most rural schools are smaller than urban and suburban schools. However, some draw students from an area that may encompass hundreds of square miles and have large student populations. A single primary school, elementary school, middle school, and high school, each with more than 800 students, may serve such a large geographic area.

Geographic isolation often means that students may have few of the opportunities and experiences found in more populated areas—for example, museums, art studios, and performing arts venues. Even basic services that people in suburban and urban areas take for granted, such as hospitals and large libraries, may not be readily available.

A high school of 100 to 200 students that is over an hour away from a medium-size town may have difficulty offering ample opportunities for what is commonly viewed as a well-rounded education. Think about it. To offer adequate coursework, a high school must employ certified subject-area teachers. Supporting an Algebra II class of 6 costs just about as much as supporting a class of 28, but districts must do so with much less financial support due to a low student enrollment count. Regardless of class size, the course requires a teacher and a classroom. Small high schools face similar constraints in offering extracurricular opportunities. It may be difficult to offer French club, debate team, football and basketball teams, and orchestra.

Hiring and retaining qualified teachers in small or large rural schools is a significant problem, even though the schools may be community-oriented centers in safe, scenic places. However, the benefits that accompany a rural area such as ready access to recreation and natural beauty may outweigh any perceived drawbacks for some.

Suburban Schools

About 40% of students in U.S. schools attend **suburban schools**. These schools most often serve students who live in single-family homes with grassy yards in areas dotted with shopping centers, places of worship, and recreational facilities. Apartment complexes and townhouses are scattered among the well-lit paved streets. Every few miles or so, there's a school. Small-town schools most closely resemble suburban schools; data from both categories are combined in this chapter.

Many people who live in the suburbs are likely to be in the middle-class to affluent socioeconomic spectrum. Their communities are basically safe places with adequate public services that provide a generally comfortable lifestyle. The schools, even in tight state budget situations, generally continue to operate at acceptable levels with tolerable class sizes, textbooks for each child in most subjects, and satisfactory building maintenance. Within suburban schools, students generally experience organization and order, extracurricular opportunities, and some degree of community participation and approval. These factors don't necessarily mean that students are learning at optimal levels, but there are some obvious advantages.

Many families choose to live in the suburbs and in small- to medium-size towns primarily because of what the schools offer their children. Reale state agents have long known that the public school options for specific residential areas have much to do with property appeal. Families desire stability and a satisfactory free education. If they can afford it, they buy homes in locations that will fulfill these desires. Do they get what they pay for? Most families would probably answer, "Yes."

Urban Schools

About a quarter of U.S. students attend urban schools. Most **urban school** settings are in sharp contrast to those of suburban schools. The facilities tend to be older, part of the fabric of downtowns that may or may not continue to be vibrant community areas. Although architecturally appealing, the older buildings are generally more expensive and difficult to maintain, and are likely to be in a state of disrepair more often than suburban school buildings.

Urban schools are likely to serve many students who live in low-income settings. As Jonathan Kozol poignantly related in *Savage Inequalities* (1991), funding differences certainly exist between some urban and suburban areas. However, some urban schools actually receive more funding per student than do suburban schools. One reason for this is that the federal government has programs that provide extra money for schools with student populations living below certain economic levels. Research supports the assertion that students from low-income families require more resources to perform at the same levels as students from middle-income families.

Many urban school settings present some unique challenges. The students in urban schools more often come to school with greater needs than can be met by the curriculum alone. Still, there are schools in urban settings that make effective teaching and learning connections.

Regardless of the school setting, the explosion of technology and social media devices is undeniable. Rather than denying the impact of this situation, some schools and school districts are embracing it with programs now commonly referred to as Bring Your Own Device (BYOD) or Bring Your Own Technology (BYOT), explored in this chapter's *SocialMEdia* feature.

All Photos: Sara Davis Powell

A few miles can make a significant difference in the school experience of students. At Wells High School in San Francisco, students look out the window to see Alamo Hill and the city skyline. Just 30 miles north of the city, students look out the window of Bolinas-Stinson Elementary at sea lions in Bolinas Lagoon.

SocialMEdia

Bring Your Own Device (BYOD) is a relatively new initiative spreading across the country. Some schools now allow students and staff to use personal mobile devices on their wireless networks for instructional purposes. Advocates say every school is participating in BYOD, but some admit it and others don't; the student devices are in schools one way or another. The choice is either to embrace and manage their use, as messy as the process may be, or to continue to try to keep the devices out of the classroom under threat of punishment.

In BYOD schools, laptops, netbooks, Smartphones, tablets, iPods, and more are being used to take notes, complete assignments, create study tools, and work collaboratively with teachers and other students. As with any new initiative, there are benefits and challenges to consider. As BYOD becomes more widespread and schools and teachers share what works and what doesn't work, the process will become manageable and productive.

Students may benefit from BYOD because they are:

- Already familiar and comfortable using their own technology; therefore, they can focus on actually learning with their devices rather than learning how to use them
- More likely to have remembered their beloved mobile devices than textbooks or notes
- More likely to continue learning outside of school hours
- More likely to have limitless access to information and resources
- Engaged by technology and more likely be more enthusiastic and excited about learning

Challenges of BYOD include:

- Creating a BYOD policy that is manageable is difficult
- Needing teacher professional development in order to optimize BYOD possibilities

- Overloading a school's wireless network
- Providing greater opportunities for cheating
- Encouraging the possibility that students may be more easily distracted while working on their own mobile devices
- Students forgetting their devices or forgetting to charge them (Will there be "loaner" devices?)
- Crating an equity gap because not all students will own the devices (Again, will there be "loaner" devices?)
- Causing an increased possibility of loss and theft.
- Needing parents to buy into BYOD and agreeing that students may take expensive technology devices to school.

If Bring Your Own Device is going to be part of the teaching and learning strategies of a school, it's important to make sure that the end justifies the means. Mobile devices can change the way teachers teach and students learn if used appropriately. Schools and teachers must work to create motivating and engaging instructional strategies that lead to increased learning. "How to" advice and lots of opinions are available on the Internet.

Point of Reflection 3.4

Which of the three settings appeals to you most as a future teacher? Do you want to teach in a setting similar to where you have lived during your K–12 years? Or would you prefer to move to a different setting?

Check Your Understanding 3.5

3.6 What Is an Effective School?

3.6 Determine characteristics of an effective school.

Effective schools meet the learning needs of the students who attend them. What are the characteristics of an effective school? Theorists and practitioners have attempted to measure schools' effectiveness for decades. Grappling with what elements characterize effective schools keeps the conversation alive. The minute we say, "Okay. This is it. If a school does this list of things in these ways, it is effective," we will box in our thinking and become stagnant. Still, although characteristics may vary in many ways, we need a picture of what effective schools may look like and what students and teachers do in them.

Characteristics of Effective Schools

In 1966, the Equality of Educational Opportunity Study, commonly referred to as the **Coleman Report**, concluded that family and community factors such as poverty and parental levels of education prevented some children from learning, and that no matter what the schools did, some children would not be successful. Appalled by this assertion, many in the education community adopted the mantra "All children can learn." President Lyndon B. Johnson responded to this problem in the 1960s with landmark legislation called the Elementary and Secondary Education Act. Among other things, this act provided extra funding, called **Title I funding**, for schools with high numbers of children from low-income homes. In the 1970s, President Gerald Ford expanded equal educational opportunity by signing Public Law 94-142, making special education services a right, not a privilege.

The **Effective Schools Movement** of the 1970s was initiated based on the belief that all children can learn. This movement was designed to locate schools deemed effective for all children and to identify common characteristics among these schools, including:

- Clear and focused mission
- High expectations for success

- Instructional leadership
- Frequent monitoring of student progress
- Opportunity to learn and student time on task
- Positive home–school relations

Lists of characteristics of effective schools are usually quite similar. Effective schools may be found in rural, suburban, and urban areas. They may be early childhood, elementary, middle, or high schools, or any combination of grade-level configurations. They serve any range of colors, classes, and ethnicities of students. School effectiveness exists where students are learning and experiencing positive personal growth, facilitated by teachers who make a difference.

In 2012, Routman (pp. 56–61) proposed that there are principles and practices that have been proven to be most critical for effective teaching and learning. She tells us that teachers act professionally in ways that increase school effectiveness by following these principles and practices, summarized here.

1. ***Rely on strong principal leadership.*** Without strong principal leadership, it is rarely possible to have long-term improved student achievement.
2. ***Raise expectations for what's possible.*** High expectations are evident when teachers, among other things, do not waste instructional time, teach students to self-monitor learning and behavior, and give relevant assignments.
3. ***Participate in professional learning communities.*** A **professional learning community (PLC)** is a school-based group of teachers and administrators who work collaboratively to share practices and data analysis of student progress to improve teaching and learning.
4. ***Develop shared beliefs.*** Sharing beliefs is important to the relationships formed and the consistency of academic rigor.
5. ***Apply an optimal learning model.*** Taking learners from watching teachers do something to doing it themselves is a proven model of effective teaching and learning.
6. ***Participate in effective coaching experiences.*** Effective teacher coaches must, first of all, be experts in content and instruction, able to demonstrate strategies and help teachers become independent practitioners.
7. ***Work toward becoming a self-sustaining school.*** A self-sustaining school is one where there is a high level of collaboration and trust, where adults rely on one another to observe and give advice, and where adults are willing to work together for the benefit of students.

Check Your Understanding 3.6

Concluding Thoughts

We make a difference when we ask ourselves and one another "And how are the children?" in conjunction with our best efforts to facilitate learning, regardless of the school venue, level, or setting. Quality teachers for every student enhances a school's effectiveness. The education of quality teachers, the hiring and retention of quality teachers, and the continuing professional growth of quality teachers are key elements of effective schools, where a balance exists between students' academic achievement and personal development.

George Albano, the 25-year veteran principal of Lincoln Elementary School in Mount Vernon, New York, can answer "And how are the children? Are they all well?" by stating that 99% of his school's fourth-graders scored at or above basic skill levels in

English, math, and science even though more than 50% are eligible for free or reduced-price lunch and 60% are African American or Hispanic. He leads an effective school where the achievement gap is nonexistent and students are in the care of competent teachers who make them feel valued. Albano puts it this way, "Success comes down to hard work; great and dedicated teachers; an integrated curriculum; lots of art, music, and physical education; the willingness to bend and break rules occasionally; and the complete refusal to let any child fail to learn" (Merrow, 2004, p. 456).

Your challenge is clear. Be the generation of teachers who figures it out—the teachers who bring us closer to quality, effective education for all students.

After reading the Chapter in Review, respond to questions about Brandi Wade and the possibility that the grade levels of her district's schools may be reconfigured in this chapter's Developing Professional Competence.

Chapter in Review

What are the purposes of public schools in the United States?

- Although often used interchangeably, there are distinctions between education and schooling. *Education* happens continually through all of life's experiences, whereas *schooling* is the formal structure of teaching and learning.
- Transmitting and reconstructing society are two complementary purposes of U.S. schooling.
- Teaching students how to participate positively in society while facilitating academic learning are two complementary purposes of U.S. schooling.
- There is no conflict between meeting individual student needs and collective student needs.
- Although schooling in the United States sustains students for today, it also prepares them for tomorrow.

What is the culture of a school?

- The culture of a school is the context of the learning experiences, as well as adult and student behaviors and attitudes.
- A school's culture can be a positive force for learning, or a negative influence that interferes with learning, and all shades in between.
- Teachers have an enormous impact on a school's culture.

How do school venues differ?

- There is a great variety of schools in the United States, from the traditional neighborhood public school to the ultimate private school—the home.
- Traditional public schools have education programs that suit most students.
- Full-service schools attend to the academic, health, and social service needs of students and families, and, in many cases, of the community.
- A magnet school is a public school with a specific theme or focus.
- A charter school is a public school that is publicly funded and independently operated. Charter schools are free from many of the regulations that apply to other public schools.
- Alternative schools are schools designed to meet the needs of students who are not successful in traditional schools.

- Private schools may or may not be affiliated with a religious organization.
- Single-gender schools, most of which are private, are schools for boys only or for girls only.
- Homeschooling is a growing trend in the United States.
- For-profit schools are run by management companies. The concept is controversial when applied to public schools.
- School choice plans provide students and parents with options in both the public and private sectors.

What is school like at different levels?

- Early childhood education spans birth through age 8, or roughly through third grade.
- Elementary education may include a variety of grade levels, with K–5 or K–6 as the most common. Early childhood and elementary overlap on the low end; elementary and middle overlap on the high end.
- Middle school education usually includes grades 6 to 8.
- High school education usually includes grades 9 to 12.

What are the three principal settings of U.S. schools?

- Urban settings are cities with large downtowns and a dense population. Urban schools are likely to have a high percentage of minority students from low-income homes.
- Suburban/town settings are distinct locations that include neighborhoods and shopping/service/cultural facilities. Suburban/town schools are likely to have a lower percentage of minorities, with most students coming from middle- or upper-income homes.
- Rural settings are areas with sparse populations and few retail stores and services. Rural schools may be all white, all minority, or integrated to some extent, depending on the area.

What is an effective school?

- Effective schools are those that meet the learning needs of the students who attend them.
- Effective schools may have a variety of characteristics, with quality teaching as the most important common element.

Developing Professional Competence

Sara Davis Powell

Thoughtfully reading this scenario and responding to the items that follow it will help you prepare for licensure exams.

Brandi Wade enjoys the fact that as a kindergarten teacher she benefits from having all the other district kindergarten teachers in her building. Recall that as a K–2 school, Summit Primary houses all the kindergarten, first-grade, and second-grade classes in the Licking Heights, Ohio, School District. However, as the district grows and diversifies, community members and individuals on the school board are talking about creating neighborhood schools, five for grades K–5, three for grades 6–8, and two high schools for grades 9–12.

Think about this dilemma from the perspectives of a variety of **stakeholders**, or those who have legitimate involvement and stand to gain or lose from the situation. Then respond to two short essay items involving the scenario. In your responses, be sure to address all the dilemmas and questions posed in each item. These items are followed by five multiple-choice questions.

1. Brandi and several other kindergarten teachers plan to present their case for keeping the district schools in their current configuration at a school board meeting. What do you think their three strongest arguments will be?
2. Do you predict the district will reconfigure the schools? If so, explain why. If not, explain your reasons for thinking the schools will remain in their current configuration.

Application Exercise 3.6: Developing Professional Competence

3. Brandi and the other kindergarten teachers think their teaching is more effective because of their collective expertise. They want to stay together. All of the following support the teachers' desire to stay together except:

   a. They can share ideas among nine teachers, rather than two or three that would result from structure changes.

   b. If there is a problem student, they have more options for classrooms for him or her.

   c. New programs are easier to implement because they can help each other.

   d. Materials are easier to manage.

4. Teachers of grades 3 to 6 in the intermediate school next door see the value of smaller schools that would be created if the county divides into school zones and also moves grade 6 to the middle school. With four grade levels, they have over 1,000 children in one building, with projected growth to 1,300 by next fall if nothing changes. Which rationale is the least important to their desire to see the district change grade-level configurations?

   a. There is no place large enough to gather all the students for special events.

   b. Research shows there is more violence and bad behavior in large schools than in small schools.

   c. Research shows that children feel a greater sense of belonging in a small school than in a large school, regardless of class size.

   d. Having grades K–5 in one building may lend to more family stability, especially for those with several children in the grade range.

5. Teachers in the current middle school that now includes grades 7 and 8 think that participation in after-school activities would increase if kids lived closer to the school they attend. It's very difficult to have after-school clubs and sports when most students are bused to school from all across the county. From a student's standpoint, which of the following would be the least important reason for creating schools that are physically more accessible to all students who attend?

   a. A school with fewer students, based on a smaller geographic area, will allow students more opportunities to be involved in a variety of activities.

   b. The schools would be more ecologically friendly because more students could walk to them.

   c. Students could go to school with others in their immediate vicinity, making it more likely that their friends live close enough to socialize on weekends or after school.

   d. In smaller schools students tend to know each other and their teachers better.

6. Many community members, including parents, believe that smaller schools with wider grade bands located throughout the county will be best for the Licking Heights district. In the proposed plan, Summit High School, which is now a full-service school with a health clinic and adult education classes, would be divided into two smaller schools. Why might two high schools, strategically located in the county, benefit students and their families more?

   a. High school sports teams would have competition within the district, allowing for more playing time for athletes.

   b. Competition between the two high schools would increase enthusiasm in the community.

   c. Research has shown that higher percentages of students in small schools get involved in activities than students in larger schools.

   d. A full-service school with a health clinic in a central location at the large school has not proven to be useful.

7. Some parents and alumni are opposed to breaking up Summit High School into two schools. Which of the following is likely the most often-cited reason for not breaking up Summit High School into two schools?

   a. A large county high school has a better chance of having an excellent record of athletic championships.

   b. A larger school provides more curricular opportunities for students.

   c. Fewer buses are needed for one location.

   d. One high school represents community cohesiveness.

Application Exercise 3.7: Developing Professional Competence

Flash Cards 3.1

Shared Writing 3.1: School Preference

Chapter 4
Curriculum, Assessment, and Accountability

Learning Objectives

After studying this chapter, you will have knowledge and skills to:

4.1 Articulate the elements of the formal curriculum.

4.2 Identify three other curricula in U.S. schools.

4.3 Summarize what is involved in classroom assessment.

4.4 Analyze how teachers evaluate student learning and assign grades.

4.5 Describe standardized tests, and how their results are used.

4.6 Explain who is accountable for student learning.

Dear Reader

Classroom teachers are curriculum designers and assessors of learning. Although teachers don't actually determine the curriculum, or what content and skills to teach, being a curriculum designer means they use a set of guidelines called standards to tell them what is appropriate at a particular grade level in a particular subject. Teachers then develop plans for teaching and learning and they design students' days so that there are opportunities to learn and practice the knowledge and skills of the prescribed curriculum.

One of a teacher's most challenging tasks is determining when and how much students learn. If teachers don't assume the role of assessor, they might design and teach lessons that they think are leading to learning when, in fact, the students aren't "getting it." To avoid unproductive teaching, educators must continually look for signs of learning—or the absence of them—to direct their teaching and improve student learning.

Who's responsible for student learning? Although common sense tells us the answer involves lots of people, including teachers, students, parents, and community members, teachers tend to get a disproportionate amount of "blame" when students don't succeed academically. Is this fair? No, of course not, because the factors that contribute to a child's success are many and complex. We teachers are responsible for much of the process that leads to learning and we gladly acknowledge this. However, when we dedicate ourselves to the teaching profession, we take on the burden of being in the public eye as the keeper and dispenser of knowledge, sharing the praise for successful student learning but also reaping the lonely blame for failure. The challenges and satisfactions of teaching make this fact a small price to pay for being one of the most important people in the lives of many children and adolescents!

Where **Do I Stand?**

Click here to complete the inventory online

The purpose of this inventory is to determine where you stand concerning what is taught and how it is taught in preK–12 schools. After reading an item, indicate your level of agreement by choosing a number and placing it in the blank before the statement. Following the inventory are directions for how to organize your responses and what they may indicate in terms of where you stand.

4 I strongly agree

3 I agree

2 I don't have an opinion

1 I disagree

0 I strongly disagree

____ 1. What students learn in school is basically what the school plans for them to learn.

____ 2. Teaching in ways that meet the needs of students with differing aptitudes is important.

____ 3. Much of what is learned in schools is unintentional on the part of teachers.

____ 4. Most of what is taught in school should be stable and not swayed by society.

____ 5. If only English language arts, math, science, and social studies were taught, schools would still fulfill their primary purposes of educating children and adolescents.

____ 6. Basing learning on real-world situations is an excellent way to teach.

____ 7. Projects provide ideal learning opportunities.

____ 8. Teacher-led class discussion is one of the most effective teaching strategies.

____ 9. The expectations of society should guide what is taught in schools.

____ 10. Although interesting, classes that don't directly address English language arts, math, science, and social studies are not important in fulfilling the primary purposes of U.S. schools.

____ 11. After-school clubs and organizations are important to the education of students.

____ 12. The teacher should be the focus of attention in the classroom.

____ 13. In the classroom, we teach who we are.

____ 14. Our vision of the future should heavily influence what is taught in U.S. schools.

____ 15. Some students should be allowed to go through some topics more quickly than other students.

____ 16. Music, visual arts, and dance should be part of a public school education.

____ 17. Teaching reading and writing is the responsibility of all teachers at all levels.

____ 18. Concentrating on one subject at a time is best for student learning.

____ 19. What is taught in schools should not be affected by cultural diversity.

____ 20. Lecture is a preferable way to teach for maximum learning.

____ 21. There are benefits associated with student collaboration.

____ 22. It is more important to master the basic subjects than to learn how to think critically.

____ 23. There is a core of knowledge that should dominate what is taught in preK–12 school.

____ 24. Student learning opportunities depend on what teachers teach.

ITEM #	*MY VIEW*	*ITEM #*	*MY VIEW*
1		2	
4		3	
5		6	
8		7	
10		9	
12		11	
18		13	
19		14	
20		15	
22		16	
23		17	
24		21	
Sum A		Sum B	

If sum A is larger than sum B, *you tend to believe there is a basic group of subjects that should dominate what is taught. The learning experiences are carefully planned and little is left to spontaneity or student interests.*

If sum B is larger than sum A, *you tend to believe in a broader scope of what should be part of student experiences. Teacher personality and demeanor figure into student learning, as do student interests.*

4.1 What Is the Formal Curriculum?

4.1 Articulate the elements of the formal curriculum.

Curriculum is the educational term for what students experience in schools. The **formal curriculum** encompasses what is intentionally taught within the stated goals for student learning. The formal curriculum, sometimes referred to as the **explicit curriculum**, is what teachers are expected to teach, what students are expected to learn, and what society expects of schools. The formal curriculum is based on three foundations: the needs of the subject, the needs of students, and the needs of society (Estes, Mintz, Gunter, 2011). These three needs align with what John Dewey conveyed in two of his most important books, *The School and Society* (Dewey, 1900) and *The Child and the Curriculum* (Dewey, 1902). The titles speak volumes, as do the texts, about the interconnectedness of society, students, and the subject matter itself. Dewey (1938) also emphasized that formal curriculum is dynamic, meaning that it is continually changing and evolving. Later in the chapter we explore three other kinds of curricula that contribute to the experiences of students in schools: informal, extra, and null.

As we consider the formal curriculum, we must acknowledge the guiding contributions of Ralph Tyler (1949), one of Dewey's students. Tyler developed what is now called the **Tyler Rationale**, proposing four questions that should be asked throughout the process of curriculum development:

1. What educational purposes should the school seek to attain?
2. What educational experiences can be provided that are likely to attain these purposes?
3. How can these educational experiences be effectively organized?
4. How can we determine whether these purposes are being attained?

Before about 1990, broad guidelines for what to teach were developed primarily by state planning committees and were based largely on textbook content, federal educational goals, and a "this is the way it's always been" attitude. Individual schools and teachers refined the state or school district guidelines to suit their particular circumstances. However, in 1989, curriculum development moved abruptly into what might be called the **era of**

standards when the National Council of Teachers of Mathematics (NCTM) published math standards for grades K to 12, the first official set of standards written for a core subject area.

Standards Influence What We Teach

Content standards define what students should know and be able to do relative to subject areas at specific grade levels. Standards help organize and guide teaching and learning in the classroom. Professional organizations of major subject areas have developed subject-specific content standards.

Two other types of standards influence curriculum. **Performance standards**, or benchmarks, designate the level of the knowledge or skill that is considered acceptable within a particular grade level. Some standards documents also include **process standards** that support content learning by explaining both how the content might best be learned and how to use the content once it is acquired. For example, the five broad areas of NCTM content standards—number and operations, algebra, geometry, measurement, data analysis/probability—are accompanied by five process standards: problem solving, reasoning and proof, communication, connections, and representation.

Because the United States Constitution does not specifically address education, what is taught and learned in U.S. schools is largely left up to individual states. By the beginning of the twenty-first–century, virtually every state had content standards in place, leading to what is called the **standards-based reform movement**, another way of expressing the era of standards.

Although most state standards are based on professional organization standards, there are variations among them. When the 2001 No Child Left Behind Act, the reauthorization of the Elementary and Secondary Education Act, required accountability, state standards and the associated standards-based testing became key to meeting this mandate. The pressure was on to show student achievement and improvement. The competitive nature of states, with their test results stacked up against one another, inevitably led to comparisons between state-determined results and results from the **National Assessment of Educational Progress (NAEP)**, often referred to as the "nation's report card." This comparison reveals major discrepancies, indicating that some state standards and tests are not as rigorous as others. Some states report high levels of proficiency among their students, only to have NAEP results imply that the state's students are not measuring up. In other words, it's easier to look good with regard to test results when standards are lower and tests are easier. This accounts, at least in part, for the increasing support for common standards.

COMMON CORE STATE STANDARDS. In this second decade of the twenty-first century, efforts aimed at the adoption of a set of common standards are in full swing. The work toward common standards, which would mean a national common curriculum in a practical sense, was initiated by two organizations that are made up of representatives from all of the states: the **National Governors Association (NGA)** and the **Council of Chief State School Officers (CCSSO)**. These organizations have joined together to work on the **Common Core State Standards Initiative**. The NGA and CCSSO (2010) tell us that the Common Core State Standards

- Are aligned with college and work expectations
- Are clear, understandable, and consistent
- Include rigorous content and application of knowledge through high-order skills
- Build on strengths and lessons of current state standards
- Are informed by other top-performing countries, so that all students are prepared to succeed in our global economy and society
- Are evidence and research based

Adoption of the Common Core State Standards in K–12 English language arts and math is voluntary for states and most have done so. Although the federal government did not write the standards, mounting research indicating state-to-state differences in standards and testing led to some federal funding being based on improvement for individual states and districts linked directly to alignment with the common, internationally competitive standards and testing.

Almost a decade after work began on the Common Core State Standards, some states are choosing to drop them. In fact, the standards have become controversial, and often for incredulous reasons. Some districts have embellished the basic Common Core by mandating particular instructional strategies that the public and many teachers mistakenly think are part of the Core. Groups of people who may not fully understand the intent or content of the standards have mounted campaigns to do away with the Common Core. For instance, North Carolina was one of the first states to enthusiastically adopt the Common Core. Then, 4 years later, the North Carolina legislature decided the standards amounted to federal interference in public education and led the state to withdraw. The state established a committee to write new standards and agreed that the new standards could be very similar to the Common Core, but would be named *North Carolina standards.* The state spent millions of dollars preparing teachers and materials to implement the Common Core, but, for a while, the state's official curriculum was put in limbo. As of 2017, North Carolina still aligns with the Common Core.

It is important for teachers to understand how the Common Core State Standards were developed and how they will be implemented. Frequently asked questions (FAQ) about the standards are shown in Figure 4.1. Take a few minutes to get a broader view of the common standards through careful reading of the questions and answers. The Common Core State Standards will likely play a major role in your teaching career.

Figure 4.1 Common Core State Standards

What are the Common Core State Standards (CCSS)?
The Common Core State Standards are standards written for K–12 English language arts and math to provide consistency of learning expectations across states. Before these standards, each individual state developed its own standards and standardized exams, resulting in widely varying topic emphases and levels of rigor in American public schools.

Who is leading the Common Core State Standards movement?
The Common Core State Standards are the result of collaboration between the Council of Chief State School Officers (CCSSO) and the National Governors Association Center for Best Practices (NGA). The CCSSO and NGA are state-based organizations that brought together teachers, school administrators, subject area experts, and education organizations from across the country to develop a common core of state standards for K–12 English language arts and math.

Why are the Common Core State Standards believed to be a valuable reform in K–12 education?
The developers of the common standards tell us they want every child to receive an education that provides tools necessary to succeed in college and beyond, no matter where they live. Because standards varied widely from state to state, consistency can only be accomplished through a set of common rigorous standards that provide clear expectations for how students, parents, administrators, education policy makers, and the community can work together toward providing the tools for success.

The Common Core State Standards make it easier for states to work together on ways to meet the standards and share helpful information and resources.

Common standards prompt textbook and digital media producers to concentrate on one set of standards and improve the resources available to all teachers and students.

The standards provide a measuring stick for student learning that is consistent from state to state. This is important for policy makers and education leaders who watch for progress on a national level.

Now that the English language arts and math standards are written, will they ever change?
Yes. The standards for K–12 English language arts and math are considered dynamic documents, meaning that they will be revised based on feedback as teachers use them and discover ways to improve them.

Will the Common Core State Standards prevent teachers from making decisions about how to teach?
No. The standards provide expectations for the knowledge and skills needed for student success. Teachers, principals, and others will decide how to help students meet the standards. Teachers will write lessons that address both the standards and student needs in their own classrooms.

Figure 4.1 *(continued)*

Figure 4.1 *(continued)*

Did teachers help create the Common Core State Standards?
Yes. Teachers participated in the development of the standards through multiple organizations including the National Education Association (NEA), American Federation of Teachers (AFT), National Council of Teachers of Mathematics (NCTM), and National Council of Teachers of English (NCTE). The CCSSO and NGA continually ask for comments and feedback.

Will more standards mean more tests?
No. The CCSS allow states to develop and share appropriate assessments. A test based on individual state standards is replaced by a test based on the common standards.

Will common standards be developed for other subjects?
No, that's not part of the plan. English-language arts and math were chosen because they are considered the basic subjects necessary for learning all subjects. Other subject areas are very important to education, but NGA and CCSSO will not develop standards in other subjects. States will continue to develop and revise rigorous and effective standards for other subjects with the help of organizations such as the National Coalition for Core Arts Standards, National Art Education Association, National Research Council, the National Science Teachers Association, the American Association for the Advancement of Science, the National Council for the Social Studies, the American Alliance for Health, Physical Education, Recreation and Dance, and the American Council on the Teaching of Foreign Languages.

Are the Common Core State Standards an attempt by the federal government to control public education?
The creation of the CCSS is a state-led endeavor, not a result of federal government efforts. However, the federal Department of Education agrees in principle with a common set of standards and uses financial incentives to encourage states to adopt the Common Core State Standards.

Based on: National Governors Association Center for Best Practices, Council of Chief State School Officers. (2010). *Common Core State Standards.* Retrieved January 10, 2017, from http://www.corestandards.org.

As with all reform efforts, there are people who are in favor of Common Core State Standards and others who object to them. Table 4.1 presents a variety of views of both advocates and critics.

Table 4.1 Advocates and critics of common core standards

Advocates Believe That Common Core Standards	Critics Believe That Common Core Standards
Provide clear and consistent goals for learning, regardless of where in the United States students may live.	Take away states' rights to determine what is taught and learned.
Prepare U.S. children for success in college and work.	Are premature and that individual state standards have not had sufficient time to succeed.
Unite teachers and students across the United States as a cooperative effort.	Do not allow for local educational values and use of local resources.
Provide common ground around which strategies and programs may be shared.	Detract from individualism of states and teachers.
Build on strengths and lessons of current state standards.	Are unwieldy and will not be enforceable.
Level the academic playing field for all students.	Will bring all states' standards down to the lowest common denominator.

OBJECTIONS TO STANDARDS. Although the standards are grade-level–specific, subject-based standards have brought unprecedented organization to what is taught and when it is taught. They are not perfect documents, however. The Common Core State Standards provide a measure of relief from the following flaws often cited for state-developed content standards:

- ***Excessive coverage:*** The sheer volume of standards in any content area may be overwhelmingly impractical.
- ***Fragmentation of learning:*** Isolated bits and pieces of knowledge and skills may not be connected and may therefore lack context and meaning.

- ***Details that obscure major ideas:*** Too many details may keep students and teachers from "seeing the forest for the trees."
- ***Broad concepts that are too nebulous:*** Standards written in broad generalities can be open to many interpretations.
- ***Lack of consistency:*** State standards and subsequent standards-based testing are uneven, with some more demanding than others.
- ***A less flexible way of teaching:*** Many experienced teachers find adherence to sets of standards inhibiting when compared to a curriculum that gives more choices.
- ***High-stakes accountability:*** Standards lead to testing, the results of which determine student grade-level retention, school status, teachers' jobs, and availability of funds, among other major consequences.
- ***Decisions influenced by disagreeing factions:*** Liberals and conservatives, religious and nonreligious, all battle for inclusion and exclusion of content, making standards "political footballs."

All of these objections and more are to be expected because any reform measure that changes what and how teachers teach and students learn is bound to be controversial. The debate is healthy and keeps the process alive and dynamic. Regardless of the controversy, standards give teachers information about what students should have learned in the past and must learn in the future. Using grade-level-specific standards for planning helps teachers fit their expectations into the bigger picture of student learning over time.

Uses and Limitations of Textbooks

Historically, one of the most influential determiners of what we teach has been the *textbook*. Now that adherence to some set of standards in the content areas is mandated by states, textbooks have lost a little of their power to shape curriculum. However, textbooks are likely to guide teaching on a daily basis if a textbook publisher responds by aligning content and skills to specific standards.

TEXTBOOKS IN THE CLASSROOM. Quality textbooks, whether paper-based or electronic, help organize and sequence course content. They provide a logical progression of topics, with content and skills that build on prior understanding and skills mastery. For instance, a social studies text will be organized chronologically so learners see how certain events impact subsequent events. A math textbook helps learners build on prior knowledge and skills in logical ways as they move, for instance, from recognition of geometric shapes to finding perimeter and then area in elementary geometry.

Teachers base much of their classroom assignments and homework on textbooks and the accompanying supplements. Supplementary materials may provide options for enrichment, remediation, extension, application, and practice of skills. They may also provide lesson plans to guide teachers, online assistance, workbooks, tests, and a variety of other resources for both students and parents.

LIMITATIONS OF TEXTBOOKS. Textbooks can be powerful—and generally positive—influences on what we teach and students learn, but they may also pose the following problems:

- Textbook content may not match standards.
- Textbooks may include too many topics, with few in adequate depth.
- There may be readability issues as the textbooks attempt to be readable for a range of abilities.
- Textbook authors may avoid interesting but controversial topics to please constituent groups.

- Textbooks may lack content or be of poor quality—problems perhaps masked by concentration on making the books colorful and appealing.
- Textbooks might exhibit bias related to conservative or liberal ideology, culture, race, gender, and the like, either overtly or by omission.

Government Influences What We Teach

Because almost everyone in the United States has attended school, most of us think we know a lot about what should be taught, as well as how to teach it. This attitude, in part, leads to the continuing influence of all levels of government on education.

Local government generally has little to do with standards and textbooks, but involved local citizens serve on school boards and, as such, have some say in how schools function. The state level of government, however, exerts a great deal of influence because most standards and other curricular decisions are made at the state level. Governors, legislators, and officials within state departments of education influence what is taught and learned in public schools.

The federal government, although not directly dictating standards, has significant influence on how schools educate students through federal legislation, most notably after the Russian *Sputnik* launch in 1957 created a sense of urgency in terms of improving U.S. education in a competitive world. After the National Defense Education Act of 1958 created math, science, and foreign language priorities, other federal legislation was passed in rapid succession that continues to influence what we teach and how we teach it, including the following:

- The Economic Opportunity Act of 1964 made vocational training a priority.
- The Civil Rights Act of 1964 prohibited discrimination, with the stated goal of equal access to quality education.
- The Elementary and Secondary Education Act of 1965 established Title I status, intended to increase funding in schools with large populations of economically disadvantaged children.
- The Bilingual Education Act of 1968 ensured the teaching of the curriculum in native languages as students learned English.
- The Title IX legislation of 1972 provided enhanced opportunities for girls to participate in athletics.
- The Individuals with Disabilities Education Act of 1975 made participation in public education by students with disabilities a right rather than a privilege.
- The No Child Left Behind Act of 2001, one of several reauthorizations of the Elementary and Secondary Education Act of 1965, required states to maintain curricular standards, test all students on the standards' knowledge and skills, and report on student achievement in disaggregated ways (separating various groups so their scores may be compared).
- The Elementary and Secondary Education Act was reauthorized as the **Every Student Succeeds Act (ESSA)** in 2016. The basic principles of this bipartisan bill state that ESSA:
    - **a.** Holds all students to high academic standards
    - **b.** Prepares all students for success in college and career
    - **c.** Provides more kids access to high-quality preschool
    - **d.** Guarantees steps are taken to help students, and their schools, improve
    - **e.** Reduces the burden of testing while maintaining annual information for parents and students
    - **f.** Promotes local innovation and invests in what works (U.S Department of Education, 2016)

Additional Influences on Curriculum

In addition to the influences previously discussed, other groups and ideologies influence the formal curriculum.

PARENTS AND THE COMMUNITY. Every community has a unique identity by virtue of the citizens who live within it, including parents who send their children to public schools. What gets the attention of the community is often a controversial issue that strikes a dissonant chord among community members. What may be considered mainstream in Miami, Florida, could be controversial in Boise, Idaho.

Parents and community members can exert influence on curriculum in a variety of ways, including voicing opinions to school personnel and school board members or local media, refusing to allow children to participate in certain activities, suggesting alternative curricular approaches, and serving on textbook adoption committees.

PARTNERSHIP FOR 21ST CENTURY SKILLS (P21). The Partnership for 21st Century Skills is a leading advocacy organization of the promotion of knowledge and skills considered necessary for success in this century. The knowledge and skills made explicit in the P21 documents are not necessarily new, but when packaged in this organization's format they make a compelling case for inclusion in the curriculum. The states that have officially become partners are all working toward including the P21 framework of knowledge and skills in their curriculum plans. Even with the development and implementation of Common Core State Standards, the Partnership for 21st Century Skills will likely continue to impact what is taught and learned in U.S. schools.

COLLEGES AND UNIVERSITIES. Students enter the doors of colleges and universities with knowledge and skills determined by the preK–12 curriculum. Simultaneously, colleges and universities affect the direction of what is taught and learned in schools primarily through the preparation of teachers, research conducted by faculty, and faculty involvement in standards development. Because of this, higher education is in the unique position of being both a recipient and a molder of curriculum.

Subjects of the Formal Curriculum

We generally consider English language arts, math, science, and social studies as the core subject areas. In early childhood and elementary settings, classes outside the core curriculum are built into the day either within the individual classroom or in special classes that meet perhaps weekly. Most middle and high schools require students to take a specific number of courses that are not part of the core. These courses, known as **related arts courses**, **exploratory courses**, or **encore courses**, are valuable components that enhance the formal curriculum and include physical education, technology, world languages, music, home arts, theater, and more.

Core Subject Areas. The subjects designated as core have basically been the same for over a century. Although much of the content has changed, English language arts (ELA), math, science, and social studies are consistently taught in early childhood, elementary, middle, and high schools.

English Language Arts. The National Council of Teachers of English (NCTE) and the International Reading Association (IRA) tell us that language development includes reading, writing, speaking, listening, viewing, and study of media. In early childhood, elementary, and middle school, much of the English language arts (ELA) curriculum focuses on skills, including reading, grammar, spelling, mechanics of punctuation and capitalization, editing, and basic research. Traditionally, reading through the fourth grade has consisted mainly of fiction (short stories and simple books). However, the Common Core State Standards for English language arts call for an equal mix of fiction and nonfiction in early childhood and elementary schools, along with an increased emphasis on writing skills.

Sara Davis Powell

Science comes alive for students, such as Amanda at Rees Elementary School, when they are encouraged to observe and interact in their world.

In middle school, the focus is on a variety of literary forms and writing. High school English language arts is primarily literature based, with continued emphasis on writing skills and research. Communication skills such as oral presentation and persuasive speech have figured more prominently in ELA classes at most levels in recent years.

Mathematics. According to the **National Council of Teachers of Mathematics** (2000), the need to understand and use math in everyday life has never been greater. From making purchasing decisions to interpreting tables and graphs, math is a vital part of the present and will be increasingly important in a more complex future. Children in early childhood settings now explore concepts involving algebra, geometry, and data analysis. Elementary and middle-level students are asked to use problem-solving strategies involving multiple variables. An increasing number of high school students are taking advantage of advanced placement math courses for college credit.

By viewing math as something students do and connect to real life, the NCTM standards ushered in a shift in math education from memorizing procedures to understanding concepts, and from emphasizing isolated mechanical ways of finding solutions to problem solving. The Common Core State Standards for math continue the emphasis on problem solving.

Science. The vision of the **National Science Teachers Association (NSTA)** is for all students to regularly experience science education that revolves around unifying themes such as order, organization, models, change, measurement, and function. To do this, teachers emphasize that science is a process involving observation, inference, and experimentation. This is a major shift away from content-specific facts toward understanding concepts through process and inquiry, with students asking questions and searching for answers.

Social Studies. The **National Council for the Social Studies (NCSS)** tells us that the primary purpose of social studies is to enable students, now and in the future, to make informed decisions that promotes the public good as citizens in our demographically diverse society. This is a definite shift from the way social studies was approached for much of the last century. Before the influence of the NCSS and the curricular changes prompted by standards, social studies was dominated by names and dates to be memorized, with little or no application of concepts to local, national, or international dilemmas.

Responding to the Common Core State Standards that only address math and English language arts, the NCSS developed the 3C Framework for Social Studies Standards: College, Career, and Civic Life. The framework includes four dimensions that emphasize the acquisition and application of knowledge.

- Developing questions and planning inquiries
- Applying disciplinary tools and concepts
- Evaluating sources and using evidence
- Communicating conclusions and taking informed action

The C3 Framework is considered necessary by the NCSS because of the loss of instructional time devoted to social studies in elementary schools due, in large measure, to the absence of end-of-grade testing in the discipline. More time is given to math and English language arts, with social studies relegated to left-over afternoon minutes of class time. NCSS intentionally aligned the C3 Framework to the language arts Common Core State Standards to encourage integration of history, civics, geography, and economics with reading, writing, speaking, and listening and language skills needed for disciplinary literacy and success in college, career, and civic life (National Council for the Social Studies, 2017).

RELATED ARTS. Related arts courses complement and enhance the core curriculum. Let's take a look at some that are frequently offered.

- **Technology** The **International Society for Technology in Education (ISTE)** is a professional organization whose mission is to provide leadership and service in the effective use of technology in education. The standards for technology are organized into categories such as basic operations, communication tools, and ethical issues. Almost all schools have computer labs used for classes in **information literacy**, a broad phrase involving recognition of when information is needed, knowing how to access information, and judging information credibility. In these labs, designated technology teachers teach whole classes of students at a time.
- **Foreign languages** The **American Council for the Teaching of Foreign Languages (ACTFL)** states that it's imperative for students to communicate successfully in a pluralistic American society and abroad. To accomplish this mission, high schools and most middle schools offer courses in a variety of world languages, most commonly Spanish and French. Because of the recognition that young children acquire a second language more readily than do young adults, many early childhood and elementary schools offer opportunities to learn a second language. The Standards for Foreign Language Learning are organized according to five goals that ACTFL calls the "Five C's of Foreign Language Education": communication, cultures, connections, comparisons, and communities.
- **Physical education and health** Leaders of physical education (PE) and health education strongly advocate for more time spent in physical activity and health-related instruction. Supporting standards are provided by the **National Association for Sport and Physical Education (NASPE)** and the **American Association for Health Education (AAHE)**. Physical education in early childhood and elementary schools may be unorganized play time, often the responsibility of the classroom teacher, or there may be a designated PE teacher who conducts whole class sessions two or three times a week for each grade level. In middle school, PE and health are likely to be rotated courses, perhaps covering 9 weeks each year, with health taught by either the PE or science teacher. In high school, students are usually required to take only one or two courses in PE and even fewer than that in health. Given the health risk factors associated with adolescence in society today, implementation of the NASPE and AAHE standards is especially important for teenagers.
- **Career and tech-prep courses** Career and tech-prep cover a broad category of courses that are usually offered in high school. Some courses are of general interest, such as basic industrial or home arts classes, and others might be career oriented, such as auto mechanics and cosmetology. The federal government supports a program called **School-to-Work**, initiated to bring real-world work-related skills and understanding to students through courses that introduce them to career possibilities.
- **Arts** The **National Standards for Arts Education** define what students should know and be able to do in the four arts disciplines: music, dance, theater, and the visual arts. The standards essentially state that by the end of high school, students should be able to communicate at a basic level in the four disciplines and be proficient in at least one art form. The availability of art experiences in music, dance, theater, and visual arts in preK–12 schools varies tremendously. In early childhood and elementary schools, the classroom teacher may be responsible for the art curriculum, or the school may have an art specialist. In middle and high schools, students usually have a variety of arts classes from which to choose and perhaps a limited number of arts activities.

Important Concepts that Add Value to Curriculum

There are some important concepts to consider as we explore curriculum. It might help to think of the formal curriculum as a cloth that covers the school day with learning opportunities. The important concepts may be thought of as threads that weave in and out of the subjects and add value, as illustrated in Figure 4.2.

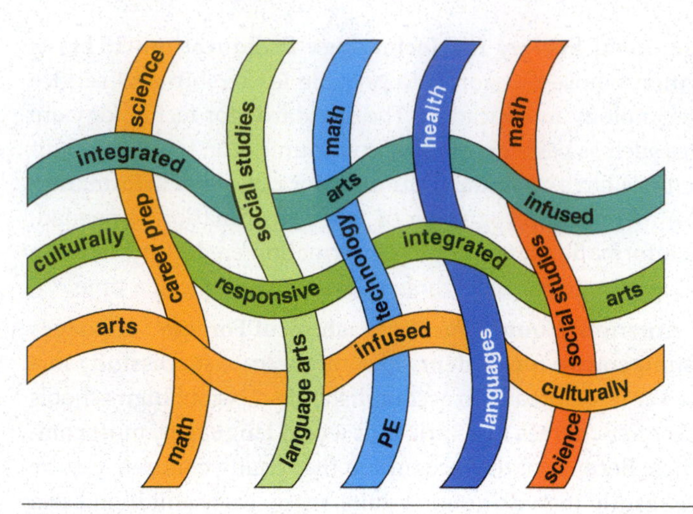

Figure 4.2 Fabric of curriculum

INTEGRATED CURRICULUM. Continuing the cloth analogy, the strength of cloth comes from weaving the threads in different directions so that the cloth holds together. When teachers include content and skills from a variety of subjects in lessons—and weave them together in meaningful ways—they are incorporating **integrated curriculum**, sometimes called **interdisciplinary curriculum**. An integrated curriculum basically involves approaching a concept from different perspectives to create learning opportunities based on connections. This is often accomplished through the use of a unifying topic or theme. Early childhood and elementary teachers do it all the time. As an example, second-grade teachers may weave a study of farm life throughout the year, aligning core and related arts subjects with the theme whenever possible. Math problems may deal with farming scenarios and science may revolve around light, rain, and soil, along with zoology. Also, the history of farming and literature about farming and farmers may be taught.

In middle school, teams of teachers may weave whole days, or even weeks, around a theme that brings together research involving real-world events and phenomena. Curriculum integration is least common in high school. However, even though high school teachers are usually organized into subject-area departments, this in no way prevents an English language arts teacher from teaching about literature through short stories, poems, and novels that reflect a topic addressed in the social studies curriculum for the grade level. For instance, if U.S. history is a course taken by most sophomores, the sophomore ELA teachers could incorporate period literature that coincides with the progressive history of the United States as taught by the history department faculty.

Connecting subjects of the formal curriculum can occur at a variety of levels of complexity. For instance, in a geometry lesson, the teacher merely mentions that the word *symmetry* is also important in art and then shows a painting that exhibits the concept. This is then followed by a well-planned series of lessons with subject-area boundaries blurred by real-world context. Teachers' efforts to make connections within the curriculum pay big dividends in terms of student interest and learning.

CULTURALLY RESPONSIVE CURRICULUM. As diversity in U.S. schools increases, the importance of and the demand for a culturally responsive perspective grows. When we approach curriculum in **culturally responsive** ways, we incorporate a **multicultural curriculum** that purposefully includes contributions and viewpoints from the perspectives of different cultures, ethnicities, races, genders, socioeconomic levels, or any other way people may differ. At its best, a multicultural curriculum is

Sara Davis Powell

Students in Mt. Airy, North Carolina, enjoy a robust program of arts education.

accurate, timely, and sensitive, yet avoids tokenism or a sense of forced inclusion (Banks, 2003).

The methods used to demonstrate cultural responsiveness and to infuse a classroom with a multicultural curriculum will depend on the grade level and subject area. In early childhood and elementary settings, celebrating historical events and holidays of a variety of cultures helps create awareness of values and traditions within the various cultures. In middle and high school, making a variety of perspectives part of your classroom discussions, and asking students to research and report on issues of interest to them that include various perspectives, can help forge an understanding of people of different cultures. One of the most effective tools for including a variety of perspectives is an emphasis on current events.

ARTS-INFUSED CURRICULUM. Including the arts in the curriculum requires awareness of opportunities, along with purposeful determination to include music, theater, dance, and the visual arts whenever possible. You don't need to be an artist or musician to display art or play music in the classroom. Encouraging students to create their own works of art to enhance a project takes exactly that—encouragement.

Teaching in Focus

Brenda Beyal, the multiage teacher at Rees Elementary in Spanish Fork, Utah, who infuses both visual arts and drama into the curriculum, encourages her students to express themselves in unique ways through what she calls a *squiggle*, a randomly drawn curvy line that forms the basis for artistic expression. Each student is given a piece of paper with the same squiggle on it and is asked to use imagination and creativity to fashion a drawing around the basic structure. While they work on their masterpieces, music plays in the classroom.

Sara Davis Powell

Application Exercise 4.1: Brenda's Room Tour

Controversy and Curriculum

Although it's hard to imagine objections to infusing arts into the curriculum, there are groups who oppose arts on the grounds that their inclusion detracts from the core subjects. Controversy and curriculum are never far apart. In a society that values opposing views and encourages diversity, the curriculum is sure to be debated. The dynamic nature of this debate is healthy, but it can also be frustrating at times for educators. Religious beliefs, censorship for a variety of reasons, and philosophical differences all influence what's included in the formal curriculum. Here are a few examples of issues that are controversial in some school districts and states with regard to what is taught in public schools:

- There is an ongoing debate over the exclusive teaching of evolution to explain the origin of human beings. **Intelligent design**—proposed by some parents and community members who oppose the teaching of evolution—includes a belief that certain features of the universe and of living things are best explained by an intelligent being (God), not by the process of natural selection espoused by evolution. Some people argue for an evolution-only curriculum; others argue for intelligent design only. Still others propose the teaching of both as theories, incurring the disapproval of many in the scientific community, including most colleges and universities, where evolution is considered factually based.
- Earlier we discussed multicultural curriculum, or the purposeful inclusion of contributions of persons of diversity and traditions that are not considered mainstream America (a loosely conceived concept). One of the arguments for more cultural responsiveness is that U.S. curriculum is too **Eurocentric**, meaning that contributions and traditions that do not originate in Europe are underrepresented. For instance, 90% of the Providence, Rhode Island, public school students in 2016 were children and adolescents of color. In contrast, a study showed that only 5% of people depicted in the school system's textbooks were non-white. Stanford University 2010–2014 research conducted in San Francisco public high schools revealed that struggling ninth-grade students who participated in a pilot program of ethnic-studies curriculum that intentionally included people of color increased attendance by 21% and improved their grade-point average by 1.4 points (The Atlantic, 2016). Those who develop curriculum for k-12 schools should use studies such as this one to create a greater balance of ethnicities.

- Should schools teach sex education? If so, what should be taught? When should topics be introduced? These are questions about which many in the United States feel strongly. The whole issue of sex education is value laden and emotionally charged. Many believe that the responsibility to teach children and adolescents about sex falls squarely on the home and religious organizations. Others contend that the school is the appropriate venue because it impacts the most students over a long period of development. With the goal of reducing teen pregnancies and sexually transmitted diseases, courts generally uphold the rights of schools to provide sex education. But the mere legality of a controversial issue such as this does not equate with widespread benign acceptance, nor does it alleviate the burden of deciding what to teach and when to teach it.

Teachers have an outlet for developing a voice about controversial aspects of teaching and learning as they share information and opinions. In this chapter's *SocialMEdia* feature, we learn more about teacher blogs. In Chapter 3, we discussed professional learning communities and the value of teachers working together to share knowledge, skill, and resources. Many teachers consider blogging as a way to connect to other teachers to develop informal learning communities. Read the feature, explore some blogs, and see if this may be a way for you to grow into and in the teaching profession.

SocialMEdia

There's probably no need to define a **blog,** but there are some considerations of interest, including:

- The word *blog* is short for *web log.*
- As a noun, a blog is an online record of opinions and information. As a verb, to blog is to post entries on a website.
- Blogs have been around since the mid-1990s and, by some estimates, almost 200 million blogs are active worldwide.
- Blogs may be individual or have multiple contributors, and most are interactive, allowing anyone to post comments and questions.

Many teacher blogs exist and serve to share information, strategies, philosophies, and frustrations. Most are initiated to communicate with other teachers outside the immediate accessibility of the blogger. Blogging can be an excellent tool of reflection. In a very real way, teacher blogging takes courage—the courage to frequently post without necessarily overthinking an issue and to honestly reflect on the profession as well as individual days in the classroom. Sometimes, revealing initial opinions, asking questions that prompt problem solving, and sharing of successes and failures lead to improved teaching and learning. In addition to sharing ideas and strategies, teacher blogging can amount to self-analysis under the watchful, and hopefully helpful, eyes of readers and contributors.

Gauging from teacher appraisals on the Internet, blogging is a very positive extension of teaching. For many teachers, blogging is an excellent source of professional development, enhancing professional growth and practice, and a means of resource sharing. You're sure to find many blogs that interest you.

Point of Reflection 4.1

What do you remember about related arts classes? Which ones did you particularly enjoy and why? Were there related arts classes you did not want to take? If so, which ones and why? Do the related arts classes you took in preK–12 have an impact how you spend your time now? If so, how?

Check Your Understanding 4.1

4.2 What Other Curricula Do We Teach in U.S. Schools?

4.2 Identify three other curricula in U.S. schools.

We've learned what goes into creating the formal curriculum for U.S. schools. Now let's look at other kinds of curricula that are part of what teachers do, or possibly don't do. Although not as obvious in as many ways as the formal curriculum—and certainly not as regulated by standards and policies—the informal, extra, and null curricula nonetheless affect teachers and students.

Informal Curriculum

The **informal curriculum** is what teachers and schools teach and what students learn that is not part of a lesson plan, a curriculum guide, or standards. It encompasses what is learned by students through attitudes, values, and various types of informal teaching situations, such as in the hall between classes, at recess, and on field trips when conversations are casual. This informal learning may be positive or negative and is often unintentional. When the formal curriculum is referred to as the *explicit curriculum*, the informal curriculum may be called the **implicit curriculum**, meaning that often it is implied and subtle. You may also hear informal curriculum and **hidden curriculum** used interchangeably. There is a distinction, however, because the informal curriculum has positive connotations, whereas the hidden curriculum has more of a negative sense, implying there may be teacher motivations that are somehow less than positive.

Another phrase equated with the informal curriculum is **wayside teaching**. John Lounsbury (1991), a noted middle-level educator and advocate for young adolescents, as well as the namesake of the John H. Lounsbury College of Education at Georgia College and State University, notes that wayside teaching is the teaching we do inside and outside the classroom through our attitudes, values, habits, interests, and creation of classroom climate. Regardless of what students learn in terms of content and skills through the formal curriculum, they learn *us*. They watch us, listen to us, and notice their surroundings; students learn more from our interactions with them than we imagine.

As an illustration of the value of the informal curriculum, consider a middle school science teacher who, wrestling with the "What should I teach?" question, decided to ask her former students what they remembered about her class and what they believed were the most important lessons. She developed a survey and received responses from students she taught in each of her nine years in the classroom. Their responses included the following:

> "The most important things I learned from you weren't in class, but during the Science Olympiad . . . ."

> "The [finest] things I learned from you have nothing to do with science."

All Photos: Sara Davis Powell

Renee Ayers, second-grade teacher at Summit Primary, develops caring relationships with her students. Here, she and Sherlonda share secrets in the positive environment Renee maintains in her classroom, part of the informal curriculum.

"The most important thing I learned from you would have to be the ability to be nice to people even if you feel like screaming . . . . The way you acted toward our class and the compassion you showed to our class [taught me this]."

"Self-confidence and how important it is."

"How important science is to society."

"How you encouraged everyone to do their best."

Several students responded that the books the teacher read aloud to them (in science class!) changed their opinions on diversity (Little, 2001, pp. 62–63). What a powerful example of positively teaching the informal curriculum!

Extra Curriculum

Activities sponsored by the school but outside the limits of the formal curriculum are considered extracurricular. Although some elementary schools offer extracurricular activities, such as jump rope and craft clubs, most extracurricular opportunities begin in middle school and expand in high school.

Extracurricular activities provide opportunities for active involvement for students, and for sponsorship and coaching for teachers. Examples include:

- Odyssey of the Mind, math and book clubs
- Debate, chess, and photography clubs
- Band and choral activities
- Athletics of all kinds, including cheerleading
- School newspaper, student government, and honor society

Recently there has been renewed interest in the factors that contribute to **school connectedness**, or student bonding and engagement. Lack of school connectedness may lead to disruptive behavior, substance abuse, emotional distress, absenteeism, and dropping out. The importance of doing what it takes to foster connectedness is magnified when we consider that some high school students—whether urban, suburban, or rural—feel "chronically disengaged" from school. A major factor that influences school connectedness is participation in extracurricular activities.

Null Curriculum

The **null curriculum** is what *isn't* taught—content and skills that perhaps simply haven't been considered or are not considered important enough to teach. Content and skills may also not be taught simply based on tradition. "We teach what we teach largely out of habit," states Eisner (2002, p. 103). The null curriculum also includes topics considered controversial, including almost anything dealing with religion, abortion, homosexuality, and other topics that are controversial in some areas but not in others.

The null curriculum may not be as important as the formal curriculum, the informal curriculum, and the extra curriculum, but it is certainly worth thinking about. What is *not* part of the school curriculum may never be considered by students, and therefore may have little to do with their futures. For instance, if teachers neglect to incorporate a culturally responsive curriculum, the failure to acknowledge and celebrate differences may contribute to prejudice and exclusionary attitudes in students.

The Partnership for 21st Century Skills promotes the teaching of some concepts that are not currently in most curricular plans. On the P21 website, teachers are told that the challenge is to purposefully incorporate the broad literacies P21 supports. A **literacy** involves the ability to analyze and apply knowledge and skills necessary to solve problems within a discipline. The Partnership for 21st Century Skills recommends that schools promote financial, economic, business, entrepreneurial, civic, health, wellness, information, and communication literacies. In many schools, these broad disciplines are not addressed and therefore are part of the null curriculum. When schools incorporate them, they will become part of the formal curriculum.

Point of Reflection 4.2

In what extracurricular activities did you participate? What impact did that participation have on you then, and now?

Check Your Understanding 4.2

4.3 What Is Involved in Classroom Assessment?

4.3 Summarize what is involved in classroom assessment.

Classroom assessment encompasses all the possible ways teachers determine what students know and can do measured against standards or other learning goals. The assessments developed and used by individual teachers are **criterion referenced**, meaning that student results indicate levels of mastery of a subject and do not depend on how other students score. In its many forms, classroom assessment serves multiple purposes that are appropriate for the variety of curricula and instructional strategies used in U.S. schools.

Purposes of Classroom Assessment

Determining student achievement and reporting grades are the most commonly understood reasons for classroom assessment, but these are not the only purposes. The National Council of Teachers of Mathematics broadened teachers' views of the purposes of assessment. Figure 4.3 illustrates NCTM's four purposes of assessment.

MONITORING STUDENT PROGRESS. Ongoing assessment allows teachers to be continuously aware of where students are in the learning process. Assessing student knowledge and skill levels before beginning a unit of study is called **diagnostic assessment** or, more commonly, **pretesting**.

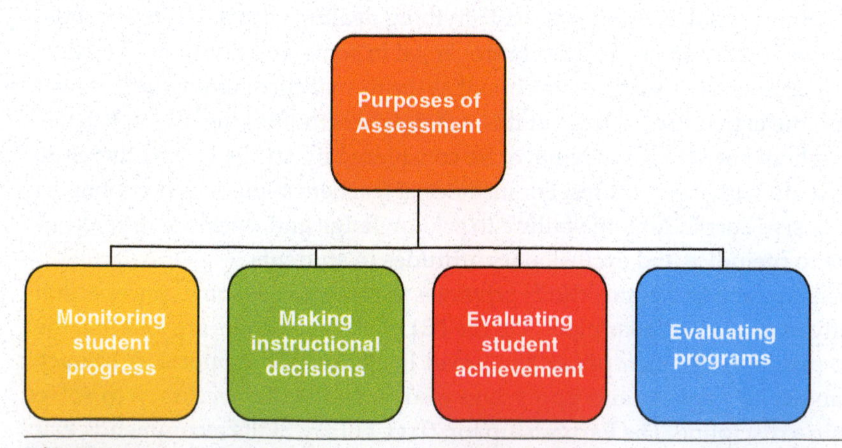

Figure 4.3 NCTM's four purposes of assessment

The results of diagnostic assessment should be used to plan the daily lessons of the unit, including multiple **formative assessments** in a variety of formats that gauge student progress. Feedback is the key to making formative assessment effective. Feedback should be timely and specific enough to make students aware of not only where they are in the learning process but also what they need to do to move forward.

MAKING INSTRUCTIONAL DECISIONS. Assessment can be a waste of time and effort if it does not influence the content, the instructional strategies, and the pacing or sequencing of classroom experiences. Effective monitoring of student progress provides the information and insight needed to make instructional decisions that promote student growth. These decisions may involve reteaching or teaching differently to help more students master the unit content and skills.

EVALUATING STUDENT ACHIEVEMENT. Assessment allows teachers to measure if, and how much, students learn. Formative assessments and their results may have a part in the measurement, but **summative assessment** is most often used to evaluate student achievement. A summative assessment is typically more formal than a formative assessment and involves judging the success of a process or product. Summative assessments most often occur at the end of a unit of study. Paper-and-pencil tests are traditional summative assessments, but they need not be the only format used. Students should be given opportunities to demonstrate what they know and are able to do in a variety of ways, such as completion of a project or performance of an authentic task, or one that actually applies the knowledge and skills. When students succeed, teachers should recognize those accomplishments.

Look closely at Figure 4.4. Notice the flow from diagnostic to formative to summative assessment. The double arrows between formative assessment and instruction indicate that formative assessment helps teachers make decisions about instruction. There is fluidity between ongoing formative assessment and what is planned in the classroom. Summative assessment occurs at the end of the formative assessment/instruction ebb and flow.

EVALUATING PROGRAMS. The fourth purpose of assessment may extend beyond the classroom. Instructional materials and formalized programs such as Scholastic 180, the literacy program used by focus teacher Deirdre Huger-McGrew at Cario Middle School in Mt. Pleasant, South Carolina, are purchased by schools and districts. The components of these programs are monitored for effectiveness, and decisions are made regarding their value based on results of various forms of assessments.

Forms of Assessment

Students learn differently and should have a variety of opportunities to demonstrate what they know and can do. Varying the assessment format ensures that differing student learning preferences and intelligences are accommodated.

Robert Marzano (2000), an educational researcher, compiled the seven basic forms of classroom assessment listed in Table 4.2. Read about each and think about whether and how it might serve a diagnostic, formative, and/or summative function.

One of the forms of assessment, teacher observation, is a given. We watch, we listen, and we make mental or written notes about student progress. Dylan Todd, one of

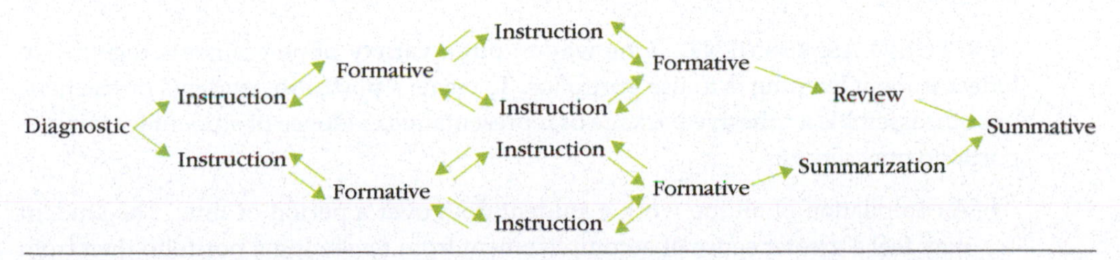

Figure 4.4 Diagnostic, formative, and summative assessment in the classroom

Table 4.2 Seven forms of assessment

Form of Assessment	Characteristics
1. Forced choice	• Multiple choice, matching, true/false, fill-in-the-blank • Can be scored objectively • Most common form of assessment • Choose from among alternatives given
2. Essay	• Good for assessing thinking, reasoning, and expression skills • Opportunity to demonstrate knowledge of relationships • Gives information on how students process knowledge • Scoring can be subjective
3. Short written responses	• Mini-essays • Brief explanations of information or processes • Scoring more objective than for essays
4. Oral reports	• Assess student speaking ability • Similar to essay but more impromptu • Require acute listening skills to score
5. Teacher observation	• Informal • Best for process-oriented and nonachievement factors • Good when linked to interview of student • Teacher notes used to record observation results
6. Student self-assessment	• Most underused form of assessment • Helps develop higher-order metacognitive skills • Assessment conference allows student to clarify own level of learning
7. Performance tasks	• Require student to construct responses, apply knowledge • Require more than recall of information • Can assess a variety of forms of knowledge and skills • Scoring dependent on task

Based on: Marzano, R. J. (2000). *Transforming classroom grading*. Alexandria, VA: Association for Supervision and Curriculum Development.

the focus students at Summit Primary School in Ohio, is repeating kindergarten, not so much for academic reasons as for social ones. Dylan Todd was a young 5-year-old when he started kindergarten. A bright little boy living in a comfortable socioeconomic status (SES) home with adoring parents, Dylan experienced expected academic growth in his first year at Summit Primary. But, as his teacher observed, he was still quite immature at the end of his initial year in kindergarten. Teacher observation, as we see in Table 4.2, is particularly effective when assessing nonachievement factors. In consultation with Mom and Dad, the decision was made to have Dylan repeat kindergarten, this time in the enrichment class.

PERFORMANCE ASSESSMENT. The last of Marzano's seven forms of assessment involves performance. This simply means that students actually show what they know and can do in ways that do not solely involve paper-and-pencil tests. **Performance assessment** may be a project, a demonstration, a creation, or anything that requires the application of knowledge and skills. You may hear the terms *alternative assessment* and *authentic assessment* used interchangeably with *performance assessment*. **Alternative assessment** is assessment that doesn't fall within Marzano's first three categories. **Authentic assessment** means that students show what they know and can do in a real-life setting or situation. Performance assessment is alternative assessment and may also be authentic.

PORTFOLIO ASSESSMENT. One way to put a variety of assessments together to reflect student learning is to use portfolios. To create a **portfolio**, students or teachers, or both, assemble a cohesive package of representative evidence of student learning. A portfolio may serve as

- A compilation of all the work a student does over a period of time. The student may feel a greater sense of accomplishment from reviewing a portfolio than from seeing individual assessments that are quickly discarded.

- A selected collection of work intended to show growth over time.
- A display tool for work samples that showcase the student's best work.

You are likely creating a portfolio, or will be soon, of products related to your education coursework. Your portfolio will show your professional growth. At some point, your instructors will evaluate your portfolio and assign a grade that indicates your achievement.

Teaching in Focus

Renee Ayers believes that ongoing assessment is vital to her teaching. The progress her second-graders are making at Summit Primary, in Summit Station, Ohio, is recorded and analyzed in multiple ways. She even finds ways for her students to view their own progress.

Sara Davis Powell

One of Renee's favorite uses of student self-assessment involves writing. She asks her second-graders to write their best about any topic they choose during the first week of school. She then tucks these little masterpieces away until the last week of second grade, when the students again choose a topic and write about it. Renee surprises her students by giving them their first week's writing to compare. She says it's one of the most joyous celebrations a 7- or 8-year-old can experience. The looks on their faces and their obvious pride in recognizing their progress are priceless!

Renee keeps anecdotal records on her students in two distinct and user-friendly ways. One method involves a clipboard and note cards. She tapes the first card to the board so the bottom of the card and the bottom of the clipboard are even. She writes a student's name on the bottom of the card. Then she tapes another card so that its lower edge lines up just above the name on the first card and writes another student's name on the bottom of that card. She continues this process, taping cards up the board to the clip. She carries this board around as she talks with students about their reading or math or a project they may be working on. In doing so she is practicing teacher observation with the added benefit of recorded notes.

Another way Renee uses a clipboard is to hold pages of sticky-back labels. She writes students' names, the date, and her observations about student learning on the labels. Later she simply puts the labels in a notebook on pages designated for each student. This is a quick way to record informal assessments all day and then easily organize them.

Of course, Renee also does more formal assessments similar to what most early childhood teachers do. But she feels that her informal assessments help her develop the kind of rapport with her students she values and give her clear insights concerning their learning.

Renee models both attitudes and techniques that promote the use of assessment as an integral part of classroom practice. She takes seriously her responsibility to understand her students' strengths and weaknesses, to know their learning profiles, and to monitor their continual progress. Her innovative approach contains ideas you can adapt to your own classrooms.

Application Exercise 4.2: Renee's Lesson and Interview

ASSESSMENT OF 21st–CENTURY KNOWLEDGE AND SKILLS

The Partnership for 21st Century Skills (2012) defines goals for assessment that reflect its philosophy and the practical advice you have read about in each of the preceding chapters. It endorses assessment that

- Promotes balance, including both standardized assessment and classroom formative and summative assessment
- Emphasizes the role of feedback as part of learning
- Uses technology and measures student mastery of 21st–century skills
- Includes development of portfolios

Given all the possible ways to assess what students know and can do, it is important to create a balanced assessment plan for the classroom. Each assessment method has appropriate uses and each has limitations. Paying close attention to which assessment is appropriate will help ensure assessments align with curriculum, instructional strategies, and the needs of students.

Point of Reflection 4.3

What forms of assessment do you remember from your K–12 experiences? Did you have preferences? If so, what aspects of the different assessments did you prefer? Why?

Check Your Understanding 4.3

4.4 How Do Teachers Evaluate Student Learning and Assign Grades?

4.4 Analyze how teachers evaluate student learning and assign grades.

Now that we have discussed the purposes and forms of assessment, let's look at how we use assessment to evaluate student learning and, ultimately, assign grades. Recall that evaluating student achievement is one of the four purposes of assessment.

Evaluation

The words *evaluation* and *assessment* are often used interchangeably, but they are not the same. Assessment is gathering evidence of student learning. **Evaluation** makes judgments about, and assigns values to, the results of assessments. For example, a student writes an essay about the effects of rail travel on the Gold Rush of the 1800s. The teacher uses the essay as an assessment of what the student learned in a unit on the events leading to the statehood of California. The assessment provides the evidence to evaluate the quality of student learning.

It is not necessary, or advisable, to evaluate all evidence of student learning. In our example of a student writing about the Gold Rush, the teacher may assess the note-taking skills of the student by checking on the completeness of note cards the student filled out during research in the library (first formative assessment). This assessment and teacher feedback help the student make corrections in the research process and move forward with the project. The teacher may simply record a check in the grade book to indicate that student progress was assessed through an examination of note cards. There's no need to make an evaluation at this point. When the student submits an outline for approval, a second formative assessment occurs. Later, the teacher may read through the essay rough draft and give feedback on it (third formative assessment), yet still not record an evaluation. In this scenario there are three formative assessments without evaluation. When the student turns in the completed essay, the teacher will use a rubric to do a summative assessment of this student's alternative performance, and then record an evaluation.

Rubrics

One of the most productive innovations in assessment is the **rubric**, an assessment tool that makes explicit what is being assessed, lists the characteristics of the different degrees of quality, and provides a rating scale to differentiate among these degrees. Rubrics add consistency to subjective evaluation and serve several distinct, yet related, purposes:

- Rubrics provide clear expectations for assignments. Therefore, they are instructional tools as well as assessment tools.
- Rubrics allow teachers to differentiate consistently among performance levels.
- Rubrics provide guidelines for student improvement.
- Rubrics make grading more transparent and consistent.

There are two basic types of rubrics. A **holistic rubric** uses one scale for an entire project. In Table 4.3 you can see that a student may receive a score of 0 to 5 according to the descriptor that most closely matches the work being assessed.

An **analytic rubric** specifies separate parts of an assessment task, product, or performance as well as the characteristics of various levels of success for each. An analytic rubric gives much more information than a holistic rubric. The sample analytic rubric in Table 4.4 could be used to evaluate a demonstration lesson you may create and deliver in a teacher preparation class.

Table 4.3 Sample holistic rubric

Score	Descriptor
5	Student clearly understands the assessment task and the product fulfills all the requirements accurately and completely.
4	Student understands most of the assessment task and the product fulfills the requirements.
3	Student understands just enough of the assessment task to fulfill most of the requirements.
2	Student has little understanding of the assessment task and fulfills a minimum of the requirements.
1	Student does not understand the assessment task and fulfills none of the requirements.
0	Student does not attempt the assessment task.

Table 4.4 Sample analytic rubric

Criterion	4	3	2	1	0
Topic choice	Relevant, interesting	Appropriate	Shallow, lacks interest	Very limited	Not appropriate
Planned assessment	Creative, matches instruction	Adequate and appropriate	Addresses only part of topic content/skills	Does not address topic	Not included
Standard(s) objective(s)	Appropriate, well written	Appropriate	Improperly written	Not appropriate	Not included
Lesson procedures	Clear, detailed, could be easily implemented by others	Clear and adequately detailed	Not detailed enough to be implemented by others	Unclear	Not included
Handout for class	Professional, detailed, few mechanical errors	Adequate detail, useful, few mechanical errors	Not enough detail, distracting mechanical errors	Not useful	Not included

Along with numbers for scoring, most rubrics include descriptors of what the numbers mean. For instance, on a 0 to 5 scale, the numbers may be interpreted as follows:

5 – Advanced		5 – Highly accomplished
4 – Proficient		4 – Developed
3 – Adequate	or	3 – Developing
2 – Basic		2 – Emerging
1 – Below basic		1 – Preparing to begin
0 – Not attempted		0 – Not attempted

Many Internet sites provide templates for the creation of rubrics for multiple content areas and performance tasks. To take advantage of all the benefits of using rubrics to evaluate classroom assessment tasks, products, and performances, teachers should:

1. Create rubrics for as many tasks as appropriate.
2. Explicitly teach students how to read and use rubrics.
3. Distribute rubrics when the task is explained or assigned.
4. Refer to the rubric when giving directions, answering questions, guiding students, and so on.
5. Provide samples of work (sometimes called anchors or **exemplars**) that fit the various criteria for scoring so that students actually see what a product that earns a particular number looks like.
6. Inform families about the use and benefits of rubrics as assessment tools so they will understand the evaluation criteria and know how to help guide their students.

Assigning Grades

A **grade** is a judgment of assessment quality, or an evaluation, with a number attached to it. The wisdom of assigning grades has been questioned for decades by many who view grades as harmful to student self-esteem and detrimental to progress. Even so, Americans expect grades and they are likely to be with us for years to come.

Perhaps the most compelling reason for grades is that they are expected by students, families, administrators, and the public in general. In *How to Grade for Learning*, O'Connor (2002) summarizes reasons for grading as follows:

1. ***Instructional uses:*** Clarify learning goals, pinpoint strengths and weaknesses, motivate
2. ***Communication uses:*** Inform students and parents about achievement
3. ***Administrative uses:*** Promotion, graduation, honors, eligibility
4. ***Guidance uses:*** Help students and parents make educational and vocational plans

GUIDELINES FOR GRADING. There are guidelines that assist teachers in making grades fair and accurate depictions of student learning, including:

1. Grade students for what they know and are able to do, without comparing them to other students.
2. Grade individual achievement more frequently than group achievement.
3. Include a wide variety of assessment methods.
4. Weight grades to reflect mastery of content and skills more than progress toward mastery.
5. Arrive at a final grade by considering outlier grades such as zeros and their effect when using mean averaging.

As you consider implementing classroom assessment, remember this mantra: "Teach what you test; test what you teach." Return often to the four purposes of assessment discussed earlier in this chapter (shown in Figure 4.3).

Check Your Understanding 4.4

4.5 What Are Standardized Tests, and How Are Their Results Used?

4.5 Describe standardized tests, and how their results are used.

A **standardized test** is one that is given to multiple groups of students, designed for specific grade levels, and typically repeated annually. These tests are administered and scored under controlled conditions, and their exact content is unknown to everyone except the test makers before they are administered.

Let's begin by comparing standardized tests and standards-based tests. A **standards-based test** is one that is devised according to the content of a specific set of standards. For instance, state standardized tests are also standards based because state content standards (now primarily the Common Core State Standards in English language arts and math) are addressed in the writing of the test items. But to say a test is standardized doesn't necessarily mean that it is standards based. The content may be derived from textbooks or various curriculum guides but not necessarily from a specific set of standards.

In the previous section, we discussed ongoing classroom assessment in varied formats that provide a broad view of learning over time. In contrast, standardized tests and their results tend to be more isolated snapshots of learning. These are often termed **high-stakes tests**—standardized tests that have far-reaching consequences, sometimes referred to as *high-stakes consequences*. A single test administered in one specific format once a year is very different from ongoing classroom assessment.

Standardized Tests in the United States

Standardized tests are given in some form in every public school in the United States. Let's explore four broad categories.

INTERNATIONAL ASSOCIATION FOR THE EVALUATION OF EDUCATIONAL ACHIEVEMENT. Founded in 1958, the **International Association for the Evaluation of Educational Achievement (IEA)** is an independent, international cooperative of national research institutions and governmental research agencies, conducting large-scale studies of educational achievement. In general, the two prominent IEA tests

- Provide achievement data to show trends in performance over time
- Foster public accountability
- Allow achievement comparisons among countries

Trends in International Mathematics and Science Study. As the only international test of math and science that compares students worldwide, the **Trends in International Mathematics and Science Study (TIMSS)** has been administered every 4 years since 1995. It is administered to fourth- and eighth-grade students, with an advanced exam given to students in their last year of high school. The United States and only nine other countries participated in the most recent administration of the advanced version of TIMSS.

In 2015, TIMSS exams were given to sample populations of fourth-graders in 49 countries and eighth-graders in 38 countries. As with any standardized assessment, IEA attempts to monitor conditions under which the TIMSS exams are given to make sure nations follow the appropriate guidelines for randomly selecting students. Rankings of the top 12 countries are in Table 4.5.

Progress in International Reading Literacy Study. As the only international test of reading proficiency that compares students worldwide, the **Progress in International Reading Literacy Study (PIRLS)** was administered to fourth-grade students only in 2001, 2006, 2011, and 2016. The PIRLS assessment tests proficiency in two specific types of reading: literary and informational. The percent of literary text items answered correctly by U.S. students on the 2011 exam was 70%, and the percent of informational text items answered correctly was 60%. These numbers align with the international averages, with correct answers on literary texts 59% and on informational texts 50%. It's important to note that results like these prompted the developers of the Common Core State Standards for English language arts to place equal weight on narrative, or literary, reading skills and on informational, nonfiction reading skills. Percentages of items answered correctly on the 2011 PIRLS for the top 10 countries are in Table 4.6. Fourth-graders in the United States scored the same as, or better than, 40 of the 45 nations participating in PIRLS in 2011.

NATIONAL ASSESSMENT OF EDUCATIONAL PROGRESS. Often called the nation's report card, the **National Assessment of Educational Progress (NAEP)** is the only standardized test systematically administered to a sampling of students across the United States. The NAEP is administered to fourth-, eighth-, and twelfth-graders in math, reading, writing, science, history, economics, geography, civics, foreign language, and a variety of the arts. The grade levels and subjects are rotated so that not every subject is assessed in every grade each year. The results are not reported by student, school, or district, but only by race, grade level, and state. The NAEP

- Allows for the achievement tracking of students at specific grade levels over time, both nationally and by individual states
- Provides a basis for state-to-state comparisons
- Allows for results tracking for a particular subject area and for comparisons among subject areas

Table 4.5 TIMSS 2015 rankings for the top 12 countries

4th- Grade Math		8th-Grade Math		4th-Grade Science		8th-Grade Science	
Rank	Country	Rank	Country	Rank	Country	Rank	Country
1	Singapore	1	Singapore	1	Singapore	1	Singapore
2	Republic of Korea	2	Japan	2	Republic of Korea	2	Japan
3	Japan	3	Chinese Taipei	3	Japan	3	Chinese Taipei
4	Russian Federation	4	Republic of Korea	4	Russian Federation	4	Republic of Korea
5	Hong Kong	5	Slovenia	5	Hong Kong	5	Slovenia
6	Chinese Taipei	6	Hong Kong	6	Chinese Taipei	6	Hong Kong
7	Finland	7	Russian Federation	7	Finland	7	Russian Federation
8	Kazakhstan	8	England	8	Kazakhstan	8	England
9	Poland	9	Kazakhstan	9	Poland	9	Kazakhstan
10	United States	10	Ireland	10	United States	10	Ireland
11	Slovenia	11	United States	11	Slovenia	11	United States
12	Hungary	12	Hungary	12	Hungary	12	Hungary

Based on: National Center for Education Statistics. (2015). Trends in International Mathematics and Science Study (TIMSS), 2015. Retrieved December 28, 2016, from https://nces.ed.gov/timss/timss2015/timss2015_table01.asp; https://nces.ed.gov/timss/timss2015/timss2015_table02.asp; https://nces.ed.gov/timss/timss2015/timss2015_table23.asp; https://nces.ed.gov/timss/timss2015/timss2015_table24.asp

Table 4.6 PIRLS 2011 rankings for the top 12 countries

Reading, 4th Grade		
Rank	**Country**	**%**
1	Hong Kong	69
2	Finland	68
3	Russian Federation	68
4	Singapore	68
5	Northern Ireland	66
6	United States	65
7	Chinese Taipei	65
8	Croatia	65
9	Denmark	65
10	England	64
International Average (45 countries)		55

Source: PIRLS 2011 Assessment. Copyright © 2012 International Association for the Evaluation of Educational Achievement (IEA). Publisher: TIMSS & PIRLS International Study Center, Lynch School of Education, Boston College, Chestnut Hill, MA, and International Association for the Evaluation of Educational Achievement (IEA), IEA Secretariat, Amsterdam, the Netherlands. Retrieved January 4, 2012 from http://timssandpirls.bc.edu/pirls2011/downloads/P11_IR_AppendixE.pdf.

Scores on the NAEP are divided into three categories: basic (partial mastery), proficient (solid performance on grade-level content/skills), and advanced (superior). Unfortunately, many students do not even achieve at the basic level. In 2015, both fourth- and eighth-grade math, reading, and science scores increased, whereas twelfth-grade scores remained about the same. In fact, in all subject areas except reading, the percentage of twelfth-graders at the proficient and advanced levels is consistently lower than the corresponding percentage for fourth- and eighth-graders. Over the years, scores at all grade levels in social science subjects such as history, civics, and geography have been lower than the scores in other areas. In all subjects, significant gaps remain between the scores of white students and those of African American, Hispanic, and Native American students (National Center for Education Statistics, 2016).

GENERAL STANDARDIZED TESTS. Mandatory testing of students using standardized tests has existed for decades. The most frequently administered general standardized tests include the California Achievement Test (CAT), the Comprehensive Test of Basic Skills (CTBS), the Iowa Test of Basic Skills (ITBS), the Metropolitan Achievement Test (MAT), and the Stanford Achievement Test (SAT). You may have taken one or more of these tests multiple times.

Many nationally published standardized tests provide detailed score reports for individual students that serve diagnostic purposes when studied by teachers. If given annually, it's possible to track a student's progress in a variety of content and skill areas within a subject.

A major thrust of national standardized tests involves comparing students, both individually and in groups. Comparison is possible because the tests are **norm referenced**, meaning that they are administered to a group of students selected because they represent a cross section of students. The scores of these representative students become the norm against which all other students are compared. Students receive percentile rankings. For instance, if Enrique's reading comprehension performance on the MAT is 78%, this means that 78% of students in his grade-level norm group scored lower than he did, and 22% scored higher. This does *not* mean that Enrique knows 78% of the content tested; rather, it means only that he did better on the test than 78 of every 100 students who took the test. Recall that classroom assessment is criterion referenced, meaning the assessment actually indicates what students know and can do rather than providing comparison data.

Two important concepts of standardized assessment are validity and reliability. If a test has **validity**, it means that the assessment measures what it is intended to measure. If a test has **reliability**, it means that the assessment yields a pattern of results that is repeated and consistent over time. Makers of standardized tests expend much effort to ensure validity and reliability and to assure the users of the tests that both of these critical components are in place.

STATE STANDARDS-BASED STANDARDIZED TESTS. The newest category of standardized tests in the United States is the state standards-based test, with items based on specific standards. All 50 states now have their own tests administered at a minimum to students in third through eighth grade. This widespread use of standards-based tests resulted from the No Child Left Behind Act of 2001, a reauthorization of the Elementary and Secondary Education Act. In the first decade of this century, NCLB dramatically changed the public education landscape in the United States in a number of ways, notably in the area of assessment.

Test results in some states are not reported in ways that are useful to teachers as they make instructional decisions. For instance, many state tests simply place students in one of four categories, such as below basic, basic, proficient, and advanced. These types of results do not provide information about performance within a particular subject area. In science, for example, the tests do not reveal whether students lack understanding in earth science, biological science, or both. Teachers and other educators have expressed disappointment that many state standards-based tests do not provide educative feedback.

State standards-based assessments are high-stakes tests because there may be drastic consequences associated with inadequate test results. For instance, the results are used to make decisions about funding and human resources, which students are promoted or held back, and who graduates and who doesn't. Based on standardized test results, states threaten (and sometimes follow through) to close schools, dismiss principals and teachers, and then reopen schools with new staffing and perhaps new programs.

Although most states have adopted the Common Core State Standards in English language arts and math, assessments of the standards still vary. States are collaborating as they implement the standards and write appropriate test items, some with the help of publishers experienced in test creation. Common testing practices may surface in the near future and be used by some states.

The Good, the Bad, and the Ugly of Standardized Testing

Many educators, parents, concerned citizens, and others loudly criticize standardized testing, particularly state standards-based standardized testing practices. Among the most well-known critics are James Popham, Susan Ohanion, Alfie Kohn, Anne Lewis, Richard Stiggins, and David Sadker. Critics of current standardized testing practices are not against assessments that are well-constructed tools for improving instruction. Their criticisms are directed at certain current practices. We hear them say, in essence, "You can't fatten cattle by weighing them," meaning that testing alone won't result in more learning.

Many teachers, parents, students, employers, and professors believe that using one test to judge what and how much is learned has questionable merit. They also agree that basing high-stakes consequences on the results of a single test is not appropriate. High-stakes consequences for those accountable for learning are attached to the results of most standardized tests, even while the tests are considered by many to be narrow measures of learning. In this chapter's *The Opinion Page* feature, we read about a school in California that, according to the writer, is meeting the needs of the student population

The Opinion Page

This Opinion Editorial appeared in the Sierra Sun, *a newspaper serving Truckee, North Lake Tahoe, and the High Sierra of California, on February 28, 2012.*

Truckee Elementary Draws Academic Strength through Diversity

by Alex Herrera

Herrera is co-president of the Truckee Elementary School Parent Teacher Organization.

Too often, trying to dispel stubborn myths can turn into an exercise in futility. But sometimes, the reality of a situation is so plain to see that correcting perception becomes a simple matter of communicating a few, basic facts. Such is the case when setting the record straight about Truckee Elementary School [TES] students' scholastic achievements.

On the basis of the 2011 results for Standardized Testing and Reporting (STAR), Truckee Elementary School has been designated a Program Improvement school. It's an often scrutinized label that belies the reality of TES, one of a vibrant and diverse community school, steered by passionate teachers who continue to develop bright, high-achieving, and confident students. And ironically, it also obscures the truth about standardized testing results—that TES students actually produce some of the best test scores in the district.

The fact is in 2011, Truckee Elementary's English-Learner sub-group ranked first in English Language Arts (ELA) and second in mathematics (out of four reporting schools). And the English-Only sub-group ranked second in ELA and third in math (out of six reporting schools). That is, both sub-groups' scores ranked near the top in the majority of tests, and they were above average in all tests. Yet TES retains PI status [a Program Improvement school], while schools with lower performing sub-groups do not.

The reason? Many schools, including several in this district, are exempt from meeting progress goals set forth by the No Child Left Behind act, either because they do not receive federal Title 1 funds, or because their sub-groups are not deemed large enough to be considered "numerically significant."

Truckee Elementary is fortunate to receive Title 1 funds other schools don't. These substantial, incremental dollars alleviate some of the pain caused by cuts in ever-tightening budgets. And as both the largest and most diverse elementary school in the district, we have more than just a handful of students in our sub-groups. As a consequence, Truckee Elementary is measured, while other schools with lower-performing sub-groups are not.

At Truckee Elementary, we don't believe any school should be measured solely by test scores. Standardized tests do nothing to reflect a child's social development, aspirations, dedication and self-esteem, factors that predict success in the real world at least as well as test scores. The strength of our school lies not in STAR rankings, but rather in the skills, passion and can-do attitude of our staff, the dedication and diversity of our student body, and the inexhaustible energy of our parents.

Still, when it comes to the unavoidable reality of mandated, standardized testing, scores do matter. And our school is not shying away from the challenge. Scores for our English Only and English Learner students sit near the top of their categories. Our school will continue to work hard to drive scores up even further, eventually dropping our Program Improvement status. That not only means maintaining the strength we've developed in core disciplines like mathematics, but in helping our English Learners close the achievement gap.

Truckee Elementary's diversity is its greatest strength, not its weakness. TES is—and will remain—a quality school our staff, students, parents, and the entire community can be rightfully proud of. However you choose to measure, there's simply no basis for any perception to the contrary.

This Opinion Page piece is an admirable balance of philosophy between those who completely malign standardized testing and those who say it is absolutely necessary. Write a well-developed paragraph in response to each of the following questions:

1. Why does Mr. Herrera believe that the results of STAR do not reflect the true nature of teaching and learning at Truckee Elementary School?
2. What opinion does Mr. Herrera voice that lets us know he doesn't object to measuring student achievement? Do you agree with his view?
3. Is Truckee Elementary the kind of school where you would want to teach? If not, explain. If so, write about your reasons.

while plagued by regulations that label the school, teachers, students, and community as underperforming. Read this opinion piece and then respond to the prompts that follow it.

There's an adage that says, "What we measure, we do." This means that assessment often determines and limits the curriculum. With test-based accountability and high-stakes consequences, this is probably inevitable. This approach is problematic because often what gets tested gets taught, and little else. For instance, announcements of which subjects will be tested at which grade levels influence how teachers allocate time, often leading them to exclude valuable curricular components for the sake of test preparation. In elementary schools in states where only math and language arts are tested, social studies and science are often relegated to 30 or fewer minutes in late afternoon. This practice leaves obvious holes in the curriculum to which students are exposed. The consequences of ignoring standards that are not tested show up in later grades when students lack prior knowledge on which the curriculum may depend. Do you recall the discussion of the null curriculum? What *isn't* taught can have far-reaching consequences.

Figure 4.5 contains statements about the good and the bad of standardized testing. Of course, the statements don't apply to all tests, just as the statements don't paint a complete picture. The issues are much too complex to be examined adequately in a chart. For our purposes, however, Figure 4.5 serves as an overview.

Standardized testing is not going away. Recognizing that reality, and making classrooms positive places in spite of testing pressures, is the challenge facing us in this age of accountability. Classroom teachers can take the reality of standardized testing and use it in beneficial ways by

- Modeling mature and reasoned responses to the assessments
- Encouraging positive attitudes in colleagues and students
- Teaching students that life is full of challenges we may not like or agree with, but that we must meet head on with our best efforts

Test-Taking Preparation

"Teaching to the test" is a phrase almost always viewed negatively. Stop and think about it for a moment: If the test is a good one that aligns with standards and contains reasonable questions, then teaching to it is a positive thing, right? "Teaching to the test" means emphasizing particular content and format. There's nothing inherently wrong with this if the practice doesn't limit the curriculum more narrowly than the

Figure 4.5 Pros and cons of standardized testing

Standardized testing is a *positive* component of public education in the United States because

- Many tests align with acknowledged learning goals (standards) and measure progress toward those goals.
- Administering the same test to large numbers of students allows for comparisons to be made and resources to be allotted where they are most needed.
- Standardized tests are cost effective because they are administered and scored uniformly.
- Without testing on a grand scale there is no way to make sure schools and teachers are doing the jobs they are assigned.

Standardized testing is a *negative* component of public education in the United States because

- The results are often misused, with consequences that are out of line with the relative importance or meaningfulness of the scores.
- The tests are often poorly constructed, with items that are not grade-level or subject-area appropriate.
- Standardized testing often reduces the curriculum by requiring teachers to concentrate on what is tested and eliminate what is not.
- Inadequate evidence is available to show a correlation between raising scores on state standardized tests and learning as reflected on the NAEP, ACT, SAT, or other nationally published standardized tests.
- Test-taking skills have an undetermined effect on raising scores, making increased learning a questionable result of better scores.
- Low-income, mostly minority, students predictably score below students with higher socioeconomic status, validating the opinion that the tests may actually test what's learned, or not, outside school.
- Teachers generally support standards, but undue pressure from high-stakes standardized tests can undermine productivity.
- Standardized tests don't measure important concepts such as cooperation, creativity, and flexibility.

standards and if it doesn't inhibit the implementation of a variety of engaging instructional practices. However, these are big "ifs" and may constitute pitfalls in the name of accountability.

Test preparation is an expectation. Creative teachers are able to weave test-preparation strategies throughout a rich curriculum and engaging instruction in ways that benefit students and expand their learning. Here are some examples of appropriate strategies:

- Practicing the format of a standardized test increases students' chances of success. If students are familiar with the way the test looks and the way answer choices are arranged on the answer sheet, the possibility of noncontent-related errors is reduced, and the test itself becomes a more accurate assessment of student knowledge and skills. For instance, if students are accustomed to listening to directions and working in silence, test day will not seem quite so extraordinary.
- If an anticipated test is in multiple-choice format, it's a good idea to occasionally provide classroom assessments in multiple-choice format.
- If short written response items are anticipated, teaching students to compose succinct, logical answers to prompts should be part of a teacher's instructional strategies.
- Almost every state provides practice materials that supposedly align with state tests. Districts and individual schools often purchase commercially produced materials designed to prepare students for standardized tests and make them available to teachers, or even mandate that they be used. If used on a limited basis, this practice is acceptable.

Check Your Understanding 4.5

4.6 Who Is Accountable for Student Learning?

4.6 Explain who is accountable for student learning.

When *A Nation at Risk* was published in 1983 by the National Commission on Excellence and Education (a commission appointed by President Reagan), America's public schools were painted as inadequate. Too many students were dropping out or graduating without basic literacy and math skills. People began asking who should be held responsible for student learning or the lack of it (NCES, 2016). Who should ask, "And how are the children? Are they all well?" and accept responsibility for the answer?

Students have the choice of listening, participating, behaving, and learning—or not. Given the finest and most equitable opportunities and full support from home, students should be held accountable for their own learning. And they are. Teachers grade them, and much of their future success rests on their school accomplishments. But students have very different starting positions when it comes to learning. Some have built-in family and community support and advantages, while others do not.

Parents and families bear a share of the accountability burden. If students are not supported in terms of adequate shelter and food, encouragement to value education, and physical and emotional surroundings conducive to studying, then families are not doing their part to promote student learning.

The adults who spend the most time with students outside the home are their teachers. Few teachers would ever deny that they are accountable for student learning, but most are quick to add they are not alone in their accountability. They expect their principals, as well as the other adults in the lives of students, to support their efforts in every way possible. The days of assuming a teacher is effective based on pleasant personality or self-declaration of competency are over. It has become absolutely necessary for teachers to follow a curriculum that is standards based. If student scores on state standards-based standardized tests are not acceptable, or at least improving, then teachers do not meet expectations.

Local school districts and school boards are also accountable for student learning. They make financial, programmatic, and personnel decisions that affect schools and classrooms.

Communities are accountable for student learning. If financial support of schools and a fundamental respect for education are not present, then communities are failing to accept their portion of accountability. Elected representatives of communities—legislators, members of city councils, mayors, and governors—all play roles in accountability because they are responsible for policies that either promote or thwart student learning.

State and federal governments share in accountability for student learning. Both levels of government pass laws and deliver mandates that directly affect schools.

So we see that "Who is accountable for student learning?" may be answered, "All of us." In other words, "And how are the children? Are they all well?" should be asked and answered over and over by everyone in the United States.

Point of Reflection 4.4

Who bears the heaviest load of accountability for student learning? If you do not believe that only one group is totally responsible, explain your view of balance with regard to accountability.

Check Your Understanding 4.6

Concluding Thoughts

Now that you know more about curriculum—what it is and where it comes from—you understand the importance of both knowing content and being enthusiastic about it. In today's educational and political environment, accountability for student learning falls most heavily on teachers.

Whether student learning occurs, and to what degree, may be gauged through classroom assessment. However, for the sake of coordination of state and national goals, a standardized system is necessary. Both classroom and standardized assessment results should guide the decisions teachers make every day in terms of curriculum and assessment. A great deal of work is still required to create a fair and equitable system that does not stifle imaginative teaching and learning but does yield results teachers can use to plan effective teaching and learning experiences.

We began this chapter by looking at assessment through the practices of Renee Ayers at Summit Primary School in Ohio. Now, as the chapter comes to an end, we join Renee as she decides to use portfolio assessment in her second-grade class. Read through *Chapter in Review* to help refresh your memory of what we have discussed, and then interact with Renee as she plans for portfolio assessment in *Developing Professional Competence*.

Chapter in Review

What is the formal curriculum?

- The formal curriculum is what is intentionally taught and stated as student learning goals.
- Standards, defined as what students should know and be able to do, serve as the framework for much of the formal curriculum.
- Adoption of the Common Core State Standards in K–12 English language arts and math is voluntary for states and, although most have done so, some states are abandoning the CCSS.
- Textbooks have a great deal of influence on the school and classroom curriculum.
- Various levels of government influence the formal curriculum.
- The formal curriculum includes both core and related arts subjects.
- An integrated curriculum involves linking curricular areas as their contents complement one another.
- A culturally responsive curriculum includes contributions and ways of viewing the world from perspectives of different cultures, ethnicities, races, genders, and socioeconomic levels.
- Infusing arts (music, theater, dance, and visual arts) into the curriculum provides opportunities for expression that motivate and engage students.
- There are multiple points of controversy related to curriculum.

What other curricula do we teach in U.S. schools?

- The informal curriculum is what teachers teach and students learn that is not part of the planned curriculum or standards.
- The extra curriculum consists of activities that are sponsored by the school but outside the formal curriculum.
- The null curriculum is what isn't taught.

What is involved in classroom assessment?

- The four major purposes of classroom assessment are to monitor student progress, make instructional decisions, evaluate student achievement, and evaluate programs.
- The three major kinds of assessment are diagnostic, formative, and summative.
- The seven basic forms of assessment are forced choice, essays, short written responses, oral reports, teacher observation, student self-assessment, and performance tasks.
- Both performance and portfolio assessment provide information on what students know and can do.
- Twenty-first–century assessment promotes balance, includes feedback, uses technology, and encourages portfolio development.

How do teachers evaluate student learning and assign grades?

- To evaluate is to make judgments about quality and quantity.
- Rubrics are instructional and assessment tools that make expectations explicit.
- A grade is an evaluation with a number attached to it.

What are standardized tests, and how are their results used?

- Most standardized tests are high-stakes tests.
- The Trends in International Mathematics and Science Study (TIMSS) and Progress in International Reading Literacy Study (PIRLS) compare student achievement among countries.
- The National Assessment of Educational Progress is called the nation's report card because it allows comparisons to be made among states.
- State standardized tests are also standards based.
- There are both benefits and drawbacks to standardized testing.
- There are appropriate ways to prepare students for standardized tests in addition to providing a rigorous and standards-based curriculum.

Who is accountable for student learning?

- Teachers, principals, and schools bear much of the burden of accountability.
- Families, the federal government, and local and state administrations are often viewed as less accountable for student learning.

Developing Professional Competence

Thoughtfully reading this scenario and responding to the items that follow it will help you prepare for licensure exams.

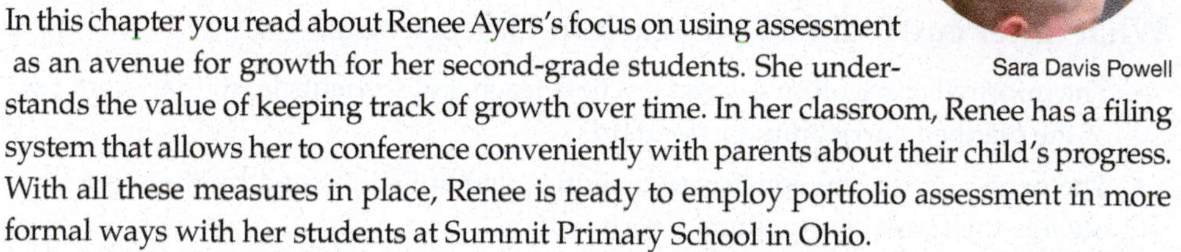

Sara Davis Powell

In this chapter you read about Renee Ayers's focus on using assessment as an avenue for growth for her second-grade students. She understands the value of keeping track of growth over time. In her classroom, Renee has a filing system that allows her to conference conveniently with parents about their child's progress. With all these measures in place, Renee is ready to employ portfolio assessment in more formal ways with her students at Summit Primary School in Ohio.

Now it's time for you to respond to two short essay items involving Renee and portfolio assessment. In your responses, be sure to address all the dilemmas and questions posed in each item. These items are followed by three multiple-choice questions.

1. Given what you know about Renee and her classroom practices, why is portfolio assessment the next logical step for her?
2. Consider the National Board for Professional Teaching Standards Core Proposition 3, which says "Accomplished teachers . . . employ multiple methods for measuring student growth and understanding and can clearly explain student performance to parents." Explain how Renee's plan addresses this standard.

Application Exercise 4.3: Developing Professional Competence

---

3. Renee is most likely planning to use portfolios to
   a. Display each student's best products.
   b. Substitute for traditional report card grades.
   c. Primarily teach students how to be organized.
   d. Show student growth over time.

4. Knowing Renee as we do leads us to predict that compiling work will be done by
   a. Students alone to teach organizational skills
   b. Renee and students working together
   c. Renee alone because she knows which pieces best accomplish the purposes of portfolio assessment
   d. Renee, in conjunction with Principal Laura Hill
5. Given what you know about Summit Primary School, how will Principal Laura Hill get the word out to all the other second-grade teachers in the district if Renee's experiment with portfolio assessment is successful?
   a. Ask Renee to explain what she experienced and her perceptions of results in a faculty meeting.
   b. Report Renee's success in a district principal's meeting.
   c. Invite all the district second-grade teachers to a special portfolio showcase event at Summit Primary.
   d. Ask Renee to write about her experiences for the district educator newsletter.

Application Exercise 4.4: Developing Professional Competence

Flash Cards 4.1

Shared Writing 4.1: Standardized Testing

Chapter 5

The Science, Art, and Service of Teaching

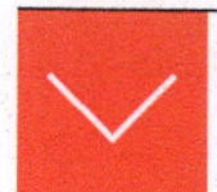

Learning Objectives

After studying this chapter, you will have knowledge and skills to:

5.1 Articulate an overview of the science, art, and service of teaching.

5.2 Explain the basic principles of classroom instruction.

5.3 Define the art of teaching.

5.4 Summarize how teachers serve students.

Dear Reader

Let's begin thinking about this chapter's content with an analogy—and a delicious one at that! Baking chocolate chip cookies requires specific ingredients, all of which are necessary. Flour is a necessary ingredient, but flour is certainly not sufficient. Butter is necessary, but it's not sufficient either. Chocolate chips are absolutely necessary, and the more the better, but no matter how many chocolate chips we have, they aren't sufficient to make mouth-watering cookies! To bake delicious cookies, all the ingredients matter. Some ingredients taste better than others when sampled alone, but when they are blended in the right proportions, the result is delightful!

Applying "necessary, but not sufficient" to teacher effectiveness reveals that the *science* of teaching (curriculum, assessment, and instruction) and the *art* of teaching (knowing how and when to use particular strategies to teach the curriculum) are necessary, but not sufficient by themselves for optimal student development. The ingredient of *service,* when added in large and individualized measure, completes the teaching recipe.

In this chapter we explore a variety of teaching and learning instructional strategies, along with two additional components of teaching—the *art* of teaching and the *service* of teaching.

5.1 What is 3D Teaching?

5.1 Articulate an overview of the science, art, and service of teaching.

Three-dimensional (3D) movies have made their mark in theaters. The 3D process adds depth that is visible when viewed through special lenses. Take a movie such as *Avatar*. In two dimensions, it's an enjoyable story with amazing computer-generated images. But when the third dimension is added, movie goers become part of the action—bobbing and weaving as objects and creatures appear close enough to touch. The audience becomes involved. *Avatar* works in 2D, but adding the third dimension enhances the perception of depth and helps make it an unforgettable adventure.

Teachers skilled in the two dimensions of teaching—science and art—are generally effective. They know the curriculum and how to teach and assess it. When the service dimension is added, students experience greater levels of cognitive, physical, emotional, social, and moral development. **Teaching in 3D,** with the whole child always in view through the lens of service, prompts students to be active participants in their own learning and growth.

Teaching has been thought of as both science and art for decades. *The New Art and Science of Teaching (2017)*, written by educator and researcher Robert Marzano, has helped revitalize acknowledgment that *teaching* is more than just the science or the knowledge of the formal curriculum and assessment, accompanied by proficiency in the use of instructional strategies. Teaching is also *art*, involving decision making based on numerous variables leading to skillful application of instructional strategies to teach the curriculum and assess learning in ways that meet the varying needs of students. Science and art are both necessary, but not sufficient, for effective teaching and learning. A third dimension is required—service. The *service* of teaching involves attitudes and approaches that promote growth in mind, body, and spirit for the present, equipping students for their journey toward responsible, respectful, and informed life and citizenship in the future.

Sara Davis Powell

As with 3D technology, teaching in 3D brings curriculum, instruction, and assessment alive for students.

Just as curriculum is the *what* of teaching, instruction is the *how*. Without effective instruction that meets the needs of learners, the most thoughtfully designed curriculum would not lead to effective learning. We teachers know there is not one single approach to instruction that works for every student in every subject all the time. Differing student intelligences, learning preferences, abilities, societal contexts, and so on, make using a variety of instructional approaches necessary to meet students' needs. Therefore, building a large repertoire of instructional strategies is vital. No need to worry—instructional possibilities are practically limitless.

"At its heart, teaching involves being able to 'unpack' something one knows well to make it accessible to and learnable by someone else" (Ball and Forzani, 2011, p. 41). This statement expresses the **art of teaching**—the ability to logically, and in a variety of ways, divide content and skills into manageable components and create experiences that lead to student learning. The **science of teaching** involves knowing the curriculum, honing instructional strategies, and becoming skilled in a range of assessment tools. Let's explore ways to implement the science of teaching to meet the needs of individual students. Doing so is truly an art!

Teaching is a service profession. Although service takes on a variety of definitions depending on context, for our purposes, the **service dimension of teaching** involves an attitude that approaches students as complete human beings. In other words, an approach to teaching from a service point of view is all-inclusive rather than focused only on academic and cognitive progress. Teachers also have the opportunity to engage students in service, as they learn about real-life issues and personal and collective responsibility. **Service-learning** occurs when student experiences combine service with a purposeful learning component.

Check Your Understanding 5.1

5.2 How is Instruction Implemented in U.S. Schools?

5.2 Explain the basic principles of classroom instruction.

A teacher provides learning opportunities that fall within a spectrum ranging from teacher centered to student centered, depending on the topic or skill, the knowledge and skill level of students, the time frame in which instruction must occur, and the teacher's instructional style. There are circumstances when lecture (perhaps the most teacher centered of all strategies) is appropriate, and there are other scenarios when student centered exploration with guidance works best. You may hear the phrases *sage on the stage* and *guide on the side* as you continue your teacher preparation. When a teacher is a *sage on the stage*, there is a lot of telling and demonstrating going on. Strategies such as lectures and **mini-lectures** (shortened, focused versions of the lecture) and teacher demonstrations are examples of *sage on the stage* teaching that can be effective strategies within a teacher's broader repertoire of teaching techniques. When a teacher is a *guide on the side*, the teacher is setting expectations, providing instructions, and serving as a resource while students do the work and exploration that lead to learning. Guiding, or facilitating, student learning leads to increased active engagement.

Big Ideas of Instruction

Let's explore some of the big ideas of instruction, along with some supporting instructional strategies that allow teachers to apply the big ideas in their classrooms. Each of the big ideas of instruction deserves, and indeed has had, entire books written about it. What you read here is an overview so that you will be aware of some of the ideas that will likely be emphasized during your teacher preparation program.

PROMOTE CRITICAL THINKING. **Critical thinking** involves observing, comparing and contrasting, interpreting, analyzing, seeing issues from a variety of perspectives, weighing variables, and then making decisions and solving problems based on these thinking skills. Can we really teach children and adolescents to think critically as they learn the standards of the formal curriculum? The answer is *yes*. Teaching critical thinking and **problem solving** is not an addition to the curriculum but rather a way of approaching the knowledge and skills we teach.

Benjamin Bloom and others at the University of Chicago first published what is now referred to as **Bloom's taxonomy** of thinking skills in 1956. Simply put, **thinking skills** are those skills that aid in processing information. These skills grow in complexity and sophistication as they progress from Level I to Level VI of the taxonomy.

Table 5.1 Bloom's taxonomy

	Categories	Key Verbs		Question Stems
Level I	Knowledge (Remembering)	Recognize Identify Recall Memorize	Retrieve List Define Duplicate	When did ______? Who was ______? Where is ______? Why did ______? Can you list four ______?
Level II	Comprehension (Understanding)	Interpret Summarize Infer Illustrate	Classify Compare Explain	How would you compare ______ to ______? What is the main idea of ______? What is meant by ______?
Level III	Apply	Implement Use Operate	Dramatize Illustrate Solve	How would you use ______ to ______? What approach would you use to ______? Can you ______ by ______?
Level IV	Analyze	Organize Integrate Focus	Categorize Differentiate Examine Test	What evidence can you find to conclude that ______? What does ______ have to do with ______?
Level V	Evaluate	Check Critique Judge	Monitor Defend Support	What is your opinion of ______? How valuable is ______ for ______? Why would you recommend ______?
Level VI	Synthesis (Creating)	Generate Plan Design	Construct Produce Develop	How would you change ______ to form ______? Can you propose a different way to ______? How would you design ______ to ______?

Based on: Anderson, L. W., & Krathwohl, D. R. (Ed.). (2001). *A taxonomy for learning, teaching, and assessing.* New York: Longman, Pearson.

Bloom's taxonomy has become an essential tool used by teachers as they plan and organize learning experiences. All the levels, as illustrated in Table 5.1, are necessary, and none should be neglected. Designing learning experiences that call only for knowledge and comprehension is cheating the minds of students who need to apply and analyze what they know, synthesize or create something new, and evaluate ideas and events. When planning lessons and assessments, teachers should use Bloom's taxonomy and the action verbs associated with each level. Questioning, an important strategy to promote student thinking, is enhanced by using the question *stems*, or question beginnings. In 2001, Anderson and Krathwohl revised Bloom's taxonomy by, among other things, using different words to describe some of Bloom's original levels and designating synthesis (creating) as a higher-thinking level than evaluation.

It's important for every teacher to understand the value of teaching and assessing at all the levels of Bloom's taxonomy. Watch as a high school science teacher explains his use of the taxonomy to increase student critical thinking.

TEACH THROUGH INQUIRY. When students pursue answers to questions posed by others or developed on their own, they are involved in **inquiry learning**. Observation, questioning, hypothesizing, and predicting are all part of inquiry-based learning, which requires students to move beyond rote memorization to become independent thinkers and problem solvers. Teaching and learning through inquiry may involve real-world contexts and discovery, and it can be accomplished in such simple ways as providing scenarios for students to explore or objects for students to manipulate. The challenge is to find or develop scenarios that inspire curiosity. Once students are curious, they're hooked! Teachers can sustain student engagement in focused, authentic learning (Ostroff, 2016).

Inquiry-based instruction is not new. All discoveries have come about as the result of questioning and answer seeking. Before students can formulate questions on their own or search for answers, they need knowledge and skills as building blocks. After these building blocks are in place, then students are ready to inquire and look for answers. Inquiry-based instruction is an effective way of teaching and learning because the ideas students create themselves are the ones they tend to retain.

A common way of implementing inquiry-based teaching is to design experiences that require students to engage, explore, explain, elaborate, and evaluate. This is commonly called the **5-E lesson plan.** For instance, an elementary teacher can tell third-graders the conditions necessary for bean plants to sprout and grow. The students can be tested and many will be able to recite the conditions, at least for the test. Using the 5-E plan, here's how the teacher might guide children through a cycle of inquiry learning:

- Take the students outdoors and ask them to observe the plants in the schoolyard (engage and explore).
- Have the students discuss with each other what they observed as the conditions for plants to grow and thrive (explain).
- Talk with the students about the possibility of an experiment involving some beans that are given the conditions the students think are needed for plants to thrive, as well as other beans that are deprived of the conditions (elaborate).
- Assist the students as they work together to create the desirable and undesirable conditions using real beans (elaborate).
- Guide the students as they observe and record bean growth and come to conclusions about what contributes to bean plants thriving, and whether their predictions were correct (evaluate).

An important element of inquiry learning is the thinking skill of questioning. Asking students appropriate questions helps them examine concepts and phenomena. When a teacher asks thoughtful questions, students also learn how to frame questions that lead to meaningful learning.

INCORPORATE STUDENT COLLABORATION. There can be significant benefits when students collaborate in a learning environment. Students may share responsibility for a project, discuss a question or prompt given by a teacher, tutor each other, help each other study for a quiz, or participate in a planned group activity. Most often, student collaboration in schools is referred to as **cooperative learning,** which, loosely defined, refers to any instance of students working together. There are several types of group formations:

- *Informal groups* meet together for a variety of tasks as needed, even as casual as a "turn and share with your neighbor" pairing.
- *Formal groups* complete designated, often long-term, tasks.
- *Base groups* consist of members who support one another with remembering and completing assignments, studying, and sharing resources.

Cooperative learning was more strictly and formally defined in the 1980s when Roger and David Johnson devised five requirements for effective student grouping practices:

1. *Positive interdependence:* Setting group goals for which all members must work to achieve; shared rewards; roles for each member, including facilitator, recorder, materials gatherer, timekeeper, and encourager
2. *Face-to-face interaction:* Students work together to explain, complete assignments, solve problems, and so on
3. *Individual accountability:* Students must complete individual tasks that contribute to the group
4. *Interpersonal skills:* Students learn to work together in socially acceptable ways
5. *Group processing:* Students reflect on how well they worked together and how effectively they accomplished their goals; students give teacher feedback on group functioning (Johnson and Johnson, 1999)

Cooperative learning is a big idea of instruction that can be successfully implemented in early childhood, elementary, middle, and high school. Watch as a geometry teacher uses cooperative groups that put students with a variety of achievement levels together.

Video Example 5.2: Informal Cooperative Learning

It's likely that you have been a member of many cooperative groups during your school experiences. Table 5.2 contains some ways teachers group and regroup students for learning.

USE TECHNOLOGY AND FACILITATE STUDENT USE. Today's students are referred to as the "Media Generation"—digital learners in "techno-drenched atmospheres" that are "gizmo-intensive" (McHugh, 2005, p. 33). "No generation has ever had to wait so little to get so much information" (Renard, 2005, p. 44). **Educational technology** is any technology-based device that assists teachers in teaching and students in learning. Even though students are growing up in a techno-drenched atmosphere, they still need guidance in navigating educational technology. They need to learn how to access what they need and decide what is important and relevant from among the seemingly endless flow of information. Students are so used to instant gratification from "on" switches that they are often frustrated when problem solving takes more time and intensive searching. Teachers are responsible for helping students make sense of technology tools, along with ways of using them to be academically productive in our technology-rich society.

Table 5.2 Cooperative learning strategies

Strategies	Description
Think-Pair-Share (T-P-S)	T-P-S involves all students in nonthreatening ways. Teachers expose students to information, give a prompt, ask a question or provide an experience, and then challenge them to think about it in a particular way and perhaps record their thoughts on paper (T). Students then choose a partner (P) and share their thoughts (S). Pyramid T-P-S involves multiple pairs of students discussing the question/prompt.
Jigsaw	This strategy involves students becoming experts on particular topics within *expert groups* and then teaching those topics to the other students in their *base groups*. Jigsaw is a powerful tool that actively involves students both in their own and other people's learning.
Role-Play	Getting students up and moving as they dramatize a scenario can make a point or prompt students to think in divergent ways. Role-playing becomes more effective with practice.
Tableau	Similar to Role-Play, the Tableau strategy involves students assuming a freeze-frame position that illustrates an event in a short story, book, or historical event. While students pose, another student in the tableau group reads a narrative that is being dramatized.

The International Society for Technology in Education (ISTE) provides detailed descriptions of the knowledge and skills related to technology use appropriate for children and adolescents. Virtually all major subject-area organizations join ISTE in promoting technology use in the classroom, as do professional organizations representing the various levels of preK–12 education.

In looking at technology available in schools, the two broad categories to consider are teaching tools and tools for teachers. Technology *teaching tools* are resources that enhance curriculum, instruction, and assessment when used by teachers to teach and by students to learn. This chapter's *SocialMEdia* segment features the use of Smartphones as educational technology. Some of the available technology teaching tools are shown in Table 5.3.

Technology *tools for teachers* are those that expedite and/or enhance the work of teachers and, consequently, curriculum, instruction, and assessment in the classroom. Examples include websites that allow for sharing of ideas, software that helps with lesson planning, and electronic gradebooks. Many technologies accommodate both categories.

INTEGRATE READING AND WRITING ACROSS THE CURRICULUM. Reading and writing are vital skills, without which life is both difficult and limited. Regardless of the subject or grade level, all educators need to be teachers of reading and writing. Infusing the curriculum with reading and writing and practice opportunities is often referred to as **reading across the curriculum** and **writing across the curriculum.**

Reading. An adage says that children "learn to read" through third grade and "read to learn" from then on. If only that were true. In early grades, when teachers expect to teach reading, they emphasize emergent literacy (getting ready to read) and beginning reading (letter/word recognition and story patterns). Often, their efforts are supported by reading specialists whose sole responsibility is teaching children to read. However, many students are not proficient readers by the end of third grade. Even if they are proficient, reading expectations become more stringent and complex, creating the need for specific literacy instruction beyond third grade. The guidelines from the Common Core State Standards for English language arts call for increased emphasis on nonfiction text throughout K–12—certainly a step in the right direction toward literacy. In middle

Table 5.3 Technology teaching tools

Technology Tool	Value in the Classroom
Word-processing software	Built-in support for writing and publishing
PowerPoint	Popular presentation program used by teachers in their classrooms to deliver instruction and by students to demonstrate skills and display project products
Smart technology	Interactive whiteboards with Internet accessibility that engage learners
Streaming video	Allows students to view video that is either stored on a site, or live, as it downloads on the computer
Instructional software	Used to learn about concepts and/or practice skills; five categories of instructional software: drill-and-practice, tutorial, simulation, instructional games, and problem solving (Roblyer, 2013)
Tablet computers	Also known as *notebooks*; smaller, more portable than laptop computers; used to access Internet, send and receive email, take photos and shoot videos, and play music
Internet	Most widely used network: World Wide Web (WWW)
Podcast	Similar to creating a radio program and then distributing it on the Internet; virtual publishing
Electronic books	emedia; iBooks; eTexts
Distance learning	Acquisition of knowledge and skills through instruction delivered using technology; learning is not place based
Digital games	Attention getting and interactive; simulations

SocialMEdia

A Smartphone can be an effective teaching and learning tool. Today's phones allow for audio, image, and video capabilities. Smartphones are different from a computer lab because the devices are personal. Students have invested a great deal of time and energy in learning how to use them and exploring possibilities. Additional reasons for using Smartphones as educational technology tools include:

- Use of a Smartphone can be engaging and motivating.
- Learning on the Smartphone can extend beyond the school walls.
- Smartphones incorporate familiar technology.

There are, however, some dilemmas involved in classroom Smartphone use:

- Not all students have a Smartphone.
- Some phones will support fewer applications than others.
- Some students may take advantage of anonymity to use phones inappropriately.
- Millions of Smartphones have been lost or stolen.
- Distractions and interruptions are possibilities.

The use of Smartphones as educational technology is a continually developing phenomenon. Sample uses include:

- Using a website such as Poll Everywhere (free for classrooms of 30 or fewer), where students can respond to questions and teachers can track instant answers
- Accessing prerecorded teacher-developed information and materials to prepare for class
- Taking advantage of the thousands of educational apps as supplements
- Collecting data and recording audio, photos, and video from experiments, fieldwork, voice messages, and so on
- Making podcasts, picture blogs, twittering, and more
- Learning and communicating collaboratively
- Accessing podcasts
- Creating mini-documentaries using the in-phone camera
- Recording field trips

Regardless of a school's Smartphone use policy, chances are that middle and high school students have them stowed away in a backpack, purse, or pocket, or perhaps left in a locker or car. Bringing this social media tool into plain sight and using it appropriately for teaching purposes may make sense for you, so long as you have a plan and permission from your administrator.

and high school there are far too many students with insufficient skills in reading and writing. Some ideas for promoting reading skills are presented in Figure 5.1.

Access to books, recreational reading, and silent reading all lead to improved skills in both decoding and comprehension. Fluent readers have the skills to be fluent writers. Conversely, students who struggle to read will also struggle to write.

Writing. Techniques for effective writing in multiple genres have not received as much attention or classroom time as reading instruction. Writing can be meaningfully integrated into all subjects at all grade levels and may be descriptive, creative, factual/informative, or expository. Teaching students to write involves many components, including sentence formation, punctuation, capitalization, word usage, style, and spelling.

Students will benefit from keeping notebooks or journals in multiple subjects to build both reading and writing skills, to increase note-taking proficiency, to record questions about content, to reflect on learning, and so on. Writing essays, biographical sketches, descriptions of events, stories, poetry, and answers to prompts fit naturally

Figure 5.1 Ways to promote reading skills

- Give students access to student-friendly, inviting, content-rich reading materials (books, magazines, newspapers, etc.).
- Read aloud to students at all grade levels to show them how to navigate through difficult text.
- Provide opportunities for silent, oral, and recreational reading.
- Use appropriate before- (explain vocabulary, predict), during- (graphic organizers, note taking, integrating prior and new knowledge), and after-reading strategies (summarizing, checking for understanding).
- Take a "textbook journey" as a class to help students understand the way the pages are set up, the purposes of the illustrations and data representations, the length and structure of the lessons and sections, the activities and exercises that follow sections, the glossary, and so on.

into English language arts and social studies classes. Writing narrative explanations of science and math procedures deepens and extends understanding.

Now that we have considered some big ideas of instruction and some strategies that bring the big ideas to life in the classroom, we are ready to explore how teachers plan for instruction.

Planning for Instruction

Curriculum is meaningless without instruction to convey it, and *instruction* is useless without curriculum. *Assessment,* the gathering of evidence of student learning, is a third component of teaching and learning that is interdependent with curriculum and instruction. All three components are vital in planning learning experiences for children and adolescents.

BACKWARD DESIGN. In their 2005 book, *Understanding by Design,* Wiggins and McTighe introduced educators to a concept that links curriculum, instruction, and assessment in meaningful and interconnected ways. This approach to planning for teaching and learning to accomplish understanding is called **backward design.** The word *backward* is used because the approach is in contrast to the way many teachers approach planning, which is to think of activities before considering the desired results of using those activities. Backward design starts with Step 1: Decide on the desired learning results (curriculum); Step 2: Identify how to collect the evidence necessary to know if the results have been achieved (assessment); and Step 3: Proceed to choosing how to help students acquire the desired knowledge and skills (instruction). These three stages, as illustrated in Figure 5.2, constitute backward design. Although some teachers view backward design as revolutionary, others call the concept just plain common sense and comment that they have used some version of it to plan their work for years.

Diagnostic, formative, and summative assessment, as discussed in Chapter 4, compose Step 2 of backward design, identifying how to collect the evidence necessary to know if desired results have been achieved. Diagnostic assessment is only possible when desired results have been identified and a plan for collecting evidence has been made—the first two stages of backward design. For instance, a teacher might plan a unit of study based on the Industrial Revolution. The teacher decides on the major concepts (content) and skills the students should understand and be able to do. The teacher then decides how to determine when the students have mastered the major concepts and skills using formative and summative assessment. A diagnostic assessment is then formulated that will diagnose what the students may already know about the topic. The teacher uses this information to plan instruction, Step 3 of backward design.

In addition to introducing the concept of backward design and expanding teachers' views of understanding, Wiggins and McTighe (2005) contend there is too much

Stage 1 Identify desired results (curriculum)

↓

Stage 2 Determine acceptable evidence (assessment)

↓

Stage 3 Plan learning experiences (instruction)

Figure 5.2 Stages of backward design

for teachers to teach and for students to thoroughly understand in content standards. They advise teachers to prioritize the standards within three categories. The most vital knowledge and skills are in the first category and are referred to as the *big ideas and core tasks,* defined as those that give "meaning and connection to discrete facts and skills" (p. 5). The next category consists of the *knowledge and skills that are important to know and be able to do.* The third category, and the one where some content may simply be mentioned or possibly eliminated altogether, consists of the *knowledge and skills that may be worthy of being familiar with but don't rise to the category of being important to know and do.* This is good advice.

LEVELS OF PLANNING. In early childhood and elementary classrooms, a daily **lesson plan** may mean planning experiences involving reading and math, with perhaps some social studies and science, a little art, and maybe some music and physical activity. In middle and high school, a daily lesson plan may mean planning for two English classes and two literature classes. *Daily* lesson planning is the planning that links teaching and learning.

A daily lesson plan should build on the lessons of previous days in cohesive ways. To assure this, daily lesson plans should be conceived within weekly plans or unit plans. A weekly lesson plan is just that—5 days of sequential lessons. A **unit of study** usually involves a theme, with daily plans within the unit addressing aspects of the theme. Weekly and unit plans should be conceived within **long-range plans** that may encompass a 9-week time frame, a semester, or a year. The best way to plan is with the entire school year's worth of standards in focus. Many schools and school districts provide **pacing guides** that outline what should be taught and when it should be taught, designating the order of concepts and skills. There are also online resources to assist in all levels of planning.

COMPONENTS OF A LESSON. Many types of lesson plan formats exist. A common one is shown in Figure 5.3. Subject-area organizations recommend specific components and particular formats that you will learn about as part of your teacher preparation program. Regardless of the format, there are lesson components that are usually considered necessary for effective instruction. Keep in mind that not every lesson will include each component, but over the course of a week, teachers generally incorporate all the components in some way.

Planning for instruction is a vital part of what teachers do. Knowing our students and their developmental levels allows us to plan our teaching appropriately to facilitate their learning. Here is a brief explanation of each of the lesson components in Figure 5.3:

- *Standards:* Standards basically set the curriculum and determine what teachers teach and students learn.
- *Lesson* ***Objectives:*** Objectives are concise statements about what students are expected to learn and be able to do as a result of the lesson.

Figure 5.3 Sample lesson plan format

Standard(s) to be addressed:
Lesson objective(s):
Lesson opening:
Procedures:
Plan for differentiation:
Opportunities for guided practice with feedback:
Independent practice:
Assessment of learning:
Closure of lesson:
Materials and resources:

- *Lesson opening:* The lesson should begin in a way that captures students' attention and creates interest. The opening can be a time to figure out what students already know about the lesson content (their prior knowledge). The information teachers gather requires them to be flexible as they adapt the lesson based on student knowledge and skill.
- *Procedures:* This is the step-by-step plan for how students will learn/explore a topic and/or skill. Procedures may include a variety of models, including cooperative learning, inquiry-based instruction, technology integration, and more, with combinations of strategies that include reading and writing and contribute to project- and problem-based learning. Class discussion, questioning, note taking, demonstration, and so on, are traditional teaching genres that may be part of the lesson procedures.
- *Plan for differentiation:* Plan on all the ways that instruction may vary based on a number of factors, primarily differing student learning needs.
- *Opportunities for **guided practice** with feedback:* It's important for students to have opportunities to work independently on applying knowledge in a nonthreatening setting (without being graded). Feedback from the teacher (or as part of an online program) as to whether the student is on the right track will prevent students from practicing incorrectly.
- *Independent practice:* This can be in or out of class and often takes the form of **homework.**
- *Assessment of learning:* How do we know if students have learned what we have articulated in the lesson objective(s)? There are multiple ways of assessing student learning.
- *Closure of lesson:* Providing a way for students to summarize what has been learned is a good way to close a lesson. The bell should not end the class period; there should be a plan to logically draw the class session to a close.
- *Materials and resources:* Planning a lesson includes gathering everything necessary for the lesson to proceed.

Not every instructional strategy is appropriate for every grade level. Early childhood is not the place for note taking, and high school is not the place for graphing solely with pictures. Some strategies, however, are appropriate for all levels of school. For instance, demonstration and cooperative learning can be used effectively in early childhood, elementary, middle, and high school classrooms.

EARLY CHILDHOOD INSTRUCTION. **Active engagement** is absolutely necessary in early childhood classrooms. Early childhood teachers need to be masters of engaging children in meaningful activities and providing an environment for creative and cooperative play. In prekindergarten, children learn prereading strategies and the meaning of numbers, among other basic concepts. In kindergarten through third grade, children *learn to read* and perform basic *problem solving.*

Sara Davis Powell

In Brandi Wade's lesson, the *objective* is for students to make judgments about the concepts of *less than, greater than,* and *equal to* as they manipulate objects. Because Brandi works with the children every day, she knows that their *prior knowledge* includes awareness of the symbolism involved with the concepts and how to count to at least 20 by assigning a number to an object (one-to-one correspondence). Using what the students already know, Brandi engages them in an activity. Here are some strategies Brandi uses in her lesson:

- *Demonstrates* counting, sorting, writing numbers, and choosing correct symbols
- Uses candy M&Ms as manipulatives, or objects to illustrate a concept
- Encourages children to work at tables where they can observe and help each other *(cooperative learning)*

Application Exercise 5.1: Brandi Wade's Lesson

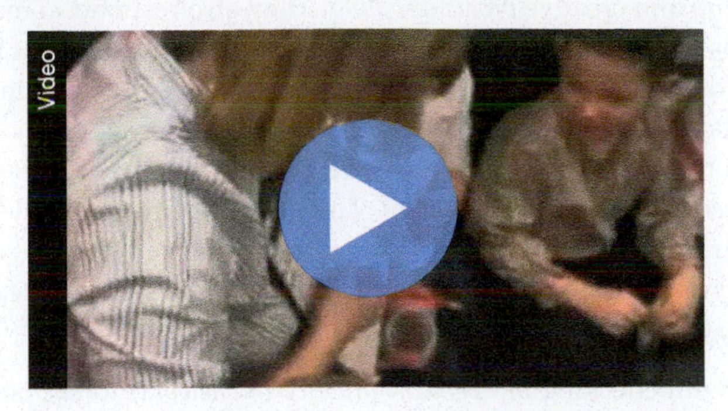

ELEMENTARY INSTRUCTION. For students in elementary classrooms, reading takes on new purposes beyond learning to decode words and reading fiction. Reading becomes a tool for acquiring new knowledge in language arts, math, social studies, science, and other subjects. Although *active engagement* remains vital, elementary children can be expected to read, study, and complete assignments with some measure of independence for brief periods of time.

In Brenda Beyal's lesson, the students experience *tableaus,* discussed earlier in Table 5.2. Here are some strategies Brenda uses to support the tableau lesson:

Sara Davis Powell

- Delivers a *mini-lecture* on author Eve Bunting
- *Reads aloud* portions of *Smoky Night*
- Uses a graphic organizer to explain what a *tableau* involves
- Incorporates *cooperative group work* as a vital part of the tableau
- *Facilitates* the work of groups

Brenda knows that her students are able to read *Smoky Night* silently and answer questions about its content. However, she wants her students to be more deeply involved with the book and, among other things, understand the author's motivations, become knowledgeable about the period of history in which the story takes place, understand the societal implications of the story, and experience some of the emotions of the characters. She chose the tableau strategy to accomplish her instructional *objectives.*

Application Exercise 5.2: Brenda Beyal's Lesson

Sara Davis Powell

MIDDLE-LEVEL INSTRUCTION. Young adolescents typically respond positively to *active learning* opportunities. They are eager to be involved in meaningful experiences that require *inquiry* and creative *problem solving*. They also respond to more traditional strategies such as *mini-lectures* and *note taking* if they have been taught to actively listen, record, and organize what they learn. Variety and frequent shifts in strategies are fundamental to engaging middle-level students.

In Traci Peters's lesson, the students review topics. They complete a worksheet, respond to *teacher questions*, and *take notes*. The new learning in this lesson involves students discovering the sum of the measures of the angles of a triangle, and then writing generalizations about what they have learned. Here are some strategies Traci uses to support the day's lesson:

- Begin class with checking *independent practice (homework)* to support and review concepts.
- *Demonstrate* and *question* using the overhead projector.
- Use *manipulatives* to discover concepts.
- Facilitate *cooperative learning* to check for understanding.
- Require a *written explanation* of learning.
- *Facilitate* small-group work.

Traci knows the value of *inquiry-based learning*. She knows that if her young adolescents *discover* the sum of the angles of a triangle they will understand the concept and remember what they learn.

Application Exercise 5.3: Traci Peters's Lesson

HIGH SCHOOL INSTRUCTION. Students in high school also respond to *active learning* opportunities. They work best when the content interests them and when they interact with the subject or topic in ways that require them to be *problem solvers*.

In Craig Cleveland's lesson, students are engaged in a thought-provoking class discussion after Craig reads a picture book to them about discrimination. The students then read a series of Jim Crow laws, with the purpose of developing role-plays that illustrate a particular law. The students act out their role-play scenarios, and then the class discusses what everyone has seen. This kind of active involvement is excellent for promoting *critical thinking*. Here are some of the strategies Craig uses in his lesson:

- *Read aloud* to the students.
- Facilitate *class discussion*.
- Deliver a *mini-lecture*.

- Use quotations to provoke *critical thinking*.
- Assign *role-play*.
- Incorporate *cooperative groups*.

Craig knows his students well. He understands that the study of discrimination through Jim Crow laws will appeal to them because of the *real-world context*. He also knows that language barriers in his classroom may be partially bridged through *role-play*.

Sara Davis Powell

Application Exercise 5.4: Craig Cleveland's Lesson

Check Your Understanding 5.2

5.3 What Is the Art of Teaching?

5.3 Define the art of teaching.

There isn't a formula for effective teaching. We can't say, for example, "I have 24 students—13 girls and 11 boys. Two have been retained a year, six have either an IEP or a 504 plan, and three are designated as gifted. I'll plug this information into a formula and out will come curriculum content; sequencing; diagnostic, formative, and summative assessment practices; and the right mixture of instructional strategies." Wouldn't it be great to have a teaching input–output machine? But no such machine exists. Every student is different, making every classroom of students different. Teachers are artists, directing learning experiences choice by choice, day by day.

Perhaps new teachers will master much of the science of teaching and may instinctively, on occasion, incorporate the art of teaching in their classrooms. However, much of the art of teaching comes with experience. But learning from experience doesn't necessarily lead to increased artistry; the learning must be intentional (Barth, 2006). Purposefully observing students and how we interact with them and the content will lead to increased artistry and awareness of what works and what doesn't. Marzano (2011) observes, "Deliberate practice involves more than just repetition, it requires activities that are designed to improve performance, challenge the learner, and provide feedback" (p. 82). Deliberate development of the art of teaching is a continual growth process involving serious reflection on classroom practice, perhaps journaling and conversations with other educators, and meaningful professional development. That's what makes it so exciting. There's always more to learn and do.

Differentiation as Artistry

Approaching instruction in a variety of ways to provide multiple paths for students to learn the content and to develop the skills of the curriculum is artistry. In 1999, Carol Ann Tomlinson gave this philosophy and practice a name: **differentiation of instruction.** Tomlinson (2014) tells us that teachers who differentiate instruction strive to do whatever it takes to meet student needs in terms of affect, readiness, interests, and learning profile. Student *affect* involves "how students' emotions and feelings impact their learning" (p. 16). Student *readiness* refers to "a student's proximity to specified knowledge, understanding, and skills" (p. 16). Student *interest* includes "that which engages the attention, curiosity, and involvement" (p. 16). And a student's *learning profile* is determined by many factors, including learning preferences, gender, and culture.

The artistry of differentiating instruction involves an array of content, a variety of processes, and choices of products when possible. The *content* is what the students should know, understand, and be able to do. *Process* consists of the ways students make sense of content, typically through activities and practice. A *product* shows what students know and are able to do; it may be, for example, a project, demonstration, test, or display.

Tomlinson wisely cautions against trying to differentiate too much, too quickly. She advises us to start slowly by recognizing one need (affect, readiness, interests, or learning profile) in our classroom, changing one part of a lesson (content, process, or product), and implementing this differentiated strategy followed by reflection on the results. As our ability and comfort levels grow in diagnosing the affect, readiness, interests, and learning profiles of our students, we can incorporate more and more instructional practices that effectively meet their needs. However, tackling too many differentiated strategies too soon in a teacher's career, or in a particular student setting, can lead to doing an activity for the activity's sake and the sacrifice of solid, well-designed teaching. Great advice.

Taking Tomlinson's advice and starting small may involve simply incorporating **manipulatives,** or objects, to represent numbers or concepts in a lesson on fractions. Differentiating may involve prompting pairs of students to complete an assignment together, allowing students to teach each other. Or perhaps differentiation will consist of giving students choices about how they want to work on the week's vocabulary words, with some individually writing definitions and others quizzing each other quietly in a corner of the room. Tomlinson's view, in general terms, of what teachers do in differentiated classrooms is outlined in Figure 5.4.

The realization that every student behavior indicates affect, interest, readiness, and learning profile, and that reading these behaviors is part of the art of teaching, can be staggering. Most new teachers find themselves concentrating on the lesson being

Figure 5.4 Differentiation of instruction

When teachers differentiate instruction, they. . .

- begin where students are
- accept and build on the premise that learners differ
- engage students through different learning modalities
- ensure that students compete against themselves more than they compete against others
- believe that students should be held to high standards
- ensure that each student realizes that success is likely to follow hard work
- use time flexibly
- are diagnosticians who prescribe the best instruction for their students

Based on: Tomlinson, C. A. (2014). *The differentiated classroom: Responding to the needs of all learners* (2ed.). Alexandria, VA: Association for Supervision and Curriculum Development.

taught with a sort of tunnel vision that may make them oblivious to student reactions. Over time, comfort with lesson procedures increases and a teacher's vision widens to include student behaviors. In other words, the teacher's classroom peripheral vision increases. At this point it's possible to use the *art of teaching* to increase the effectiveness of *the science of teaching*.

Understanding that students learn best in different ways, watch to see a third-grade teacher teaching vocabulary using students' natural tendency to move. Recall from Chapter 2 that this is the kinesthetic learning modality. In this way, the teacher differentiates instruction.

Video Example 5.3: Teaching Vocabulary with Movement

High Expectations As Artistry

The art of teaching leads us to make decisions centered on students and their needs. For decades, research has indicated that teacher expectations determine how they interact with students. High expectations for some students lead teachers to treat them differently from how teachers treat the students for whom they have low expectations. Expectations matter.

Addressing expectations as part of the art of teaching is vital. It's easy to say, "I have high expectations for all my students" and then behave very differently toward individuals. Here's what we need to realize: *High* expectations do not necessarily mean the *same* expectations. When teachers are realistic, they know that student aptitudes and readiness vary greatly. Having the same expectations for all students isn't fair to any student. Our expectations should be based on all the variables that contribute to learner differences: affect, readiness, interests, and learning profile. Expectations should be individualized and always set high for each student, with a clear vision of growth and success. We must be cautious, however, to avoid stereotyping when we consider variables such as socioeconomic status or race—factors that may lead to unfair and debilitating lower expectations.

All teacher behaviors communicate expectations to students and, in turn, influence students' expectations of themselves. Teacher expectations of a student often become a self-fulfilling prophecy. Teacher and author LouAnne Johnson remarks, "When my students believe that success is possible, they will try. So my first priority in any class is to help my students believe in themselves and their ability to learn" (2005, p. xiii).

Marzano (2011) states that there are four distinct steps we can take both to be aware of our expectations and to purposefully adjust our behavior. The first step is to *identify students for whom we may have lower expectations.* Second, he urges us to *identify similarities among students* so that we recognize potential. This leads us to identify possible biases that should not impact expectations. Once we've done this soul-searching, the third step is to *identify how we treat the students from whom we expect less.* Then as the fourth step, we do what's necessary to *behave toward students based on our high and thoughtfully individualized expectations.*

High, individualized expectations for each and every student affect not only academic achievement but also student social-emotional health and well-being. While developing and maintaining these expectations, teachers are using artistry that assumes the best of students and leads them to optimal learning and growth. By doing so, teachers are serving the whole student, cognitively, physically, emotionally, socially, and morally.

Point of Reflection 5.1

Do you recall teachers who attempted to teach the same content in different ways? If so, what type of strategy addressed your learning needs and preferences most? If not, what is one strategy you wished you could have experienced more in K–12?

Check Your Understanding 5.3

5.4 How Do Teachers Serve Students?

5.4 Summarize how teachers serve students.

Most teachers naturally see students and their profession through a service lens; to do so intentionally increases the potential impact of this third dimension of teaching. Note that a service approach does not in any way conflict with academic learning or accountability. It's not an add-on, but rather an integral part of a teacher's day. Service primarily manifests itself in the unplanned, spontaneous, and unavoidable area of the curriculum that is rarely written in a lesson plan, but that strongly influences every part of teaching and learning—the informal curriculum. In addition, teachers serve students by providing them with opportunities to serve others, to experience the satisfaction of giving back in ways that increase their knowledge and skills, while doing positive things locally and beyond.

Teachers Serving Students

Like it or not, who we are and what we do have an impact on our students. By virtue of being the teacher, our words, actions, nonverbal communication, and attitudes become part of every academic lesson we plan and implement, as well as every teacher–student encounter and interaction. We impact the informal curriculum, both intentionally and unintentionally. We might go so far as saying teachers *are* the informal curriculum. If we are positive, caring, excited about learning, fair, and organized, students learn that

- optimism is more productive than pessimism;
- cooperation and empathy matter;
- structure and enthusiasm enhance learning; and
- responsibility is personal and valuable (Powell, 2015).

Teaching in Focus

Sara Davis Powell

Chris Roberts is an adventurer. He travels extensively, climbs mountains, and rafts in white water. He could do lots of things with his life—and he does. But his career choice is teaching 8-, 9-, and 10-year-olds at Rees Elementary School in Spanish Fork, Utah.

It takes only a few minutes in Chris's multiage classroom to recognize how his energy and wide range of interests influence how he interacts with students. He teaches all the core elementary subjects, as well as the dance component of the arts emphasis at Rees. When asked what he gets out of teaching, Chris says, "I like to play, I love these kids, and learning is the most exciting thing in the world."

You won't find in his lesson plans any references to the fascinating displays in Chris's classroom. Nor will you find "Tell the kids about my last dive off the Yucatan" or "Let my students know that life is a wonderful adventure." When Chris infuses his hobbies, interests, and travel into his classroom, he is teaching what was defined earlier as the *informal curriculum*—lessons that aren't in the curriculum standards. The cartoons with philosophical messages, the inspirational stories and poems, the giant topographical map of Utah, the newspaper and magazine clippings about people who triumphed over unimaginably difficult circumstances, and the personal family photographs—all of it speaks to who Chris is and what he values.

Application Exercise 5.5: Chris Roberts's Room Tour

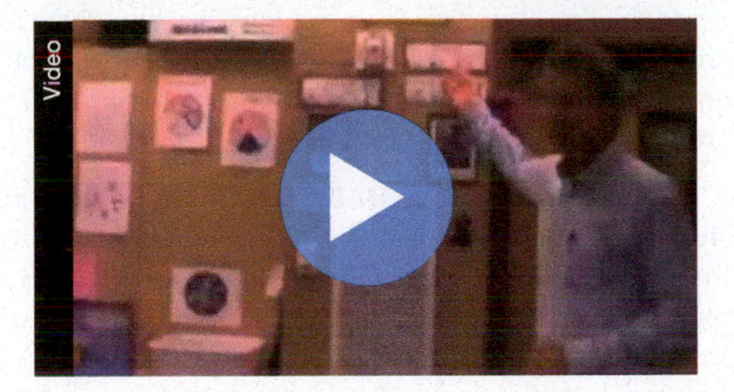

On the other hand, if we are negative, lack interest in students and subjects, or exhibit a general disdain for our work, students are likely to mirror these qualities. If our classrooms are a mess, if the school building is dilapidated, and if the community is unsupportive, students learn that they may not matter very much.

There are as many aspects of the service dimension of teaching as there are instructional strategies and combinations of strategies. Although we focus here on six ways teachers serve students, once you understand the service dimension, you will naturally add to them based on your personality and the students you serve. After we explore these six ways, we discuss the purposes and methods of involving students in service and service-learning.

1. FORM RELATIONSHIPS. Relationships matter. Promoting positive relationships means making connections with students with an interested mind and a caring heart. Relationships happen between individuals; viewing students as individuals is necessary. This means, to the extent possible, we should get to know our students, and, in turn, allow them to get to know us. We need to be real people with dreams, flaws, and lives outside school.

Positive relationships may be formed through simple acts such as quickly learning student names, greeting students with a smile, having real conversations, acknowledging circumstances that affect student lives, and demonstrating care at every turn. Teacher–student relationships are also fostered when students know they can count on us to protect them—academically, emotionally, and socially. Refusing to tolerate any sort of harassment among students builds the trust necessary for positive relationships.

Empathy—the capacity to see situations from another's point of view—is something we should both exhibit and teach. The better we know our students, the greater our capacity for empathy. The more we model empathy and talk about it with students, the more likely they are to empathize with each other and with us, making relationship bonds stronger and more beneficial.

Building relationships leads to increased student engagement and achievement. When students sense they are valued in classroom relationships, they are more willing to cooperate and engage in the classroom. Students who sense they belong have more inner resources to use to be successful. They know they are cared for.

2. CREATE A CLIMATE OF RESPECT. A climate of respect begins with a teacher deliberately modeling acceptance. It's obvious to students when a teacher accepts students for who they are and where they are in their growth journey; it's also obvious to students when a teacher doesn't. Unconditional acceptance fosters self-acceptance and leads to students accepting each other, and to take risks, make mistakes, and keep growing.

When students sense acceptance, they are more willing to express themselves. A climate of respect exists when a teacher values what students have to say. Giving students choices, asking for their opinions, teaching them to reflect on their own learning, and giving meaningful writing assignments help develop **student voice.** When students are treated with respect, two valuable things happen: Their self-worth grows and they are more likely to respect the teacher.

3. MODEL PRODUCTIVE HABITS. When you think about how many waking hours students spend in school from kindergarten through high school, it becomes clear that they spend as much, if not more, of their formative years with teachers as with family members. Students watch us as we work and express our personal interests. It's a valuable service for teachers to model productivity.

In an article "One to Grown On/Watching Us Work," Tomlinson (2012) tells us that teachers who model productive habits of successful, well-adjusted adults and use opportunities to prepare students for their futures

- Respect students.
- Assume students have abilities.
- Hold high expectations.
- Teach students to work smart.
- Discuss stepping stones to successful futures.

As we teach the prescribed knowledge and skills, it is possible to boost development of students into fulfilled citizens with productive work ethics.

4. EMPHASIZE CIVICS AND CITIZENSHIP. The 2015 National Assessment of Educational Progress results show that civics education ranks last among the subjects tested. Not only do teachers need to teach more about government and the principles of democracy but they also must provide opportunities for students to practice these principles, and be given the empowerment to do so.

The habits of good citizenship must be modeled in our schools by the adults who inhabit them. Civics education can enhance these habits. This is not the sole responsibility of social studies teachers; just as with reading and writing, all teachers share this responsibility. Every day in every newspaper across the country, we find articles about how "we the people" live together and make decisions. Be informed and lead discussions on topics that are current and interesting. This may take as little as a 30-second mention or a 10-minute discussion. Bring up issues and ask for student opinions and solutions. This is practicing citizenship. Damon (2012) tells us that there are at least four commonsense ways to foster civics and citizenship knowledge and action:

1. Talk about current, as well as past, civic leaders. Yes, we can learn from George Washington and Nathan Hale, but how about from more recent government figures such as Hillary Clinton and Colin Powell?
2. History courses shouldn't necessarily be chronologically based. How about using concepts and themes to blend the past and the present?
3. Foster patriotism by emphasizing the best of America's traditions.
4. Make sure students know how our government works. Knowledge is power in the development of civic participation and pride.

Retired U.S. Supreme Court Justice Sandra Day O'Connor states, "Knowledge of our system of government is not handed down through the gene pool. . . . The habits of citizenship must be learned . . . . But we have neglected civic education for the past several decades, and the results are predictably dismal" (Coley and Sum, 2012). In 2009, O'Connor founded *iCivics*, combining her passion for civics and the availability of technology for teaching. *iCivics* is a nonprofit group providing free online educational games and lesson plans focusing on structures of government, citizenship rights and responsibilities, and the U.S. Constitution. Teachers across the country are taking advantage of *iCivics* resources to engage students.

5. PROMOTE CHARACTER BUILDING. Schoolwide emphasis on character development has gone in and out of favor for decades, depending in large measure on school leadership and community expectations. Three-dimensional teachers help students build character, regardless of school programs intended to do so. Many components of character education are accepted as valuable to most Americans. Very few would be opposed to students learning to be more honest, hard-working, and responsible. These desirable traits support academic learning, and they may be even more long-lasting and beneficial than the subject-area standards in the curriculum.

One character trait addresses desirable student-to-student interactions—**civility.** When we practice civility, we treat others the way we want to be treated. Defining civility, pointing out instances of civility as well as examples of incivility, and modeling civility by not tolerating any form of harassment in our classrooms are part of a teacher's service to students.

A classroom and school climate of civility will exist only when students are empowered to do what's right, both individually and collectively. Because most student-to-student interactions occur outside the hearing of adults, we need to help students understand that when two, three, or more of them stand up against harassment, bullying of any kind, or inequities, they become a force for civility. To demonstrate the power of standing together, pick up a student's wooden pencil and break it with both hands. Then gather five or six pencils from students and try to break them, together, in the same way. You won't be able to. Chances are students will remember this demonstration of strength in numbers when civility is practiced together.

6. COMMUNICATE POSITIVELY. Teachers communicate all day long, verbally and nonverbally. Nonverbal communication may be body language, gestures, eye contact, touching, writing, or electronic in expression. What we say, what we don't say, and the constant stream of messages we convey affect students. These messages are powerful: A careless or sarcastic comment may slip and be forgotten by us, yet may cut to the heart of a student. A disdainful look read by a student as a comment on his worth may long be remembered.

On the other hand, a thoughtful question asked with genuine interest or a smile in the hall and a friendly greeting may make a student's day. Simple gestures like a pat on the shoulder, an email sent to mom saying project work is going well, eye contact during a conversation—this communication takes very little time or effort, but it could change the direction of a day or a lifetime for a child in crisis.

To communicate with optimum effectiveness requires an element we often neglect—listening. There's a difference between hearing and really listening. Simply hearing will not give us the clues we need to thoughtfully and appropriately respond. When communicating with students, a disposition of service requires us to *respond* rather than *react* to words and events. This takes self-control, and lots of it. Reactions are quick and brash. Responses take more time to formulate, with both reason and thoughtfulness. Remember, however, that sometimes all a student wants is a listening ear and some validation of feelings and concerns. In this regard, listening is a form of communication; silence can be powerful.

We have discussed just six aspects of the service dimension of teaching. This chapter's *The Opinion Page* feature is based on one of the most appealing aspects of the teaching profession. We get to "start over" every school year! Aspects of the previous year that worked well can be enhanced and implemented again. Approaches that were less than successful may be changed or abandoned. In "Let's Resolve to Improve School Year," the guest writers give valuable advice for beginning a new school year. Because the service dimension of teaching should grow and develop with experience, it's valuable to consider additional ways to be three-dimensional teachers.

The Opinion Page

This Opinion Editorial appeared in the *Omaha World-Herald* on August 8, 2012.

Let's Resolve to Improve School Year

by Gene A. Budig and Alan Heaps

Budig, a McCook, Neb., native, was president/chancellor of three major state universities. Heaps is a vice president of the College Board in New York City.

According to the academic calendar, it's a new year. August and September are the months when K–12 and higher education institutions gear up for the start of school.

Here in the United States—as well as in many other countries—the beginning of the new year is accompanied by a number of traditions. One of the most popular is the making of resolutions: promises to ourselves and others that we will behave well (or better) in the months ahead.

The practice of making new year's resolutions is not a new one. Four thousand years ago, the Babylonians started each year by paying their debts and returning borrowed objects. Two thousand years ago, the Romans asked forgiveness from their enemies. Five hundred years ago, medieval knights took a vow to reaffirm their commitment to chivalry.

In recent times, the new year's tradition has been altered to favor a more tailored approach to resolutions, each of us focusing on behavior that fits our individual situation. According to a U.S. government website, popular resolutions here in America include to drink less alcohol, eat healthier food, enroll in more education, find a better job, get fit, lose weight, manage debt, reduce stress, quit smoking, do more recycling, save money, take a trip, and/or volunteer to help others.

It is estimated that almost half of adult Americans make new year's resolutions. It is also estimated that one-quarter drop their resolutions within a week. One-third drop their resolutions within one month. Slightly more than half (54 percent) drop their resolutions within six months.

In the spirit of new beginnings, we talked with a few colleagues and developed a list of educator resolutions for the upcoming academic year.

Be innovative: Our world is rapidly changing. In many ways, possibilities are limited only by our imaginations. But many of our schools look and work the way they did a hundred years ago. We need to implement bold ideas for improving our classrooms.

Be students ourselves: All of us can find something to learn, whether it's about new teaching methods, classroom technology or even a new personal hobby. Let's be continuous learners so we can see the teaching process through the eyes of students.

Broaden the enterprise: We live in a world where the many parts of our lives are interconnected. This is also true of students, all of whom have intricate and powerful ties to their communities, families and personal histories. Let's reach out to student families and community members.

Lead the discussion: No one knows education better than educators. While our judgment is far from infallible, we need to better assert our opinions and knowledge. Let's lead the debate by raising the issues we believe important.

Admit our weaknesses: There are problems in education, and some of them are of our own making. Let's admit this and work to fix them.

Communicate more: Teachers are good at talking to teachers. Counselors are good at talking to counselors. Principals are good at talking to principals. But we're not as good at communicating among the levels and with others. Let's communicate with the broad spectrum of educators and others.

Be role models: Students look not only to what we say but also to what we do. They emulate our behavior in things both big and small. Let's behave in ways we would want our students to follow.

Set high expectations: Our students are a pretty remarkable group. They can achieve almost anything with the right supports. Let's give all students the credit and respect they deserve.

It's about the students: Most importantly, this year, let's remember that education is not about the teachers, the administrators or the lawmakers. It's about the students. If we keep our focus on the students and their welfare, we will have done much to improve the conversation about our schools.

These resolutions are tough ones. But educators are committed to their profession and their students. We hope that educators will work hard to be in that 46 percent who keep their resolutions for more than six months.

Assignment: Much of the content of this Opinion Page piece relates directly to what you have read in this chapter. ***Choose three of the nine resolutions and write a well-developed paragraph for each****, discussing aspects of the chapter that support them.*

Service-Learning

There is a difference between volunteerism and service-learning. Volunteerism entails choosing to give time or effort to serve or support a cause without the expectation of receiving anything in return. Volunteerism is noble; there are many choices for which we all may volunteer. We want students to see us modeling volunteerism as we encourage them to do the same. Service-learning, however, goes beyond volunteering, and, indeed, may not be voluntary on the part of students. When a planned learning component is added to service, we have created a service-learning opportunity with the goal of enhancing students' social, academic, and civic skills and sensibilities.

To illustrate the difference between volunteerism and service-learning, think about students volunteering to serve the community by cleaning out a streambed. This is certainly a service. But if the students collect the trash and debris, analyze what they find to determine polluting effects, and then share the results with the community, they are learning while serving and providing valuable information that may solve a community problem.

GUIDELINES FOR SERVICE-LEARNING. The National Youth Leadership Council recommends that service-learning experiences include the eight specific components in Figure 5.5. The individual components may exist within a project to varying degrees, but should be part of the design for service-learning projects.

Many school districts believe so strongly in the benefits of service-learning that they are making participation in the experience a requirement for graduation. For instance, the Service-Learning Initiative of Chicago Public Schools requires 40 hours of service-learning experience as part of what's necessary for high school graduation. Chicago Public Schools simplified guidelines for acceptable service-learning experiences into

Figure 5.5 National Youth Leadership Council service-learning guidelines

Service-learning should:

1. Be meaningful and personally relevant service.
2. Link to curriculum to meet learning goals and content standards.
3. Incorporate reflection that leads to analysis of self and individual relationships to society.
4. Promote understanding of diversity and mutual respect among all participants.
5. Provide participants with a strong voice in planning, implementing, and evaluating projects.
6. Be collaborative with the intent of being beneficial and meeting community needs.
7. Include ongoing monitoring of progress.
8. Have sufficient duration to result in specific outcomes.

Based on: National Youth Leadership Council. (2008). K-12 Service-Learning Standards for Quality Practice. Retrieved from http://www.nylc.org/sites/nylc.org/files/files/Standards_Oct2009-web.pdf

three components. Within these three components we see implications for the more rigorous standards in the National Youth Leadership Council (2008).

1. Students *prepare* by
   - learning about issues
   - building the skills they will need
   - developing an action plan for service
2. Students *act* by
   - engaging in meaningful service
   - making a difference in their community
   - realizing connections to classroom curriculum
3. Students *reflect* by
   - analyzing and making sense of their experiences
   - discussing, journaling, and presenting

Let's add a fourth component: *Students celebrate!* We want students to realize their success and be proud of themselves.

Service-learning opportunities vary based in part on the age of students; interests of teachers and students; collaborations in place among schools and community organizations; and, of course, community need. There are ongoing needs such as homeless shelters, park and road cleanup, and nursing homes. There are also crises to which students and teachers can find ways to respond. In October 2012, *Hurricane Sandy* devastated much of the Northeast, destroying homes, roads, and schools; about 6 weeks later, 26 children and adults were killed in a horrific attack on Sandy Hook Elementary School. *Sandy,* then Sandy Hook—our hearts broken twice in a matter of weeks. As teachers, we should create service-learning opportunities for ongoing community needs, but also be ready to act quickly to help our students be aware of crises (age-appropriately), providing meaningful ways to help students respond as they serve in some capacity. For instance, if you teach on an eighth-grade team, you might have a year-long recycling service-learning project. Suddenly in April, a community suffers massive damage from a tornado and rainstorm, leaving a middle school flooded with no classroom supplies. Your team could organize a campaign to collect school supplies and get them to the students who are meeting in a makeshift school in an abandoned strip mall. Each student could write a personal note expressing her or his best wishes to the students who are victims of the storm. The victims, in turn, may be encouraged to express their thanks for the well wishes and the supplies. Could the school district afford to provide school supplies for the rest of the year? Yes, probably. But the human desire to help, and the human desire to show gratitude, will both be enhanced as students learn organization and communication skills.

Service-learning possibilities are many, with some of the more common projects listed in Figure 5.6.

An outstanding source of projects and lesson plans is the Service-Learning Ideas and Curricular Examples (SLICE), a resource provided by the National Service-Learning Clearinghouse (2012). Service-learning projects may also be conducted within the framework of an established organization or movement. See examples in Figure 5.7.

Some schools have an annual *Day of Service.* Teachers prepare students for the day by facilitating their research in the area of service; using guest speakers; taking field trips; and, in general, helping students understand what they will experience and why it's important. A day of service may involve road or parks cleanup, a walk/run to raise money for a cause, or a day spent with senior citizens. From 2008 to 2016, former First Lady Michelle Obama was the chairperson of Youth Service America's *Global Youth Service Day* occurring every April. These events were the largest service events in the world. Teachers and students can plan service projects with the help of Youth Service America.

BENEFITS OF SERVICE-LEARNING. The benefits of service-learning are numerous for both the community and the students who participate. Members of the community may receive valuable assistance with ongoing or crisis-related problems, become the

Figure 5.6 Examples of service-learning

Need	Project	Possible learning components
Deteriorating buildings, homes, neighborhoods	Paint structures or create murals to beautify town, neighborhood, or school buildings	– Planning project – Scale drawing
Loneliness of elderly	– Write letters, make holiday cards – Choral or instrumental concerts – Visits with residents of nursing facilities – Reading to seniors – Create oral histories	– Communication skills – Knowledge of history
Homelessness	– Tutor children after school – Collect school supplies and clothes – Collect toys and books for clinics near homeless shelters	– Organization skills involved in project planning – Knowledge of economy – Understand job requirements and availability – Understand housing options and dilemmas
Hunger	Plant, maintain, and harvest a community garden; give food to needy	– Knowledge and skills for plant growth – Understanding environmental concerns – Math skills needed for garden design – Respect for growing systems
Hunger	Collect and distribute food	Verbal and writing skills to communicate need and collection plan

Figure 5.7 Sample established organizations as context for service-learning

Organization	About the organization
Alex's Lemonade Stand Foundation (ALSF)	Alex (1996–2004) started a front yard lemonade stand to raise money for cancer research; now a national fundraising movement
Project Learning Tree	Program of the American Forest Foundation; uses the forest to engage students in environmental concerns and solutions
Veterans History Project	The American Folklife Center collects, preserves, and makes accessible the personal accounts of American war veterans
National Student Campaign Against Hunger and Homelessness (NSCAHH)	Largest student network fighting hunger and homelessness in the country
Service for Peace	Established in 2002 by international youth volunteers from across the U.S. to help participants develop a sense of responsibility for others, confidence in their own ability to make a difference as they work together with people from backgrounds different from their own
PeaceJam	International education program originating in Colorado in 1993; purpose is to create young leaders committed to positive change in themselves, their communities and the world through the inspiration of Nobel Peace Laureates
Project Linus	Founded in 1996 to provide blankets for children who are seriously ill or have experienced trauma

recipients of additional assistance because of the spotlight created by student attention, and be encouraged to make needed changes as a result of student enthusiasm and innovation. Students who participate in service-learning may experience life-long personal and academic benefits that align with 21st–century knowledge and skills such as collaboration, communication, and leadership. They may

- Develop critical thinking and problem-solving skills.
- Increase their understanding of the curriculum.
- Gain hands-on experience.
- Explore values and beliefs.
- Increase their exposure to, and understanding of, diverse cultures and communities.
- Learn more about social issues, both their causes and possible remedies.
- Discover skills and interests in a potential career path.
- Make connections that could lead to jobs or internships.
- Increase their commitment to serving others.

With an impressive list like this, it's hard to imagine *not* planning service-learning opportunities for students. In Figure 5.8, read about a very meaningful service-learning emphasis at Chardon Middle School.

Figure 5.8 Chardon Middle School service-learning experience

Sara Davis Powell

On Tuesday morning, September 11, 2001, the United States came under attack as four commercial airplanes were hijacked. The unsuspecting airliner crews and passengers became victims of suicide missions carried out by 19 al-Qaeda terrorists, members of an Islamist militant group founded by Osama bin Laden in 1988. Three of the planes were used to strike targets on the ground, including the World Trade Center buildings in New York City and the U.S. Pentagon. Nearly 3,000 people tragically lost their lives.

The fourth plane, United Airlines Flight 93, was in route from New Jersey to San Francisco when four al-Qaeda terrorists hijacked the plane by breaking into the cockpit and redirecting the flight toward Washington, DC, with the intent of crashing into the U.S. Capitol. Several passengers were able to call family and friends on the ground and learned of the hijacker's intentions. They courageously fought the hijackers and, in the process, Flight 93 crashed near Shanksville, Pennsylvania. Because of the actions of the 40 passengers and crew aboard the plane, the attack on the U.S. Capitol was thwarted.

Let's look at how Tim Bowens and his colleagues and students have used service-learning to learn more about, and memorialize, Flight 93 heroes. In his own words, Tim tells us how this particular service-learning emphasis fits within the Chicago Public Schools service-learning guidelines.

1. Students *prepare:*
   - Every year in Chardon, Ohio, our middle level students learn about the horrific events of September 11, 2001. Annually our 6th graders visit the Flight 93 Memorial in Pennsylvania where they learn about the importance of the heroism of the passengers and crew of Flight 93 through presentations at the site by families of passengers and crew members, as well as students who were in nearby schools on 9/11.
2. Students *act:*
   - After years of visiting temporary memorials for Flight 93, students and their community raised over $10,000 to help build the permanent memorial now at the site of the crash.
   - During the 2010–2011 school year we worked with a local arts organization to create an oral history project. Nearly 30 individuals were interviewed concerning the events of 9/11, and specifically about Flight 93. The interviews were transcribed and made into a theater production.
   - In 2012 teachers and students worked with artist Augusto Bordelois to create two murals made of thousands of pieces of colored mosaics. The murals are on permanent display on two staircases in Chardon Middle School. One represents 9/11 and the other is dedicated to Flight 93. Mr. Bordelois spent time preparing the students by showing how art and history are connected. He relayed examples of how important historical events (ex. Washington crossing the Delaware) have been interpreted by artists. He also demonstrated the significance of monuments and memorials. This tied beautifully to our 6th grade curriculum as we study ancient civilizations and their enduring impact/contributions. Look no further than the Egyptian pyramids for meaningful symbols and memorials.
3. Students *reflect:*
   - Since the murals are there for all to see (the artist feels they will stand even if the school was demolished–that's how well-constructed they are), students can take pride in them as they walk by in the years to come. They know that future generations of students will learn from their service-learning project.
   - Teachers can use the murals as an introduction to 9/11 and for instruction prior to visiting Shanksville each spring.
   - One of the more moving aspects of being at the Memorial occurs when we leave the site. We ask students to be silent and just quietly reflect on all they see. Now when students return to school, the murals bring that back.

Based on: Email communication with Tim Bowens, November 24, 2012.

Point of Reflection 5.2

Do you recall a teacher who obviously served students in one or more of the six ways discussed? Describe what you remember and how you responded to the extra effort of the teacher.

Point of Reflection 5.3

What service-learning projects were you involved with in grades K–12? Describe one project and how participation affected you.

Check Your Understanding 5.4

Concluding Thoughts

John Goodlad, following his landmark study of American high schools, wrote that the typical classroom is a site where "boredom is a disease of epidemic proportion" (1984, p. 9). What a devastating indictment.

Can you picture a classroom full of students deeply immersed in learning rather than entrenched in boredom? Asking, "And how are the children? Are they all well?" leads us to make engaging teaching that leads to optimum student learning our ultimate goal. Now that you know more about instruction—its limitless variety and potential—your ability to envision student engagement has increased. Recognizing that the art of teaching involves knowing how and when to apply instruction based on student needs and preferences, and understanding that teaching is a service profession, helps us become 3D teachers, ready to address the cognitive, physical, emotional, social, and moral development of our students.

We began this chapter by considering Chris Roberts and his classroom at Rees Elementary in Utah. Now, as the chapter comes to an end, we join Chris as he uses his knowledge of curriculum and instruction to support multiage grouping. Read through *Chapter in Review* to help refresh your memory of what we have discussed, then interact with Chris as he confronts a challenge in *Developing Professional Competence.*

Chapter in Review

What is 3D teaching?

- Three-dimensional teaching involves the science, art, and service of teaching.
- The service dimension of teaching involves an attitude that approaches students as complete human beings, with cognitive, physical, emotional, social, and moral components.
- Curriculum is the *what* of teaching, and instruction is the *how.*
- Building a large repertoire of instructional strategies is vital.

How is instruction implemented in U.S. schools?

- Backward design is an approach to planning for teaching and learning that starts with deciding on the desired learning results, then identifies how to collect the evidence of learning, and concludes with choosing appropriate instructional strategies.
- Content priorities include first, vital knowledge and core tasks; then, what is important to know and do; and finally, what is worth being familiar with.
- There are big ideas of instruction that serve to ground and provide a framework for teaching and learning.
- Multiple strategies of instruction allow for variety in how the curriculum is taught.
- Thoughtfully planning for instruction is vital for effective teaching and optimal student learning.
- Some instructional strategies are appropriate for students of all levels.
- Choosing instructional strategies for each of the four levels of school requires thoughtful consideration.

What is the art of teaching?

- The art of teaching is the ability to logically, and in a variety of ways, divide content and skills into manageable components and create experiences that lead to student learning.
- There is no formula for effective teaching. Every student is different, making every classroom of students different.
- The artistry of differentiating instruction involves an array of content, a variety of processes, and choices of products when possible.
- Expectations should be based on all the variables that contribute to learner differences: affect, readiness, interests, and learning profile. Expectations should be individualized and always high for each student, with a clear vision of what constitutes growth and success.

How do teachers serve students?

- Teachers serve students when they form relationships, create a climate of respect, model productive habits, emphasize civics and citizenship, promote character building, and communicate positively.
- Service-learning occurs when students' experiences combine service with a purposeful learning component.
- Service-learning requires students to *prepare* by learning about issues and developing an action plan, then to *act* by engaging in meaningful service and realizing connections to classroom curriculum, and to *reflect* by analyzing and making sense of their experiences.
- The benefits of service-learning are numerous for both the community and the students who participate.

Developing Professional Competence

Sara Davis Powell

Thoughtfully reading this scenario and responding to the items that follow it will help you prepare for licensure exams.

The district school board where Chris Roberts teaches is considering doing away with multiage classrooms. We read about multiage classrooms in Chapter 3 as we explored a variety of configurations for teaching and learning in U.S. schools. We also know from the interviews with Chris and his teammate Brenda that they have successfully taught for years in classrooms occupied by third-, fourth-, and fifth- graders. We hear Chris admit in his interview, however, that he doubts he gets to all the content standards of the three grade levels as he teaches in a multiage setting each year.

Chris believes strongly in exposing students to the world through a variety of means. His extensive travels, his love of the arts, and his selection of books for the classroom provide opportunities for him to infuse teaching and learning with real-world context. Through this context, Chris knows that his students are learning valuable lessons.

It will be difficult to defend multiage grouping to the school board, but Chris is convinced the configuration works for his teaching team.

Now it's time for you to respond to two essay items involving the scenario. In your responses, be sure to address all the dilemmas and questions posed in each item. These items are followed by five multiple-choice questions.

1. Chris has decided that he will attend the next school board meeting and present his reasons for continuing multiage grouping. This item is about his preparation. Who should he speak with to help him prepare to do this? What elements of his classroom practice should he emphasize? About what should he be very knowledgeable before addressing the board? Consider the following InTASC Standards and how Chris might use them as he prepares to address the school board:

   Standard #2: The teacher uses understanding of individual differences and diverse cultures and communities to ensure inclusive learning environments that enable each learner to meet high standards.

   Standard #3: The teacher works with others to create environments that support individual and collaborative learning, and that encourage positive social interaction, active engagement in learning, and self-motivation.

   Standard #4: The teacher understands the central concepts, tools of inquiry, and structures of the discipline(s) he or she teaches, and he or she creates learning experiences that make these aspects of the discipline accessible and meaningful for learners to assure mastery of the content.

   Standard #5: The teacher understands how to connect concepts and use differing perspectives to engage learners in critical thinking, creativity, and collaborative problem solving related to authentic local and global issues.

   Standard #7: The teacher plans instruction that supports every student in meeting rigorous learning goals by drawing upon knowledge of content areas, curriculum, cross-disciplinary skills, and pedagogy, as well as knowledge of learners and the community context.

   Standard #9: The teacher engages in ongoing professional learning and uses evidence to continually evaluate his or her practice, particularly the effects of his or her choices and actions on others (learners, families, other professionals, and the community), and adapts practice to meet the needs of each learner.

2. Chris knows how important his introduction is in terms of getting the board to listen to him and find him credible. What should he say in his opening remarks?

Application Exercise 5.6 Developing Professional Competence

3. Chris states that he probably doesn't get to all the state standards in his classroom. He may be able to clarify which, if any, of the standards he doesn't address by
   a. Reading summaries of the standards provided in the state document
   b. Matching the textbooks he uses to the standards
   c. Taking the time to look very closely at the standards for each grade level and create one document that sequences the standards
   d. Asking someone from the state to observe his classroom

4. Chris knows that he will be questioned about the range of ages in his classroom. Which of the following statements is *least* appropriate for making a case for multiage grouping?
   a. My teaching style works because kids will learn what interests them.
   b. Chronological age does not necessarily determine learning readiness.
   c. Sometimes students learn much from each other and the age disparities often work in favor of peer teaching.
   d. In multiage classrooms teachers can guide learning over a 3-year period to make sure there is consistency and continual progress.

5. Which of the following will be *least* helpful to Chris as he prepares to make his case before the school board?
   a. Brenda and Tim
   b. Parents of students in his class
   c. Mike Larsen, the principal
   d. Utah Superintendent of Education

6. What information might be *most* convincing if he had time to research it?
   a. The number of other schools using multiage grouping
   b. A comparison of the success in sixth grade of the students from multiage grades 3–5 settings and the students in self-contained classes in grades 3–5
   c. A survey of parents of children in grades K–2 to see how many will request a multiage setting when their children reach third grade
   d. A comparison of how Utah fares relative to other states on the NAEP exam

7. Which pair of big ideas of instruction should Chris emphasize as the *most* powerful justification for having third-, fourth-, and fifth-graders in one classroom?
   a. Promoting critical thinking and differentiating instruction
   b. Incorporating student collaboration and promoting critical thinking
   c. Differentiating instruction and incorporating student collaboration
   d. Teaching through inquiry and using technology

Application Exercise 5.7 Developing Professional Competence

Flash Cards 5.1

Shared Writing 5.1: Service-Learning

Chapter 6

Creating and Maintaining a Positive and Productive Learning Environment

Learning Objectives

After studying this chapter, you will have knowledge and skills to:

6.1 Explain ways teachers create a positive learning environment.

6.2 Identify routines that contribute to maintaining a productive classroom environment.

6.3 Compare and contrast how teachers establish expectations, incentives, and consequences.

6.4 Analyze ways to develop a classroom management plan.

Dear Reader

Students are motivated to learn when the learning environment is positive and productive. The converse is also true. The absence of a positive and productive learning environment stifles motivation and learning. Thinking through the concepts in this chapter is a vital first step in creating a classroom environment that engages students and enhances learning.

We used to talk about *classroom management* as the task that involved corralling students into a state of attention and then directing them to do what we wanted. Not so long ago, the picture-perfect scenario of good classroom management was 30 students all seated in rows; all with sharpened pencils, tablets (paper ones!), and textbooks opened to page 234 and all giving rapt attention to the person standing in the front of the room. That worked for some of us as learners, but it certainly won't work in most classrooms today. The concept of *learning environment* is so much broader and richer than classroom management.

Learning is messy. Engaging students in their own learning is crucial. Creation of a learning environment that is stimulating, structured to include participation, marked by respect and civility, and led by a teacher who is both 100% present and armed with comprehensive lesson plans and differentiated strategies will make the environment positive and productive. It's not too soon to begin thinking about the learning environment you want to create in your future classroom as you continue your journey toward becoming a teacher.

Where Do I Stand?

 **Click here to complete the inventory online**

This inventory focuses on creating and maintaining a positive and productive learning environment. As you think through the following statements that prompt you to consider your own views, indicate your level of agreement by choosing a number and placing it in the blank before the statement. Following the inventory are directions for how to organize your responses and what they may mean in terms of where you stand.

4 I strongly agree

3 I agree

2 I don't have an opinion

1 I disagree

0 I strongly disagree

____ 1. Without a positive and productive learning environment, teaching has little effect.

____ 2. The learning environment is basically determined by levels of student cooperation and student misbehavior.

____ 3. Some students may find that their school and classroom are the cleanest, safest, and most attractive environments in their lives.

____ 4. It is necessary for the teacher to be able to easily approach each individual student in the classroom seating arrangement.

____ 5. Displaying only exemplary student work in the classroom is a more effective motivator for all students than displaying something each student has done, thus including mediocre work.

____ 6. For a classroom community of learners to function optimally, a teacher must create a safe environment—academically, emotionally, and physically.

____ 7. To create and maintain a positive and productive learning environment, teachers must be able to focus directly on one student or small group and block out the whole group for distinct periods of time.

____ 8. When routines are in place in the classroom, teachers have more time to teach, and students have more time to learn.

____ 9. Creating and maintaining a positive, productive learning environment encompasses more than the traditional notion of classroom management (the establishment and enforcement of rules and disciplinary actions).

____ 10. There is no single recipe for effective classroom management that works all the time in every classroom.

____ 11. Families of students have little to do with the learning environment.

____ 12. Teachers do not necessarily have to stay within established school rules/expectations when creating them for an individual classroom.

____ 13. If teachers depend exclusively on extrinsic incentives (those that come from or depend on others), they are taking on the full responsibility for motivating their students.

____ 14. Praise is generally not a powerful extrinsic motivator for students.

____ 15. Consequences should focus on the behavior, not on the person.

____ 16. When an individual behaves appropriately because of intrinsic motivation or an internal desire, the behavior not only lasts but it also spreads to other aspects of life.

____ 17. When it comes to extrinsic and intrinsic incentives, teachers should choose one approach and stick with it for consistency.

____ 18. Student self-monitoring, or when students assume control of their own behavior, helps develop a sense of ownership of actions.

____ 19. A very important step in creating a positive and productive learning environment is initiating and maintaining contact with students' families.

____ 20. Specific praise related to a particular action is more effective than general praise like saying, "Nice job."

____ 21. Knowing students well—their cultures, their home settings, their abilities/disabilities, and more—is vital in understanding how to help them behave in respectful and responsible ways.

____ 22. Proactive prevention through engaging instruction is the best approach to classroom management.

____ 23. Consequences should match the inappropriate behavior as often as possible.

____ 24. Misbehavior involving physical violence, loud or threatening verbal abuse, vandalism, theft, and possession of illegal substances or weapons dictates the involvement of administrators.

____ 25. Unobtrusive intervention, or strategies that don't interfere with learning, is rarely effective in curbing misbehavior.

____ 26. Verbal interventions can resolve minor problems if delivered quickly, calmly, and in ways that match the offense.

____ 27. Detention is most effective when it involves isolation and requires the student to give up time he or she would rather spend elsewhere.

____ 28. Developing a classroom climate marked by a sense of community is a good thing to do, but it has little to do with student behavior or misbehavior.

____ 29. When a student misbehaves and a consequence is assigned and completed, the student deserves to be given a fresh start.

____ 30. Even though some students require unique services to optimize their learning potential, they must be held to the same behavior expectations as other students to achieve consistency.

Now record your item responses in columns A and B. Subtract each B response from 4 because B indicates levels of disagreement with negative concepts. Record this new number, a positive indicator, in the C column. Find the sums of columns A and C, and then divide Sum A by 20 and divide Sum C by 10 to determine A and C.

ITEM #	***COLUMN A*** ***MY RESPONSE***	***ITEM #***	***COLUMN B*** ***MY RESPONSE***	***COLUMN C*** ***Subtract each response in Column B from 4 and record the difference here.***
1		2		
3		5		
4		7		
6		11		
8		12		
9		14		
10		17		
13		25		
15		28		
16		30		
18				Sum =
19				Sum ÷ 10 = C C =
20				
21				
22				
23				
24				
26				
27				
29				
	Sum =			
	Sum ÷ 20 = A A =			

Add A and C and then divide by 2. Plot this number on the number line to see where you fall on a continuum of your prior understanding of concepts related to a positive and productive learning environment. Then carefully read this chapter to learn more about the learning environment.

My Prior Understanding of Concepts Regarding the Learning Environment

0__________1__________2__________3__________4

Little prior understanding — Developing understanding — Ready for deeper consideration of concepts

6.1 How Do Teachers Create a Positive Learning Environment?

6.1 Explain ways teachers create a positive learning environment.

Creating and maintaining a positive and productive learning environment is complex and compelling—complex because there are multiple variables to consider, and compelling because without a positive and productive learning environment, teaching has little effect. New and experienced teachers alike are often puzzled by the whole process. They sometimes think of the learning environment in narrow terms of student cooperation and student misbehavior. But the learning environment is so much more. When teachers expand their view to include the elements discussed in this chapter, it becomes clear that creating and maintaining a positive and productive learning environment is indeed a puzzle, one with many interlocking pieces that depend on one another to form a complete, stable picture.

Some of the most important pieces of the learning environment puzzle are shown in Figure 6.1. A positive and productive learning environment that includes these vital components doesn't just happen. It takes planning, continuous effort, and a watchful eye.

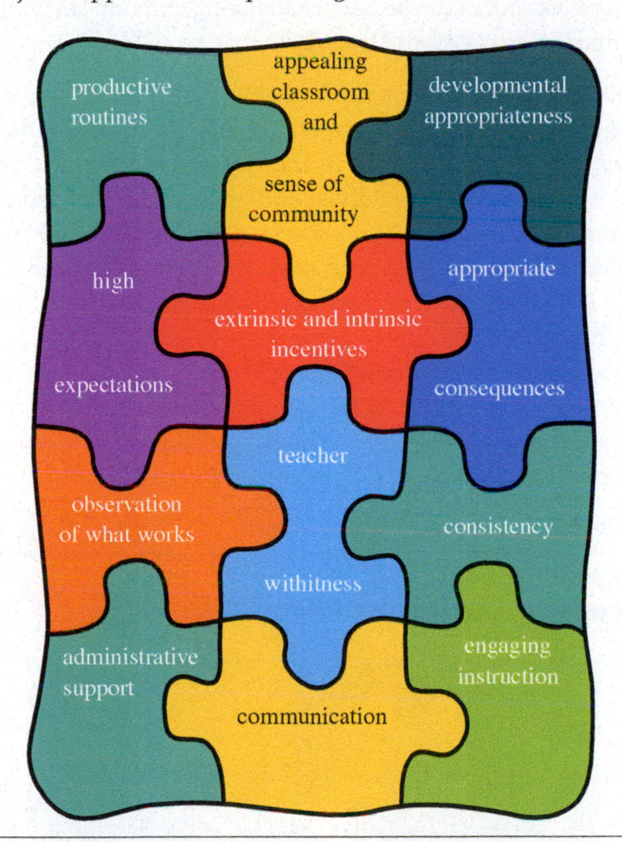

Figure 6.1 A positive and productive learning environment

Application Exercise 6.1: Figure 6.1: A positive and productive learning environment

Physical Space

A welcoming, well-organized, student-friendly environment goes a long way toward helping accomplish both learning and affective goals. John Dewey's wisdom concerning the physical surroundings of learning includes his statement that "any environment is a chance environment so far as its educative influence is concerned unless it has been

Sara Davis Powell

Deirdre's classroom at Cario Middle School takes on a homelike appearance with the addition of furniture other than desks.

deliberately regulated with reference to its educative effect" (1944, p. 19). This statement tells us that our classrooms themselves matter. The learning environment can actually enhance teaching and learning when we deliberately and thoughtfully arrange and decorate with student well-being in mind.

Teachers seldom have much to say about which classroom they are assigned or the general condition of the school building. You may have gone to school in well-kept, relatively modern buildings; in older stately surroundings; or in dilapidated structures beset with never-ending maintenance problems. Your teachers may have had clean, comfortable spaces to decorate, or they may have fought off bugs and fungus in a dingy, poorly lit room plagued with a leaky roof. Teachers are responsible for making the most of room assignments. Even under dismal circumstances, designing a classroom can be both challenging and fun. Do it for your students, and do it for yourself. The classroom truly is "home away from home."

HOME AWAY FROM HOME. As a teacher, you will spend 8 to 9 hours a day for almost 200 days every year in your classroom. Early childhood and elementary students will spend almost all their days in the classroom with you, whereas middle and high school students will generally spend about a sixth of their school time in any one classroom. The classroom atmosphere is important for all students, but it is particularly influential for students who may, through circumstances beyond their control, find that school and their classrooms are the cleanest, most welcoming environments in their lives.

If space allows, adding a comfortable couch, chairs, lamps, rugs, plants, curtains, and other homey items does wonders for inviting students in to learn. Focus teacher Deirdre Huger-McGrew of Cario Middle School, South Carolina, created a reading center in her classroom with a couch, chairs, tables, and lamps.

Application Exercise 6.2: Deirdre's Room Tour

SEATING ARRANGEMENT. The arrangement of desks and tables in a classroom depends on a number of variables, including the level of the school, the subject(s) taught, and available floor space and furniture. Traditional rows of desks are fine for whole-group instruction, whereas clusters of desks or students sitting together at tables helps facilitate group work. Ideally, the arrangement will be flexible enough that seating can accommodate various instructional strategies.

PROXIMITY. Whatever the seating arrangement, one vital element to keep in mind is **proximity**, the accessibility of teacher to students. The teacher needs to be able to approach each student quickly and easily, without having to negotiate narrow pathways that could lead to stumbling or a complex maze that makes it difficult to work one-on-one with students. Students also need to have visual access to boards and screens.

WALL SPACE AND INTEREST CENTERS. Creative teachers often find ways to entice students to come into the classroom and browse. Walls and tables offer tremendous opportunities to create spaces that students will want to explore just to see what's up.

A simple yet potentially powerful use of wall space is the organized display of student work. Preprinted posters may be appropriate on classroom walls, but they should not be used to the exclusion of regularly updated student work. Displaying student work fosters student ownership of the classroom. Some teachers display only exemplary work, such as tests that received As or perfectly colored maps. This practice stops short of being optimally effective if half or more of the students never see their work displayed because their achievement on traditional assignments never rises to the top of the class. Ingenious teachers who know students well incorporate creative assignments that give average and even below-average achievers opportunities to excel. It is well worth the time to arrange physical classroom space thoughtfully. Doing so will shape in many ways the interactions of the people who inhabit the classroom and contribute to building classroom community.

Video Example 6.1 shows how Angelica Reynosa takes advantage of wall space in her classroom.

Building Community

A **classroom community** is not just a place but also a way of actively learning together. Dewey (1944) expands on this thought by telling us that people in a community are "like-minded," having common beliefs, understandings, and aims (p. 4). Maintaining what Dewey calls like-mindedness can be thought of as maintaining **classroom climate**, the everyday environment in which teachers and students work together.

Let's look at four ways teachers can maintain a classroom climate that builds community among themselves and their students: demonstrate care, develop trust, teach unconditionally, and embrace technology use.

DEMONSTRATE CARE. A teacher must care about curriculum, instruction, assessment, society, the past, the present, the future, and—most of all—students. A caring classroom centers on relationships—between teacher and students and among the students themselves. Taking a personal interest in students is the first step in developing caring relationships. Respectfully approaching students as individuals is key to this process. So how do we get to know individual students? Early childhood and elementary classrooms of 15 to 30 students allow teachers to know students and their families well.

The numbers are manageable, and teachers have most of the day, every day, to develop relationships. Middle and high school teachers are challenged by both numbers and time because they may have 60 to 120 students a year in their classes for only a small portion of each school day. A few of the many ways teachers can get to know students include:

- Begin the year with a getting-to-know-you activity.
- Take time to talk informally with students.
- Be involved in extracurricular activities.
- Purposefully ask questions, remember answers, and follow up often.

DEVELOP TRUST. For a classroom community of learners to function optimally, trust is an absolute necessity: trust between teacher and students, and trust among students. A safe environment—academically, emotionally, and physically—is necessary. Maslow's hierarchy of needs indicates that physiological needs, safety, love, and belongingness form the basis for meeting higher-order needs. All of these needs must be met by a classroom characterized by trust.

In a trust-filled classroom, students are more comfortable with the environment and willing to take risks that lead to learning. They know that if they attempt a task and don't succeed, they will be encouraged to try again and will be given tools that increase the likelihood of success. Students are more willing to ask and answer questions, knowing they won't be ridiculed or demeaned in any way. Trust fosters learning. Craig Cleveland, our focus teacher at Roosevelt High School, California, believes that teacher–student relationships characterized by trust and respect encourage students to take more risks that lead to learning. In his own words . . .

> Educators first teach who they are. Their dispositions, views of life, and how they perceive their students are picked up on and learned by the students before the first quiz. The opportunity for excellent student performance in the classroom is directly related to how the teacher interacts with the students. I believe that teachers must be fair, have no favorites, and be liberal in providing needed help. Kindness is the fundamental rule for communication between student and teacher. Kindness is hopeful, encourages students to do better, and shows respect for others. Khammany (one of our focus students) comes from a supportive family where she is loved. She thrives in a classroom environment where her ideas are listened to and respected. I believe that students are more willing to take risks in class when they know that their contribution will be appreciated.

TEACH UNCONDITIONALLY. When we practice **unconditional teaching**, we accept students for who they are, not for what they do. It's an attitude that conveys clearly to students that they matter to us, no matter how many times they may fail to achieve or misbehave. Unconditional teaching requires that we allow students to begin fresh, that we don't take their misbehavior or lack of effort personally. We are adults who do what we can to help students grow. Alfie Kohn (2005) maintains that unconditional teaching involves

- Showing students we are glad to see them
- Showing students we trust and respect them
- Displaying an appealing informality
- Spending time with students even when we don't have to
- Asking about students' lives outside of school and remembering their answers
- Finding something appealing about each student

EMBRACE TECHNOLOGY USE. It has been estimated that in approximately 1 minute, 42,000 people will update their Facebook status, 36,000 tweets will be sent, and 15 hours of video will be uploaded to YouTube. Even more astonishing is that 1.18 billion people log onto Facebook daily (Zephoria, 2017). Throughout this text you read about social media and how to use the tools to enhance professional development and in classroom teaching strategies. Social media is part of our lives, whether we choose to recognize it or not. In addition to Facebook, Twitter, and YouTube, social media tools outside of school—such as Ning communities, Google Groups, Etherpad, Wordle, and VoiceThread, to name a few—are connecting both adults and students.

Marc Prensky (2010), author and founder of Games2train, reports that when teachers think that virtual relationships, or those that exist online, are somehow less real or important than face-to-face ones, we are barriers to our students' progress by limiting their relationships and harming the learning community. A computer, to be of optimal value, must be personalized so it becomes an extension of a student's personal self and brain, customized to be a tool of expression and communication.

Checking technology tools at the door of the school or telling students to keep smartphones turned off while in the school building is not going to stop texting and other technology-enhanced communications from happening. Smartphone communication is the new form of note passing. Try as we might to prevent it, note passing persists, just in ever-changing formats. To fight it is to lose.

School-provided technology, typically classroom computers, have filters in place with the purpose of protecting students from admittedly dangerous situations. But when students leave school, the filters are gone and they face the perils alone. Teachers need to teach students about the devastating possibilities of **cyberbullying**, for instance, by teaching them **cybercitizenship**. Using an abstinence stance when it comes to social media cheats our students of wisdom we could convey.

As teachers, we should be open and willing to learn as we explore the possibilities presented by social media that can help build community in creative and ever-expanding ways. This *SocialMEdia* feature introduces Twitter as a teaching and learning tool.

SocialMEdia

The learning environment is most effective when all students are engaged and participating. Teachers can use a variety of social media to make this a reality, including Twitter.

Twitter is a micro-blogging communication network made up of participants using messages of up to a maximum of 140 characters, called Tweets. Teachers have experimented for several years with ways to use Twitter for teaching and learning. There are hundreds of comments online about Twitter in the classroom, so there is no shortage of ideas. Twitter is useful in and out of the classroom because it can be used with any Internet-connected computer as well as on Internet-accessible mobile devices. For this reason, Twitter may be the most democratizing of current social media tools because it's readily available and does not require specific tools. With the 140-character restriction, students who lack confidence in their writing skills are not as intimidated by Twitter. Keep in mind, however, that not only is this restriction motivating, but it is also challenging in many circumstances because students are forced to express themselves with economy of words. It's very often more difficult to say something meaningful in fewer, rather than more, words.

Organizations such as ASCD Learn. Teach. Lead. use Twitter for a wide variety of purposes, including spreading information about professional development opportunities, keeping participants posted about what's happening at conferences, communicating among teachers about teaching and learning, and following noted educators to learn about their most current ideas and research projects.

Here are 10 ideas for using Twitter in K–12 learning environments:

- Encourage students to work together, sharing ideas and completing projects.
- Bring current events into the classroom in real time.
- Reach out to experts in particular fields.
- Practice communicating in a new language, including English for English language learners.
- Communicate assignments and changes in plans.
- Ask students to read an article or chapter and then summarize it in 140 characters.
- Pose a prompt and ask students to tweet responses.
- Create a discussion group using a hashtag so all are included.
- Follow a famous person connected to the curriculum and report on his or her life to the class.
- Develop "Twitter pals" with students tweeting another student in a different location or with different demographics to learn about diversity.

In addition to all the learning environment benefits, Twitter can also be a great way to communicate with other teachers to share questions and ideas. Getting started with any new technology is usually the most difficult step. Excellent information regarding every aspect of Twitter can be found on the Web.

Withitness, Overlapping, and the Ripple Effect

As a result of observation and analysis, Jacob Kounin (1970) described what effective classroom managers do. To create and maintain a positive and productive learning environment, teachers must practice **withitness**. This term refers to awareness of what's going on in the whole classroom that enables the teacher to step in when needed to keep the environment positive. Teacher withitness often surprises students because they perceive the teacher must have eyes in the back of his or her head. Withitness allows teachers to do what Kounin calls **overlapping**, which means multitasking, or taking care of several things at once. A teacher who has withitness and the ability to overlap can help a small group with an assignment, see a student pestering another student, and give a "cut-it-out" look while answering a question and checking the clock to see how much time remains in the class period.

In addition, Kounin says effective classroom managers understand the **ripple effect** that occurs when one action leads to or directly affects another action. He states that the cut-it-out look given to one student may help deter another student from the same off-task behavior. This is a positive ripple effect. Similarly—but with negative results—if the teacher interrupts the whole class, loudly saying, "Jeremy, stop that right now. You do nothing but continually disturb," other students may perceive that the teacher overreacted and begin to display the same pestering behaviors.

Kounin's research has yielded the commonsense view that teachers who know what's going on, who can switch from one activity to another smoothly, and who can maintain positive momentum will be successful in maintaining a productive classroom environment. As you continue reading this chapter, keep withitness, overlapping, and the ripple effect in mind.

Using Time Wisely

One constant in schools is time itself; however, how we spend that time is variable. Although some communities have increased the length of the school day, and even the number of days in a school year, most have 180 school days a year, and about 7 hours a day, for having an impact on students. This "180/7" configuration is based on tradition and not necessarily on what we know about teaching and learning. The length of the school year and the hours in a school day are often political pawns and are not likely to change before you enter your first classroom as a teacher.

Our challenge is to maximize the time we have with students. Early childhood and elementary teachers may have 7 hours a day with students, but that doesn't mean they have 7 hours of **instructional time**, the time available for teaching and learning. Middle and high school teachers may have 60 minutes in each class period, but that doesn't mean they have 60 minutes in which to actually implement instruction. If we are not careful, too much time is spent in nonproductive ways or at least in ways that do not promote academic learning. Given administrative demands such as collecting lunch money, taking attendance, responding to interruptions, and getting students where they need to be throughout the day, we often sense that the amount of time available for instruction is limited. Recess, transitions from class to class, lunch, and so on—all legitimate uses of time—further limit instructional time.

One study yields some fairly shocking results concerning the breakdown of the time allotted for the school day. The minimum school day in most elementary schools consists of 6 hours, or 360 minutes. After subtracting time for recess, lunch, and transitions, the time left for academics is about 4.5 hours, or 270 minutes. In the schools studied, researchers found that teachers actually used about 3 hours, or 180 minutes, for actual instruction. Of these 180 minutes, only about 120 resulted in productive learning time, or **time on task** (Weinstein, Romano, and Mignano, 2011). What this amounts to is about 2 hours a day, out of 6, spent on meaningful application of the formal curriculum.

This is unacceptable. But before we view this finding too negatively, keep in mind that the informal curriculum is also very important. Interaction time between a teacher and students has positive effects on student learning in terms of relationship building and motivation—two concepts we know make a positive difference in student learning. However, a teacher's goal must be to spend more than a third of a school day in meaningful teaching and learning. Be very conscious of our responsibility to maximize the valuable commodity of time in the classroom.

Check Your Understanding 6.1

6.2 What Routines Contribute to Maintaining a Productive Classroom Environment?

6.2 Identify routines that contribute to maintaining a productive classroom environment.

A **routine**, sometimes referred to as a *procedure*, is an expected action that occurs in a given circumstance to accomplish a task efficiently. When routines are in place in the classroom, teachers have more time to teach, and students have more time to learn.

Practicing Routines

It is important to practice routines in the first weeks of school. In this way, the routines become habits. Three important reasons for using routines that help preserve instructional time are getting student attention, responding to interruptions, and transitioning from one activity to another.

STUDENT ATTENTION. When students are engaged in class activities, and the teacher wants to make an announcement, give directions, or remind students of the time, an attention getter is necessary. Some teachers turn the classroom lights off and on or simply speak loudly enough to be heard. An excellent method for getting attention involves the teacher raising a hand and students doing likewise. Students know to stop talking as their hands go up. Once there is silence, the teacher talks while students listen. If rehearsed repeatedly during the first weeks of school, this method (and a variety of others you'll observe in field experiences) will become automatic. Having one method, practicing it, and consistently using it will return big dividends.

RESPONDING TO INTERRUPTIONS. Class interruptions constitute a real frustration for teachers. The most frequent culprit is often the public address (PA) system. The routine of students instantly "freezing" will allow the announcement to be heard and any necessary action to be taken quickly.

Students at all levels have legitimate reasons for leaving a particular class to go somewhere else in the building. Perhaps it's a resource class, a special counseling group, a remedial reading class, or a gifted and talented program. The students involved need to practice the routine of watching the clock and leaving when it is time or watching the doorway for someone who may arrive to escort them. These comings and goings should not be allowed to interrupt the whole class. Students occasionally need to go to the restroom or get a drink of water during class time. Teachers should establish routines for these occasions as well.

When a visitor (an administrator, teacher, student, or parent) enters the classroom, the routine of students noticing and working more quietly will allow the teacher to respond without interference. This routine will not come naturally for students; it must be practiced.

TRANSITIONS. When students change activities or locations they are in **transition**, the time when most classroom disruptions happen. In early childhood and elementary schools, children may transition between learning activities three or four times before going to recess or a special area class such as music or physical education. Then it's back to the classroom until lunch, perhaps followed by another recess, then back to class. Teachers typically have routines for all these transitions.

In middle and high schools, the transitions between classes provide opportunities for misbehavior. Students may be in crowded, rushed circumstances, where social dilemmas can easily surface. A routine for *teachers* that can decrease the likelihood of misbehavior involves merely standing outside their classroom doors during transitions.

Routines in the Four Levels of School

The nature and number of classroom routines vary depending on the school level. Early childhood and elementary classrooms have many more elements to which routines apply than middle school classrooms, and high school classrooms have even fewer. But there are some elements at all four levels that call for routines. For instance, attendance must be taken one or more times daily. Distribution of materials and entering and leaving the classroom also occur daily. Let's take a look at some of the routines of our focus teachers.

EARLY CHILDHOOD. Brandi Wade and Renee Ayers, our focus teachers at Summit Primary School in Ohio, implement routines in their classrooms for activities such as:

- Paying attention
- Gathering supplies
- Moving about the room
- Working in groups
- Playing with, and putting away, games and toys
- Reacting to interruptions
- Going to the restroom
- Lining up and moving through the building
- Sharpening pencils
- Keeping desks in order
- Filing and retrieving folders

Brandi and Renee provide a personal routine for each student in the form of classroom jobs that help develop responsibility. These routines/jobs make life in the classroom run more smoothly and increase instructional time. Some of the jobs include board eraser, floor patrol (uses small broom and dust pan), computer helper (turns off computers at the end of the day), and gardener (waters plants).

Renee tells us that her second-grade classroom space is limited and she needs to use every inch of it in optimal ways. Routines and classroom jobs for her students maximize efficiency. Each morning, Renee follows a routine that organizes her students. She uses a pocket chart (plastic hanging chart with clear pockets) to display her daily classroom schedule in terms second-graders can read. She changes the activities as needed so the students know ahead of time what to expect. A sample of the contents of Renee's pocket chart is shown in Figure 6.2.

Figure 6.2 Second-grade pocket chart schedule

9:30 Welcome/Morning Work
Calendar/Morning Message
Self-Selected Reading
Working with Words
Rest Room Break/Snack
Writing
11:55 Music
12:35 Lunch
1:05 Recess
Guided Reading
Rest Room Break
Math
Science/Social Studies
4:00 Dismissal

Application Exercise 6.3: Renee's Room Tour

ELEMENTARY. Many elementary teachers deal with classroom elements that require routines similar to those found in early childhood classrooms. Students in grades 3 through 5, however, are developmentally able to adhere to more complicated routines and to do them without direct prompting from the teacher. Chris Roberts and Brenda Beyal work as a team at Rees Elementary School in Utah. They have established similar routines because they share third-, fourth-, and fifh-grade students throughout the day. Chris and Brenda expect their students to come and go between classrooms and throughout the school responsibly. Within each classroom the routines vary, but basically, the two teachers deal with these activities:

- Gathering/Using materials
- Turning in homework assignments
- Paying attention
- Working in groups
- Borrowing library books
- Dismissal procedures for walkers, bus riders, and car riders

MIDDLE SCHOOL. Because Deirdre Huger-McGrew at Cario Middle School in South Carolina has one small group of students half a day and another small group for the other half, she finds it relatively easy to get her middle school students to follow routines that make the classroom run smoothly. These routines revolve around the following activities:

- Class-to-class transitions
- Computer use
- Gathering and returning materials
- Restroom and water breaks

Traci Peters, seventh-grade math teacher, also at Cario Middle School, believes in the value of structure. The routines she establishes include:

- Passing in and handing back papers
- Borrowing supplies from the bins in the room
- Obtaining restroom passes, used only during the first and last 5 minutes of class

Traci is extremely organized. Not only does each desk have a number but each critical math resource has a number. A student in Traci's class knows that his seat number must match his calculator, protractor, and ruler number. There is a chart on Traci's wall that assigns students to write a summary of the day on the "What did I miss?" board, to which absent students go when they return to class. These routines save valuable instructional time in Traci's classroom.

Video Example 6.2 shows how Traci uses her classroom space.

Video Example 6.2: Traci Peters' Room Tour

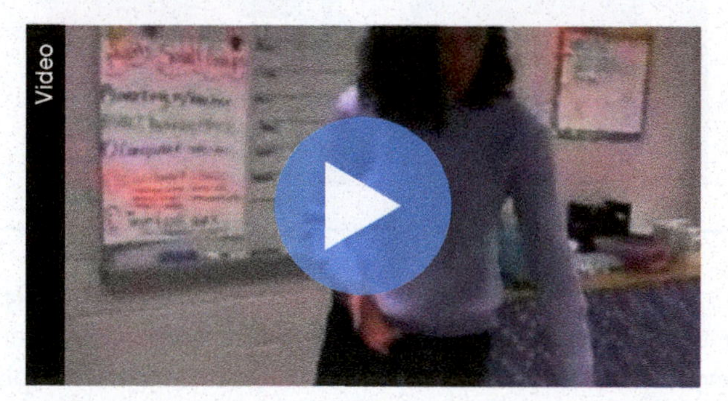

HIGH SCHOOL. Students in high school can be expected to understand routines. There are generally fewer to deal with, but they are no less important than those used in the earlier grades. Craig Cleveland and Angelica Reynosa, focus teachers at Roosevelt High School in California, have routines addressing these activities:

- Entering and leaving class
- Checking out and returning materials
- Responding to class interruptions, such as announcements, hand-delivered messages, and visitors

Craig's classroom routines revolve around group work and his classroom library. He teaches his students how to work together in the beginning of the school year, focusing on collaboration and cooperation. Then for the rest of the school year the students know the routine and follow it. They also know where to go in Craig's classroom to get the reading material that interests them or that is assigned. There are books on every wall in the classroom. Craig uses house gutters mounted on the wall to serve as book shelves, making book and magazine covers visible to attract students.

Application Exercise 6.4: Craig's Room Tour

Establishing developmentally appropriate routines and then teaching and practicing them increases the effectiveness and efficiency of the classroom. Also necessary for classroom effectiveness and efficiency are developmentally appropriate expectations, incentives, and consequences.

Check Your Understanding 6.2

6.3 How Do Teachers Establish Expectations, Incentives, and Consequences?

6.3 Compare and contrast how teachers establish expectations, incentives, and consequences.

When you read the title of this chapter, you may have thought it was just a fancy way to refer to a chapter on **classroom management**, the establishment and enforcement of rules and disciplinary actions. You should now see that creating and maintaining a positive, productive learning environment encompasses much more than the traditional notion of classroom management. There is no single recipe for effective classroom management that works all the time in every classroom. Teachers have always struggled with this part of their work.

Expectations, a word with positive connotations, will be used in place of *rules*, a word with negative connotations. **Incentives** will be used in place of the overused and value-laden word *rewards*. **Consequence** implies more natural ramifications for wrongdoing than does the word *punishment*, which can be arbitrary. The three concepts of expectations, incentives, and consequences are interdependent. However, for the sake of organization and clarity, they are addressed separately here.

Before discussing expectations, incentives, and consequences, think about the concepts of prevention and intervention. When it comes to student misbehavior, teachers have only two options: *They can either prevent it, or they will need to intervene.* Obviously, prevention is more desirable. Remember that the best way to prevent behavior problems in the classroom is through engaging instruction.

Sara Davis Powell

This teacher needs to establish behavioral expectations to help maintain productive routines such as class transitions.

Expectations

Teacher expectations have an impact on students in significant ways as they affect students' academic performance and behavior. Teacher expectations may become self-fulfilling prophesies for some students. Therefore, it is vital to set and communicate high expectations.

ESTABLISHING BEHAVIORAL EXPECTATIONS. How do teachers establish expectations that are foundational, including *physical* norms for preserving the health and safety of students, *moral* norms pertaining to respect for others, and *societal* norms for politeness and individual responsibility? The answer, in large measure, depends on the developmental stages of the students. With young children, most expectations have to be made very explicit—for example, "Don't bother classmates," "Share materials," and "Don't tease one another." For older children and adolescents, many expectations can be summed up with statements such as "Treat one another with respect."

Establishing behavioral expectations is generally a teacher task. However, proponents of what is sometimes called a **democratic classroom**—one that promotes choice, community, authentic learning, and relevant, creative curriculum—encourage student participation in the establishment of behavioral expectations. Other influences affect the task, including expectations previously established by the school district and those held by the grade level or the whole school staff. There are few circumstances in which an individual teacher should set expectations less stringent than grade-level, team, or whole-school expectations. However, teachers can certainly add to, or make more stringent, their own classroom expectations. For instance, if school expectations include a "no gum" rule, then a teacher cannot allow gum chewing in the classroom. But if there is no schoolwide rule against gum chewing, a teacher may nonetheless establish the expectation that students will not chew gum in a particular classroom.

Here are some examples of behavior—some mild, some moderate, and some severe—that fall short of most teachers' behavioral expectations:

- Talking or moving around the classroom at inappropriate times
- Disturbing others (of course, there are thousands of ways students might do this!)
- Being tardy and having excessive absences
- Exemplifying off-task behaviors (missing materials, working on an assignment that is not the current task, daydreaming, or sleeping)
- Leaving the classroom without permission
- Cheating, lying
- Using obscene or vulgar language
- Defacing property
- Being verbally or physically noncompliant (refusing to do what is asked)
- Stealing and vandalizing
- Fighting or inflicting violence
- Being under the influence of illegal substances

SAMPLE EXPECTATIONS. Why would students choose to live up to classroom expectations? Many do so because they are accustomed to living up to expectations at home or in other settings. Some students require specific incentives to comply with expectations. Most students fall somewhere in between.

Some teachers choose to keep their lists of expectations short and general, as illustrated in Figure 6.3. Notice that none of the sample lists of expectations mention cheating, lying, vulgar language, vandalism, theft, substance abuse, or violence. As stated earlier, many teachers lump preventing all of these negative actions under the word—*respect*—assuming that if students show respect, they won't engage in any of these behaviors.

Incentives

An incentive is a reason for doing something. For instance, a first-grade student may stay in line while walking to music class (expectation) because the teacher told the class if everyone stayed in line, the music teacher would be pleased (incentive). Keep in mind that incentives that motivate one individual may have little effect on another. If the first-grade student doesn't like music or the music teacher, pleasing that teacher would not serve as an incentive. Teachers are responsible for understanding their students well enough to provide the bases for incentives that will motivate students in terms of behavior, academics, and personal growth.

The two basic kinds of incentives are extrinsic and intrinsic. **Extrinsic incentives** are those that are imposed or that originate outside the individual. **Intrinsic incentives** are those that come from within and result from students' natural drives.

EXTRINSIC INCENTIVES. Most theorists (and indeed probably most of your professors) downplay the value of extrinsic incentives in the classroom. And they are right. Extrinsic incentives are less desirable than intrinsic incentives. Extrinsic incentives depend on people other than the student. For instance, if a fourth-grade teacher offers a popcorn party on Friday if the class has fewer than five names recorded for misbehavior during the week, then students depend on one another to behave and on the teacher to keep his or her word. They apply peer pressure, again external, to achieve the Friday incentive. Do you think the students will be just as motivated to behave acceptably the next week without the promise of a popcorn party? Probably not. When extrinsic incentives are taken away, positive results are less likely to be reinforced. When teachers employ extrinsic motivation, they are taking on the full responsibility for motivating their students. Even so, extrinsic incentives are common in all levels of school.

Figure 6.3 Sample lists of classroom expectations

1. Pay attention.
2. Listen when others talk.
3. Treat each other with courtesy.

---

1. Work all class period.
2. Complete all assignments.
3. Stay in the area you are assigned.
4. Show respect at all times.

---

1. Respect each other and the teacher at all times.
2. Talk quietly so as not to disturb others.
3. Ask for help by raising your hand.
4. Follow all classroom procedures.

---

1. Arrive on time for class every day.
2. Have all materials needed to participate fully.
3. Maintain a respectful attitude.

---

1. Respect yourself.
2. Respect others.
3. Respect property.

In early childhood and elementary classrooms, extrinsic incentives may include:

- Extended time for recess
- A movie at the end of the day or week
- Special food treats
- Free time for students to explore classroom centers on their own
- Music to accompany an activity
- More time to engage in a favorite activity
- Stickers, certificates

At some point in your field experiences you will likely encounter extrinsic incentives in the form of a **token economy**, a system of distributing symbolic rewards (tokens) for appropriate behavior and withholding or taking away rewards for inappropriate behavior. At a designated time, students can exchange their tokens for something they value. Principal Susan McCloud at T. C. Cherry Elementary School in Bowling Green, Kentucky, reports that the culture of Cherry changed remarkably when her teachers began concentrating on positive behavior and incentives rather than negative behaviors and punishment. One major aspect of the change was the establishment of a token economy, in which students accumulated Cherry Pit Points that they could later "spend" at the Cherry Pit Store. Principal McCloud says this token system gives the students a sense of power and control when they think, "'Hey, I can behave and if I do, I get things that I want'" (2005, p. 49).

A primary influence for young adolescents revolves around friends. Many middle-level teachers capitalize on this developmental trait by promising socializing time at the end of a class period or at the end of a week in exchange for appropriate behavior. High school teachers take advantage of adolescent tendencies in the same way. In middle and high school, extrinsic incentives tend to be less tangible and more social in nature, such as the use of praise as a motivator.

PRAISE. Praise may be a powerful extrinsic motivator for some students. It is extrinsic because it depends on someone else, the praiser. There are important guidelines for optimizing the value of praise. Specific praise is more effective than general praise. For instance, saying to a student, "Your participation in today's activity helped your whole group stay on task. Thanks, Marcus," is more valuable than simply saying, "Nice work" as Marcus's group leaves the classroom. Using the student's name is important. Whether to praise in private or in public depends in large measure on the developmental level of the students. Most early childhood and elementary students enjoy being praised in front of their classmates. Young adolescents and high school students are often embarrassed by public praise. A compliment in private is generally more motivational and increases the likelihood of the desired behavior being repeated.

LOGIC OF EXTRINSIC INCENTIVES. In a perfect world, extrinsic incentives would not be necessary. We would all behave appropriately because it's the right thing to do. We would all work hard to reach our potential and to benefit others. Real teachers in real school settings understand the theories that reject extrinsic incentives; they also understand that much of society runs as smoothly as it does because of extrinsic motivation. Ask how many people who work in service industries (fast-food restaurants, dry cleaners, etc.) actually get out of bed and go to work because they are internally motivated to do their jobs. How they do their jobs—their attitude, attention to quality, and drive to be successful—may indeed be intrinsically motivated. But chances are that most go to work to earn money.

Ideally, students complete assignments and behave appropriately because they want to (intrinsic motivation). But there are tasks (drill and practice, assignments with no readily apparent value) and behaviors (walking in a straight line, being quiet when a visitor enters) that simply may not be internally motivating for some students in some settings. When it comes to extrinsic and intrinsic incentives, most teachers use a mixture to meet the real needs in their real classrooms.

INTRINSIC INCENTIVES. For lasting results, intrinsic incentives, such as the satisfaction of completing an assignment that is challenging, or behaving appropriately in an assembly, have the most value. Helping students understand why a particular behavior is desirable builds an internal "want to" that is motivating. When an individual behaves appropriately because of intrinsic motivation, chances are the desired behavior not only lasts but spreads to other aspects of life with positive results.

The best classroom management involves **student self-monitoring**. This is the ultimate intrinsic incentive because when students assume control of their own behavior, they develop a sense of ownership. Sounds good, doesn't it? We all want this for our students and our classrooms. However, helping students move toward this ideal when they may be accustomed to being told what to do, when to do it, and how to do it, with the promise of rewards for compliance, is a difficult task. Teaching for obedience is much easier than teaching for responsibility. Methods of accomplishing student self-monitoring are beyond the scope of this text, but this discussion may plant the seed that will give you the intrinsic motivation to think about, read about, and plan for a classroom full of self-monitoring students. Patrick Sutton, a focus student attending Cario Middle School in South Carolina, appears to have mastered a healthy measure of self-monitoring.

Application Exercise 6.5: Patrick's interview

Akin to intrinsic motivation is the concept that when student needs are met, misbehavior is less of an issue. When student needs are met, students behave appropriately because (1) they want to and (2) there's little need to do otherwise. Glasser's *Choice Theory* (1998) says that five basic needs constitute the source of all intrinsic motivation: survival, love and belonging, power, freedom, and fun. Glasser contends that giving students what they need will get teachers what they want: student responsibility and more appropriate behavior.

As with other aspects of teaching, teachers must remember that their classrooms are likely to include diverse groups of students. What is valued and what is motivating may be quite different from classroom to classroom, and student to student. Knowing students well—their cultures, their home settings, their disabilities, and more—is vital in understanding how to help them behave in respectful and responsible ways. Now let's turn our attention to what takes place when students do not respond favorably to incentives.

Consequences

Proactive prevention strategies, coupled with a system of incentives that helps students self-monitor their behavior, is the best approach to classroom management. But when expectations are not met, and prevention isn't enough, teachers must intervene. Intervention usually involves consequences. There are two guidelines teachers should follow to help ensure that consequences are reasonable, fairly applied, and not overly reactive, punitive, or exclusionary. First, *consequences should match the inappropriate behavior.* Second, *consequences should focus on the behavior, not on the person*, thus preserving both the student's dignity and the teacher–student relationship.

MATCHING CONSEQUENCES TO MISBEHAVIOR. Consequences should match misbehavior both in appropriateness and in severity. Although it would be impossible to design a distinct consequence for every type of misbehavior, teachers should attempt to match consequences whenever possible. For instance, if a student writes on desks or lockers, an appropriate consequence would involve cleaning during a school-required detention. If a student wastes class time, spending free time making up class work would be appropriate. If teasing and hurt feelings are involved, perhaps an apology and reading a short story about how hurtful teasing can be may be effective. Most schools have a standard list of consequences ranging from mild to severe. As with expectations, these consequences need to be applied in the classroom. Teachers can go beyond schoolwide agreed-upon consequences by developing and implementing consequences tailored to the misbehavior of their own students.

UNOBTRUSIVE INTERVENTIONS. The variability of both students and misbehavior dictates a wide range of consequences, beginning with consequences that do not disrupt instruction. There are both nonverbal and verbal ways to address relatively minor behavior problems such as student inattention; minor off-task behaviors such as daydreaming, doing something other than what is expected, and not using proper materials; leaving a designated area; pestering another student; and many others.

Nonverbal **unobtrusive interventions** include moving closer to the offending student (proximity), giving a disapproving look, stopping mid-sentence for a moment to gain student attention, and making an established gesture. To be effective, nonverbal interventions take thought and proactive behavior on the part of the teacher. The best way to learn about nonverbal interventions is to watch and listen carefully as experienced teachers make them work. You'll have opportunities to do this during field experiences in your teacher preparation program. Chances are that unobtrusive intervention will be enough for most students, most of the time, if the environment is respectful and students are engaged in learning.

Verbal interventions can resolve minor problems if delivered quickly, calmly, and in ways that match the offense. From saying, "Everyone needs to listen," to using the offending student's name in a classroom scenario, to a class discussion about why a particular behavior is inappropriate, teachers' words can make a difference. Whatever is said should purposefully lead students back to focus on instruction or learning activities.

Simply asking a student to move to another part of the classroom temporarily, or permanently, may solve some minor misbehavior problems. Withdrawing privileges is another tactic some teachers use successfully.

TEACHER-PRESCRIBED CONSEQUENCES. Teachers must move beyond unobtrusive nonverbal and verbal intervention when misbehavior warrants. The timing of this escalation depends on a number of variables, including school level, student needs, and assessment of possible damage or danger involved with the misbehavior.

Time-out is a consequence often used in early childhood and elementary classrooms. Students are isolated, usually within the classroom, and not allowed to participate in whatever is going on. Time-out works well as a consequence if not overused and if classroom instruction and activities are engaging, making isolation undesirable.

Detention is a consequence often used at all grade levels. It is most effective when it involves isolation and requires the student to give up time he or she would rather spend elsewhere. Some teachers, teams of teachers, and whole schools find that lunch detention works well. Students assigned to lunch detention are separated from others and required to eat lunch alone in silence. After-school detention is typically used for completion of assignments or for school-related chores such as cleaning or helping in some way. Weekend detention, sometimes called Saturday school, is generally reserved for more serious or repeated offenses.

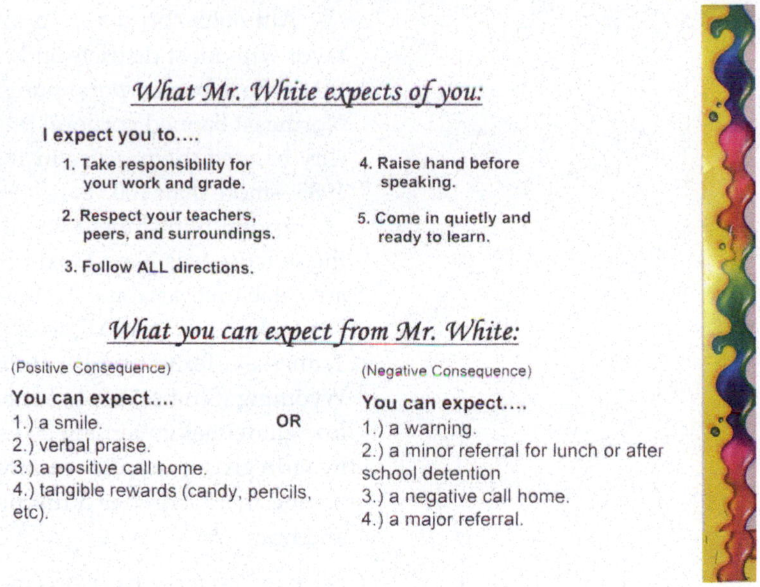

Boynton and Boynton (2005) describe **processing** as the concept of sending a student out of the classroom for the purpose of reflection and to consider better choices. Students may be sent to another classroom, the hallway, the library, or a designated room, sometimes called a behavior improvement room (BIR). Processing is appropriate for minor misbehavior that occurs repeatedly or student disruptions that aren't resolved through unobtrusive nonverbal or verbal interventions.

What Mr. White expects of you:

I expect you to....

1. Take responsibility for your work and grade.
2. Respect your teachers, peers, and surroundings.
3. Follow ALL directions.
4. Raise hand before speaking.
5. Come in quietly and ready to learn.

What you can expect from Mr. White:

(Positive Consequence)

You can expect....

1.) a smile.
2.) verbal praise.
3.) a positive call home.
4.) tangible rewards (candy, pencils, etc).

OR

(Negative Consequence)

You can expect....

1.) a warning.
2.) a minor referral for lunch or after school detention
3.) a negative call home.
4.) a major referral.

Setting expectations and consequences, and then making them public and explicit, helps bring order and civility to the classroom.

SERIOUS CONSEQUENCES. Some misbehavior calls for consequences beyond what an individual teacher may assign. Misbehavior involving physical violence, loud or threatening verbal abuse, vandalism, theft, and possession of illegal substances or weapons dictates the involvement of building-level administrators who may elect to involve law enforcement. Such serious misbehavior often results in suspension, either in school or out of school, or expulsion. Classroom teachers should not attempt to handle such misbehavior alone. A supportive and decisive administrator can be one of the most valuable assets to teachers and the classroom management process.

Chances are that most people in the United States would be surprised to know that **corporal punishment**, or physical punishment, is still allowed in 19 states today (Anderson, 2015). Interestingly, the perceived need for such punishment dates back to the early days of the country. Figure 6.4 provides a portion of a teacher's journal dated 1776 that describes a "bad boy" and the philosophy of the day about "curing" the student. Most teachers will recognize at least some of the traits described by Master Lovell in at least a few of the students they have known. Reviewing the history of educational practices provides a perspective showing that the struggles teachers face in today's classrooms are not necessarily new.

Figure 6.4 Master Lovell's journal

A Bad Boy is undutiful to his father and mother, disobedient and stubborn to his master, and ill natured to all his playmates. He hates his books and takes no pleasure in improving himself. . . .

He is always in mischief, and when he has done a wrong, will tell twenty lies to clear himself. He hates to have anyone give him good advice, and when they are out of sight, will laugh at them. He swears and wrangles and quarrels with his companions, and is always in some dispute or other. . . .

He is frequently out of humor, and sullen and obstinate, so that he will neither do what he is asked, nor answer any question put to him. In short, he neglects everything that he should learn, and minds nothing but play and mischief. He grows up a confirmed blockhead, incapable of anything but wickedness and folly. . . . [T]o make a bad boy into a good one, he should be thrashed daily for some reason or other, and locked securely in a closet. There he can meditate upon his sins and thus avoid his fate.

Source: Loeper, J. L. (1973). *Going to school in 1776*. New York: Macmillan.

Although corporal punishment has vocal critics and its practice has fallen out of favor with most districts and educators, some people still believe it is warranted. The first state to ban corporal punishment was New Jersey in 1867. Many large cities in the Northeast banned corporal punishment before their states did so. Notably, New York City banned the practice in 1870, whereas the state of New York did not ban it until 1985—more than 100 years later. Educators may use paddling, the most common form of corporal punishment, in all the Southern states, plus others. The last state to ban the practice was New Mexico in 2011. The states that still allow corporal punishment are: Alabama, Arizona, Arkansas, Colorado, Florida, Georgia, Idaho, Indiana, Kansas, Kentucky, Louisiana, Mississippi, Missouri, North Carolina, Oklahoma, South Carolina, Tennessee, Texas, and Wyoming. It is most prevalent in Texas and least prevalent in Wyoming (Strauss, 2014). School districts that practice corporal punishment must follow guidelines governing its use that have resulted from court cases. These guidelines include giving specific warnings that a behavior may result in physical punishment, having more than one adult present, and ensuring that the punishment is reasonable and humane.

FOCUS ON THE BEHAVIOR, NOT THE PERSON. Children and adolescents are developing and growing. Their misbehavior often results from fleeting moods, spontaneous impulses, and poor decision making linked to immaturity.

Constructive Correcting. How teachers correct students makes a difference. If done constructively, the chances of a student walking away hating the teacher and planning to misbehave again, but not get caught, are diminished. Assigning consequences in ways that serve as student learning experiences is both productive and constructive—productive in that students sense that they are viewed as individuals, and constructive in that students may use the experience to build their understanding of why certain behaviors are unacceptable. Correcting students in constructive ways can turn something negative into a growth experience. For instance, a consequence for using the word *retard* in a joking manner may be viewing a video about children with Down syndrome that explains their intellectual disabilities and the coping strategies they are taught. The disrespect shown by using *retard* as a slang word will hopefully be corrected with increased understanding.

Starting Fresh. When focus is placed on the misbehavior rather than on the student, it is possible for the student to see beyond the incident and consequence to the possibility of a fresh start. Chris Stevenson (2002), noted expert on middle-level education, advises that teachers should have an attitude that says to students, "Redemption is always close, not closed" (p. 219). In other words, when a student misbehaves and a consequence is assigned, the student deserves to be given a fresh start. This helps students build **resilience**, the ability to bounce back and meet life's challenges.

Family Communication. When communicating with the family of a student who misbehaves, it is vital to focus on the misbehavior, not the person. In essence, if a student is maligned rather than the misbehavior, then the family is maligned, with a negative effect on the family–school relationship. A wise teacher emphasizes the positive and the potential before discussing the misbehavior.

If a teacher has already had a positive family communication, such as a complimentary note sent home or a pleasant meeting at Back-to-School Night, then a phone call about a behavior problem may work wonders. For some students, just the threat of a call is enough. For other students, a call home is meaningless. For instance, parents may not be available for a call (and students know this) or parents may have received many such calls and may not care or may feel helpless to remedy the situation.

Parent or family conferences can be effective if they are handled professionally and result in an agreed-upon, enforceable plan to correct the problem. We should not expect families to come up with the plan. Before the conference teachers need to think through elements of possible plans that will be effective and not interfere with teaching and learning.

This *The Opinion Page feature* is about a principal who obviously understands the big picture of expectations and consequences. Teachers can learn a great deal from this principal's design of a consequence that fits the misbehavior.

Now that we have considered ways to create a positive learning environment; how routines contribute to a productive learning environment; and some of the basics of expectations, incentives, and consequences, we are ready to explore developing a classroom management plan.

The Opinion Page

This Opinion Editorial appeared in the *Inter-Mountain*, a newspaper serving the Potomac Highlands area of West Virginia, on May 30, 2012.

Students Must Learn from Their Mistakes

by staff writer

Next month, a group of Pendleton County High School graduates will host a Fun Day for area youth to raise money for the custodian staff and fire department. They'll also spend two days of their summer vacation helping clean up around the school.

This is the same group of 25 to 30 students who, a few weeks ago, broke into their school, scattered corn, straw, and yarn, wrapped toilets in Saran wrap and tin foil, and smeared Vaseline and shaving cream throughout the building. What started out as a planned prank of decorating some classrooms with balloons and streamers got "out of hand" the students and their Principal Tim Woodward say. The school's custodian described the result as "a mess, a total mess."

Classes were canceled the following day to allow time for cleanup.

Law enforcement isn't pressing charges, unless school system officials decide otherwise. Some parents think their children deserve a stern punishment.

Woodward decided against suspending the students, saying that would cause them to miss their graduation. Instead, he elected to impose "restorative discipline restitution"—hence the additional summer projects. This, he says, "actually teaches the student."

Had they been suspended from graduation, they may have felt remorse on that day or regret in years to come. They may even have quite a tale in explaining why they didn't get to attend the ceremonies. What they would be without is a lesson of value.

While many may not agree with Woodward's decision, it appears he is on the right track. There's no excuse for what the students did. It was simply wrong. Now, it's in their best interest and that of those who affiliate with them in the future to learn from their mistakes. It may even be something they can teach their children.

This Opinion Page piece commends an act of common sense on the part of the principal. Write a well-developed paragraph in response to each of the following questions:

1. In what ways does the consequence fit the misbehavior? Why do you think some parents did not agree with the principal's choice?
2. How does the principal demonstrate consideration for the whole child? What does this have to do with resilience?
3. In what ways does the punishment contribute to constructive correcting? Explain the use of the phrase "restorative discipline restitution."

Point of Reflection 6.1

What classroom expectations, or rules, do you remember in your K–12 experiences? Were they clear and rational, or were they ambiguous and didn't make sense to you? On what do you base your opinion?

Check Your Understanding 6.3

6.4 How Can I Develop a Classroom Management Plan?

6.4 Analyze ways to develop a classroom management plan.

Considering elements that contribute to a successful classroom management plan will create an awareness of what to look for in field experiences throughout your teacher preparation program as you observe teachers dealing daily with learning environment issues. This section looks briefly at what selected theorists and researchers have to say about classroom management; the necessity of considering students' special needs, societal context, and developmental stages; and some general guidelines for planning and implementing classroom management.

Prominent Theories of Classroom Management

If you presented a classroom management scenario to a room full of teachers and asked them how they would respond, you'd no doubt hear as many solutions as there were teachers. A single foolproof recipe for classroom management simply doesn't exist. Many new teachers are dismayed to hear this because a recipe or formula would make life much easier. But take heart! Teachers can take advantage of what experienced theorists like those in Table 6.1 have to say, as well as research-based strategies, to garner ideas to consider in developing personalized classroom management plans.

Consider the Students

We have already discussed the importance of considering all aspects of students' lives when planning for curriculum, instruction, and assessment. This outlook is equally important in planning for the learning environment.

SPECIAL NEEDS. Students with special needs, those requiring unique services to optimize their learning potential, usually also require specific guidelines for classroom

Table 6.1 Overview of selected theories of classroom management

Theorist	Model	Basic Beliefs
Skinner	Behavior modification	Teachers use positive and negative reinforcements or rewards and punishments to modify or shape students' behavior.
Glasser	Choice therapy and quality schools	Schools help satisfy students' psychological needs and add quality to their lives. Teachers teach, manage, provide caring environments, and conduct class meetings in a way that adds quality to students' lives.
Gordon	Teacher effectiveness training	Teachers teach self-discipline, demonstrate active listening, send "I-messages" rather than "you-messages," and teach a six-step conflict resolution program.
Canter	Assertive discipline	Teachers and students have rights in the classroom. Teachers insist on responsible behavior and use a hierarchical list of consequences to manage behavior.
Kounin	Instructional management	Teachers use effective instructional behaviors (teaching techniques, movement management, and group focus) to influence student behaviors.
Curwin and Mendler	Discipline with dignity	Teachers protect the dignity of students. Teachers are fair and consider individual situations (as opposed to rigid rules), list rules that make sense to students, and model appropriate behaviors.
Gathercoal	Judicious discipline	Teachers provide behavioral guidelines for property loss and damage, threats to health and safety, and serious disruptions of the educational process. They also demonstrate professional ethics and build a democratic classroom.

Based on: Manning, M. L., & Bucher, K. T. (2013). *Classroom management: Models, applications, and cases*. Boston: Pearson Education, Inc.

management. The best way to find out what the guidelines are for a student who has special needs is to talk with the person in your school who has oversight responsibility for the student's education. Most often this is one of the special educators in your building. You will be referred to the student's individualized educational program, which will contain information about any variances from what are considered normal, reasonable incentive-and-consequence systems necessitated by the student's disability. The Individuals with Disabilities Education Act (IDEA) includes provisions for the development of a management plan through a team of educators using a process known as **functional behavioral assessment (FBA)**. This process looks for events and actions that may lead to misbehavior and devises strategies to help students abide by classroom expectations.

SOCIETAL CONTEXT. Students don't leave their home lives on the schoolhouse steps at 8 a.m., to be picked up at 3:30 p.m. when they leave the classroom. The societal context in which they are growing up colors their attitudes, aptitudes, and reactions. You name it, they bring it with them into the classroom. The answer to the familiar questions, "And how are the children? Are they all well?" should guide the development and implementation of a classroom management plan.

What motivates one child to follow routines and expectations may be meaningless to another. Students' perceptions—regardless of whether the source may be culturally or socioeconomically based—influence their reactions to expectations, incentives, and consequences. Some of the everyday areas about which perceptions may differ include eye contact, physical closeness to others, competition, and receiving attention (Manning & Bucher, 2013).

DEVELOPMENTAL APPROPRIATENESS. Understanding human development is absolutely essential when writing and implementing a classroom management plan. Let's take a look at how three of our focus teachers maintain learning environments through classroom management plans that both match their personal styles and respond to the developmental stages of their students.

Chris Roberts, multiage teacher at Rees Elementary School in Utah, tells us he does his best to have unconditional love for students. His students feel that love and do their best to work hard and learn all they can. His classroom doesn't have "rules"; rather, it has "agreements." Chris believes this language change is important. He says kids are smothered in rules. He and his students meet together a lot in the beginning of the year and do experiential activities to build teamwork. They talk about how they want their "village" to be. They write down their discussions and sign an agreement that they will do their best to show respect for each other and property. They continually assess how they are doing all year long. Chris regularly writes letters to his students, telling them he appreciates the positive things they are doing.

Brenda Beyal, Chris's teammate, believes in talking with students to set expectations, much like Chris does. As with other classroom elements when student input is sought, teachers have some non-negotiables. Brenda's non-negotiables are in Figure 6.5. Her list may contain some principles you haven't thought about.

Figure 6.5 Brenda's guidelines for classroom management

1. Build trust from the moment students walk through the door.
2. Protect trust all year long.
3. Play with students on the field and in the classroom (sports, checkers, educational games, etc.).
4. Don't send students away to be disciplined unless absolutely necessary. If you do, you give away their respect for you and your role.
5. Don't ever be degrading. This ruins your relationship with students.
6. Set up clear expectations with consequences that apply when students make bad choices.
7. Make students take responsibility. Keep their problems, their problems.
8. Be sympathetic but firm, fair, and consistent.

Figure 6.6 Cario Middle School student expectations

1. Conduct yourself in an orderly manner.
2. Be on task.
3. Respect yourself and others.
4. Take care of all property.
5. Promote safety in everything you do.

Focus teacher Traci Peters at Cario Middle School in South Carolina, invests a lot of time in getting to know her 7th-grade students and attending school events to support their participation. Building relationships is foundational to Traci's classroom management plan. Traci and her students abide by the five basic behavior guidelines agreed on by the entire staff of Cario Middle School and listed in Figure 6.6. The Charleston County School District requires teachers to give conduct grades for each student in every 9-week grading period. Employing a system commonly found in many schools, Traci gives demerits for misbehavior. She has a system for converting demerits into letter grades. She also uses a "three strikes, you're out" policy, meaning that after three demerits in her classroom in a quarter, a student goes outside her classroom management plan and talks with a building-level administrator. Traci says, "Basically, I give kids a chance to be kids, but at the same time I expect them to respect me and those around them." She tells us that parent communication is a major help in managing a middle school classroom.

Most high school students understand behavioral expectations and the rationale behind them. If adolescents ages 15 through 19 are disruptive in the classroom, they usually know exactly what they're doing and, in some cases, do it because they know they can get away with it or perhaps because they want to be suspended. Students who are disruptive in high school are often sent out of the classroom, instructed to see an administrator, and may be given **suspension**, which consists of being sent off school grounds for a specified length of time. This severe consequence should be reserved for extreme cases. Roosevelt High School in California publishes school rules as well as its Student Code of Conduct in a student handbook. The school rules on which Roosevelt teachers build their classroom expectations are shown in Figure 6.7. The Code of Conduct covers expectations for a safe environment, closed-campus rules and exceptions, the necessity of ID tags, absences, the use of electronics, and a sexual harassment policy. In addition, the Fresno [California] Unified School District maintains a zero-tolerance policy for possession of firearms, weapons of any kind, explosives, and controlled substances, and attempted or actual harm to another person. Immediate suspension occurs for these violations, many times resulting in **expulsion**, or permanent removal from school.

Our focus teachers at Roosevelt High seldom have misbehavior in their classrooms that a certain look or a private word won't remedy. They are instead often faced with the dilemma of students not engaging in learning. So, rather than overt misbehavior, a lack of desire or enthusiasm for the whole educative process often challenges them. This can be an even more perplexing problem than dealing with students who are disruptive.

Figure 6.7 Roosevelt High School behavior guidelines

Roosevelt High School students are required to conduct themselves in an appropriate, acceptable manner at all times when present in school, in classrooms and hallways, on school grounds, and at school-sponsored events. Students are to:

1. Treat others with consideration and dignity.
2. Respect the property of others.
3. Be punctual and prepared for class.
4. Follow the direction of all staff.

Incorporate 21st Century Skills

The Partnership for 21st Century Skills' framework consists of four categories of student outcomes: *Core Subjects; Learning and Innovation Skills; Information, Media, and Technology Skills;* and *Life and Career Skills*. Life skills are applicable to maintaining a positive and productive learning environment. The five major components of Life and Career Skills are listed in Figure 6.8 Let's briefly examine each component.

FLEXIBILITY AND ADAPTABILITY. Being flexible and adaptable doesn't mean passively going with the flow. Partnership for 21st Century Skills suggests that we teach students to respond to change in ways that make growth a priority and to use feedback constructively. This means that students need to develop resilience that helps them deal with both praise and criticism. Teaching students to be adaptable involves giving them experiences in different roles, responsibilities, and schedules.

Although we can control many elements in the classroom, it is inevitable that something will interrupt the flow of teaching and learning. For instance, in an elementary classroom, a teacher may purposefully orchestrate a disruption in an event students helped plan, such as an afternoon outdoors looking for plant samples. The teacher might lead the students to plan the event on a day when she knows the field is scheduled to be mowed. When she tells the students about the mowing on the morning of their planned outing, they will be disappointed. She can have the students get into small groups and brainstorm how they might be flexible and adaptable and still accomplish their goals. Then students should share and discuss their possible alternatives. This is a life skill that is very much a part of a productive classroom environment.

INITIATIVE AND SELF-DIRECTION. The components addressed in these life and career skills include managing goals and time, working independently, and being self-directed learners. All of these components play major roles in maintaining a positive and productive learning environment. Independent, self-directed learners will be able to manage time as they accomplish their goals. Helping students become this ultimate vision of who we want them to be isn't necessarily something that becomes part of daily lesson plans. It is a teacher attitude that weaves in and out of every formal and informal encounter we have with students. For instance, a high school civics teacher might plan for students to complete a semester-long project. Many steps are built into the project, beginning with a whole-class activity involving brainstorming, followed by small-group work for those with similar interests. Then the individual student, armed with skills from working with two different-sized groups, sets off independently to work through the assignment step by step at his or her own pace. The teacher is deliberately creating experiences that lead to initiative and self-direction.

SOCIAL AND CROSS-CULTURAL SKILLS. This area is all about two vital aspects of a classroom community: relationships and communication. Showing respect in a variety of circumstances and with a broad spectrum of people—based on age, gender, ethnicity, abilities, political persuasions, religion, and all the ways we may differ—is key. Every day in the classroom, teachers have the responsibility to model acceptance and respectful communication. They model when to speak and when to listen, when to be open minded, and then when to stand on reasoned ground.

Figure 6.8 Twenty-first–century life and career skills

- Flexibility and adaptability
- Initiative and self-direction
- Social and cross-cultural skills
- Productivity and accountability
- Leadership and responsibility

One way to foster social and cross-cultural skills is purposefully grouping and regrouping students in ways that expose them to all the diversity a particular setting can offer. Some demographics are rich in diversity; others are not. Even where race and socioeconomic circumstances are similar, students display diversity in learning styles, abilities, motivation, and achievement. Teachers need to look beyond the obvious and into the subtle, and then group students, teaching them how to communicate and work together in positive and productive ways.

PRODUCTIVITY AND ACCOUNTABILITY. Producing results and fulfilling responsibilities, or being accountable, are vital attributes of success. When students experience success through being productive and accountable, success will likely lead to more success. It's a cycle we often have to orchestrate the first or second time around until students experience what it's like to actually be productive. We certainly have to be close guides for younger students to first succeed, and then recognize success in the form of productivity so they understand the cycle and will want to replicate it. But adolescents often need this close guidance as well. Our hovering will have to take different forms to be effective, but that's part of understanding the development of our students. If adolescents have little experience with productivity and accountability, we have to make the elements obvious, actually *plan* for them to succeed, and then help them reflect on the big picture of the relationship between hard work and success.

LEADERSHIP AND RESPONSIBILITY. There's a reason why social studies standards begin with the study of self and family in kindergarten; extend to the study of neighborhoods and community in first grade; and then progress to an overview of local, state, and national dimensions before concentrating on U.S. History in fifth grade. From there, a broad view of history is tackled, followed by in-depth study of how our world works regarding people, geography, politics, and so on. Children and adolescents develop from a narrow perspective on life and their world to an understanding of interdependence, built in large measure through the guidance of their teachers.

Integrity and ethical behavior, two attributes we hope will be part of all aspects of leadership, don't necessarily happen naturally. Pointing out moral dilemmas and then prompting students to make choices and act in responsible ways is a positive and healthy part of the informal curriculum. For instance, when a dispute arises on the playground—and it most certainly will—rather than assigning a consequence based on what appears to be a rule infraction or simply a child being mean, a teacher might plan a class debriefing of the situation with students asking questions of the kids involved in the dispute, attempting to get at the cause of the problem. In this way, students begin to think through situations, look at possible causes and solutions, recognize volatile circumstances, and learn to take responsibility and lead others in that direction as well. Although this all sounds quite straightforward and simple, it takes incident after incident, solution seeking over and over again, to internalize the lessons. As adults, this is a lifelong learning task, and for children, we can't start too soon to help them develop leadership and responsibility skills.

General Guidelines for Developing a Classroom Management Plan

We have discussed some of the most important elements of developing and implementing a classroom management plan. Certain guidelines are non-negotiable when establishing such a plan. Although it is impossible to address all of them within the scope of this text, here are several important ones:

- *Always stay within school and district policies and guidelines.*
- *Use positive rather than negative statements when establishing expectations.* Students need to know what they *should do,* not just what they *shouldn't do.* For instance, the

expectation "We will show respect for others when working together or apart" is more likely to gain compliance than "We will not be disrespectful of others when working together or apart." Plant positive thoughts in students' minds that promote productive habits of appropriate behavior.

- *Consistently apply expectations and consequences.* Some teachers set an expectation and have different consequences based on the number of times a student's behavior is outside the expectation. This sort of consequence layering in no way undermines the consistency of consequences.
- *Look for students' redeeming characteristics.* Everyone has them. Looking for the good in students helps us like them more and perhaps find some things in common with them.
- *Explore conflict resolution and peer mediation.* This approach involves students trained as go-betweens to help other students work through their differences and agree to disagree amicably. Look for such programs as you observe and interact in schools.
- *Communicate and document.* Once established, a teacher's classroom management plan should be explicitly taught to students, the building administrators should receive a written plan, and parents and families should be informed of it. An aspect of communication often neglected by teachers is documentation, or record keeping. When a consequence is applied, document it.
- *Ask for help.* There are some behavior issues that classroom teachers should not handle alone. Physical violence, overt bullying, and verbal abuse of students or adults cannot be tolerated in a classroom setting. Episodes of this nature must be dealt with immediately by administrators.

Don't be Part of the Problem

Think back to your days in prekindergarten through twelfth grade. Can you remember a classroom behavior problem actually getting worse because of something a teacher did or didn't do? Were you ever in a class when student misbehavior escalated so that it was almost out of control even as the teacher yelled for attention? How about out-of-control behavior in the presence of a teacher who repeatedly used "shhhh" to ask for silence? Neither approach works.

Purposefully embarrassing students should never be a teacher tactic. The result may be serious psychological damage to the student. Another likely result is the student's loss of respect for the teacher who has displayed his or her own version of misbehavior.

Avoid making threats without following through. This practice can have disastrous results in a classroom.

A teacher repeatedly saying, "If you don't stop that I'll . . . " may cause the immediate misbehavior to escalate, and it guarantees future problems because students won't believe the teacher will follow through.

Teachers should never allow a classroom confrontation to escalate into a power struggle. When a student loses control of his or her temper and directs remarks at a teacher, and the teacher reacts in kind, the opportunity to be a mature, reasonable role model is lost. No one wins. Giving a student time to calm down and gracefully save face will provide a chance for student and teacher to talk about the situation. In some exaggerated cases, avoiding a power struggle prevents physical violence and gives time for administrators to get involved in a resolution.

As a last bit of advice, don't take student behavior personally. Remember that students come into your classroom with all that nature and nurture has dealt them. Although your actions and attitudes can in large measure determine the classroom learning environment, human beings at times defy prediction. When a student lashes out at you or a classmate or a circumstance, chances are the behavior is due, at least in part, to life outside the classroom walls. We do our best to prevent behavior problems, respond in ways that stem escalation, and still there will be times when we feel as though we have failed. Students are not acting out to show their dislike or disdain for us or the curriculum . . . don't take it personally.

Point of Reflection 6.2

Do you remember teachers you thought were part of the problem when it came to the learning environment? Describe one or two and their actions.

Check Your Understanding 6.4

Concluding Thoughts

Students learn much more than academic subjects in our classrooms. They learn how to exist in society. They learn the limits of what they can and can't do in terms of behavior. A positive and productive learning environment is safe—physically, emotionally, and academically. When students feel safe, they are more likely to participate, learn, and grow.

Creating and maintaining a positive and productive learning environment is hard work. Teachers can learn how to cultivate appropriate relationships with students, how to establish routines that foster productivity, and how to thoughtfully develop classroom management plans that are effective. With diligence and consistent monitoring, a positive and productive learning environment can be maintained.

Well-managed classrooms are marked by civility. Some students come to school without a clear idea of what civility looks like because they don't live in the midst of it. Teachers must model civility, orchestrate an environment that fosters it, and then expect nothing less of students.

After reading the *Chapter in Review,* interact with Brenda Beyal as she struggles to mentor a new teacher in this chapter's *Developing Professional Competence.*

Chapter in Review

How do teachers create a positive learning environment?

- The physical layout, appearance, usefulness, and overall appeal of the classroom either enhance the learning environment or detract from it.
- Care and trust help teachers and students build a sense of community.
- Teacher awareness, ability to multitask, and recognition that one action directly affects another are valuable assets in creating a positive learning environment.
- Time is a constant that should be used wisely to promote learning in schools.

What routines contribute to maintaining a productive classroom environment?

- The types of routines needed vary by school level, but their importance at all levels cannot be overemphasized.
- Students need to practice routines so they become productive habits.

How do teachers establish expectations, incentives, and consequences?

- Successful classroom management is a prerequisite for successful teaching and learning.
- The best prevention of behavioral problems is engaging instruction.
- Many issues and situations require teachers to establish behavioral expectations, incentives for achieving these expectations, and consequences for not fulfilling them.

How can I develop a classroom management plan?

- Prominent theories and classroom observations provide background and strategies for new teachers to use when formulating management plans.
- Teachers should consider student needs and development when formulating a plan.
- Classroom management plans are most effective when expectations are stated positively; when expectations, incentives, and consequences are applied consistently; and when teachers model appropriate behavior.

Developing Professional Competence

Sara Davis Powell

Thoughtfully reading this scenario and responding to the items that follow it will help you prepare for licensure exams.

Brenda Beyal is an experienced teacher who values relationships with students and has confidence in her classroom management procedures. She was asked by Principal Mike Larsen to mentor Elizabeth, a new teacher who came to Rees Elementary School with a very strong academic record that included graduating with a 4.0 grade-point average and a master's degree in teaching reading. Mike was very excited to give Elizabeth an opportunity to teach a self-contained fourth-grade class as her first teaching assignment. Brenda was happy to be her mentor, but when Elizabeth arrived at Rees she wasn't keen on the idea of someone actually assigned to help her be successful, and she let others know it.

Brenda was friendly and offered to help Elizabeth set up her room and guide her through the fourth-grade curriculum and materials she would use. She politely listened but showed little interest. For classroom management, Elizabeth posted preprinted posters with rules and warnings. Brenda explained that Rees has basic expectations that involve respect and that she may want to meet with her students to talk about what respect might look like in the classroom and allow the children to have some input. Elizabeth said no, and told Brenda that her training was as a Skinnerian behaviorist.

One afternoon in October, after hearing repeatedly from students that Elizabeth's students were not happy and several parents had complained to the principal, Brenda overheard a conversation in the hallway. Elizabeth told her student Marcus that she was at the limit of her patience, that he was nothing but trouble, that she now knew how to treat him for the rest of the year, and that his parents would be very disappointed in him. Brenda knew it was time to talk with Elizabeth even though she had resisted her attempts before.

Now it's time for you to respond to two essay items involving the scenario. In your responses, be sure to address all the dilemmas and questions posed in each item. These items are followed by three multiple-choice questions.

1. Refer to Brenda's guidelines for classroom management in Figure 6.5. Name two guidelines for which it is likely too late for Elizabeth and this year's fourth-graders. Name two guidelines that Elizabeth may have in place, given what you know from this scenario. Explain why you selected each of the four guidelines.

2. What problems does Elizabeth invite for the rest of the year by telling Marcus that she knows how she will treat him? Explain.

Application Exercise 6.6: Developing Professional Competence

3. Which guideline for developing positive teacher–student relationships do you think Elizabeth most likely violated in her encounter with Marcus?
   a. Engaging instruction
   b. Clearly defined parameters of acceptable student behaviors
   c. Use of effective monitoring skills
   d. Appropriate consequences

4. Elizabeth told Brenda that she is a Skinnerian behaviorist. This means that:
   a. She must have studied B. F. Skinner and believes that children will behave if they understand what's right.
   b. In her study of Skinner she learned that rewards and punishment will shape student behavior.
   c. In graduate school she learned that Skinner believed in verbally reprimanding students and humiliating them to gain obedience.
   d. She is a trained specialist in behavior management.

5. Based on what she heard in the hall, Brenda is afraid that Elizabeth's style of classroom management will possibly destroy which quality she believes in building?
   a. Resilience
   b. Self-determination
   c. Students' love of learning
   d. A healthy sense of competition among students

Application Exercise 6.7: Developing Professional Competence

Flash Cards 6.1

Shared Writing 6.1: Classroom Expectations

Chapter 7

History of Education in the United States

Learning Objectives

After studying this chapter, you will have knowledge and skills to:

7.1 Identify major influences, issues, ideologies, and individuals in 17th-century American education.

7.2 Identify major influences, issues, ideologies, and individuals in 18th-century American education.

7.3 Identify major influences, issues, ideologies, and individuals in 19th-century American education.

7.4 Identify major influences, issues, ideologies, and individuals in 20th-century American education.

7.5 Articulate major influences, issues, ideologies, and individuals in 21st-century American education.

Dear Reader

History is neither dull nor dry. Real people in real places used problem-solving techniques to address real issues as they arose—and made history in the process. These people were as alive as you are today. History is nothing but problem solving, a skill often relegated to math class only. But think about it: Life presents dilemmas and we deal with them, or problem solve. This then leads to more dilemmas as the results of our previous actions confront us and we gain more insight. This is history in the making!

You've probably heard the saying, expressed by many in various ways, that if we don't pay attention to history, we are doomed to repeat it. Educators tend to be among the worst perpetrators of proving the truth in this saying. We seem to recycle old ideas every 25 or 30 years, even though they didn't work the first time around. One reason for this sad state is that we, as teachers, fail to know the history of our profession and the practices that are part of it.

This chapter is an overview of the history of education in the United States. Knowing the major influences, issues, ideologies, and individuals will give you some perspective as you explore education in this nation. Every philosophy and trend that guided educational processes was forged or in place because of what theorists and teachers thought was right at the time. You will likely find some of what you will read to be antiquated, or worse, immoral. But remember that every generation has a perspective that the previous one did not. The United States has not always considered equal opportunities for all children to be a guiding force in what we do in schools. Study the history of education in America, learn from it, and contribute solutions to challenges, rather than repeat the mistakes of the past, as we move forward.

Where Do I Stand?

 **Click here to complete survey online**

This inventory helps you begin thinking about elements of your philosophy of education. After reading an item, indicate your level of agreement by choosing a number and placing it in the blank before the statement. Following the inventory are directions for how to organize your responses and what they may indicate in terms of where you stand.

4 I strongly agree

3 I agree

2 I don't have an opinion

1 I disagree

0 I strongly disagree

____ 1. It is vital that we teach personal responsibility in school.

____ 2. Students must be disciplined, hard workers in order to learn.

____ 3. The classroom should be a model of democracy.

____ 4. Memorization is a learning strategy that should be employed frequently in classrooms.

____ 5. Schools should use intense study of the classics to strive for excellence in students.

____ 6. Making a lesson interesting to students is important to their learning.

____ 7. Learning is worthwhile only if it increases a student's sense of self.

____ 8. The school and teachers should determine what is learned, without regard for student interests.

____ 9. A major goal of public education is positive social change.

____ 10. Choices and electives have no place in the curriculum.

____ 11. A teacher should be a facilitator of learning.

____ 12. Rules are very important in the classroom and must be adhered to at all times.

____ 13. Teachers teach the whole child, not just the intellectual aspects.

____ 14. An important part of teaching involves instilling students with a sense of responsibility for humanity.

____ 15. Part of the responsibility of a teacher is to be an intellectual and moral role model.

____ 16. Active engagement is important for learning.

____ 17. Curriculum should be established that does not easily or often change, but may shift because of changes in society.

____ 18. Cooperative learning is an instructional tool that should be used often in the classroom.

____ 19. There is a set curriculum of basic core knowledge that all Americans should know.

____ 20. Individualism and freedom of choice are paramount in successful classrooms.

____ 21. Teachers are primarily dispensers of knowledge.

____ 22. Learning takes place through experiences.

____ 23. The wisdom students need may be obtained through study of the writings of great thinkers down through history.

____ 24. Standards and testing are of the utmost importance in schools.

____ 25. Traditional teaching methods, primarily those that are teacher directed, work best.

____ 26. Choices in what and how to learn are important.

____ 27. Curriculum should be established that does not change regardless of shifts in society.

____ 28. Standardization, tracking, and testing should have a minor role, if any, in the classroom.

____ 29. Student differences are not important when determining what and how to teach.

____ 30. Exploration and discovery are major factors in student learning.

Place the number you chose representing your level of agreement beside each of the following item numbers. Then find the sum of each column.

ITEM	MY #	ITEM	MY #
2		1	
4		3	
5		6	
8		7	
10		9	
12		11	
15		13	
17		14	
19		16	
21		18	
23		20	
24		22	
25		26	
27		28	
29		30	
Sum A =		Sum B =	

- *If Sum A is larger than Sum B, your views of schools and teaching tend to be more* ***teacher centered****. We examine two philosophies within the teacher-centered category.*
- *If Sum B is larger than Sum A, your views of schools and teaching tend to be more* ***student centered****. We examine three philosophies within the student-centered category.*

You may sense a need to alter some of your responses as you learn more, and that's a very healthy thing to do. The more we know, the more we grow.

7.1 What Were the Major Influences, Issues, Ideologies, and Individuals in 17th-Century American Education?

7.1 Identify major influences, issues, ideologies, and individuals in 17th-century American education.

Schools in the 17th century were established by the Europeans who settled along the eastern coast of what would become the United States of America.

Context for Change

The founding of Jamestown, Virginia, in 1607 by roughly 100 men is used to mark the formal beginning of North America's colonization. Previous voyages to the New World were mostly prompted by the hope of finding riches. The English Puritan religious sect that settled in Plymouth, Massachusetts, 13 years later included men, women, and children. Families came to begin new lives in a place where they hoped to be free to worship their God in their chosen ways. Culturally, the first colonists had their roots in England; religiously, the first colonists opposed the Church of England because it lacked tolerance for any doctrine other than its own. The Church of England in the 17th century was an extension of the English government. To escape being forced to abide by the Church of England's doctrine, the Puritans, who held that the Bible in its literal (or pure) form is the source of all wisdom, sought to establish English-style colonies with their own biblical interpretations to guide them. However, they were not particularly more tolerant than the Church of England they had escaped. For instance, because one of the prominent Puritans of the 17th century, Roger Williams, espoused separation of church and state, he was banished from the Massachusetts Bay Colony to what is now Rhode Island.

The Puritans believed that people were basically sinful and that children would remain so if they could not ward off Satan by reading the Bible and faithfully upholding its principles. To the Puritans, children were merely small adults who needed to learn scripture. Play was considered a waste of time, and discipline was stern (Pulliam and Van Patten, 2013). This attitude carried over into early American schools.

Some of the events of the 17th and subsequent centuries are depicted on the timeline in Figure 7.1. Notice that selected events of American history are alongside momentous events in U.S. public education to provide context for what you read in this chapter. Refer to Figure 7.1 often as you progress through the centuries.

Figure 7.1 Education in Historical Perspective

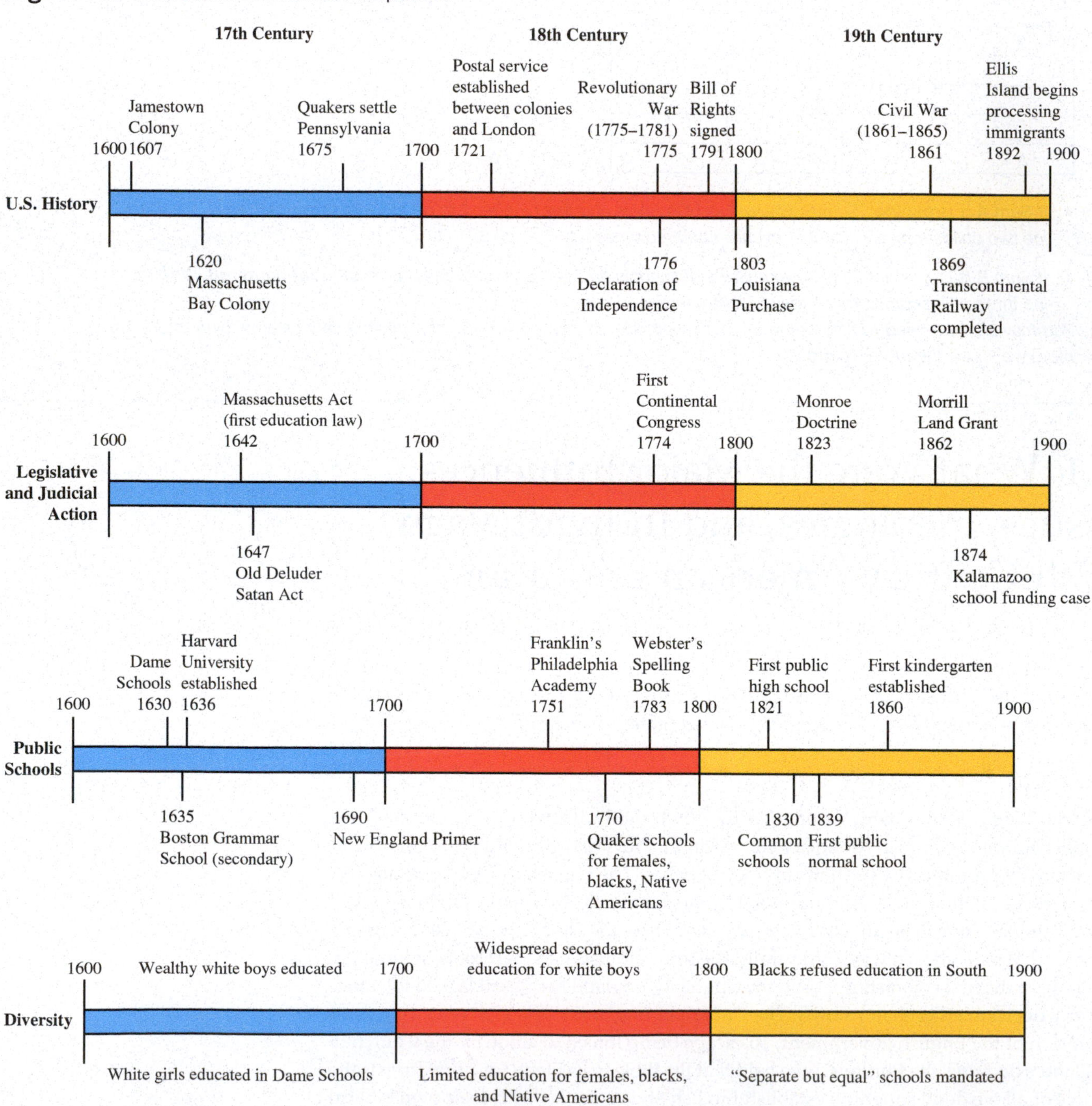

17th-Century American Schools

The early colonists recognized the need to provide schooling for their children, at least for their male children. They also knew that learning a trade was perhaps best accomplished by working with an expert artisan. Later, as colonies flourished in New England, more formal types of schools grew in number and variety in the mid-Atlantic area and the South.

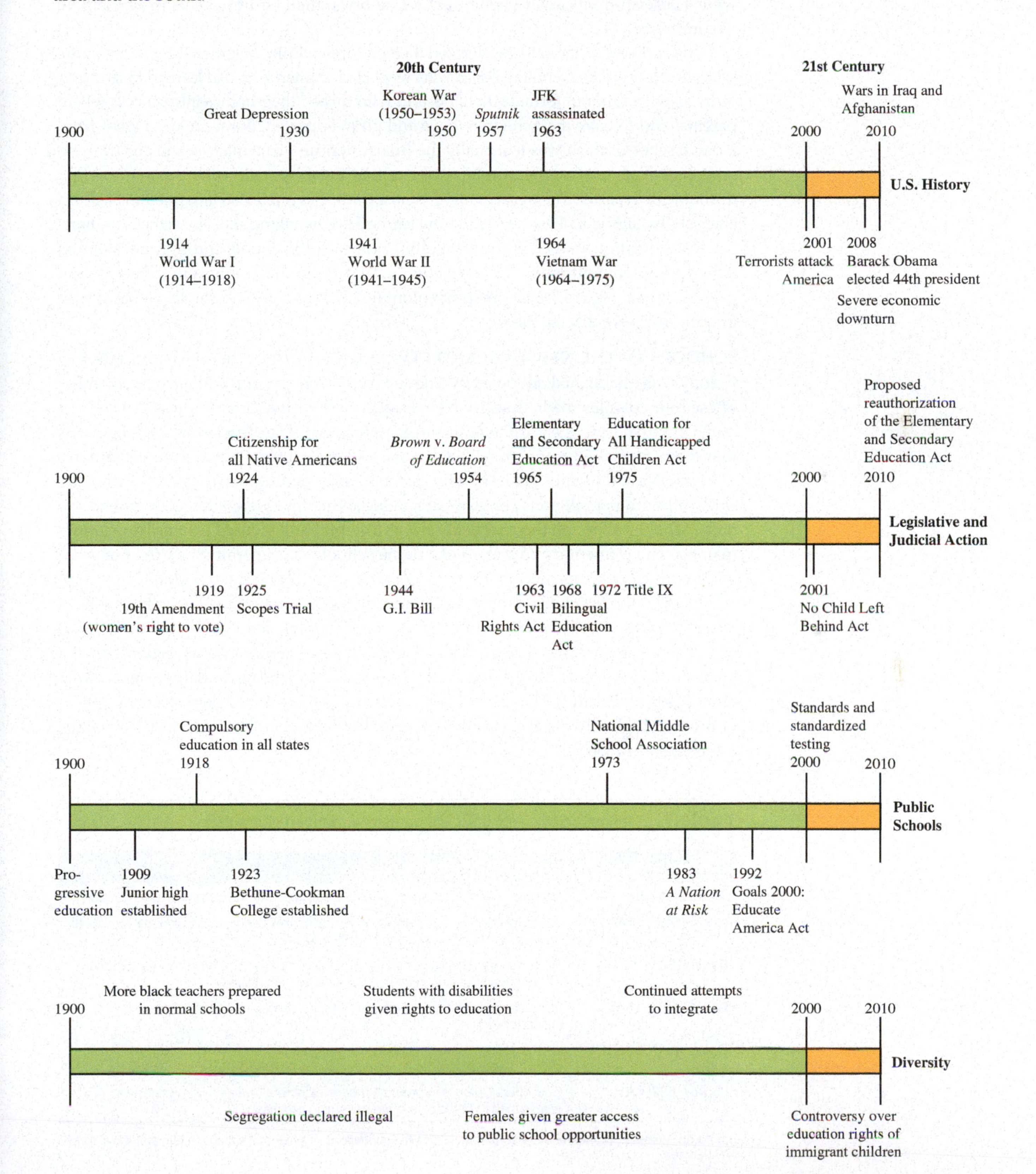

EARLY COLONIAL SCHOOLS. Having left England and suffered the hardships of the transatlantic voyage to the New World, the Puritans established an early type of schooling influenced both by European theorists, some of whom are listed in Table 7.1, and by Puritan religious beliefs and social customs. Although the first colonial schools were established for religious purposes, by teaching students to read and write, the schools helped the secular aspects of society to develop and prosper as well. These students, overwhelmingly white boys, then had the skills to participate in commerce.

The earliest Puritan settlers educated their children within their own homes, but **dame schools** soon became common. *Dames* were respected women who had learned to read and write, usually without formal schooling, and who turned their homes into schools where parents paid to have their children (boys and girls) educated. Some children went from a dame school, which was essentially the first American elementary school, or from no schooling at all, to an apprenticeship that required them (virtually all boys) to move into the home of a master. The master taught them a trade and often also taught them basic literacy skills. Girls usually stayed home and learned homemaking skills from their mothers.

As education moved from individual homes into schools throughout colonial America, notable differences in education emerged among colonies in different geographic areas. Figure 7.2 is a map of colonial America showing the three basic geographic areas we discuss next.

SCHOOLS IN THE NEW ENGLAND COLONIES. In 1630, the Massachusetts Bay Colony was established, followed by Rhode Island, Connecticut, and New Hampshire. These four colonies made up early New England. Their inhabitants tended to be very much alike, sharing the Puritan faith and English roots. They tended to settle in towns that made formal education a relatively easy endeavor. Dame schools were commonplace for New England children, who learned basic reading, writing, and arithmetic skills, all within a religious context. Girls in New England were allowed to attend the dame schools, although their curriculum was different and focused primarily on homemaking. The elementary education of a dame school was generally the extent of what girls received in terms of formal schooling for much of the colonial period.

In 1635, the first **Latin grammar school** was established in Boston for boys whose families could afford education beyond the dame school. The word *grammar* is associated with elementary school today but was a term for secondary schools in the 17th century. Students learned higher levels of reading, writing, and arithmetic, along with classical literature. The Latin grammar schools were considered the forerunners of modern high schools and specifically prepared boys to attend Harvard University, established in 1636.

Table 7.1 Influence of major theorists on early American education

Theorist	Summary of Influence
Erasmus (1466–1536)	Need for systematic training of teachers; liberal arts education includes classics
Luther (1483–1546)	Education necessary for religious instruction; education should include vocational training; need for free and compulsory education
Calvin (1509–1564)	Education serves religious and political establishments; elementary education for all; secondary education for leaders; emphasis on literacy
Bacon (1561–1626)	Education should advance scientific inquiry; provide rationale for development of critical thinking skills
Comenius (1592–1670)	Learning must come through the senses; general body of knowledge (*paideia*) should be possessed by all
Locke (1632–1704)	Goal of education is to promote the development of reason and morality to enable men to participate in the governing process

Based on: Webb, L. D., Metha, A., & Jordan, K. F. (2017). *Foundations of American education* (8th ed.). New York, NY: Pearson.

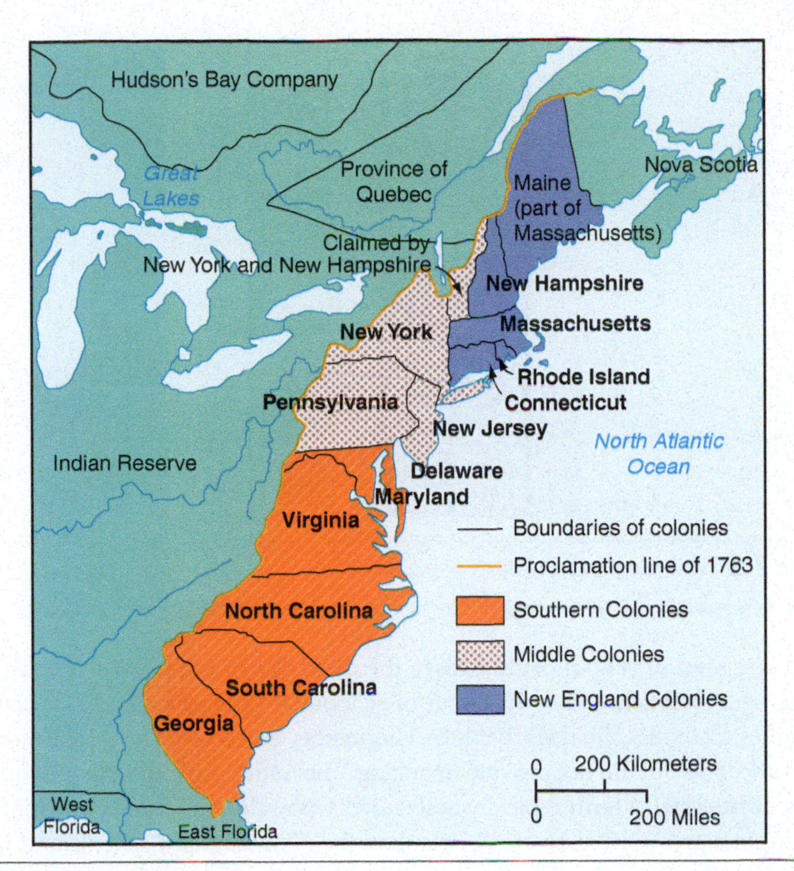

Figure 7.2 The original 13 colonies

Only the wealthiest New Englanders went beyond dame schools. Schooling opportunities and apprenticeships for white boys from poorer families were either less desirable or nonexistent. Girls, African Americans, and Native Americans had even fewer opportunities for educational advancement.

Some Puritan leaders recognized the benefits of educating all children, at least all white children. The **Massachusetts Act of 1642** was the first **compulsory education law** in the New World. Although the law required all white children to attend school, it did not specify how or where children would get an education. Nor did the law provide funding, making it the first **unfunded mandate,** a legally enforceable law without provision for monetary support. Five years later, the **Massachusetts Act of 1647,** also known as the **Old Deluder Satan Act** because education was considered the best way to fight the devil, established that every town of 50 or more households must provide a school. Again, no funding was attached, and either parents or the whole community contributed to supporting a school and a teacher. These two acts, along with Puritan determination, led to the New England colonies having about the same literacy rate as England by 1700.

The *New England Primer* was first published in 1690 for children in upper elementary and secondary levels. The book was a perfect example of the interrelatedness of education and religion in colonial New England. Published for over 150 years with few substantial changes over its lifetime, the *New England Primer* included a spelling guide based on the alphabet denoted in brief rhymes and pictures. It also included the Lord's Prayer, the Apostles' Creed, the Ten Commandments, a list of the books of the Bible, and the numbers 1 to 100. Figure 7.3 contains a sample from the *New England Primer*.

SCHOOLS IN THE MIDDLE COLONIES. New York, New Jersey, Pennsylvania, and Delaware made up the middle colonies. Their population was much less homogeneous than that of New England. Settlers came from Sweden, the Netherlands, Germany, France, and other parts of Europe, along with people of the Quaker faith who primarily settled in Pennsylvania.

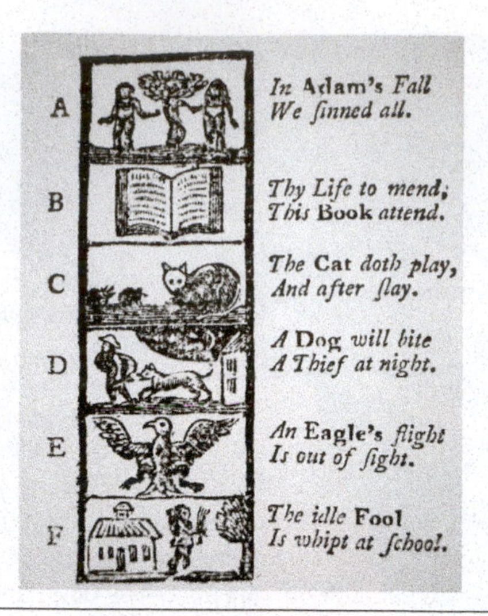

A
In Adam's Fall
We ſinned all.
B
Thy Life to mend,
This Book attend.
C
The Cat doth play,
And after ſlay.
D
A Dog will bite
A Thief at night.
E
An Eagle's flight
Is out of ſight.
F
The idle Fool
Is whipt at ſchool.

Figure 7.3 *New England Primer*

Based on: American School/Private Collection/Peter Newark American Pictures/Bridgeman Images

No one kind of school could satisfy the diversity of the middle colonists. Each religious sect established its own brand of schooling: Lutherans, Presbyterians, Jews, Mennonites, Catholics, Quakers, Baptists, Huguenots, and so on. The colonies attempted to license schools but did not provide financing. The middle colony schools were mostly private, or *parochial,* a term typically associated with religion. These parochial schools often taught a greater variety of subjects than the New England schools and included topics such as business, bookkeeping, and navigation.

SCHOOLS IN THE SOUTHERN COLONIES. Like the middle colonies, the southern colonies were settled by diverse groups, but the settlers were even more widespread geographically. In Virginia, Maryland, Georgia, and the Carolinas, more so than in New England or the middle colonies, opportunities for education were based almost exclusively on social class. Children of plantation owners and wealthy merchants either attended private schools or were taught at home by tutors. These privileged students went from elementary to secondary schools either in the South or in Europe. Children who lived on small farms or children of laborers experienced whatever education was available through charity schools run by people who believed education should be more widely available, apprentice programs, or church schools. The children of slaves received no formal education in the southern colonies during the 17th century.

Teachers in Colonial America

During the 17th century there was no formal system of teacher preparation. The closest parallel would have been apprentices assigned to Quaker teachers, who themselves lacked formal training in the education of both children and teachers. In dame schools the teachers were widows or housewives who could read and write to some unspecified degree of proficiency. Men who taught in the first elementary schools often did so for very short periods of time before beginning official training for the ministry or law.

Many teachers were indentured servants who taught in exchange for passage to the New World. Often, people were teachers because they were not successful in other occupations; some were even of questionable character or conduct. Teachers in the secondary schools (Latin grammar schools) enjoyed more status than those in elementary-level schools. They often had more education themselves, and many had college training.

Many teachers in both the 17th and 18th centuries participated in the curious custom of **boarding 'round.** To save lodging money, towns required teachers to live with the families of their students for 1 week at a time. This practice did nothing for the dignity of the teacher or the profession. Pay was low, about what farmhands made, and without permanent homes, teachers often thought of themselves as expendable part-time employees.

Today, the majority of what students know about history is taught by K–12 teachers. Far from expendable, teachers use every resource at their disposal to enhance student learning. One social media tool that is proving useful in all subjects, but particularly in teaching history, is *Google Docs*. Through this Internet tool, teachers can create virtual packets of information, including primary source documents, videos, photos, lists of resources, and so on, to go with the standards they are teaching. *Google Docs* are instantly available to all students on a variety of Internet-accessible devices. Read more about *Google Docs* in this chapter's *SocialMEdia* feature.

SocialMEdia

Google Docs, a free web-based suite of services offered by Google, was introduced to the public in 2010. This productive tool allows you to create and edit documents online while collaborating in real time with other users. It's simple and intuitive to use. There's no software to purchase and never a charge for creating or uploading documents, presentations, spreadsheets, forms, and drawings that may be kept personal, shared for others to view, or shared for others to work on collaboratively with you. There's even a chat feature.

For teaching and learning, there are many ideas for using *Google Docs* in the classroom, including:

- Teachers can load primary sources and photos, and students have access to them instantly.
- Students can work on writing projects, with peers and/or teachers adding comments and edits.
- A team of students can work on a project from anywhere in real time, with all participants seeing additions and questions at the same time.
- Surveys and forms can be easily created and completed, with results available on a spreadsheet.
- Thousands of templates are included for drawing, forms, surveys, and so on.
- Collaborative brainstorming is possible, with participants adding information in creative webs to show connection of ideas.
- Students can do homework and assignments together.
- Student DropBoxes can collect student work and organize it for teachers.

You can find a *Google Docs* tutorial on YouTube.

Check Your Understanding 7.1

7.2 What Were the Major Influences, Issues, Ideologies, and Individuals in 18th-Century American Education?

7.2 Identify major influences, issues, ideologies, and individuals in 18th-century American education.

The first half of the 18th century was characterized by geographic expansion on American soil and the maturation of the economic and political climate. In perspective, it was relatively calm in terms of history and schools when compared to the second half.

Context for Change

Representatives to the First Continental Congress (1774) in Philadelphia met originally to discuss how to claim their rights as British citizens in America. However, the Declaration of Independence soon followed, as did the writing of the U.S. Constitution, and then the Bill of Rights. The United States of America was rapidly taking shape.

Future leaders, such as Benjamin Franklin (1706–1790) and Thomas Jefferson (1743–1826), were born and grew up not only to pave the way for the new nation but also to influence the direction in which 18th-century education was heading.

Benjamin Franklin (1706–1790)

B Christopher/Alamy Stock Photo

A pudgy, bookish man with long curly hair and little square glasses, flying a kite in the middle of a thunderstorm, is the image most have of Ben Franklin. Inventor and philosopher extraordinaire, Franklin contributed to American education in many valuable ways. In the mid-18th century, he espoused educating America's youth in the practical and useful arts and trades. In addition to the traditional study of reading and math, Franklin was the first to propose the study of history that included not just past politics and wars but also customs and commerce. He founded the Library Company of Philadelphia in 1731 to promote reading by subscription to help tradesmen and farmers become as intelligent as gentlemen of other countries. In his *Proposals Relating to Education of the Youth of Pennsylvania* (1749), Franklin said that wise men view the education of youth as "the surest foundation of . . . happiness" (Franklin, 1931, p. 151).

Franklin (1749/1931*); Good (*1964*).*

18th-Century American Schools

In 1751, Benjamin Franklin established the Franklin Academy, a school that was oriented toward real-world, useful learning. The Franklin Academy offered mathematics, astronomy, navigation, accounting, bookkeeping, French, and Spanish. One significant contribution of the Franklin Academy was its provision for students to choose some courses, the forerunner of today's electives.

Private **academies** sprang up across the nation. These schools were designed to teach content intended to prepare students to participate in business and trade. They met not only intellectual needs but also economic needs. In addition to these academies, **town schools** were established for whole communities. Although some schools still limited curriculum to reading, writing, and the classics, specialized schools in the form of academies became popular.

Thomas Jefferson had political, practical, and intellectual motives for his interest in and attention to education. He believed that education was essential to the maintenance of a viable republic. Education, in Jefferson's view, would increase production and preserve health. In 1779, he proposed the Virginia Bill for the More General Diffusion of Knowledge, which provided for broader availability of education for more children. Jefferson's bill did not pass the Virginia legislature, but it raised awareness of the need and potential value of education among both lawmakers and the public (Good, 1964).

Thomas Jefferson (1743–1826)

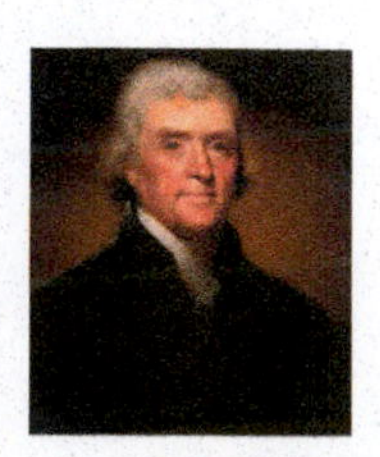
John Parrot/Stocktrek Images/Alamy Stock Photo

As author of the Declaration of Independence and serving as the third president of the United States (1801–1809), Thomas Jefferson believed that only through education could people preserve freedom and promote their own happiness. Historian S. Alexander Rippa (1997) said of Jefferson that "none has so consistently viewed public education as the indispensable cornerstone of freedom" (p. 55). Jefferson believed that government must be by the consent of the governed, and he wanted those governed to read. In fact, he suggested to President John Adams that anyone who was given the opportunity to learn to read but didn't, should not be allowed to vote. President Adams disagreed with this idea.

Disappointed by the refusal of the Virginia House of Burgesses to pass his Bill for the More General Diffusion of Knowledge, Jefferson spent the years following his presidency establishing the University of Virginia (UVA). It was truly his university in the beginning. He designed both the curriculum and the buildings, bought the trees and designed the landscaping, purchased the library books, chose the faculty, and admitted the first class of students. Thomas Jefferson died on July 4, 1826, 1 year after UVA opened and exactly 50 years following the adoption of the Declaration of Independence.

*Good (*1964*); Rippa (*1997*)*

In the 18th century many Quakers came to America . They believed that education should be all-inclusive. In 1770, Quakers in Philadelphia established a school for elementary students that included girls, African Americans, and Native Americans. In the South, however, formal education for African and Native Americans was nonexistent, despite a high literacy rate for white men and women. In Virginia, for example, 9 of 10 white men, and 2 of 3 white women were able to read (Button and Provenzo, 1989).

Noah Webster (1758–1843) had a profound influence on 18th-century American schools, particularly because of his writing. His most important work was the *American Spelling Book,* published in 1783. Some scholars say Webster had more influence on American education than anyone else in the 18th century and have referred to him as "Schoolmaster of the Republic" (Webb, Metha, and Jordan, 2017).

Several colleges were established in the colonies prior to the American Revolution, among them Yale University in 1701, the University of Pennsylvania in 1753, Brown University in 1764, and Dartmouth College in 1769. At first, theology was the most popular degree; later, other majors such as law, medicine, and commerce increased in popularity (Cohen, 1974).

18th-Century Teachers

As was true in the 17th-century, teachers in the 18th century continued to be undervalued in most of colonial America. In Loeper's (1973) *Going to School in 1776,* we find accounts of teachers who plowed fields and did menial tasks during the summer to support themselves in the winter while teaching. One in particular, Mistress Robbins, was hired to be a teacher at the age of 17 because she could read from the Old Testament without stumbling over the big words. Once hired, she found her responsibilities included physically taking care of the schoolhouse. She had to resort to severe corporal (physical) punishment to control the older boys whom she reported as threatening, lawless, and profane. Because of low pay, Mistress Robbins was forced to live with her students' families or, as it was called, to *board 'round.*

Education as a Priority

Education received a boost in priority with the passage of the **Northwest Land Ordinance of 1787,** which divided federally owned wilderness land into townships and required the building of schools. Article Three of the Ordinance proclaimed, "Religion, morality, and knowledge being necessary to good government and the happiness of mankind, schools and the means of education shall be forever encouraged."

Education is not directly mentioned in the **U.S. Constitution ratified in 1788.** However, the Tenth Amendment in the Bill of Rights states, "The powers not delegated

Noah Webster (1758–1843)

More than any other education statesman of the late 18th and early 19th centuries, Noah Webster reshaped the English language and literature into America's own. He was intensely patriotic and believed that the United States needed not only political independence from Europe but also cultural independence. The enormous success of Webster's *American Spelling Book*, which included moral stories, lists of words, and a pronunciation guide, put an end to the importing of English books to be used as textbooks. Webster believed in free education for all American boys and girls. Interestingly, he saw the education of women as an absolute necessity because they are the first teachers of children. A Yale graduate, member of the Massachusetts legislature, lawyer, writer, scholar, and businessman, Noah Webster had a tremendous impact on American education.

Good (1964); Gutek (2011); Webb et al. (2017)

B Christopher/Alamy Stock Photo

to the United States by the Constitution, nor prohibited by it to the states, are reserved to the States respectively, or to the people." Thus, from the inception of the United States to the present, except for the occasional federal mandate, states have grappled independently with educational issues.

As the new nation of the United States of America approached the 19th century, a surge of energy was directed toward education. Leaders and policies emerged that would place American education squarely in the foreground of thought and action.

Check Your Understanding 7.2

7.3 What Were the Major Influences, Issues, Ideologies, and Individuals in 19th-Century American Education

7.3 Identify major influences, issues, ideologies, and individuals in 19th-century American education.

The 19th century was one of unprecedented growth, both geographically and governmentally.

Context for Change

In 1800, American geography lessons included maps showing 17 states. By the end of the century, maps of America boasted 45 states. During this century, the United States established a functioning and flourishing economy, endured a protracted test of the strength of its union (the Civil War), and matured into a stable, respected political entity.

With the election of President Andrew Jackson in 1828, the birth of the Democratic Party brought changes to American politics, turning a nation governed largely by an aristocratic society to one based in greater measure on government of, by, and for the people. Westward expansion propelled by the continuing desire for individual independence and opportunity took the growing nation all the way to the Pacific Ocean.

Cultural and economic differences between an increasingly industrialized North and an agrarian South grew and festered in the 19th century. The rift erupted into the Civil War in 1861 as southern states seceded from the Union and formed the Confederacy.

Although the most commonly perceived reason for the Civil War is slavery, other actual issues surrounding the onset of hostilities revolved around states' rights and economics. Over 600,000 Americans on both sides lost their lives before the North and South were reunited in 1865.

Of all the issues facing the American population as the nineteenth century drew to a close, the most significant were associated with the Industrial Revolution. Poverty-level wages, a workforce that would soon include too many children, unchecked immigration, and abysmal working conditions all reflected poorly on the country's ability to cope with the abuses actually brought about by its wonderful spirit of inventiveness. Each of these issues would have to be faced and solved, and the educational system revamped to meet the needs of the more commerce- and industry-based society that was on the horizon.

19th-Century American Schools

The 19th century in the United States was characterized by a wide variety of schools. There were town schools, primarily in the northern states; charity schools, run by churches and philanthropic groups; and widely varying dame schools serving as small venues for local education. Religious schools grew as families banded together with others of the same denomination and country of origin. Academies of all descriptions, some prestigious and some humble, flourished in the first half of the 19th century. In the South, most educational opportunities still belonged to the wealthy; in the West, most frontier children did not attend school. The obvious lack of consistency and opportunity did not mirror the ideals of America's founders, who saw education as a means to accomplish the goal stated in the Preamble of the U.S. Constitution to "promote the general Welfare."

On the post–Civil War education front, one fact was crystal clear: Both the classical educational system popular in the Northeast and the one-room schoolhouse approach adopted during western frontier days were increasingly incapable of meeting the needs of the country. Let's look at some of the categories of schools developed in 19th-century America.

COMMON SCHOOLS. The system of free public schools that exists today had its beginnings in the common schools movement, first established about 1830. **Common schools** were community-supported elementary schools for *all* children established in response to a variety of economic, social, and political factors. This was a radical departure from previous schooling that catered primarily to wealthy males. Think about it— *all* children. Because free public education for all children was a new concept, common schools were debated, with many citizens seeing their value and others remaining skeptical, as illustrated in Table 7.2. Horace Mann was the champion of common schools. In fact, he was widely regarded as a champion of children in general and of the basic American ideal of opportunity for all.

Table 7.2 Merits of and objections to the common school from various viewpoints

Group	Merits
From the viewpoint of . . .	**Common schools provided . . .**
The working class	Avenues for social and economic mobility
Some in business and industry	An increase in the supply of literate and trained workers
Social groups	Means of controlling crime and social unrest
People of the frontier	Symbols of civilization and ways to keep literacy and citizenship alive in the wilderness
Group	**Objections**
From the viewpoint of . . .	**Common schools were objectionable because . . .**
Private school proponents	Free schools meant fewer private school students
Some in business and industry	A decrease in the workforce of children who opted for school instead of jobs
Some political leaders	Apprehensions that an overeducated citizenry might question authority

Application Exercise 7.1: Table 7.2 Merits of and objections to the common school from various viewpoints

In common schools, and most other schools of the 19th century, the works of William Holmes McGuffey had the most significant impact on what children learned. McGuffey's books differed from the unimaginative literature of previous centuries and included stories that promoted truth, honesty, and hard work.

W. H. McGuffey (1800–1873)

Mary Evans Picture Library/The Image Works

Far from the overly pious and drab books that first appeared in American schools and painted a dreary picture of the worth of children, W. H. McGuffey's six-volume set of *McGuffey's Readers* included stories and poetry that appealed to the interests of students. The volumes were geared to specific levels and paved the way for the separation of elementary school into grade levels. The volumes sold over 1 million copies between 1836 and 1906 and helped students learn to read and study while instilling in them virtues such as patriotism, morality, and a work ethic. McGuffey, as a minister, professor, and college president, indelibly left his mark on American education.

McNergney and McNergney (2009); Webb et al. (2017)

As common schools increased in number, their inconsistencies became more and more apparent. Some were housed in acceptable buildings with adequate supplies and appropriate heating and lighting. Other common schools were housed in dilapidated, poorly heated and lit, filthy surroundings.

SECONDARY SCHOOLS. When the English Classical School opened for young men in Boston in 1821, it marked the beginning of the public high school. In 1824, the school's name was changed to the Boston English High School. In 1838, a coeducational high school opened in Philadelphia. This school offered three tracks: a classical (Latin) curriculum (4 years), a modern language curriculum (4 years), and an English curriculum (2 years) (Webb et al., 2017).

Before the Civil War, high schools were almost exclusively found in the North and always in cities. Because children could learn to read in common schools, and reading was considered sufficient education by many citizens, high schools were slow to grow in number.

In the aftermath of the Civil War, with Reconstruction and rapidly growing industrialization, economic growth spurred the establishment of more schools—not just common schools but also secondary schools. High schools began to flourish about 1850, and by 1870, they had replaced academies as the dominant secondary school. In 1874, a case in the Michigan Supreme Court called the **Kalamazoo case** established that the legislature could tax for support of both common and secondary schools, propelling public high schools into school systems in every state.

Sara Davis Powell

The common school movement made it possible for some African American children to be educated in public schools.

KINDERGARTEN. Early childhood education in the United States developed after elementary (common schools) and high schools (secondary schools). In Europe, Swiss educator Johann Pestalozzi (1746–1827) developed the theory of child-centered education and the concept of individual differences among children. German educator Friedrich Froebel (1782–1852) agreed with Pestalozzi, but he took child-centered education further. Froebel was a proponent of an activity-based curriculum in an early childhood setting, where children are encouraged to be creative and expressive. This setting was called a *kindergarten*, or "children's garden." The first kindergarten in the United States was established in 1860 in Boston. By 1873, kindergartens had become part of many public school systems (Chartock, 2004).

Friedrich Froebel (1782–1852)

When the first English-speaking kindergarten in the United States opened in Boston in 1860, it was the direct result of the work of Friedrich Froebel, widely viewed as the father of the kindergarten or "children's garden." Froebel thought of young children as flowers that would blossom into healthy adults if given the opportunity to be creative in an active curriculum. His emphasis on self-development and self-expression is the theoretical basis for early childhood education.

Johnson, Musial, Hall, Golnick, and Dupuis (2011)

C.W. Bardeen/Library of Congress Prints and Photographs Division

With the establishment of kindergarten, common school, and high school, the need for specially prepared teachers grew.

Teacher Preparation

Before Horace Mann's proposal that teachers receive special training, few completed any form of secondary education. Teachers were inadequately and inconsistently prepared. Notable exceptions were the teachers prepared at the Troy Female Seminary, the first institution of higher learning for women in the United States, established in Troy, New York, in 1821 by Emma Willard (1787–1870). The first **normal school,** a publicly funded institution dedicated exclusively to preparing teachers, was established 18 years later, in 1839 in Lexington, Massachusetts. Catherine Beecher (1800–1878), along with Horace Mann, was instrumental in making teacher preparation a priority in normal schools.

As the first specially prepared teachers entered their classrooms, they seldom encountered children with disabilities, children of color, or children of poor immigrants. This situation would change with time.

19th-Century Education for Children with Disabilities, Minorities, and Immigrants

The 19th century was marked by meager, yet important, advances in education for children with disabilities, children of color, and children of poor immigrants.

CHILDREN WITH DISABILITIES. Social mores of the day demanded that any educational opportunities for children with disabilities be separate from those for children without disabilities. A few innovative schools were established in the 19th century for students with certain disabilities. In 1817, Thomas Gallaudet established the first school

Emma Willard (1787–1870)

While boarding schools were teaching girls how to be polite, proper wives who could serve tea and make genteel conversation, Emma Willard was formulating plans for a school to teach girls and women useful, solid skills in homemaking as well as content and pedagogy to enable them to be teachers or to enter other professions. In 1821, she established the Troy Female Seminary, the first institution of higher learning for girls. Before the first normal school was established in 1839 by Horace Mann and others, the Troy Seminary had prepared over 200 teachers. Willard is also credited with the establishment of home economics as a legitimate subject area. She wrote textbooks, traveled extensively, and was a lifelong activist for women's rights.

Chartock (2004); *Good* (1964); *Webb et al.* (2017)

Everett Collection/ Alamy Stock Photo

Horace Mann (1796–1859)

Everett Collection Historical/ Alamy Stock Photo

Widely known as the Father of American Education, Horace Mann had a profound influence not only on early American schools but also on modern schools. He believed that regular attendance in schools with quality teachers would serve to equalize opportunities for poor, African American, and disabled children. He vigorously advocated for common schools.

As attorney and state legislator turned education advocate, Mann established the first *normal school* in 1839 in Lexington, Massachusetts. Normal schools proved to be incredibly important as 2-year colleges specifically designed to prepare teachers. Mann was not afraid of controversy as he pushed for separation of church and schools—not a popular stance in 19th-century America. Even as an avowed religious man, he was often criticized from church pulpits. As the first secretary of education for the Massachusetts Board of Education, which he helped establish in 1837, and throughout his life, Horace Mann spoke eloquently and worked tirelessly as a champion of schools and students.

Not only was Horace Mann an advocate for free quality education but he also worked for the abolition of slavery and the limiting of alcohol as a social problem. In addition, he was a vocal supporter of women's rights.

*Chartock (*2004)

Catherine Beecher (1800–1878)

Historical/Corbis via Getty Images

Although Catherine Beecher's sister, Harriet Beecher Stowe, author of *Uncle Tom's Cabin*, may have more name recognition, Catherine had a great impact on the establishment of teacher training schools, or normal schools. In 1832, she established the Western Institute for Women, partially because she saw a need for better educated teachers. The institute was not publicly funded and did not prepare teachers exclusively, but it spawned other institutions of higher learning for women. In 1839, Beecher, along with Horace Mann and others, started the first publicly supported normal school for teacher preparation.

*Holmes and Weiss (*1995)

for the deaf in Hartford, Connecticut. In the mid-19th century, physician Samuel Howe was influential in the establishment of the first school for blind children: the Perkins School for the Blind in Watertown, Massachusetts (Cubberly, 1934). Mental and behavioral disabilities were not addressed in 19th-century schools.

NATIVE AMERICAN CHILDREN. In 1824, the U.S. government established the Bureau of Indian Affairs and began placing whole tribes of Native Americans on reservations. Most of what little formal schooling Native American children received was provided by missionaries, whose efforts were fueled by a desire to convert the children to Christianity. The missionary schools were not consistently organized or maintained (Chartock, 2004).

A further goal of most efforts to educate Native American children in the 19th century was **assimilation,** the attempt to make the children more like white children, the dominant culture, or, in the terms of the time, "civilizing" them. The American government built boarding schools in the latter part of the 19th century and forced thousands of Native American children to leave their homes and live in these boarding schools where attempts were made to diminish their culture in favor of the white, English-speaking social norms of the time. The boarding schools proved to be complete failures, as the Native American students ran away or returned to their reservations immediately after graduation (Webb et al., 2017).

MEXICAN AMERICAN CHILDREN. At the end of the Mexican American War in 1848, vast territories comprising what are now Arizona, California, Colorado, Nevada, New Mexico, and Utah came under U.S. control. The Mexican families who stayed in these

Teaching in Focus

Sara Davis Powell

Angelica Reynosa, a world history teacher at Roosevelt High School, California, knows that her task of helping sophomores understand historic events and their impact on today's world is a complex one. Most of the 31 students in Angelica's class are new to the United States. Some of them may have picked up English through classes at Roosevelt or simply from living in Fresno, California. Many live in homes where only Spanish is spoken. These students haven't grown up steeped in the U.S. social studies curriculum and reciting the Pledge of Allegiance each morning since they were 5 years old. As a second-generation American herself, Angelica understands at least some of her students' challenges.

Angelica has always loved to study history. She views the subject she teaches as a living, breathing entity that's filled with problem-solving scenarios and intrigue. Her teaching philosophy dictates that she engage her students, not merely give out reading assignments. The objective of the lesson featured later in Application Exercise 7.3 is "Students will participate in an activity that will help them grasp the reasons for the rise of Marxist theory. They will experience the 'haves' and 'have-nots' of the capitalist system and critically evaluate the benefits and drawbacks of capitalism and socialism." That's an ambitious objective, one that takes a great deal of thought and planning.

Many of Angelica's students fall into the have-nots, similar to the people Angelica describes in her lesson. They may be in the United States illegally, crowded into the homes of extended family while their parents look for work or hold low-paying jobs. There's so much Angelica wants them to understand about the world.

territories after the United States took over suffered discrimination much like that experienced by the Native Americans. Like Native Americans, Mexican Americans were targets of efforts at assimilation. For much of the 19th century, most Mexican American children had few, if any, educational options. When they did attend school, teachers generally tried to Americanize them, or assimilate them into the dominant culture by insisting they learn and use English and give up some of their customs (Webb et al., 2017).

Almost 2 centuries later, in 21st century America, we still find that language assimilation is desirable for productive citizenship. Angelica Reynosa, one of our focus teachers at Roosevelt High School, teaches history in a bilingual classroom. Recall from Chapter 2 that bilingual education provides classroom instruction in two languages.

AFRICAN AMERICAN CHILDREN. Although the education of Native American and Mexican American children was far from ideal and was inconsistently implemented, at least it didn't face legal objection by state or federal governments. The same cannot be said about the education of African American children in the 19th century. For example, when Prudence Crandall admitted an African American student, Sarah Harris, to the school she founded in Connecticut in 1830, the school was forced to close. Crandall reopened the school for girls and enrolled 15 African American students from other states. The Connecticut legislature subsequently passed the **Black Law,** a law that specifically forbade schools intended to educate African Americans from other states without the permission of local authorities.

Prior to the Civil War, **Black Codes** were enacted, predominantly in the South, prohibiting the education of slaves. Some white people feared that educating slaves would give the slaves a sense of self-importance and they might begin to think they were created equal and had certain inalienable rights—as stated in the Declaration of Independence. In 1850, with increasing numbers of free African Americans in the North desiring education, the Massachusetts Supreme Court upheld the decision in *Roberts v. City of Boston* that separate-but-equal schools did not violate the rights of African American children. This ruling solidified the practice of *separate but equal,* meaning that separate schools for black and white children supposedly offered the same opportunities for all children. This assumption proved to be false, with schools for African

Prudence Crandall (1803–1889)

North Wind Picture Archives/The Image Works

Way ahead of her time, and incredibly courageous, Prudence Crandall believed strongly in the rights of African American students to an education. Her Quaker roots and her own education under a noted abolitionist, Moses Brown, helped shape her steadfast belief in equal opportunity. In 1830, Crandall founded a school for neighborhood girls in Canterbury, Connecticut. When she admitted an African American girl, Sarah Harris, Crandall and her school became the target for vandalism and ostracism. White parents withdrew their daughters. When Crandall established a school populated entirely by African American girls, it was destroyed by outraged whites. Sarah Harris went on to teach many years in Louisiana, thus carrying on Prudence Crandall's legacy.

Pulliam and Van Patten (2013)

American children receiving less funding and being housed in inferior facilities (Kaplan and Owings, 2011). At the end of the 19th century, the practice was reinforced by the ruling in a similar case, *Plessy* v. *Ferguson*.

Following the Civil War, the Bureau of Refugees, Freedmen, and Abandoned Lands, more commonly referred to as the *Freedmen's Bureau,* made efforts to help African Americans find ways of making a living and settle into a free lifestyle. The Freedman's Bureau opened 3,000 schools in the South to educate African American children. By 1869, about 114,000 African American students were being educated in these schools. Along with typical school subjects, these new schools added industrial training in an effort to prepare African American students for employment (Gutek, 2011). In addition, many ex-slaves formed their own education associations that sponsored schools exclusively for African American children, staffed exclusively by African American teachers. By 1870, southern African Americans had established over 500 of these schools, resembling the earlier common schools movement (Kaplan and Owings, 2011). Hampton Institute, founded in 1868, was an institution of higher education that emphasized industrial skills and teacher preparation for African Americans.

The most famous graduate of the Hampton Institute was Booker T. Washington. Following graduation, he became Hampton's first African American teacher. Washington was a major supporter of vocational education for African Americans. He viewed learning practical skills as a way of advancing socially and economically in the United States. In 1881, Washington founded the Tuskegee Institute in rural Alabama. By 1890, Tuskegee had 88 faculty members and more than 1,200 students, making it one of the larger colleges in the South (McNergney and McNergney, 2009).

L.W. Hine/Library of Congress Prints and Photographs Division

The doctrine of *separate but equal* was evident in the United States until well past the middle of the 20th century.

ASIAN AMERICAN CHILDREN. Although their numbers were smaller than immigrants from Mexico, there were children of Asian parents in U.S. schools in the nineteenth century. Most were Chinese, who began to arrive mid-century and filled a need for laborers in an increasingly industrialized United States. The Immigration Act of 1882 slowed the arrival of people from China. In the latter part of the century, traders from India began arriving, mostly on the East Coast of the United States. Until 1886, people from Japan could not leave their country. Once the restriction was lifted, Japanese (mostly men) moved to the United States and began to fill the void for inexpensive labor created by the Chinese government's

Booker T. Washington (1856–1915)

As a steadfast believer that education was the way to advance socially and economically, Booker T. Washington spent his life furthering educational opportunities for African American students. First graduating from, and then teaching at, the Hampton Institute, Washington later founded the Tuskegee Institute in Alabama in 1881. Throughout his career, Washington promoted his message that African Americans needed vocational skills to get and keep good jobs. Washington led the Tuskegee Institute until his death in 1915.

Chartock (2004); McNergney and McNergney (2009)

Frances Benjamin Johnston/Library of Congress Prints and Photographs Division

crackdown on emigration. (Note that to *emigrate* means to leave one's country. When people emigrate, they become *immigrants* in their destination country.)

CHILDREN OF POOR IMMIGRANTS. The United States is a nation of immigrants. The country's motto, *E Pluribus Unum,* means "from many, one." The issue of how to educate the *many* and have a strong *one* is not new. From 1870 to 1900, the United States experienced an influx of almost 12 million immigrants, many from Mexico, Asia, and Eastern Europe, and many whose primary language was not English (Boyer and Stuckey, 2005).

Many immigrants were very poor, but their skills were needed in the rapid industrialization of the United States. As the economy grew, so did the tax base for supporting free elementary schools and high schools. The number of free public schools increased dramatically as the country attempted to cope with its industrial growth and, with the many coming to its shores, to become one nation.

Most poor immigrants in the 19th century had no means of providing for their families when they first arrived in the United States, generally in the already heavily populated cities of New York and Chicago. **Settlement houses** were established by reformers to address the problems of urban poverty. These were community service centers that provided educational opportunities, skills training, and cultural events. Jane Addams (1860–1935), who was raised in a wealthy Quaker home, established Hull House, the most famous of the settlement houses, in Chicago in 1889.

Higher Education

In 1862, President Lincoln signed a congressional bill called the **Morrill Act.** Through this act the government granted states 30,000 acres of land for every senator and representative it had in Congress in 1860. The income the states could generate from

Jane Addams (1860–1935)

Raised in a wealthy home with an abolitionist Quaker father, Jane Addams set her sights on becoming a doctor. However, because of back problems, she quit her studies and determined to dedicate her life to helping the urban poor. She founded Hull House in an old, run-down Chicago mansion. Located in the middle of an immigrant neighborhood, Hull House provided education for both children and adults. Addams recruited college-educated young women to work at Hull House. Many later used what they learned there to propel them to make their own contributions to social reform. For years Hull House served as a model for other successful settlement houses, which numbered almost 100 by 1900.

Addams tirelessly promoted women's suffrage (right to vote) and was president of the Women's International League for Peace and Freedom from 1919 until her death in 1935. In 1931, she received the Nobel Peace Prize.

Boyer and Stuckey (2005)

Hulton Archive/Getty Images

this land was to be used to support at least one college. The **Second Morrill Act of 1890** further stipulated that no grants would be given to states where college admission was denied because of race unless the state provided a separate-but-equal institution. As a result of the Morrill legislation, 65 land-grant colleges were established, including the universities of Maine (1865), Illinois (1867), and California (1868); Purdue University (1869); and Texas A&M (1871) (Rippa, 1997).

As colleges flourished, more progressive ways of educating children and adolescents also began to grow. The discussion of 20th-century education begins with progressive education, first introduced at the close of the 19th century.

Check Your Understanding 7.3

7.4 What Were the Major Influences, Issues, Ideologies, and Individuals in 20th-Century American Education?

7.4 Identify major influences, issues, ideologies, and individuals in 20th-century American education.

Varying population patterns, American inventiveness, wars, and technology made the 20th century one of extremes.

Context for Change

In the 20th century, America survived two world wars; numerous regional conflicts in Korea, Vietnam, and elsewhere; and a protracted period of dire economic stress. It also thrived in years of unprecedented economic prosperity. The populace of the United States grew increasingly aware of its own diversity. Periods of rampant racial tension necessitated healing and both legal and educational responses on a national level.

Technological advances took Americans to the moon and beyond, enhanced communication of all sorts, and brought about global awareness unimagined in other centuries. In schools, the beginning of the century ushered in more of the components of John Dewey's progressive education into classrooms.

Progressive Education

In 1896, John Dewey established the first laboratory school at the University of Chicago to test the principles of **progressive education.** The progressive method was very different from the traditional 19th-century approach to education. What started with students learning in cooperative groups and letting their interests guide what they learned about traditional subjects grew into a major movement with far-reaching implications. The influence of John Dewey was tremendous as the United States moved from the 19th to the 20th century.

The progressive movement gained momentum during the first quarter of the 20th century and flourished until the end of World War II. The influences of progressivism are still evident today in the 21st century. The basic principles of progressive education are summarized in Figure 7.4. These principles show the sharp contrast between the philosophy of progressivism and the established ways of conducting school discussed earlier. John Dewey's primary focus was the implementation of schooling as a means of social reform and the improvement of life for Americans.

Figure 7.4 Basic principles of progressive education

1. Education is life, not just preparation for life.
2. Learning should be directly related to the interests of the child.
3. Learning through problem solving should be emphasized more than rote memorization of subject matter.
4. The role of the teacher is to facilitate learning more so than to direct it.
5. Cooperation among students should be emphasized more than competition.
6. Democracy should be practiced to encourage the free interplay of ideas that leads to growth.

Based on: Kneller, G. F. (1971). *Introduction to the philosophy of education.* New York: Wiley.

Junior High and Middle School

The need for a bridge between elementary and high school became apparent as the high school developed into a 4-year institution and the courses taught there became more standardized in content. Educators began to delineate the kinds of preparation necessary for high school success. High school teachers and administrators asked for basic preparation in algebra and English before high school. Writers such as G. Stanley Hall began recognizing a period of life called *adolescence* and acknowledging that adolescence was different from childhood. This new viewpoint led to a change in the configuration of schools; elementary schools shifted from eight grades to five or six, and the remaining two or three grades became junior high schools. Later in the century, junior high most frequently encompassed grades 7 through 9.

In the 1960s, another concept of schooling was formed to meet the unique needs of young adolescents: the middle school. Rather than viewing grades 5 to 8 or 6 to 8 as merely a time of preparation for high school, middle school philosophy called for recognition of the unique developmental qualities of young adolescents and use of developmental appropriateness in the school, in both curriculum and instruction.

Montessori Method

Although Maria Montessori (1870–1952) was developing a philosophy of early childhood education in Italy and other parts of Europe in the beginning of the 20th century, the Montessori method was not widely implemented in the United States until the 1950s. Today, many Montessori principles can be found in early childhood settings across the United States.

John Dewey (1859–1952)

Think about all the things that happened in the United States during John Dewey's life, from the Civil War to the Korean War. He lived and wrote a very long time. In terms of education, many consider Dewey the most influential American of the 20th century. He was a professor of philosophy and pedagogy at the University of Chicago and at Columbia University. In Chicago, Dewey's son attended a school run by an ardent follower of Pestalozzi and Froebel. Dewey was so impressed with the approach of the school that he began researching, thinking, and writing about it. What we know today as progressive education was given an intellectual foundation by Dewey.

Dewey wrote more than 500 articles and 40 books, among which *The School and Society* (1900) and *The Child and the Curriculum* (1902) (see Dewey, 1991) had perhaps the greatest impact on American education. In his laboratory school at the University of Chicago, he implemented progressive education and introduced projects such as carpentry, weaving, sewing, and cooking into the curriculum. Dewey believed that education should be experiential and child centered, rather than subject driven. He proposed that education is best served when the whole child is considered, including all the aspects of development.

Library of Congress Prints and Photographs Division

John Dewey believed that democracy should be practiced not only in the governance of the United States but also in the day-to-day life of a school. Children should be free to question, investigate, and make changes in their environments. Learning the principles of democracy early in life would serve them well later as adults.

Dewey (1991); Rippa (1997).

Maria Montessori (1870–1952)

Interfoto/Personalities/ Alamy Stock Photo

A compassionate medical doctor, Maria Montessori established a children's house, a kind of school within a house, for poor children in early 20th-century Italy. As people recognized the transformation in these children, they began studying Montessori's methodology and opening other children's houses, later referred to as *Montessori schools.* As Maria Montessori herself said, "The task of the child is to construct a man [or woman] oriented to his environment, adapted to his time, place, and culture" (1967, p. xiv). She believed that children are capable of integrating aspects of the world around them through the use of their senses. Children ages 3 to 6 are the ideal participants in the Montessori method. Montessori insisted that children's environments be carefully constructed to allow them to sense their learning with materials, such as letters made of sandpaper and colored objects to count.

Chartock (2004); Good (1964); Montessori (1967)

Influential African American Leaders

W. E. B. Du Bois believed that African Americans should pursue higher education to become leaders in politics and education. He sharply disagreed with Booker T. Washington's philosophy that African Americans would best serve themselves and their race by pursuing vocational arts and skills to prepare them to compete with white people in the workplace.

Mary McLeod Bethune was influential in both education and government policy. Her long career as a teacher, as well as a college instructor and founder, took her from her home in South Carolina to college experiences in Chicago; to Florida, where she founded Bethune-Cookman College; and all the way to Washington, DC, where she served as an adviser to President Franklin D. Roosevelt in the 1930s (Chartock, 2004).

W. E. B. Du Bois (1868–1963)

Cornelius M. Battey/ Library of Congress Prints and Photographs Division

A champion of equality for Africans and African Americans, W. E. B. Du Bois spent his life as a scholar, a writer, and a reformer. In 1895, he was the first African American to earn a doctorate from Harvard University. From 1895 through the 1950s, he was a college professor and a civil rights activist. He organized worldwide conferences of black leaders. Du Bois considered Africa the homeland of all black people and wrote about the dual citizenry of black people who had left Africa in his 1903 book, *The Souls of Black Folks*. In 1907, he cofounded the National Association for the Advancement of Colored People (NAACP). Disillusioned by lack of progress for people of African descent in the United States, Du Bois embraced socialism. At age 93, he joined the Communist Party and moved to Ghana, where he died at age 95.

Boyer and Stuckey (2005)

Mary McLeod Bethune (1875–1955)

Library of Congress, Prints and Photographs Division, Carl Van Vechten Collection

Born in South Carolina of former slave parents, Mary McLeod Bethune was educated in a Presbyterian mission school and attended Moody Bible Institute in Chicago. The school in her hometown of Mayesville, South Carolina, was for whites only. Although Bethune originally wanted to be a missionary to Africa and was often quoted as saying the drums of Africa still beat in her heart, she dedicated her life to educating African American students. She established a school in Florida that became a normal school to train female African American teachers. Later, the school evolved into Bethune-Cookman College, a 4-year coeducational college with mostly African American students.

In the midst of her work with education, Bethune became good friends with Eleanor Roosevelt, who drew her into government service—specifically the National Youth Administration (NYA), a branch of the Works Progress Administration (WPA) created by President Franklin D. Roosevelt. In 1935, Bethune founded the National Council of Negro Women, an umbrella group for all organizations working on behalf of African American women.

Boyer and Stuckey (2005)

The Last Five Decades of The 20th Century

1950s. The *Leave It to Beaver,* white-bread world of Ward and June Cleaver and their two sons was experienced by many families in the United States and was considered a desirable social paradigm during the period of unprecedented economic growth and prosperity following World War II. In 1957, however, the "all's right with the world" syndrome was shaken by the Soviet launch of *Sputnik,* the first satellite to venture into space. The **National Defense Education Act of 1958** called for strengthening of science, math, and foreign language programs. Teachers were given training in the use of new methods and materials in hopes of bringing American student learning up to, and beyond, the levels of learning in other countries.

Another major factor in the American schools of the 1950s was the increasing pressure to desegregate. After all the years of separate-but-equal schools, the Supreme Court upheld the complaints of the National Association for the Advancement of Colored People (NAACP) made on behalf of a Kansas family in the now famous ***Brown* v. *Board of Education*** ruling of 1954. Chief Justice Earl Warren declared that segregating children based solely on race was wrong and illegal. Some schools integrated peacefully, but others did not. Still other segregated schools made little or no attempt to change at all.

In some parts of America, schools and school districts appear to be re-segregating, not because of laws or policies related to race, but because of socioeconomic differences. This chapter's *The Opinion Page* feature is written by an editor of a Dallas, Texas,

The Opinion Page

This Opinion Editorial appeared in The Dallas Morning News, *on May 5, 2013.*

Choosing Separate and Unequal Texas Schools

by staff writer

Sunday's Page One story about the re-segregation of public schools is sobering but can't be surprising to anyone who lives, breathes and sees. It's not something that has happened overnight or that is linked to racist policies. Rather, it is socioeconomic reality: Those with the means move away from problems and toward places where they believe their children can best succeed. To many, that means moving out of the struggling Dallas Independent School District to places such as affluent, far-northern Frisco. . . . When DISD was forced to desegregate in 1970, the district was 60 percent white. Now, it's less than 5 percent white. At a third of DISD campuses, whites make up 1 percent or less of the student body. In the last 15 years, the number of white students in DISD has dropped from 16,019 students to 7,417. Meanwhile, during that same period, the white population at Frisco ISD has gone from 2,873 to 22,973.

This isn't as much about race and ethnicity as it is class and poverty. As the series points out, some minority parents are also making the choice to flee traditional public schools by enrolling their children in charter schools.

Unlike the segregationist policies that led to the landmark Brown vs. Board of Education ruling in 1954, this re-segregation can't be addressed with a simple court ruling. It's not about laws that try to keep certain students out. It's about parents choosing to move students out. As DISD board President Lew Blackburn points out, "some racial overtones" may be part of the problem. But there's also a legitimate perception that districts such as DISD are doing a lousy job of educating students.

Regardless of the culprit, the result is the same: Kids from poorer families, who tend to be minorities, are relegated to underperforming schools because, unlike their better-off contemporaries, they have few real educational options. Such divides threaten the cohesion of a well-functioning society. We know it doesn't have to be this way. Even within DISD, examples abound of high-achieving schools with diverse populations, such as Woodrow Wilson High School and the School for the Talented and Gifted.

One part of the solution is adequate funding for schools, which the state Legislature has done a woeful job of providing. But that is just one piece of the puzzle, along with engagement by parents, commitment from students, higher expectations from teachers, and the most effective educational strategies from administrators. It underscores the need for effective education reforms, crafted around accountability, such as those being advanced by DISD Superintendent Mike Miles.

Desegregation in the 21st century won't be the result of court rulings, but rather, turning urban districts into centers of innovation that make them academic destinations parents want to move to, not away from. Texas Commissioner of Education Michael Williams emphatically states, "If we don't [close the racial achievement gap], then those people who believe demographics is destiny will be right. But we're not going to allow them to be right. We can still be a state that is going to be more Hispanic, more African-American and still outperform every other state in the country."

This *Opinion Page* paints a realistic portrait of many urban school districts. It tells us schools in the Dallas Independent School District have become more and more dominated by minority students as white families have moved to suburbs where they perceive their children will receive a better education. Write a well-developed paragraph in response to each of the following questions:

The writer says re-segregation isn't linked to racist policies, but to socioeconomic reality. Prior to 1954, could this statement be made about segregated schools? Why or why not? What changed policy?

1. Why does the writer link school reform with accountability? How are the two interdependent?
2. What does "demographics is destiny" mean? Why is Commissioner Williams so determined to not let the statement be true?

newspaper who believes the urban Dallas Independent School District is a victim of socioeconomic segregation, resulting in the majority of white families moving away from the city and into the suburbs.

While the launching of *Sputnik* triggered immediate changes in American education, and desegregation came to the forefront as an ongoing issue with significant moral implications, another, quieter, yet very important change was also taking place in the 1950s. Educators began to examine curriculum more carefully as a result of the thinking of Ralph Tyler (1902–1994). Tyler proposed that data concerning the needs of the learner, the needs of society, and the needs of the subject area should all be considered in the process of developing curricula. Tyler believed that learning should have both specific objectives and appropriate assessments.

Another influential person in American education, Benjamin Bloom (1913–1999), headed a group that composed what has become known as Bloom's taxonomy of learning objectives. The taxonomy was introduced in 1956 and continues to influence how educators think about and write learning objectives today.

1960s. The 1960s were characterized by a more outspoken U.S. citizenry. The election of a young, vibrant president, John F. Kennedy, gave rise to a sense of idealism among younger voters. After the assassination of President Kennedy in 1963, Lyndon Johnson attempted to continue in this vein with what he called the War on Poverty and the creation of the Great Society. Both the Kennedy and Johnson administrations allocated large amounts of money to break the cycle of poverty in the United States (Boyer and

Ralph Tyler (1902–1994)

The Ohio State University Archives

Upon his death, a news release from the Stanford University News Service called Ralph Tyler "the grand old man of educational research." Ralph Tyler's contributions to education were many, but his legacy is centered on curriculum development. Of the 16 books and over 700 journal articles he wrote, the one with perhaps the most impact was his first, *Basic Principles of Curriculum and Instruction*, published in 1949.

Tyler's commonsense approach to curriculum development involved

- Determining the goals of the school;
- Selecting learning experiences useful in attaining the goals;
- Organizing instruction around the experiences; and then
- Deciding how best to evaluate the learning.

Tyler conducted a groundbreaking longitudinal analysis of 30 schools and the careers of their students called the Eight-Year Study (1933–1941). This study focused on the opportunities students had who stayed in school rather than joining the workforce during the Depression.

Tyler is also responsible for initiating the National Assessment of Educational Progress (NAEP) test in the 1960s, which is still the only test that evaluates the U.S. school system itself rather than the success of the students in it. Ralph Tyler was often heard to make two statements: "I never wanted to be anything but a teacher" and "I never met a child who couldn't learn."

McNeil (2002); *Stanford News Service* (1994); *Tyler* (1949)

Benjamin Bloom (1913–1999)

Special Collections Research Center, University of Chicago Library

Following the 1948 convention of the American Psychological Association, Benjamin Bloom chaired a team that examined the cognitive, affective, and psychomotor domains of educational activity. From their work came what today is known as *Bloom's taxonomy.* As part of his work at the University of Chicago, Bloom observed that about 95% of all classroom questions were at the knowledge (recall) level. The taxonomy provides a way to structure both activities and questions that run the gamut of intellectual processing.

Bloom also did extensive work in the area of assessment. He was influenced by Ralph Tyler and recognized that comparing students wasn't as important in terms of assessment as helping students master the learning.

Benjamin Bloom's work has been both condensed and expanded over the years by scholars and practitioners. His contributions to education are meaningful and enduring.

Bloom (1956); Eisner (2000).

Stuckey, 2005). For example, the **Vocational Education Act of 1963** quadrupled the amount of money allocated for vocational education.

The following year, the **Civil Rights Act of 1964** stipulated that if schools discriminated based on race, color, or national origin, they would not be eligible for federal funding. Similarly, in a series of court battles, the Supreme Court continued to strike down school segregation.

In 1965, Congress passed the Elementary and Secondary Education Act (ESEA), which provided extra money for school districts with low-income families. Project Head Start was also established to boost the early learning of children ages 3 to 6 from low-income homes. The **Bilingual Education Act of 1968** (Title VII of the ESEA of 1965) validated children's native language and provided funds to assist non–English-speaking students, who were dropping out of high school at a rate of about 70%. The dramatic increase in numbers of Mexican and Mexican American children in the schools as a result of both legal and illegal immigration has created an ongoing challenge for educators that the Bilingual Education Act only partially addresses.

1970s. During the first half of the decade, the country's attention was focused on the Vietnam conflict and the administration of President Richard Nixon. Public trust in establishment institutions was repeatedly shaken, resulting in a general lack of confidence in schools and teachers. The number of students in public schools decreased during the 1970s, while private schools and homeschooling grew. Public school students' test scores dropped. Many perceived a need to implement a back-to-basics curriculum, and demands for accountability increased.

At the same time, some good things happened in 1970s education. Title IX of the Education Amendment Acts, which prohibited discrimination based on sex in any education program receiving federal funding, took effect in 1972. Additionally, in 1979, President Jimmy Carter elevated the federal Office of Education to a department, making its secretary a member of his cabinet.

The Education for All Handicapped Children Act (Public Law 94-142) passed in 1975. This important legislation granted children with disabilities the right to an education that meets their needs in the least restrictive environment.

It wasn't until the 1970s that the U.S. policy toward Native Americans changed from one of assimilation to fostering self-determination, encouraging Native Americans to take charge of their own education, whether on reservations or in other public schools. Today, even though there are more Native Americans under age 20, proportionally speaking, than in the general white population, a smaller percentage of Native Americans participate in formal education (Ornstein and Levine, 2006). In other words, in the whole Native American population, there is a greater percentage of people under the age of 20 when compared to the white population. Yet there is a smaller percentage of these young people in school when compared to white young people.

1980s. During the 8 years of Ronald Reagan's presidency (1981–1989), federal funding for elementary and secondary education declined by 17%. Even so, the quality of education received renewed attention for two basic reasons. The first reason was concern over economic competition with Japan. Many Americans believed that the United States had begun to compare unfavorably with Japan, in part because of inferior schools.

The second reason for the renewed attention to education was the release in 1983 of a report commissioned by President Reagan called ***A Nation at Risk: The Imperative for Educational Reform***. The language of the report was strong, referring to public education in the United States as a "rising tide of mediocrity." In response, various proposals for reform and improvement surfaced. *The Paideia Proposal* (1982) by Mortimer Adler called for a core curriculum based on Great Books. The 1989 Carnegie Council on Adolescent Development report, *Turning Points: Preparing American Youth for the 21st Century*, validated the middle-level philosophy of the Association for Middle Level Education, which called for small learning communities, the elimination of tracking, and careful guidance.

Restructuring became a buzzword in education. Some of the efforts included year-round schools, longer school days, longer school years, and more funding for technology.

1990s. The 1990s could be labeled as the era of standards. Along with the standards came tests designed to determine whether students had met the standards. The emphasis shifted from the input of education (what teachers do, funding, support) to the output of education (student learning). President Bill Clinton brought increased attention to education as he promised to be an effective "education president." He formalized Goals 2000, an initiative begun by his predecessor George H. W. Bush during his administration (1988–1992). Although the goals were admirably lofty, they were also unrealistically high and have, for the most part, been unfulfilled.

In the 1990s, teachers began taking on leadership roles in schools and in school districts. There was more collaboration among parents, the community, students, administrators, and teachers. Record enrollments resulted in a teacher shortage. President Clinton, in addition to providing federal support for the recruitment of 100,000 new teachers, joined policymakers in asking states to raise teacher standards (Webb et al., 2017).

Application Exercise 7.2: Identifying Important People in the History of U.S. Education

Point of Reflection 7.1

Do your views align with some of the basic principles of progressive education in Figure 7.4? If so, which ones and why? Do your views differ from those of progressive education? If so, how?

Check Your Understanding 7.4

7.5 What Major Influences, Issues, Ideologies, and Individuals Are We Experiencing in 21st Century American Education?

7.5 Articulate major influences, issues, ideologies, and individuals in 21st-century American education.

Almost two decades of this new century have passed. Our nation has experienced turbulence on every front.

Context for Change

The new century was ushered in with fears that proved to be unfounded as we anticipated what was called *Y2K*, or *Year 2000*. Many gathered around televisions to watch as the year 2000 dawned in countries around the globe, complete with celebrations and massive displays of fireworks—and an eerie sense of anxiety about events such as worldwide computer blackouts and destruction of all sorts that were prophesized but never materialized.

Less than two years later, on September 11, 2001, our worst fears did materialize in the form of the disastrous day now simply known as *9/11*. When terrorists killed thousands of Americans on our own American soil, our way of life changed, both politically and practically. The subsequent conflicts and political unrest in Iraq and Afghanistan continued to take their toll. The administration of George W. Bush (2000–2008) was one of turmoil and intense disagreement over issues related to war, economics, and governmental controls. The economic downturn that began during the Bush years strangled American prosperity and perpetuated a downward spiral of failed businesses and unemployment that made life very difficult for many in the first decade of the new century. Rampant mistrust and suspicion plagued America.

The election in 2008 of America's first African American president, Barack Obama, brought jubilation for some and a newly expressed animosity for others. The abrupt change from a conservative Republican administration to what many viewed as a liberal Democrat occupant in the White House put American's political tolerance for bipartisan decision making and action to the test. Even with the election of President Obama for another term in 2012, the inability of the two major parties to work together continued. The election of Donald Trump as president in 2016 ushered in an era of one-party dominance, with escalating strife and division in the United States.

No Child Left Behind

The defining education-related legislation of the first decade of the 21st century was the **No Child Left Behind Act of 2001 (NCLB).** The act was the reauthorization of the Elementary and Secondary Education Act (1965) and called for accountability of schools and school districts to states, and of states to the federal government. No Child Left Behind was formulated as a response to evidence that students were being promoted without mastering concepts and were graduating without basic literacy skills. The Elementary and Secondary Education Act was reauthorized as the **Every Student Succeeds Act** in 2016.

21st-Century Knowledge and Skills

As noted in previous chapters, the Partnership for 21st Century Skills (P21) exerts considerable and growing influence in schools across the country. But it's not just an organization that is influencing what we teach and learn; it's the underlying concept that our world is changing and schools need to change as well.

In each "Context for Change" section in this chapter we get a sense for the complexity of life in the United States and around the world. The goal of teachers and schools should be to provide educational experiences that reflect this complexity as we equip students to live productively and positively. The present, and therefore history as well, is shaped by human responses to dilemmas. It's all about problem solving—a 21st-century skill that is more relevant now than ever before.

In this century, information will continue to grow at exponential rates. Teaching students how to figure out what they need to know, where and how to access it, and how to use it effectively should be emphasized in teaching and learning. Then wrapping this package in appreciation for, and the ability to accomplish, collaboration will help students thrive in the 21st century.

21st-Century Schools

In most schools in the United States it would be difficult to recognize change between the 1990s and the first decade of the 21st century. In some schools the classrooms may not have changed much physically or in terms of learning experiences since long before 1990. Yet in other schools innovative technology such as SMART Boards, tablet and laptop computers, LCD projectors, and more tell the story of mushrooming technological advances.

Virtual schools are becoming more widespread as educators use technology to deliver and reinforce teaching and learning. Books of all kind are available electronically, and communication with classrooms around the globe changes the way we view instruction. Although teaching is still viewed as place-based in a classroom for most educators, the possibilities of using whole communities and cyberspace as learning environments are taking education into uncharted dimensions. What an exciting time to become a teacher!

Addressing Racial and Ethnic Diversity in the 21st Century

If asked how we are addressing racial and ethnic diversity in public schools, the short answer may be "Not very well," and certainly not with consistency. For instance, in 2009 Orfield's research showed that 55 years after the Supreme Court declared that separate is not equal in *Brown* v. *Board of Education,* U.S. schools were more segregated than before the Court ruling (Orfield, 2009). Of the defining issues in American education, perhaps none is so challenging as finding ways to address racial and ethnic diversity. Figure 7.5 shows the percentage of students by race and ethnicity in regions of the United States.

Although American public schools have been relatively successful in educating immigrants from Europe and Asia and helping them achieve at least middle-class status in the United States, generally speaking, our schools have been much less successful in doing so for African American and Hispanic students. Figure 7.5 reveals that in 2013 the percentage of African American and Hispanic students together was about the same as the percentage of white students in public schools. Given that over 80% of public school teachers are white is inherently problematic. Children and adolescents need role models that look like them and their families. Watch Video Example 7.1: Racial Diversity and listen as a black teacher talks about the impact of his race on students.

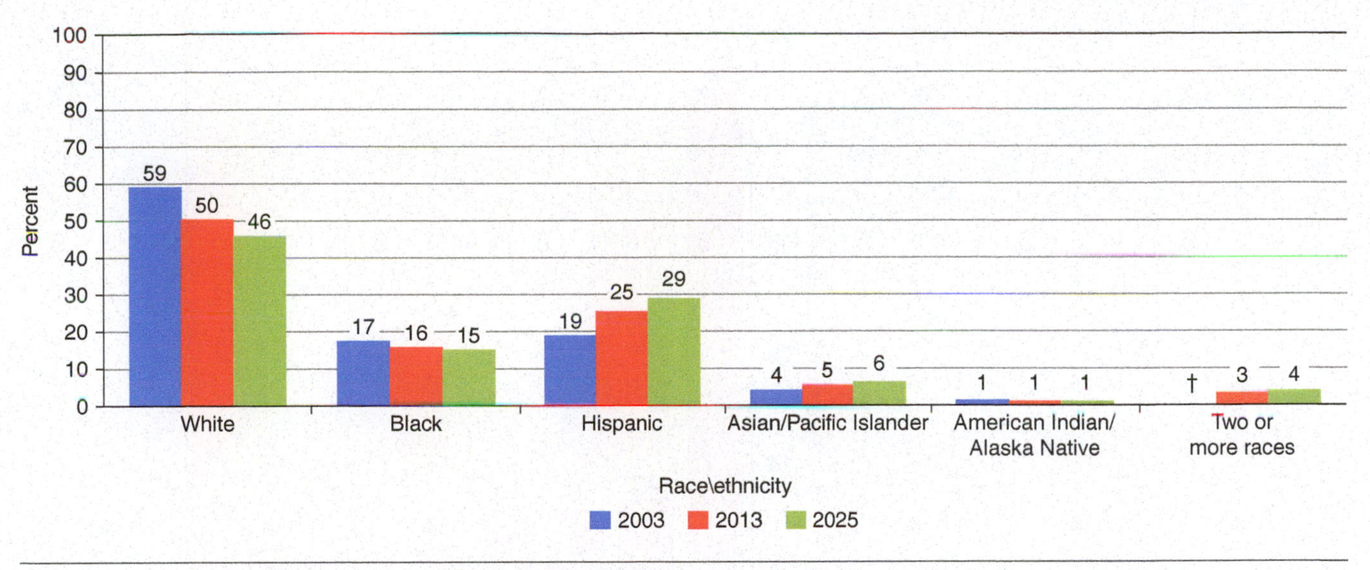

Figure 7.5 Public school student enrollment percentages by race/ethnicity, 2003, 2013, and 2025 projection

† Not applicable.

Based on: U.S. Department of Education. (2016). National Center for Education Statistics, Common Core of Data (CCD), "State Nonfiscal Survey of Public Elementary and Secondary Education," 2003–04 and 2013–14; and National Elementary and Secondary Enrollment by Race/Ethnicity Projection Model, 1972 through 2025.

Video Example 7.1: Racial Diversity

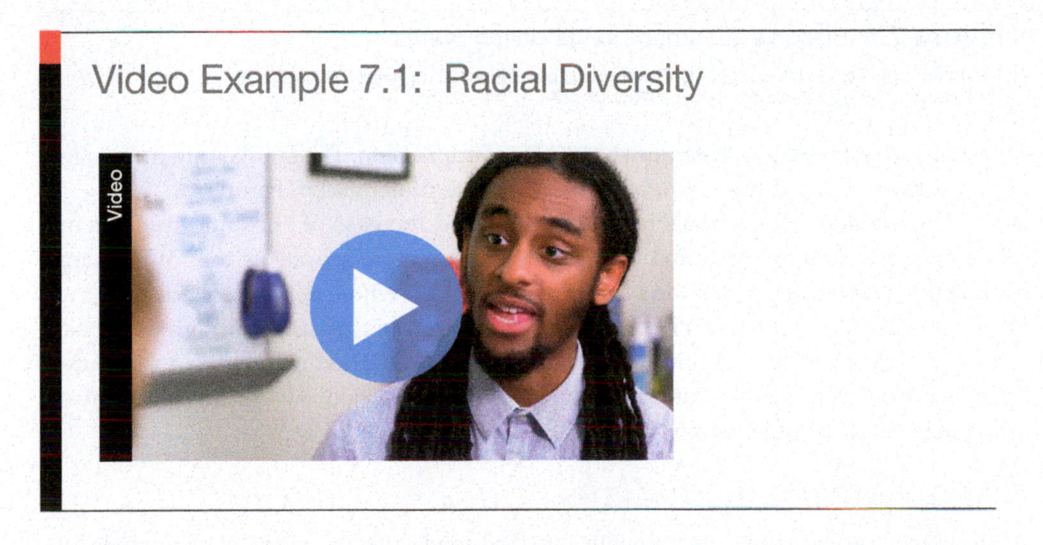

African American Students

Laws have been passed and policies have been made with the intent of fully integrating U.S. schools. In our country's history, African American students have suffered outright with purposeful discrimination, including laws that forbade their education. Today, there are no such laws, and yet in some locations and in some circumstances, we still find differences in opportunities for black students compared with white students (Banks and Banks, 2016).

One of our focus students at Cario Middle School, Patrick Sutton, is an excellent student with what appears to be an intact sense of confidence. For Patrick, as an African American student, the doors of opportunity seem to be open wide. His positive experiences at Cario are what we should desire for all students, regardless of their race or ethnicity.

Hispanic American Students

At the end of the first decade of the 21st century, there were over 45 million Hispanic people living in the United States. Some families have been here for centuries, and the

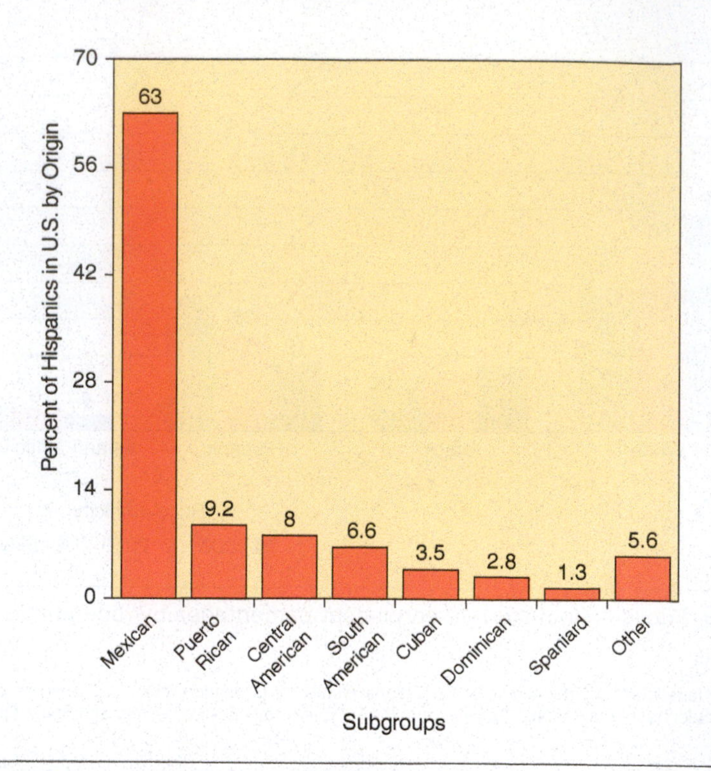

Figure 7.6 Hispanic subgroups in the United States

Based on: U.S. Census Bureau. (2011). The Hispanic population: 2010. Retrieved August 30, 2013, from http://www.census.gov/prod/cen2010/briefs/c2010br-04.pdf

vast majority have come to escape some form of oppression. The families are from many countries, and thus have a variety of ethnicities, as illustrated in Figure 7.6.

The dilemmas for schools regarding the rapid increase of Hispanic students are complex. Perhaps the dilemma with the most impact on schools is that of language diversity. How do we teach the standards to children who can't understand what we say or write? Currently our schools attempt to answer this question through three basic programs: English as a second language (ESL), bilingual education, and structured English immersion (SEI). Our efforts are inadequate, particularly for any child raised in a non–English-speaking home.

Asian American Students

About half the world's population falls into the broad category of Asian. The people live in China, Japan, India, Pakistan, Vietnam, Korea, Samoa, Cambodia, Laos, and many more countries. Asian Americans have vastly different experiences both before emigrating and when in the United States either legally or illegally (U.S. Census Bureau, 2009).

Students from China, Japan, and India generally achieve at high levels in U.S. schools, whereas students from Southeast Asian countries such as Vietnam and Cambodia tend to struggle. Many children who come to America from war-torn, trauma-filled areas find their problems within U.S. education exacerbated, or made worse, by their life experiences. Again, language is a major barrier to success. In large cities and small towns across America, teachers who speak only English work daily with children who speak a great variety of languages in their homes and struggle to communicate in English in order to learn even small bits and pieces of our curricular standards. Read what focus teacher Angelica Reynosa says about her role as an advocate for Hispanic students in *Teaching in Focus.*

Middle Eastern American Students

So often targets of prejudice in our post-9/11 world, students of Middle Eastern descent are entering our schools in increasing—yet still relatively small—numbers. They may be from countries including Egypt, Jordan, Iraq, Iran, Syria, Lebanon, and Saudi Arabia.

Teaching in Focus

Angelica Reynosa, World History, Roosevelt High School, California. *In her own words. . . .*

Sara Davis Powell

I can't imagine being anywhere else professionally than in a school. My husband and I are both teachers. It is a wonderful life!

I teach in a school where minority populations are the majority. Most of my students, and indeed most of the students at Roosevelt, are Latino Americans. Some were born in America; others have been here for only a few weeks. Some have families with established careers; others have families who are undocumented workers. Regardless, they are the faces of an ever-growing Latino presence in America. Some of my students, like Hugo, have secure, loving homes headed by parents who risked their lives to come to America. Hugo will be successful. He knows it's his legacy. He attends school regularly, and he is learning English quickly.

I see my job as not only a teacher of a course for high school credit but also as an advocate for the well-being of my students, most of whom are in bilingual classes so they can learn their subjects while learning to be fluent in English. As a Spanish speaker, I am able to teach both history and coping skills in English communication. Find your special niche in education. You have unique talents and gifts that will be valuable to students. Search for those talents and develop them for the sake of the students.

Application Exercise 7.3: Angelica's Lesson and Interview

the religion of people referred to as Muslims. But in reality, more Middle Eastern Americans align with Christianity than with Islam.

Cultural norms of Middle Eastern American students are often noticeably different from the mainstream. They may talk more loudly with what sounds like an odd intonation, hold hands with same-sex friends, not consider being late a sign of disrespect, not hold females in as high regard as males, and so forth. Because these norms are counter to what we generally expect in U.S. schools, life in school may be more difficult for some. Even so, students of Middle Eastern heritage tend to do quite well in school, go to college at a higher than average rate, and live productive lives in the United States (Banks and Banks, 2016).

Your future classroom will be filled with a diverse student population. Remember that students display diversity in many ways, not just in race or ethnicity. But chances are you will have at least two races or ethnicities represented. Welcome the challenge! Our differences make us stronger.

Be Aware of Education History in the Making

Time gives us perspective. We can look at the history of American education and determine which of the various influences, issues, ideologies, and individuals have most affected the course of schools, teachers, and students. What is less than obvious is which of these influences, issues, ideologies, and individuals are making a difference or initiating significant change right now. Fifty or 100 years from now, it will likely be evident.

Education issues come and go, often in predictable cycles. The notable individuals involved in education at any given point are numerous. Sifting through them to determine who has significant and long-term influence generally only happens with time.

Table 7.3 History in the making

Individual	Theory, Field of Research, Written Works
Mortimer Adler	Paideia Proposal; core curriculum based on Great Books
James Banks	Multicultural education
David Berliner	Educational researcher; teacher effectiveness
Marva Collins	Tireless advocate for all children; founder of Westside Preparatory School
James Comer	Comer Model; emphasis on social context of teaching and learning
Larry Cuban	Expert on change in education
Linda Darling-Hammond	*The Right to Learn;* teacher quality and preparation
Marian Wright Edelman	Children's Defense Fund; advocate for all children
Elliot Eisner	Arts education; curriculum reform
Jaime Escalante	Outstanding high school math teacher in urban Los Angeles
Paulo Freire	*Pedagogy of the Oppressed;* education gives power to the poor
Howard Gardner	Multiple intelligences theory
William Glasser	Choice theory of human behavior
John Goodlad	*A Place Called School;* democracy and education; teacher education
Maxine Greene	Existentialism; *Landscapes of Learning*
E. D. Hirsch	*Cultural Literacy: What Every American Needs to Know*
Ivan Illich	Social reconstructionism; *Deschooling America*
Herbert Kohl	*36 Children;* the value of teachers and teaching differentiated instruction
Jacob Kounin	Classroom management
Jonathan Kozol	*Savage Inequalities: Children in America's Schools;* study of urban children
Sonia Nieto	Multicultural and bilingual education
Nel Noddings	Caring in the classroom; teacher reflection
Theodore Sizer	Coalition of Essential Schools; necessity of community in school environment; *Horace's Compromise*
Robert Slavin	Success for All program; early intervention
Kay Toliver	Outstanding teacher in urban New York City
Carol Ann Tomlinson	Differentiated instruction
Grant Wiggins/Jay McTighe	*Understanding by Design;* development of curriculum, instruction, and assessment

The danger of listing contemporary movers and shakers in any field is the inevitable omission of names. Given that risk, Table 7.3 is an attempt to provide a partial list of individuals and their contributions that are currently influencing American education. You will no doubt hear and read about these people as you pursue a degree in teaching.

Reading professional journals, continuing to take courses, attending conferences, having conversations with colleagues—all these activities will help you stay abreast of the individuals in the forefront of our work as teachers. History is in the making all around us. In classrooms across the United States, excellent teachers are the real heroes of education. If you decide to be a teacher, then the history of American education has been changed,

Point of Reflection 7.2

Do you anticipate a diverse classroom with a sense of excitement or a nagging dread? Explain your answer. Is there anything in your background that uniquely prepares you for a diverse classroom? If so, explain.

Check Your Understanding 7.5

perhaps not in ways that will make it into history books, but definitely in ways that will influence the lives of the hundreds, maybe thousands of students in your future classroom.

Concluding Thoughts

This brief look at the history of education in the United States has been written from a majority culture viewpoint (white, middle class) primarily using sources having the same lens. Encapsulating 400 years into one brief chapter involves choices that have inherent limitations. Be aware of this when you consider any aspect of history. Understand that there's always more to the story.

American education has been more reactionary than trailblazing, more foundational than earthshaking. In an ideal world, educators would be ahead of dilemmas, and the teaching and learning in U.S. schools would lead the way toward solutions to our country's problems. And, indeed, this is true, but in a subtle way. The adage "Teachers make all other professions possible" elevates teachers to indispensable heroes, although they are largely unheralded as such.

The history of education in the United States parallels the history of the country. Although once relatively simple and perceived as manageable, education in the United States is now incredibly complex and often unwieldy, with issues to match. In spite of the lessons to be learned from studying the history of American education, there remain unacceptable conditions for learning in some schools, unequal opportunities for children based on such factors as socioeconomic status and race, and international test results that show mediocre performances by U.S. students. Together we will face many challenges as we strive to effectively build on the past to do a better job of educating in—and for—the future, always asking, "And how are the children? Are they all well?"

We began this chapter by considering Angelica Reynosa's classroom and teaching responsibilities at Roosevelt High School in Fresno, California. As she teaches world history, she is often reminded that the plight of many of her students resembles some in history who have suffered hardships but who also possessed hope for a better life. Now as the chapter comes to an end, we rejoin Angelica as she considers ways to make history relevant for her students.

Read through *Chapter in Review* to help refresh your memory of what we have discussed, then interact with Angelica as she plans learning experiences for her students in *Developing Professional Competence.*

Chapter in Review

What were the major influences, issues, ideologies, and individuals in 17th-century American education?

- Many of the original colonists came to America seeking religious freedom and established schools to bolster their beliefs.
- Colonial schools primarily served white males.
- Education differed greatly among the New England, middle, and southern colonies.

What were the major influences, issues, ideologies, and individuals in 18th-century American education?

- Private academies served as secondary schools that went beyond what was taught in dame schools and town schools.
- Influential leaders such as Benjamin Franklin, Thomas Jefferson, and Noah Webster contributed to the expansion of educational opportunities.
- Education became a state responsibility by virtue of not being addressed in the Constitution.

What were the major influences, issues, ideologies, and individuals in 19th-century American education?

- Common schools were the first public, free American elementary schools.
- Following the Civil War, the first high schools began to flourish to meet the new economic demands of an increasingly industrialized United States.
- Kindergarten, with an activity-based curriculum, became common by the end of the 19th century.
- Teacher preparation institutions called *normal schools* were created to respond to the need for more teachers with increased and consistent preparation.
- Few educational opportunities existed for children with disabilities, children of color, or children of poor immigrant parents.
- Land-grant colleges were established as a result of the Morrill Acts.

What were the major influences, issues, ideologies, and individuals in 20th-century American education?

- John Dewey and the philosophy of progressive education fostered more active student participation in a school system based on democratic principles.
- Junior highs, and then middle schools, bridged the gap between elementary and high schools.
- Interest in science and math education increased following the launch of *Sputnik*.
- In 1965, Congress passed the Elementary and Secondary Education Act (ESEA), which initially provided extra money for school districts with low-income families, and now applies to a variety of education reforms.
- During the 1970s, the Education for All Handicapped Children Act and Title IX increased educational opportunities for all children.
- *A Nation at Risk* served as a wake-up call for education in the United States.
- Curriculum standards emerged in the 1990s as the defining criteria for the quality of teaching and learning.

What major influences, issues, ideologies, and individuals have we experienced so far in 21st-century American education?

- The first decade of the 21st century in America was filled with turmoil.
- The No Child Left Behind Act of 2001 called for increased accountability at local and state levels and emphasized the need for all children to learn.
- The Partnership for 21st Century Skills (P21) has exerted, and continues to exert, considerable and growing influence in schools across the country.
- Some schools have remained virtually unchanged for decades; others reflect the technology and strategies available for teaching and learning in the 21st century.
- Although some strides have been made in a quest to provide equal opportunities for learning to all children in the United States, there is still much to do.
- In some locations and in some circumstances, we still find differences in opportunities for black students compared with white students.
- The Hispanic student population is rapidly growing, but our ability to improve their learning and their language skills is not keeping up with their need.
- Students from China, Japan, and India generally appear to be achieving at high levels in U.S. schools, whereas students from Southeast Asian countries such as Vietnam and Cambodia struggle.

- Cultural norms of Middle Eastern American students are often noticeably different from those of mainstream Americans, necessitating an even greater need for understanding on the part of teachers.
- Teachers should assume the responsibility of staying current with major shifts in educational concepts and trends. Time provides perspective. As history unfolds, those most influential will emerge in prominence.

Developing Professional Competence

Thoughtfully reading this scenario and responding to the items that follow it will help you prepare for licensure exams.

Sara Davis Powell

Angelica Reynosa wants her students to see the big picture included in the world history curriculum and wants to help them grasp the significance of how various forms of government enhance or inhibit people's lives. She wants them to understand how knowledge of history is meaningful for their futures and how it can give them perspective about their roots and cultural struggles.

Now it's time for you to respond to two short essay items involving the scenario. In your responses, be sure to address all the dilemmas and questions posed in each item. These items are followed by three multiple-choice questions.

1. The class you observed is bilingual. How did Angelica approach the lesson both to teach the content and the English language? Why is Angelica's own ethnicity important to the teaching and learning process in her classroom?
2. As Angelica considers her students and her responsibilities, she reflects on these two NBPTS and InTASC standards. Why is each especially important to her, given that she teaches in a bilingual classroom?

   NBPTS Standard 5 Teachers are members of learning communities.

   InTASC Standard 9 Professional Learning and Ethical Practice

   The teacher engages in ongoing professional learning and uses evidence to continually evaluate his or her practice, particularly the effects of his or her choices and actions on others (learners, families, other professionals, and the community), and adapts practice to meet the needs of each learner.

Application Exercise 7.4: Developing Professional Competence

3. Why is the establishment of colonies in the 17th century in what is now the United States relevant to many of Angelica's students?
   a. The people who came to America from Europe did so to find refuge from a government that they found to be oppressive.
   b. It's been 400 years and we now have perspective on the early days of the United States.
   c. Many Hispanics came to America then as they do now.
   d. Mexico was experiencing a similar fight for independence in the 17th century.

4. Why is it important for Angelica's students to understand how various people throughout history have suffered oppression?
   a. They need to see that they are not alone.
   b. They will be encouraged to see how people have overcome difficulties.
   c. They need to understand it so they won't perpetuate it.
   d. It is vital to understand that history repeats itself.

5. In the lesson you observed, what purpose does the candy serve?
   a. The candy randomly given and taken shows students that they actually have very little control over their lives.
   b. They are learning to cleverly hoard candy and keep it from being taken away, much as they will need to do in a capitalistic country.
   c. The candy is an incentive to participate fully in the rock-paper-scissors activity.
   d. The candy is randomly given and taken away, showing that in governments without freedom there is little control over one's destiny.

Application Exercise 7.5: Developing Professional Competence

Flash Cards 7.1

Shared Writing 7.1: Importance of History

Chapter 8

Philosophical Foundations of Education in the United States

Learning Objectives

After studying this chapter, you will have knowledge and skills to:

8.1 Articulate why a philosophy of education is important.

8.2 Explain how two prominent teacher-centered philosophies of education affect teaching and learning.

8.3 Compare and contrast how three prominent student-centered philosophies of education affect teaching and learning.

8.4 Develop your own personal philosophy of education.

Dear Reader

When it comes to a philosophy of education, there's no avoiding it. Every decision, every action, and every interaction come from a philosophy, whether we've thought about it, written it, or never even considered it. One thing's for sure—we live it.

The Greek word *philo* means "love," and *Sophos* means "wisdom." **Philosophy,** then, means "love of wisdom." Philosophy is a means of answering fundamental questions. It's not a boring, stuffy subject, but rather a vibrant way of discovering and expressing ways of being and behaving. A teacher's **philosophy of education** is the teacher's "love of wisdom" regarding teaching that expresses itself every day in the classroom.

This chapter provides only a very brief overview of some of the components of philosophy that apply to teaching and learning. Don't be put off by the terminology. Think about the meanings and implications of the words that label the areas of philosophy we discuss: *essentialism, perennialism, progressivism, social reconstructionism*, and *existentialism.* Consider the concepts seriously and internalize them. Each area has a down-to-earth definition and is illustrated with words that are familiar. Take it personally and pay attention to how each philosophy affects teaching and learning. You'll learn a lot about yourself. This won't happen with a quick read-through and a glance at the figures. The chapter is relatively brief, allowing time to read it twice or even three times, purposefully reflecting on the content to make it personally meaningful.

If you've ever considered questions such as "Who am I?" or "What's my purpose in life?" you have engaged in philosophical thought. Every attitude and action is determined by some deeper basic beliefs, conscious or unconscious. To bring a philosophy to the surface of your consciousness requires consideration of your values and views about life. It necessitates reflection on circumstances, reactions, assumptions, intentions, and so on.

Few teachers have a defined philosophy of education. If asked, most may shrug and say, "I've never thought about it," or "I don't have time for that kind of stuff." But if you study a teacher's attitudes and actions over even a relatively brief period of time, you can probably make some accurate statements about the philosophy that impacts what you observe.

8.1 Why Is a Philosophy of Education Important?

8.1 Articulate why a philosophy of education is important.

A philosophy of education is a living, dynamic part of who we are in the classroom. Allan C. Ornstein (2003) expresses the far-reaching impact of a philosophy of education when he writes,

> Philosophy enters into every important decision about curriculum, teaching, instruction, and testing .... The methods and materials a teacher chooses to use in a classroom reflect a professional judgment, which reflects philosophy .... In short, choices reflect philosophy—and whether we recognize our own philosophy in education, it is out there and it influences our behavior and attitudes in classrooms and schools. (p. 17)

Because teacher preparation puts you in a position to think about decisions relative to teaching, prospective teachers are usually asked to write a philosophy of education. This means you will look closely at established philosophical viewpoints, you will analyze what these viewpoints mean to teachers and their work, and then you will either state with which philosophy you agree or with which combination you most closely align. The philosophy of education you write before entering the classroom as a teacher will be based on limited experience and will be a work in progress. But it's a start, and it's an important one. It's healthy and productive for teachers to teach according to combinations of philosophies. This creates balance and produces commonsense, responsive decisions in the classroom. Read focus teacher Craig Cleveland's reasons for developing a philosophy of education then watch his interview as he expresses his personal philosophy.

People change and grow, often in response to personal experiences. Your philosophy will change and grow. In Figure 8.1, read about Karen Heath's experience of writing an initial philosophy of education as a college assignment and her subsequent experiences leading her to revisit her philosophy.

Teaching in Focus

Craig Cleveland, history teacher, Roosevelt High School, California. *In his own words ....*

Much of what you need to know about effective teaching and learning is found within yourself already. The environment and circumstances in which you learned powerful and life-changing lessons may have been in school or elsewhere in life. The relevant and meaningful lessons your students learn will need to be both inside and outside the school if education is going to have the power to transform them into thoughtful mature people.

Sara Davis Powell

Essential to creating a learning environment in the classroom is a researched and clearly articulated philosophy about how learning happens. When such a philosophy is in place, teachers are able to make sound and reliable instructional decisions and refinements.

Continuing my education in a graduate program, reading professional literature, regularly reflecting on my teaching with an eye toward improvement, and having ongoing conversations with friends and colleagues help make more concrete my beliefs about how learning happens. A ninth-grade student of mine made the insightful statement, "Learning is natural." I believe learning is natural when the learner has interest and a voice as a participant within the learning environment of school.

Application Exercise 8.1: Craig's Philosophy

Philosophy Trees

Our discussion of each philosophy is accompanied by a diagram of a tree. The analogy of a philosophy of education to a tree is appropriate in many ways. The tree trunk represents teaching. The root system is a particular philosophy of education, or a combination of philosophies, providing the strength and foundation of the tree. The philosophy literally grounds the tree. The branches of the tree represent the work of teachers. Each trunk-attached branch supports smaller branches with plentiful leaves that represent teaching and learning.

Figure 8.1 Karen Heath, 2005 Vermont Teacher of the Year

Sara Davis Powell

One of the ubiquitous rites of passage for preservice teachers is the completion of a philosophy of education. When I was a senior in college 22 years ago, having just completed my student teaching, one of the final requirements before being certified was to complete such a document. I was still a student, and much of what I thought about and wrote was largely theoretical. I wrote about the need for children's differences to be recognized, the importance of process in education, and freedom within a structured environment. "A Personal Philosophy of Education," as it was titled, went subsequently into a box in an attic while I ventured across the country and, a few years later, settled into a home in Vermont where the box was moved to a new attic, gathering dust with other college relics.

Last year when I was nominated to be Teacher of the Year, I was called upon once again to produce a philosophy of education. I sat down one weekend and wrote about what I believe to be the most important aspect of education—the heart. Years of experience have taught me that in order to be an effective teacher, my heart must be in it fully, from devotion to subject matter, to striving to keep up with best practices, and, most importantly, to having a heart connection to the children, as that is the only sure avenue to effective student learning.

It took a bit of digging, but I found the old college box, and at the very bottom of it lay my original philosophy of education. I took it like a treasure into the afternoon sun in our yard and carefully read not just a philosophy, but also the mind-set of an idealistic 21-year-old. Surprisingly, I still agreed with everything I had written, but there was a distinct lack of mention of anything having to do with relationships. I guess that is the aspect of teaching that I have truly learned over time.

Though my first written document sat untouched for 23 years and my newest one was just composed, I have always carried with me a philosophy of education. It brings stability to my work as initiatives and programs come and go. From a fairly benign population of children in a wealthy college town to an inner-city Boston high school, my philosophy is the backbone of what I do as a teacher. It directs what and how I teach and, most importantly, how I interact with my students. It is the core of who I am as a teacher.

Based on: E-mail communication with Karen Heath, January 18, 2007.

Many aspects of a tree's growth are directly analogous to teaching and learning. Do you recall seeing a cross section of a tree trunk? Elementary students learn that you can count the rings to determine the age of a tree because each year of growth not only takes a tree skyward but also wraps another layer of life around it. So it is with teaching experience. Each year, previous experiences aren't shed but rather are wrapped in new experiences.

Trees have two kinds of roots: anchor roots, which grow deeper with time and hold the tree upright against most winds, and feeder roots, which shoot out in all directions and draw in nourishment. Have you ever noticed a makeshift fence or stakes with colored tape around the base of a tree when construction was nearby? The purpose of this barrier is to let workers know that digging closer would likely damage the tree. Although a tree can survive the loss of some feeder roots, the diameter of the feeder and anchor root system is generally the same as the diameter of the canopy of the tree's branches and leaves. Cutting away feeder roots will diminish the canopy in like proportion. The size and stability of the philosophical root system determine the effectiveness of the teaching and learning canopy. Your anchor matters; your philosophy of education affects all aspects of your success as a teacher.

Teacher-Centered and Student-Centered Philosophies

When we refer to an aspect of education as **teacher centered,** the teacher is prominent in the classroom, determining, and being the center of, curricula and instructional strategies. When the curriculum and instructional strategies are **student centered,** the students have choices concerning what to learn and the instructional strategies actively involve students in their own learning. The five philosophies discussed here fall neatly into these two categories. Essentialism and perennialism are teacher-centered approaches, whereas progressivism, social reconstructionism, and existentialism are more student centered, as illustrated in Figure 8.2. Keep this in mind as you read about the five philosophies. Also think about early childhood, elementary, middle, and high school classrooms as you consider each philosophy of education.

Check Your Understanding 8.1

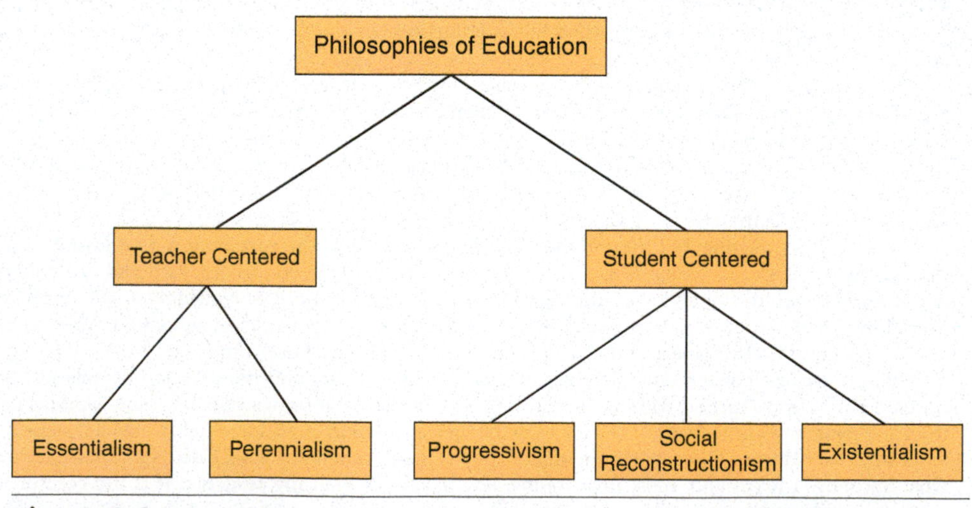

Figure 8.2 Teacher- and student-centered philosophical approaches

8.2 How Do Two Prominent Teacher-Centered Philosophies of Education Affect Teaching and Learning?

8.2 Explain how two prominent teacher-centered philosophies of education affect teaching and learning.

Essentialism and perennialism are often considered "old school." Very few teachers in public schools, and perhaps a limited number in private schools, adhere faithfully to either, but there are elements in each with which most teachers would agree and attempt to emulate. Essentialism and perennialism have much in common.

Essentialism

Essentialism is a philosophy of education based on the belief that a core curriculum exists that everyone in the United States should learn. This core can shift in response to societal changes but should always be basic, organized, and rigorous. When you hear someone praise the concept of "back to basics," chances are that person is an essentialist.

Essentialism is an ancient philosophy, but it grew in popularity in the 20th century in the United States as a backlash to progressivism, the educational philosophy begun by John Dewey. Whereas progressivism puts student interests at the center of curriculum and instruction, essentialism puts little stock in what students want in terms of what and how they learn. Essentialism gained impetus from the launching of *Sputnik* by the Soviet Union in 1957 and again from the publication of *A Nation at Risk* in 1983—two events we discussed in Chapter 7. Supporters of the essentialist philosophy are vocal about their view that schools have dumbed down the curriculum with nonessential courses, resulting in lower test scores (Ravitch, 2000). Essentialists favor high expectations for students, along with testing to measure mastery of standards.

An essentialist philosophy of education puts the teacher front and center as an intellectual and moral role model. Direct instruction is encouraged, but other instructional methods are used if they have proven effective. Students are expected to listen and learn as they follow the rules of the classroom.

One prominent proponent of essentialism is E. D. Hirsch, author of *Cultural Literacy: What Every American Needs to Know* (1987). Hirsch lists events, people, facts, discoveries, inventions, art, literature, and more that he believes all Americans should know about to be culturally literate. Another proponent of essentialism is Theodore Sizer (1932–2009), founder of the Coalition of Essential Schools, a group of about 200 schools that pledge to promote the essentialist goals of a rigorous curriculum based on standards. Sizer (1985) insists that Coalition of Essential Schools students clearly exhibit mastery of content as well as evidence of developing thinking skills.

Take a few minutes to study the essentialism tree in Figure 8.3. Visualizing how teachers might translate the elements of essentialism into their classrooms will help you understand this philosophy of education.

Perennialism

Perennialism is a philosophy of education based on a core curriculum, and in that regard it is similar to essentialism. The difference lies in what constitutes the core. The word *perennial* means "everlasting" and is often used when talking about plants.

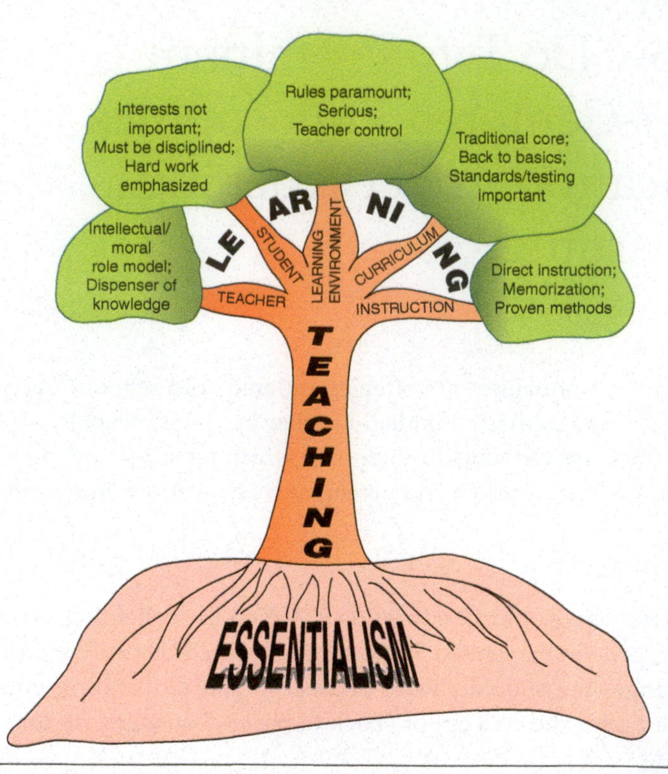

Figure 8.3 Essentialism tree

A perennial flower blooms in season, is dormant for a time, and then blooms again, year after year. A flower that is not a perennial is an annual that must be replanted each year. Perennialism, as a philosophy of education, says there is a curriculum with themes and questions that endure and are everlasting. In contrast, the curriculum of essentialism is considered basic and core, but its components may change as society changes and, as such, the essentialist curriculum is more comparable to an annual.

Perennialists believe that even as life changes and times change, the real substance and truths of life remain the same. The wisdom students need may be obtained through the study of **Great Books,** the writings of those considered to be the great thinkers through the history of Western civilization, such as Homer, Shakespeare, Melville, Einstein, and many others. Perennialists do not endorse choices in the curriculum or elective courses, and they ascribe to a rigid curriculum for elementary, middle, and high schools.

Teachers who practice perennialism as a philosophy of education want to be in control of the classroom. They dispense knowledge and lead discussions of classics that require rigorous, logical thought by students. Differences in students are rarely considered, as all are expected to learn from the classics (Webb, Metha, and Jordan, 2017).

Mortimer Adler (1902–2001), author of the *Paideia Proposal* (1982), is perhaps the best known recent proponent of perennialism as a philosophy of education. The word *paideia* refers to a state of human excellence. Adler said that schools should use intense study of the classics to strive for excellence in students (Pulliam and Van Patten, 2013). Adler founded the Great Books of the Western World program at the University of Chicago in 1930.

Take a few minutes to study the perennialism tree in Figure 8.4. Visualizing how teachers might translate the elements of perennialism into their classrooms will help you understand this philosophy of education.

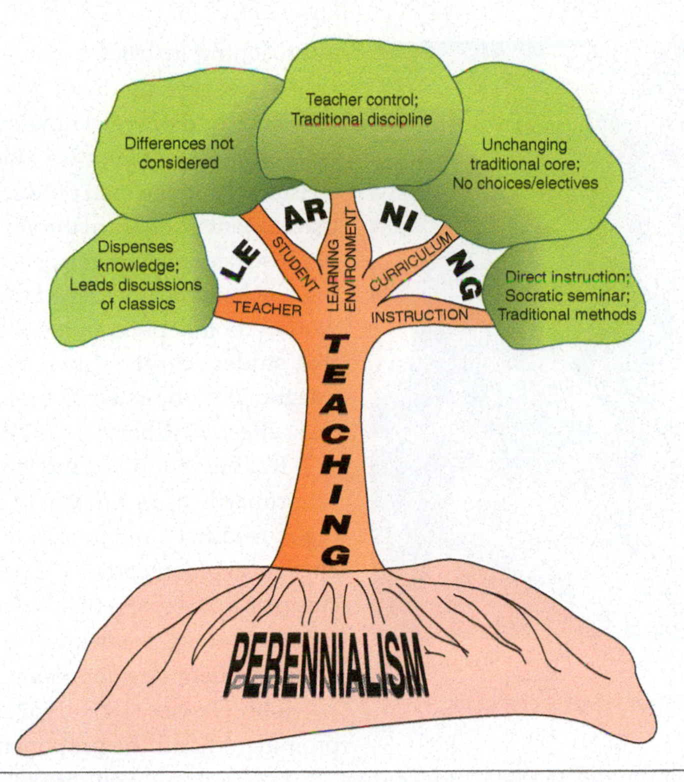

Figure 8.4 Perennialism tree

Point of Reflection 8.1

Do you identify with some of the elements of essentialism and perrenialism? If so, which ones? Are there some aspects that do not appeal to you? If so, which ones?

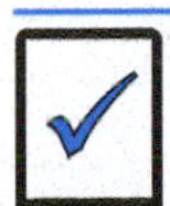

Check Your Understanding 8.2

8.3 How Do Three Prominent Student-Centered Philosophies of Education Affect Teaching and Learning?

8.3 Compare and contrast how three prominent student-centered philosophies of education affect teaching and learning.

Progressivism

Progressivism is a student-centered philosophy of education that focuses on a curriculum of interest to students. To progressivists, education is more than preparation for the future—it is life itself. The progressive philosophy of education endorses experiential learning full of opportunities for student discovery and problem solving.

Constructivism and pragmatism are philosophies of education that fall within the broader philosophy of progressivism. **Constructivism,** an inquiry-based way of

Sara Davis Powell

Encouraging students to engage in learning and express themselves is part of the philosophy of progressivism.

approaching instruction, builds on progressivism because students are challenged to construct, or discover, knowledge about their environments. Process is valued in progressivism, often more than product. The theory is that students who learn through the processes of construction, discovery, and problem solving will be better able to adapt to a changing world. Another philosophy, **pragmatism,** says that student-centered perspectives that are integrated with firsthand experiences are the most effective (Chartock, 2004).

Teachers who ascribe to progressivism act primarily as facilitators of learning, serving as resources and guides to students who engage, explore, gather evidence, draw conclusions, and express themselves. Real-world problem solving is intended to promote individual student development (Gutek, 2005).

John Dewey (1859–1952) was the most prominent of all the proponents of progressivism, beginning in the late 19th century and continuing well into the 20th century. Dewey supported a balance between valuing established content with structured learning activities and planning experiences that interest, motivate, and actively involve students. Although progressivism fell out of favor in a call for more academic rigor in the late 1950s, many tenets of the philosophy continue to be part of today's most widely used instructional strategies.

Take a few minutes to study the progressivism tree in Figure 8.5. Visualizing how teachers might translate the elements of progressivism into their classrooms will help you understand this philosophy of education.

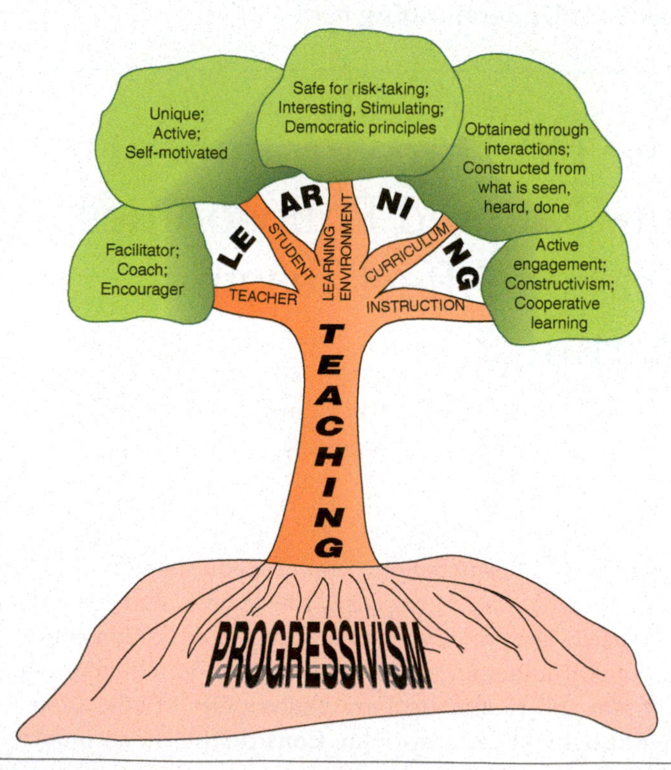

Figure 8.5 Progressivism tree

Examining the progressivism tree reveals that the progressivist teacher often facilitates student discovery and critical thinking rather than serving as a dispenser of knowledge. In Video Example 8.1, we observe a fourth-grade teacher working with a small group of students as they grapple with the differences between a food web and a food chain. Watch and listen as the teacher skillfully, and in a non-intimidating way, helps the students think about what they know and draw their own conclusions.

Video Example 8.1: Learning Facilitation

Many teachers are choosing to involve students in their own learning through technology tools. The use of tablets in the classroom is growing rapidly in popularity and potential effectiveness. This chapter's *SocialMEdia* feature looks at the benefits of classroom tablets, as well as the dilemmas their use may present.

SocialMEdia

Although public education is traditionally slow to adopt new technology, the use of tablets in the classroom is proving to be the exception. Some estimates put tablet sales to schools as doubling each year for several years. However, integrating them into the curriculum is still in the infancy stage. Teachers using tablets see them as valuable tools for teaching and learning, with potential to have greater impact with time.

Tablets make sense in every kind of school, but particularly in rural areas, providing virtual field trips, conversations with experts from around the world, advanced placement courses, and more. In some areas there aren't enough towers to make Internet access possible in homes. Even without Internet, programs can be loaded on tablets to give access to students in rural areas.

Let's look at some benefits of tablet use for teaching and learning:

1. Students are comfortable with the technology. Teachers may have difficulty adjusting to tablets, but students don't. Tablets are portable, colorful, connected, and interactive.
2. Tablets are now readily available, made by a number of companies, each with strong and weak points. Apple's iPad, Amazon's Kindle Fire, Barnes & Noble's Nook, Google's Nexus 7, and other Android tablets are among the most popular. The Microsoft Surface has some advantages because of its detachable keyboard, solving the typing issue of other touch-only tablets. Increased competition will likely drive prices lower.
3. Innovative software is continually being developed specifically for tablets. There are applications for tablets in all subject areas. For example, in science there are apps that allow students to explore and label the stars and constellations. Images from digital microscopes may be shared on tablets. Also, tablets can bring history to life through interactive ebooks and videos, with primary sources accessible. Students can keep up with happenings around the world on tablets. For students with special needs, curriculum may be tailored through specific apps that help them learn in ways that suit their strengths.
4. Cameras on tablets allow individual exploration, creativity, and the capacity for more engaging presentations.
5. Because of access to the Internet, information on tablets does not go out of date as it does in a textbook.
6. Tablets can store thousands of books, allowing students virtually limitless data storage capacity.
7. Tablets provide class interactivity. Students can communicate with teachers and other students, share ideas, and work on projects.

There are drawbacks to using tablets in the classroom that will undoubtedly be remedied with innovation and time. Here are some of the challenges of classroom tablet use:

1. The initial cost of tablets for a whole school is expensive. When questioned, cost is a factor for most individuals in positions to make the tablet-or-no-tablet decision. However, a New York City Council member has suggested replacing textbooks with tablets for 1,700 schools. She contends that this can happen when New York City stops purchasing textbooks.
2. So far, most tablets do not have built-in keyboards. The touch screen is not considered efficient for lengthy writing. It is still more difficult for students to respond to data on a tablet than on desktop or laptop computers.
3. Monitoring student activity on tablets is a dilemma for many teachers that may be solvable using a tablet that is loaded with only what teachers want on them. The Kuno educational tablet allows content to be stored locally on the device. If a school doesn't want Internet access on the tablets, but only curriculum for the various subject areas, programs such as the CurriculumLoft, a web-based storage system for digital curriculum, will make this possible.
4. Breakage, loss, and theft pose dilemmas.
5. Perhaps the biggest challenge from a teacher's standpoint is finding ways to make tablets, or any technology for that matter, part of daily instruction, not just a motivating add-on. The possibilities are many.

Chances are you will enter the teaching profession with classroom tablets both commonplace and productive.

Social Reconstructionism

More than any other philosophy of education, **social reconstructionism** looks to education to change society, rather than just teach about it. Social reconstructionism as a philosophy of education calls on schools to educate students in ways that will help society move beyond all forms of discrimination to the benefit of everyone worldwide. This philosophy addresses such topics as racial equality, women's rights, sexism, environmental pollution, poverty, substance abuse, homophobia, and AIDS. Proponents of other educational philosophies often avoid such topics, thus relegating the topics to the null curriculum, discussed in Chapter 4.

According to some educators, Theodore Brameld (1904–1987) founded the philosophy of social reconstructionism following World War II. Brameld (1956) based the philosophy on two premises: (1) people now have the capacity to destroy civilization and (2) people have the potential to create a civilization marked by health and humanity. The basic tenets of social reconstructionism, however, go back to the early Greeks and, more recently, to Karl Marx, who called for a social revolution that would bring about equity among all people (Jacobsen, 2003).

Teachers who ascribe to social reconstructionism promote active student involvement in societal problems. They plan experiences for students to explore issues and possible solutions, but avoid moralizing. They promote democracy and the freedom to make choices while helping students discover the consequences of particular lines of reasoning and action. All of this occurs within an educational context that focuses on reading comprehension, research techniques, analysis and evaluation skills, and writing as a form of persuasive communication.

Major proponents of social reconstructionism as a philosophy of education include George Counts (1907–1974), Paulo Friere (1922–1987), and Ivan Illich (1926–2002). In his book *Dare the School Build a New Social Order?* (1932), Counts wrote about his view that schools should equip students to deal with world problems. Friere wrote in *Pedagogy of the Oppressed* (1970) about his personal experiences in working with poor illiterate peasants that led him to the philosophy that education is the key to empowering the poor to control and improve their lives. In his book *Deschooling Society* (1971), Illich promoted a radical view. He wrote that schools as we know them should be eliminated because they do nothing to decrease poverty. He contended that schools actually prevent what he saw as real education, a process he viewed as happening in more informal ways. Although "deschooling" American society is not likely to happen, the social reconstructionism views of Illich have prompted important questions about the role of public education (Chartock, 2004).

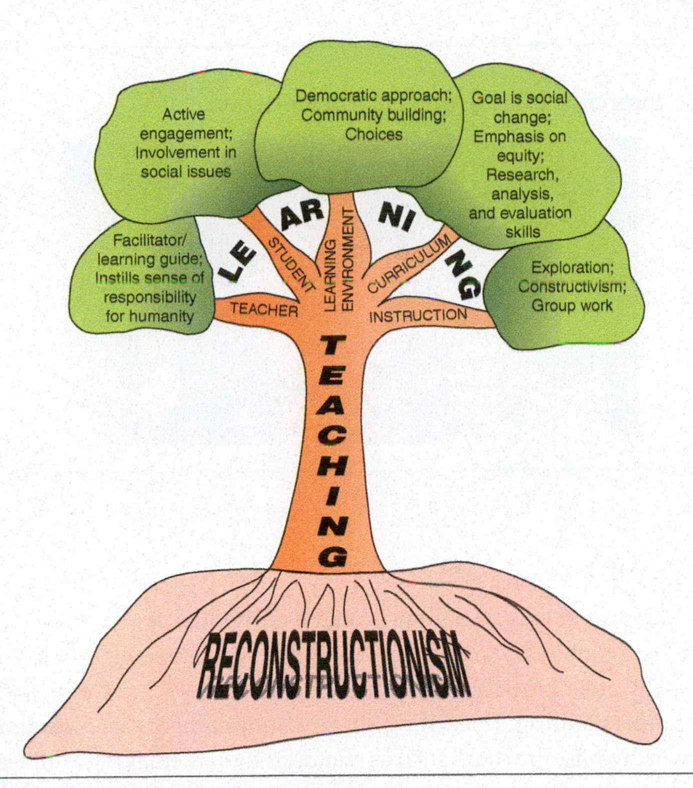

Figure 8.6 Social reconstructionism tree

Take a few minutes to study the social reconstructionism tree in Figure 8.6. Visualizing how teachers might translate the elements of social reconstructionism into their classrooms will help you understand this philosophy of education.

Brenda Beyal, focus teacher at Rees Elementary, considers her philosophy a healthy mix of progressivism and social reconstructionism, as you can read in *Teaching in Focus* and see in her interview.

Teaching in Focus

Brenda Beyal's passionate approach to teaching is evident in every aspect of her work—curriculum choices, teaching methods, relationships with students, interactions with colleagues, and the learning environment she has created in her classroom. In her interview, Brenda tells us she considers her choice to teach a "calling." She had planned to be an engineer until she took a course that addressed the needs of children with disabilities. That's when she knew teaching would be her life's work. She has taught for over 20 years, most of them spent in a multiage classroom at Rees Elementary, south of Salt Lake City, Utah.

Sara Davis Powell

Brenda's classroom is very student friendly, with tables and a couch rather than desks in rows; a large classroom library with books for all reading levels on a wide range of topics; multiple cabinets of art supplies; display boards of student work; and an area filled with Native American art, posters, and artifacts that have personal meaning to Brenda because of her Native American heritage.

Brenda was one of the originators of the multiage concept at Rees Elementary. She wanted to have longer-term relationships with individual students. She saw the benefits of children at different stages of maturation being together for several years. Brenda also liked the idea of collaborating with other teachers in creative ways. With colleagues Chris and Tim, Brenda maintains an arts-infused curriculum by teaching all three classes of multiage students an art form. Her specialty is visual arts, evident by the amount of artwork in her classroom.

Each day is filled with opportunities, according to Brenda, who finds purpose and beauty all around her as she fulfills her calling. Watch Brenda's interview to learn more about her and her classroom.

Application Exercise 8.2: Brenda's Philosophy

Existentialism

The primary emphasis of **existentialism** is on the individual. As a philosophy of education, existentialism contends that teachers teach the whole person, not just math, reading, science, or any other particular subject. Each student searches for personal meaning and personal understanding. If learning about a subject increases a student's sense of self, then it's worthwhile. Practices such as standardization, tracking, and testing do not fit into an existentialist viewpoint. Because meaning is personal, each student has the freedom and the subsequent responsibility to make his or her own choices. Existentialism rejects traditional education. Few schools practice existentialism as an educational philosophy, and most that do are private. However, there are teachers in both public and private classrooms who practice some elements of existentialism.

The existentialist teacher honors individual students by arranging for learning experiences from which each student may choose. The classroom atmosphere is supposed to be stimulating and full of choices. The student's job is to make choices and

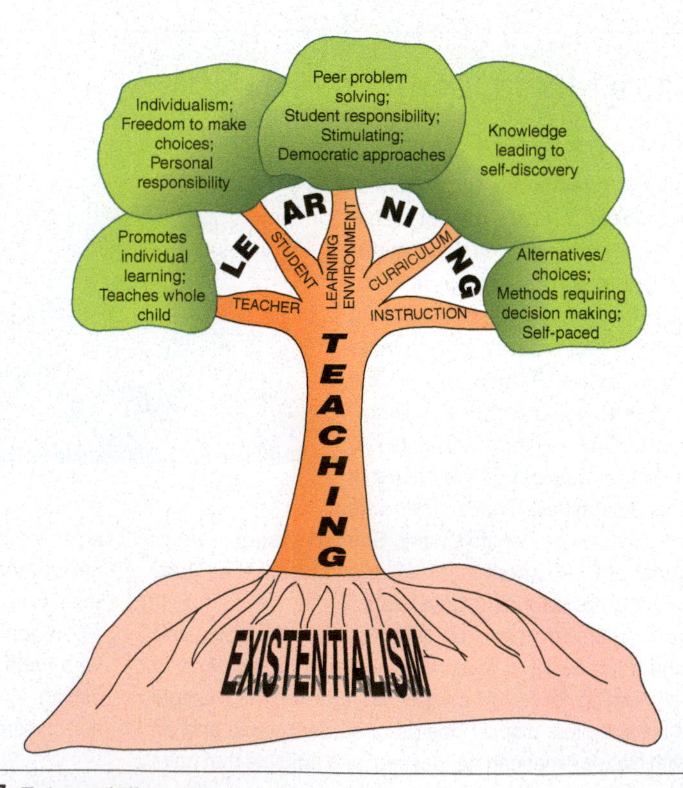

Figure 8.7 Existentialism tree

then take responsibility for those choices. Teachers and students have a great deal of individual contact, participating in learning that is self-paced and self-directed (Greene, 1978). A teacher who follows existentialism as a philosophy of education teaches best by being a role model, and demonstrates the importance of a discipline by pursuing academic goals related to the subject area.

A. S. Neill (1883–1973) was one of the most influential proponents of existentialism. He founded the Summerhill School in England following World War I. Learning by discovery was the primary feature of Summerhill. The student as an individual was emphasized and exploration for the sake of learning had few restrictions (Neill, 1960).

Maxine Greene (1917–2014) was the most well-known proponent of existentialism. She referred to a heightened level of personal awareness as "wide-awakeness." Greene refuted critics of existentialism who said that the philosophy in practice allows children to run free and out of control. She maintained that freedom has rules that allow others to be free as well (Greene, 1995).

Take a few minutes to study the existentialism tree in Figure 8.7. Visualizing how teachers might translate the elements of existentialism into their classrooms will help you understand this philosophy of education. Then read what Chris Roberts, one of our focus teachers at Rees Elementary School, says that reflects his philosophy of education.

Teaching in Focus

Chris Roberts, Grades 3–5 Multiage Classroom, Rees Elementary School, Utah. *In his own words . . . .*

I heard or read somewhere that "you teach who you are." I know, after teaching 29 years, that there is a lot of truth in those five words. I've had students return to visit me years after they've been in my class and I get invited to many of their weddings. As we catch up on the years that have passed, none of them talk about their reading or math; they tell me about me. Their memories don't focus on the great unit I taught on Native Americans, but rather on the time I told them about a trip I went on or a belief I have about life. I don't think you can be an excellent teacher if your own life is boring or "unexamined," as Henry David Thoreau would caution. Children will naturally be less interested in learning from someone they find uninteresting. Don't let the classroom, and pressures you will surely face, rule your life. Live a full life. Share with your students what you learn and experience on your amazing path.

Sara Davis Powell

Application Exercise 8.3: Contrasting philosophies of progressivism and perennialism

Point of Reflection 8.2

Do you identify most with the elements of progressivism, social reconstructionism, or existentialism? Explain your reasoning.

Check Your Understanding 8.3

8.4 How Do I Begin to Develop My Own Personal Philosophy of Education?

8.4 Develop your own personal philosophy of education.

When it comes to developing a philosophy of education, balance is important. If you found yourself aligning with parts of one and parts of another as you read about the prominent philosophies of education, and thinking, "How will I weigh all this and decide?" you are certainly not alone. Very few educators can place themselves squarely in one camp or another. Picking and choosing from among the components of several philosophies is referred to as taking an *eclectic approach*. This entails balance. It's natural for teachers to lean toward one philosophy or approach more than another, but subscribing to only one philosophy will not serve the needs of all children.

Other Philosophies

Before considering the development of a personal philosophy of education, let's look briefly at some other "isms" that may impact educational philosophy.

Idealism is a philosophy based on the belief that ideas are the only reliable form of reality. Idealists believe that because the physical world changes continually, ideas are what should be taught. Taking the opposite stance, **realism** is based on the belief that some facts are absolutes whether recognized by all or not. Realists contend that the only way to know these absolutes is to study the material world.

Romanticism, or naturalism, contends as a philosophy of education that the needs of the individual are more important than the needs of society. Many early childhood and elementary educators incorporate into their classrooms the tenets of romanticism that state that young children are born good, pure, and full of curiosity, and that their individual interests should be validated with opportunities to explore and manipulate elements of their environment.

Postmodernism grew out of a sense that those in power control those who don't have power. Postmodernists believe this control is manifested through major institutions such as schools. The decades of the 1960s and 1970s were times of unprecedented outcries for justice and equality through the civil rights movement, the feminist movement, and a renewed concern for the poor. Postmodernist philosophy grew as a response to these cultural stirrings. The postmodern curriculum includes perspectives on history and literature by a variety of authors representing different lifestyles. Proponents of postmodernism contend they are attempting to strike a balance of power among all people and that intellectual growth from multiple perspectives is one avenue for doing so. Critics of postmodernism contend that the philosophy seeks to promote political purposes rather than intellectual purposes (Ozmon and Craver, 2008).

You will likely encounter other philosophies as you participate in future teacher preparation courses. The ones you have read about so far provide many choices for you to consider as you begin the process of forming your own philosophy of education. This chapter's *The Opinion Page* feature expresses a philosophy of education. The writer has definite opinions about a particular aspect of education that should be included in the opportunities afforded students.

Your Turn

Now it's your turn to grow a philosophy tree. The root system will consist of an anchor philosophy—that is, the philosophy with which you most closely align. There's no need to ascribe to every tenet of this anchor philosophy, but it should express most of

The Opinion Page

This Opinion Editorial appeared in the Las Vegas Sun, *on January 15, 2012.*

Education Should Include Opportunities in Sports, Activities

Jocelyn Jordan commutes to Western High School to play for the girls' basketball team because her school doesn't have a squad . . . sometimes she makes it on time, sometimes she doesn't.

Jordan, a sophomore at Northwest Career Technical Academy, is at the mercy of public transit. Her journey requires her to catch two buses; she sometimes jogs in at the end of practice because of a late bus. When practice or games are over, which can be well into the evening, it's back to the bus stop to go home. She tries to do her homework on the bus so she isn't up too late after finally getting home.

Teammate Tenaya Williams, a sophomore guard at Western, understands that. She takes the bus home, a trip of 3.1 miles. She knows the distance because she has walked the route and measured it.

But, admirably, these young women aren't looking for sympathy—they know that's the price they have to pay for playing high school basketball.

"If you really care about something, you will walk 3.1 miles for it," Williams said. "It's cool. I don't mind having to take the bus or walk."

That is a commendable attitude. It certainly isn't easy for a student to try to juggle school and a sport, particularly when she knows she won't be home until late and may still have to cram in homework. It makes for long days and not much sleep. That's hardly a recipe for student success, and not too long ago, students had a better option. The Clark County School District used to provide bus service to help students who were staying late for extracurricular activities but that service was ended about a decade ago in a round of budget cutting.

The lack of bus service dampens student participation in sports and after-school activities. "I guarantee you a majority of the schools would get more kids involved if we had activity buses," [said] Ray Mathis, the district's executive athletic director. . . . "There are a lot of kids in that situation across the district."

Western is part of the district's "turnaround" effort. It is one of three low-performing high school campuses that are receiving extra money and attention as officials try to boost performance. As part of that effort, school officials should find a way to provide students the opportunity to participate in sports and extracurricular activities by offering some sort of way home.

This may not be a priority in a district that has struggled with low test scores, and it can be easy for some people to wave off sports and activities as "extras," saying schools should be focusing on the basics and raising student achievement. Academics is vitally important, and it's true that raising student performance has to be the priority. But that shouldn't be seen as exclusive of sports and activities. Sports and extracurricular activities are an important part of a student's education. Involvement in activities helps students connect with the school. They also teach important lessons that can't be replicated in a classroom—consider the friendships found among teammates or the bonds formed when students come together in a club to accomplish a task.

Without lessening the importance of academic achievement, life is much more than filling in the right bubble on a standardized test. Any turnaround won't be complete until students have the opportunity to receive a well-rounded education, and that includes the ability to participate in sports and extracurricular activities.

And sometimes that includes help getting there.

This Opinion Page piece expresses a philosophy of education, not necessarily one that fits neatly in one of our five philosophies, but rather a mix of philosophies. Write a well-developed paragraph in response to each of the following questions:

1. Choose two philosophies from this chapter that align with what *The Opinion Page* expresses. Write about each, briefly explaining why you chose it.
2. Do you support the opinion expressed in *The Opinion Page*? If so, why? Do you have personal experiences that lead to your support? If you do not agree with *The Opinion Page*, give your reason(s).
3. Do you agree that it's the school district's responsibility to provide transportation for students who choose to be involved in extracurricular activities? If so, why? If not, why not?

your current beliefs about teaching and learning. Other philosophies may be part of the feeder root system. The branches and leaves of the tree's canopy will be a mix of what you believe about the roles of the teacher, students, the learning environment, the curriculum, and instruction. Keep in mind that the deeper and wider the philosophical root system, the stronger and more stable the trunk will grow and the richer and more extensive the canopy will be.

One approach to help begin examining your own philosophy is to study the content of Table 8.1 carefully. Considering the responses to the important and broad questions in the table is a way to explore your own philosophical views. There are many questions that may be asked, with each philosophy of education contributing unique responses.

Table 8.1 Questions and philosophical responses

Question	Essentialism	Perennialism	Progressivism	Reconstructionism	Existentialism
What is real?	Elements of core curriculum; may change	Elements of core curriculum; unchanging	What can be verified through the senses	What can be verified through research and analysis	Based entirely on the individual's perspective and experience
How do we acquire knowledge?	From a combination of the classics and science	From the never-changing classics	From individual experiences and discovery	From individual and group searches for meaning and justice	Through individual quests; making choices
What is valuable?	Core of knowledge that responds to some societal shifts	Changeless core of knowledge	Determined by individual interacting with own culture	Whatever makes society more just and equitable	Whatever leads to greater self- knowledge
What makes sense?	Classics provide generalizations; specifics are deduced; observation and analysis of specifics may lead to generalization	Deductive reasoning from truths of classics	Discovered through problem solving	Weighed against potential benefit or harm to society	Whatever enhances individual freedom and increases personal responsibility

Application Exercise 8.4: Table 8.1: Questions and philosophical responses

Another approach to growing your philosophy tree is to spend some time thinking about your favorite teachers in early childhood, elementary, middle, and high school. Why did you admire them? What made them special? Your answers need to go beyond "She was so nice" or "He just stands out in my mind." To help you think through the reasons particular teachers had positive effects on you, use the chart in Table 8.2. Think about how this person appeared to view his or her roles as a teacher, including relationships with students, the creation of the learning environment, and approaches to curriculum and instruction. Table 8.2 will help organize your recollections.

A sincere, honest start to the development of a philosophy of education will help you grow into the teaching profession. Having opportunities to talk about your philosophy and listen to your classmates, your instructor, and teachers in the field will make you more comfortable articulating your stance. The more you think, talk, and listen, the more confident you will become that you are grounded in your reasons for how you approach your role, your students, the learning environment, curriculum, and instruction.

Figure 8.8 is a tree waiting for you to make it your own. Your philosophy tree can be a valuable component of the teaching portfolio you will no doubt develop as part of your teacher preparation.

Table 8.2 My favorite teachers' philosophical bents

Teacher's Name	Teacher's Role	Interactions with Students	Learning Environment	Curriculum	Instruction	Aligned with Which Philosophy?

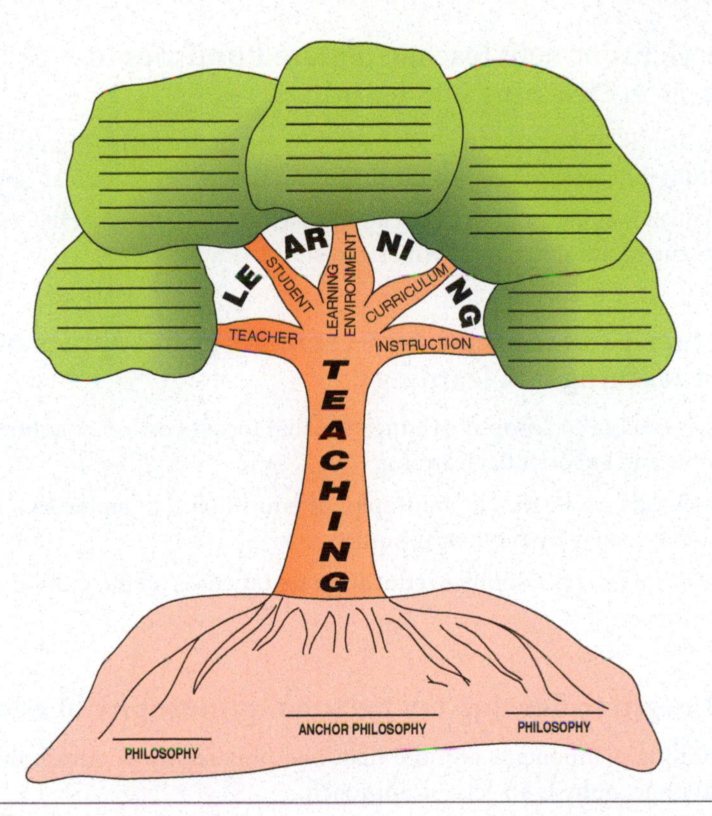

Figure 8.8 My philosophy tree

Check Your Understanding 8.4

Concluding Thoughts

Chances are that a philosophy of education is not something you've ever seriously considered. Now you have some background about major philosophies of education. You have been prompted to think about, and tentatively declare, which philosophy represents your primary beliefs about teaching and learning. You also know that an eclectic approach is not only natural but will actually benefit the diverse groups of students you will encounter.

Thoughtful teachers are not necessarily swayed by gimmicks and fads. They have basic beliefs about teaching and learning that guide their practice, and they can articulate the bases for their decisions. These are teachers who will positively affect student learning throughout their careers. This applies equally to early childhood, elementary, middle, and high school teachers. A carefully considered philosophy of education provides a solid foundation for professionals in the classroom.

After reading the *Chapter in Review*, read more about Brenda and respond to items in this chapter's *Developing Professional Competence.*

Chapter in Review

Why is a philosophy of education important?

- We all have philosophies that guide our decisions, attitudes, and actions.
- A teacher's philosophy of education affects every decision about teaching.

How do two prominent teacher-centered philosophies of education affect teaching and learning?

- Essentialism is a philosophy of education based on the belief that there is a core curriculum that is responsive to the times and that every American should know.
- Perennialism is a philosophy of education based on the belief that there is a changeless core curriculum that every American should know.

How do three prominent student-centered philosophies of education affect teaching and learning?

- Progressivism is a philosophy of education that focuses on a curriculum of interest to students and experiential learning.
- Social reconstructionism is a philosophy of education that endorses a curriculum that benefits society by promoting equity.
- Existentialism is a philosophy of education that focuses on the individual's search for meaning.

How do I begin to develop my personal philosophy of education?

- Incorporating components of more than one philosophy of education into your personal philosophy is an eclectic approach.
- Growing an effective philosophy tree requires a strong root system with philosophical grounding to enhance both teaching and learning.

Developing Professional Competence

Sara Davis Powell

Thoughtfully reading this scenario and responding to the items that follow it will help you prepare for licensure exams.

Brenda Beyal ascribes to a very student-centered philosophy of education, as we have seen in her interview and what we have read in *Teaching in Focus*. She knows the content she teaches and works very hard to be the best teacher she can be. The one thing that continually bothers Brenda is the fact that we are in an era of standards, where curriculum is prescribed and teaching is on a fast-paced schedule. Add to this the week of standardized tests she must monitor every spring, and we find Brenda seeking balance for her students and innovative ways to accomplish what is expected of her while paying attention to individual student needs.

One of Brenda's favorite authors is Vito Perrone (1991). Here is an excerpt that is particularly poignant for her:

> To engage students constructively, the school day needs more continuities, not more fragmentation. Work that can truly be valued takes time, sometimes hours and days. It is hardly reasonable to expect a child to complete a fine piece of artwork in ten- or twenty-minute intervals, twice a week, or produce a well-organized, thoughtful description, a poetic or narrative story within ten minutes. Teachers know this but claim that in this current basic skills, testing, "academic" environment, they don't have the time any more for work of that quality. (p. 33)

Now it's time for you to respond to two short essay items. In your responses, be sure to address all the dilemmas and questions posed in each item. These items are followed by two multiple-choice questions.

1. Perrone writes about "continuities." What kinds of activities do you think Brenda would put in this category? Explain two continuities you would expect to see in her classroom.
2. How might Brenda incorporate balance into the day as she teaches the standards while valuing quality and creativity?

Application Exercise 8.5: Developing Professional Competence

3. What do you think Brenda may consider sources of fragmentation of her teaching day?
   a. District administrative guidelines that outline the time to be spent each day on language arts, reading, math, science, and social studies.
   b. Her students go to dance/movement class with Chris Roberts in the morning and to music/ theater class with Tim Mendenhall in the afternoon.
   c. She has an early lunch time with her class.
   d. Rees incorporates two recess times a day.
4. Brenda attributes her agreement with Perrone's point about what is valuable in schoolwork to her Native American heritage. What might be the best of these four options for Brenda to let students know about her opinion?
   a. She could teach the students some of the soothing chants and tunes Native American mothers sing to their children.
   b. She could share artifacts and talk with students about how they are preserved.
   c. She could tell them stories about patience and perseverance from Native American folklore.
   d. She could explain to students the meaningfulness of the sundial and how Native Americans have historically honored the sun.

Application Exercise 8.6: Developing Professional Competence

Flash Cards 8.1

Shared Writing 8.1: : Basic Philosophical Questions

Chapter 9

The Societal Context of Schooling in the United States

Learning Objectives

After studying this chapter, you will have knowledge and skills to:

9.1 Explain how family, community, and society impact students in the United States.

9.2 Describe how socioeconomic status affects students in the United States.

9.3 Articulate how health issues negatively impact students in the United States.

9.4 Analyze how issues involving race affect students in the United States.

9.5 Identify the effects of bullying, theft, and violence on students and schools in the United States.

9.6 Summarize how truancy and dropping out affect youth in the United States.

Dear Reader

This chapter is about the realities that touch the lives of students in our classrooms. Although these issues don't affect all students or families in a negative way, they do reach into all settings—urban, suburban, and rural. They affect all races and all ethnicities in both affluent neighborhoods and impoverished ones. And they affect U.S. citizens as well as noncitizens.

The issue of poverty has far-reaching negative effects on students and their success. It's hard for most of us to understand what it's like to move when the rent comes due. Yes, the negative influences of poverty can be overcome, but it's a difficult road to travel. Even so, teachers can help children and adolescents travel it more productively. Issues involving childhood and teen obesity, substance abuse, and risky sexual behavior are also serious challenges that will likely be with us for a long time. We are working on impacting student choices. The guarded good news is that drug, alcohol, and tobacco use, as well as many risky sexual behaviors, have either leveled off or are declining. Helping children and adolescents make wise choices continues to be a major teacher responsibility.

Brown v. *Board of Education*, the landmark case that led to school desegregation, was decided 60 years ago, and yet we still deal with issues revolving around race. All too often, violence, theft, and bullying exist in society and in schools. Creating respectful environments of civility is the responsibility of teachers who are watchful and wise.

Where Do **I Stand?**

 **"Click here to complete the inventory online."**

This inventory focuses on professionalism—a way of life that should permeate your relationships and propel reform that benefits teaching and learning. As you think through the following statements that prompt you to consider your own views, indicate your level of agreement by choosing a number and placing it in the blank before the statement. Following the inventory are directions for how to organize your responses and what they may mean in terms of where you stand.

4 I strongly agree

3 I agree

2 I don't have an opinion

1 I disagree

0 I strongly disagree

____ 1. Professionalism entails meeting responsibilities head on, as well as taking full advantage of opportunities involving teaching and learning.

____ 2. One of the most valuable aspects of a teacher preparation program is the opportunity to spend time in schools.

____ 3. Becoming a professional entails reflecting on field experiences in schools.

____ 4. After graduation, a teacher candidate has time to develop professional attitudes and actions.

____ 5. Being positive is a choice. It doesn't mean glossing over difficulties but rather approaching each day with possibilities in focus.

____ 6. Core courses, although interesting, have little bearing on teacher preparation.

____ 7. It is very important to respect the adults and students in your school.

____ 8. Spending time in schools is peripheral to learning to be a teacher.

____ 9. Becoming a professional involves field experiences that let you see reality, reflect on what you see, and formulate possible solutions to the dilemmas you observe.

____ 10. Learning what not to do as a result of seeing its actual, or potential, damage is powerful.

____ 11. Being realistic about schools is counter to being positive about the possibilities of quality education.

____ 12. When we fulfill our responsibilities, and take advantage of our opportunities involving relationships, we are doing so for the children and adolescents we teach.

____ 13. We learn valuable lessons in professionalism only from positive role models.

____ 14. Teachers who take responsibility for student learning take no excuses—from students, parents, or themselves.

____ 15. Part of professionalism entails teaching the whole child, requiring that we accept students for who they are rather than what they do.

____ 16. When conditions outside the classroom are severely impaired, making a positive difference for kids within our classrooms is close to impossible.

____ 17. When we take responsibility for teaching all students unconditionally, regardless of the circumstances, we will necessarily have high expectations for them.

____ 18. The way schools care about children is reflected in the way schools care about the children's families.

____ 19. Parental involvement is actually an interference in many instances.

____ 20. Parental involvement matters to student achievement.

____ 21. Teachers need to grasp the reality of parental concern and tenaciously find ways to involve them.

____ 22. Professional courtesy dictates that teachers not observe one another in their classrooms because of the possibility of being judgmental.

____ 23. Whatever the barriers to parental involvement, teachers need to strive continually to break them down by cultivating an invitational attitude.

____ 24. Part of being a professional teacher is knowing what is available and, along with administrators and counselors, making sure families are aware of how to access community services.

____ 25. Although teachers have responsibility for the welfare of students in their classrooms while in school, they bear little responsibility for their relationships with students' families.

____ 26. Professional growth is an absolute necessity for teacher effectiveness.

____ 27. There is always something to be learned when teachers get together, regardless of the perceived quality or relevance of what is formally presented.

____ 28. Teachers have a responsibility to join professional organizations to help build the teaching profession.

____ 29. Classrooms and groups of children benefit from engaging lessons, but this does not promote the professionalism of teaching.

____ 30. When a teacher tries an instructional strategy that works well with a particular topic or with a specific group of students, sharing the experience with other teachers is an act of professionalism.

Now record your responses, find the sum of each column, and then divide each sum by 10 to determine A, B, and C.

ITEM #	*MY RESPONSE*	*ITEM #*	*MY RESPONSE*	*ITEM #*	*MY RESPONSE*
1		17		4	
2		18		6	
3		20		8	
5		21		11	
7		23		13	
9		24		16	
10		26		19	
12		27		22	
14		28		25	
15		30		29	
Sum = ÷ 10 =	= A	Sum = ÷ 10 =	= B	Sum = ÷ 10 =	= C

Now subtract C from 4 because C indicates levels of disagreement with negative concepts. This new number becomes D, a positive indicator.

Add A, B, and D and divide the sum by 3. Plot this number on the number line to see where you fall on a continuum of professional attitudes.

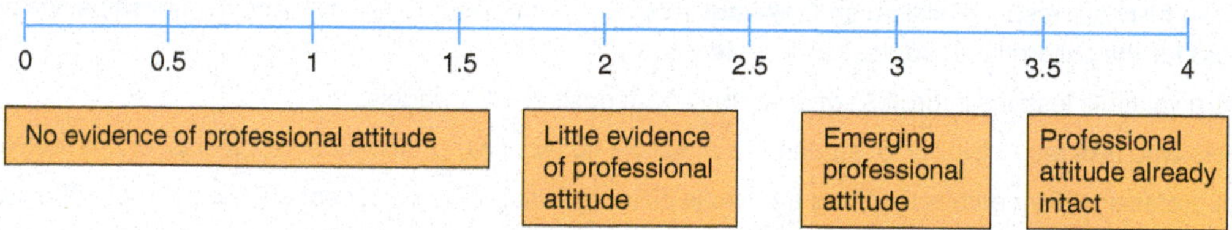

Does your place on the number line accurately reflect where you think you are with regard to teacher professionalism? If so, why? If not, why not?

9.1 How Do Family, Community, and Society Impact Students in the United States?

9.1 Explain how family, community, and society impact students in the United States.

The most basic societal unit of humankind is the family. Families exist within communities, and communities make up the larger building blocks of any society. This relationship, as illustrated in Figure 9.1, creates a pattern of influence that is undeniable. When children are very young, the family has the most direct influence. As they grow,

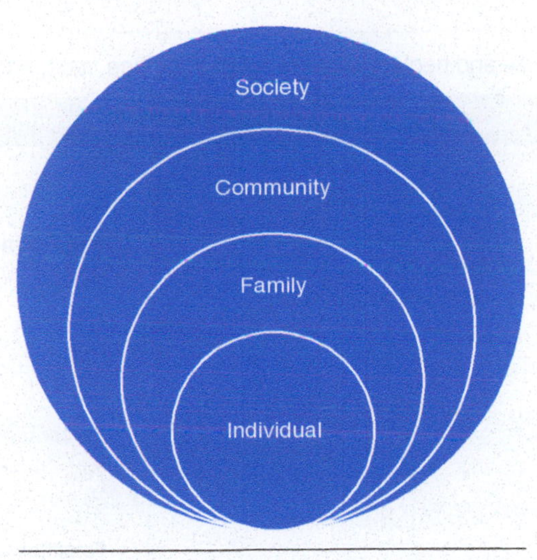

Figure 9.1 Individual, family, community, society

the community plays a bigger role in children's lives. The influence of society grows immensely stronger with age.

For some children, family life is idyllic and supportive; for others, it is not. Some children's families live in communities that are peaceful and caring; others live in the midst of destruction and violence. Although they all live within the same society, some children in the United States are shielded from some negative influences by family and community, and others are not.

Family

Family is a source of diversity. Regardless of what a family may look like or the societal pressures a family may experience, members of families can support student success—or thwart it.

Many children and adolescents are victims of neglect and abuse, which places them squarely in the at-risk category. **Child abuse** is any act that results in death, serious harm, or exploitation; **child neglect** is a form of abuse resulting from a failure to act in the best interest of the child. Almost five children in the United States died as a result of abuse or neglect *each day* in 2014. The United States has the worst record of child abuse–related deaths among all industrialized nations (Child Welfare Information Gateway, 2016). This fact should alarm all of us. Table 9.1 consists of percentages of child fatalities by abuse or neglect in 2014 by gender, age, race, and perpetrator. Tragic, indeed. Note in Table 9.1 that more than four African American children per 100,000 died of abuse or neglect, whereas fewer than two per 100,000 Hispanic and white children died of abuse or neglect. Children of two or more races had the next highest number of fatalities after African American children with more than two per 100,000. More fatalities were male than female, and 79% of perpetrators were parents. It is also appalling to realize that 90% of the fatalities due to child abuse and neglect in 2014 were those most vulnerable: children under the age of 3.

For a case of abuse or neglect to be included in government statistics, it must be reported, meet the established definition, and be investigated. Allegations of child abuse and neglect received by agencies of the U.S. Department of Health & Human Services (DHHS) go through a screening process to determine if child maltreatment is likely. If it is, the allegation is turned over to Child Protective Services (CPS) and considered a report of child abuse or neglect. According to Childhelp (2016), a prevention and treatment of child abuse organization, more than six million children were reported as victims of abuse and neglect, with approximately 700,000 children verified as victims of child abuse or neglect in 2014. This number of children would fill 10 modern

Table 9.1 Child abuse and neglect fatalities by gender, age, race, and perpetrator, 2014

Gender	Percentage
Male	59
Female	41
Age	**Percentage**
0–3 years	78
4–7 years	12
8–11 years	5
12–17 years	5
Perpetrator	**Percentage**
Father or mother or both	79
Nonparent (may be caregiver or relative or other)	21
Race	**Fatalities per 100,000**
African American	4.36 per 100,000
American/Alaskan Native	1.46 per 100,000
Asian	0.64 per 100,000
Hispanic	1.54 per 100,000
Pacific Islander	1.14 per 100,000
White	1.79 per 100,000
Two or more races	2.23 per 100,000

Based on: Child Welfare Information Gateway. (2016). *Child abuse and neglect fatalities 2014: Statistics and interventions*. Retrieved April 20, 2017, from https://www.childwelfare.gov/topics/can/
U.S. Department of Health & Human Services. (2016). *Administration for Children and Families, Administration on Children, Youth and Families, Children's Bureau*. Child maltreatment 2014.

football stadiums. Although this number is disturbing, we are told it is only the tip of the iceberg. Some forms of neglect, as well as both sexual and emotional abuse, have few recognizable symptoms to a casual observer. Maltreatment can remain undiscovered for an entire childhood. The recorded cases could actually represent millions of victimized children and adolescents. By some estimates, as many as 60% of deaths by abuse are not reported as abuse cases (Childhelp, 2016).

It is difficult to determine the scope of the toll that child neglect and abuse take on children and adolescents in the United States. For many, it's hard to imagine the reasons or the results of such cruelty. For some students, teachers and school personnel are their most trusted adults.

WHAT CAN SCHOOLS AND TEACHERS DO? School personnel are among those required to report suspected abuse. Also included are social workers, health-care workers, mental health professionals, child-care providers, medical examiners or coroners, and law enforcement officers. Teachers should report suspicions to administrators or guidance counselors. Any citizen may report suspicions of abuse to any Child Protection Services agency or to Childhelp at 800-4-A-CHILD (800-422-4453).

As a teacher, you may be the adult who comes between a child and a lifetime of suffering or, worse, death. Knowing the signs of neglect and abuse is an important first step. Figure 9.2 lists the signs provided by Child Welfare Information Gateway.

Community and Society

Previous chapters have discussed the concept of community as it refers to relationships in a classroom or school. In this section, however, **community** refers to the neighborhood, town, city, or county in which a student lives. The members of a community are

Figure 9.2 Recognizing child abuse

The following signs may signal the presence of child abuse or neglect.

In general, the **child:**

- Shows sudden changes in behavior or school performance.
- Has not received help for physical or medical problems brought to the parents' attention.
- Has learning problems (or difficulty concentrating) that cannot be attributed to specific physical or psychological causes
- Is always watchful, as though preparing for something bad to happen.
- Lacks adult supervision.
- Is overly compliant, passive, or withdrawn.
- Comes to school or other activities early, stays late, and does not want to go home.
- Is reluctant to be around a particular person.
- Discloses maltreatment.

In general, the **parent:**

- Denies the existence of—or blames the child for—the child's problems in school or at home.
- Asks teachers or other caregivers to use harsh physical discipline if the child misbehaves.
- Sees the child as entirely bad, worthless, or burdensome.
- Demands a level of physical or academic performance the child cannot achieve.
- Looks primarily to the child for care, attention, and satisfaction of the parent's emotional needs.
- Shows little concern for the child.

In general, the **parent and child:**

- Rarely touch or look at each other.
- Consider their relationship entirely negative.
- State that they do not like each other.

Here are the signs of child physical, sexual, and emotional abuse, as well as the signs of neglect.

Signs of Physical Abuse

Consider the possibility of physical abuse when the **child**:

- Has unexplained burns, bites, bruises, broken bones, or black eyes.
- Has fading bruises or other marks noticeable after an absence from school.
- Seems frightened of the parents and protests or cries when it is time to go home.
- Shrinks at the approach of adults.
- Reports injury by a parent or another adult caregiver.
- Abuses animals or pets.

Consider the possibility of physical abuse when the **parent or other adult caregiver**:

- Offers conflicting, unconvincing, or no explanation for the child's injury, or provides an explanation that is not consistent with the injury.
- Describes the child as "evil" or in some other very negative way.
- Uses harsh physical discipline with the child.
- Has a history of abuse as a child.
- Has a history of abusing animals or pets.

Signs of Neglect

Consider the possibility of neglect when the **child:**

- Is frequently absent from school.
- Begs or steals food or money.
- Lacks needed medical or dental care, immunizations, or glasses
- Is consistently dirty and has severe body odor
- Lacks sufficient clothing for the weather
- Abuses alcohol or other drugs

Consider the possibility of neglect when the **parent or other adult caregiver:**

- Appears to be indifferent to the child.
- Seems apathetic or depressed.
- Behaves irrationally or in a bizarre manner.
- Is abusing alcohol or other drugs.

(continued)

Figure 9.2 *(continued)*

Signs of Sexual Abuse

Consider the possibility of sexual abuse when the **child:**

- Has difficulty walking or sitting.
- Suddenly refuses to change for gym or to participate in physical activities.
- Reports nightmares or bedwetting.
- Experiences a sudden change in appetite.
- Demonstrates bizarre, sophisticated, or unusual sexual knowledge or behavior.
- Becomes pregnant or contracts a venereal disease, particularly if under age 14.
- Runs away.
- Reports sexual abuse by a parent or another adult caregiver.
- Attaches very quickly to strangers or new adults in their environment.

Consider the possibility of sexual abuse when the **parent or other adult caregiver:**

- Is unduly protective of the child or severely limits the child's contact with other children, especially of the opposite sex.
- Is secretive and isolated.
- Is jealous or controlling with family members.

Signs of Emotional Maltreatment

Consider the possibility of emotional maltreatment when the **child:**

- Shows extremes in behavior, such as overly compliant or demanding behavior, extreme passivity, or aggression.
- Is either inappropriately adult (parenting other children, for example) or inappropriately infantile (frequently rocking or head-banging, for example).
- Is delayed in physical or emotional development.
- Has attempted suicide.
- Reports a lack of attachment to the parent.

Consider the possibility of emotional maltreatment when the **parent or other adult caregiver:**

- Constantly blames, belittles, or berates the child.
- Is unconcerned about the child and refuses to consider offers of help for the child's problems.
- Overtly rejects the child.

Based on: Child Welfare Information Gateway, 2013. *What Is Child Abuse and Neglect? Recognizing the Signs and Symptoms.* Retrieved August 31, 2013, from https://www.childwelfare.gov/pubs/factsheets/whatiscan.cfm

those who live within a specific geographic vicinity, those with whom students may come in contact through everyday activities such as shopping or when seeking services.

Most towns, cities, and counties provide services such as medical facilities; utilities (electric, gas, and water); welfare and Medicaid; some form of counseling or assistance; law enforcement; recreation opportunities; and schools. Available services vary. Some students and their families live in communities that support healthy lifestyles. In these communities, traditional measures of success—economic stability, nonviolent approaches to problem solving, and education—are valued and promoted.

Unfortunately, many students live in communities that are not only nonsupportive but also may be harmful to them. Some neighborhoods and communities are filled with violence and drugs, where children and adolescents are exposed to unhealthy lifestyles. For many children, negative influences of society will be mitigated by positive forces, such as supportive families, higher socioeconomic status, or membership in the majority race. Other children will suffer proportionately more from negative societal influences due, at least in part, to poverty.

WHAT CAN SCHOOLS AND TEACHERS DO? Regardless of the community in which a student lives, there are havens that provide private and government services. Teachers need to be knowledgeable about the services available to students and their families and provide them with information about how they can use those services to improve their lives.

Given the content of this chapter, you may be wondering why our first Teaching in Focus features Brandi Wade, a kindergarten teacher. The answer is actually simple: Social issues do not suddenly appear in the lives of adolescents. The societal context

Teaching in Focus

Sara Davis Powell

Her 14 years in the classroom have allowed Brandi Wade, one of our focus teachers at Summit Primary School in Ohio, to see her first group of kindergartners graduate from high school—or not. She has watched her students progress through primary, elementary, middle, and high school. She has seen some cope and thrive, and others become involved in destructive lifestyles. One thing Brandi knows for sure is that success is more likely for some than for others. Thus, she continually adjusts and differentiates.

In early December, Brandi decided that she needed to change some of her routines and instructional strategies. She had lived with her kindergartners 5 days a week for more than 3 months, and she knew some of them were not yet thriving. Her experience had taught her that treating these 5- and 6-year-olds the same was not going to meet their needs.

Brandi's decision to make some general changes in her classroom—including a new seating arrangement, a new rule-and-consequence system, a heavier reliance on one-on-one instructional strategies, and a buddy plan—came because of her consideration of the students in her class.

Brandi's realistic view—that some of her students will struggle more than others—lowers neither her hopes nor her expectations for all her students. Regardless of the strikes against them, Brandi maintains that her children can and will learn. She knows that challenges for her children may come in many forms. Students raised in poverty face particular challenges. Children who are minorities face other challenges. Children who live in relative wealth, but with few restraints or little structure, are challenged in other ways. All of Brandi's students need academic and interpersonal skills, along with self-confidence and the ability to make reasoned decisions. All are, or will be, at risk in some way. Revisit Brandi's room tour and watch her interview to gain more insight into how she implements her philosophy of education.

Application Exercise 9.1: Brandi's room tour and Interview

of students' lives surrounds them from birth. By the time children are in kindergarten, many influences have already shaped them. Brandi is very aware of the fact that her students enter kindergarten with individual histories as well as their present circumstances. They do not come to her, as educators once believed, as blank slates. Many already have strikes against them not of their own making, such as poverty or a family that doesn't value education. Brandi understands the saying, "There's nothing so unequal as the equal treatment of unequals." Think about this.

Point of Reflection 9.1

How familiar are you with child and adolescent abuse and neglect? Do you have personal experiences with abuse or neglect? Do you know people who are or were victims? Briefly explain.

Check Your Understanding 9.1

9.2 How Does Socioeconomic Status Affect Students in the United States?

9.2 Describe how socioeconomic status affects students in the United States.

We may think we know what "poor" looks like: the house, the car, the neighborhood, the need for a warm coat and school supplies, hunger, and meals supplied through Title I free breakfast and lunch programs. But Richard Rothstein (2008), a researcher who analyzes poverty and how it affects people, tells us to look more deeply to see the multitude of effects that may accompany poverty. If two groups of students attend the same quality school, but one group is distinctly disadvantaged in terms of socioeconomic status (SES), the group with low SES will achieve at lower levels. This is true not only according to Rothstein but also according to statistics kept in almost every school setting. "Each of these disadvantages makes only a small contribution to the achievement gap, but cumulatively, they explain a lot" (Rothstein, 2008, p. 8). Rothstein lists some of the disadvantages, stating that children in low-SES settings may have:

- No routine medical and dental care, leading to more absences
- Increased likelihood of asthma, often resulting in sleeplessness, irritability, and lack of exercise
- Lower birth weight, resulting in many possible health issues
- Lead poisoning and iron-deficiency anemia, each leading to cognitive and behavioral difficulties
- More mobility when the rent comes due, resulting in less school continuity
- Greater family stress due to employment uncertainty, often resulting in arbitrary discipline
- Fewer adult role models with professional careers
- More likelihood of living in single-parent homes
- Fewer family vacations, trips to museums and zoos
- Fewer opportunities for dance lessons, music instruction, organized sports teams, cultural awareness, and other activities that build confidence

Keep in mind that these are generalizations, and not stereotypes. Individual students living in poverty may display some, all, or none of these characteristics. In addition, Eric Jensen (2009, p. 19), veteran educator and expert researcher concerning brain function, tells us that "children raised in poverty are more likely to display

- 'acting-out' behaviors
- impatience and impulsivity
- gaps in politeness and social graces
- a more limited range of behavioral responses
- inappropriate emotional responses [and]
- less empathy for others' misfortunes."

Table 9.2 shows the percentages of children living in homes with incomes below the poverty line. Nationally, this percentage is 22%, with New Hampshire at the lowest

Table 9.2 Percent of children in families living in poverty by state, 2015

States	Percentage of Children Living in Poverty
New Hampshire	**11%**
North Dakota	**12%**
Maryland, Minnesota, Utah, Vermont, Wyoming	**13%**
Hawaii	**14%**
Alaska, Colorado, Connecticut, Iowa, Massachusetts, Virginia	**15%**
New Jersey, Washington, Wisconsin	**16%**
Delaware, Kansas, Maine, Nebraska	**17%**
Idaho, South Dakota	**18%**
Delaware, Illinois, Montana, Pennsylvania, Rhode Island	**19%**
Missouri, Oregon	**20%**
California, Indiana, Nevada, Ohio	**21%**
Oklahoma, Michigan, New York	**22%**
Florida, North Carolina, Texas	**23%**
Georgia, South Carolina, Tennessee	**24%**
Arizona, West Virginia	**25%**
Kentucky, District of Columbia	**26%**
Alabama, Arkansas	**27%**
Louisiana	**28%**
New Mexico	**29%**
Mississippi	**31%**

Based on: Annie E. Casey Foundation. (2016). *Kids count: A state-to-state comparison of economic wellbeing.* Retrieved March 14, 2017, from http://www.aecf.org/m/resourcedoc/aecf-the2016kidscountdatabook-2016.pdf#page=23

percentage (11%) and Mississippi having the highest percentage (31%). The total number of children under age 18 living in poverty is almost 16 million (Kids Count, 2016) (Annie E. Casey Foundation, 2016). Some say that emphasis on the disadvantages of poor children gives educators excuses for why these children don't learn at the levels of other children. On the contrary, awareness of these and other disadvantages provides teachers a more realistic view of what our mission involves. Excuses are unacceptable; knowledge and understanding are invaluable.

Mark Rank, researcher of the dilemma of poverty and children, tells us that half of all children in America will live in households that make use of food stamps at some time in their first 18 years of life. Even more startling is the fact that nearly

90% of African American children will have this experience. "Taken as a whole, the negative impact of poverty on children's overall health status is reflected in the fact that it has been estimated that poverty among American children raises the direct expenditures on health care by approximately $22 billion per year" (Rank and Hirschl, 2009, p. 998).

Homeless Children and Youth

Perhaps the most devastating impact of poverty is homelessness. On any given night in January 2016, there were approximately 120,000 homeless children in the United States, with more than 4,000 of them unaccompanied by someone over age 18. By some estimates, the United States has more homeless children and women than any other industrialized nation (Project HOME, 2017). The federal government defines *homeless children and youth* as those who lack a fixed, regular, and adequate nighttime residence. The children and youth may share overcrowded temporary housing (76%) or live in emergency or transitional shelters (14%) or in motels (7%) due to lack of alternative adequate accommodations. About 3% of the children in homeless families have little to no shelter and may spend nights in cars, parks, public spaces, abandoned buildings, substandard housing, bus or train stations, or similar settings (National Center for Homeless Education, 2016). Just reading these statistics is troubling; imagine what life must be like for the children who live them.

In the 2014–2015 school year, the U.S. government estimates that there were more than 1.2 million homeless children enrolled in public schools. This number is an underestimate of the total homeless children population, with more than 40% of the entire homeless population composed of families. The severe economic downturn of 2008 resulted in an 11% increase in the number of homeless children from 2008 to 2016. Many families that had homes in 2008 or 2009 lost them and became homeless. Causes of homelessness among children fall into three interrelated categories: family problems, economic problems, and residential instability. Regardless of the cause, recent evidence confirms that homelessness among families is increasing (National Center for Homeless Education, 2016).

The **McKinney-Vento Act of 1987** was strengthened and received new interest in 2016 when President Obama reauthorized the Elementary and Secondary Education Act as the Every Student Succeeds Act. McKinney-Vento is part of the federal government's response to homelessness. The act addresses the problems homeless children and youth face in enrolling, attending, and succeeding in school. Because of this act, homeless students are assured of:

- Equal access to the same free, appropriate public education as those who are not homeless
- A public preschool education
- Comparable educational services, including transportation and meals
- A mainstream school environment, free from being stigmatized in any way (Office of the Federal Register, 2016)

Homelessness is a devastating experience for families—it disrupts every aspect of family life, causes physical and emotional damage, interferes with children's education and development, and often results in the separation of children from parents.

Although generalizations may be useful for understanding children and planning learning experiences, it is important not to lump all low-income or homeless students together as a group and design programs based on only one element of their lives—their socioeconomic status. This kind of categorizing flies in the face of all we know about student learning differences and the value of getting to know students individually.

WHAT CAN SCHOOLS AND TEACHERS DO? When we consider ways to meet the needs of children and adolescents living in poverty, we must focus on their strengths with eyes that see possibilities. Here are some things to keep in mind when working with families and children in low-income homes:

- Have high expectations for all children, rememberingVygotsky's zone of proximal development (discussed in Chapter 3) and recognize that progress is incremental, with steps forward and steps backward, or no steps at all, impacted by many of the elements of poverty.
- Provide resources for children living in low-income settings. Lists of supplies needed for each grade level may cost from $20 to $40 per child. For some families, especially those with multiple children, this is a major burden. We should know about our students' home lives before we meet them by talking to former teachers and knowing addresses. A note saying you have some extra supplies and that families should not worry about the published list will forge a trusting bond with families.
- Have extra clothing on hand and hygiene supplies available in a "secret" closet and let students know they are welcome to "shop" when they have privacy in the classroom.
- Make sure your school has community resource information for families and that they communicate this to families in need.

Here are examples of educators who recognize their responsibility to care for all children and, in particular, those in economic distress.

- Doug is a middle school science teacher who keeps granola bars in his desk drawer for students who are so hungry that they fall asleep in his class. He also goes to the cafeteria for free breakfast with students who are hungry but may be embarrassed to go in alone.
- George is a high school teacher who collaborates with social workers to get clothes for students who need them and allows homeless students to leave school materials with him.
- Mary is principal of a middle school where local businesses contribute classroom supplies instead of asking students and parents to provide them. For Christmas, her staff gave bags to homeless students filled with practical items and gift certificates to grocery stores. They report that the toughest students soften and begin to trust the adults at school.

What we do in our classrooms to promote learning may indeed affect the future conditions of the students we teach and, ultimately, their children, the next generation of students. In a very real way, we *can* affect the economic conditions in which children grow. Jensen (2009) tells us that children who live in poverty have had major negative influences on their lives and feel hopeless. He contends that one of the most meaningful things we can do for children in poverty is to give them hope. "Hope changes brain chemistry, which influences the decisions we make and the actions we take. Hopefulness must be pervasive, and every single student should be able to feel it, see it, and hear it daily" (p. 113).

One of our ethical responsibilities as teachers is to raise public awareness of our students' accomplishments and realities. In doing so we can help eliminate harmful stereotyping and inform our communities about ways they may help our children grow strong and healthy in mind, body, and spirit. Read about one educator's efforts to raise public awareness in this chapter's *The Opinion Page* feature.

The Opinion Page

This Opinion Editorial was published in the La Crosse Tribune, *Wisconsin, on December 25, 2012.*

Poverty in Schools Is Community Problem

by Rick Blasing

Rick Blasing is a counselor at Lincoln Middle School, SOTA II and Coulee Montessori in La Crosse, Wis.

When you consider what it must be like to be a child living in poverty, what do you envision?

Do you visualize a sad, sullen young person, an individual who cannot even consider the possibility of a happy life for himself? Do you see an individual who may be poorly fed, ill-clothed or whose eyes reflect a profound sadness?

When we see this young person in the community, we cannot fully know whether the possible signs of poverty we observe are a consistent life-condition. However, in the schools and in our classrooms, educators quickly learn of the dire conditions in which far too many of our community youth exist.

Through daily contact, teachers quickly recognize the signs of those who might be lacking sleep or who might be disconnected from their peers. These children become quickly evident to the caring educator, who can recognize a youngster who lacks not only material things but also the essential components and necessities needed for a healthy brain and body, a sense of self-esteem and a positive vision for their future.

Students who live in poverty parachute into the school environment from their "other world" on a daily basis, always striving to display a semblance of normalcy. It can be a tortuous and damaging existence for them, and it can assault their young sense of self and distort what they see as their own value and place in society.

For many, the school and classroom offers at least a temporary respite from the fundamental things lacking in their young lives.

Our community is indeed rich in resources. We are wealthy beyond measure when it comes to the amount of dedicated people who work to make things better for others. Working in the schools, I'm often heartened by the degree of dedication and selfless generosity demonstrated by parents and guardians who contribute their time and talents, educational materials, and pantry items to help with the great work going on. It's truly humbling and encouraging to witness this.

It's exciting to see an increasing degree of collaboration between groups and agencies in our region, which are searching for new ways to help those children and their families in our community. At a gathering in August, the city of La Crosse, La Crosse County and the La Crosse School District hosted the La Crosse Community Summit: Rebuilding for Learning II community conversation.

This event brought together city and county professionals, educators and other community stakeholders with the goal of creating and implementing a web of organized learning supports to address those societal barriers to learning.

While children in poverty certainly have the ability to achieve at the same level and reach the same academic benchmarks as their peers, their initial ability to effectively focus and learn can be severely hampered when their basic human needs are not being met.

A more recent community conversation about children in poverty took place in October at Viterbo University. Co-sponsored by AMOS (a local interfaith community coalition), the D.B. Reinhart Institute for Ethics in Leadership at Viterbo, the La Crosse County Human Services Department and Family Policy Board, [the] League of Women Voters of the Greater La Crosse Area, and the Wisconsin Council on Children and Families, this gathering provided a meaningful discussion involving strategies for helping children and families in poverty. Through these invaluable community conversations, we learn about the ways we can work together for greater common good.

During this season of giving and sharing, it's a timely reminder that we remain focused on those families in our society needing resources, assistance, job-training and employment opportunities to better their economic situation and prospects for the future. It is imperative we do what we can to provide the children with the necessary resources and nutrition so that they can effectively learn and grow while in our schools—giving them all of the benefits that a good education provides.

It has been said that it's the moral test of a nation in how it treats those who are in the dawn of life or in the twilight of life. Let us aspire to meet that moral test and, to that end, work to eliminate the poverty that hurts the lives of so many families and children in our community.

This Opinion Page piece is poignant and compelling. It is a statement of a community's dedication to ask "And how are the children? Are they all well?" They want to answer that they are doing what they can to give every child opportunities for positive development, regardless of their circumstances. Write a well-developed paragraph in response to each of the following questions and prompts:

1. Relate what you know about Maslow's hierarchy of needs to what Rick writes in this *Opinion Page*. Elaborate on which needs must be met first, and which will be met more easily as a result.
2. The imagery of students "parachuting" into the school environment makes a point. Why is this message so important for teachers to understand?
3. What are some ways you might make the most of what Rick calls the "temporary respite" of your classroom?

Let's take a look at a sixth-grade classroom where most of the students receive free or reduced-price lunch, indicating low socioeconomic status. Watch Video Example 9.1 to see enthusiastic students mirror their teacher's dispositions toward teaching and learning as expressed in his interview.

Video Example 9.1: Success and Low Socioeconomic Status

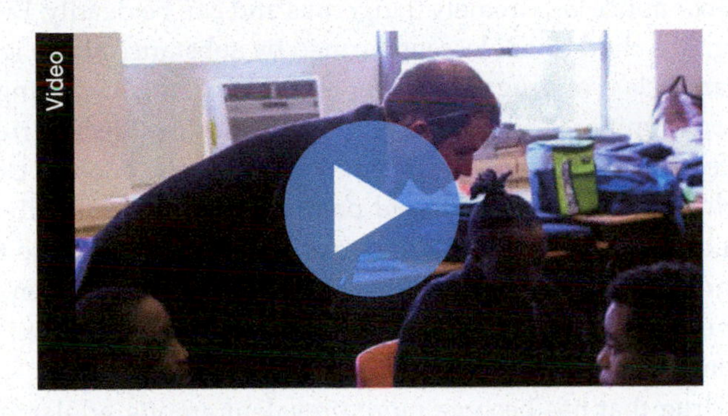

Point of Reflection 9.2

With what socioeconomic status (SES) group(s) are you most familiar? How did your own SES affect your school days?

Check Your Understanding 9.2

9.3 How Do Health Issues Affect Students in the United States?

9.3 Articulate how health issues negatively impact students in the United States.

Some health issues pose immediate and obvious dangers to children and adolescents. For instance, underage alcohol consumption and abuse of both legal and illegal drugs alter mental states and lead to overt behavioral changes. Other health issues are just as insidious, but their effects are incremental; their negative consequences occur gradually and are generally not accompanied by alarm. For instance, tobacco use and obesity among children and adolescents rarely push adults' panic buttons, but they may lead to deadly consequences.

Rates of substance abuse—specifically, alcohol, legal and illegal drugs, and tobacco—are either stable or not rapidly rising overall. About 5% of 12- to 17-year-olds abused or were dependent on alcohol or drugs in 2015, compared to 8% in 2008 (Kids Count, 2016). Early sexual experiences are declining, with a teen birth rate that has fallen dramatically in recent decades. However, some health professionals say that the overall health of children and adolescents is worsening because of dramatic increases in obesity rates.

Substance Abuse

Substance abuse is a pattern of alcohol, tobacco, or drug use that can lead to detrimental and habitual consumption, very possibly with impaired functioning at school and work, along with legal difficulties. The guarded good news is that substance abuse among children and adolescents has not recently escalated. The bad news continues to be that substance abuse is extremely dangerous and can be deadly. Even if the statistics show leveling, one child or adolescent harmed by substance abuse is one too many.

Opioids are a class of drugs becoming more prevalent, and rising to epidemic levels in some communities. This class of drugs includes the illegal drug, heroin, as well as powerful legal pain relievers available by prescription such as oxycodone, hydrocodone, codeine, and morphine. Opioid pain relievers are generally safe when taken as prescribed by a doctor, but they are frequently misused because they can produce euphoria in addition to pain relief. Opioids can lead to dependence and even fatal overdose. When prescription opioids aren't available, heroin is used with devastating results (National Institute on Drug Abuse, 2017).

Another drug that has become more prevalent among adolescents is marijuana. As states declare it legal among adults, it becomes very easy for adolescents and even children to access, use, and abuse. The possible repercussions of marijuana use during adolescence when the brain is still developing include:

- Increased risk of mental health issues
- Decline in school performance
- Impaired driving
- Potential for addiction
- Difficulty thinking and problem solving
- Difficulty with memory, coordination, and maintaining attention (Centers for Disease Control and Prevention, 2016)

When do children and adolescents begin drinking alcohol and using drugs? Although most research studies begin with eighth-graders, elementary teachers and principals know that experimentation with alcohol, drugs, and tobacco begins even earlier. The average boy takes his first drink at age 11; the average girl, at age 13. Each year there are almost 200,000 emergency room visits due to underage drinking, and annually over 4,000 deaths are attributed to underage drinking (Centers for Disease Control and Prevention, 2016). Information relevant for teachers to know about alcohol and drug use is shown in Table 9.3.

Table 9.3 Alcohol and drug use of ninth- and twelfth-graders

Alcohol and Drug Use of Ninth- and Twelfth-Graders	Percent of Ninth-Graders	Percent of twelfth-graders
Ever drank alcohol	51	73
Currently drink alcohol, occasionally to often	23	42
Ever used marijuana	26	50
Currently use marijuana, occasionally to often	15	28
Ever used cocaine	3	7
Ever used ecstasy	3	6
Ever used heroin	2	2
Ever took steroids without a doctor's prescription	4	3
Ever took prescription drugs without a doctor's prescription	13	20
Were offered, sold, or given an illegal drug on school property	22	20

Source: From Youth Risk Behavior Surveillance System. Centers for Disease Control and Prevention (CDC). (2016)

The heartbreaking stories of automobile accidents involving intoxicated or high adolescents at the wheel spur groups such as Mothers Against Drunk Driving (MADD) and Students Against Destructive Decisions (SADD; formerly Students Against Drunk Driving) to continue their awareness campaigns. Teenage drunk driving kills about eight teens a day. Of all teen deaths in car accidents, 60% are related to alcohol or drugs. Statistics show that a teenage boy with a blood alcohol level of 0.05, below the level to be considered legally drunk, is 18 times more likely to be in a single car accident than nonimpaired boys. For girls, the number is even worse. A girl with a blood alcohol level of 0.05 is 54 times more likely to cause a single-car crash (Alcoholism Information and Resources, 2010). Staggering statistics.

Both cigarettes and smokeless tobacco continue to pose health dangers for children and adolescents, although teenage use of tobacco has decreased from about 40% in 1996 to about 12% in 2016. One reason for the decline in cigarette smoking is the advent of electronic cigarettes that are still harmful because they contain nicotine. Nicotine in tobacco or in ecigarettes affects the structural and chemical changes in developing brains of children and adolescents, making those who smoke more vulnerable to alcohol and drug addiction, as well as mental illness. Even with the overall decline in tobacco use, nearly 3,200 people younger than 18 years of age smoke their first cigarette each day. This is significant because 90% of adult smokers began the habit before the age of 18. Smokeless tobacco is almost exclusively used by males, with about 500,000 boys currently at risk for mouth cancer and addiction because of smokeless tobacco (National Institute on Drug Addiction for Teens, 2017). Data about teens and tobacco are shown in Table 9.4.

Other drugs are somewhat common among adolescents, but in much lower levels than alcohol, cigarettes, or marijuana. Synthetic marijuana, also known as K–2 or Spice, is sometimes more readily available than real marijuana. When manufacturers can't get a particular ingredient, they substitute chemicals, adding to the dangers of this synthetic drug. Abuse of inhalants—the drug of choice for some younger teens because of availability—is decreasing. However, according to a large-scale research report, 11% of students had sniffed glue, breathed the contents of aerosol spray cans, or inhaled paints to get high one or more times during their lives (United States Department of Health and Human Services [USDHHS], 2012).

Children and adolescents often have an unfounded sense of immortality. Do you remember thinking, "Well, sure, some people are hurt by this, but it won't happen to me"? The students in your future classrooms will likely often have this attitude. They grossly underestimate the serious consequences of abusing alcohol, drugs, and tobacco.

WHAT CAN SCHOOLS AND TEACHERS DO? In 1995, the Supreme Court ruled that schools can arrange to randomly test student athletes for drugs. In 2002, another ruling included those who voluntarily participate in activities such as cheerleading, band, debate, and so on. Schools that conduct random student drug testing hope to decrease

Table 9.4 Tobacco use

Tobacco Use	Ninth Grade	Twelfth Grade
Ever tried cigarette smoking	25	38
Currently smoke cigarettes frequently	2	5
Currently use smokeless tobacco	6	7
Ever used electronic vapor products	37	51
Currently use electronic vapor products	20	28

Source: From Youth Risk Behavior Surveillance System. Centers for Disease Control and Prevention (CDC). (2016)

abuse among students in two ways. First, schools hope random testing will serve as a deterrent to drug use. Second, they hope to identify adolescents who already have drug problems and refer them for counseling and treatment.

Teachers need to be informed about the warning signs—often sudden, negative changes in behavior and academic performance—of alcohol and drug abuse. We need to be articulate when it comes to describing the consequences of substance abuse of all kinds. We must take the problem seriously. Here are some suggestions for positively influencing students:

1. Develop strong relationships with students and understand their unrealistically optimistic perceptions concerning substance abuse.
2. Become a trusted mentor for individual students at risk for using alcohol, drugs, and tobacco.
3. Don't just give statistics. Expose students to graphic videos of the consequences of risky behavior, introduce them to families that have suffered the consequences of substance abuse, have students with recovery stories speak with your class, and so on.
4. Promote honest discussions about real-world issues, including substance abuse.
5. Use active instructional techniques such as role-playing to teach refusal skills.
6. Make information available about community services related to prevention and intervention of substance abuse.

Sexuality-Related Concerns

Fewer never-married 15- to 19-year-olds are having sexual experiences now than in the 1990s. They are starting later and experiencing fewer partners. However, the use of birth control remains disturbingly low and is decreasing. See Table 9.5 for some trends of sexual intercourse among teenagers.

TEEN BIRTHRATE. Although pregnancy among girls ages 10 to 14 is especially tragic, only about 1 in every 1,000 girls in this age group becomes pregnant. As illustrated in Figure 9.3, except for the first half of the 1990s, the teen birthrate for 15- to 19-year-olds has declined since 1960, with slight increases in 2008. A decrease in sexual intercourse among adolescents has contributed to the decline (Centers for Disease Control and Prevention [CDC], 2016). However, as of 2015, the progress is uneven, with some states reporting far higher rates of teen birth per 1,000 teenagers than others. Massachusetts had the lowest rate at 9 per 1,000 teens, and Arkansas had the highest rate of 38 per 1,000 teens. The national average was 22 (National Campaign to Prevent Teen and Unplanned Pregnancy, 2016).

Table 9.5 Trends in sexual activity as reported by 15- to 19-year-olds (percentages), 1991–2015

Survey Question	1991	1995	1999	2003	2007	2011	2015
Have you ever had intercourse?	54	53	50	47	48	47	41
Did you have intercourse before age 13?	10	9	8	7	7	6	4
Have you had intercourse with more than 4 people?	19	18	16	14	15	15	12
Did you use any form of birth control during your last intercourse experience?	17	16	15	14	15	13	15

Based on: Centers for Disease Control and Prevention (2012). *Trends in the Prevalence of Sexual Behaviors and HIV Testing National YRBS: 1991–2011*. Atlanta, GA: Author. Retrieved March 10, 2013, from http://www.cdc.gov/healthyyouth/yrbs/pdf/us_sexual_trend_yrbs.pdf; and Centers for Disease Control and Prevention. (2016). *Youth risk behavior surveillance system*. Atlanta, GA: Author. Retrieved March 25, 2017, from https://nccd.cdc.gov/youthonline/App/Results.aspx?LID=XX

Figure 9.3 Pregnancy rates per 1,000 teens, ages 15 to 19, 1940–2011

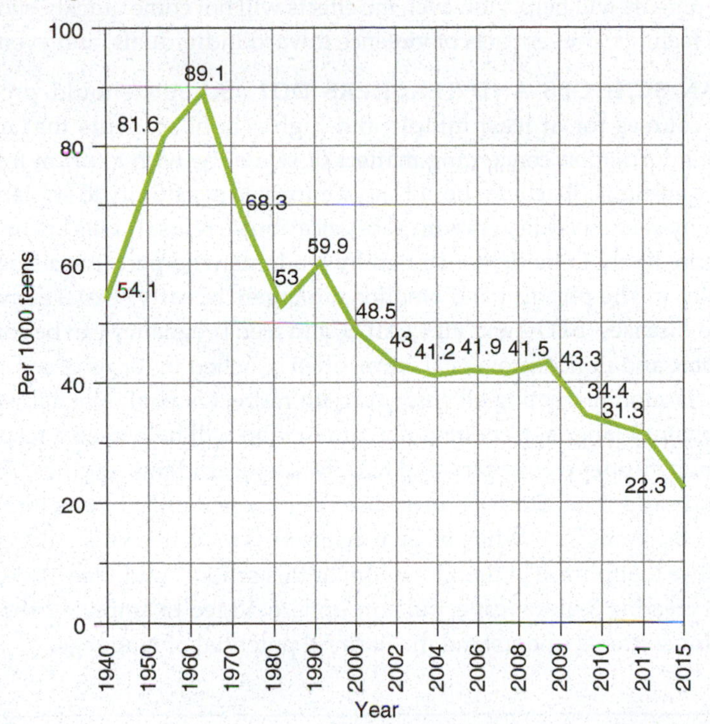

Based on: Centers for Disease Control and Prevention. (2010). *Teen birth rates drop in 2008 following a two-year increase*. Atlanta, GA: Author; Hamilton, B. E., & Ventura, S. J. (2012). Birth rates for U.S. teenagers reach historic lows for all age and ethnic groups. *NCHS Data Brief, 89*. Hyattsville, MD: Hamilton, B. E., Martin, J. A., & Ventura, S. J. (2012). Births: Preliminary data for 2011. *National Vital Statistics Reports*, 61(5). Hyattsville, MD: Ventura, S. J., Mathews, T. J., & Hamilton, B. E. (2001). Births to teenagers in the United States, 1940–2000. *National Vital Statistics Reports*, 49(10). Hyattsville, MD: Centers for Disease Control and Prevention. (2016). *Youth risk behavior surveillance system*. Atlanta, GA: Author. Retrieved March 25, 2017, from https://nccd.cdc.gov/youthonline/App/Results.aspx?LID=XX

Nationally, an average of 52 of every 1,000 girls ages 15 through 19 became pregnant in 2015. The rate for black girls was 93; for Hispanic girls, 74; and for white girls, 35. There are, of course, many consequences of teenage pregnancy and teen births, including:

- Only 38% of girls who give birth before age 18 graduate from high school by age 22.
- Only about 2% of teen mothers graduate from college.
- Daughters of teen mothers are 3 times as likely to become teen mothers themselves.
- Teen mothers are twice as likely to not seek prenatal care in the first trimester.
- When teen mothers who move out of the family home, 67% live below the poverty line.
- Children born to mothers younger than 18 score significantly worse on measures of school readiness in math and reading. (National Campaign to Prevent Teen and Unplanned Pregnancy, 2012, 2016)

HOMOSEXUALITY. Homosexuality is not, in and of itself, a health concern. However, sexual orientation is an issue that evokes strong sentiments that spill over onto school grounds. "Tragically, public schools have become front lines in the culture war over homosexuality—and the biggest losers are the kids caught in the crossfire of incendiary rhetoric and bitter lawsuits" (Haynes, 2006, p. 3). In an effort to find a process that will allow educators and students alike to civilly discuss issues of sexual orientation, a document titled "Public Schools and Sexual Orientation: A First Amendment Framework for Finding Common Ground" was endorsed in 2006 by organizations including the American Association of School Administrators and the Association for Supervision and Curriculum Development. Will documents such as this end teasing and harassment aimed at adolescents who are, or are perceived to be, homosexual? Perhaps eventually official documents will help. However, the effects will not come quickly enough to spare many hurt feelings, prevent acts of violence toward individuals, and even suicides.

WHAT CAN SCHOOLS AND TEACHERS DO? Schools should provide health education courses for at least middle and high school students that include open and honest information concerning matters of sexuality, with a forum for asking and answering questions. Teachers should show informed sensitivity to students grappling with sexuality-related issues. As with substance abuse, refusal skills are important, and they are more likely to be demonstrated by students who perceive a sense of control over their lives. The physical and emotional dangers of early sexual activity, sexually transmitted diseases (STDs) and HIV/AIDS, and teen pregnancy can be communicated in nongraphic and noncontroversial ways, often couched in terms of self-respect.

In the classroom, treating all students with respect is vital. Not allowing students to use derogatory language about sexual orientation will help keep a respectful atmosphere. Among upper elementary and middle school students, saying "That's so gay" is a sign of disapproval. Students often use the phrase lightly, but its implications can deeply hurt those students who perceive themselves to be homosexual. Simply saying, "We don't use that phrase in this classroom or this school" and then sticking to it is an example of creating a more respectful atmosphere. Video Example 9.2 shows how one teacher helps students understand the harmful potential of language.

Video Example 9.2: Promoting Understanding

Some schools have established sex education programs and clinics that provide access to birth control information and devices; others primarily advise abstinence. Both programs are controversial. Many districts support special schools for pregnant students and new mothers. These schools help young women stay in school and graduate. Teenagers should be assisted in the development of skills in communication and sexual decision making so that sex does not just "happen." As teachers, we can help make teens aware of the consequences of sexually risky behaviors.

Childhood Obesity

Americans rank obesity as a health problem second only to cancer. Childhood obesity has more than doubled in children and tripled in adolescents in the past 40 years. One third of children and adolescents in the United States are considered overweight or obese (Centers for Disease Control and Prevention, 2017). The commonly held definition of **obesity** involves the body mass index (BMI), a measure of how much a person weighs relative to height, as illustrated in Table 9.6.

Former First Lady Michelle Obama chose childhood obesity as a cause to champion. Her program "Let's Move" is a nationwide campaign with the goal of solving the problem of childhood obesity in a generation and empowering children born today to

Table 9.6 Computing body mass index (BMI)

BMI	Status
Below 18.5	Underweight
18.5–24.9	Normal
25.0–29.9	Overweight
30.0–39.9	Obese
40 and above	Morbidly obese

Note: BMI = (weight in pounds × 703) ÷ [(height in inches) × (height in inches)].

Based on: Data from Craig, G. J., & Dunn, W. L. (2007). Understanding human development (p. 248). Upper Saddle River, NJ: Prentice Hall.

reach adulthood at a healthy weight. "The physical and emotional health of an entire generation and the economic health and security of our nation is at stake" (2010).

Mrs. Obama traveled the country promoting healthy habits in schools, communities, and families. She asked school food services to cut calories and offer more fresh produce. It is estimated that as many as half of school-age children eat about half their daily calories at school; what is served in the cafeteria matters.

What's considered normal weight for children and adolescents varies with their age. But take a look at a line of children walking down an elementary hallway or adolescents gathered around the school commons. It's obvious which students are grossly overweight or on their way to becoming so.

Researchers are studying the causes and consequences of childhood obesity. Some obvious problems include:

- Easy access to far too many fast-food restaurants
- Fewer recess and physical education minutes allotted during the school day
- Some schools are still serving basically hamburgers and pizza and allowing unhealthy drinks and snacks to be sold in schools
- Excessive time spent watching television and playing video games
- Social media obsession that limits physical activity
- Sugary snacks and cereals eaten rather than fruit and vegetables
- Parents working long hours and relying on less-than-healthy meals
- Too few outdoors experiences that include movement

Table 9.7 consists of information concerning dietary and activity behaviors of teenagers. The data are provided by the *Youth Risk Behavior Surveillance System,*

Table 9.7 Dietary and activity behaviors (survey results by percentage)

Dietary Behaviors (during the 7 days prior to the survey)	Ninth Grade	Twelfth Grade
Did not drink water	4	4
Did not eat breakfast on all 7 days	60	66
Did not eat fruit or drink 100% fruit juices	6	5
Did not eat vegetables	7	6
Drank a can, bottle, or glass of nondiet soda or pop	74	72
Drank a can, bottle, or glass of a sports drink	60	53
Physical Activity	**Ninth Grade**	**Twelfth Grade**
Were not physically active at least 60 minutes per day on 5 or more days	46	57
Played video or computer games or used a computer 3 or more hours per day, for something that was not school work on an average school day	45	40
Watched 3 or more hours per day of television, on an average school day	26	25
Did not attend physical education classes on 1 or more days	29	64

Source: From Youth Risk Behavior Surveillance System. Centers for Disease Control and Prevention (CDC). (2016).

an important study conducted in 2016 by the Centers for Disease Control and Prevention.

The consequences of childhood obesity include serious health issues such as type 2 diabetes, heart disease, sleep disorders, asthma, joint dysfunction, and mental health problems. What used to be considered adult-only health problems are now serious health problems for adolescents and even children. As a result of weight issues, today's children may live shorter and less healthy lives than their parents. Serious social and psychological problems are also consequences of childhood and adolescent obesity. Being teased, loneliness, low self-esteem, and other consequences result from being a severely overweight child or teenager.

Although researchers are not saying that obesity causes lower academic performance, the link between obesity and lower achievement may reveal serious academic consequences. Seriously overweight children are twice as likely to be in special education and remedial classes from an early age. A study of approximately 11,000 kindergartners found that overweight children had significantly lower reading and math scores when compared to children in the normal weight range. These academic difficulties continued through first grade (Story, Kaphingst, and French, 2006).

Mrs. Obama is quick to point out that childhood obesity is not the fault of the children themselves. The kids don't choose what's offered in the school cafeteria for breakfast and lunch. They are not responsible for foods loaded with sugar and fat or super-sized portions, nor do they determine how much time is allotted for recess and physical education. Yes, they may choose to watch TV and play video games or surf the Internet instead of running around outside, but it's the adults who make all the alternatives available (Obama, 2010).

WHAT CAN SCHOOLS AND TEACHERS DO? In 2004, Congress passed the Child Nutrition Reauthorization Act, mandating that all schools participating in the federal school meal program develop comprehensive wellness policies focusing on the following:

1. What children and adolescents eat in school:
   - Provide more nutritious school breakfasts and lunches.
   - Limit à la carte items to healthier foods.
   - Reduce or eliminate vending machines or stock only nutritious foods.
2. How physically active students are in school:
   - Provide daily physical education (PE) in elementary and middle school.
   - Increase high school PE requirements and provide more extracurricular physical activity options.
3. In-school health and nutrition education
4. Set an example of healthy living

Teachers can encourage all the elements of a wellness policy by serving as role models for healthy living. Eating nutritious, balanced meals and snacks in school and showing evidence of an active lifestyle that includes exercise will go a long way toward influencing students. Teachers can help prevent childhood and adolescent obesity by being vocal advocates for students' health. Chris Roberts is one of the focus teachers at Rees Elementary School in Utah. Not only does he live a very active life, but he also requires his third-, fourth-, and fifth-graders to participate in movement to music and to the beating of drums.

Application Exercise 9.2: Chris Roberts's lesson

Suicide

Every 13 minutes someone dies of suicide in the United States. The ultimate health issue and absolute tragedy for young adolescents (ages 10 to 14) and adolescents (ages 15 to 19) is suicide. It remains the third-leading cause of death among teens, trailing only accidents and homicide. The rate of suicide for adolescents has nearly tripled since 1960 (Mental Health America, 2016). Girls attempt suicide twice as often as boys, but boys complete the act four times as often as girls. Girls tend to attempt suicide by overdose or cutting. Boys tend to choose more lethal means such as jumping from heights, hanging, and firearms, which account for 60% of all teen suicides. Percentages of girls and boys and suicide attempts as reported in the CDC's 2016 *Youth Risk Behavior Surveillance System* are in Table 9.8.

The reasons behind teen suicide are complex. When teens go through times of stress and major life changes such as parents divorcing, moving away from familiar surroundings, and family financial dilemmas, they may experience extreme anxiety. Unrealistic academic and social expectations can lead to a sense of inferiority and disappointment. When students are bullied for any reason, they become frustrated and lose hope of happiness. Students who are gay, lesbian, or transgender, or who are questioning their sexuality likely experience stress, with or out without bullying. Because adults often dismiss the trauma of adolescence, comforting themselves with the belief that all kids always go through phases and moodiness, we may miss important signs of depression prompting suicidal thoughts that are overwhelming.

Adolescent depression is increasing at an alarming rate. In fact, some research says that as many as 20% of teenagers may suffer from clinical depression at some point. Recent surveys indicate that as many as one in five teens suffers from depression (Mental Health America, 2016). **Depression** is a mental illness characterized by a deep sense of sadness and a loss of interest or pleasure in activities. Students who are depressed are 14 times more likely to make a first suicide attempt. In fact, over half of all adolescents who suffer from depression eventually attempt suicide (American Psychiatric Association, 2005). Refer to the long list of signs that adolescents are possibly considering suicide in Figure 9.4. It is our responsibility to read the symptoms, remember them, and watch for the behaviors in our students.

WHAT CAN SCHOOLS AND TEACHERS DO? Suicide is a senseless tragedy. For many of us it's difficult to imagine being distressed to the point of absolute hopelessness.

Table 9.8 Suicide information

Suicide (during the 12 months before the survey)	Male	Female
Felt sad or hopeless almost every day for 2 or more weeks in a row so that they stopped doing some usual activities	20	40
Seriously considered attempting suicide	12	23
Made a plan about how they would attempt suicide	10	19
Attempted suicide	6	12

Based on Centers for Disease Control and Prevention. (2015). Suicide: Facts at a glance. Atlanta, GA: Author. Retrieved March 25, 2017, from https://www.cdc.gov/violenceprevention/pdf/suicide-datasheet-a.pdf

Figure 9.4 Signs teens are considering suicide

Teens who are thinking about suicide might:

- Talk about suicide or death in general
- Give hints that they might not be around anymore
- Talk about feeling hopeless or feeling guilty
- Pull away from friends or family
- Write songs, poems, or letters about death, separation, and loss
- Start giving away treasured possessions to siblings or friends
- Lose the desire to take part in favorite things or activities
- Have trouble concentrating or thinking clearly
- Experience changes in eating or sleeping habits
- Engage in risk-taking behaviors
- Lose interest in school or sports
- Suddenly perform poorly in school
- Withdraw from friends and activities
- Experience sadness and hopelessness
- Lack enthusiasm, energy, or motivation
- Display anger and rage
- Overreact to criticism
- Exemplify poor self-esteem or guilt
- Be indecisive, forgetful, restless, or agitated
- Change eating or sleeping patterns
- Abuse illegal or legal substances that harm

Source: Kids Health, 2015; Mental Health America, 2016.

But it happens. Adolescents do this unthinkable deed and leave family and friends to suffer the devastation of "why." As educators, we can help. Here are some guidelines for dealing with adolescents at risk for suicide attempts:

- Understand and recognize factors that may indicate suicidal tendencies.
- If you suspect suicidal tendencies, always notify others such as a mental health professional or a school counselor who may, in turn, contact family members.
- Be willing to listen rather than lecture.
- Find ways to involve students in service learning that takes them "outside" themselves.
- Reassure adolescents that depression and suicidal tendencies are treatable.

Other Risky Behaviors

Over 15,000 students in 21 large urban areas responded to extensive surveys about their behaviors. The 2016 Youth Risk Behavior Surveillance Survey (YRBSS) is the largest public health surveillance system in the United States, monitoring a broad range of health-risk behaviors among high school students, some of which are listed in Table 9.9. Obviously, many of these behaviors don't just magically begin when students step inside the high school hallways. Education and modeling will impact younger students and perhaps serve as preventive measures.

Table 9.9 Some adolescent health issues

Some Adolescent Health Issues (in 12 months prior to survey unless otherwise specified)	Ninth Grade	Twelfth Grade
Ever had asthma	23	22
Did not see a dentist (for a check-up, exam, teeth cleaning, or other dental work during the 12 months before the survey)	24	27
Did not have 8 or more hours of sleep, on an average school night	66	78
Had a sunburn (after being outside in the sun or after using a sunlamp or other indoor tanning device)	55	56
Never or rarely wore a bicycle helmet	79	84
Never or rarely wore a seat belt	6	6
Rode with a driver who had been drinking alcohol (in a car or other vehicle one or more times during the 30 days before the survey)	20	20
Drove after they had been drinking alcohol (during the 30 days before the survey)	6	10
Texted or emailed while driving a car or other vehicle (on at least 1 day during the 30 days before the survey)	16	61
Carried a weapon on school property (such as a gun, knife, or club, on at least 1 day during the 30 days before the survey)	3	4
Were in a physical fight	28	17
Were electronically bullied (counting being bullied through email, chat rooms, instant messaging, websites, or texting)	16	14
Were bullied on school property	23	16

Point of Reflection 9.3

Has suicide touched your life? If so, in what way(s)?

Check Your Understanding 9.3

9.4 How Does Racism Affect Students in the United States?

9.4 Analyze how issues involving race affect students in the United States.

Even though race has been discredited as a legitimate, precise way to categorize people, "race and racism profoundly structure who we are, how we are treated, how we treat others, and our access to resources and rights" (Mukhopadhyay and Henze, 2003, p. 669). **Racism** is a form of prejudice that stems from a belief that one race is superior to another. Racism may be perpetuated by individuals or even by governmental policies (Gollnick and Chinn, 2013).

Discrimination

It's illegal to discriminate by race in American public schools. So that should be the end of the discussion, right? You will never find a public school policy that says, "If you are a racial minority, you must attend schools with peeling paint and inadequate, poorly maintained bathrooms," or "If you are a child of color you may not experience advanced classes or be in gifted programs." No, this would be against the law.

However, official policies of nondiscrimination often do little to remedy discrimination in the day-to-day realities of the children and adolescents of color who make up about 40% of students in U.S. public schools. Even in classrooms where a rich racial diversity exists, subtle forms of racism may be at play. The most subtle may be silence, with no ill intent on the part of the teacher. Polite and Saenger (2003) tell us that "the most pernicious and pervasive silence in . . . school classrooms is the silence surrounding the subject of race" (p. 275). Children are aware of physical differences of race at a very early age. Avoiding the subject doesn't make children's questions go away; they simply go unasked and unanswered. If children are not given opportunities to explore their own identities, as well as those of others around them, they will move from elementary to middle to high school carrying increasingly "complex feelings about race and racial issues, including pride, ignorance, anger, shame, ambivalence, and alienation" (Lewis-Charp, 2003, p. 25).

Another subtle form of discrimination in schools is what has become known as the **soft bigotry** of low expectations. Whether these expectations are the result of an assumption about abilities and intelligence, of previous experiences with students of various races, or of some other factor, having low expectations for some students amounts to racism. Landsman (2006) says, "I believe that a true test of any country's morality is whether it gives all children a fair and equal chance to achieve their potential as human beings" (p. 29).

Immigration and Classroom Success

The presence of immigrant children and adolescents in our classrooms helps all students understand that people view the world differently. They contribute to our classrooms by increasing our knowledge and appreciation of diversity and by providing our classrooms with richer learning experiences.

One in every five students has a parent who was born outside the United States. A quarter of these children were also born outside the United States. By some estimates, immigration will account for 96% of the future increase in the school-age population over the next 50 years (U.S. Census Bureau, 2008). This is a societal fact that will affect, if it doesn't already, every teacher. Deb Perryman, an advocate for immigrant students, tells us about her experiences in Figure 9.5.

Teachers often need to make an extra effort to understand how immigrant children may respond to many aspects of school in the United States. Without sensitivity to differences, racism may become part of their classroom experiences. Ariza (2002) gives us some examples of differences that may be manifested in a classroom with children who are immigrants or the children of immigrants:

- Manes is a student from Haiti whose parents have gone to great lengths and considerable risk to ensure an education for their children. In Haiti, teachers rarely send communications home with students. Weeks after sending home notes that required parental attention and signatures, a frustrated teacher assumes Manes's parents don't care. However, they simply didn't know to look in Manes's book bag for notes and papers requiring their attention.
- Hong, a student from Southeast Asia, has had a cold and sore throat. A common ethnic remedy in her country of origin is to rub a coin up and down on an area that is causing illness to draw out the pain. When Hong arrives at school with what appear to be bruises on her neck, the teacher suspects child abuse.
- Mohammad, a son of recent immigrants from the Middle East, is Muslim. Normally an active, cheerful child, he became withdrawn and wanted to change his name

Figure 9.5 Deb Perryman, 2004 Illinois Teacher of the Year

Sara Davis Powell

I teach the very fine students of Elgin High School in Illinois. EHS is an urban school serving 2,200 students speaking 56 languages. Official records show that 50% of our kids are living at or below the poverty level.

I remember the stories my grandparents told me of the hard times they had coming to the United States from Ireland. They faced name calling and worked dangerous jobs for low wages. I am thankful for all of the risks they took because I have so many opportunities. I remember my great grandpa yelling at the top of his lungs during dinner. He wasn't mad but nearly deaf after many years working as a boiler maker. That is the first time I can remember thinking to myself, "I will never treat another person the way my grandparents have been treated."

The immigration process is very complicated. As of May 2005 Illinois has a law (HB 60) that is providing possibilities for thousands of students. It buys time for those students seeking citizenship to actually complete the process while continuing their education. It gives me hope and, best of all, gives hope to students who are children of immigrants.

I have a set of twins I am working with now. When they entered the United States from Mexico 10 years ago, their parents went to the Immigration and Naturalization Service and began their road to citizenship. They have diligently tried to meet every stipulation and deadline, only to find themselves basically still on square one because of the bureaucracy involved, along with our overloaded, and understaffed, naturalization system. Now the boys are ready for college and the family is threatened with deportation.

I will continue to champion the cause of protecting immigrant children from arbitrary harm. I will ask the hard questions. When will we accept the next wave of immigrants without prejudice? When will we realize that every generation before us has come to the land of opportunity to get/create jobs and live productively?

Source: From e-mail communication with Deb Perryman, January 13, 2007.

following the 9/11 tragedy in 2001 so that no one would associate him with his religion or with terrorists.

- Maria, a 7-year-old whose family is from Colombia, routinely carries a baby bottle filled with milk in her lunch box. Her classmates teased her, and her teacher asked if she had mistakenly put her baby brother's bottle in her lunch. She was humiliated. The teacher later discovered that it is both proper and commonplace in some areas of Colombia for primary school children to drink from bottles.

Immigration and the laws addressing it continue to be a major source of contention and animosity in the United States. Regardless of the political infighting and social stigmas, the immigrant children and adolescents in our classrooms are just that— children and adolescents. They deserve the same care and consideration teachers give to all other students.

WHAT CAN SCHOOLS AND TEACHERS DO? Joseph White and James Cones, the authors of *Black Men Emerging* (1999), tell us there are three basic steps to confronting racism.

1. *Explore the issue of racism intellectually.* Read about racism and minority groups and discuss what you read with other teachers. Attend sessions at conferences that explore issues of racism and how to combat it in the classroom.
2. *Engage in dialogue about racism.* Start conversations with families, students, and the community about racial issues. Be open to frank talk and serious exchange of ideas.
3. *Immerse yourself in other cultures.* If you are white, attend an African American church service or a Kwanza celebration where you can join in and begin to understand traditions and perceptions. If you are Jewish, attend a Christian service. If you are non-Hispanic, join in Cinco de Mayo festivities.

In our classrooms, we need to be sensitive to each and every student, listen to interactions and guard against racial slurs of any kind, hold high and individualized expectations for each student, and continually seek to understand and appreciate differences that may accompany race.

Point of Reflection 9.4

What is your racial identity? How has this identity affected you as a student? How does your own racial identity impact your beliefs about, and attitudes toward, those with racial identities other than your own?

Check Your Understanding 9.4

9.5 What Are the Effects of Bullying, Violence, and Theft on Students and Schools in the United States?

9.5 Identify the effects of bullying, theft, and violence on students and schools in the United States.

School is a relatively safe place to be. Considering that more than 55 million students attend school each day, the chances of one of them being a victim of a violent act are small. However, crimes against students by other students continue to be problematic, even though the occurrence of violence and theft in schools has decreased since the mid-1990s (Dinkes, Kemp, and Baum, 2009).

Recent data indicate that school-age students are victims of all kinds of minor crimes about as often at school as away from school. However, with serious violent crimes such as rape and murder, the difference between in-school and out-of-school victimization is dramatic, with school the least likely place for harm (Dinkes et al., 2009).

Physical threat is not the only aspect of victimization to consider. The insidious nature of bullying causes real harm to students who are bullied, to those who perpetrate the bullying, and even to the bystanders who see it happening and do nothing to help.

Bullying

In the aftermath of the 1999 Columbine High School tragedy, people across the United States asked, "How could something like this happen?" Psychologists, counselors, principals, teachers, and parents, as well as the print and electronic media, began to speculate about what might have led Dylan Klebold and Eric Harris to kill their schoolmates and a teacher and then turn their guns on themselves. From conversations with people who knew Dylan and Eric, the conclusion was drawn that they were adolescents who felt alienated from other students and from school.

Although the extreme violence of Columbine cannot be entirely explained by examining student relationships, interest in interactions among students has grown. Bullying, often considered as simply "what kids do," has become a topic of concern. **Bullying**, or relationally aggressive behavior, is "a type of emotional violence where individuals use relationships to harm others. Examples include exclusion from a group and rumor spreading" (Ophelia Project, 2005, p. 3). In addition, bullying may involve physical aggression, such as shoving, tripping, and taking personal items. "Bullying is a weapon of people driven by the need for power. Bullying can be a single interaction—verbal, physical, or emotional—but it is always crafted to cause fear and to exert power" (White-Hood, 2006, p. 30). Bullying may be linked to current and future psychological and behavioral difficulties, including depression, dropping out of school, substance abuse, risky sexual behavior, abnormal eating habits, delinquency, and suicide. "Sticks and stones may break my bones, but words will never hurt me" may be the least accurate adage ever. Words hurt; inappropriate images ruin lives.

Almost everyone has been teased or called names at some point, and most people have teased others or been guilty of name-calling. When teasing becomes malicious and repetitive, when its intent is to embarrass, hurt, or isolate, it crosses the line into bullying. When rumors are intentionally spread to destroy the reputation of another, gossip becomes bullying. Most teachers can identify students who bully, as well as those who seem to be magnets for taunts and subtle forms of relational aggression. Figure 9.6 is an overview of the most frequent forms of bullying, according to students—one in three of whom report being bullied.

CYBERBULLYING. A particularly insidious form of bullying accomplished through social media sites, text messages, emails, chats, and websites is **cyberbullying**. The purpose of cyberbullying is to intentionally embarrass, harass, intimidate, or make threats through mean messages, rumors, pictures, videos, or fake profiles. Cyberbullying may happen 24 hours a day, 7 days a week, and likely victimizes children and adolescents when they are alone. Messages and images can be either posted anonymously to one person or widely distributed, and may be harsher because the bullier is probably anonymous. Not knowing who the cyberbullier is can add to the anxiety. Here are some instances of cyberbullying:

- Tricking someone into revealing personal or embarrassing information and then sending it to others
- Posing as the victim and sending mean or untrue messages as him or her
- Forwarding mean messages
- Making fun of others on a website
- Using websites to rate others as sexiest, prettiest, ugliest, and so on, often in vulgar, insulting ways
- Posting photos without consent
- Creating fake online profiles on websites such as Facebook, Myspace, Twitter, and others, to make fun of people

By definition, cyberbullying occurs only among children and adolescents. When adults exhibit similar behaviors, it's considered cyber-harassment or cyber-stalking—a behavior that can have legal consequences. The same groups of children and adolescents who are more susceptible to noncyberbullying—those who are lesbian, gay, bisexual, or transgender (LGBT) youth and those with disabilities or who are socially isolated—are most likely to be victims of cyberbullying. However, many incidents involve students considered otherwise mainstream but who may be the object of jealousy or a grudge. This chapter's *SocialMEdia* feature addresses cyberbullying—a very

Figure 9.6 Frequent forms of bullying

Being made fun of: 21%
Being the subject of rumors: 18%
Pushed, shoved, tripped, or spit on: 11%
Threatened with harm: 6%
Excluded from activities on purpose: 5%
Coerced to do something they did not want to do: 4%

Based on: Dinkes, R., Kemp, J., & Baum, K. (2009). *Indicators of school crime and safety: 2009* (NCES 2010–012/NCJ 228478). Washington, DC: National Center for Education Statistics, Institute of Education Sciences, U.S. Department of Education, and Bureau of Justice Statistics, Office of Justice Programs, U.S. Department of Justice.

Social MEdia

Teachers should learn to recognize and prevent cyberbullying. They should help kids know how to respond when it occurs. Some instances are easy to recognize because the messages are direct and mean. Other instances involving impersonations, posting of personal information, and videos sent to a select group may be much more difficult and time-consuming to detect.

Some signs of cyberbullying may be similar to, or the same as, signs of other victimization or extreme stress. Even so, it's important for teachers to watch for symptoms and then determine their causes. A victim of cyberbullying may:

- Be overly protective or secretive about online activities
- Turn off the screen when someone comes near
- Become withdrawn or show signs of depression
- Be anxious or overly stressed
- Stop using the computer and other technology
- Suddenly avoid or change friends
- Lose interest in activities or school

The profile of someone who cyberbullies may not be overtly different from that of any other adolescent since the reasons for this harmful activity may be jealousy or a grudge—two things that are part of the human condition. A cyberbullier may:

- Be overly protective or secretive about online activities (same as the bullied)
- Turn off the screen when someone comes near (not unlike the bullied)
- Appear nervous or secretive when using social media
- Spend excessive amounts of time on the computer

Teachers may help prevent cyberbullying by:

- Implementing and enforcing a school anti-bullying code of conduct
- Having students sign an anti-bullying and anti-cyberbullying pledge (to not participate and to speak up if someone is being bullied)
- Creating a safe place for students to voice concerns or problems
- Talking with students about cyberbullying: what it is, the impact it has, and its consequences
- Making it clear that cyberbullying will not be tolerated
- Working with students to help raise cyberbullying awareness within the school through student-led clubs, assemblies, or posters (National Crime Prevention Council, 2017)

Teachers should tell students

- *Never* post or share personal information, or that of a friend, online (including full name, address, telephone number, school name, parents' names, credit card or Social Security number).
- *Never* share Internet passwords with anyone, except your parents.
- *Never* meet anyone face-to-face previously known only online.

If students suspect, or are certain, cyberbullying is occurring, teachers may advise them to:

- Tell an adult they trust about what's going on.
- Not delete any of the emails, texts, or messages. They can serve as evidence.
- Keep a record of incidents.
- Not forward any mean messages that spread rumors.
- Not plot revenge—it won't solve anything.
- Report the incident to the administrator of the website.

Cyberbullying hurts. It can be dangerous physically, emotionally, and socially. Cyber-safety is everyone's responsibility.

real problem that deserves teacher vigilance to recognize, prevent, and teach responses that lead to cyber-safety.

THE BULLY, THE BULLIED, AND THE BYSTANDER. An excellent resource for teachers on the topic of bullying is Barbara Coloroso's 2008 book, *The Bully, the Bullied, and the Bystander*. The **bully** doesn't generate as much attention as the act of bullying, but perhaps should. Until we understand why and how a child becomes a bully, we will not be effective in deterring bullying. Bullies may have been, or are, victims of bullying themselves. For the most part, bullies are seeking power. They exert power by harming others, by intimidating, and by being dominant.

The **bullied** are victims of the act of bullying. We've all known them; perhaps you yourself were one. The bullied are targets. Some may be the youngest; the smallest (or largest); victims of previous trauma; submissive; outstanding in some way (often academically); the kid with low self-esteem; annoying; racially/culturally different; one with physical or mental disabilities; kids with acne or a hearing aid; those who are lesbian, gay, bisexual, transgender, or who are questioning (LGBTQ) their sexual orientation—or simply the kid in the wrong place at the wrong time. In fact, a survey of LGBTQ students revealed that 9 out of 10 experienced harassment in school (USDHHS, 2013). Whatever their situations, children and adolescents who are victims of bullying may

- Become withdrawn
- Begin using alcohol and drugs as escape mechanisms
- Skip school
- Be unwilling to attend school or other activities
- Suddenly stop caring about grades
- Have lower self-esteem
- Develop health problems

The **bystander** is anyone who witnesses bullying. A bystander has choices to make: simply watch, walk away, join in, or intervene (Coloroso, 2008). As adults, we think we would, of course, intervene and help the bullied. It's easier for us than it is for peers of the bully and the bullied. This is where the culture of a school or classroom either can make it tougher to bully or allow bullying to continue unchecked. A culture of openness, respect, and civility will make it harder for bullying to occur. A culture of free-for-all, disrespect, and empty threats will perpetuate bullying.

WHAT CAN SCHOOLS AND TEACHERS DO? In 2004, Congress amended the Safe and Drug Free Schools Act to include bullying and harassment. This addition requires all schools that receive federal funding to actively prevent bullying and to respond to all instances of it. School districts are developing policies and mandating antibullying programs. Books such as *Odd Girl Out: The Hidden Culture of Aggression in Girls* (Simmons, 2002) and *Best Friends, Worst Enemies: Understanding the Social Lives of Children* (Thompson and Grace, 2001) shed new light on the ramifications of relational aggression for both the aggressor and the victim. Books like these and established anti-bullying programs indicate that many times bullies were themselves bullied at some point or perhaps abused in some way by family members. Most scenarios are complex. Even when teachers don't understand all the circumstances and are not trained to work through the psychological maze of causes for episodes of bullying, they can take steps to help prevent bullying in classrooms and schools. These steps include the following:

- Watch for bullying and take it seriously. Don't be an idle bystander.
- Train all adults in the school, including office and custodial personnel, bus drivers, and teacher assistants to recognize and respond when bullying occurs.
- Be an obvious presence. Early childhood and elementary teachers should monitor the playground. Middle and high school teachers should be visible and vigilant in the hallways, at lunchtime, at bus drop-off areas, at extracurricular events, and so on.
- Do everything possible to help students develop genuine self-esteem that will prevent bullying driven by the victim's lack of confidence. An intact self-esteem will also prompt victims of bullying to better withstand the torment and to seek assistance.
- Incorporate lessons, formally or informally, that help students internalize the belief that bullying and relational aggression in all forms are harmful and absolutely wrong.
- Implement prescribed anti-bullying programs with sincerity and purpose.

Research indicates that bullying may be the last significant step before the bully or the victim turns to more physically dangerous behavior, such as physical violence against other students.

Violence and Theft in Schools

The most common forms of violence in schools are physical fights, with about equal fault among fighters, and simple assault involving a perpetrator and a victim. Both forms of violence involve boys about twice as often as girls. The good news is that between 1993 and 2009, the percentage of high school students reporting being in a fight on school grounds dropped from 16% to 11%. A larger percentage of black and Hispanic students report being in fights than Asian and white students. Fighting is reported more often in urban settings than in suburban and rural settings (National Center for Education Statistics, 2011).

Incidents of theft in schools include purse snatching, pickpocketing, and stealing property from another's desk and/or locker. In 1995, about 8% of middle and high school students reported something stolen from them while at school. The rate of theft in school has decreased steadily since then, with only 3% reporting theft in 2009 (U.S. Department of Justice, 2011).

Deaths at school due to violent acts are rare, considering that there are more than 55 million students in school each day. In 2009, there were 33 violent deaths in public schools. Even though the numbers are relatively small compared to the total population, 2012 proved to be an especially brutal year for violent deaths in schools. In February, a single gunman at Chardon High School, Ohio, fatally shot three students. In December, a young man armed with assault weapons killed 20 first-grade students and six adult staff members at Sandy Hook Elementary in Newtown, Connecticut. These horrific events break our hearts and cause us to wonder what could possibly go through someone's mind that would lead them to commit a crime so heinous against students and their families. In our rage and despair, we look more closely at counseling, at recognition of severe psychological problems, at the availability of weapons, increased school security, and so on, as we ask why something so awful could happen. Communities respond to their grief in a variety of ways, knowing that they are by and large helpless to find adequate remedies. In Figure 9.7, we read, in his own words, teacher Tim Bowens' account of one way the Chardon, Ohio, community responded to their February 2012 tragedy.

WHAT CAN SCHOOLS AND TEACHERS DO? To help ensure the safety of students from early childhood through high school settings, schools have formulated a variety of

Figure 9.7 Chardon Middle School and Project Linus

On February 27, 2012, a former student of Chardon High School in Chardon, Ohio, entered the school and fatally shot three students and wounded several others. I was on bus duty one afternoon some time after the shootings at Chardon High School when I saw students walking by with blankets around their shoulders. There were multiple designs – soccer balls, rainbows, stars, and so on. Kids were being kids that day, and it was great to see. They found both comfort and peace from the blankets lovingly made by volunteers who were concerned for their well-being following the tragic events of that awful day in February. I learned this was a program called Project Linus that provided each student at Chardon High School with a blanket. When my colleague Julie Kenny and I began planning a Day of Service for our school, this seemed like a perfect service project. The shootings at Chardon High made all our students grow up quickly, and gave them empathy for others who experience trauma and tragedy. An ugly and unpredictable reality came to their doorstep. After the lockdown, when they left our building to the safety and security of their parents' arms, they learned about the tragedy that would change so many lives.

The goal in all of our projects has been for our students to see and reach beyond the walls of our school. During the Day of Service, students created blankets in small groups with the assistance from teachers. While creating the blankets, students had an opportunity to work together to make something special that would bring comfort to other students. It was especially fun to watch the 8th grade boys attempt something so foreign to many of them. It was important for our students to give back in light of all who reached out to our district and our students in the days following February 27. Our lovingly made blankets were delivered by Project Linus volunteers to children in area hospitals in hopes that they would bring a smile and some comfort to those who are suffering.

Source: From email communication with Tim Bowens, November 24, 2012.

plans and policies, ranging from programs that foster respect among students to overt ways of increasing security, such as installing surveillance cameras and metal detectors, requiring ID badges, locking school entrances during school hours, and using drug-detection dogs in random sweeps. Some school districts have adopted **zero tolerance** policies, meaning there are nonnegotiable consequences for certain infractions. For instance, the consequence for fighting may be automatic suspension for 3 days. Possession of a weapon may result in automatic expulsion.

Between the horrific events at Columbine, Sandy Hook, and Chardon, many schools responded to the threat of violence. Controlled access to the building during school hours went from 75% to 90%, the requirement that students wear badges or picture IDs went from 4% to 8%, the use of security cameras went from 19% to 55%, the provision of telephones in most classrooms went from 45% to 72%, and the requirement that students wear uniforms went from 12% to 18% (Dinkes et al., 2009).

Individual teachers may have the greatest effect on school safety and security by being aware and watchful. Although violent episodes may occur, they are relatively infrequent. When students take weapons to school or there is a student fatality on school grounds, it is often front-page news—probably because it doesn't happen very often and, when it does, most people are appalled by it. Rather than being frightened day in and day out, think through how you would respond to a variety of scenarios, primarily how you would get help from nearby teachers, administrators, counselors, school security officers, and the like. Most schools have plans in place to address violence when it occurs.

Bullying and violence don't have a single source or cause. They originate from complex situations that didn't begin in an instant and won't be fixed quickly or with a single solution. A multifaceted approach is needed that emphasizes civility, tolerance, and respect for dignity and life, as well as the inclusion of commonsense security measures.

Point of Reflection 9.5

Do you recall being bullied? If so, how did it happen? Did you know students who were relentlessly bullied in school? Did you know students who bullied others? How did you feel toward those who bullied others? How about toward those who were bullied?

Check Your Understanding 9.5

9.6 How Do Truancy and Dropping Out Affect Youth in the United States?

9.6 Summarize how truancy and dropping out affect youth in the United States.

Dropping out of school has been called "the silent epidemic" by researchers at the Bill and Melinda Gates Foundation—"silent" because it has been covered up and ignored for decades, and "epidemic" because the problem has reached near-panic proportions (Bridgeland, DiIulio, and Morison, 2006). One of the most accurate predictors of dropping out is truancy.

Truancy

Nonattendance of compulsory education, not including excused absences generally granted for health reasons, is called **truancy** (Focus Adolescent Services, 2006). Truancy is often referred to as "cutting class" or "skipping school." According to the Los Angeles Office of Education, not only does truancy indicate who is most at risk for dropping out but also it correlates strongly with juvenile delinquency. In Van Nuys, California, a 3-week sweep of the city for truant middle and high school students correlated with a 60% drop in shoplifting arrests. School officials concluded that when they're not in school, many truancy-prone students are committing crimes (Focus Adolescent Services, 2006).

On any given day, about 5% of students are absent from U.S. schools. At some schools, however, the rate is often closer to 20%. Absenteeism for any reason causes students to fall behind. With too many absences, students may feel lost in class, resulting in low self-esteem and a sense of resignation. Families suffer the consequences of truancy as they watch someone they love drift toward academic failure. Communities suffer, not just because of crime, but because of the possible loss of productive, self-sufficient citizens.

According to a study by the Center for Social Organization of Schools at Johns Hopkins University, when truant students were asked why they skipped school, about half said they just didn't want to go to school, about a fourth said they felt pushed out or bullied, and the remaining fourth reported external problems, many of them family related. The researchers found this information encouraging because they contend that 75% of the truancies, or all except those attributed to external problems, can be altered by school actions. We must give students schools that are safe and free of bullying (MacDonald, 2004).

WHAT CAN SCHOOLS AND TEACHERS DO? Schools need to maintain accurate attendance records and communicate all absences to families. Although it sounds obvious, many schools do not call students' homes to ask about students who don't show up. Often parents and guardians don't know there's an attendance problem until it appears insurmountable.

Teachers must develop relationships with students that let them know they matter. Engaging, relevant instruction and a "we miss you when you're gone" attitude go a long way toward doing away with the "I just didn't want to go" syndrome expressed by so many truant students. Catching the problem in the truant stage will help prevent the travesty of dropping out.

Dropping Out

The reality is that each year over a million students who begin ninth grade with their peer group will not walk across the stage at graduation 4 years later. About 7,000 students drop out of school every single day (Alliance for Excellent Education, 2009). Honestly acknowledging how many students are school **dropouts**, or do not graduate from high school in 4 years—and most will leave high school if they don't graduate in 4 years—is the first step to fixing the problem. And there definitely is a problem.

Prior to 2005, students who left school but indicated that they would seek a general equivalency diploma (GED) or who simply never returned to school after numerous absences were not considered dropouts. For decades, states reported grossly inflated high school completion numbers, with many above 90%. The U.S. Department of Education mandated in 2010–2011 that all states use the same definition of **graduation rate**, meaning students who successfully complete high school in four years. State graduation rates using this definition are in Table 9.10. Now we can more accurately compare state data and track progress over time, which has been substantial, with almost all state percentages rising since 2011. In fact, the U.S. average graduation rate in 2010–2011 was 79% and in 2014–2015 rose to 83%.

From a racial and national standpoint, Asian students topped the graduation rates, with 89% finishing high school in four years, followed by white students at 87%, Hispanic students at 76%, and black students at 73%. The Bureau of Indian Education, a division of the Bureau of Indian Affairs, educates more than 41,000 American Indian and Alaska Native children in 183 elementary and secondary schools on 64 reservations in 23 states. The graduation rate of these students is 70% (U.S. Department of Education, 2016).

Table 9.10 High school graduation rates by state, 2014–2015

Rank	State	Graduation Rate
1	Iowa	91%
2	New Jersey	90%
3	Alabama Nebraska Texas	89%
4	Kentucky Maine Missouri New Hampshire Tennessee Vermont Wisconsin	88%
5	Connecticut Indiana Maryland Massachusetts North Dakota West Virginia	87%
6	Delaware Illinois Kansas Montana North Carolina Virginia	86%
7	Arkansas Pennsylvania Utah	85%
8	South Dakota	84%
9	Oklahoma Rhode Island	83%
10	California Hawaii Minnesota	82%
11	Ohio	81%
12	Michigan South Carolina	80%
13	Georgia Idaho New York Wyoming	79%
14	Florida Louisiana Washington	78%
15	Arizona Colorado	77%
16	Alaska	76%
17	Mississippi	75%
18	Oregon	74%
19	Nevada	71%
20	New Mexico	69%
21	Washington, DC	59%

Based on: U.S. Department of Education (2016), EDFacts/Consolidated State Performance Reports. Retrieved April 7, 2017, from http://www.governing.com/gov-data/high-school-graduation-rates-by-state.html

Why do students drop out of school? The reasons are often complex, with Figure 9.8 listing eight of them. You can mix and match the reasons to form plausible scenarios. For instance, boredom in a particular class may lead a group of students to identify with one another and to ditch school occasionally; skipped classes may then lead to academic problems, more absences, and finally dropping out. However, there's actually

Figure 9.8 Top reasons dropouts identify for leaving school

High school dropouts say they . . .

- Were not motivated or inspired to work hard (69%)
- Found classes to be uninteresting (47%)
- Were failing in school (35%)
- Started high school poorly prepared (35%)
- Would have been required to repeat a grade to graduate (32%)
- Had to get a job and make money (32%)
- Became a parent (26%)
- Had to care for a family member (22%)

Source: Bridgeland, J. M., Dilulio, J. J., & Morison, K. B. (2006). *The silent epidemic: Perspective of high school dropouts.* Retrieved April 8, 2006, from http://www.ignitelearning.com/pdf/TheSilentEpidemic3-06FINAL.pdf

good news in Figure 9.8. The most cited reasons for dropping out are largely within our control; they are school related. Although we can't change much of the societal context of our students, we can change what happens within the walls of our classrooms. In the following "What Can Schools and Teachers Do?" section, there are steps to take to increase graduation rates and, in doing so, have tremendous impact on the lives of our students as well as on the economic viability of our nation.

Dropping out often results from a slow process of disengagement, with costly ramifications that may last a lifetime. The negative consequences included in Figure 9.9 are primarily economic. However, the cognitive, social, emotional, physical, and moral impact of dropping out is often devastating for individuals, families, communities, and our country.

Dropping out of high school today is to a student's social health what smoking is to his or her physical health. It is an indicator of a host of poor outcomes to follow, ranging from low lifetime earnings, to high incarceration rates, to the likelihood that the dropout's children will also drop out of high school and start the cycle anew.

WHAT CAN SCHOOLS AND TEACHERS DO? There are no simple solutions to the problem of students dropping out of school. But much of the dilemma is solvable with purposeful effort that focuses on the whole child. Addressing an isolated problem area

Figure 9.9 Negative consequences of dropping out

- Nearly half of dropouts ages 16 to 24 are unemployed (Thornburg, 2006).
- Dropouts typically earn less than graduates: The average earnings difference is estimated to be $9,000 a year and $260,000 over the course of a lifetime (Dynarski, Clarke, Cobb, Finn, & Rumberger, 2008).
- Dropouts contribute only about half as much in taxes as do high school graduates (Dynarski et al., 2008).
- If U.S. high schools and colleges raise the graduation rates of Hispanic, African American, and Native American students to the levels of white students by 2020, the potential increase in personal income would add more than $310 billion to the U.S. economy (Alliance for Excellent Education, 2009).
- Increasing the graduation rate and college matriculation of male students in the United States by just 5% could lead to combined savings and revenue of almost $8 billion each year by reducing crime-related costs (Alliance for Excellent Education, 2009).
- Dropouts draw larger government subsidies in the form of food stamps, housing assistance, and welfare payments (Dynarski et al, 2008).
- Dropouts constitute a disproportionate percentage of all prisoners and of prisoners on death row; 67% of the latter did not complete high school (Thornburgh, 2006).
- Dropouts have worse health outcomes and lower life expectancies than high school completers (Dynarski et al., 2008).

Source: Alliance for Excellent Education. (2009). *High school dropouts in America*. Retrieved June 7, 2010, from http://all4ed.org/files/GraduationRates_FactSheet.pdf; Dynarski, M., Clarke, L., Cobb, B., Finn, B., & Rumberger, R. (2008). *Dropout prevention*. Retrieved June 8, 2010, from http://ies.ed.gov/ncee/wwc/pdf/practiceguides/dp_pg_090308.pdf; Thornburgh, N. (2006, April 17). Dropout nation. *Time*, pp. 30–40.

will likely not be enough, but addressing several areas of concern may produce the desired result of keeping students in school.

In most instances, the students who drop out are capable of succeeding academically: Most are passing when they drop out, and 70% are confident they could complete the program of study (Education Vital Signs [EVS], 2006). Educators don't need to dumb down the curriculum. Efforts to retain students should center on some, or all, of the following suggestions:

1. Know the warning signs. For instance, sixth-graders who don't regularly attend school, receive poor marks for behavior, or fail math or English for any reason have only a 10% chance of graduating (EVS, 2006). So, even a group of sixth-graders can be targeted for intervention.
2. Establish ninth-grade academies. Many schools have found success in separating ninth-graders and providing them with extra counseling and support.
3. Consistently provide engaging curricula and instruction.
4. Maintain a safe environment and a welcoming climate.
5. Ensure an adult advocate for every student at every grade level. This person may be a classroom teacher, counselor, mentor, or administrator who has a specific responsibility to stay connected to the student.
6. Improve home and school communication.
7. Provide flexible school configurations of both time and space that address the preferences and developmental needs of students.

School Connectedness

As this chapter concludes, you may find the societal context of schooling quite discouraging. We have primarily looked at aspects of life that affect our students in negative ways. Note that in each *What can schools and teachers do?* section, the recurring message is that we must know our students well, be vigilant, and do everything within our power to help students grow and thrive. The guarded good news is that some negative aspects of societal dilemmas appear to be getting better.

Application Exercise 9.3: Societal Context Issues

School connectedness occurs when students sense they belong, that adults and students care about them as whole people. When students sense they are connected to the school, they tend to have more positive health and academic outcomes. Students recognize when their teachers give them time, interest, attention, and emotional support. Students who feel connected to their school are

- More likely to attend school regularly, stay in school longer, and have higher grades and test scores
- Less likely to smoke cigarettes, drink alcohol, or have sexual intercourse
- Less likely to carry weapons, become involved in violence, or be injured from dangerous activities, such as drinking and driving or not wearing seat belts
- Less likely to have emotional problems, suffer from eating disorders, or experience suicidal thoughts or attempts (Centers for Disease Control and Prevention, 2009)

Desirable outcomes, aren't they? Teachers have the power to promote school connectedness for students.

Check Your Understanding 9.6

Concluding Thoughts

There's a saying, "We cannot control the wind, but we can adjust our sails." The societal issues that negatively affect students are complex and multidimensional. They don't begin with us, and most won't be completely resolved through us. However, with that reality in view, we can begin to focus on positive steps to prevent or halt risky behaviors and their impact on children and adolescents. Controlling the wind may not be within our reach as teachers, but it is indeed possible to adjust both our own and our students' sails.

After reading the *Chapter in Review*, read about Brandi's dilemma involving child neglect and respond to items in this chapter's *Developing Professional Competence*.

Chapter in Review

How do family, community, and society impact students in the United States?

- Families, communities, and society in general can support student success or thwart it.
- Children and adolescents who are victims of child abuse or neglect are at risk physically, emotionally, socially, and academically.
- Communities can provide vital services for students and their families.

How does socioeconomic status affect students in the United States?

- The privilege gap between the haves and have-nots is a societal dilemma with far-reaching ramifications for children and adolescents.
- Children in low-income settings have many disadvantages that affect achievement in school.
- The most devastating impact of poverty is homelessness.

How do health issues affect students in the United States?

- The rates of most forms of substance abuse have recently decreased, yet even one child or adolescent harmed by substance abuse is one too many.
- Children and adolescents often have an unfounded sense of immortality, which makes them feel they will not be harmed if they use substances such as inhalants, alcohol, legal and illegal drugs, and tobacco.
- Risky sexuality-related behavior can result in emotional distress, sexually transmitted diseases, and unplanned pregnancy.
- Teasing and harassment about homosexuality can be the root of distress for students in and out of school.
- Childhood obesity is near epidemic proportions and has long-term negative effects on students and society.
- Suicide is the third leading cause of adolescent deaths, with contributing factors that may be recognizable, leading to intervention.

How does race affect students in the United States?

- Racism is a form of prejudice stemming from the belief that one race is superior to another.

- Racism may take the form of inaction through silence or of low expectations for certain students.
- Immigrants and their children require special attention to ensure success in school.

What are the effects of bullying, theft, and violence on schools and students in the United States?

- Bullying can be verbal, physical, or emotional, and it is intended to exert power and cause harm.
- Violent acts in school include simple assault (usually fighting), sexual assault, and aggravated assault (definite perpetrator and victim), and they occur most frequently in urban areas and among high school students.

How do truancy and dropping out affect youth in the United States?

- Truancy is a reliable predictor of dropping out.
- When students drop out, there are long-term negative effects for themselves, their families, their communities, and the country.
- Reasons for dropping out are many and complex, with financial-, self–esteem-, and crime-related consequences.

Developing Professional Competence

Thoughtfully reading this scenario and responding to the items that follow it will help you prepare for licensure exams.

Sara Davis Powell

One thing Principal Laura Hill at Summit Primary School is adamant about is making sure there is a visible adult at home when her kindergarten students and first- and second-graders are dropped off by the bus after school. The drivers are instructed to bring children back to school if an adult does not appear in the yard or doorway. Consistently, an adult welcomes Caroline each afternoon.

Caroline, who is in Brandi Wade's kindergarten class, is quiet and shy. As you read in the beginning of the chapter, in December Brandi rearranged physical aspects and instructional strategies in her class based on her observations of the children. During the first couple of months of the year her concern for Caroline grew. Although her mom came to Back-to-School Night and raised no red flags for Brandi, she sees some indications that all may not be well at Caroline's house.

In her 12 years as a classroom teacher, Brandi has seen bruises and burn marks on children and has reported them to the principal, who took appropriate action. After the fact, she has known of sexual abuse of her students, but she has never had suspicions. Brandi sees no obvious signs of abuse with Caroline but rather subtle hints of something wrong. On the playground, there are times when she notices that Caroline appears to be sore when she walks. Brandi has also noticed that when a man is around, Caroline clings to her. One day during free drawing time, Caroline drew a picture of a man that was more anatomically accurate than a kindergartner might depict.

Now it's time for you to respond to two short essay items involving the scenario. In your responses, be sure to address all the dilemmas and questions posed in each item. These items are followed by three multiple-choice questions.

1. There is always a danger that stepping into a domestic problem may actually make it worse. Perhaps nothing wrong is taking place. Given this, should Brandi share her concerns about Caroline as the holidays approach or wait until the children return after winter break? Explain your response.

2. Brandi takes the portion of the following InTASC Principle 10 very seriously. She always tries to understand the context of her students' lives. This particular situation with Caroline, however, is a new challenge and one that makes her feel inadequate to handle. What might Brandi do to help Caroline feel safe in school and not to fear the men who are part of the school environment?

InTASC Knowledge, Principle 10

The teacher seeks appropriate leadership roles and opportunities to take responsibility for student learning, to collaborate with learners, families, colleagues, other school professionals, and community members to ensure learner growth, and to advance the profession.

Application Exercise 9.4: Developing Professional Competence

3. Even though there are no overt signs of abuse, what should Brandi immediately do?
   a. Continue to watch Caroline and document what she notices.
   b. Talk with Principal Hill about her observations and leave it to the principal to pursue the situation.
   c. Try to get Caroline to confide in her.
   d. Ask a family in Caroline's neighborhood if they notice anything suspicious about the family.
4. One day Caroline mentions that her mother has a boyfriend who lives with them. What should Brandi do with this information?
   a. Brandi should wait and see what else happens.
   b. Brandi should call Caroline's mom and ask for a parent conference.
   c. Brandi should tell Principal Hill immediately.
   d. Brandi should ask Caroline if she likes him.
5. The children like to post their drawings on a large bulletin board in Brandi's classroom. She encourages them to do so. On the day she sees Caroline's drawing, what is the best way to avoid having the picture of the man posted?
   a. She could ask the children to put their drawings in their desks and then take Caroline's after the children leave for the day.
   b. She could say she will choose the drawings that will be posted for the day.
   c. She could say they don't have time to post at the moment and she would just like to keep the children's drawings for now.
   d. She could post all the drawings in an effort to let Caroline know she has done nothing wrong.

Application Exercise 9.5: Developing Professional Competence

Flash Cards 9.1

Shared Writing 9.1: School Preference

Chapter 10

Ethical and Legal Issues in U.S. Schools

Learning Objectives

After studying this chapter, you will have knowledge and skills to:

10.1 Define characteristics of an ethical teacher.

10.2 Determine how laws affect schools, teachers, and students.

10.3 Summarize the legal rights of teachers.

10.4 Articulate the legal responsibilities of teachers.

10.5 Interpret how the law impacts the relationship between school and religion.

10.6 Describe the legal rights of students.

Dear Reader

Teachers hold a unique position in a community. In our trust are the children, the dearest resource of love and hope for each generation. It's an awesome responsibility and an opportunity for service, challenge, and fulfillment that few professions provide. Along with responsibility and opportunity come legal and ethical guidelines.

Please carefully consider the topics in this chapter. Even though very few teachers have legal issues over the course of their careers, avoiding problems and circumstances that may put your career in jeopardy requires a healthy dose of common sense and an understanding of the laws that directly relate to teachers and schools. We teachers are citizens and, as such, enjoy the same rights as other citizens. However, because teachers represent their schools, there are policies and expectations that affect what we do and what we say both inside the schoolhouse and in the community. The more we know about laws, policies, and expectations, the better.

Ethical guidelines are not legislated. Because teachers spend their days with children and adolescents who bring their experiences, families, and cultures to school with them, situations are often not simply black or white, but are tinged with subtle shades of gray. Most dilemmas and decisions you will make as a teacher have no laws, or even school policies, to guide you. This is where a sense of ethics will be very important.

The United States has laws for a reason—they make it possible for people to live together as a nation. Laws prompt civility in neighborhoods, towns, cities, states, and across the country. We gain perspective and more fully understand how laws impact the daily work of teachers by examining actual people and events that have helped shape the fabric of laws that affect education. The cases in this chapter are not fictional. They are real. Read carefully and think about the implications for your future career in an early childhood, elementary, middle, or high school classroom. But first, consider how ethical standards play a major role in the teaching profession.

10.1 What Does It Mean to Be an Ethical Teacher?

10.1 Define characteristics of an ethical teacher.

Laws tell us what we can and can't do. **Ethics** tell us what we should and shouldn't do. Ethics are standards of conduct based on moral judgments. Because ethics are grounded in personal belief systems, what is ethical in one person's view might not be ethical from another's perspective. Although most of the time what is lawful is also ethical, and what is ethical is also lawful, this is not always the case from everyone's viewpoint. For instance, abortion is legal in the United States, but many U.S. citizens consider it unethical. For some people with strong anti-abortion beliefs, acting on personal ethics may mean becoming involved in unlawful forms of protest against a legal activity.

Professional Ethics

Most professions have codes of ethics. The largest teacher organization, the National Education Association (NEA), has a code of ethics you may read on the NEA website. The NEA Code of Ethics is divided into two sections: teacher commitment to students and teacher commitment to the profession. The code lists actions teachers "shall not" take to fulfill obligations to students and the teaching profession.

It is important for teachers to understand that the "shall nots" of teaching serve as guidelines to help us avoid unethical situations and their consequences. However, there are also many "shalls" involved in practicing ethical teaching, as we discuss throughout this entire text. If these positive elements are internalized, practicing ethical teaching becomes habitual. Ethical teachers *shall:*

- Purposefully serve as positive role models for their students
- Put students' best interests ahead of other considerations
- Involve families often and positively
- Support colleagues and work collaboratively
- Create and maintain a productive learning environment
- Diversify instruction to address student differences

Derek Boucher teaches modern world history and U.S. history at Roosevelt High School in Fresno, California, where focus teachers Angelica Reynosa and Craig Cleveland teach. He is also the reading intervention teacher for sophomores and juniors, many of whom are English language learners. It is in this capacity that Derek feels a keen sense of responsibility toward building his students' literacy skills. He tirelessly searches for ways to engage his students in reading. Derek believes that to transform students into readers, it is important to make reading both satisfying and focused on meaning. He selects books and magazines that will capture student imagination, as he voraciously reads professional literature to help him grow as a teacher. Derek exemplifies characteristics of an ethical teacher's approach to teaching and learning. Watch Video Example 10.1 and listen for ways he is a role model, puts students first, and creates and maintains a productive learning environment by diversifying instruction to address student differences.

Video Example 10.1: Derek as an Ethical Teacher

Laws do not dictate actions such as Derek's; ethical attitudes and beliefs prompt them. Let's bring these concepts into the reality of the classroom by examining what it means to be an ethical teacher. Regardless of what else our students learn, they learn *us*. We either represent, or *mis*represent, ethical behavior in the classroom.

Ethics for Teachers

An ethical teacher is guided by a set of beliefs that leads to attitudes and actions focused on what's best for students. Being ethical means taking the high road and behaving professionally in the midst of big issues as well as in everyday decision making in the classroom.

Howe (1996) tells us that six characteristics form a conceptual basis for making ethical decisions. The first characteristic, *appreciation for moral deliberation*, means understanding that situations are complex and that part of our obligation is to ensure that the rights of all involved are protected. The second characteristic, *empathy*, refers to the ability to put oneself mentally in the place of others to appreciate a variety of perspectives. *Knowledge*, the third characteristic, is necessary to have a clear view of the dilemma at hand. Dealing with knowledge requires *reasoning*, the fourth characteristic, and *courage*, the fifth characteristic, is needed to act on that reasoning. Finally, the sixth characteristic, *interpersonal skills*, allows teachers to communicate effectively with others about their ethical deliberations. These six characteristics are described in Figure 10.1. Characteristics 2 through 6 are self-explanatory. This doesn't diminish their value, but we know what they look like in practice more often than we do characteristic number 1.

Cultivating an "appreciation for moral deliberation," as Howe puts it, is a career-long area of growth for teachers. When we have big decisions to make, we generally see the right and wrong sides pretty clearly. We know there are consequences for our choices and we usually recognize many of them. This is a good thing. But what about the seemingly little decisions and actions, the things we do, or don't do, on a regular basis? Is it possible that these less-than-life-changing situations have "complex moral dimensions" and require that we have a "realization that care is needed to protect the rights of all parties"? Bringing higher-order thinking and problem-solving skills to bear on all dilemmas, big and small, is what teachers must do.

Figure 10.1 Six desirable characteristics for teachers as they make ethical judgments

1. Appreciation for Moral Deliberation—ability to see complex moral dimensions of a problem and realization that care is needed to protect the rights of all parties
2. Empathy—ability to "get inside the skin of another"
3. Knowledge—facts to enable us to put issues in context
4. Reasoning—reflecting systematically on an issue and moving step by step to a conclusion
5. Courage—the willpower to act in what we perceive to be the right way, rather than just the comfortable way
6. Interpersonal Skills—communicating about issues sensitively and tactfully

Based on Howe, K. R. (1996, May/June). A conceptual basis for ethics in teacher education. Journal of Teacher Education, 37, 6.

In Table 10.1 you'll find some sample attitudes and decisions leading to actions, along with questions a teacher might consider. Could a teacher be dismissed because of these? Maybe, but probably not. Would a teacher's reputation suffer in the eyes of some? Maybe, and probably so. Every teacher could name similar—as well as very different—scenarios from personal experience, if prompted to think about it. Perhaps there's the dilemma: *if prompted to think about it.* When our actions go unexamined, we are less likely to consider moral deliberation and therefore not be the ethical teachers we might otherwise become.

Table 10.1 Recognizing ethical dilemmas

Attitudes/Decisions/Actions	Thinking It Through
With a wink, I say to a few students that I think I'm coming down with something. I return 48 hours later with an obvious skier's sunburn.	Is it OK to indicate to students that I am going to call in sick when I'm really planning to go on a ski trip? What lesson are they learning from me about responsibility and honesty?
A spelling bee competition is planned for tomorrow in which all the students in each class must participate. I have three students who are English language learners. I really want to win this bee because I am a candidate for my school's Teacher of the Year award. I casually mention to the three students that tomorrow would be a great day to stay home and enjoy the new-fallen snow because it's Friday before winter vacation and they won't miss much.	Have I let my desire to look good get in the way of doing what's right for my students? Without these three students, my fifth-grade class has the best chance of winning our grade-level spelling bee. Winning will be a big boost for my students. So am I justified in encouraging these three students to stay home? After all, it's Friday before winter vacation and not much will go on that's academic in nature besides the spelling bee. They won't miss much—or will they?
On a field trip to a local museum I decide to buy each student a cold drink from a vending machine. I drop in two quarters and out pops not just one soda, but three. I laugh and say this must be my lucky day.	It's only a dollar loss for the vending company, but am I setting a good example for students? If I think that cheating the system makes me lucky, what message am I giving my students?
I just started a landscaping business that hopefully will occupy my weekends and give me extra income. I have developed an advertising flyer that I will distribute in the community. Because I haven't made much money yet, I decide to use the school copier late one afternoon to make a thousand flyers.	The students will likely never know I did this. But if another teacher walks into the workroom and sees what I'm doing, will my reputation be somewhat affected?
A parent generously donated $200 for me to buy a classroom set of a novel to use in spring semester. She determined the donation amount by going to a local bookstore. Knowing that I would get a 10% teacher discount, she gave me a check rather than buying the books herself. I go online and find the books for $150 and order them. I decide that it was my ingenuity that resulted in the discount and decide to keep the extra $50 for my trouble.	It's unlikely that anyone will ever know about this, so why should I care? After all, I work very hard as a teacher and this is just a small perk. Is $50 worth living with a small voice inside that says I should have spent the money on something for my classroom?
It's time for the first-quarter grades to be submitted just as football season has become very exciting. Our team is looking promising as a contender for the district championship. Mike has a 68% in my class, making him ineligible to play in a big rivalry game Friday night. He's had a lot to do with practice every afternoon and he's a really good guy. I decide to make his grade a C– instead of a D.	I didn't make this adjustment for several other students who struggled, or maybe didn't struggle enough, to make a C–. Because I insist that all my students keep up with their grade averages, Mike will know that I changed his grade. What message am I sending him about doing just enough to get by and then receiving "gifts"? If he brags about this, what about the other students, both those who didn't get the extra boost and others who do fine in my class but will know that I fudged on Mike's grade? Will some parent discover what I have done and complain to my principal?
It's time once again to promote the sale of wrapping paper to earn money for school projects. I send a letter home encouraging parents to join in. I email parents each day reminding them to help their students sell the paper. I promise the students a party, but only for those who bring in orders for $100 of paper. The students feel the pressure, as do the parents.	Because my class is composed of kids from a wide range of socioeconomic-level homes, am I unduly putting pressure on some families who don't know many people with discretionary money to spend on fancy wrapping paper? If I still like the party idea, how might I design the party incentive so that particular students would not be ostracized?
Because fund-raising efforts have been disappointing in recent years, and our school improvement team wants to landscape the courtyard, our principal decides to give each student who brings a $20 donation 10 points to be used on any test in any class during the quarter.	At first I buy into this plan, not considering the fairness or morality of it. Then a student comes to me and complains that being able to give $20 will be difficult. Suddenly I see this initiative as very unfair and fundamentally misguided. Should I express this to my principal? Should I tell my students that I won't honor the 10-point bonus?

When we habitually apply ethical thinking and actions (the "shalls" referred to earlier) to situations, we are contributing to the development of students who ideally will do the same. As we model morally sound decision making, it is helpful to have a vision of desirable traits we want to promote in those we profoundly influence through ethical teaching. In writing about her vision of young adolescents, Donna Marie San Antonio (2006, p. 7) simply and eloquently describes some desirable traits. We want students to be

- Smart but not arrogant
- Flexible but not easily deterred from their hopes and dreams

- Compassionate toward others but not overly accommodating
- Self-confident but not too preoccupied with themselves
- Proud but not exclusive

Helping students build these traits is a tall order and one we must fulfill with ethical attitudes, decisions, and actions. The results will be positive and cumulative.

Point of Reflection 10.1

What are your memories of teachers who promoted ethical behavior? Describe a scenario from your PreK–12 school experiences.

What are your memories of teachers who displayed unethical attitudes and actions? Describe a scenario from your PreK–12 school experiences.

Check Your Understanding 10.1

10.2 How Do Laws Affect Schools, Teachers, and Students?

10.2 Determine how laws affect schools, teachers, and students.

The U.S. government, its legal system, and the laws that affect schools, teachers, and students are based on a balance of rights and responsibilities. The government and legal system achieve a viable balance of power through the interaction of the three branches of government: executive, legislative, and judicial. Since the founding of the United States of America, four basic sources of law have directly impacted the everyday work of all teachers: the U.S. Constitution, federal laws, state and local laws and policies, and case law.

U.S. Constitution

The Constitution does not specifically mention education. However, certain amendments directly impact teachers and schools.

FIRST AMENDMENT. The First Amendment to the U.S. Constitution guarantees, among other things, freedom of speech and religion and prohibits government (i.e., public school) advancement of religion. Freedom of speech, as guaranteed in the First Amendment, applies to schools. As you read this chapter you'll recognize how often the First Amendment is cited as a guide in decision making on educational issues. The Association for Supervision and Curriculum Development (ASCD) established the **First Amendment Center** to provide resources to assist schools in implementing the guiding principles of the First Amendment.

FOURTH AMENDMENT. The Fourth Amendment protects citizens from unreasonable search and seizure and, in doing so, protects the basic privacy and security of all people, including students' rights to privacy. For instance, do students have the right to keep whatever they want in a locker assigned to them? Under what circumstances can adults examine the locker's contents? This topic is discussed later in the chapter.

FOURTEENTH AMENDMENT. The Fourteenth Amendment protects the rights of due process and guarantees equal protection to all citizens. For teachers, this amendment pertains to job security and the right to be heard if charges are made against them. Later in the chapter we examine how this amendment affects both teachers and students.

The general guidelines of the U.S. Constitution—specifically the First, Fourth, and Fourteenth Amendments— provide the framework for the federal laws that affect schools, teachers, and students.

Federal Laws

The federal statutes written and passed by Congress (the legislative branch of the U.S. government) have a major impact on the daily work of teachers and the operation of schools. Here are examples of federal laws impacting education:

- The National Defense Education Act (1958) established curricular priorities, placing math, science, and foreign languages at the top.
- The Civil Rights Act (1964) officially ended generations of overt racial segregation in public schools by declaring, "No person in the United States shall on the grounds of race, color, or national origin, be excluded from participation in or be denied the benefits of, or be subjected to discrimination under any program or activity receiving federal financial assistance." Unfortunately, however, segregation still exists in public schools in many areas.
- The Elementary and Secondary Education Act (1965) was originated to benefit children in low socioeconomic settings. This act created Title I funding and has been reauthorized several times.
- The Bilingual Education Act (1968) proposed that students be taught in their native languages while they learned English.
- Federal Title IX legislation (1972) opened many doors, specifically to girls, by prohibiting discrimination based on gender.
- The Individuals with Disabilities Education Act (1975, 1990, 2004) guarantees the rights of students with disabilities to a free education in the least restrictive environment.

Another federal law you've read about is the 2001 reauthorization of the Elementary and Secondary Education Act (ESEA), known as No Child Left Behind. This federal law has significantly impacted schools thus far into the 21st century. In 2016, ESEA was again reauthorized as the Every Student Succeeds Act (ESSA).

State and Local Laws and Policies

The Tenth Amendment of the U.S. Constitution stipulates that anything not specifically addressed by it becomes a state issue. Consequently, laws and policies affecting education vary from state to state, and from district to district within each state. Some of the issues addressed by state and local laws and policies include curriculum standards and assessment mandates, as well as funding and governance. The guidelines for teacher certification are also left up to states, with some federal stipulations.

Case Law

Many legal decisions concerning education are based on precedents—what has been done in the past and what the judicial system has decided with regard to specific rights and responsibilities. The cases brought before the courts are deliberated and settled based on what the U.S. Constitution says, what federal law dictates, and what state and local governing bodies have established. All of these aspects are considered, ideally with heaping doses of common sense, as decisions are made by the courts.

Case law is based on the doctrine of *stare decisis*, a Latin phrase meaning "let the decision stand." This means that once a decision is made in a court of law, that decision sets a precedent for future cases of a similar nature until challenged or overturned. There is a large body of federal case law on which state and local cases rely for precedents. A decision made by the U.S. Supreme Court establishes case law until either the Supreme Court changes the ruling or an amendment to the Constitution alters the decision. Unfortunately, many school and local government officials have not abided by this principle. Because the Supreme Court doesn't have an enforcement arm, continued court action is sometimes necessary to bring school districts into compliance. For instance, the famous *Brown* v. *Board of Education* (1954) court decision ruled that separate schools are not equal and opened many schoolhouse doors for African Americans. Occasionally during the last 60-plus years, however, decisions have been made that do not comply with the *Brown* results, and more court action is needed.

Throughout this chapter, discussions of the legal rights and responsibilities of teachers, the rights of students, and the relationship between schools and religion will cite sample case law. In this chapter's *The Opinion Page* feature, we read about actions that allegedly conflict with case law.

The Opinion Page

This Opinion Editorial appeared in The Stamford Advocate, *Connecticut, on March 8, 2013.*

A Return to School Segregation?

by Wendy Lecker

Wendy Lecker is a columnist for Hearst Connecticut Media Group and is senior attorney for the Campaign for Fiscal Equity project at the Education Law Center.

From *Brown* v. *Board of Education* to Connecticut's landmark case, *Sheff* v. *O'Neill,* to the language of the Connecticut constitution, the law has been clear. Children have a constitutionally guaranteed right to a public education that is not impaired by isolation based on race, ethnicity, national origin or disability. Therefore, it is unconstitutional to develop and fund education programs that intentionally or unintentionally limit access to educational opportunities based on racial or ethnic backgrounds, or disabilities. Yet recently, it was announced that schools exclusively for "gifted" children will be opening in Windham, New London, and Bridgeport. Whether intended or not, the proposal takes Connecticut back to the ugly era of school segregation.

These three districts plan to pull what they characterize as "gifted" children from their schools and create separate schools "to highlight and encourage the potential" of these particular students. The schools are modeled after the Renzulli Academy in Hartford, named for UConn professor Joseph Renzulli, and serving "gifted" children in kindergarten and in fourth through ninth grades.

Admission to this school is based on Connecticut Mastery Test scores, grades and a teacher recommendation, although a representative at the school explained that the scores are the "big part" of admissions. Decades of research have proven that standardized tests are an unreliable and inaccurate measure of student achievement and do not measure student potential. In fact, the data reveal that the strongest correlation is between test scores and socio-economic status.

The gross injustice of relying on these tests scores is apparent at the Hartford Renzulli Academy. In 2011, the school had no ELL (English Language Learners) or any students with disabilities. In 2012, the school had but one ELL student and only 6 of the 120 students were classified as students with disabilities. The notion that you cannot be "gifted" if you do not speak English or if you need special education services is absurd.

Beyond the faulty admissions criteria, segregating so-called gifted children into a separate school contravenes what we know about a child's educational development. Children blossom at different times. A child who may not display his gifts at 10 may develop them at 13, given the appropriate access to learning. Conversely, a child who may read at an advanced stage at age 5 may find that her classmates have caught up to her developmentally by age 7, thus erasing her perceived "gift." Cementing children into a classification at one age, and denying them access to higher-level learning deprives those in the lower level of that chance to blossom. Until now, even Joseph Renzulli asserted that his gifted pedagogy was designed to work in all school settings for all children.

The most disturbing issue of all is that creating separate schools for "gifted" children violates Connecticut law and policies prohibiting school segregation. While the equal protection clauses in most state constitutions only bar discrimination, Connecticut's expressly bans segregation as well as discrimination. In *Sheff* v. *O'Neill,* our Supreme Court ruled that segregation has pernicious effects on children whether that segregation is intentional or unorchestrated, and ruled that the state must act to prevent and eradicate school segregation.

Connecticut's state Board of Education recognized that segregation has a destructive effect on children's educational opportunities. In its 2010 resolution against tracking, the board wrote that grouping by ability "limits achievement and stifles expectation and opportunity for college and successful competition in the workplace" because it denies those in lower levels access to a more challenging curriculum and higher expectations. The board unanimously disapproved any practice that permanently groups students for instruction. As the board noted, the practice of tracking disproportionately burdens poor, African-American and Latino students.

The state board resolved that any school district that assigned students to a particular level based on assessed or perceived readiness had to disclose this fact to parents and report to the state the research proving that this separate placement was necessary, the length of time it planned to deny children in lower levels access to learning with higher-achieving peers, and the demographic characteristics of those children denied access to higher-achieving peers. Now, only three years later, officials stand silent as Connecticut abandons its commitment to desegregation. Indeed, it appears that our leaders are acting to speed re-segregation.

In recent years the state has dramatically increased funding for privately run charter schools that routinely exclude non-English-speaking students and students with disabilities. And now, we have a proposal for "gifted only" schools, equipped with "gifted only" water fountains, "gifted only" bathrooms and "gifted only" lunchrooms.

Something is very wrong here.

This *Opinion Page* piece is an impassioned statement against student segregation. The writer knows the law and is observing instances that she perceives as Connecticut schools not adhering to either the spirit or the letter of the law. Write a well-developed paragraph in response to each of the following questions:

1. Ms. Lecker, the author of this opinion piece, expresses her dismay at the proposed admissions criteria for the three schools designed exclusively for gifted children based largely on results of Connecticut's state assessment, the Connecticut Mastery Test. Do you agree or disagree with her opinion of the use of this primary criteria? Why?
2. The 2010 resolution against tracking, or grouping by ability, was a bold step for Connecticut's Board of Education. What does the statement that tracking "disproportionately burdens poor, African-American and Latino students" mean? Did you experience tracking? If so, how did you feel about it? If you never experienced tracking, what is your opinion of the practice?
3. Who would most likely challenge the proposed schools exclusively for gifted children? Briefly explain three legally based actions or events that will likely be persuasive in court.

Before addressing the rights and responsibilities of teachers and students, consider the relationship between laws and ethics. Take a few minutes to examine Figure 10.2 that shows how laws and ethics differ in a number of ways, yet still share the two linking characteristics.

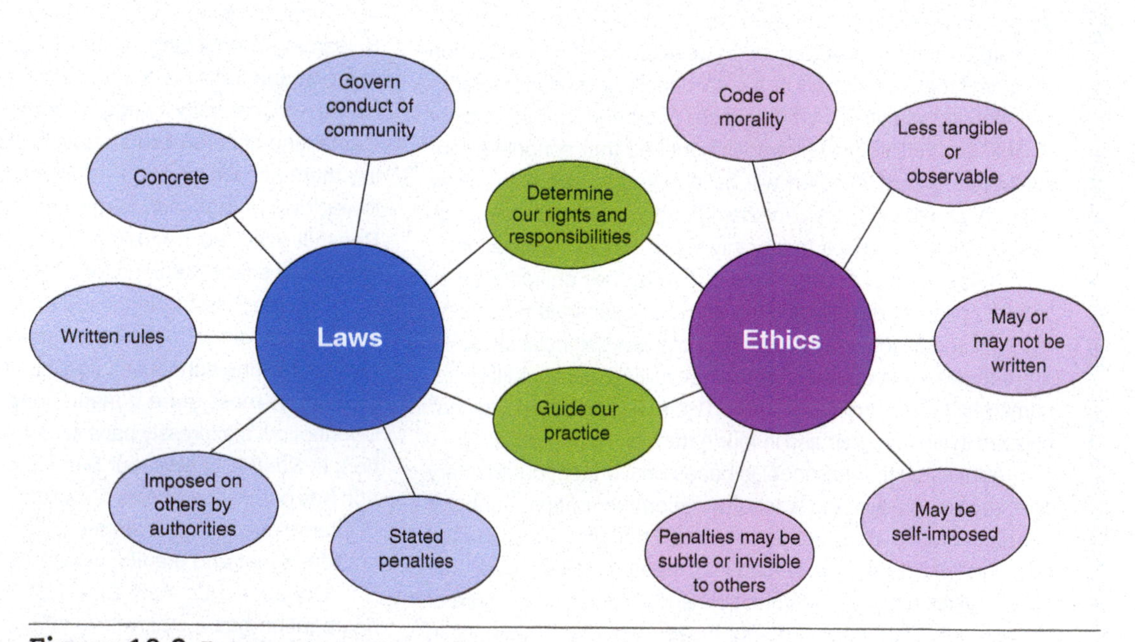

Figure 10.2 Relationship of law and ethics

Application Exercise 10.1: Figure 10.2 Relationship of law and ethics

Check Your Understanding 10.2

10.3 What Are the Legal Rights of Teachers?

10.3 Summarize the legal rights of teachers.

Teachers in the United States are entitled to the same rights as other Americans. Most teachers will never find themselves in positions where their legal rights are threatened. The day-to-day realities of teaching rarely involve legal challenges. However, some rights are occasionally tempered by the opinions of either the community or the court when there is concern that teachers' individual rights may impact classroom effectiveness. In addition, certain legal rights apply specifically to the teaching profession.

Employment Legalities

Being employed by a school district entails understanding your rights and responsibilities. You will sign a contract, possibly have tenure in your future, and have procedures for filing grievances if things go wrong or if dismissal is threatened.

TEACHING CONTRACTS. A **contract** is an agreement between parties that states the rights and responsibilities of each. A teacher signs an initial contract and then signs again each year to continue in the same position. Teaching contracts typically include a formal offer of employment, the salary, and a description of the position. When you sign a teaching contract, you state that you will abide by district policies. It is very important to read carefully and understand the policies and the contract. Both are extensive and may be written in complex language. Don't hesitate to ask for an explanation.

Contracts are binding on both parties. If you sign a contract and then back out or take a different job, or if the district backs out, you or the district can be sued for damages involving **breach of contract**.

TENURE. Continuing contract status is known as **tenure**. Most districts require teachers to serve successfully for about 3 years before offering them a continuing contract, or tenure. During these first 3 years or so, teachers can be dismissed for suspected incompetence or because of a general **reduction in force** of the district teacher population. Such a reduction may result from lower student numbers, budget cuts, or program cancellations. Reductions in force (RIFs) may also apply to tenured teachers. However, the general rule of "riffing" is that the last hired are the first to go.

A teacher with tenure is entitled to a contract each year unless the district has reason not to renew it or the teacher decides to go elsewhere. In most states, tenure doesn't guarantee a particular position in a particular school, but it does guarantee employment in the district.

Some object to the concept of tenure because it requires more steps to dismiss an ineffective teacher who has tenure. However, even teachers with tenure cannot keep their jobs if they are shown to be incompetent, display immoral behaviors, are **insubordinate**, or are involved in any of a wide array of behaviors considered unprofessional conduct.

DISMISSAL. Teachers have been dismissed for many reasons, some of which sound outrageous to us today. Historically, teachers have been dismissed for not attending a particular church, for wearing pants in public (a female teacher), for marrying or becoming pregnant during the school year, and even for moving to a neighboring town. More recently, the courts have ruled for dismissal due to, among others, the following reasons:

- Insubordination
- Neglect of duty
- Conduct unbecoming a teacher
- Incompetence
- Physical or mental health problems
- Engaging in illegal activities
- Causing or encouraging disruptions

Some teacher offenses are considered by the courts to be remediable, meaning that given assistance and time, a teacher may be able to correct the problem and be effective in the classroom. For instance, if a district begins dismissal procedures because a tenured teacher's classroom management skills are considered very poor, the court will likely say the teacher has a right to try to remediate those skills. On the other hand, some actions are considered irremediable in that they are so unprofessional that a district is not obligated to provide assistance. Conviction in a criminal case and having a sexual relationship with a student are two examples of actions for which districts may begin immediate procedures toward dismissal.

A teacher's role-model effectiveness is based both on work and personal behavior. It relates to your reputation among students, staff, and in the community. Here are two overriding questions asked when considering dismissal:

- Is the educational process significantly disrupted by the teacher's action?
- Is the teacher's credibility significantly harmed among students, colleagues, families, and the community?

DUE PROCESS. When a tenured teacher is threatened with dismissal, the steps the district must take to pursue the charges against the teacher are called **due process.** Due process is an important principle that requires guidelines to be followed to ensure that individuals are protected from arbitrary or capricious treatment by those in authority. The procedures of due process vary by state, but generally a teacher must be:

- Notified of the proposed charges
- Given reasonable time to examine evidence
- Told who will be called as witnesses and given the right to legal representation
- Provided with a hearing before an impartial jury, panel, and/or judge
- Given the opportunity to call witnesses and cross-examine the district's witnesses
- Afforded a decision based on evidence
- Provided a transcript of the proceedings
- Given the right to appeal

Even though due process has been in force for many years and will likely continue to be part of the profession, outcomes of hearings based on due process may vary by location and according to the times.

UNIONS AND COLLECTIVE BARGAINING. Although not exclusively related to getting and keeping a job, collective bargaining is a right practiced in most states by teacher unions. States often allow unions to negotiate with school boards concerning elements of teacher contracts and working conditions. The two major teacher organizations that act as unions are the National Education Association (NEA) and the American Federation of Teachers (AFT). States have their own affiliates of the NEA or the AFT to represent teachers in more local ways. Individual teachers and groups of teachers can file grievances, or formal complaints against a district. The NEA and the AFT, or their state affiliates, often represent teachers who file **grievances**. As unions, these two important teacher organizations can also call for teacher strikes when collective bargaining does not result in changes that satisfy the large groups of teachers who affiliate with the unions.

Freedom of Expression

There are many ways to express opinions and beliefs, including symbolic, written, and verbal expression. Symbolic expression generally involves making a statement by what is worn—a style of clothing, a political button, some color combinations, an armband, a ribbon, and so on. Some symbolic statements are socially acceptable, even desirable. For instance, ribbons showing support for breast cancer research or bracelets commemorating important days in history are considered appropriate. However, wearing an armband to protest an ongoing war, or wearing a shirt with inflammatory or offensive words or pictures, may be legal outside school but ruled unacceptable for teachers in school. These acts can serve as possible grounds for dismissal. Wearing shirts with religious messages are also grounds for dismissal. In 2001, a case determined that a teacher could not wear a "Jesus 2000" shirt because of its religious message (*Downing* v. *West Haven Board of Education*). For teachers, freedom of symbolic expression has limits, especially if it disrupts the school or classroom or makes it appear that the school endorses a specific viewpoint.

As with symbolic expression, written and spoken expression must not interrupt the education process. Teachers have the right to express themselves through letters to the editor, written articles, conversations, speeches, and debates. Since the often-quoted case of *Pickering* v. *Board of Education*, 1968, the courts have generally ruled on the side of teachers' rights to freedom of spoken and written expression, even when that expression involves harsh criticism of personnel connected to education. In *Pickering*, an Illinois teacher wrote a sarcastic letter to the editor criticizing the school superintendent and school board for funding practices. U.S. Supreme Court Justice Thurgood Marshall stated that the problem was one of balance between personal rights of the teacher and the district's right to promote efficient public service through its employees. The court ruled in favor of Pickering and his right to openly debate questions without fear of retaliatory dismissal.

If a teacher's expression is intended to incite unprofessional behavior, the courts may rule against the teacher, as in *Stroman* v. *Colleton County School District*, 1992. The teacher was dismissed because he asked other teachers to call in sick as a form of protest. The Supreme Court ruled in favor of the school district on grounds that encouraging others to lie is unprofessional.

Academic Freedom

Academic freedom is a form of expression that allows teachers to use their judgment in making decisions such as what to discuss, what to assign as readings, and what teaching strategies to employ. Like the other freedoms, academic freedom has limits that courts have upheld in many cases.

One recurring issue involves the courts' attempts to balance the right of academic freedom with a district's desire for students to learn a specific curriculum. Districts and states set the curriculum teachers must teach. When teachers exercise academic freedom and go beyond or eliminate parts of this curriculum, problems occur because either (1) including the additional topics does not leave time for the prescribed curriculum or (2) the nonprescribed topics are controversial and may be deemed inappropriate.

In this era of standards and high-stakes testing, failing to teach the prescribed curriculum is likely to become evident when student test scores decline, but it may take years for a pattern of lower scores to emerge. The line between what is appropriate in the classroom, and what is not, is the most common cause of disagreements between districts and teachers with regard to academic freedom. Some of the topics deemed inappropriate in the public school classroom when they are not part of the curriculum include sexuality-related issues, gun control, abortion, some political issues, and any topic involving offensive language. For instance, in *Keefe* v. *Geanakos*, 1969, a Massachusetts high school English teacher assigned an article from the *Atlantic Monthly* that contained offensive language. He was fired because he would not agree to never give the assignment again. A court decision gave Keefe his job back and stated that because some of the school's library books contained the same words and students would likely not be shocked by them, parental complaints about the words did not dictate what was proper in the classroom.

Some teaching methods may be deemed inappropriate if a teacher cannot substantiate the approach using professional opinions and research. Even if the teacher takes a case to court to try to acquire the right to use a method and loses, dismissal is seldom based on the attempt to use the strategy. In *Murray* v. *Pittsburgh Board of Education*, 1996, a teacher used a motivational technique called "Learnball" with at-risk high school students involving dividing the class into teams. Competition between teams involved rewards, such as listening to the radio and shooting baskets with foam balls. The school board ordered the teacher not to use the method. Murray sued the board but lost. The courts determined that the school board had the right to set policy against specific teaching methodologies.

Table 10.2 consists of court cases and some thoughts about their implications for you as a teacher. In each case in Table 10.2, teachers lost their positions. Don't dismiss a case because it seems to be from a long time ago. The alleged misconduct and subsequent court decisions are still relevant as case law. Take your time as you read about real cases.

The general direction of court cases today that consider dismissal tends more toward defending a teacher's personal liberty than in the past. Table 10.3 consists of cases decided in favor of the teacher.

Let's take another look at Derek Boucher and how he fulfills the role of an ethical teacher by taking advantage of the 1968 verdict in *Pickering* v. *Board of Education*. Derek not only reads professional literature, he also makes his opinions known through writing about issues from a teacher's perspective. Video Example 10.2 Professional Involvement provides an opportunity to hear him speak briefly about this activity.

Video Example 10.2: Professional Involvement

Table 10.2 Teacher dismissal cases and implications

Case	Explanation	Implications for Teachers
Walthart v. *Board of Directors* Iowa, 2005	Teacher had knowledge that her minor son and his teenage friends were consuming alcohol on her property, but failed to intervene. Court held that her ability to be a role model was damaged.	This happens more frequently than we realize. Not only is it against the law, but, for a teacher, it represents incredibly poor judgment.
Nancy J. Zelno v. *Lincoln Intermediate Unit No. 12 Board of Directors* Pennsylvania, 2001	Teacher had 3 DUI offenses and 2 offenses for driving while her license was suspended. She was incarcerated on weekends during the school year and remained incarcerated through the summer until her sentence was completed.	Engaging in illegal activities by drinking while driving shows a blatant disregard for safety. Teachers should never be in this position. Your personal life can indeed impact your reputation and status as a role model.
Gaylord v. *Board of Education, Unified School District, Morton County* Kansas, 1990	Teacher called in sick after his request for a day off was denied.	Not only is this *insubordination* but it also shows a serious lack of good sense. Teacher work schedules are reasonable when compared to most professions. Always try to arrange travel and activities on weekends or days designated as teacher holidays.
Stroman v. *Colleton County School District* South Carolina, 1992	Teacher circulated a letter to encourage his fellow teachers to engage in a "sick-out" to protest change in methods for paying teachers and perceived budgetary mismanagement.	This is a clear case of *causing or encouraging a disruption*. There are legitimate ways to express concern. Encouraging others to lie is unprofessional and a sure way to lose both respect and a teaching position.
Ware v. *Morgan County School District* Colorado, 1988	High school music teacher took a misbehaving student outside and used obscene language to tell him he was a disgrace to the band.	This is wrong on so many levels and is definitely *conduct unbecoming-a teacher*. First, telling a student he is a disgrace is never appropriate. His actions may be disgraceful, but he is not a disgrace. Second, use of profanity around or directed at a student is never acceptable. It is offensive and unprofessional.
Krizek v. *Cicero-Stickney Township High School* Illinois, 1989	Teacher was dismissed for showing an R-rated movie to her class. She apparently told her students they would be excused if their parents objected, but did not communicate directly with parents. The court upheld dismissal, saying the movie was a planned event, and not an inadvertent mistake, and that the teacher's methodology was problematic.	All schools require parental permission in writing for students to watch R-rated movies. This fact can't be ignored; doing so constitutes *neglect of duty*. If you ever have doubt about an activity, take that doubt as a sure sign that you should ask an administrator for advice.
Faulkner v. *New Bern-Craven County Board of Education* North Carolina, 1984	Teacher was found to habitually and excessively use alcohol. He even consumed some form of alcoholic beverages at school, or, at least, had the odor of alcohol on his breath at school during instructional hours after warnings against doing so.	Drinking alcohol is legal for adults, but doing so in excess in a community harms a teacher's reputation for using good judgment. Certainly consuming alcohol at school is absolutely wrong. This is a case of *conduct unbecoming a teacher*, with personal behavior affecting perception of professional competence.
School District No. 1 v. *Cornish* Colorado, 2002	Teacher refused to teach the approved math curriculum because she considered it inadequate to meet state standards. She also did not provide lesson plans per the principal's resulting directive.	Teachers are not in a position to dictate school curriculum. Refusal to teach the designated curriculum amounts to *insubordination*. If we think it's lacking, we can supplement as necessary, while making our opinions known to those in authority. There is a fine line between doing what we know is best for students and being insubordinate in the face of mandates.
Crosby v. *Holt* Tennessee, 2009	Teacher had an inappropriate relationship with a female student, sent inappropriate emails over the school's system to a married female teacher, and gave misleading information during investigation of the allegations.	This case has three elements, each of which alone would be grounds for dismissal. An inappropriate relationship with a female student constitutes an *illegal activity;* using the school's email system to send inappropriate emails to a married female teacher is *conduct unbecoming a teacher;* and giving misleading information is *insubordination*. Concerning the inappropriate relationship with a female student, sometimes all it takes is an accusation by a student who is, for some reason, unhappy with you to set legal wheels turning. Male teachers, in particular, must be very careful to never be alone with a student and should not make remarks that may be misconstrued as sexual harassment.

Based on: Schimmel, D., & Stellman, L., & Fischer, L. (2011). Teachers and the law (8th ed.). Upper Saddle River, NJ: Pearson. LaMorte, M. W. (2012). School law: Cases and concepts (10th ed.). Upper Saddle River, NJ: Pearson.

Table 10.3 Cases decided in favor of teachers retaining positions

Case	Explanation	Implications for Teachers
Pickering v. *Board of Education* Illinois, 1968	Teacher wrote a letter criticizing local school board actions. He was dismissed and the state supreme court upheld the decision. When Pickering took the case to the U.S. Supreme Court, the decision was overturned and he kept his job.	This is a good-news case! As teachers, we are entitled to our opinions, even when they are critical of our school. We may express opinions in the same ways as any other citizen and should do so. Everyone benefits when teachers are active citizens. However, keep in mind that for every action there is a reaction. When we have strong opinions, it's tempting to blurt them out, sometimes in unprofessional ways. Expect not-so-pleasant repercussions. There is a time and a place to express ourselves—and always professionally.
Lusk v. *Estes* Texas, 1973	Teacher testified in school board meeting that his principal and coworkers were mentally and sociologically unqualified to deal with modern, complex, multiracial student bodies. The teacher's opinion received widespread media coverage. The teacher was dismissed, but reinstated when the court said his opinions were relevant to the Dallas community.	Because of the *Pickering* ruling (above), this case was decided in favor of the teacher. Did he have evidence that his statements were founded in fact? Maybe, maybe not. But he had a right to make the statements because his view was relevant to the well-being of his community. As with the *Pickering* implications, we generally get more mileage from our efforts if we act with respect. The responsibilities of citizenship can be heavy.
Keefe v. *Geanakos* Massachusetts, 1969	Teacher assigned an article for his high school students to read and later discuss. The article contained some offensive language, some of which Keefe said out loud in class. He was dismissed, but a district court overturned the dismissal when it was discovered that the same language could be found in some school library books.	This case speaks to academic freedom. Yes, we may be free to speak offensive language in class if it is part of an academic lesson. The question is "Should we?" The courts defend such language if used in a literary sense or part of a current events discussion, but offensive language when discussing the Pythagorean theory is probably unnecessary. Always consider your community and your students.
Scruggs v. *Keen* Virginia, 1995	Teacher supervised study hall and was asked by two female students her opinion of interracial dating. After parental complaints about her negative statements, the teacher was dismissed because she was told her job was to teach math and her comments were potentially disruptive. A federal court ordered that she be reinstated because her job in study hall was to guide students as best she could and was not expected to stand mute when asked about an important social issue of the day.	Discussing topics considered controversial by some is best done with other adults. Perhaps a way around giving opinions you sense may not be aligned with the questioner is to turn the question around with "Well, what do you think?" We can act as sound boards for students without injecting our opinions. It's hard, but it gets easier with practice.

Teachers' Personal Lives

A teacher has a right to a personal life. However, the concept of teachers as role models entails more limits than people in other professions may experience. These limits have been upheld in the courts, with some limits more clearly defined than others. As late as the 1960s, teachers were quickly and without challenge fired for adultery, drunkenness, homosexual conduct, unmarried cohabitation with the opposite sex, or becoming pregnant while single.

PERSONAL CONDUCT AND JOB PERFORMANCE. The notion that teachers can be automatically fired for what is considered by the community as immoral behavior was rejected by the California Supreme Court in *Morrison* v. *State Board of Education,* 1969. The court found that grounds for dismissal must include evidence that the personal conduct of a teacher adversely affects job performance. The court also said it was dangerous to allow the terms *immoral* and *unprofessional* to be interpreted too broadly. It was established that immoral conduct means vastly different things to different people. For example, to some individuals, immoral behavior includes laziness, gluttony, selfishness, and cowardice, and unprofessional conduct for teachers may include signing controversial petitions, opposing majority opinions, and drinking alcoholic beverages. In *Morrison,* the court ruled that a teacher should not be fired because someone disapproves of the teacher's personal life unless it directly relates to his or her professional work, and that today's morals may well be considered absurd in the future. In recent decades, the courts have generally ruled that teachers have the right to privacy with regard to procreation, marriage, child rearing, and other activities in the home.

Since 1969, other cases have been brought to courts by teachers who felt they were wrongly dismissed. The courts continue to look for evidence that particular conduct adversely affects job performance. In *Eckmann* v. *Board of Education*, 1986, an Illinois teacher was fired when she became pregnant while unmarried and decided to raise the child as a single parent. The judge found in favor of the teacher and said that she had a due process right to conceive and raise her child, even out of wedlock, and without school board intrusion (Schimmel, Stellman, Conlon, and Fischer, 2011).

As with personal conduct, if a district wants to fire a teacher for health reasons (e.g., obesity, disabilities, or AIDS), it must show a direct link between the health problem and impaired classroom function.

There's so much to know about laws and their impact on our profession. A good way to immerse yourself in the cases and their implications is to create a wiki among your cohort of students interested in becoming teachers. A wiki allows you to build notes concerning the laws to further your understanding. This chapter's *SocialMEdia* feature is all about wikis for professional development, as well as how they can be used for teaching and learning in your classroom.

Social MEdia

The word *wiki* means "quick" or "fast" in the Hawaiian language. A wiki can bring people together quickly in a simple, easy-to-use format. In the world of social media, a wiki is a shared space for collaboration on the Internet. Wikis are easily editable, encouraging members of the wiki group to comment on what others ask and write. Wiki tools are similar to regular word-processing tools. Users can upload documents, create links to other sites, and embed video. This technology's interactive nature makes wikis ideal for both teacher professional development and for classroom teaching and learning.

A community of teacher-learners can share questions, experiences, and practices through a wiki. Through wikis, teachers may

- Plan units of study together.
- Share what works in the classroom.
- Discuss problems with students; give and receive advice.
- Learn new practices and discuss their value.
- Share logistical information, such as field trip requirements and trip planning progress.
- Compose reports or letters to send to parents.
- Create a storage place for ideas and instructional materials and strategies.

Wikis can also be valuable tools for teaching and learning. Through wikis, students may

- Access class information posted by the teacher.
- Organize projects with shared responsibility anytime and anywhere they have Internet access.
- Create study guides using each other's knowledge.
- Write a group report.
- Share editing responsibilities for either group assignments or individual writing.
- Keep an ongoing list of vocabulary words, along with real-world word usage and ways of remembering definitions.
- Share what occurred in class with absent students.
- Ask questions about something that's being studied and receive answers written by students, for students.

Wikis may be developed for free by going through services such as **TeachersFirst**, a Wikispaces site dedicated to teachers and students. In fact, wouldn't it be a good idea for you and your cohort of future teachers to create a wiki dedicated to sharing your experiences in teacher education?

MISCONDUCT WITH STUDENTS. The most clear-cut decisions involving the firing of teachers on moral grounds involve misconduct with students. When a teacher's personal life or habits intersect those of a student in illegal or morally questionable ways, it is relatively easy for a school district to dismiss a teacher for:

- Sexual relations with students
- Profane, abusive language directed at students
- Allowing students to drink alcohol
- Encouraging students to be dishonest

Table 10.4 consists of cases involving teachers' personal lives, with their positions in jeopardy. In each case, the teacher was terminated.

There are many court rulings that do not result in the threat of dismissal or any sort of action against the teacher. These cases decide certain issues and teachers continue to teach, abiding by the decisions. Table 10.5 includes cases in which teachers keep their positions.

Table 10.4 Teachers' personal lives dismissal cases and implications

Case	Explanation	Implications for Teachers
Cooper v. *Eugene School District* Oregon, 1986	Teacher converted to the Sikh religion and explained to her students that she would now wear a white turban and, occasionally, all white clothing. Her administrator said she violated both state and district policy against teachers being demonstrative of a particular religion and dismissed the teacher. The court upheld the school's decision.	Public schools must, by law, remain religiously neutral. Teachers need to understand that although we are free to have different beliefs, we still represent the school system. We can practice whatever faith we wish, or none at all, but we can't appear to promote any particular belief system. This is difficult when we have strongly held beliefs, but it is part of separation of church and state that helps keep all of us free to worship, or not, as we desire.
Spanierman v. *Hughes* Connecticut, 2008	Teacher established a MySpace page, originally in an attempt to communicate with students about homework and other school issues. However, over time the page also contained objectionable material as the communications took on more of a social rather than academic nature. Following complaints from teachers who accessed the site, the teacher was dismissed. A U.S. District Court upheld the dismissal.	There have been very few cases so far involving teachers and social media, but more are sure to come. In this one, the teacher's initial intentions appear to be legitimate. We must remember that what we do online is not private. There is danger in electronic communication; use it wisely. This means being careful with student and parent communication, as well as what you post on Facebook and other personal-oriented sites. Never post anything you wouldn't want your principal, parents, or students to see. They might!
Oleske v. *City School District Board of Education* Ohio, 2001	Teacher was dismissed for telling sexually oriented jokes to eighth-grade students. A state court upheld the dismissal, saying that teachers should recognize that this behavior detracts from their role model status.	Some new teachers have a tendency to want to be "friends" with students in ways that make them popular. This is very understandable, but it can lead to unacceptable behavior.
Flaskamp v. *Dearborn Public Schools* Michigan, 2004	Teacher began a romantic and sexual relationship with a former student that was discovered about a year after graduation. She was dismissed. The court upheld her dismissal and stated that there must be at least two years between graduation and the beginning of a personal relationship between teacher and former students.	If you are 21 when you begin teaching, your students may be 17 or 18, creating a relatively small age difference. This court ruling is an important one to understand. At this point in your life, the chronological age may be close, but you will be a college graduate with a career and adult responsibilities.
Katz v. *Ambach* New York, 1984	Teacher was dismissed after it was proven that he kissed sixth-grade girls, patted them on the behind, and permitted obscene jokes and profanity in the classroom. The court upheld the dismissal.	Male middle and high school teachers must be especially careful not to create any appearance of inappropriateness. The teacher in this case went well beyond the "appearance."
Board of Education v. *Wood* Kentucky, 1986	Teachers were fired for having a summer party with two 15-year-old students present. At the party the teenagers smoked marijuana. The two teachers were fired after arguing that school was not in session and their rights to privacy were breached. The court determined that smoking marijuana with students is immoral and criminal behavior and upheld the dismissal.	You are a teacher during the school year *and* in summer, or whenever school is not in session. If you go to the same pool or participate in the same activities as students during holidays, you don't shed your responsibility to be an adult role model.
Jefferson Union High School District v. *Jones* California, 1972	Teacher was fined for possession of marijuana while on vacation. The arrest and fine appeared in a Honolulu newspaper and someone in the teacher's hometown saw it. He was dismissed when it was discovered and the court upheld his firing.	Even on vacation we are subject to tougher standards than many of our peers. This reality is part of teaching. Be mindful that our behavior follows us, even when it may seem unlikely.

Table 10.5 Cases involving personal lives decided in favor of teachers

Case	Explanation	Implications for Teachers
Morrison v. *State Board of Education* California, 1969	Teacher participated in a brief homosexual relationship with another teacher. He was dismissed but reinstated due to a court decision in his favor citing that the behavior does not directly affect job performance.	Remember that this case was relatively shocking in 1969. Today, we assume personal rights when it comes to sexuality. Because we are role models, using discretion in our demonstration of romantic involvement, whether heterosexual or homosexual, is best for our communities.
Thompson v. *Southwest District* Missouri, 1980	Teacher dismissed because she lived with her boyfriend, not publicizing it, but also not making it a secret. When the school board dismissed her for immorality, they made a public display of it. The court found that living with her boyfriend did not diminish the teacher's classroom effectiveness and ordered her reinstated.	As with *Morrison*, this seems a bit frivolous now as most of us would not question a teacher's right to live with whomever he or she pleases. The court not only ruled in favor of the teacher but also chastised the school district for making the teacher's personal choices public knowledge.
Eckmann v. *Board of Education* Illinois, 1986	Teacher was fired when she became pregnant while unmarried. The court ruled that she had a right both to raise her child and keep her teaching position.	There was a time not so long ago when even married women were asked to stop teaching when their condition became evident. Now schools more closely mirror the world outside the schoolhouse door.

Table 10.5 *(continued)*

Case	Explanation	Implications for Teachers
Nichol v. *ARIN Intermediate Unit* Pennsylvania, 2003	Teacher wore a small cross to her elementary school and was dismissed based on a district/state policy. The policy prohibited school employees from wearing religious dress, emblems, or insignia (specifically crosses and Stars of David) while performing their duties in public schools. A federal court found the policy unconstitutional and the teacher was reinstated.	Given that teachers are not allowed to wear in-your-face symbols of their faith, small pieces of jewelry are exempt. States and districts cannot make policies that are unreasonably restrictive.
Randle v. *Indianola Municipal Separate School District* Mississippi, 1975	Teacher married a controversial civil rights advocate and was not rehired. A federal court of appeals declared that a school district cannot refuse to hire or rehire based on with whom a teacher decides to affiliate.	As with *Keyishian*, the court declared that teachers may marry or affiliate with anyone they wish. The limitation is whether the affiliation interferes with the person's function as a teacher.
Weaver v. *Nebo School District*, Utah, 1998	Teacher and volleyball coach was dismissed because of negative reaction to her sexual orientation. She had received letters from the school district instructing her to not make any comments to students, staff members, or parents about her homosexuality. The court ruled there was no job-related basis for the dismissal and ordered that she be reinstated.	Think about how our freedoms have increased in fewer than two decades. We don't have to hide our affiliations, opinions on societal issues, or political beliefs. As representatives of schools, however, our first consideration should be our students and the messages we send them, both consciously and unconsciously. Always be mindful that how you demonstrate your personal choices will impact impressionable and developing students.

Point of Reflection 10.2

Do you think the role of teacher carries with it personal restraints? Would you be willing to alter your lifestyle somewhat to conform with what a particular community considers moral and professional behavior?

Check Your Understanding 10.3

10.4 What Are the Legal Responsibilities of Teachers?

10.4 Articulate the legal responsibilities of teachers.

Teachers have many responsibilities, some dictated by laws and others by state, district, or school policies. Some responsibilities are governed by ethical and professional guidelines.

Liability

To be **liable** means to be responsible for. We generally hear the term in a negative sense, such as "He was found liable for the accident" or "That will raise my liability insurance premium." In a positive sense, though, liability is what teaching is all about—accepting responsibility for students while they are under our supervision. This is why we study aspects such as child development, subject matter, instructional and assessment strategies, guidelines for health and safety, and school law. However, being held liable when something goes wrong is far from positive. Depending on the severity of the issue, liability for a situation can end a career.

Teachers serve ***in loco parentis***, meaning "in place of parents." They are bound by law to care for and protect children in the school setting as a parent would and are held to a standard of reasonableness. Teachers, schools, and districts are sometimes sued over issues related to liability. For a school employee to be considered liable for something, the following four components must be proven to be present:

1. The person has a legal duty to protect students.
2. The person fails to act within reason and provide the appropriate standard of care.
3. There is a causal connection between the person's conduct and the result of the injury.
4. Actual damage occurs to the injured person. (LaMorte, 2012)

In the case of *Mancha* v. *Field Museum of Natural History*, 1971, students ages 12 to 15 went on a field trip with teachers to the Chicago Natural History Museum. The students were allowed to view the exhibits on their own. One student was beaten up by teenagers from another school. In this case, the teachers had a legal duty to protect students (1), and there was actual damage (4). The court had to decide if the teachers failed to act within reason and provide an appropriate standard of care (2) and if there was a causal connection between the teachers' conduct and the injury (3). The teachers were not held liable for the student's injuries because the court determined there was minimal risk at the museum, and the teachers could not reasonably have been expected to directly supervise them.

In a similar case the same year, an eighth-grader sustained a severe eye injury when a student threw rocks during a baseball game. The teacher involved in *Sheehan* v. *St. Peter's Catholic School*, 1971, had accompanied the students outside but then returned to the building. The courts determined that the teacher left the area and therefore was not properly supervising the students. She was found liable for leaving students alone in a potentially dangerous setting.

Teachers can take some precautions that will lessen the causal connection between their actions and any harm that may come to students. Here are a few to consider:

- Be 100% present when with students. Limit personal distractions and remain focused.
- Think through situations and, if possible, avoid those that have unusual potential for danger.
- Establish routines and rules that make safety a habit among students.
- Remind students of appropriate behavior to help them remain safe.

Accidents happen—in the classroom, the hallway, the cafeteria, the science lab, the gym, on school grounds, and on field trips. Using good judgment in the *in loco parentis* role will be enough for most teachers. But occasionally students are injured and teacher liability may be questioned. Liability insurance is a good idea. Teacher organizations offer reasonably priced policies that are recommended even for student teachers. These organizations often also provide legal assistance to members who find themselves involved in a school-related lawsuit.

In Table 10.6 we read about cases brought against teachers involving teacher liability. As with the other tables, take time to consider the implications after reading the brief facts of each case.

Copyright Laws

Copyright laws provide guidelines for authorized use of someone else's intellectual property and are intended to protect the rights of creators of intellectual property by preventing others from copying or distributing it without permission. Intellectual property includes written material, original audio and visual work, and computer programs.

Copyrighted materials may be used under three conditions: the user has permission from the copyright owner, the work is in the public domain, or the use is considered

Table 10.6 Teacher liability cases and implications

Case	Explanation	Implications for Teachers
Kaufman v. *City of New York* New York, 1961	Teacher was supervising in the gym when two boys knocked heads while playing basketball and one was seriously injured. The court ruled that any amount of supervision could not have prevented the accident and that the school and teacher were not liable.	This teacher was where he was supposed to be when the accident occurred, which released him from liability for the injury. Never do anything less than be where you are supposed to be at all times. Ducking around the corner to make a phone call or answer a text when you are supposed to be paying attention to students in your care, is never wise.
Morris v. *Douglas County School District* California, 1965	Teacher took a class of first-graders to the beach for an outing. The children were walking on the edge of the water when a large log rolled up with a wave and seriously injured a child. The court found that the teacher was liable because this kind of injury was not uncommon and the teacher was responsible for the safety of the young children in her care.	Use good judgment! Of course first-graders will want to be as close as possible to the water, if not in it. Apparently large logs forcefully coming to shore on this particular coastline are a frequent occurrence. Do your research and anticipate dangers to help avoid student injury, a suit against you, and, if not a suit, the sense of guilt that accompanies a child being injured.
Mancha v. *Field Museum of Natural History* Illinois, 1971	Teachers allowed 12- to 15-year-old students to "self-guide" during a field trip to a museum. When not in their sight, a boy was beaten by other boys not part of the field trip. The parents sued, but the court determined that it was very unlikely that this sort of incident would happen, making it unforeseeable. The teacher was not held liable for the student's injuries.	The students are old enough to self-direct on this common type of field trip. The key here is that the teachers did not take unreasonable risks in the museum and they were present. Always think through what you are planning to make sure you are showing good judgment.
Sheehan v. *St. Peter's Catholic School* Minnesota, 1991	Teacher accompanied 20 girls outside for recess, sitting them on benches on the third base line while eighth-grade boys played baseball. She then returned to the building. In her absence, some boys started throwing pebbles at the girls and one girl was hit in the eye and seriously injured. The court determined this sort of behavior could be foreseen and found the teacher liable for not properly supervising the students.	The only reason to leave children placed in your care is to go for help if an emergency occurs. Otherwise, no matter how important a call may be or the need to retrieve something you forgot or your need to run in for "just a minute" for any reason, don't do it.
Eisel v. *Board of Education of Montgomery County* Maryland, 1991	Two guidance counselors were informed by high school students that one girl had made a suicide pact with another. The counselors met with the girl, who denied any plan to commit suicide. She subsequently did kill herself and the parents sued the counselors. The court agreed that, in matters potentially dealing with life and death, the counselors were obligated to contact the parents. The counselors were held liable.	Unfortunately, it is relatively common to hear talk of suicide, especially among girls. Although teachers are not charged with being guidance counselors, we are, however, responsible for student well-being. The verdict in this case is not common, but the court decided that the counselors knew that the threat was more than a rumor and had the obligation to call the parents. As a teacher, remember that this kind of parental contact should be handled by counselors and administrators.
Santiago v. *Cooper* Tennessee, 2006	Teacher conducted kindergarten recess indoors because of inclement weather. The students played with age-appropriate toys, with one boy hitting another in the eye with a plastic hammer. The child lost vision in the eye that was hit. After mounting medical bills, the teacher was sued. The court did not rule in favor of the family because the teacher was present and supervising.	The teacher felt very bad about what happened, but because she was there and the toys were plastic, she was not found to be liable. Had she gone to the restroom or to get a cup of coffee and left the children, she would have likely been held liable. Never leave students alone while you are in charge of them.
Davis v. *Monroe County Board of Education* Georgia, 1999	Teachers were aware that a fifth-grade girl was being physically and verbally harassed by a classmate, according to the court ruling. She and her parents repeatedly reported it to the school, but it continued. The family filed a lawsuit, and 6 years later the U.S. Supreme Court ruled the school failed to act appropriately to protect the girl.	This ruling determined that educators can be held liable if they do not respond to complaints of physical and verbal harassment. Teachers often concentrate on lessons and forget to use their peripheral vision to monitor student relations.

"fair use." A work is in the **public domain** if it is more than 75 years old or is published by a government agency. **Fair use** allows the nonprofit reproduction of certain materials in the classroom without permission of the copyright owner (Schimmel et al., 2015). Generally, fair use stipulates that the material copied must be for educational purposes and that the amount copied must fall within certain guidelines, some of which are listed in Figure 10.3. Teachers may not, however, make copies of consumable products such as textbooks, workbooks, and standardized test materials. If copies could be freely made of these kinds of materials, then their creators and publishers would lose money because the need for them would diminish.

Because teachers often want students to create work using certain computer software, it is important to know that computer software is copyrighted and that fair use

Figure 10.3 Guidelines for classroom copying

1. A single copy may be made of any of the following for your own scholarly research or use in teaching:
   - a chapter from a book
   - an article from a periodical or newspaper
   - a short story, short essay, or short poem
   - a chart, graph, diagram, drawing, cartoon or picture from a book, periodical, or newspaper.
2. Multiple copies (no more than one per student) may be made for classroom use if each copy gives credit to the copyright holder and passes three tests.
   - The brevity test includes guidelines such as poems of fewer than 200 words and prose of fewer than 2,500 words.
   - The spontaneity test generally says that you are inspired to copy and use material for the sake of teaching effectiveness and there was not time to ask and receive permission.
   - The cumulative effect test generally restricts the length of time copied material is used and how many instances of copying take place in a period of time.
3. Teachers cannot copy individual works and put them together to serve as an anthology.
4. Students cannot be charged for the photocopying of copyrighted works.

Based on: Underwood, J., & Webb, L. D. (2006). *School law for teachers: Concepts and applications*. Upper Saddle River, NJ: Merrill/Prentice Hall.

guidelines do not apply. Some software publishers allow one backup copy to be made, but more than this is illegal. Additionally, commercially produced videos may not be copied. Copies made of television programs can be kept for 45 days and then must be erased or destroyed.

With the Internet serving as a major research tool in classrooms today, teachers must be aware that what is on the Internet is not in the public domain. Because the Internet is international, laws governing its use are somewhat unclear. Following fair use guidelines is a safe way to use Web resources.

Whether using written works, audiovisual materials, computer software, or information from the Internet, teachers must take copyright laws seriously. School districts have policies based on fair use guidelines. A school's media specialist is often a helpful, knowledgeable source of information about what is lawful and what is not. Teachers should ask for advice if there is any question about how they plan to use any form of intellectual property.

Reporting Suspected Child Abuse

A teacher who has a reasonable suspicion of child abuse or neglect has a legal obligation to report it to a school counselor or administrator, who in turn will report it to a social services agency or the police. Teachers don't have to be certain that they are correct. They are granted immunity and may not be sued for reporting their suspicions (Schimmel et al., 2015).

It is a good idea for teachers to keep lists of signs of abuse and neglect handy for easy reference. Teachers should never become too busy to be observant. Physical abuse may be visually evident and difficult to miss. However, sexual abuse may be subtle in terms of symptoms, and emotional or mental abuse may be even more difficult to detect. Reviewing the signs periodically, watching for behavioral or emotional changes, and reporting suspicions of abuse or neglect to administrators or school counselors will help protect students. This is a teacher's legal and ethical responsibility—and simply the right thing to do.

Teacher responsibilities obviously include protecting their students however and whenever they can. Teacher responsibilities also include safeguarding students' rights.

Check Your Understanding 10.4

10.5 How Does the Law Impact the Relationship between School and Religion?

10.5 Interpret how the law impacts the relationship between school and religion.

The First Amendment makes it clear that the founders of the United States did not want government to have any say in how or whether citizens worship. Because public schools are government entities, they may neither establish religion nor interfere with the free exercise of it. As clearly stated as it is in the U.S. Constitution, the issue is anything but clear cut in practice. Few topics are as charged with emotion and passion, and hence with such potential to polarize people, as religion.

Let's establish some basic "dos and don'ts" for teachers and students with regard to religion and education. In 1998, President Clinton asked then Secretary of Education Richard Riley to prepare guidelines based on law and court decisions to help educators determine the rights of students and staff regarding religion and public schools. Twenty years later these guidelines have not changed. For easy reference, these guidelines are adapted into a question and answer format in Figure 10.4.

Religion and Compulsory Education

Compulsory education laws require students to attend school through a certain age. *Pierce* v. *Society of Sisters*, 1925, established that compulsory education laws could be met through attendance at private or parochial schools. In the 1970s, Amish families asked to be exempt from compulsory education beyond eighth grade on the grounds that attendance in upper grades would have a negative effect on their traditions and way of life. The Supreme Court ruled in their favor in *Wisconsin* v. *Yoder*, 1972. This ruling is known as the "Amish exception." If non-Amish parents wish to isolate their children from public or private school (under age 16), they must show that school will somehow destroy their religion. Homeschooling is a legal option with very few requirements or constraints. Because families aren't required to supply a reason for homeschooling, it is unknown how many families use their right to homeschool their children as a way to avoid compulsory education laws.

Prayer In School

Students may pray silently or quietly in small groups in school—but that's it. Legally, there can be no school-sponsored public prayer, not even nondenominational prayer (Schimmel et al., 2015). This prohibition includes prayer at gatherings such as graduation ceremonies, football games, and assemblies. In *Santa Fe Independent School District* v. *Doe*, 2000, a Texas school district allowed students to vote on whether to have prayer and who would deliver it before football games. Groups of Mormon and Catholic students, alumni, and parents filed a suit claiming the district was violating the First Amendment. The U.S. Supreme Court ruled against the district, contending that the school would be endorsing a specific religion depending on who delivered the prayer.

Some communities choose to violate the First Amendment principle of separation of church and state by endorsing prayer in school-related settings. If challenged, they would likely lose in court. Some school boards even begin their meetings with prayer, often careful not to use language that would offend Christians or Jews. However, these prayers may offend Muslims, Buddhists, and other religious groups, as well as atheists. Regardless of who is present, organized verbal prayer is not legal in public education meetings.

Figure 10.4 Guidelines for religious expression in public schools from the U.S. Department of Education

Can students pray in school?
Yes. Students may pray individually or in a group as long as they are nondisruptive. For instance, students may pray before meals or tests to the same extent they may engage in comparable nondisruptive activities.

Can students read religious materials and discuss religion among themselves?
Yes. Students may read and talk about religion to the same extent as they may read and talk about anything else in school.

Can students meet to express their religious beliefs during the school day and on school grounds?
Yes. Students may meet for nondisruptive purposes during their lunch periods or other noninstructional time during the school day, as well as before and after the school day. This includes religion-related meetings.

Is it legal to have organized prayer at sporting events or other school functions?
No. Under current Supreme Court decisions, school officials may not mandate or organize prayer at any school-sponsored event or graduation.

Can teachers participate in religious meetings while at school?
No. Teachers and school administrators, when acting in those capacities, are representatives of the state and are prohibited from soliciting or encouraging religious activity, and from participating in such activity with students.

Can teachers teach about religion in schools?
Yes. Teachers may teach *about* religion, including the history of religion; comparative religion; the Bible (or other scripture) as literature; and the role of religion in the history of the United States and other countries. Teachers may also prompt students to consider religious influences on art, music, literature, and social studies.

Can teachers display religious-related holiday items or encourage the celebration of religious holidays in school?
No. Although public schools may teach *about* religious holidays, including their religious aspects, and may celebrate the secular aspects of holidays, schools may not observe holidays as religious events or encourage students to do so.

Is it acceptable for students to express religious beliefs in school assignments?
Yes. Students may express their beliefs about religion in the form of homework, artwork, and other written and oral assignments free of discrimination based on the religious content of their work. The assignments should be graded according to the standards the lesson is intended to address.

If a lesson may be considered offensive by a student and/or the student's family, can the student opt not to participate?
Yes. Schools can excuse individual students from lessons that are objectionable to the student or the students' parents on religious or other conscientious grounds.

Can students opt out of a particular dress code or uniform for religious reasons?
Legally, the answer is no. However, schools have discretion to interpret this in ways that make sense in their communities.

Can students wear religious messages or symbols on their clothes?
Yes. The restrictions are the same as for any other comparable messages. Schools cannot single out religion-related messages and symbols to prohibit.

Based on: Riley, R. W. (1998). *Secretary's statement on religious expression*. Retrieved May 5, 2017, from http://christiananswers.net/q-eden/religiousexpression.html

Religious Organizations Meeting on School Grounds

If a school building is used before or after hours for organizations of any kind, it may also be used for organizations that are religious in nature. In *Good News Club* v. *Milford Central School*, 2001, the Supreme Court ruled that a private Christian organization for children ages 6 to 12 in New York could use a public school for weekly after-school meetings. Although some lower courts have ruled that teachers may be involved in student religious organizations on their own time, generally school employees may not sponsor the groups (Schimmel et al., 2015).

RELIGIOUS HOLIDAYS. Observing specific religious holidays in class is not allowed. This is a visible and controversial aspect of mixing school and religion. The longest traditional school breaks or vacations (other than summer) occur during Christian celebrations—December break at Christmas and spring break at Easter. What was once called "Christmas Break" is now generally referred to as the "Winter Holiday." The traditional holiday student presentation once called the "Christmas Program" is now the choral/band event that may be referred to as the "Holiday" or "Winter Program." Students may sing Christmas songs with religious messages, such as "Silent Night," but these songs may not dominate the program.

Holiday displays that depict Christian or Christmas symbols may be used if they are balanced with other cultural symbols such as a Jewish menorah. The displays must be temporary and help show diversity. Parents and students may request to be exempt from activities focused on holidays.

RELIGION AND CURRICULUM. Must schools do away with all reference to religion to separate church and state? The answer is no. It is permissible to teach about religion but not with the purpose of convincing students that a particular belief should be followed. Use of the Bible, Talmud, Koran, and other religious books for teaching literature and history is permissible so long as one is not endorsed over another.

Perhaps the greatest point of tension concerning religion and curriculum is the theory of evolution. In the so-called "Scopes Monkey Trial" in 1925, a high school teacher was convicted of violating a Tennessee regulation against teaching anything that contradicted the biblical Genesis account of the creation of humans. Although the conviction was overturned on a technicality, controversy over the teaching of evolution in schools has continued. In 1982, Louisiana passed the Balanced Treatment Act, which required the teaching of both creationism and evolution. The U.S. Supreme Court ruled the act illegal because it endorsed creationism, a Christian view, to the exclusion of other views. Some school districts, and even whole states, have attempted to give equal time both to what some Christians believe about creation as embodied in the literal translation of the Bible and to evolution. Some districts have attempted to outlaw the teaching of evolution or to require a disclaimer stating that it is only a theory, one of many that try to explain the origin of humans.

Point of Reflection 10.3

Did you or your family ever have religion-based views that conflicted with events at your school? Were your views conservative (i.e., opposition to dancing, nonacceptance of evolution, nonparticipation when certain movies were shown, etc.)? If these questions don't apply to you, describe someone you've known whose religion-based views may have conflicted with school or school policy.

Check Your Understanding 10.5

10.6 What Are the Legal Rights of Students?

10.6 Describe the legal rights of students.

Students do not leave their constitutional rights at the schoolhouse door. You may notice that there isn't a section of this chapter devoted to students' legal responsibilities. If there were, the section would be brief. Students have the responsibility to go to school as long as it is compulsory (usually to age 16, but to age 18 in some locations). That's about it in terms of legal responsibilities. Although we hope students take responsibility for their learning and behavior, unless their behavior is deemed illegal or extremely disruptive, there are no other laws binding them.

Freedom of Expression

Before 1969, students were not recognized as having First Amendment rights to freedom of expression. The U.S. Supreme Court's decision in *Tinker* v. *Des Moines Independent Community School District*, 1969, provided a clear message that a student is entitled to freedom of expression. In this case, three students wore armbands to school to protest the war in Vietnam and were punished for doing so. The *Tinker* case reversed the school's stance and has been cited repeatedly since 1969. However, court challenges since *Tinker* have served to balance the rights of students to express themselves and the necessity of limiting personal freedom to ensure the safety and well-being of others. For students, understanding the need for this balance is a lesson in the principles of democracy.

FREEDOM OF SYMBOLIC EXPRESSION. The *Tinker* decision so influenced how students are viewed in relation to freedom of expression that it is known as the *Tinker doctrine*. This doctrine extends to symbolic freedom. Students are allowed to express their views symbolically through what they wear as long as it doesn't disrupt the educational process.

Dress Codes. Since the 1960s, numerous lawsuits have been initiated over the restrictions imposed by dress codes, but the U.S. Supreme Court has not ruled on the issue. In 1972, Justice Black wrote that the U.S. Constitution doesn't require the courts to bear the burden of supervising clothing or hairstyles.

However, schools are concerned about immodest dress and unusual hairstyles because they could disrupt the educational atmosphere of the classroom as well as lead to more serious issues. For instance, violence generated by gangs and groups such as the "trench coat mafia" (the students associated with the 1999 Columbine school shootings) has prompted educators to identify and attempt to ban insignia clothing and hats associated with specific groups. Some of the expressions of style that cause concern in schools include:

- T-shirts depicting violence, drugs, sexual messages, etc.
- Sagging pants or jeans
- Colored bandanas
- Words shaved into scalps
- Brightly colored hair
- Exposed underwear
- Tattoos and piercings

These forms of symbolic expression are not protected by the First Amendment because they may contribute to school unrest; most dress codes outlaw some or all of them. However, because some of the items are associated with particular cultures, it is difficult for schools to designate them without appearing to be biased. Rules designating skirt length, requiring belts, and prohibiting exposed midriffs are more generic but still hard to enforce. Students often enjoy expressing personal taste in their choices of clothing and shoes.

Uniforms. Dress codes are often ambiguous, leaving much room for interpretation. They can infringe on learning time if teachers are expected to watch for and report violations. Thus, some schools and entire districts choose to impose a uniform policy, giving students several modest, relatively plain choices of clothing. Currently, more than half the states have schools with uniform policies. Some large cities, such as Long Beach, Chicago, and San Antonio, require at least elementary students to wear uniforms. In 2002, Memphis, Tennessee, became the nation's first large public school district to adopt a uniform policy in all 175 schools.

Public schools that impose uniform policies must provide an opt-out clause for parents who don't want their children to participate. For instance, some parents may not want their children to wear a uniform because it conflicts with the clothing traditions of their religion. Other parents may request to be exempt simply because their children don't want to wear the uniform and are persistently making that clear. Private schools do not receive government support and, unlike public schools, may impose a uniform policy on all students without allowing them to opt out.

FREEDOM OF SPEECH. The freedom of speech implied in *Tinker* was challenged in 1986 when a student made a speech containing sexual innuendo in a high school assembly. He was reprimanded and subsequently sued the school, claiming that his freedom of speech was denied. The case, *Bethel School District No. 403* v. *Fraser,* 1986, went to the U.S. Supreme Court, where the adolescent lost. The court ruled that a school does not have to accept indecent or offensive speech.

Although students enjoy free speech, it does have limits. An individual student's freedom of speech, as well as freedom of the press, must be balanced against the school's ability to maintain a safe and civil atmosphere, where all students and teachers are shown respect.

FREEDOM OF THE PRESS. School publications have long been fertile ground for disputes about students' rights to express themselves. In attempts to make school newspapers relevant and truly student owned, students tend to write about what's on the minds of classmates, no matter how controversial. However, it is clear from court decisions such as *Hazelwood School District* v. *Kuhlmeier,* 1988, that teachers and administrators may exercise editorial control over school publications. The court upheld an educator's right to delete certain student writing from school-sponsored publications.

For all three forms of expression—symbolic, speech, and written—students' rights must be balanced with what is in the best interest of the school population. The adults in charge—school board members, district personnel, administrators, and teachers—must be vigilant and protect student rights while also protecting those who may be adversely affected by the exercise of those rights.

The Right to be Protected

Freedom of expression refers to what students may do. The right to be protected is freedom from actions that may be imposed on students.

SEARCH AND SEIZURE. The Fourth Amendment provides for citizens to be secure from unreasonable search and seizure. This right applies to students in schools—to a point. The courts have attempted to balance a student's right to privacy and the school's need to know. The key term is *reasonableness*. In *New Jersey* v. *T.L.O.,* 1985, two high school girls were accused of smoking in the bathroom. After finding drug paraphernalia in her purse, T.L.O. was turned over to juvenile court. Her family sued for invasion of privacy. The U.S. Supreme Court ruled against her and maintained that the search and seizure were reasonable.

In most cases, the courts have ruled against schools that arbitrarily and routinely search lockers, use drug-sniffing dogs, and search through students' clothes. Privacy is upheld as a right unless a search is deemed reasonable. But school lockers are part of school property. If there are reasonable suspicions of contraband in lockers, they may be searched.

Drug testing as a form of search of students remains controversial among the general public. However, since about 2000 most court decisions have ruled that drug testing is permissible for all students who participate in extracurricular activities, making no distinction, for example, between basketball and debate teams.

If there is reasonable suspicion for a search, the search itself must be reasonably conducted. Age and gender need to be considered. Walking through a metal detector or putting a book bag through a detector is noninvasive and considered reasonable if there have been problems with weapons at the school. Searching lockers, either by hand or using dogs, is more invasive but reasonable if there is suspicion. Asking students to empty their pockets and take off coats may be called for and is reasonable. However, strip searches are very invasive and should only be done if there is probable cause (more stringent than reasonable suspicion) and by proper authorities, not by teachers. The courts have been split on the legality of strip searches. In elementary school, strip searches are typically supported by the courts, whereas in middle and high school, they are sometimes not supported by court decisions. This kind of intrusive search should not be done by teachers alone under any circumstances.

SEXUAL HARASSMENT. According to the American Association of University Women (AAUW) (2005), **sexual harassment** is behavior with sexual implications that is neither wanted nor welcome. It interferes with a person's life. Sexual harassment may include obvious looks with lewd intent, taunts with sexual innuendo, touching, kissing, groping, and any actions or behaviors that have sexual connotations. The AAUW conducted a survey of eighth- and eleventh-grade students in 1993, and again in 2001, to gauge the extent of sexual harassment in schools. The survey revealed that 80% of students in both grade levels experienced sexual harassment. The results served as a wake-up call for schools as sexual harassment came into the public eye. However, a positive change is that in 2001, 69% of respondents, as opposed to only a small percentage in 1993 reported knowing about school policies against sexual harassment and the consequences for harassing. Awareness has increased, but the problem persists.

When students report incidents that appear to be sexual harassment, teachers must take their complaints seriously. The ruling in *Davis* v. *Monroe County Board of Education*, 1999, determined that educators can be held liable if they do not respond to complaints of sexual harassment. A fifth-grade girl in Georgia was groped and verbally harassed by a classmate. She and her parents repeatedly reported it to the school, but it continued. The family filed a lawsuit, and 6 years later the U.S. Supreme Court ruled in a 5-to-4 decision that the school failed to act appropriately to protect the girl.

Teachers must also be conscious of their own behavior with students to prevent it from being misconstrued as harassment. In the 2001 AAUW survey, 7% of the respondents said that teachers sexually harassed them. Teachers must be constantly aware of how students may perceive their actions.

When sexual harassment is detected, the school is likely to take disciplinary action. The range of possibilities, governed by both common sense and lawful procedures, is broad.

DISCIPLINARY ACTION. The U.S. court system has been clear that schools have the right to administer a variety of punishments based on policy. Relatively minor rule infractions call for relatively minor consequences or punishment that may be administered at the classroom or school level. Rule infractions that are more serious require more serious consequences.

CORPORAL PUNISHMENT. Fewer than half the states allow corporal punishment. Individual districts may choose not to allow corporal punishment even if allowed by the state. People who are in favor of corporal punishment say it's necessary and educationally sound, while those who oppose it call it archaic, cruel, inhumane, and unjustifiable (LaMorte, 2012).

In *Ingraham* v. *Wright*, 1977, the Supreme Court found that corporal punishment does not violate the tenets of the Constitution and is legal in states that have not banned the practice. The most common restrictions in states that permit corporal punishment are that only an administrator can spank or paddle a student, and there must be an adult witness. Teachers can lose their jobs if they violate state laws or local policies related to corporal punishment (Schimmel et al., 2015).

EXCLUSIONARY DISCIPLINE. Exclusionary discipline, or discipline that takes students out of school, such as suspension and expulsion, carries with it the need for student due process, or steps that protect student rights (Pauken, 2006). Excluding students from school through suspension or expulsion has been ruled a denial of property rights to an education. *Suspension* is time out of school that may range from 1 day to less than a semester but is usually 10 or fewer days. *Expulsion* is more permanent and is generally for a semester or for an indefinite period.

Exclusionary punishment carries possible long-term consequences that may exceed the seriousness of the original offense. Any time away from school can be harmful to students in many ways. For instance, if a brief suspension causes a student to miss an exam, grades will suffer. Being out of school more than 10 days makes it almost impossible for a student to catch up. An expulsion almost always means a grade must be repeated. For some students, a lengthy suspension or expulsion may make admission to certain colleges difficult or impossible.

Students are entitled to due process when exclusionary punishment is imposed or when the rule infraction and resulting punishment will become part of a student's permanent record. In the case of *Goss* v. *Lopez*, 1975, several Ohio high school students were suspended for up to 10 days without receiving a hearing. The students maintained complete innocence and were never informed of what they were accused of doing. When a federal district court agreed with the boys in their suit against the school, administrators appealed to the U.S. Supreme Court, where the decision went in favor of the students again. The justices wrote that students have a property right in school and that they may not be withdrawn without due process that includes

- Written notification of time and place of hearing, along with a description of the procedures to be followed
- List of evidence to be presented and names of witnesses
- Description of the substance of witnesses' testimonies
- Taped or written record of the proceedings and findings
- Notification of the right to appeal (Schimmel et al., 2015)

STUDENT RIGHT OF NONPARTICIPATION. Students have a right to refuse to participate in some activities. The following rights have been upheld in the courts:

- Students may refuse to recite the Pledge of Allegiance.
- Students may refuse to dance, even when it is part of the physical education curriculum.
- Students may have other literature substituted for the planned curriculum if they object for religious or other reasons.
- Students may opt out of certain courses (usually dealing with sex education) if they and their parents object to content.
- Parents may refuse to follow guidelines that require students to be immunized.

This list will no doubt grow as parents and students have their voices heard in the courts. Administrators and teachers need to be aware of students' rights to nonparticipation, or at least question the legitimacy of insisting on compliance with school policies and traditions.

STUDENT RECORDS: ACCESS AND PRIVACY. The **Family Educational Rights and Privacy Act (FERPA) of 1974**, commonly called the **Buckley Amendment,** allows parents and guardians access to their students' academic records and requires written parental permission for the records to be shared with anyone else. When students turn age 18, they have control over who sees their records.

The Buckley Amendment establishes the minimum standards regarding privacy of records, with some states and districts going beyond to allow students access to their own records. Some items, however, are not subject to student or parent viewing. For instance, teachers' grade books, notes kept by teachers for their own use, and the private notes kept by school law enforcement teams typically remain inaccessible to others.

The extent to which student records must be kept private was tested when an Oklahoma parent challenged the long-standing practice of students grading one another's work in *Owasso Independent School District* v. *Falso*, 2002. The parent sued an Owasso school, saying that peer grading was embarrassing and often inaccurate. Because of conflicting court actions, the case ended up in the U.S. Supreme Court, which ruled unanimously that day-to-day grading is not covered by FERPA.

RIGHT TO NONDISCRIMINATION. Students may not legally be discriminated against by public schools. Discrimination cases that have been tested in U.S. courts have resulted in the following principles:

- Students of any race, religion, or disability may attend U.S. public schools.
- Students who are married, are parents, or are divorced may attend the same public schools as those who are not.
- Students with HIV/AIDS pose no significant risk to others and may attend public schools.

Not only are all students guaranteed the right to attend public schools but the right has also been extended to extracurricular activities.

Table 10.7 includes sample court cases involving student rights. Teachers need to be as informed as possible about what the courts have decided.

Table 10.7 Cases involving student rights

Case	Explanation	Implications for Teachers
Tinker v. *Des Moines Independent Community School District.* Iowa, 1969	This case involved three students who wore armbands to protest the war in Vietnam. They were suspended and subsequently sued the district. In this monumentally important case, the U.S. Supreme Court ruled that students do not "shed their rights to freedom of speech or expression at the schoolhouse gate." The *Tinker* case has been cited repeatedly since 1969.	The rights of teachers and students differ inside the schoolhouse. When teachers express their views, they have a legally captive audience of people: their students. Therefore, their overt display of opinions is not allowed. However, students have the right to express their views in peaceful, nondisruptive ways.
Goss v. *Lopez* Ohio, 1975	Several high school students were suspended for up to 10 days without receiving a hearing. The students maintained complete innocence and were never informed of exactly what they were accused of doing. When a federal district court agreed with the students in their suit against the school, administrators appealed to the U.S. Supreme Court, where the decision went in favor of the students again. The justices wrote that students have a property right to school attendance.	Often teachers will be aware of, or even report, grave discipline infractions of students. Within a day or two, the students are back in school, leaving teachers disgruntled with administrators. We need to realize that sometimes principals are not in control of when students are in or out of school.
New Jersey v. *T.L.O.* New Jersey, 1985	Two high school girls were accused of smoking in the bathroom. One admitted it, and one (T.L.O.) denied it. In the principal's office, T.L.O. was asked to empty her purse. In it were cigarettes, cigarette-rolling paper, marijuana, a pipe, a roll of money, and a list titled "People who owe me money." The student was turned over to juvenile court. She sued the school for invasion of privacy. The U.S. Supreme Court ruled against her and maintained that the search and seizure were reasonable.	It's very tempting at times, especially in middle and high school, to look the other way when we suspect students are engaging in the kinds of activities implied in this case. But try to resist the temptation. When you smell smoke, or detect alcohol or marijuana, or see things happening in the halls or school grounds that appear to involve substance abuse or violence, tell an administrator. Their eyes can't be everywhere. They depend on aware teachers to help keep the school safe and healthy.

Table 10.7 *(continued)*

Case	Explanation	Implications for Teachers
Bethel School District No. 403 v. *Fraser* Washington, 1986	The freedom of speech implied in *Tinker* was challenged in 1986 when a student made a speech containing sexual innuendo in a high school assembly. He was reprimanded and subsequently sued the school, claiming that his freedom of speech was denied. The court said that schools have the right to censor communication in schools to avoid disruption.	If language and innuendo are not tolerated in a school assembly, then they should never be tolerated in your classroom. This sort of problem is most prevalent with adolescents who, at times, seem very adultlike. Teachers cannot tolerate, and certainly cannot condone, offensive student language.
Hazelwood School District v. *Kuhlmeier* Missouri, 1988	Articles written by students for a high school newspaper were deleted by the principal. The main topics of the articles were teen pregnancy and divorce, and they contained references to sexuality that the principal thought inappropriate for younger students. In addition, even though their names were changed, the principal was concerned that students written about in the articles were identifiable. The Supreme Court ruled in favor of the district, stating that educators may exercise substantial control over school-sponsored publications and events.	Schools have the right to censor controversial articles in school publications. Of course this is important for those who sponsor publications, but it's also important for all teachers. Students will often push the limits and need to understand that educators can censor writing. If in doubt, always ask an administrator.
Isaacs v. *Board of Education of Howard County* Maryland, 1999	A high school girl was not allowed in school because she wore a head wrap to celebrate her cultural heritage, in violation of the "no hats" rule. A judge ruled in favor of the school for the following reasons: 1. Hats increase horseplay and conflicts. 2. Hats block teachers' and students' views in classrooms. 3. Hats allow students to hide drugs and other contraband. 4. Hats foster a less respectful learning climate. The judge concluded that it was unrealistic to expect schools to make hat-by-hat decisions.	This is becoming more and more controversial as cultural and religious diversity increase. Had this case made it to the U.S. Supreme Court, the outcome may have been different. However, if there is a schoolwide "no hats" rule, teachers must comply and report infractions, even if you think a student should be allowed to wear a head covering.

Point of Reflection 10.4

Did your schools have dress codes or uniforms? What do you remember about them? Did you feel that your freedom of expression was restricted by what the schools said you could and couldn't wear?

As a future teacher, do you like the idea of dress codes or uniforms? Why or why not? Are uniforms more important at certain levels of school?

Check Your Understanding 10.6

Concluding Thoughts

Controversial issues—such as sex and AIDS education, Internet usage, school choice, high-stakes testing, school uniforms, protection for LGBTQ students, and funding for public education—continue to emerge and will no doubt prompt legal questions. The courts will interpret the Constitution or rely on case law to settle such disputes. Teachers need to stay current on how laws affect what takes place in classrooms and schools.

When you choose to teach, you make a commitment to a service profession. You take on the serious responsibility not only to abide by laws but also to continually promote what is ethical for students and for yourself, both in the big issues as well as in the seemingly minor issues that test you every day. You commit to thoughtful and deliberate decision making, to showing the courage to do what's right for students, and to having the good sense to ask for advice and guidance when needed.

Read through *Chapter in Review* to help refresh your memory of what we have discussed, and then interact with Brenda as she confronts challenges in *Developing Professional Competence.*

Chapter in Review

What does it mean to be an ethical teacher?

- Laws tell us what we can and can't do. Ethics tell us what we should and shouldn't do.
- The National Education Association provides a professional code of ethics for educators.
- To be an ethical teacher means to be guided by a set of beliefs that leads to attitudes and actions focused on what's best for students.
- Six characteristics that help teachers make ethical decisions include appreciation for moral deliberation, empathy, knowledge, reasoning, courage, and interpersonal skills.
- Ethical attitudes, decisions, and actions involve both major and seemingly minor issues.
- It is important to have a vision of the characteristics we want to help cultivate in our students.

How do laws affect schools, teachers, and students?

- The laws that affect schools, teachers, and students are based on a balance of rights and responsibilities.
- Four basic sources of law directly impact the work of teachers: the U.S. Constitution, federal laws, state and local laws and policies, and case law.

What are the legal rights of teachers?

- The legalities of employment include contracts, tenure, and dismissal.
- Due process involves a set of guidelines that must be followed to ensure that individuals are protected from arbitrary or capricious treatment by those in authority.
- Teachers enjoy the same rights as other citizens, including freedom of expression—whether symbolic, written, or spoken—but with restraints based on the responsibilities of teaching.
- Academic freedom is a form of expression that allows teachers to use their judgment concerning what and how to teach.
- Teachers have some restrictions on their personal lives that other people do not have because of the nature of the teaching profession.

What are the legal responsibilities of teachers?

- Teachers serve *in loco parentis* and are responsible to care for and protect the students they supervise.
- Among other things, teachers have the legal responsibility to avoid liability, abide by copyright laws, and report suspected child abuse.

How does the law impact the relationship between school and religion?

- The First Amendment says that government (public schools) can neither establish religion nor interfere with the free exercise of it.
- Public prayer is illegal in public school. Religious organizations may meet and pray in school facilities outside regular school hours.
- It is permissible to teach about religion but not with the purpose of persuading students to believe in a particular religion.

What are the legal rights of students?

- Court decisions attempt to balance the rights of students to express themselves and the necessity of limiting personal freedom to ensure the safety and well-being of others.
- Students have freedom of symbolic expression, speech, and the press.
- Student privacy is protected from unreasonable search and seizure.
- Students have the right not to be sexually harassed.
- Students have due process rights when facing serious disciplinary action.
- Students and parents have rights concerning privacy and access to records.
- Students may not legally be discriminated against by public schools.

Developing Professional Competence

Thoughtfully reading this scenario and responding to the items that follow it will help you prepare for licensure exams.

Sara Davis Powell

Brenda Beyal, a teacher in a multiage classroom, enjoys the fact that her school, colleagues, and students are open-minded and accepting of differences. She also enjoys the status of her school as an arts-focused elementary. The arrival of fifth-grade twin girls in Brenda's classroom one afternoon in May proved to be both a challenge and an opportunity.

Amira and Farah were the first children of traditional Muslim parents to attend Rees Elementary School. These 11-year-old twins walked into Brenda's classroom one Friday morning in May, only weeks before the end of the school year. They wore loose-fitting pants and long tunic tops, along with scarves on their heads that completely covered their hair. Amira and Farah smiled sweetly and took their seats at a table with three other children. Brenda welcomed them and invited the girls to introduce themselves to the class, hoping their English would be understandable since they greeted her politely with "Good morning, Mrs. Beyal." Amira went first and explained that her name means *princess* in Islam. Then Farah followed suit by saying that her name means *happiness*.

Brenda had been told she would have two new students, but she had not been told that the girls were part of a very traditional Muslim family and that there would be some challenges because of their presence as the first students of Islamic faith. Here are some of the challenges Brenda faced:

- A school rule states that headgear may not be worn in the school building. The girls wore *hijab*, traditional Muslim headwear.
- Amira and Farah arrived in the middle of Ramadan, a Muslim month in which believers fast during daylight hours.
- Amira and Farah are required to pray five times a day, and two of the times fall within the school day.
- The parents of Amira and Farah talked with Principal Larsen and told him they are aware that his school is known for the arts. They have concerns because (in their tradition) dance serves no purpose and needlessly causes girls and boys to come in contact, and they find some music offensive. In addition, Muslim children are not allowed to draw human figures.
- Sentiment in the United States toward people of the Muslim faith can be less than favorable, especially following the events of 9/11 in 2001.

Think about Brenda's challenges and opportunities to help all her students learn from, and about, each other's similarities and differences. Respond to three short essay items involving the scenario. In your responses, be sure to address all the dilemmas and questions posed in each item. These items are followed by two multiple-choice questions.

1. Is it legal for Amira and Farah to pause twice each day for prayer and refuse to eat lunch during Ramadan? If not, why? If so, how might Brenda explain this to her students?
2. Should the school rules about headgear be relaxed to allow Amira and Farah to wear *hijab*? If not, how should Brenda handle the situation? If so, how might Brenda explain this rule variation to her students?
3. Brenda's class has spent more time than most learning about the 9/11 devastation that occurred before the children in her class were even born. Brenda's Uncle Alfred was a firefighter who died attempting to rescue others in Tower II and she tells his story and shows family photos to personalize the event each September. Brenda anticipates there will be questions from students, perhaps expressed privately to her, about whether the new girls are part of the group responsible for the tragedy. What is the primary point Brenda should make with her students? Explain your response.

Application Exercise 10.2: Developing Professional Competence

4. After the bus announcements were made at the end of the school day, Amira and Farah told Brenda that their father would pick them up at the front door. Knowing that the cars are moved quickly through the pick-up line, what might be best for Brenda to do?
   a. Call the office and ask Principal Larsen to escort the girls to their car.
   b. Ask teammate Chris Roberts if her remaining students waiting for transportation can go to his classroom so she can escort the girls to their car.
   c. Ask one of her students who is also a car-rider to go with the girls to their car.
   d. Quickly call a teacher who has car-rider duty and ask her watch for the girls and make sure they get to their car.
5. When Brenda goes home the day the twins arrive, which choice is perhaps the most helpful as she considers the following day with her class?
   a. Talk with her husband about how to best handle the new situation.
   b. Go to the library to find out what she can about the Muslim religion.
   c. Look up *Ramadan* on the Internet to anticipate what to expect the girls to do during this holy month.
   d. Arrange to meet with Principal Larsen early the next morning.

Application Exercise 10.3: Developing Professional Competence

Flash Cards 10.1

Shared Writing 10.1: Ethical Teachers

Chapter 11
Governing and Financing Public Schools

Learning Objectives

After studying this chapter, you will have knowledge and skills to:

11.1 Explain how the federal government influences public education in the United States.

11.2 Summarize the state's role in public education.

11.3 Describe how school districts function.

11.4 Analyze the management structure of individual schools.

11.5 Identify how other entities impact the governance of public schools in the United States.

11.6 Explain how public schools are financed.

11.7 Describe how funds for education are spent.

Dear Reader

As professionals, we need to understand where, when, and how decisions are made that affect our schools and classrooms, and, ultimately, our students, families, and communities. Perhaps in a perfect world, these decisions would be made by people who have firsthand experience with teaching and learning, people who understand the complexity of the processes that lead to the development of engaged, curious, and productive citizens who never stop learning and whose actions reflect civility. However, in the United States we often find ourselves bogged down in bureaucracy, with levels of government imposing policies that not only are difficult to comprehend but also may make us feel powerless to influence.

Public education costs a lot of money. People not directly involved with teaching and learning often say schools spend too much yet achieve minimal results. True, money doesn't buy learning, but it does provide the facilities, programs, and personnel that help make education accessible to all. Developing an overview of governance and finance now will help you put in context what you read in the newspaper or see on TV about issues such as school board proceedings, hiring of administrators, legislative decisions, and test score reports. Compared to learning about student development and instructional strategies, the content of this chapter may seem dry. However, understanding the governance and financing of public education increases our professionalism and helps us be more effective advocates for children and adolescents.

11.1 How Does the Federal Government Influence Public Education?

11.1 Explain how the federal government influences public education in the United States.

Before we address the influence of the federal government, take a look at the overall structure with four levels of governance of public education shown in Figure 11.1.

Because education is not addressed in the U.S. Constitution, it has historically been interpreted as a state's responsibility. However, the federal government's involvement in the functioning of schools through the institutions and agencies shown in Figure 11.2 has increased in recent decades.

Presidential Influence

Almost every presidential candidate in the 20th century included education in his or her campaign platform; most had boldly articulated plans and promises. From its establishment in 1857 until 1980, the U.S. Department of Education served in an advisory capacity with little impact on public schools. President Ronald Reagan (1980–1988) was the first president to experience the department as a cabinet-level agency, resulting from action taken by President Jimmy Carter's administration in 1979. Since 1980, the influence of the U.S. Department of Education has steadily increased. President Bill Clinton (1992–2000) worked vigorously toward achieving the objectives of *Goals 2000,* an ambitious list of goals for students in U.S. public schools. President George W. Bush's legacy (2000–2008) regarding education is the No Child Left Behind Act of 2001, discussed throughout this text. At the end of President Barack Obama's eight years in the White House (2008–2016), the Elementary and Secondary Education Act (ESEA) was reauthorized again as Every Student Succeeds Act (ESSA) to replace the No Child Left Behind Act.

Congress and the Courts

The U.S. Congress has passed many influential laws regarding education, and the federal court system has made numerous rulings affecting education. For example, the Bilingual Education Act of 1968 made provisions for English-language instruction. The Education for All Handicapped Children Act of 1975 was the first to guarantee a free public education for students with disabilities. The No Child Left Behind Act of 2001 impacted K–12 schools, teachers, and students, although assessments of

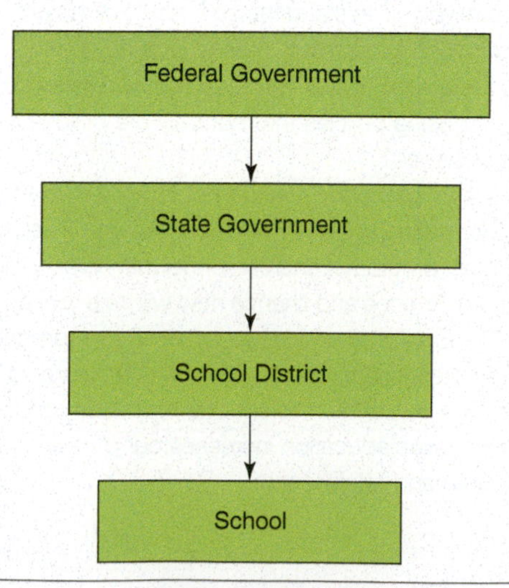

Figure 11.1 Overview of U.S. public school governance

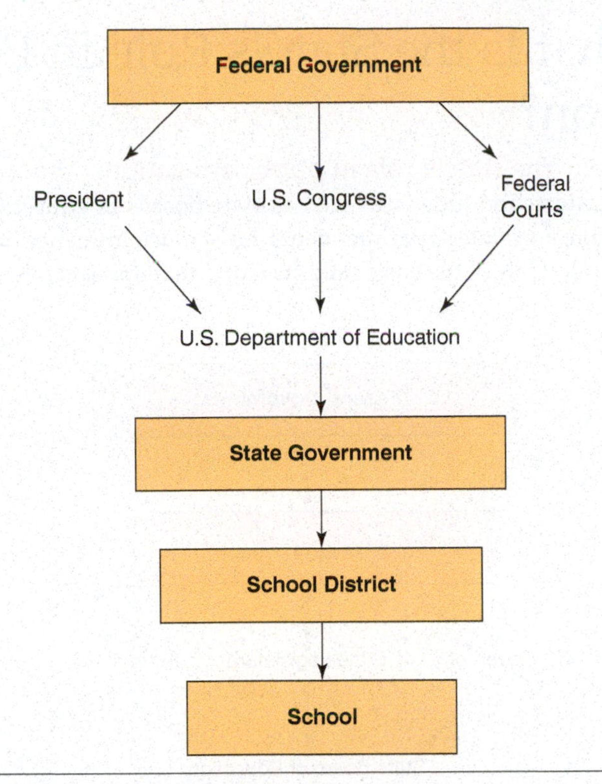

Figure 11.2 Federal government role in U.S. public school governance

its success were both mixed and impassioned. In 2016 the original Elementary and Secondary Education Act of 1965 was reauthorized as the Every Student Succeeds Act (ESSA), replacing No Child Left Behind. The ESSA places more authority for education-related decisions in the hands of states and local school districts. U.S. courts hear and rule on cases that directly and indirectly impact schools and the work of teachers. In Chapter 10 we examined the influence of case law on education.

U.S. Department of Education

The U.S. Department of Education has had some influential secretaries over the years. The term *secretary* as used here indicates the head of a presidential cabinet–level department. The secretary of education is chosen and appointed by the president, making the position political. The secretary of education influences policies established by the U.S. Department of Education, which has a sizable budget and exercises its power through these policies and programs. The federal government sponsors programs that impact schools and students such as Head Start and the National School Lunch Program, both of which benefit children in low socioeconomic settings.

Funding provided to schools by the federal government is distributed in the form of assistance to implement approved programs and to conduct educational research. These funds are also used as leverage to help ensure that state departments of education both comply with specific federal mandates, such as guidelines and policies related to attempts to equalize educational opportunities for all children, and comply with the use of widespread testing programs. In some cases, states may choose whether to comply with U.S. Department of Education policies. However, the federal government withholds funds from states and their schools when they choose not to comply.

Check Your Understanding 11.1

11.2 What Is the State's Role in Public Education?

11.2 Summarize the state's role in public education.

Governors, legislators, and judges, as well as state boards of education, state departments of education, and state superintendents, have much influence on public schools. Figure 11.3 is an overview of the basic state structure that impacts schools in the United States.

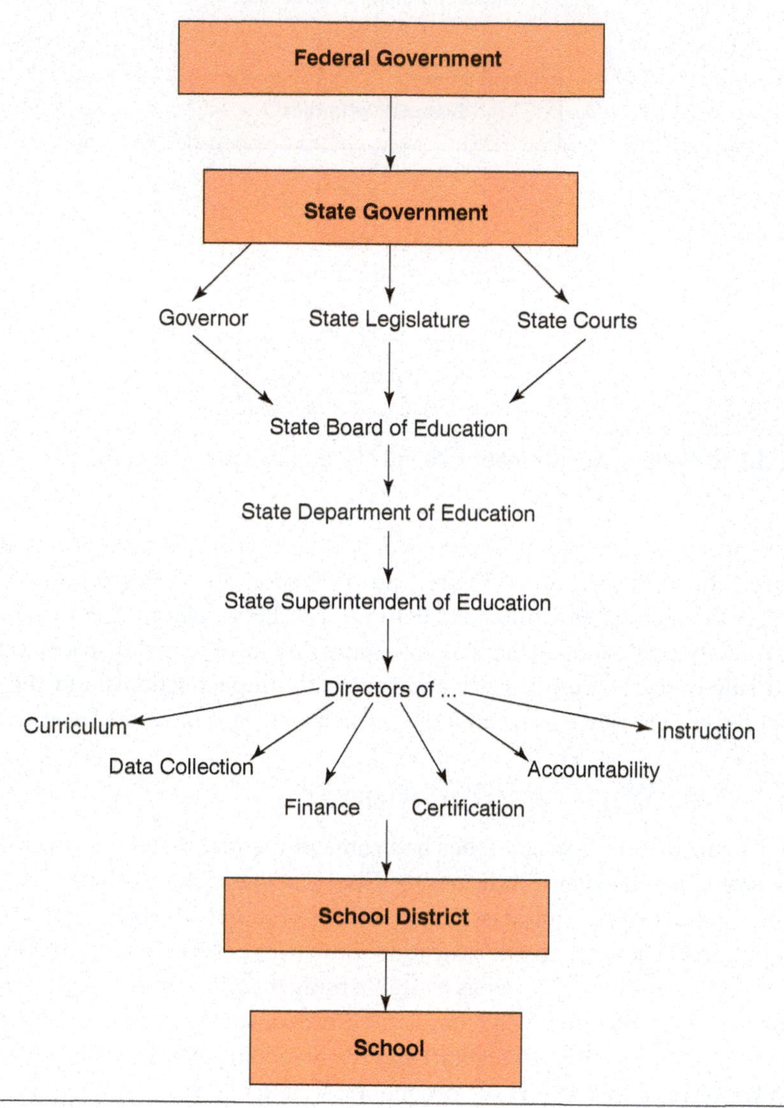

Figure 11.3 State government role in U.S. public school governance

Application Exercise 11.1: Figure 11.3 State government role in U.S. public school governance

Balance of Power at the State Level

States govern under a balance of power with three major branches of government, similar to what exists at the federal level. Governors have executive authority; legislatures have lawmaking authority; and state courts uphold and interpret laws, as well as establish constitutional guidelines.

GOVERNORS. Governors, as leaders of state governments, potentially have tremendous influence on public schools. A governor's attitude toward education has far-reaching power on policies and laws. In many states the governor appoints the state's superintendent of education, as well as members of the state board of education. In addition, governors make budgetary recommendations that impact schools.

The National Governors Association (NGA) was founded in 1908 and serves as the collective voice of the nation's governors. The NGA Center for Best Practices is an online clearinghouse that provides governors and the public with information about public education, including such topics as disparities in academic achievement, turning around low-performing schools, and quality of teaching. The organization describes policy options for states, identifies how states cope with dilemmas pertaining to education, helps governors establish and maintain quality education in their states, and counsels them on how to work effectively with state legislatures. Recall that the NGA was one of two organizations originating and propelling the development of the Common Core State Standards.

STATE LEGISLATURES. Members of state legislatures have significant influence on public education. State legislators affect schools as they determine:

- State laws that impact every aspect of public education.
- How state chief officers of education and state school board members are selected.
- Responsibilities of state-level school officials.
- How taxes are used to support schools.
- The general direction of the curriculum.
- The length of the school day and year.
- Aspects of teacher employment, including issues involving tenure, retirement, and collective bargaining.

There are no requirements in terms of educational background or experience for state legislators. Teachers and school administrators frequently question the wisdom of decisions made in the legislature. Having conversations, inviting legislators to visit schools, and writing letters are vehicles for influencing legislative viewpoints.

STATE COURTS. When state laws require interpretation, or when there is a conflict between state laws and federal regulations or the U.S. Constitution, state courts impact public education. State courts hear arguments and make decisions about school compliance with state laws that are often written in broad terms.

State Board of Education

Almost every state has a **state board of education**, generally composed of seven to nine volunteers who are either elected or appointed by the governor. State legislatures give state boards oversight authority; in other words, state boards act in regulatory and advisory capacities. State boards of education make major decisions concerning the operation of public schools as they

- Set goals and approve standards and assessments for schools.
- Establish the standards by which schools are accredited (allowed to function).
- Advise the governor and the legislature on educational issues.
- Make many of the decisions about how state funds are used.
- Represent and report to the public on education issues.
- Serve as the governing body of the state department of education.

The state board of education is primarily a policy-making body with broad responsibilities. The many detailed responsibilities that deal with education on a statewide basis are overseen by the state's department of education.

State Department of Education

A **state department of education** (also known as *state office of education* or *department of public instruction*) operates under the guidance of the governor, legislature, and state board of education. These state agencies are large, with a complex array of responsibilities and employees. Governors, state legislators, and state board members may not have expertise in education. However, most of those who hold nonclerical positions within a state department of education are professional educators. There is one notable exception. The chief state officer, or state superintendent of education, is likely to be either publicly elected or a political appointee and does not have to be a professional educator.

STATE SUPERINTENDENT OF EDUCATION. The one person with responsibility for managing the state department of education is called the **state superintendent**, chief state education officer, or commissioner of education. This person may either be elected by the voters or appointed by the governor or state school board, depending on the state's policy. The state superintendent position is both public and political. She or he is in charge of the bureaucracy that is usually centralized in the state's capital city, and travels throughout the state as the acknowledged authority on how schools operate and are assessed for effectiveness.

STATE DEPARTMENT OF EDUCATION RESPONSIBILITIES. The state superintendent of education generally has a large staff of individuals with varied expertise. The people who work as department directors are in charge of divisions within the state department that address, among other issues,

- Teacher certification (or licensure)
- Curriculum standards and accountability
- Instruction (usually a director for each content area)
- Special education
- School levels (high, middle, elementary, early childhood)
- Technology
- Charter schools
- Teacher professional development
- State budget funds
- Communication and public relations
- Collection and reporting of school data

Although not a common occurrence, a state department of education may take over the operation of a school—or even an entire school district—that is deemed unsatisfactory.

Check Your Understanding 11.2

11.3 How Do School Districts Function?

11.3 Describe how school districts function.

A **school district** is an organizational structure of local schools defined by geographic boundaries. Figure 11.4 provides an overview of the basic structure that exists in most school districts.

School districts have at least one **feeder system** of schools—that is, early childhood/elementary schools that feed into middle schools that feed into a specific high

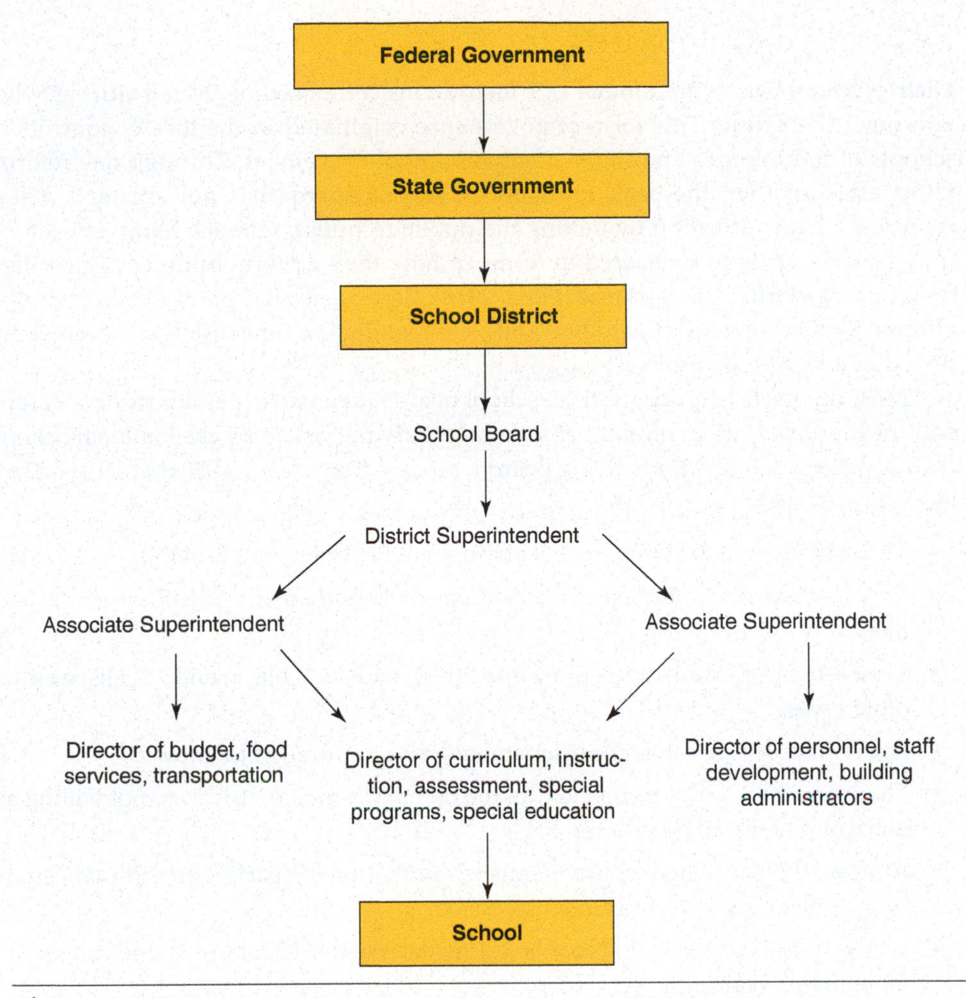

Figure 11.4 School district role in U.S. public school governance

Application Exercise 11.2: Figure 11.4 School district role in U.S. public school governance

school. There are over 15,000 school districts in the United States. In the early to mid-20th century, there were almost 10 times as many. The decrease occurred as people realized it was more efficient to combine small districts and share services and administration. Interestingly, the entire state of Hawaii is one school district, whereas the state of Texas has more than 1,000 separate districts.

School districts vary greatly in size, from one building that houses all grade levels, as in Gilpin County School District in Colorado with about 300 students, to New York City public schools, with over 1 million students. Small and large districts both have distinct advantages as well as limitations. Small and medium districts have the advantage of accessibility. Teachers feel as though they can be heard in policy matters, and parents often sense a distinct connection to the schools and faculty. In very large districts, teachers may sense that they are far removed from where policy decisions are made. Large districts generally have the advantage of availability of numerous services and specialists who oversee the many aspects of life in schools and classrooms. In small and medium districts, individuals tend to have an array of duties, and fewer curricular and service options are offered. Regardless of size or complexity, each district has a school board and a superintendent who function as leaders of central administration.

District School Boards

District school boards are unique U.S. institutions composed of elected citizens who volunteer their time. This form of governance originated in the locally controlled schools of the colonies and in the common school movement. Through one reform effort after another, the basic structure of school boards has not changed. They represent democratization by linking the public to public schools. Many educators find school boards to be flawed in terms of how they govern, but most agree that they serve a worthwhile purpose (Hess, 2010). Because local schools are profoundly affected by district school board decisions, we spend more time discussing them than the other levels of governance.

Most members of public district school boards are neither parents nor educators and they receive little or no compensation. A study published by the National School Boards Association (2011) involving board members from about 2,000 districts yielded the following information.

- There are more male (56%) school board members than female (44%).
- Very few board members are under the age of 40 (only 4%), with 35% over the age of 60.
- Most school board members are white (81%), with 12% black, and 7% Hispanic or other races.
- Fewer than 40% of school board members have children of their own.
- The school board reports that 92% of the parents in their districts are not willing to serve on the school board.
- Almost all (96%) school board members say that their districts provide safe environments for teachers and students.
- A large majority (88%) of school board members have lived in their communities more than 5 years.
- Almost all (90%) school board members say they will continue to live in their districts indefinitely.

BOARD ELECTIONS. It can be costly to campaign for a school board seat, especially in medium to large districts (at least 20,000 students). The two basic kinds of school board elections are at-large and single-member elections. In **at-large elections**, voters may choose any candidate regardless of the area in the district the candidate represents. If there are five distinct areas in a school district, each will have specific candidates who live in the areas, but *every* voter in the *entire* district may vote for their choices regardless of where they live.

In **single-member elections**, only those who live in a specific area can vote for the representatives in their area. The single-member process has the potential to elect more representative school board members because neighborhoods are more likely to have candidates and voters who share ethnicity and socioeconomic status.

BOARD RESPONSIBILITIES. District school board members are responsible for setting policies that affect the operation of schools. Some of the most important concerns and responsibilities of school board members from small, medium, and large districts are funding, student achievement, teacher quality, improving technology, and special education. Dealing with these concerns and fulfilling other duties require numerous meetings and research. Among other responsibilities, school board members

- Decide how much money will be spent on teacher salaries, facilities improvement, and instructional materials.
- Hire and fire personnel, both professional and classified (clerical, custodial, etc.).

- Approve and evaluate programs that may affect some or all schools, teachers, and students within the district.
- Make curricular decisions within state guidelines.
- Determine organizational policy.

SCHOOL BOARDS AND THE PUBLIC. Controversy is never far from school boards. Members are easy targets for both oral and written chastisement by the community. It is a rare moment indeed when school board members are not perceived by some segment of the population as incompetent, downright stupid, or even evil. As trustees of public schools, their often-unappreciated position requires them to make hard decisions. When one group feels slighted or excluded, the board hears its complaints, but must still make decisions that may not be satisfactory to those affected. When it makes fiscal (monetary) sense to close a school, parts of the community storm the board with emotionally charged, often valid, objections. The board listens and makes decisions. When community groups work diligently to help improve education for all students and present research and suggestions, the board listens and makes decisions. When teachers take positions on issues such as board choices to transfer administrators, or program alterations, they make their case to the school board. Again, the board listens and makes decisions.

An ongoing challenge for school boards is to be both accountable and **transparent**, meaning that decisions are made with full disclosure of information and reasoning. With technology today, there is little justification for data not to be available to the public. Methods for making information gathered by school boards easily searchable are also possible. But this organizational structure, almost as old as the United States itself, will likely be slow in following any new guidelines calling for complete transparency. With all this responsibility, and frequent community wrath, why would any citizen want to be a school board member? Many do it as a service to the community. They have a genuine interest in doing what they can to benefit local schools and students. Others seek the position to gain power and visibility, to further political ambition, or to advocate for a specific cause. Regardless of their motivations, school board members dedicate long hours to the governance of public schools, including the hiring of a district superintendent.

District Superintendent and Staff

A **district superintendent** functions as the school district's chief executive officer. The superintendent is hired by the board and serves at its pleasure, which means the board can also dismiss the superintendent. The superintendent is expected to advise the board and carry out board policies. As largely noneducators, board members often choose an educator as superintendent to keep schools running smoothly on a day-to-day basis. The relationship between the board and the superintendent can become awkward when school board members go beyond policy making into what is considered the authority of the superintendent. When board members get involved in day-to-day operations, it is often referred to as **micromanagement**. If tensions develop over policies or decisions, a school board may dismiss a superintendent. Generally, before things escalate to this point, the public is involved and meetings are held to discuss the situation. These can be trying times for communities. If a superintendent is dismissed, a very public search process is usually conducted to find a replacement. Generally, a community is invigorated at the prospect of new leadership and will rally around the person hired to lead the public schools. A "honeymoon" period is seen as a positive time, with the new superintendent greeted and embraced while getting to know schools and school personnel and all the community **stakeholders**, or those who will be ultimately affected by public school district governance. In a rather sarcastic—yet realistic—way, this chapter's *The Opinion Page* feature describes the Charlotte Mecklenburg School

District's "honeymoon" with new Superintendent Dr. Heath Morrison, hired by the North Carolina district in 2012.

The Opinion Page

This Opinion Editorial appeared in the Charlotte Observer, *North Carolina, on May 9, 2012.*

What Were You Thinking, Supt. Morrison?

by Mark Washburn

Mark Washburn writes television and radio commentary for the Charlotte Observer.

It is our pleasure to welcome you, Heath Morrison, to our wonderful community.

Now that your salary as new superintendent of schools has been negotiated, it is time to talk about your benefits package, which we think you will find is superior.

For the first nine to 12 months of your employment, everyone in town will be gracious and fawning. We will listen to your ideas with eyes a-sparkle and jaws a-droop. We will tell you again and again how thrilled we are to have a smart cookie like you. We will find magic money in the budget to carry out your clever initiatives. We will compare your leadership abilities to those of Gandhi. We will surprise you with ice cream on Fridays.

At the 13-month mark, we will recognize you're getting weary of vast adoration. We will then start a program we call "gracious wondering." For a time, not exceeding two years, we will wonder about the progress our school system is making. In the latter part of this phase, we will hold mock tribunals and invite you to testify about why things are the way they are. Our former superintendents have all found this to be a time of introspection and personal growth. This will be facilitated by our supportive and caring school board. You have met them by now and know what a wise and harmonious group they are.

At the four-year mark, you will become fully vested in the executive incentive package called "unrelenting demonization." Your annual performance review will be a glorious spectacle of pursed lips, sour faces and slowly shaken heads. Around town, your name will be synonymous with epic failure. Parents and teachers will be united in the notion that *Something Must Be Done*.

In year five, we will celebrate the nadir of your career. You will be considered personally responsible for unsatisfactory test scores (no matter what they are, they will be unsatisfactory), every breach of classroom discipline and whatever clunkers are drafted by the Bobcats.

At this juncture, you will be hired by another district and slink out of town. For both of us, the cycle will begin anew. It will, in short, be just like the reign of any school superintendent anywhere.

We cannot tell you how excited we are to have you aboard. We have felt an emotional void since our last superintendent mysteriously vanished. We look forward to you providing a service to our community that we think you'll find is absolutely critical.

This Opinion Page piece reveals a familiar reality through the use of sarcasm. Mr. Washburn has obviously observed the coming and going of a number of district superintendents. Write a well-developed paragraph in response to each of the following questions:

1. Mr. Washburn writes this piece to Dr. Morrison. He refers to his benefits package as the reception he will receive from the community. In his first year as superintendent, why do you think the community will be so welcoming? What need, or perceived need, must the community have?
2. Overall, what sort of community attitude is Mr. Washburn predicting for the middle of Dr. Morrison's time in Charlotte? What circumstances are community members likely ignoring when they appear to put exclusive blame on leadership?
3. "Nadir of your career" refers to the lowest point of Dr. Morrison's time as superintendent. Do the last three paragraphs say more about a leader and his or her ability or us as community members? Explain your opinion.

In small districts, superintendents may handle almost *all* oversight responsibilities. The larger the district, the more necessary it is for the superintendent to delegate. Medium-to-large districts have associate or assistant superintendents who handle specific duties such as supervision of the different levels—early childhood, elementary, middle, and high. They work with district curriculum and instruction directors to coordinate efforts. Larger districts also have associate superintendents in charge of areas such as personnel, facilities, and finance.

People in the community sometimes complain there are too many administrators and non-classroom teachers doing supervisory work rather than directly teaching children. Before making this judgment, citizens should recognize how complex it is to operate school districts and individual schools in ways that free teachers to teach and students to learn.

Point of Reflection 11.1

Were your K–12 experiences in a small, medium, or large district? What advantages or limitations because of the size of your district were you aware of? Did you attend school from kindergarten through twelfth grade in one feeder system, or did you move frequently?

Check Your Understanding 11.3

11.4 What Is the Management Structure of Individual Schools?

11.4 Analyze the management structure of individual schools.

Now we consider individual schools, the places where teachers and students interact. Within the school building, the management structure often depends on both the size and the level of the school. Figure 11.5 lists some of the people who may contribute to the management of local schools, including the one constant person in almost all building-level management structures: the principal.

Principals

The **principal** oversees every aspect of school life and is responsible to the district for all that occurs at the school. The principal's role involves oversight of administrative tasks such as facility maintenance, attendance, discipline, parent and community relationships and communication, transportation, and all manner of paperwork. Principals also have the role of instructional leader, with knowledge of, and experience with, the teaching and learning process. Instructional leaders make positive suggestions and

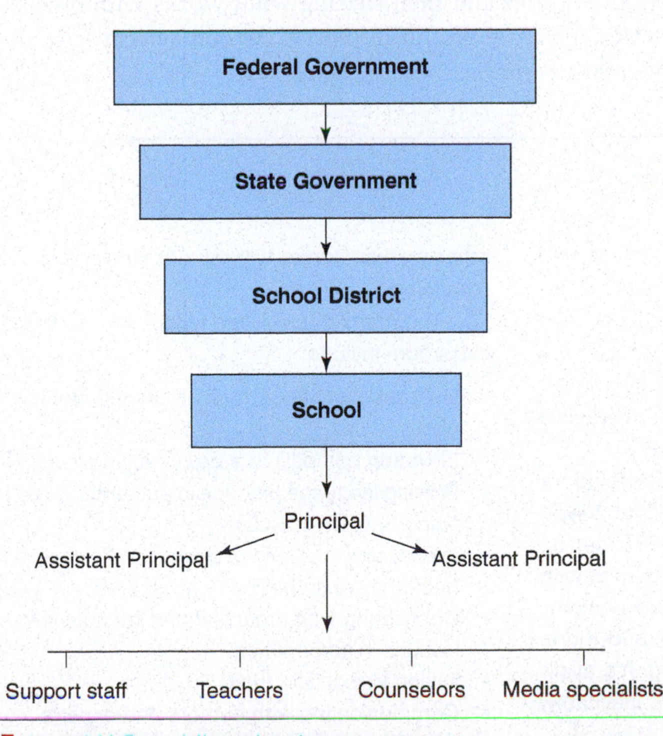

Figure 11.5 Local U.S. public school governance

model practices that enhance student learning. A principal who is an instructional leader focuses teachers on improved learning for all students. Many principals who are confident in their administrative and instructional leadership skills believe in the benefits of sharing leadership with teachers and members of the community.

SITE-BASED MANAGEMENT. In *Leadership Capacity for Lasting School Improvement* by Linda Lambert (2003), we are told that the most effective principals build leadership capacity in teachers and others who are sincerely interested in student learning. **Site-based management** is a form of local school governance that puts much of the decision-making power regarding curriculum, textbooks, student behavior, staff development, budget, and hiring in the hands of teachers, family members, and the community. Principals who want to share leadership and management of schools employ at least some of the actions listed in Figure 11.6. Serving on a site-based management team gives teachers deeper insight into the role of the principal.

Figure 11.6 Building leadership capacity

Principals who build leadership capacity in teachers and others

- Consider community values as they develop a shared vision.
- Consistently keep the focus on teaching and learning.
- Find ways to dismiss ineffective teachers by using district evaluation systems.
- Make decisions using community input.
- Tirelessly seek and secure resources and support for the school.

Based on: Lambert, L. (2003). *Leadership capacity for lasting school improvement*. Alexandria, VA: Association for Supervision and Curriculum Development.

From the list in Figure 11.6, perhaps the most fundamental thing principals do to empower teachers to take responsibility for student learning is the second statement: *Consistently keep the focus on teaching and learning*. In other words, student learning takes precedence and empowered teachers do what's best for them. As you consider the technology in the *SocialMEdia* features so far, and their potential impact on learning, you can be a leader in your school by finding technologies that excite and motivate your students and then sharing what works with other teachers. This chapter's *SocialMEdia* feature is a hit in most classrooms because of the face-to-face encounters students experience.

SocialMEdia

Web conferencing is a way to connect students with people and places around the world. The technology may be accessed using the tools (computer, webcam, and microphone) already available in most classrooms. Enhancing the ability to use web conferencing not only with individual students but also whole classes requires tools such as tablet computers and interactive whiteboards.

Currently, the leading facilitator of web conferencing for education is Skype, a free online communication tool. *Skype in the Classroom* is a valuable resource, providing set-up guidelines, a help center for questions, ways to connect with teachers around the world who seek classroom connections, sample lesson plans for using web conferencing, and more. *FaceTime* is another vehicle for web conferencing. It's available on iPhones, iPads, and other Mac technology. Inevitably, other manufacturers will roll out similar and more innovative technology.

The many possibilities for using web conferencing in the classroom include:

- Cultural exchanges that otherwise would probably never occur
- Elevating pen pals to a new, exciting level
- Proving language practice in authentic ways, including practicing English for ELLs
- Introducing students to people and places in the setting of a book they're reading or a geographic area they're studying
- Connecting with organizations such as NASA for tours and lessons in aeronautics
- Taking virtual field trips
- Communicating with authors and experts

Other benefits of using web conferencing include:

- Rural schools are using web conferencing to connect them with opportunities enjoyed by urban and suburban learners because of their proximity to museums, zoos, concerts, and more. On the flip side, urban and suburban students can virtually experience what rural life is like.
- Teachers can hold parent conferences with web technology and parents can view student performances.
- Teachers can connect with each other and with worldwide experts to learn new content, theory, and instructional practices. Web conferencing is an excellent professional development tool.

Many skills can be taught through Skype that span subject areas and provide authentic use of knowledge and skills. As students plan web conferences, they learn to:

- Set goals and formulate questions to be addressed.
- Communicate to arrange the session.
- Execute logistics of the session.
- Use appropriate etiquette and clear speech.
- Reflect on their experiences.

Testimonials from teachers who have taken the time and energy required to use web conferencing in their classrooms say it's more than worth the effort. These are exciting possibilities for your future classroom!

Principals have multiple responsibilities and answer to various constituencies, including superintendents, community members, families, and teachers. They are often privy to information that impacts their decisions, some of which they cannot share with their staffs. Too many teachers tend to pass judgment on a principal's decisions and sometimes hold grudges. As a new teacher, you need to realize that you won't always understand why or how decisions are made. Your best path is to be supportive of your principal and helpful to the programs and people aligned with your school's mission.

UNDERSTANDING THE ROLE OF THE PRINCIPAL. As you begin your teaching career, your principal will have a major impact on you. Your memories of the principals you have experienced may factor into how you view your first principal when you become a teacher. He or she will select you and ask the school board to hire you, will determine the grade level or subject you teach, will likely assign a teacher mentor for you, will evaluate your teaching performance, and will make the decision whether to offer you a contract for the following year.

Principal Laura Hill at Summit Primary School takes all her responsibilities very seriously. We met her in Chapter 3 when we discussed schools. Watch Video Example 11.1 Principal Hill's Responsibilities through the lens of understanding her role. Listen for what she says about the school district's role in the grade-level configuration of Summit Primary School.

Video Example 11.1: Principal Hill's Responsibilities

Figure 11.7 illustrates gender, age, and racial characteristics of school principals at the elementary and secondary (high school/middle school) levels. An update is needed for this information from a 2009 study to see if there are changes, but no one has undertaken this task. We will view the data with an assumption that the percentages are basically the same today.

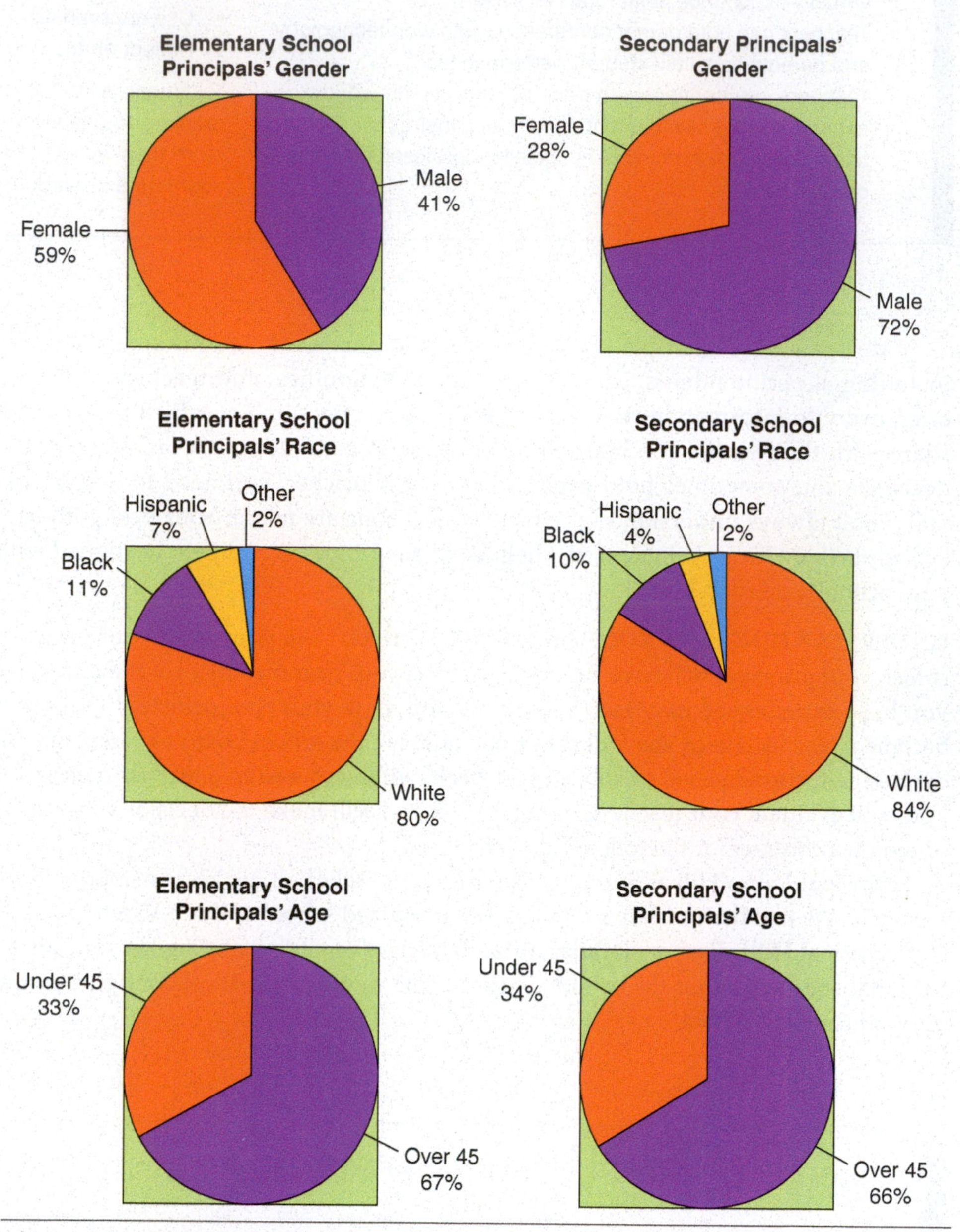

Figure 11.7 Characteristics of elementary and secondary school principals

Based on: U.S. Department of Education. (2009). *Characteristics of public, private, and Bureau of Indian Education elementary and secondary school principals in the United States.* Washington, DC: Author.

You will notice that the overwhelming majority of these school leaders are white, and, overall, male, and over the age of 45. Just as there is a need for a more diverse teaching force, there is also a need for principals who more closely mirror student gender, racial, and ethnic characteristics. One such principal is Maria Romero at Roosevelt High School. Watch Video Example 11.2 Principal Romero and Student Ethnicity to hear her description of the Roosevelt students and how she responds when asked about her own ethnicity.

Video Example 11.2: Principal Romero and Student Ethnicity

Assistant Principals

The position of assistant principal entails a variety of duties. If there is only one in a school, then the responsibilities may be general and similar to the principal's, or as

All Photos: Sara Davis Powell

Assistant principals may be perceived as stern in their role as student disciplinarian, and yet be approachable supporters of teachers.

specific as the principal chooses to make them. When there are multiple assistants, they generally have designated areas of responsibility. For instance, a medium-size elementary school (400 to 700 students) may have a principal and one assistant who may do various aspects of the principal's job, depending on day-to-day needs. A large middle school (more than 1,000 students) may have a principal and two or three assistants, each responsible for a grade level. A principal of a large high school (more than 1,500 students) may have more than three assistants who specialize in areas such as student discipline, athletics and extracurricular activities, transportation, and materials. Teachers often work with assistant principals. A teacher in a large school may be more connected with the assistant principal(s) than with the principal.

Teacher Leaders

The phrase **teacher leader** has come to mean in many circles that a teacher has taken on additional responsibilities such as chairperson of a grade level of teachers or perhaps a subject-area specialist who works with other teachers to help them improve their knowledge and/or skills. But some individuals can be leaders in their schools, as well as in their districts and states, simply by being dynamic, well-informed classroom teachers. They don't need official titles to impact other educators around them, their own students, and other students in their buildings and their communities.

A growing number of teachers with specialized training are relieved of some or all their classroom teaching duties to lead a grade level or be an in-school subject area expert. For instance, a school may have an instructional coach, a teacher who works with individual teachers as they improve or add to their toolboxes of instructional strategies. Another school may have a math specialist who teaches math to all fourth- and fifth-graders, regardless of their homeroom. These specially designated teacher leaders may become part of the school management team along with the principal and assistant principal(s).

Point of Reflection 11.2

What do you remember about your schools' principals? Were they accessible or did they seem aloof? Did you view them as disciplinarians to be feared or as friendly adults who were helpful to teachers, parents, and students?

Check Your Understanding 11.4

11.5 What Other Entities Impact the Governance of Public Schools in the United States?

11.5 Identify how other entities impact the governance of public schools in the United States.

The decisions about policies and laws by the individuals and groups discussed so far in this chapter are influenced by many constituencies. Among them are parents, businesses, universities, and special interest groups.

Parents

Parents, including stepparents, foster parents, and guardians, have the potential to be among the most important partners in the education of children. Parents are influential in the lives of their own children and, if they are informed and involved in schools, can make a positive difference in the lives of many children in their local schools. One question is "How can they do this?" But perhaps even more important to ask is "Why don't they do it more often?"

One way for parents to be involved in the life of the school is through the **Parent Teacher Association** (PTA), a national organization with millions of members at thousands of schools across the country. School PTAs (sometimes called PTOs—Parent Teacher Organizations) have varying degrees of impact. Some groups boast large numbers of members whose only involvement is the payment of small annual dues ($2 to $10). Other groups have very active members who volunteer to help at school in a variety of ways. Although individual PTAs contribute to school life, rarely do they impact decision-making bodies.

Parents can volunteer in schools and classrooms and impact the quality of students' school-related experiences. They also have opportunities to serve on committees that address school issues. In some school districts, parents are encouraged to be part of site-based management groups called School Improvement Councils (SICs) or Local School Councils (LSCs). Being part of an SIC or LSC is a serious responsibility that far too few family members are willing to accept. Parents are usually busy providing for their families and often feel that their time is too limited to commit to membership in a site-based management group. Some parents may be intimidated by the process or may feel they are not qualified to represent other families.

Businesses

Businesses have a vested interest in education. Having competent employees is a major key to business success, and these employees are likely to be products of public education. Large businesses and their chief executive officers are increasingly becoming involved in **education summits**, or organized meetings to advocate for school improvement. This is a positive step because business leaders can potentially support schools and students in meaningful ways.

Business leaders can be influential in supporting educational initiatives. Some businesses offer scholarships to promising students. Other businesses, whether locally owned or national franchises, form partnerships with schools to sponsor events, such as science fairs, and contribute resources to enhance school activities. Additionally, some large businesses give employees paid time off to volunteer in schools and may match funds their employees donate to school organizations.

Universities

Schools of education and teacher educators have an important influence on schools because most classroom teachers are prepared on university campuses. Future teachers learn about the concepts discussed in this text and more as they go through teacher preparation programs. The more teachers know, the better prepared they are to take active roles in influencing policies and working toward school improvement.

Teacher educators have the knowledge, and ideally the will, to exert influence by expressing their views to school administrators, school board members, and legislators. They can serve on School Improvement Councils, curriculum revision and textbook adoption committees, and, in general, be active in local, state, and national education associations. University professors also impact schools through research focused on classroom programs and practices and by facilitating staff development. These activities can form the foundation for recommending policy changes and promoting effective practices.

Special Interest Groups

When a group of people join together with a common mission and work to have an impact, they are often called a **special interest group**. An example would be a group composed of parents of children who have special needs. Informal groups of parents of children with autism or Down syndrome, for example, may band together to help ensure more effective services for their children.

Sometimes community members join forces to form local **watchdog groups**, meaning they keep an eye on school district accountability by examining policies and practices. These groups often fund or conduct research on issues, articulate findings and viewpoints, and lobby school board members and state legislators to bring about change. Special interest groups offer effective services by asking hard questions and being persistent in their search for answers.

Check Your Understanding 11.5

11.6 How Are Public Schools Financed?

11.6 Explain how public schools are financed.

Free public education—think about it. What a remarkable and noble concept. But is public education really free? Hardly. It's true that students don't pay tuition. However, their parents often pay fees for specific items, such as science equipment, gym clothes, band instruments, workbooks, and athletic uniforms, as well as vague charges for grade-level fees. Parents are also asked to supply certain materials each school year. But these expenses barely make a dent in what it costs to provide K–12 education. So where does all the money come from?

Most of the funding for public education comes from federal, state, and local governments in the average proportions shown in Figure 11.8. It's interesting to note how these three major sources of funding have shifted over the years, from local funding as the primary source in the early part of the 20th century, to local and state sources currently sharing funding responsibilities at approximately the same levels today.

Note that the title of Figure 11.8 includes the word *average*. Public education funding varies widely among states that determine their own funding formulas. For instance,

- In Vermont, 89% of public education funding comes from the *state*; in South Dakota, it's 26%.
- In Illinois, 65% of public education funding comes from *local sources*; in Hawaii, it's 2%.
- In Mississippi, 16% of public education funding comes from the *federal government*; in New Jersey, it's 4% (U.S. Department of Education, 2016).

These variations occur for complex and shifting reasons. The end result is wide disparity among states in overall funding support for the public education of over 55,000,000 students in the United States.

Federal Funding

The federal government budget is supported through income taxes, investments, and various charges for services and goods. Federal government contributions to public education account for only about 2% of the U.S. government budget.

The federal government supplies a little over 10% of the total education budget. Although this doesn't sound like a lot, federal contributions have a major impact on public schools because the money is allocated as **categorical grants**, or funds earmarked for specific purposes. Programs such as Head Start, Title I, the Bilingual Education Act, and the Education for All Handicapped Children Act are examples of categorical grants. As a group, these and other grants are referred to as **entitlements**, meaning that certain

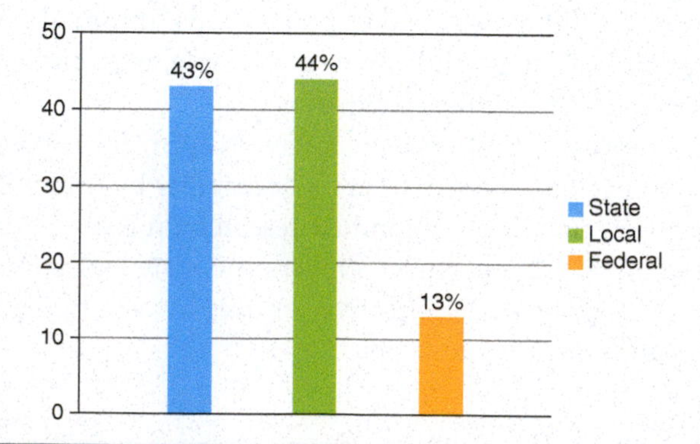

Figure 11.8 Average percentage of revenues received from federal, state, and local sources for public elementary and secondary schools

Based on: Federal Education Budget Project School Finance (2013). *Federal, State, and Local K–12 School Finance Overview.* Retrieved September 8, 2013, from http://febp.newamerica.net/background-analysis/school-finance

segments of the population have specific needs and the federal government deems these individuals as entitled to extra assistance.

The Reagan administration attempted to diminish the influence of the federal government on schools while still funding their efforts. In the 1980s, some federal funding changed from categorical grants to **block grants**, which provide funding with few restrictions for its use. This type of funding allows states and school districts the freedom to use the money in ways that meet their specific needs.

The No Child Left Behind Act of 2001, as a reauthorization of the 1965 Elementary and Secondary Education Act, involved federal funds tied to school improvement as prescribed by the act's specific guidelines. Schools were required to meet the mandates of NCLB to receive the funds. In most cases, states attempted to protect federal funding by complying with the mandates.

State Funding

About half the funding for public education comes from state sources. State money for schools is basically raised through taxes, such as:

- State income tax based on personal earnings
- State corporate tax based on company earnings
- State sales tax added as a percentage of the cost of goods and services
- **Excise tax**, or tax on luxury items such as boats and travel trailers
- **"Sin" tax** on items some consider vices, such as alcohol and cigarettes

As of 2013, 43 states had lottery games with portions of the funds specifically earmarked for education (U.S. Government, 2013). Although lottery-based funding may sound appealing and, indeed, has been used productively in many instances, there are inherent problems. First, gambling through state-run lotteries appears to attract a disproportionate number of low-income people who often have little schooling. Many disagree with the concept of a lottery system for this reason. Second, although lottery funding is initially viewed as extra money to supplement other, more stable sources, over time having this easy source of funds often leads to the reduction of more stable funding. In other words, a state's attitude may be "We have all this lottery money so we don't need to give schools as much from the state budget." This is risky business, from both state and local standpoints, considering the uncertainty of a lottery's ability to provide money consistently for schools.

In tough economic times, difficult budgetary decisions must be made at all levels. This often proves especially difficult at the state level. When money is tight, some services and programs must be cut. Because education is such a large part of a state's overall budget, the decision to withdraw funding from schools is both public and painful. Most states occasionally face shortfalls. California serves as an example of where some citizens have gone from passive disapproval to aggressive action. More than 60 individual students and their families, 9 school districts from throughout the state, the California School Boards Association, the California State PTA, and the Association of California School Administrators filed a lawsuit against the state based on their view that the current educational finance system is unconstitutional. Through *Robles-Wong* v. *State of California*, filed in 2010, the plaintiffs asked that California's finance system, specifically its funding policies for education, be changed. They asked that the state determine the cost to adequately fund public education to meet both the state's own program requirements and the needs of the students. It's disheartening to report that in August 2016, in a 4–3 vote, the California Supreme Court stated that the state has no obligation to guarantee the level of funding for education nor to guarantee a specific level of public education for children and adolescents. Now that you know more about case law, this should be a particularly disturbing court decision (California School Board Association, 2016).

Local Funding

The source of local funding for schools is primarily **property taxes**. Values of property are determined, and a small percentage of the assessed amount (usually less than 1%) is collected annually and used for local services. Most goes to schools. On the surface, using property taxes to finance education seems reasonable. After all, everyone benefits from an educated citizenry. However, as illustrated in Figure 11.9, many people believe an alternative method of funding public education should be imposed. In 1978, California was the first state to put a limit on how high property taxes could go. California's Proposition 13 was a model for other states. Now almost all states impose what is called a **tax cap** on local property taxes, or an upper limit to taxation.

IMPACT OF RELIANCE ON PROPERTY TAXES. Let's consider what reliance on property taxes for almost half of public school funding might mean for different communities. A district composed of middle- to upper-socioeconomic suburban neighborhoods with prospering retail stores and a couple of thriving industries will likely generate a healthy amount of money with a relatively low percentage of the assessed property value. In this case, people who own homes and businesses pay what might be considered reasonable taxes on their property and appear to have adequate funding for schools. Now think about a district in a very rural area, with a lot of land, but few homes, with families who drive out of the area for jobs or who work in the few businesses located in the district. In this case, home and business owners may have to pay a much larger percentage of the assessed value of their property to support schools. There may simply not be enough property value to generate adequate funding. Finally, consider a densely populated urban area, with many people who are renters in high-rise buildings and often living on government subsidies such as welfare. An area such as this may have large numbers of children but very few home or property owners. In some urban areas, business and industry provide an adequate tax base, but in others the base is very low, resulting in inadequate school funding.

Figure 11.9 Sample community responses to property taxes and their use to fund schools

PatrickWatson/Pearson Education, Inc.

We moved into this home in 1968. We made the last of our monthly mortgage payments the same year we both retired. Our pensions were supposed to give us enough income to stay right here for as long as our health allows. But year after year the value of the house goes up, with all the new stores and shopping centers popping up in the area. Our property taxes have doubled. If they go much higher, we may have to move. We raised our kids, and now they're raising their own. I'm all for good schools, but not if we lose our home.

I have a good job that allows my wife, who used to be a third grade teacher, to homeschool our two kids. We live in an upscale neighborhood and are very happy with our lives. But what we're not happy about is the way our property taxes are skyrocketing. I believe in public education, but we can afford to homeschool while the kids are young, and then they'll go to our church's private 6–12 school. Why should I have to pay exorbitant property taxes for schools I'll never use?

PatriciaMarks/Shutterstock

Imtmphoto/Fotolia

I don't have kids and never plan to. I like my life as it is, with good friends and a job that calls for me to travel to interesting places. I bought a great downtown loft apartment with payments I can afford. However, now that this area of downtown is being revitalized, the value of my place is on the rise, along with escalating property taxes. I understand that most of this money goes for public schools. Well, the school a few blocks away sure doesn't look like much of my money, or anyone else's, is being spent there. If that school represents how this school district is spending my money, I'll vote for any decrease of the spending cap.

Relying on property taxes to provide a substantial portion of support for public education can create a funding gap that further exacerbates socioeconomic differences. And, as we know, where there are socioeconomic gaps, there are almost certainly achievement gaps. In states with tax caps, it may not be possible for communities to raise the percentage of the tax on assessed property value, even when most people believe it should be done to support their schools. They are stuck with the limit, despite what may be unfair and nonproductive funding. If you hear or see an expression such as "Drop the cap, end the gap," you'll better understand the meaning of this slogan. Read more about the funding gap in Figure 11.10. With all the problems inherent in using property taxes as the primary source of local funding, alternatives are often sought.

LOCAL FUNDING ALTERNATIVES. Some communities are attempting to support public education through an increase in sales taxes. For instance, when the sales tax is raised from 6% to 7%, an extra penny is collected for every dollar spent on taxable goods. This translates into a sizable amount of money. For a school district, such an increase could mean less dependency on property taxes as the source of local funding.

Another way school districts acquire funds is to borrow money through what is called a bond issue, the sale of bonds to raise an amount of money stipulated for specific projects. When using a **bond referendum**, the school board asks voters in their district to approve the borrowing of the money (the bond) that will be repaid over a period of time. Bond offerings can be for hundreds of millions of dollars. In some states, boards are not required to ask voters for permission to borrow money for schools. The request may need only city or county council approval.

PRIVATE DONATIONS. In addition to federal, state, and local funding, many districts and individual schools receive private gifts of either money or goods. These gifts rarely account for more than 3% of the total amount of school funding. Individuals and foundations may contribute to a specific program or project and have a significant impact on that particular segment of school life. However, states, districts, and schools should be cautious about considering private gifts when planning budgets. These sources are often one-time donations or may prove to be unstable.

Figure 11.10 The funding gap

"Closing the achievement gap is a familiar theme these days. But lurking behind the achievement gap is another contentious issue: funding. Excellence in education doesn't come without a price tag." This statement by Amy Azzam, associate editor of *Educational Leadership*, begins her 2005 special report on *The Funding Gap 2004*, a study conducted by the Education Trust.

The study used the financial data from the U.S. Census from each of the more than 14,000 school districts. The focus of the study was on funding disparities by state between high-poverty and low-poverty districts, as well as between high-minority and low-minority districts. The results revealed that more than half the states provide less money to high-poverty districts than to low-poverty districts. This translates into less money for high-minority areas since there tends to be a higher concentration of minorities in high-poverty areas.

The disparities become even more glaring when we consider the fact that it costs more for high-poverty districts to meet the same standards as low-poverty districts, by some estimates as much as 40% more. Education Trust found that with this cost adjustment, 36 states provide an average of $1,348 per student less for high-poverty versus low-poverty districts. Some states have disparities as high as $2,500 per student.

Given the study results, Education Trust recommends that states:

- reduce reliance on local property taxes
- spend extra money to help low-income children
- do away with funding gaps among individual schools within districts

Azzam closes her report by stating "Closing the achievement gap starts with closing the funding gap. Only by providing the necessary resources can states help ensure quality education for all students."

Based on: Azzam, A. M. (2005). The funding gap. *Educational Leadership, 62*(5), 93.

Point of Reflection 11.3

What is your view of the connection between spending on education and student achievement? On what do you base your opinions?

Check Your Understanding 11.6

11.7 How Are Funds for Education Spent?

11.7 Describe how funds for education are spent.

Just as the ability to generate money varies greatly from state to state and district to district, the amount each state spends on public education varies as well. Rather than totals per state, the number that is most meaningful is the amount of money spent per pupil.

Expenditure Per Pupil

The average amount of money spent from federal, state, and local sources on an individual student is called the **expenditure per pupil**. A comparison of expenditures per pupil by state is found in Figure 11.11. Keep in mind as you look at this figure that the cost of living, and consequently the cost of education, varies from state to state and region to region. Does almost three times the learning occur in New York, where expenditures per pupil are over $20,000, as in Utah, where per pupil spending is about $6,500? The answer, of course, is *no*. Look back at Figure 11.10, which points out that children living in poverty require 40% more spending. Spending more to educate students who need extra services to succeed in school is being responsive to differences that often relate to race, socioeconomic status, and levels of disabilities. There are so many variables to consider, including issues such as the percentage of teachers who are experts in their teaching fields, state-of-the-art instead of dilapidated facilities, and whether class sizes are small instead of large. These all cost money.

The national average expenditure per pupil has continually increased. As with any large enterprise, everything required to fund education becomes more expensive. When gas prices rise, so does the cost of bus transportation. When construction costs rise, so does the cost of building new schools. The more diversified student populations become, the more expensive it is to hire personnel to meet their needs. It is understandable that public education is criticized for increased spending when there appears to be little progress in terms of test scores. But it is a complicated issue as schools continue to struggle with the connection between spending and levels of learning.

Allocation of Education Funding

With any large endeavor, there are administrative and other costs that affect, either directly or indirectly, the cause or people served. So it is with education. It would be wonderful if 90% of an education budget could go directly into the classroom to pay teachers, buy books and supplies, and provide the latest technology. But as you saw earlier in this chapter, support for the work of individual teachers in their classrooms requires (at least as the education system is currently configured) people in district and state positions. Some of the current programs with the greatest impact require national-level support as well.

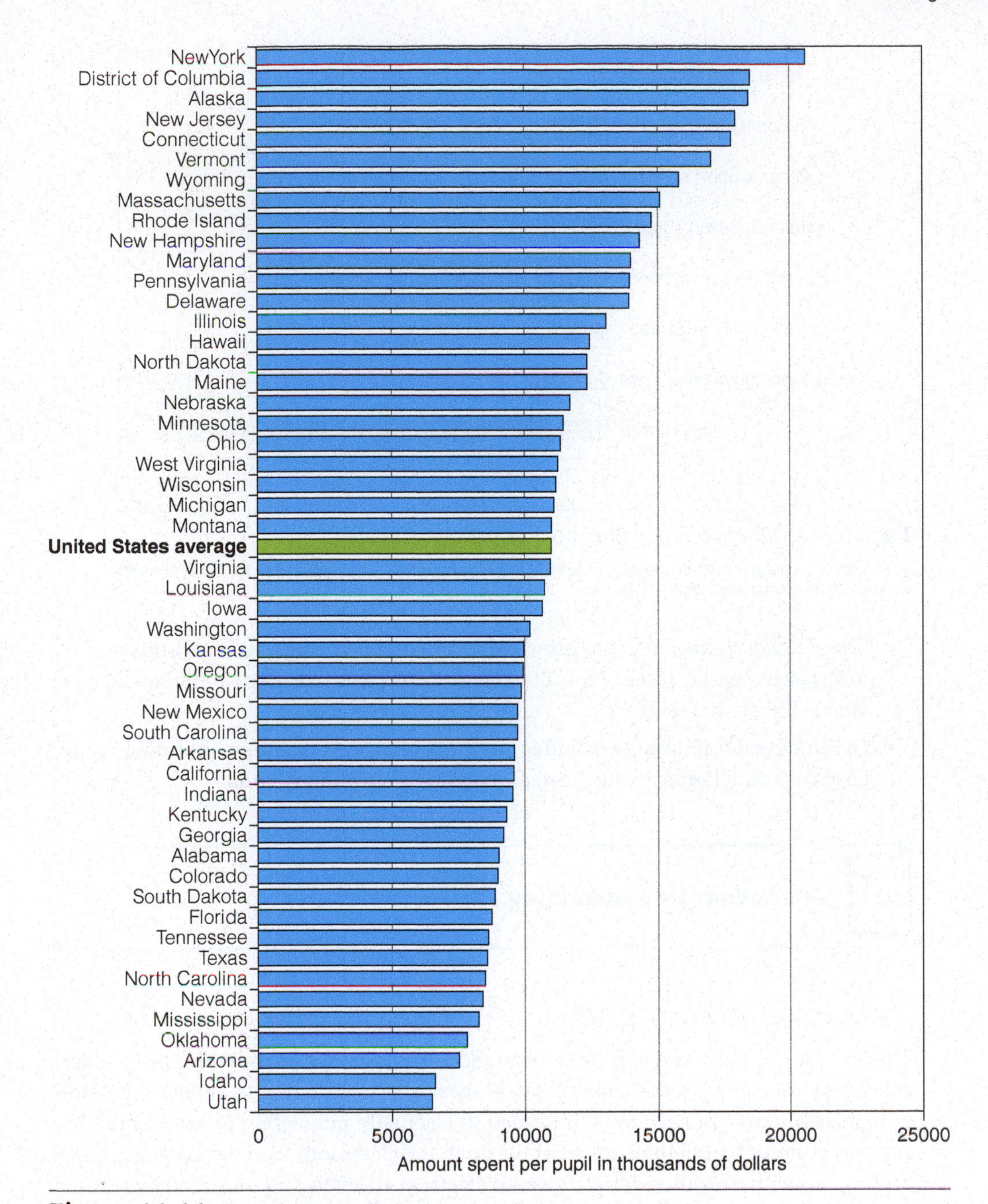

Figure 11.11 Average expenditures per pupil by state, 2014

Based on: U.S. Census Bureau. (2016). Public education finances: 2014. Retrieved May 13, 2017, from https://www2.census.gov/govs/school/14f33pub.pdf

Figure 11.12 shows the overall expenses of U.S. school districts. With about 15,000 school districts, the allocation of 64% directly to instruction is impressive, with most spent for teacher salaries. The rest buys books, classroom supplies, technology, and so on.

- *General administration* includes district-level administrators.
- *Student transportation* mainly involves school buses. The buses must be purchased, maintained, and filled with gas. Drivers must be paid.
- *Instructional staff support* includes curriculum and instruction specialists, teacher training, and teacher assistants.
- *Student support services* include school psychologists, nurses, behavior specialists, home liaisons, and others who work with students with needs, special and otherwise (not including special education teachers).

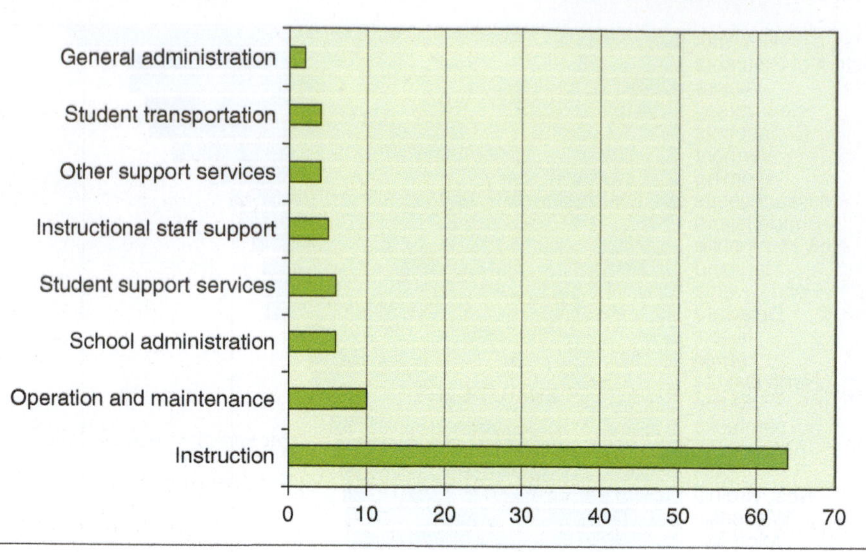

Figure 11.12 How funds are spent at the district level

Based on: U.S. Census Bureau. (2016). Public education finances: 2014. Retrieved May 13, 2017, from https://www2.census.gov/govs/school/14f33pub.pdf

- *School administration* refers to principals and assistant principals and funds needed to support their positions. Note that over twice as much is spent at the school level versus the district level.
- *Operation and maintenance* includes anything related to facilities—building repair, custodial staff, lights, water, heat, air-conditioning, and grounds.

Check Your Understanding 11.7

Concluding Thoughts

The only way teachers can hope to understand and possibly influence the more political aspects of education in the United States—basically what happens outside the individual classroom—is, first, to be informed. It's actually interesting to learn about the support systems that help us do what we do in the classroom. You can be engaged by keeping up with education-related current events at all levels and informed by reading education journals and books. The second step to affecting the bigger picture of education is to have the will to be involved—to step outside the classroom doors and advocate for children in the larger arena of the community, the district, the state, and the nation.

After reading the Chapter in Review, consider strategies that may be helpful to Chris Roberts as he plans to present a new arts program for approval in this chapter's Developing Professional Competence.

Chapter in Review

How does the federal government influence public education in the United States?

- The president, the U.S. Congress, and the federal court system endorse specific programs and make and enforce laws that impact schools.
- The U.S. Department of Education initiates programs and mandates the compliance of states using federal money as leverage.

What is the state's role in public education?

- Each state has its own unique governance system.
- State governors, legislatures, and court systems all impact the functioning of education within the state.
- A state board of education is a volunteer policy-making body that has oversight responsibilities.
- A state department of education functions under the leadership of a state superintendent and many administrators who work to support schools and teachers.

How do school districts function?

- A school district is made up of schools defined by geographic boundaries.
- District school boards set policies that affect the operation of schools.
- A district superintendent is the chief executive officer of a school district and may have a staff with specified duties.

What is the management structure of individual schools?

- The principal oversees every aspect of a school and answers to the district for all that occurs.
- Assistant principals and teacher leaders play important roles in school management.

What other entities impact the governance of public schools in the United States?

- Parents and families have the potential to positively impact student success in school.
- Businesses have a vested interest in effective schools that prepare their employees and consumers. Business–school partnerships benefit both parties.
- Universities and teacher education faculty prepare teachers and impact education.
- Special interest groups are composed of concerned citizens who work for the benefit of specific causes within schools.

How are public schools financed?

- On average, state and local funding share about 87% of the funding burden equally, with federal funds accounting for most of the rest.
- Federal funds are either earmarked for specific purposes in the form of categorical grants or given for states to use at their discretion in the form of block grants.
- State funds are generated primarily through sales taxes and income taxes.
- Most local funds usually come from property taxes, a controversial source.
- Private donations provide boosts to specific programs and efforts but account for a very small percentage of total school funding.

How are funds for education spent?

- The amount spent on each student, the expenditure per pupil, varies greatly from state to state.
- Over half the money spent on public education goes for expenses related to classroom instruction. The rest is spent on support services, including administration, facilities, and transportation.

Developing Professional Competence

Sara Davis Powell

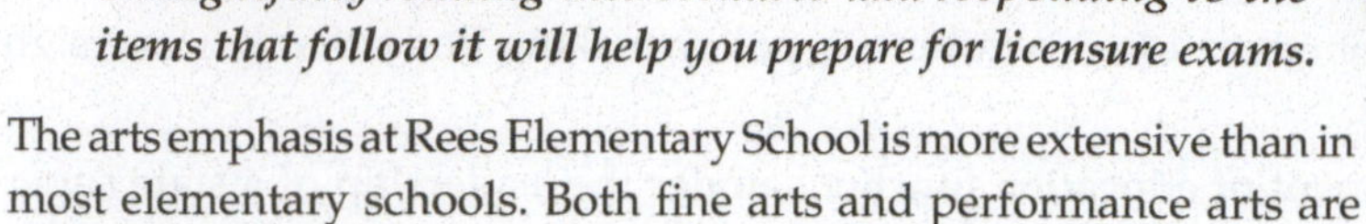

Thoughtfully reading this scenario and responding to the items that follow it will help you prepare for licensure exams.

The arts emphasis at Rees Elementary School is more extensive than in most elementary schools. Both fine arts and performance arts are part of the everyday world of Rees students. They learn about art and "do" art during the school day, with evidence of this on display throughout the school. But as the student population begins to shift, the teachers become aware of more and more of their students going home to empty houses and remaining there for several hours before their parents get home from long days at work. Focus teachers Chris and Brenda decide it's time to take art beyond the 3 p.m. afternoon dismissal bell. To do this will take time and money.

Chris Roberts has a good idea about what's involved in working through the public school governance system, thanks to his experiences with the initiation of multiage classrooms. He has volunteered to take on the task of finding support for the idea of "Afternoon Arts" and finding funding to make it happen. He understands the meaning and value of these two pertinent standards:

InTASC Standard 10

The teacher seeks appropriate leadership roles and opportunities to take responsibility for student learning, to collaborate with learners, families, colleagues, other school professionals, and community members to ensure learner growth, and to advance the profession.

NBPTS

Accomplished teachers can evaluate school progress and the allocation of school resources, in light of their understanding of state and local educational objectives.

Now it's time for you to respond to two short essay items involving the scenario. In your responses, be sure to address all the dilemmas and questions posed in each item. These items are followed by three multiple-choice questions.

1. Describe the kind of support Chris might want from his principal, the district arts director, community members, and families. Address each separately.
2. The teachers who believe in the potential of "Afternoon Arts" will likely want to be part of the program. Should they be paid for the 3 hours a day required, or should the intrinsic value of the program and what it may mean to kids who need it be enough reward for their efforts? Justify your response.

Application Exercise 11.3: Developing Professional Competence

3. Rees Elementary has a state arts grant, but this funding will be withdrawn next year, given an economic shortfall. Which of the following would *not* be a possible source of funding for "Afternoon Arts"?
   a. Community businesses contributing to the program
   b. District funding designated for at-risk students
   c. Federal categorical grant
   d. Federal block grant

4. What challenges do you anticipate that may stem from the fact that Rees Elementary is in Utah?
   a. Utah is a rural state and incorporating the arts may be difficult.
   b. Utah's per-pupil expenditure is comparatively quite low.
   c. There may be resistance among the new families in the Rees attendance zone.
   d. There are few models of arts programs.
5. In what order would Chris want to present the "Afternoon Arts" program to individuals and groups to gain approval and possible funding?
   a. Principal, district arts director, community businesses, families
   b. Families, principal, district arts director, state curriculum director
   c. Principal, community businesses, families, district arts director
   d. Principal, district arts director, state curriculum director, families

Application Exercise 11.4: Developing Professional Competence

Flashcards 11.1

Shared Writing 11.1: Your Principal and You

Chapter 12

Professionalism in Relationships, Reality, and Reform

Learning Objectives

After studying this chapter, you will have knowledge and skills to:

12.1 Explain how I can develop as a professional.

12.2 Analyze how I can develop and maintain professional relationships.

12.3 Identify some realities of teaching.

12.4 Summarize my role as a professional in education reform.

Dear Reader

Teaching is a lifestyle, a career that occupies both your head and your heart. It takes both content knowledge and skills to teach children and adolescents. It also takes a level of care and concern beyond that of most other professions to apply knowledge and skills in ways that engage and inspire. As teachers, we must develop a level of professionalism to guide our interactions with students, families, the community, school personnel, and each other. These interactions may surround content, logistics of the school, public relations, and more.

So long as we have public education, we will have efforts to improve it. Most widespread initiatives are not started by teachers, but the responsibility to implement the reform *du jour* is usually ours. This is a reality. Sometimes realities are negative and encumbering, leaving teachers to swim upstream to do what's best for students. But swim we will, because the teaching profession is what holds our nation together and gives it hope for the future.

12.1 How Can I Develop as a Professional?

12.1 Explain how I can develop as a professional.

Professionalism is necessary in all that teachers do. There is no on-off switch for professionalism based on circumstances. We never stop growing as professionals; opportunities are everywhere to hone the science, art, and service of teaching. When faced with realities that are negative in nature, we respond in professional ways to make a positive difference. When inevitable reform initiatives come our way, we are professional in our participation, reflection, and assessment of potential for benefits and actual results.

Professionalism entails meeting responsibilities head on, as well as taking full advantage of opportunities involving teaching and learning. Responsibility and opportunity have a symbiotic relationship. You may recall from biology that when organisms are symbiotic, they have a mutually close relationship that is advantageous to both.

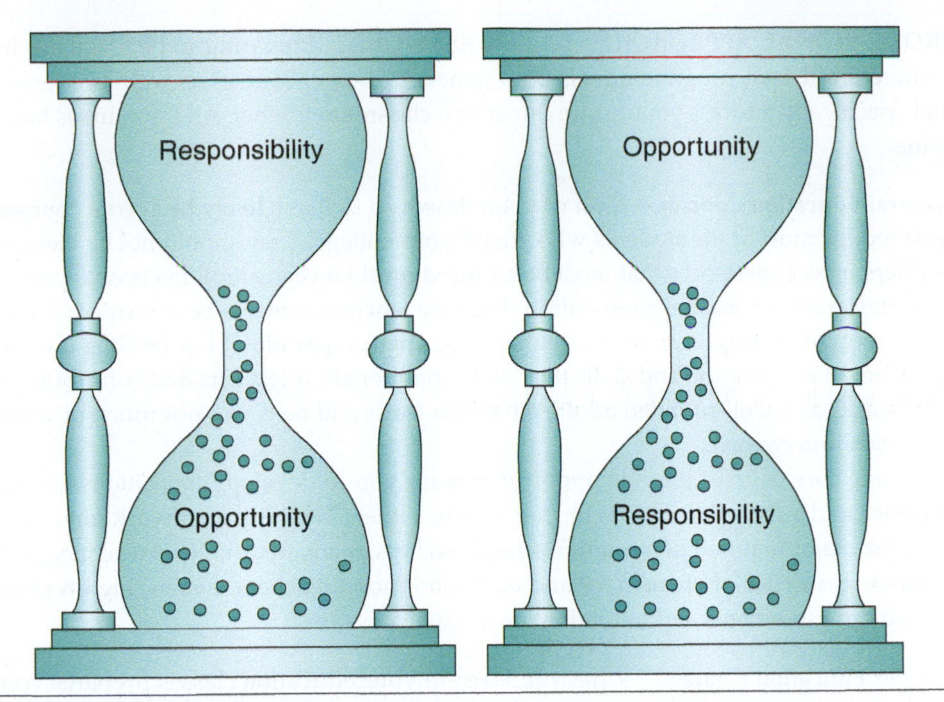

Figure 12.1 The relationship between responsibility and opportunity

Responsibilities and opportunities are so close that they flow into one another. When responsibilities are fulfilled, opportunities are created; when opportunities are recognized and acted on, they often incur responsibilities.

The close and mutually advantageous relationship between responsibility and opportunity is illustrated in Figure 12.1. Like the sand flowing from one chamber into the other in an hourglass, when responsibility is on top and is being fulfilled, it flows into opportunity. Similarly, when we make the most of opportunities, we are turning the hourglass over and watching each grain of our efforts create new responsibilities. This concept applies to each section of this chapter. Think of it often as you read.

Professionalism During Teacher Preparation

It's not too early to approach every aspect of becoming a teacher with ever-developing professional attitudes and actions. There are ways to do this at every stage of teacher preparation and while teaching. In Application Exercise 12.1, Beth Thompson, principal of a large Title I middle school, shares some advice for teacher candidates as they prepare to teach.

Application Exercise 12.1: Beth Thompson's Advice

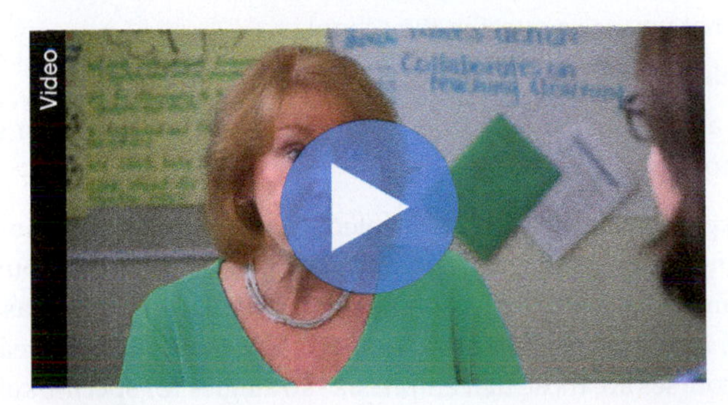

PROFESSIONAL APPROACHES TO COURSEWORK. Preparing to be a teacher in a university-based program entails both general, or core, courses as well as courses that specifically address your future career as a classroom teacher. All the courses have value.

General Education Courses. Most of your classes so far have likely been core courses required for most of the students who attend your college. They should not be viewed as fillers or as experiences that must be endured until you can enroll in classes specifically designed for teacher preparation. Because teachers need to be informed, interested, and interesting, core courses enhance teacher preparation by providing a wide spectrum of information and skills that are foundational for teachers and contribute to your status as a well-rounded adult. What you learn will help you put much of what you teach into context.

Some core courses provide opportunities for you to develop dispositions, or the attitudes and values you carry with you for life. Others lay the groundwork for a content area major required of most high school teachers, many middle-level teachers, and a growing number of elementary and early childhood teachers, depending on state licensure requirements and individual university programs.

Teacher Education Courses. What you learn in your education classes prepares you for your professional life. This realization should inspire you to pay attention, complete all readings, participate in class group work (with enthusiasm!), and keep up with assignments. You should do what is necessary to *own* the knowledge and skills, not simply *borrow* them until the end of the semester. This means internalizing and reflecting on what you learn through reading, lecture, class discussion, and experiences in real schools. Put more into your course assignments than required. Apply the content and skills to everything you know and are learning about schools, students, and teaching.

PROFESSIONAL APPROACHES TO FIELD EXPERIENCES. One of the most valuable aspects of a teacher preparation program is the opportunity to spend time in schools. **Field experiences**, or **practicum experiences**, involve observing and/or participating in actual classrooms. You may have the opportunity for field experiences in early childhood, elementary, middle, and high school classrooms before you are required to declare your chosen level of certification. You may also have a chance to observe in related arts and special education classes. Ideally, you will have the opportunity to visit rural, suburban, and urban schools. These experiences will help you decide who, what, and where you may want to teach.

Here are some general guidelines for approaching field experiences in a professional manner. Following these guidelines with enthusiasm will make your field experiences, in schools with real teachers and real students, much more meaningful.

1. Know your instructor's expectations.
2. Dress and behave with respect.
3. Remember that you are a guest in the school.
4. Keep a detailed log of your experiences, even if it is not required.
5. Spend time after each field experience reflecting on your time in schools. Write questions about what you observed.

Early field experiences will likely be devoted to **structured observations**. This means you will be looking for specific things and responding to prompts that purposefully call attention to certain aspects of the classroom. Field experiences that are associated with, or embedded in, **methods courses** will likely incorporate your first teaching experiences. Methods courses are those that emphasize strategies for specific subjects and will probably incorporate opportunities to actually apply what you are learning.

Student teaching, or clinical practice, is the capstone internship experience of your teacher preparation program. This one- or two-semester experience will allow you to use what you have learned in your courses and practiced in your other field experiences. You will get to know a group of students well as you gradually take over full teaching duties. Your student teaching experience will probably require the hardest work you've ever done. The experience will give you an idea of what teaching is really like and if the profession is work you really want to do. You will have opportunities to learn new skills, benefit from observing experienced teachers, and begin to grow into your own approach to teaching and learning.

As with other field experiences, there are commonsense things you can do to make the most of student teaching. Here are some professional attitudes and actions that will be valuable to you:

1. ***Keep a Journal.*** You will probably be asked to do this by your supervising instructor. Keeping a journal will help you reflect and learn more from your experiences.
2. ***Keep Up.*** You will be very busy, with more responsibility and pressure than you've ever experienced. There will be lesson plans to write, materials to gather, and paperwork to complete—all this while you are learning your craft, your profession. Don't let any aspect slide, and don't get behind.
3. ***Be Positive.*** We choose our attitudes. Being positive is a choice. It doesn't mean glossing over difficulties, but rather approaching each day with possibilities in focus.
4. ***Be Realistic.*** Being realistic is not in conflict with being positive. It is acceptance that some of your lessons will not go as planned, nor are you going to solve all the problems of the students in your classroom. You are learning to be a teacher.
5. ***Confide in Someone You Trust.*** You will find that no one understands what you are experiencing as completely as another clinical intern. You should also confide in your supervisor.
6. ***Be Respectful.*** Dress and speak respectfully; be respectful of the adults and students in your school. Earn their respect.

You will probably be required to develop a cohesive package of your representative products, commonly referred to as a **teacher preparation portfolio**. This portfolio may either document growth or display best work, depending on its purpose. A teacher preparation portfolio may be composed of items such as lesson plans, student artifacts, sample assessments, journal entries, sample letters to parents, and your resume. A portfolio that documents growth will help you see areas of progress and detect areas of either weakness or lack of experience. A portfolio that displays your best work can be used to document accomplishments and may be an excellent tool when you begin looking for a teaching position.

States require one or more exams to be passed before licensure or certification is granted. Take these exams seriously and take them when your instructors advise you to. This is one aspect of teacher preparation you don't want to neglect. Your future depends on passing scores.

ALTERNATIVE PATHS TO THE CLASSROOM. Many states provide alternative paths to the classroom specifically targeted to adult career changers. These programs have different names and different requirements, but all serve to fill U.S. classrooms with qualified teachers. In North Carolina, the term used for this alternative path is *lateral entry*; in Florida, it's *professional development certification program;* and in California, there are a number of paths, with explanations found through the California Commission on Teacher Credentialing. Details about alternative paths are available through state departments of education.

Most alternative paths require completion of a 4-year bachelor degree. Beyond that, the state requirements to enter the public school classroom vary from requiring a major in the content area to be taught and/or passing scores on content or teaching methods-related exams. In addition, most states require additional proof of certain teaching competencies.

Professionalism as a Teacher

Professional growth is an absolute necessity for teacher effectiveness. Professional self-growth leads to improved teaching quality and student achievement. In addition to professional opportunities to grow with help from your colleagues and participation in professional organizations, a wealth of literature addresses the many aspects of teaching and learning. Reading articles and books pertinent to content and students, and then using the ideas and advice, is another way for teachers to continue to grow professionally. Collegial conversations allow for sharing both questions and possible solutions.

Teachers are required to renew their certification or licensure every five years or so. Most states require six hours of graduate coursework or selected professional development participation measured in continuing education units (CEUs) or a combination of the two. Each state designates how CEUs fulfill the requirements for maintaining certification or licensure.

PROFESSIONAL DEVELOPMENT. ***Professional development*** is a phrase used to describe efforts to help teachers improve their knowledge and skills. Some districts refer to professional development as in-service training, staff development workshops, or teacher retreats. Many opportunities for professional growth will be presented to you. Some are required and others are optional.

You will likely hear more than a few teachers complain that a professional development workshop or staff retreat is sure to be a waste of time. They may have become jaded by ineffective sessions, or they may not be open to exploring new ideas. But remember this: There is always something to be learned when teachers get together, regardless of the perceived quality or relevance of what is formally presented.

Teachers don't have to go somewhere or be in a particular place to learn more about their craft. Twenty-first–century technology allows teachers to access knowledge in a variety of ways, presenting options for ongoing and specifically tailored professional development.

Some schools and districts are using the ***Moodle*** format for elearning. Moodle (Modular Object-Oriented Dynamic Learning Environment) is a course management system that allows teachers to share information and plans. Other elearning vehicles include wikis, blogs, and Ning. Although face-to-face professional development will always have a place in teachers' careers, online learning has the capacity to reach more teachers in convenient, immediate ways.

ADVANCED DEGREES. Teachers can continue their professional education by seeking advanced degrees. Combinations of on-site and distance learning often allow coursework to fit more easily into a teacher's schedule. Master of education degrees are offered at numerous universities. Secondary teachers often seek advanced degrees in the subject area they teach; elementary teachers may seek advanced degrees in a more generic area such as curriculum and instruction. Not only does more in-depth study of content, curriculum, and instruction enrich teaching, but it also opens leadership doors.

NATIONAL BOARD FOR PROFESSIONAL TEACHING STANDARDS CERTIFICATION. One of the most recognized, state-endorsed opportunities for professional growth is certification through the **National Board for Professional Teaching Standards (NBPTS)**. The organization was created in 1987 to emphasize what teachers should know and do to positively affect student learning. The philosophical foundation of NBPTS (2016) is composed of five core propositions:

- Teachers are committed to students and learning.
- Teachers know the subjects they teach and how to teach those subjects to students.
- Teachers are responsible for managing and monitoring student learning.
- Teachers think systematically about their practice and learn from experience.
- Teachers are members of learning communities.

In addition to the five core propositions, NBPTS has specific standards that must be met in each of the categories of certification. There are 25 certification areas that align with content and the levels of school, including early childhood, middle childhood (elementary), early adolescence (middle school), and adolescence and young adulthood (high school). As of 2016, over 112,000 teachers were certified through NBPTS (NBPTS, 2016).

TEACHER EVALUATION AS OPPORTUNITY FOR PROFESSIONAL GROWTH. It is perfectly normal to be apprehensive about being evaluated, especially in your first few years in the classroom. Evaluations should be viewed as opportunities for professional growth. There is always more to know and new skills to develop, even for experienced teachers.

The methods school districts use to evaluate teachers vary. Most involve elements such as observation of teachers with students, opinions of administrators concerning planning for instruction, evidence of collaboration with colleagues, attendance at professional development sessions, and classroom management skills. New teachers are usually assigned a mentor teacher who will informally observe and do formative assessments, which are ongoing classroom visits to look at how new teachers function. Formative assessments result in no formal affirmation or unfavorable consequences; rather, they are used to promote growth.

Teachers usually receive an annual summative evaluation, one that will be accompanied by a written report of performance (as measured using whatever criteria the state and district choose) that forms the basis for continuing employment decisions. This summative evaluation will be conducted by a building-level administrator who may use a detailed form on which a kind of "score" is kept of both if, and to what extent, a teacher does certain things associated with effective instruction. Some evaluations are much less prescriptive, with the evaluator taking detailed notes about what's observed and then writing a description from the notes. Either method will be the basis for follow-up conferences. Teacher evaluation will be discussed in more depth later in the chapter.

Contributing to the Teaching Profession

The teaching profession is bolstered every time an engaging lesson is taught or learning is facilitated in whatever way is appropriate for students. In this respect, effective teachers routinely contribute to the profession. In addition, there are specific activities that reach beyond the classroom to have a positive impact on the teaching profession.

TEACHER INVOLVEMENT IN PROFESSIONAL ORGANIZATIONS. The effectiveness of any organization depends in large measure on its membership. Teachers are responsible for the effectiveness of professional teacher organizations, whether large and politically aggressive, like the National Education Association (NEA) and the American Federation of Teachers (AFT), or small, like a district social studies council organized to provide resources and information for area social studies teachers. In most cases, membership in professional organizations is voluntary, although there are instances when teachers may feel pressured into joining specific groups.

Subject-area organizations, such as the National Council of Teachers of English (NCTE) and the National Council of Teachers of Mathematics (NCTM), provide valuable information and resources. Being a member helps teachers do what they do more effectively; every teacher who belongs makes the subject-area organization stronger. Most states have their own subject-area organizations that are affiliates of the national subject-area groups. State membership fees are generally less and conferences are more accessible because they are held within the individual state. Membership in state organizations is a good place to begin.

It is important for teachers to take advantage of the opportunities professional organizations provide. In turn, teachers should feel a responsibility to join professional organizations to help build the teaching profession.

TEACHER INVOLVEMENT IN THE SCHOOL. Being an active participant in the collegiality of a school is a positive way to be involved. For new teachers, this may mean benefiting from a strong mentor relationship with experienced teachers and maintaining a helpful, open spirit. When you become more confident in your new role, you will have opportunities to be part of committees and task forces with specific decision-making and action responsibilities.

Focus teacher Renee Ayers is involved in her school in many ways, including serving as a mentor to new teachers. Read what she says in *Teaching in Focus.*

Teaching in Focus

Renee Ayers, Grade 2, Summit Primary School, Ohio. *In her own words. . . .*

Sara Davis Powell

Many wonderful people supported and helped me during my first years of teaching: the clever curriculum director who told me about the "question chair" to stop interruptions during reading groups; the kind principal who cheered me on even when I was in tears in his office; the caring special education teacher who would come to my classroom during her planning period to tutor a student with special needs; the 30-year-veteran teacher next door who taught me all of his "sing to learn" songs; and the school counselor who assisted me in doing hands-on science experiments with 27 second-graders. I look back with such fondness as I consider the people who nurtured me.

As I grew in my career I decided I had a responsibility to pass this support on to other new teachers. In my sixth year of teaching I became a praxis mentor with every intention of going into my protégés' classes and dishing out all my experience and advice. What I found from this experience was that by observing and supporting first-year teachers, I had created an opportunity for myself to learn. Every protégé has become a resource and friend to me. Their enthusiasm is contagious, their teaching practices are fresh, and their ability to persevere through the extreme pressure and demands of a first classroom never ceases to amaze me.

TEACHER INVOLVEMENT IN THE DISTRICT. Every district functions within state guidelines and with the use of state funds. Being informed about how your district functions begins with paying attention to who is in leadership roles and how the chain of influence works. After teaching for a few years you may have opportunities to participate in district-level committees that may make decisions and take actions such as

- Textbook selection (within state guidelines, if applicable)
- Curricular planning to incorporate state standards
- Recommendations for creating activities to involve parents

Extending teacher influence at the local and district levels is what **systemic involvement** is all about. It is possible and desirable—although it consumes time and energy—for teachers to have an impact on both adults and students well beyond the classroom door. You can grow into many of these responsibilities and opportunities with time and experience.

CONTRIBUTIONS TO THE PROFESSIONAL KNOWLEDGE BASE. When a teacher tries an instructional strategy that works well with a specific topic, or with a certain group of students, sharing the experience will help other teachers. This sharing can happen in a team or grade-level meeting, through a Moodle or other online vehicle, at a meeting of a professional organization, or in an article written for an education journal. Teachers who try a new strategy, develop a way to gather evidence concerning its effects, interpret the evidence, and make inferences from it are conducting a kind of research referred to as **action research**. Reporting findings and continuing inquiry add to the professional knowledge base.

Point of Reflection 12.1

Are you excited about field experiences? What aspects do you anticipate enjoying most? What aspects do you anticipate will cause some level of anxiety for you? Why?

Check Your Understanding 12.1

12.2 How Do I Develop and Maintain Professional Relationships?

12.2 Analyze how I can develop and maintain professional relationships.

As a service, or "helping," profession, teaching involves relationships more than almost any other profession. From students, to families, to the community, relationships are key to success. Within the profession, other adults in our schools and in the district present opportunities for mutually advantageous relationships. When we fulfill our responsibilities and take advantage of opportunities involving relationships, the children and adolescents we teach benefit. Building and maintaining strong relationships helps us ask and answer the recurring questions, "And how are the children? Are they all well?" in resoundingly positive ways.

Relationships With Students

For teachers, students are absolutely at the top of the list of professional responsibilities and the primary focus of opportunities. We are responsible for student learning as we maintain high expectations for them.

TAKING RESPONSIBILITY FOR STUDENT LEARNING. The common link among teachers who consistently reach students whom others might consider unreachable is that they take responsibility for student learning. We may not be able to change conditions outside school that impinge on student achievement, but we can absolutely change what happens in our classrooms to increase learning.

Teachers who take responsibility for student learning take no excuses—from students, parents, or themselves. They find ways to engage students in learning. They use instructional strategies appropriate for both the content and the learners, and they model respect and enthusiasm.

HIGH EXPECTATIONS. When we take responsibility for teaching all students unconditionally, regardless of the circumstances, we necessarily have high expectations for them. Providing learning experiences that allow students to be successful will increase their sense of **self-efficacy**, or the belief that they can achieve. High expectations can foster this sense of competency. Unlike sometimes empty techniques that focus on building self-efficacy with words but are devoid of actual accomplishments, the concept of self-efficacy must be based on accomplishments. As students master a concept or skill, we must encourage them to attempt even more difficult tasks. In this way, our high expectations for students lead to their own high expectations for themselves.

Relationships With Families

Involving families in the life of the school benefits the educational process in many ways. Parents are a child's first teachers. During the critically important years between birth and age 5, parents (and their choice of child-care providers) have a great impact on children. In addition, for the rest of childhood and adolescence, parental modeling and attitudes influence students' success in school. Throughout this section, the words *parents* and *families* are used interchangeably to acknowledge the multiple ways people come together in a home.

Multiple studies show that parental and family involvement increases academic achievement and attendance rates and leads to more positive attitudes and behavior of students in the classroom. That's a formula for success! Although all students benefit from parental involvement, studies show that low-income and culturally diverse students are particularly more likely to succeed when family members communicate with, and are active in, the life of the school.

INVOLVING FAMILIES. Family involvement can take many forms, from consistently encouraging students to complete homework, to attending parent–teacher conferences, to volunteering regularly in the school or classroom, or even to serving on a district school board. Providing a schedule of involvement opportunities is useful and may include:

- Parent volunteer opportunities that include materials preparation and working with students who may need extra help
- Parent–student–teacher events, such as family math night and career exploration workshops
- Student performances, such as chorus and band concerts, sports events, and club activities

Through participation, parents show support for both students and teachers. In turn, they gain a sense of connection with the education of their children.

FAMILY COMMUNICATION. Events such as Back-to-School Night, Open House, and parent conferences provide opportunities for teachers to talk about their curriculum, classrooms, and students. New teachers should ask experienced teachers about the format and general procedures for these events.

In addition to schoolwide and regularly scheduled forms of communication, there are many other ways teachers can invite families to participate in their students' education, including:

1. ***Welcome Letter.*** Sending a letter to families at the beginning of the school year is a good way for you to introduce yourself, inform parents about policies and procedures that are specific to your class, tell parents about volunteer opportunities, and let parents know how and when to reach you.
2. ***Classroom Newsletter.*** Weekly or monthly newsletters sent home with students can keep parents informed and give them ideas for how to encourage students to complete school assignments and homework. Make sure the written communication you send home is error free.
3. ***Phone Calls.*** Not all phone calls home signal trouble at school. Using the telephone to communicate good news is powerful. Imagine a parent hearing, "Good afternoon, Mrs. Lawson. This is Annie Morgan, Brandon's math teacher. I just wanted to tell you that Brandon took the lead today in his group's problem-solving activity. I

was so proud of how he worked with the other students to come up with a unique solution!" Now imagine the smile that spreads across Mrs. Lawson's face, especially if Brandon is often the object of not-so-positive school communication. The teacher has taken an important step toward gaining Mrs. Lawson as a partner in Brandon's education and support should she need assistance in the future to help correct an undesirable trait Brandon might demonstrate. She has also encouraged Brandon to continue his positive behavior.

Some phone calls home may be for reasons that include a negative change in a student's achievement or attitude, unacceptable behavior, and incomplete or missing work. These calls need to be handled professionally. If possible, it's best to have negative discussions in person so there can be face-to-face dialogue, but the initial call may be an invitation for such a meeting. Always prepare for phone calls, positive or negative, beforehand.

4. ***Electronic Communication.*** Parent and teacher communication via email has become the norm. It can be done day or night, without disturbing the receiving party. When using email, don't be sloppy. Use a salutation, as well as uppercase and lowercase letters. Do not use faddish abbreviations. The guidelines for both written and telephone communication apply to email communication as well.
5. ***Classroom web page.*** Most schools provide space for individual teacher or classroom web pages. These are often used for assignments and reminders. Be creative, but most of all, be up-to-date. When web pages contain beginning-of-the-year greetings in November, it gives parents and others a very negative impression.

Video Example 12.1 includes a couple of important pieces of advice regarding teacher relationships with families from a sixth-grade language arts teacher in a Title I school.

FAMILY–STUDENT–TEACHER CONFERENCES. For many beginning teachers, as well as a fair share of experienced ones, conference time is anticipated with dread. Rather than viewing conferences as responsibilities to be endured, approach them as opportunities to cultivate a partnership with families for the sake of the students.

One of the most helpful ways for new teachers to become comfortable with family–student–teacher conferences is to sit in when experienced teachers are talking with families and students. Ask teachers you admire if it would be possible for you to be a silent observer. You will pick up phrases, mannerisms, and strategies that will help guide your own conferences.

Some conferences include only adults; others include students. Many teachers are finding great benefits in student-led conferences, with students talking directly to family members and teachers merely onlookers.

FAMILY BARRIERS TO INVOLVEMENT. Some barriers to family involvement result from the attitudes and actions of parents and families, and some from the attitudes and actions of teachers. Three barriers seem prevalent among parents and families who hesitate to become involved.

Socioeconomic Barriers. Regardless of socioeconomic status, culture, language, or educational background, there are many legitimate barriers to family involvement, including:

- Families in low-income settings may be more mobile than other families. Communication sent through the mail may not reach these families. Families may have a phone one week, but not the next. Many low-income homes do not have access to the Internet, so e-mail communication is not an option.
- Transportation may present a challenge for low-income families. Some families depend entirely on public transportation, making getting to and from their students' schools very difficult.
- Finding or paying for child care can be difficult as well, so younger siblings may need to accompany parents and guardians to school functions.
- Work can be a barrier to family involvement at any socioeconomic level. Often in low-SES families, both parents or guardians work two or three jobs, and their time is extremely limited. At the other end of the socioeconomic spectrum, parents or guardians who are highly paid professionals may also have severe limitations on their time. In both cases, showing up at school between 8:00 am and 4:00 pm may be virtually impossible.

Cultural and Language Barriers. Children do not choose the culture in which they are born. Their families may value education, or they may consider formal education unnecessary beyond the stage of being able to read and write at survival levels.

The language of a student's family may be a major barrier to involvement. The families of three of our focus students speak little English in their homes. Hector, our fourth-grade student at Rees Elementary, is the only one in his family who speaks fluent English. He is the link between his family and the school. At Roosevelt High School, Hugo speaks very little English himself, and his parents speak even less. Khammany, also at Roosevelt High School, is fluent in English, but her mother speaks no English at all. Engaging these parents in the life of the school is difficult. Video Example 12.2: Khammany's Mom's Interview illustrates communication difficulties likely when parents have limited English skills.

Video Example 12.2: Khammany's Mom's Interview

Educational Background Barriers. If parents or guardians were not successful in school, they are unlikely to be enthusiastic about stepping through the doors of their children's schools. If they quit school in sixth or eighth grade, for example, or if they never graduated from high school, they may be intimidated and hesitant to talk with teachers, believing that they themselves are incapable of helping students with anything academic.

Table 12.1 consists of strategies for teachers and schools as they work toward increasing family involvement.

Table 12.1 Strategies to overcome barriers to family involvement

Barrier	Strategy
Frequent address changes	Organize student families into small groups, being careful to include a family that is rooted in the community. Devise ways to help these small groups stay in touch, with the more settled family taking the lead in communicating with the teacher when families move.
Disconnected phones	Using the group idea just described, establish a phone tree as a source of class information. In this way teachers learn about phone problems, perhaps before there is a need to call the family on a more urgent matter.
Lack of transportation	Make school events compatible with public transportation schedules. Have a teacher ride along on a route where many of the students live to serve as a welcoming guide to and from the event.
Time barriers	Schedule family–student–teacher conferences at times that accommodate more parents and guardians. Split sessions could be 3:00–5:00 pm and 7:00–9:00 p.m. Provide ways for working parents to volunteer time, perhaps with weekend and evening projects that also involve students.
Child-care dilemmas	Provide child care onsite during school events and planned conference times. High school classes and organizations can be responsible for taking care of children while parents and guardians involve themselves in the life of the school.
Cultural differences	Acknowledge different perspectives and incorporate activities, artwork, and celebrations that draw families into the life of the school.
Language barriers	Find people who will serve as interpreters at events and conferences. Advertise the presence of interpreters to let families know they will be able to communicate with teachers. Translate newsletters and forms into the languages spoken and read at home.
Limited education	Warm, friendly teachers who use jargon-free language in their communications help encourage family involvement. Providing after-school homework help can ease family guilt over not knowing how to help their children with assignments.

TEACHER BARRIERS TO FAMILY INVOLVEMENT. Teacher-generated barriers to family involvement are less legitimate than family-generated barriers. A teacher's failure to invite family involvement may stem from timidity, lack of conviction that family involvement matters, or lack of effort.

Timidity. Some teachers become nervous when they anticipate speaking to, or with, parents or guardians. You may hear them say, "I can be up in front of my sophomores all day long, but bring in their parents, and I freeze." A skilled communicator with students can become a skilled communicator with adults. Experience makes it easier.

Some teachers are uncomfortable having other adults watching and listening to them. They might worry about facing questions and possible criticism. They may find the presence of parents and guardians in their classrooms inhibiting and intimidating. This form of timidity can be overcome by planning excellent learning experiences for the classroom and being at your best every day with the attitude that families are your partners. The more hands and minds the better when it comes to increasing student learning.

Not Believing Families Matter. Some teachers appear to be unconvinced that family involvement matters. They do not actively reach out to the parents and guardians of their students to seek their involvement. Traci Peters is not one of them. She believes strongly in the value of parent and guardian involvement, as expressed in *Teaching in Focus*.

Teaching in Focus

Traci Peters, Grade 7 Math, Cario Middle School, South Carolina. *In her own words. . . .*

Sara Davis Powell

When parents send you their children, they are sending you the best ones they have. They're not keeping their brighter, better behaved children at home. They are sending you their "babies," even in middle school. In an instant, teachers become the ones who spend more time each day with these children than the parents. Most parents want to be informed and involved, and they want what is best for their child. Parents and teachers are on the same side—the student's side. As teachers, we need to reach out. There are many benefits to parental involvement for students, teachers, and the parents themselves.

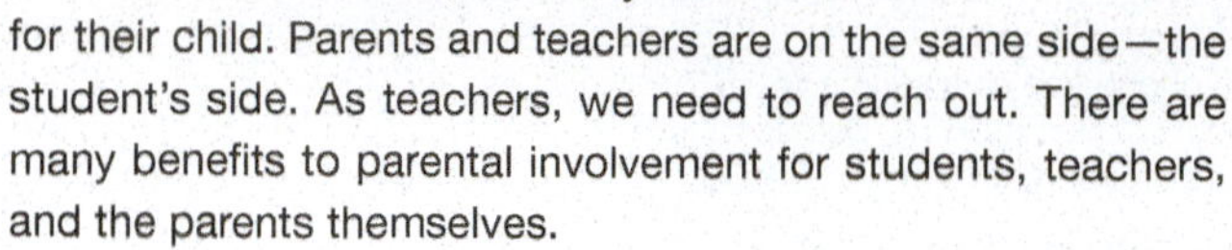

There are many ways to involve parents, from simple occasional email communication and a classroom newsletter, to more complex strategies such as home visits and family math nights. What matters is that we establish positive connections between the classroom and the homes of students. If you think of it as a give-and-take relationship, you may find very practical benefits to parental involvement. They can simplify some of your tasks by doing things such as copying and preparing materials, shopping for "fun with food" day, and displaying student work in the classroom or in the halls. They will enjoy their involvement and support your efforts in the classroom!

Lack of Effort. The most disturbing teacher barrier to family involvement in schools and classrooms is lack of effort. There is no legitimate reason not to make that call, write that note, or invite parents and guardians into the classroom. If you are convinced that family involvement matters and that they are your allies in the education of students, you will draw parents and guardians into—rather than excluding or even alienating them from—the educational process. Not only is this good for children and adolescents, it's also very rewarding, according to teacher Brenda Beyal in *Teaching in Focus.*

Teaching in Focus

Brenda Beyal, Grades 3–5 Multiage Classroom, Rees Elementary School, Utah. *In her own words. . . .*

Sara Davis Powell

Tucked away in a drawer I have a note that was given to me by a parent over 10 years ago. I take it out on occasion when I am having a particularly hard time with a school situation, or when I'm feeling ineffective. I read the salutation, "Dear Respected Madam." This is one of the most gracious openings to a note that I have ever received. The note is from parents who had just emigrated from India. They had asked for help with a small matter, and I was able to help solve a dilemma for them.

The words still send a surge of renewal and recommitment within me for my chosen profession—teaching. Families and parents can make emotional deposits into our teaching lives, and then some can make deep withdrawals. As a teacher, I hold on to the unintentional deposits that parents make, and, with their help, I let the withdrawals slip away from my teaching so they will not keep me from making powerful teaching and learning connections.

Whatever the barriers to parental involvement, teachers need to break them down and cultivate an invitational attitude. Parents are part of the larger community. When we engage families as active participants in the life of the school, we are reaching out to the community.

Relationships With the Community

Education is a public enterprise. Pick up a newspaper and you will find something in it that features or refers to schools and teachers. The community reads and hears about schools, forming impressions along the way. Teachers, and those who work in and with schools, are acutely aware of how public their endeavors are. For most people in a community, the sum total of their knowledge about schools is what they know from the media and what they hear from their personal acquaintances about teachers, students, and classrooms. For this reason, teachers have the responsibility to be public relations agents for schools. We must put our best professional selves forward to represent education—in community groups, in places of worship, in social gatherings, in the grocery store—everywhere we go.

The community can provide support, resources, and services that are valuable lifelines for students and their families. Individuals can volunteer their time, give money and materials, and share their expertise as student mentors and guest speakers. Corporations can fund programs and events, offer employees release time to volunteer in schools, and provide political support for needed policy changes. Teachers should know what is available and, along with administrators and counselors, make sure families are aware of how to access community services such as health clinics, family counseling, and tutoring. When school, families, and the community work together, students receive optimum benefits, as illustrated in Figure 12.2.

Professional Relationships With Colleagues

"One incontrovertible finding emerges from my career spent working in and around schools: The nature of relationships among the adults within a school has a greater influence on the character and quality of that school and on student accomplishment than anything else" (Barth, 2006, p. 9). This bold statement was made by Roland Barth, highly respected former teacher and principal and founding director of the Principals' Center at Harvard University. He continues by saying, "In short, the relationships among the educators in a school define all relationships within the school's culture" (p. 9). Is it possible that as a teacher, your relationship with another teacher down the hall affects these other relationships? Yes, according to Barth, who tells us we must find a way to confront this "elephant in the room": the relationships that loom so large within the school but are seldom addressed. The four basic relationships among teachers as defined by Barth are *parallel play*, *adversarial relationships*, *congenial relationships*, and *collegiality*.

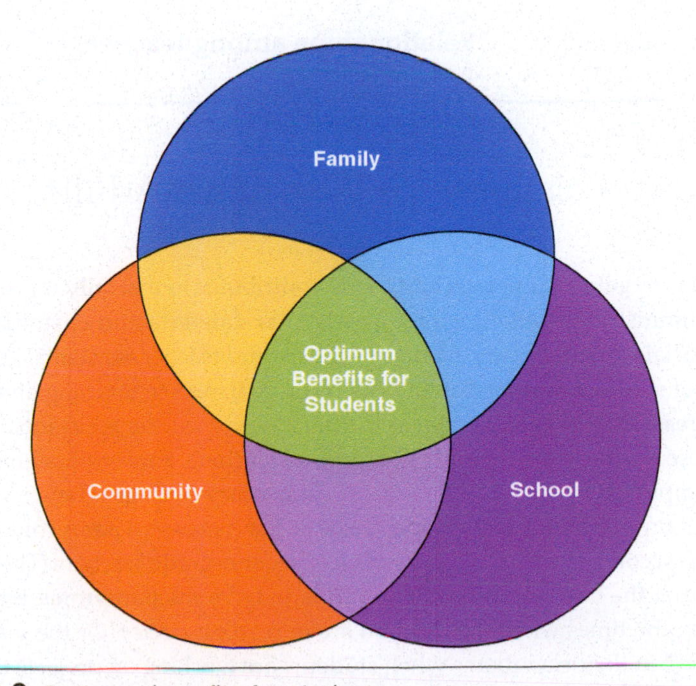

Figure 12.2 Optimum benefits for students

PARALLEL PLAY. When children sit on the floor just inches from one another, so absorbed in their own toys that they never acknowledge each other's presence or offer to share or play together in any way, we say they are engaged in parallel play. This behavior is considered normal development for 1- and 2-year-olds. Sadly, a sort of *teacher* parallel play is the norm in many schools. Too often teachers close their doors, hoard their lessons and materials, and infrequently share their tools of the trade—their knowledge of curricula and repertoire of instructional strategies. This isolating approach robs teachers of potential individual and collective growth.

ADVERSARIAL RELATIONSHIPS. Barth tells us that one reason so many teachers engage in a sort of parallel play is that they are attempting to avoid adversarial relationships, or those relationships characterized by blatant criticism, talking behind the backs of others, and unwarranted and destructive competition. This amounts to unprofessional behavior.

CONGENIAL RELATIONSHIPS. You will no doubt develop congenial relationships with many of your colleagues. You will enjoy one another's company. People of different ages, personality types, interests, cultures, and races are teachers. You will find some with whom you have much in common and others very different from yourself. Developing congenial relationships makes school more fun. Students can sense when their teachers enjoy the people around them. That's being a role model in one of the most practical ways.

COLLEGIALITY. Relationships with other teachers that promote growth through sharing of professional expertise are **collegial relationships**. Barth (2006) quotes famous baseball manager Casey Stengel: "Getting good players is easy. Getting 'em to play together is the hard part" (p. 11). There are lots of "good players," or competent teachers, in schools. Developing collegiality means getting teachers to "play" together. When Barth visits schools and looks for signs of collegial relationships, he looks for three components:

1. Educators talking with one another about practice and sharing craft knowledge
2. Educators observing one another while they are engaged in practice
3. Educators rooting for one another's success

Application Exercise 12.2: Relationships among teachers

Professional Relationships With Other Adults in the School

It's a good idea to get to know each adult who contributes to the daily work in schools, including administrators, administrative assistants, cafeteria and custodial workers, counselors, social workers, nurses, media specialists, and teacher assistants. They all have the interests of students as priorities and can be our partners in teaching and learning.

Paraprofessionals are also known as teacher aides or teacher assistants. The people who hold these positions are typically not certified teachers. Paraprofessionals are most commonly employed in early childhood and elementary settings. They may be in one classroom full time or may rotate among teachers. For instance, a paraprofessional may be assigned to second grade in a school with five second-grade teachers. These teachers may decide that the best use of another adult is to have the paraprofessional join the classes during the times when the children are in reading circles. Or the teachers may want extra help in their classrooms when students are working on projects that require the use of multiple materials.

Some schools are fortunate to have paraprofessionals who have worked for 20 or 30 years in schools. They may know the community well and be valuable assets. If you are fortunate enough to have a teacher assistant in your classroom, treat him or her with respect. You have professional knowledge that may exceed that of a paraprofessional in some ways, but chances are your assistant has a lot of experience with students and families. Learn from them even as you direct their participation with the students in your classroom.

Point of Reflection 12.2

Do you believe what a teacher does in the classroom can overcome obstacles to learning that students face outside the classroom, such as poverty, lack of family involvement, and a background deficient in content and skills? Why or why not?

Check Your Understanding 12.2

12.3 What Are Some Realities of Teaching?

12.3 Identify some realities of teaching.

Teaching is complex. As with any endeavor that's multifaceted, being a teacher has its wonderful aspects and rewards layered on top of, and in between, the hard realities that make the profession challenging. But the benefits and satisfaction of effective teaching are more than just layers—more importantly, they are *foundational* when we understand that what we do day-to-day makes our country stronger and our way of life richer, and gives opportunities to children and adolescents that only education can provide. Remember this as you read about challenges that will likely be part of your reality as a teacher.

Bureaucratic Overload

It takes administrators and district personnel to make schools function. We need them to do all the things they do to keep schools open and functioning and to keep us in our classrooms, teaching. However, the paperwork and recording responsibilities in response to administrative demands can seem overwhelming at times. Teachers must keep up with periodic school/district/state testing and all it involves, including test preparation and monitoring as well as interpreting and using results. Increasing numbers of students with special needs require not only additional planning but also documentation.

Wise administrators will keep meetings to a minimum and make the ones that are unavoidable, meaningful and useful. However, with each new initiative comes the need for explanations and training, follow-up, and record keeping. Meeting fatigue is a common teacher ailment and the cure seems to elude us. Be patient and remember that when teachers gather, there's always something to learn from each other.

When Teacher Preparation Doesn't Match Reality

It's very likely that you will see and hear things in schools that are contrary to what you are learning in teacher preparation. In real classrooms, the variables are many and teachers, as human beings, do not always approach responsibilities and opportunities in the best possible ways, or even in ways that seem acceptable. One of the purposes of field experiences is to let you observe reality, reflect on what you see, and formulate possible solutions to the dilemmas that you witness.

Perhaps you will see what you consider poor instruction. You will probably hear a teacher or two scream at children or humiliate a child in front of the class. It is difficult to watch this type of behavior and yet say nothing. Remember: You are the guest. It is not your place to correct a teacher or act indignant in the face of teacher behavior you view as inappropriate. Also realize that you do not know the whole picture. You are seeing a snapshot. The time to express your dismay, or even outrage, is in your college class or student teaching seminar with an instructor and classmates. We learn a great deal from observing incorrect methods and behavior. Learning what *not* to do by seeing its actual or potential damage is powerful.

Many new teachers enter the classroom full of ideas and enthusiasm for all they have learned in teacher preparation. The problems begin when new teachers find it difficult to use the strategies they know are research-based and, in theory, beneficial to teaching and learning. The reasons for this dilemma are complicated and include occasional low levels of administrative support, class size that limits the kind of engagement necessary, lack of resources and materials, and extreme emphasis on test preparation. Professional teachers work toward balance between doing the things they must do and finding ways to optimize student learning.

Classroom Management

It is valuable to understand the theories of structuring and maintaining a classroom that result in optimal student behavior. Much has been written on the topic. However, when new teachers are asked about the most trying aspects of teaching, classroom management inevitably surfaces on the list.

Most teachers agree that the only way to become comfortable with what theories tell us, or experienced teachers advise, is to actually be in a classroom—on-the-job learning. This means your first couple of years may be frustrating as you get your classroom "sea legs." Most of the students will behave reasonably and respond to reminders of the correct things to do. However, you will likely encounter students who don't behave appropriately, who try your patience and push you to *react* to them rather than calmly responding. You aren't alone. This happens at times to every teacher. The better we know our students, the more prepared we can be to respond to discipline issues. Stay cool, stay focused, and stay consistent. Don't hesitate to ask for advice and help.

Changing Demographics

In numerous places in this text we've explored the changing demographics of the United States. Even though multicultural opportunities make us stronger and enrich our classrooms, the challenges are undeniable. This is reality.

Although children and adolescents from many ethnicities and cultures are coming to the United States, the predominant minority ethnicity is Hispanic. In 1960, only 3.5% of the U.S. population was of Hispanic ethnicity; in 2014 the percent was 17.7, accounting for over 52 million people. The rate of emigration of people of Hispanic ethnicity to the United States, however, has consistently slowed since 2007 (Pew Research Center, 2016a). Many of these new U.S. residents are living in states that previously had very little Hispanic presence, such as Georgia, South Dakota, Mississippi, Wisconsin, Pennsylvania, Tennessee, Virginia, and North Carolina. More Hispanic immigrants are also moving to rural areas and small towns. In 2016, the fastest-growing population of Hispanic immigrants was found in North Dakota (Pew Research Center, 2016b).

Large cities and suburban areas are making progress, although in some places the strides are minimal, to help Hispanic children and adolescents achieve academic goals by providing English-language learning opportunities through bilingual classes, English as a second language programs, and structured English immersion. In many rural areas and small towns, these programs are problematic due to limited teaching staffs and funding. Communication with families becomes particularly difficult when there are few bilingual teachers and translators.

Involving families in the education of their children is an important teacher responsibility. Hispanic parents are valuable resources for teaching and learning. "The Hispanic family structure epitomizes the values normally associated with high academic performance . . . clear boundaries and rules, and the sort of open communication that allows parents to inquire about school" (Cattanach, 2013, p. 23). Often, however, the level of engagement with which Hispanic parents are comfortable consists of making sure students are in school, with homework at least attempted. Families need encouragement to increase engagement with the school and the classroom to help their children fulfill their academic potential. As schools adjust to the demographic shift that's frequently accompanied by low socioeconomic status, they are faced with not only teaching the students but the families as well.

Undocumented students graduate from high school each year. Many states have recently declared that these same adolescents may attend public colleges at in-state tuition rates. Only six states have passed laws stating that undocumented adolescents may not receive in-state tuition—Alabama, Arizona, Georgia, Indiana, Missouri, and South Carolina (National Conference of State Legislatures, 2015).

A generation of teachers in U.S. classrooms never faced substantial language and culture differences. They are now trying to adjust. Your classroom will likely be very diverse and your career will begin with challenges inherent in multilingual, multicultural students.

Budget Issues

Rarely is there enough money to fund what needs to be done to facilitate the learning results we want to see. In particular, states and school districts have struggled with budget issues since the economic downturn of 2008. Some districts have announced each April that teachers and teacher assistants will be laid off, often only to hire them back in August when funds somehow appear. The threat of losing a job is stressful, and when it happens year after year, it is definitely counterproductive. The actual reductions in force are devastating not only to the individuals who lose their jobs but also to those who remain and are forced to do more with larger numbers of children for the same or less compensation. Classes get bigger, resources become scarce, and morale plummets. This is a sad reality.

Some states and districts are choosing to deal with the budget crisis by **furloughing**. This is when teachers or assistants are asked not to work for a certain number of days and they lose their salary for those days Not giving step raises is another way districts save money. There are teachers who have not received a raise in 4 or more years. Some districts are closing schools or consolidating smaller schools to save operating budget funds. Many districts have dismissed teacher assistants and other support personnel who help teachers do their job of teaching students. This is devastating news for early childhood teachers.

Public Education Under Attack

Public education is perceived by many as an endangered species. Political events beginning in 2016 and subsequent budget cuts and emphasis on school choice have generated increased public awareness, as well a fair amount of public outrage.

Public schools are venerable institutions of democracy in the United States. The vast majority of the over 55,000,000 students in school every day are in public school classrooms. As Thomas Jefferson famously expressed, our democracy depends on an educated citizenry. Ways of providing that education are sometimes contentious.

School choice, whether part of public options or private venues, will likely never be fairly distributed to children and adolescents who live in low socioeconomic settings. Choice requires information and transportation, two components often in short supply in many homes across the country. Providing school choice in and of itself is a noble endeavor. But until options are available to all children and adolescents through both information and transportation, most will not have choices.

When funding is diverted from public schools that serve low-income families to schools that do not serve this population, and information and transportation are not made available to all students, the *have-nots* will continue to attend neighborhood schools that many *haves* would not attend willingly. These underresourced schools are labeled as failing and the downward spiral continues.

Evaluating schools is necessary. However, publishing letter grades that often reflect raw data and rankings rather than information on levels of improvement further exacerbates the issue. Public perception and confidence are eroded and those who have information and transportation opt for education choices.

This reality of purposeful or indirect attacks on public education is complicated. The attacks didn't start yesterday, and chances are they won't be alleviated any time soon. As a teacher candidate, please understand that there's nothing black or white about this issue. There are not necessarily villains, but there can certainly be heroes. Common sense, a broad and deep view of what's best for the United States and those who inhabit our country, and the will to do our best for all children and adolescents are imperative.

Point of Reflection 12.3

Which reality of teaching discussed in this chapter concerns you most? Why?

Check Your Understanding 12.3

12.4 What Is My Role as a Professional in Education Reform?

12.4 Summarize my role as a professional in education reform.

To reform is to change, to make different, or to attempt to improve. The word **reform** in education usually involves funding allocations, school choice, new instructional programs, and basically the promotion of one ideology or another. People who propose reform in K–12 education do so with the goal of improving student learning. To be sure, reform initiatives change the way some aspects of schools operate, either permanently or for a period of time until the particular ideology falls out of favor. There have been many reform efforts in the last few decades and there will be many more in the future. Some will advance student learning and others will not. Fragmented efforts, without a view the big picture of teaching and learning, will fail.

So how do professional teachers respond to calls for reform? Public schools continue to be works in progress. Reform of one sort or another will always be with us. Professional teachers know this. They also care deeply about students and the teaching profession and support ideas and efforts intended to increase learning. If a particular reform doesn't appear to make sense for the students they know well, they speak up concerning their objections, they work cooperatively with others even as they try to influence the course of events, and they continually keep the question "And how are the children?" at the forefront of all discussions. Being an informed professional is a position from which you can positively impact reform.

The following reform efforts are briefly and simply described. This is just a sampling. Each is actually quite complex and teacher professionalism propels us to learn more about the issues.

Reform of Teacher Evaluation

There are both renewed interest in teacher evaluation and growing sentiment that some evaluation systems are not working. There are two distinct purposes of teacher evaluation: *measuring* teachers and *developing* teachers. Although some models attempt to do both, their attempts are, or are perceived to be, one-sided in purpose. Strictly measuring teacher effectiveness allows for decisions concerning rehiring or dismissing and decisions about whether to promote. An interesting adage says, "You can't fatten a cow by weighing it." By the same token, you can't develop more effective teachers simply by measuring them.

What's the point of measuring a teacher's effectiveness if there's no component for helping that teacher improve? If dismissal is the goal, then simply measuring effectiveness may have an end result that's good for students. But if teachers are going to remain in the classroom as almost all do after being evaluated, then *developing* teachers needs as much attention as *measuring* them. Most teacher evaluation models attempt to incorporate balance through observing teachers in their classrooms using structured instruments and rubrics and examining test scores of their students, or incorporating value-added concepts.

VALUE-ADDED TEACHER EVALUATION. When student test scores are used to evaluate teacher effectiveness, it is referred to as **value-added teacher evaluation**. This simply means that teachers either have helped students learn more as measured by test scores (value added), or they haven't. Isn't this what effective teaching is all about? Of course!

So why is this premise—that students of effective teachers will improve their standardized test scores—controversial? Let's explore some "big picture" issues associated with value-added teacher evaluation. Many educators who seriously consider the value-added concept of teacher effectiveness seem to agree on at least four flaws:

1. Experience indicates that a teacher's success from year to year as measured by standardized test scores varies, often by quite a bit.
2. Test scores vary by students assigned to teachers. For instance, teachers with large numbers of English-language learners and students with special needs typically have slower test score gains than teachers with other students. Attempts to control for these differences are inadequate.
3. The impact of an individual teacher is tempered by forces outside the teacher's control. Neighborhoods, homes, societal pressures, and other factors influence learning.
4. Not all teachers have students subjected to standardized testing. This includes most primary grade teachers and related arts teachers whose subjects are not tested.

TEACHER OBSERVATION. Just as there are issues with using value-added measures for teacher evaluation, the credibility of observations of teachers as they work depends on many factors, including the perspective and training of the observer, the frequency and timing of the observations, the preconceived notions of the observer concerning the teacher, and more. These are important variables for teachers and observers. If two teachers teach the same subject(s) and their students are from the same demographics, having different observers is often seen as subjective.

In large environments, it's inevitable that one observer will not conduct all the observations. A straightforward rubric helps, and so does a planned conference following the observation to discuss the rubric and the lesson observed. This process, along with recommendations for improvement and the time and resources to move forward, may lead to valuable professional development.

The good news is that recent research reveals that effective evaluation can enhance the effectiveness of the teachers evaluated. Feedback from evaluations can spark self-reflection and provide a focus to professional development (Ritter and Barnett, 2016). Obviously, much work is needed to create teacher evaluation models that accomplish both purposes of evaluation, measurement and development, and result in stronger, more effective teachers.

TEACHER PROFESSIONALISM REGARDING EVALUATION. Knowing that someone is watching us teach, and taking notes on what we appear to do right and wrong, can be quite nerve-wracking. Like it or not, you will be evaluated. Philosophically, we know it's necessary and valuable, but in practice we often dread it. Some of the dread goes away when the evaluator knows what effective instruction looks like and has the ability to give feedback that is specific and thought provoking. Remember: When we are evaluated, we have the opportunity to grow, to become better teachers. That's the professional attitude toward evaluation. We may still not like it, but at least we understand the purpose and are assured we will learn from the experience.

Performance-Based Pay

Performance-based pay, a hot topic in education, involves paying teachers more when they produce whatever results are designated as desirable. The issue elicits many opinions from many people. But, by most accounts, we aren't much closer to figuring out how to judge teacher performance accurately and fairly, and how to reward it, today, than we were in 2000, or 1960. Is it what we observe teachers doing that counts? Are extra duties worth extra pay? Should teachers in hard-to-staff schools be paid more? Do high school science and math teachers, or special education teachers, deserve more money than fifth-grade teachers? Or is the bottom line how teachers affect student test scores?

Performance-based pay for teachers is not a new concept. Every 20 years or so the idea surfaces, some districts and states try it, flaws in the system emerge—and the idea is once again abandoned. But performance-based pay makes sense, doesn't it? Simply put, the teachers who do the best jobs should be paid the most. From a business-model perspective, where production may be relatively easy to measure, performance-based pay may be incentive enough to see sustained positive results. In education, if performance-based pay increases were given for longer working hours or more graduate degrees, measurement would be easy. However, if sustained positive results are seen in student learning, the questions remain: "How do we quantify student learning?" and "Which parts of student learning, by whatever measure we use to judge it, are directly attributable to the teacher who has had the students in class for 9 months?" Consider these scenarios:

- If a teacher's fourth-grade students show marked improvement in math, who's to say that the foundation for the increased learning wasn't built in third grade and simply all came together in fourth grade?
- If tenth-graders demonstrate improved writing skills, is it due at least in part to the ninth-grade teacher's concentration on mechanics that the tenth-grade teacher used in the process of teaching about idea development? Should the tenth-grade teacher be rewarded but not the ninth-grade teacher?

Can you see how complex the issue of performance-based pay becomes?

COMMON SALARY MODEL. The traditional way to pay teachers is on an established scale that uses years of services and education level as the only variables. Teachers qualify for steps that determine salary. For instance, if you begin teaching with a bachelor's degree, you will be on the bottom of the scale. Each year you will receive a step raise based on years of service. If you receive a graduate degree, you will receive a raise and be on a different path than those with bachelor's degrees. You will continue to receive longevity raises, but your pay will be higher than teachers without graduate degrees.

Some teacher salaries are enhanced because of extra duties assumed such as coaching, sponsoring a student organization, working on a school-based project, or mentoring new teachers. For some teachers, the only feasible way of making more money is to become an administrator. This is very unfortunate because we lose excellent classroom teachers to positions not directly involved in classroom and student interactions. But it's a fact of life in K–12 public education.

CONTROVERSY OVER PERFORMANCE-BASED PAY. Performance-based pay will continue to be debated and attempted as part of ongoing efforts of educational reform. Some states are developing aggressive plans for performance pay. Note that many initiatives are put in place not by educators but rather by legislators. Table 12.2 lists some of the beliefs of advocates and critics of performance pay based on measures of student learning.

Table 12.2 Advocates and critics of performance pay based on student learning

Advocates' Beliefs about Performance-Based Pay	Critics' Beliefs about Performance-Based Pay
Can be a catalyst for change	Amounts to tweaking, rather than fixing, the problem of uneven or lagging achievement
Increases student learning	Penalizes teachers who do not directly teach the tested subjects
Motivates teachers who aren't trying hard enough	Encourages teaching to the test, thereby narrowing the curriculum
Makes teaching more competitive and increases effectiveness	Fails to instill systemic responsibility for increasing student learning
Is a fair way to differentiate among varying levels of teacher effectiveness	Perpetuates measuring success by test scores alone

TEACHER PROFESSIONALISM AND PERFORMANCE-BASED PAY. Because pay based on performance has been attempted several times over the past 5 or 6 decades, almost always unsuccessfully, there may be considerable pessimism among veteran teachers who have seen plans come and go. Still, professionals remain optimistic that ways will be found to judge their competency, at least in part, on the degree of learning experienced by their students. They know, however, that the current method of measuring student learning solely by standardized test scores does not present the whole picture of their teaching effectiveness. Even so, professionals encourage exploration in education that may positively impact teaching and learning.

The Opinion Page features Dr. Tom Watkins, former Michigan state superintendent of schools. He emphasizes that all decisions about school reform should be based on how teaching and learning are affected.

State Reform Efforts

Whole states may be involved in sweeping changes, all with the purpose of reforming schools to increase student learning. The 2012 Louisiana reform initiative propelled by Governor Bobby Jindal is an example. One of the most notable changes was making vouchers available to all students in the state, thus encouraging parents to exercise

THE OPINION PAGE

This Opinion Editorial appeared in the Kalamazoo Gazette, *Michigan, on December 30, 2012.*

Future of State, Nation Inextricably Linked to Quality of Our Teachers

by Tom Watkins

Tom Watkins served as Michigan's state superintendent of schools from 2001 to 2005. He is an advocate for public education and sensible school reforms, and a 2010 Upton Sinclair Award winner from Ednews.org. He is a U.S./China business and educational consultant.

Business owners know you must engage your employees in the change process. Training our adults to be competitive on the world stage and educating more of our children to be able to collaborate and compete globally is the key to the country's future prosperity.

Education holds the key to our collective futures. The city, state, and nation that creates an effective system of learning will thrive. Our goal should be to make Michigan and America the brain bank of the world where everyone wants to come for deposits and withdrawals.

Yet, rather than seeking ways to develop a shared vision and common agenda to make this happen, political and ideological battles sharpen and continue to beat down the very people we need to build up—our teachers.

Teachers are key.

The voice of the classroom teacher must be heard, especially around issues of classroom discipline, instructional design, and delivery above the reform chatter. Our public schools are the true Statue of Liberty in this great country of ours—taking the tired, hungry, poor kids who speak English as a second language, and children with disabilities to give them hope and opportunity. Our great teachers are the torches lighting the way for us all.

Rhetoric from the state and our nation's capital has never educated a single child. It is our teachers who know their subject matter, who have a passion for teaching and learning, and who are provided the support and tools from administration, that we must invest our resources and energy moving forward. As Michigan's state superintendent of schools from 2001 to 2005, I had a simple measuring stick against which ALL decisions made by the Department of Education and state Board of Education were judged: "Show me how this helps our teachers teach and our children learn."

We need to engage teachers in the process of reform to attract and retain the very best in the classroom. The state Board of Education, in an overt effort to engage teachers, invited the annually selected Michigan Teacher of the Year to have a seat, but more importantly, a voice at the state board table. The teachers' voice is always the last heard prior to policy being enacted.

So as the New Year rings in, rather than hammering our teachers down, let's snap that symbolic hammer in half and turn it instead into a ladder that helps lift up our schools, teachers, and most importantly, our children. Do our schools and teachers need to constantly evolve, embrace change and adapt to a disruptive world where ideas and jobs can and do move around the globe effortlessly? Of course. Yet, without the ability to tap the energy, talents, skills, and passions of these great educators that are touching our collective futures every day, we are missing a major ingredient necessary to soar in the 21st century knowledge economy.

Research and common sense reinforce that quality teachers matter. In the education enterprise, we must always remember that teachers have the lead role (along with parents and students). The teacher is Diana Ross and the rest within the school building are singing "doo-opp." We need to actively seek ways to engage teachers and make them a key member of any education reform effort.

If you can read this, thank a teacher!

But if you are a policy-maker (governor, legislator, school board member, superintendent, principal), consider re-evaluating how you can harness the talents of the master-link in the learning process—our great teachers.

The future of our state and nation is inextricably linked to the quality of our teachers.

This *Opinion Page* piece is a thoughtfully and professionally written case for the value of teachers in our schools, states, and nation. Dr. Tom Watkins, a veteran educator, speaks from a foundation of experience and expertise. Write a well-developed paragraph in response to each of the following questions and prompts:

1. Dr. Watkins writes, "Political and ideological battles sharpen and continue to beat down the very people we need to build up—our teachers." Summarize what you have read so far in this chapter that supports his view of the political and ideological battles that affect teaching and learning.
2. We are told that all decisions should be measured by "Show me how this helps our teachers teach and our children learn." Choose one reform initiative discussed in this chapter that you think has the potential to measure up and explain why. Then choose one reform initiative that you predict will not measure up and explain your reasons for choosing it.
3. There are so many analogies and metaphors in this *Opinion Page* that convey meaning. Choose one that particularly speaks to you and discuss why.

choice in their students' schools. Another voucher bill allowed individuals or corporations to fund private-school tuition grants, with the donors then recouping most of the money through a rebate from the state general fund. Governor Jindal's education agenda also included establishing statewide oversight of early childhood education programs that receive public money. These ideas and actions are pro-school choice and pro-charter/private schools.

As you can imagine, many teachers and administrators in public schools were not fans of Governor Jindal's reform efforts. Included in his plan was a partial abolishment of teacher tenure, something that's also happening in other states. His plan linked teacher compensation partially to student performance assessed through state tests. Some aspects of the plan were tested in courts, as well as tried in the court of public opinion. The unrest reported by some in Louisiana is perhaps a lesson in what may result from too much change too fast, and change without educator buy-in. It's too early to know if learning will increase because of the governor's reform agenda.

District Reform Efforts

Almost all school districts initiate reforms and make changes they contend will increase student learning. One that comes along every decade or so is the effort to change the school calendar. After all, we are no longer an agrarian-based society with all hands needed to plant and harvest crops. Most current calendars are still based on this paradigm of 9 months on and 3 months off to work in the fields. Many new calendar paradigms make sense for increasing student learning. For instance, the schedule that would have students in school for 9 weeks and then off for 3 weeks would eliminate what many term the **summer slide**. In the 9-week on/3-week off model, and others with similar patterns, the breaks are frequent, but not long enough to adversely affect knowledge and skill retention. The shorter breaks would provide opportunities for enrichment and remediation as needed.

Three months of no formal learning is especially detrimental to economically disadvantaged students. Some research documents that summer break is anything but a vacation for students in low-income homes who struggle to have enough to eat and safe surroundings. Every summer these same students lose approximately two to three months of reading progress, and their peers in average to above average economic settings actually gain a bit of reading proficiency. Studies show that almost all students regress in math skills (National Summer Learning Association, 2017).

The district level is often where reform initiatives blossom because of local involvement and investment in successful schools. One example of a community joining forces to increase student learning and well-being is happening in La Crosse, Wisconsin. The district consists of 12 elementary schools, 6 middle schools, and 3 high schools. Of these 21 schools, 10 are charter or choice schools, including an elementary school and a middle-level Montessori school, an early childhood center, and two vocational and arts schools. The district serves about 7,000 students with about 600 teachers. The students are 79% white, 10% Asian, 7% black, and 3.5% Hispanic.

The La Crosse collaborative group composed of over 150 community participants and 30 unique agencies and cultural/ethnic groups has conducted three La Crosse Community Summits. The goals of the summit participants include:

- Identify and address, in a systematic way, gaps in support systems for families.
- Identify the barriers to learning in our community.
- Create a deeper level of trust and communication that will enhance the academic growth of the children in our schools.
- Create a comprehensive web of organized learning supports designed to remove barriers to learning.

The University of Wisconsin–La Crosse is assisting with information gathering and analysis. This is an example of a very admirable collaboration that will have a positive impact on teaching and learning (School District of La Crosse, 2017).

TEACHER PROFESSIONALISM IN STATE AND DISTRICT REFORM. Professionalism, when faced with state and district reform efforts, leads teachers to find out as much as possible about initiatives and to explore how they can be part of positive results. After teaching for 10 or more years, many teachers are tempted to respond, "Been there, done that." And, indeed, they may have. Ideas for reform tend to be cyclical. Many are tried with few or no results, only to be repackaged years later and tried again. However, professional teachers look very carefully at proposals for elements that may be right for current circumstances in education or improved to the point of being valid this time around. Professional teachers choose to be involved as much as possible in decision making. They reflect on efforts, avoid negativity, and do what they can to improve teaching and learning.

Standards and Assessment Controversy

Now that the dust has settled resulting from the introduction of the Common Core State Standards (CCSS), fewer states are using the standards, opting instead for more state-generated tests. Many states that initially adopted the CCSS did so in order to receive additional money through the Obama administration Race to the Top initiative. Some state legislatures resented the perceived link of the standards to the federal government, even though Common Core resulted from actions by the National Governors Association rather than the U.S. Department of Education. The original 48 states to adopt CCSS by 2012 had dropped to 37 in 2016 (Education Week, 2017).

Two consortiums developed standardized tests to align with the Common Core State Standards: Partnership for Assessment of Readiness for College and Careers (PARCC) and Smarter Balanced Assessment Consortium (SBAC). In 2016, 21 states used one or the other. The rest of the states used state-specific assessments for at least grades 3–8 (Gewertz, 2017).

TEACHER PROFESSIONALISM CONCERNING STANDARDS AND ASSESSMENT. States and districts use the knowledge and skills specified in the Common Core State Standards or their standards of choice as targets on which to build their grade-by-grade and subject-by-subject curricula. The CCSS do not propose to tell teachers how to teach. Instructional strategies can be chosen or developed by individual teachers or groups of teachers to best promote teaching and learning.

Although choices in instruction are, for the most part, still made by teachers, the choice whether to give or not give standardized assessments is not. Professionalism with regard to standards involves making the standards come alive for our students. We do this by knowing their interests and needs, by developing lessons and experiences that are standards-based and developmentally appropriate, and by then engaging learners in knowledge and skills that build on prior learning. Professionalism related to standardized assessment leads teachers to face the testing in positive ways and to emphasize to students that the exams provide ways for them to show what they know and can do.

Instructional Reforms

At any given time in U.S. schools, dozens of reforms involving instruction are evident. Some may tweak methodology but be touted as revolutionary, and others may truly amount to a paradigm shift. Often the new strategies are abandoned before having a real opportunity to make a difference; others continue to be practiced long after being shown to not have a positive impact on learning.

The **flipped classroom** is an example of a paradigm shift. In a flipped classroom, students watch a video of a teacher giving a lecture or demonstration after school as homework. They then come to class ready to interact with the knowledge and skills. The traditional classroom/homework model is turned upside down, or *flipped.* This instructional hot topic has been around for several years and has gained momentum. The popularity of the model is based on the opportunity to use class time for discussion, activities, collaborative projects, application of knowledge, and practice of skills. Teachers who have committed to flipping their classrooms have generally become outspoken advocates of the model.

Some critics of the flipped classroom say it relies too heavily on lecture—rather than students sitting in a classroom, they instead sit in front of a computer screen. Teachers who like flipping counter this criticism with the benefits of using their time with students to actively engage them in their own learning. Another criticism is that some students don't have reliable access to computer technology apart from school. Jon Bergmann, flipped classroom advocate and technology director in Kenilworth, Illinois, reports beginning flipped classrooms in his school in 2007 and burning DVDs for students without Internet access. Another solution may be to make computers available to students before and after school. Critics ask, "If students won't do traditional homework, what makes us think they will sit in front of a screen and listen to a lecture?" An additional negative is that if every teacher "flips," students may watch lectures for a couple of hours a night. Countering this is advocates' claim that flipping individualizes learning because students can watch the lecture or demonstration as many times as necessary to "get it." This *SocialMEdia* feature presents more information about flipping your classroom and some of the tools available to help you get started.

SocialMEdia

Flipping your classroom doesn't have to be an everyday or long-term commitment. The tech tools already available to you allow you to do a trial run, thanks to social media and technology for teaching and learning. You can start small by using your Smartphone to make a brief video of you explaining a concept, demonstrating a math procedure, creating a mini-lecture about a character in a novel or historical setting, and more. Then post the video on the class website or class wiki. Ask students to view the video before class. During class, engage students in exploration of the topic with which they are already familiar because of what they watched before class.

Flipping your classroom doesn't require expensive equipment. *Jing* allows you to *capture* anything you find on your computer, including both still shots and video. You can annotate what you've captured with the software tools provided to point out particular aspects of the photo or video. Videos are limited to 5 minutes. To create a longer video, *Snagit* will come in handy. Once you have captured what you want students to see and hear, the piece can be saved to your computer. The next step is to share what you've created. With a free Jing account you receive a *Screencast* account that turns what you've created into a link. This link can be shared in any way you want. Jing incorporates a history function that saves all your episodes so you can easily help students review lessons they may have missed or need for remediation purposes. User-friendly videos and texts help you get started using Jing and Screencast to add to your instructional toolbox for many purposes or to use to flip your classroom.

TEACHER PROFESSIONALISM AND INSTRUCTIONAL REFORM. Not all instructional strategies will be appropriate for your classroom. We've discussed many variables that make you and your students unique. These variables must be considered when deciding if and when to use instructional strategies. Occasionally, a school district will adopt a specific package of strategies and dictate that all teachers use them. You won't have a choice. The professional teacher will remain open-minded and present evidence that particular strategies either are working or are counterproductive. If the initiative continues, you will know your students well enough to tweak or supplement to keep learning moving forward.

Reform Based on International Comparisons

When international test results for U.S. public school students are compared to the results of other countries, United States students as a whole are never at the top. However, we are almost always in the top 10. There are those who berate the public education U.S. students receive based on the misguided beliefs that (1) test scores are the most revealing measure of student learning and (2) there is an even playing field, thus validating comparison data.

Trends in International Math and Science Study (TIMSS) and Progress in International Reading Literacy Study (PIRLS) are two international tests administered to random cohorts of students in about 50 countries. Each time TIMMS and PIRLS data are published, there's a renewed call for reform in U.S. schools. In the last century, there was a flurry of interest in education in Japan due to their consistently high scores. Legislators and education delegations traveled to Japan to observe and talk with Japanese educators in a quest to learn new methods that might be translatable into U.S. reform. Articles were written and calls for emulation of Japanese methods abounded—and then went away. It became clear that the United States is *not* Japan, that our challenges are different from those of Japan, a country whose test results we envied.

In this century, the "new Japan" is Finland. Finnish students have outscored U.S. students for decades in all subject areas. Teams of U.S. educators and elected officials have flocked to this Nordic country to observe and gather data about which Finnish practices are responsible for their achievements. But once back home, most have reluctantly said, in essence, "Yes, the Finns have the right idea, but the paradigm shift would be just too huge to work here." Let's explore Finnish public education.

In 1971, Finland rejected the evaluation-driven, centralized model of education that exists in most of the Western world, and even in the country's neighbor, Norway. Finnish education for children and adolescents is organized in three levels. In level 1, children must attend a year in preprimary education at age 6 and it may be in a state school or a daycare setting. The second level is called *basic* education for ages 7–15. More than 90% of Finnish students go on to the third level, upper secondary education, which may be either general or vocational. Completion of a 3-year program makes students eligible for higher education. Public education is primarily supported financially by the country and is free to all students, ages 7 to 19, as are most higher education options. All students receive free meals while at school and free transportation (Finnish National Agency for Education, 2017).

Finland has one core curriculum for basic school, but local administrators may add to it. The Finnish National Board of Education provides the objectives and learning outcomes of the different subjects and study modules for general upper secondary education. Teachers are trusted to develop instructional methods that suit the learning needs of their students, and are encouraged to try new methods and share their successes. Teachers decide how to assess students, determining who is ready to move on and who is not. In fact, there is only one standardized exam in Finnish schools and it determines which secondary education students are prepared to enter, general or vocational level.

In Finland, teaching is an attractive career choice where teachers are recognized as the key to quality education. Getting into a university teacher education program is very competitive, with only about 10–30% of applicants chosen to enroll. Teachers in Finland, for basic school and both tracks of secondary school, must obtain a master's degree to be hired because once they are in a classroom, they are given high degrees of autonomy, meaning they make many decisions as to what and how to teach. Teachers receive continuing education (at least 2 hours a week) throughout their careers, with all expenses paid. There is no merit or extra performance-based pay and no alternative routes to teaching (Finnish National Agency for Education, 2017).

Students in Finland do not have homework in basic school. They have about 4 hours of classroom time, 190 days a year. Children ages 7–15 have at least an hour of unstructured recess a day, along with lots of arts and crafts. The prevalent philosophy is that if children don't play, they won't learn. The difference between weakest and strongest students in Finland is the smallest in the world. There is no ability tracking until secondary school and underachievers are not retained. Although schools have the latest in technology, students rarely use computers or tablets in regular classroom instruction. Students with special needs are taught in regular classrooms when possible. If their disabilities make it too difficult for them to learn to their potential in a broad setting, they are taught by specialists in a small setting. Students with exceptional academic talent are taught in regular classrooms where every student experiences the same curriculum (*Business Insider*, 2017).

Returning from a visit to observe Finnish schools, Texas teacher Shannon Frank (2016) tells us, "Teaching in Finland is not about creating the best students with the best SAT scores who know the most about history, physics, or algebra. It is about creating globally competent, critical thinkers who are ready to be successful in their post-graduation life." Please take the time necessary to absorb the data in Table 12.3. You'll see that although we have some elements in common with Finland (life expectancy, ages of children in schools), our differences present challenges that likely account for why our TIMSS and PIRLS results generally don't measure up to those of Finland. Of particular note are population numbers, immigration rates, racial groups and languages, total hours spent in school, poverty rates, and teacher pay.

Should we simply stop trying to learn from successes and failures of other countries? Of course not. Should we temper what we observe based on our unique determination to provide equal opportunities for all students in a country rich in diversity, yet often thwarted by economic challenges that sometimes stand in our way? Yes. Solutions to some of our most vexing issues in U.S. teaching and learning lie in innovation and common sense, and our willingness to continually seek ways to better serve children and adolescents. Our future depends on it.

Table 12.3 Comparison of U.S. and Finland education

Criteria	Finland	U.S.
Population	5,300,000	318,892,103
Population growth rate	.05%	.77%
Median age	43	38
Life expectancy	80	80
Net immigration rate	.62/1000	2.5/1000
Poverty rate	5%	16%
Racial groups	>95% white	64% white; 12% black; 16% Hispanic; 8% other
Languages	Finnish 94%; Swedish 5%	English 82%; Spanish 11%; 7% other
Age children begin school	7	5–7
Compulsory education until age	16	16–18 (varies by state)
Mean years in school	9	12
Ages 7–15 hours in school/year	675	about 1,000
Age 16+ hours in school/year	913	about 1,000
Requirements to teach	Master's degree	Bachelor's degree
Teacher pay relative to others with similar postsecondary preparation	+14%	−23%
High school (or equivalent) graduation rate	93%	82%

Based on: Central Intelligence Agency. (2016). The world factbook. Retrieved May 31, 2017, from https://www.cia.gov/library/publications/the-world-factbook/geos/fi.html and https://www.cia.gov/library/publications/the-world-factbook/geos/us.html

TEACHER PROFESSIONALISM REGARDING INTERNATIONAL COMPARISONS. Professionals will always welcome new ideas. We may become frustrated when comparisons are made that we know are invalid due to the unique nature of public education in the United States. We understand that as a public endeavor, U.S. public education is subject to policies set by people who are not trained as educators and who have no experience in the classroom except as students. We differ from other countries in multiple ways, many of which revolving around what we consider our finest attributes such as compulsory education for all students regardless of their ethnicity, first language, socioeconomic status, or intellectual potential or achievement record.

There's a fine line between being realistic and making excuses. Teachers should err on the side of being realistic, but without closing the door on ideas that might work. We have so much to learn *about* learning. It's an exciting time to be a professional educator!

Reform in Perspective

Veteran teachers will tell you about initiatives and reform efforts that lasted maybe a year, maybe two, with extensive buildup and preparation—some with a flurry of activity, but few with lasting positive effects. This doesn't mean we shouldn't keep trying. It does mean we need to be steady, professional educators who care deeply about all students and their learning, even as initiatives and reform efforts come and go.

In his book, *So Much Reform, So Little Change*, Charles Payne (2008) laments the fact that so many reform efforts end in disappointment. Educators and, unfortunately, elected officials come up with, or push, ideas and programs that look good on paper, and may make sense from a business perspective, but fail to view schools and school systems from the human perspective. Payne tells us that relationships and trust-building are foundational, rather than side issues. They matter to the success of any reform.

As part of his "School Reformers' Pledge of Good Conduct," Payne urges us to approach any effort to improve schools without a hint of doing anything behind the principal's back or showing disrespect for school leaders. We should also not expect change overnight. In other words, to contribute to the success of efforts aimed at school improvement, we need to be professionals.

Often the most effective reform is accomplished day by day through the attitudes and actions of teachers who live and teach in ways that are guided by professionalism. Such is the case with focus teacher Traci Peters at Cario Middle School, South Carolina. In *Teaching in Focus,* Traci writes directly to you, giving advice based on her years as an effective, happy teacher.

Teaching in Focus

Traci Peters, seventh-grade math, Cario Middle School, South Carolina. *In her own words . . .*

Dear Teacher Candidate,

What an exciting career you have chosen. I can assure you that your years as a teacher will be filled with memories that last a lifetime! Many things change each year as a new group of students enter your life. Yet many things must stay the same. Here are just a few things on my "have to do each year" list:

Sara Davis Powell

- Love your students as if they were your own children, even the ones that know just what buttons to push. In order to love them, you have to get to know them. So talk to them about things other than the textbook!
- Laugh with your students. If you don't enjoy teaching, then why do it? Middle school kids are especially funny and definitely want all the attention they can get.
- Follow a routine every day. This doesn't mean that you have to do the same thing every day, but it does mean that kids like structure.
- Stay organized—it saves lots of time and frustration!

- Plan with your colleagues. It'll make for more exciting lessons and give you some much needed "adult time." Don't forget to ask for help when you need it!
- Respect your students and their parents, and, in turn, they will respect you. Most importantly, respect yourself. A happy teacher makes a happy class!
- Be consistent with your discipline, from day to day and from student to student. Be sure you don't overuse the word "no" when "yes" is sometimes more appropriate. Remember to reward good behavior, and be sure the consequence fits the not-so-good behavior.

Good luck to you in your first year of teaching. Be confident that you will make a difference in your students' lives and that all of your hard work does pay off!

Sincerely,
Traci

As this text comes to an end, let's revisit reasons for teaching. In conversations with teachers, they often talk about why they teach. They share anecdotes and reflections about their students and classrooms. This is a compilation of some thoughts recently gathered.

I teach because . . .

- Children are our most precious resources for the future.
- The quality of education determines the character of our community and our society.
- I get to be with other teachers who are creative, hopeful, patient, and collaborative.
- When a student understands something after struggling with a concept, that's the best feeling of all.
- My students have the potential to impact our world in positive ways.
- I learn my subject better every day by digging deeper to make science come alive for my students.
- I laugh multiple times every day when either I make a silly joke or a student makes a funny comment that gets us all laughing.
- Being around kids everyday helps me stay young and keep up with current trends and ideas.
- I enjoy a measure of autonomy when it's just my students and me; I feel like an artist working on an immensely valuable canvas.
- The school schedule fits perfectly with my family life, allowing me to do something very important as a professional and as a wife and mom.
- It's a way to make a difference, hopefully over and over.
- Teaching is more than a job, it's a meaningful career.
- I have always loved math and I want to engage my students in actually doing math, not just learning procedures.
- There's never a dull moment!
- I like to learn!
- I want to pass along my passion for literature.
- It's my way of serving my community and my country.

Check Your Understanding 12.4

Concluding Thoughts

It's possible to spend an entire career in the position of teacher and never accept the inherent professional responsibilities that accompany the position. How unfortunate and sad for the individual who chooses to go through the motions but never invests the commitment and care necessary to be a true professional.

On the positive side, it is possible to spend an entire career accepting responsibilities to students, families, community, colleagues, the educational system, the profession, and self-growth. Fulfilling each responsibility brings opportunities to affect students' lives and to enjoy a career filled with challenge and satisfaction.

Congratulations on completing this text and the course that made it required reading! For those of you who are sure that teaching is in your future, or who are still seriously considering the profession, you have quite an adventure ahead of you. If this is your first course in teacher preparation, you now probably have a sense of what's ahead in your college program. With each step toward becoming a teacher, your passion for teaching and learning will likely grow.

If, however, you have decided that teaching is not for you, thank you for opening your mind to what education in the United States is like and to the needs of the more than 50 million students who attend preK–12 schools. You are more informed than most of the nation's public. Expressing your opinions will be easier (and hopefully more valid) now that you have a greater understanding of the challenges and opportunities that lie within U.S. schools. Be an advocate for children and their futures—and thus for the future of us all. Please frequently ask, "And how are the children? Are they all well?"

Each page in this text is written by the hands, and from the heart, of a teacher. To be a teacher is to live in a world of possibility—to know that what we do matters. Join us.

After reading the *Chapter in Review,* read about Deirdre's plan to recruit minority teachers for Cario Middle School and respond to items in this chapter's *Developing Professional Competence.*

Chapter in Review

How can I develop as a professional?

- When professional responsibilities are fulfilled, opportunities are created; when opportunities are recognized and acted on, their benefits incur responsibilities.
- As a student, all coursework is valuable, along with field experiences.
- Clinical practice, or student teaching, is the capstone internship experience of your teacher preparation program.
- It is important for teachers to balance their professional and personal lives by developing interests and friendships that promote healthy lifestyles.
- The teaching profession is bolstered every time an engaging lesson is taught or learning is facilitated in whatever way is appropriate for students.
- Teachers have a responsibility to extend their influence beyond the classroom and into the school arena and perhaps the district, state, and even national arenas.
- Teachers have many opportunities to add to the teaching knowledge base through research, writing, and participation.

How do I develop and maintain professional relationships?

- Teachers should develop and maintain a sense of responsibility for student learning.
- Parental involvement increases academic achievement and attendance rates and leads to more positive attitudes and behavior.

- The community provides valuable support and services for children and their families.
- To be collegial requires overt efforts to create and maintain mutually beneficial relationships.

What are some realities of teaching?

- The paperwork and recording responsibilities in response to administrators can seem overwhelming at times.
- It's very likely that you will see and hear things in schools that are contrary to what you are learning in teacher preparation. In real classrooms, the variables are many and teachers, as human beings, do not always approach responsibilities and opportunities in the best possible ways, or even in ways that seem acceptable.
- Most teachers agree that the only way to become comfortable with what theories tell us, or experienced teachers advise, is to actually be in the classroom—on-the-job learning.
- Your classroom will likely be very diverse and your career will begin with challenges inherent in multilingual and multicultural students.
- Rarely is there enough money to fund what needs to be done to facilitate the learning results we want to see.
- Public education is perceived by many as an endangered species for a variety of reasons.

What is my role as a professional in education reform?

- Professional teachers support ideas and efforts intended to increase learning.
- Being an informed professional is a position from which to impact reform.
- Professionals remain optimistic that ways will be found to judge their competency accurately and fairly.
- Professionals encourage exploration in education that may positively impact teaching and learning.
- Teacher professionalism pushes us to be great teachers and leaders, to promote innovation and continuous improvement, and to help our students become ready for college and careers.

Developing Professional Competence

Thoughtfully reading this scenario and responding to the items that follow it will help you prepare for licensure exams.

Sara Davis Powell

Cario Middle School is a suburban school with a population of about 75% white students, 20% black students, and the rest a mix of students of Asian and Hispanic ethnicities. Of the 67 teachers at Cario, only 2 are African American. This has always bothered Deirdre a little, but now that she teaches the CARE students, most of whom are black, she has become even more aware of the lack of diversity of the teachers with whom she works.

Deirdre received a master's degree from the College of Charleston located about 15 miles from Cario. The college has a large teacher preparation program, with teacher candidates recruited by local schools because of their proven ability. Deirdre has decided she wants to do some recruiting herself, primarily among the nonwhite teacher candidates. To do so, she has some decisions to make.

Now it's time for you to respond to two essay items involving the scenario. In your responses, be sure to address all the dilemmas and questions posed in each item. These items are followed by three multiple-choice questions. Consider the following teacher standards as you respond.

> ***InTASC Standard 9, Professional Learning and Ethical Practice***
>
> The teacher engages in ongoing professional learning and uses evidence to continually evaluate his/her practice, particularly the effects of his/her choices and actions on others (learners, families, other professionals, and the community), and adapts practice to meet the needs of each learner.
>
> ***AMLE Standard 5: Middle Level Professional Roles***
>
> Middle level teacher candidates understand the complexity of teaching young adolescents, and they engage in practices and behaviors that develop their competence as professionals.
>
> ***InTASC Standard 10, Leadership and Collaboration***
>
> The teacher seeks appropriate leadership roles and opportunities to take responsibility for student learning, to collaborate with learners, families, colleagues, other school professionals, and community members to ensure learner growth, and to advance the profession.

1. Deirdre is not sure her desire for more nonwhite teachers at Cario will be met with enthusiasm from her colleagues. She knows they won't object, but they likely won't share her passion. How might she approach them? What information could she present that would make her case in a professional way? Why is it important for the teachers at Cario to know about Deirdre's recruitment? How does InTASC Standard 9 apply?
2. Deirdre thinks that some teacher candidates may be swayed toward Cario if they meet some of the parents of students who are in the racial minority. How should Deirdre go about arranging a meeting? Who would need to be involved? How does InTASC Standard 10 apply?

Application Exercise 12.3: Developing Professional Competence

3. What should Deirdre do before she begins planning the recruitment effort?
   - **a.** She should talk with several instructors at the College of Charleston to gauge whether they will be open to her efforts.
   - **b.** She should discuss her desires with Cario principal Carol Bartlett.
   - **c.** She should determine the percentage of nonwhite teacher candidates at College of Charleston.
   - **d.** She should contact the NAACP to ask if there are established procedures.
4. From whom will Deirdre need to seek support for her recruiting activities?
   - **a.** The dean of the College of Charleston School of Education, Carol Bartlett, the NAACP, and the state department of education
   - **b.** Carol Bartlett, the NAACP, and the state department of education
   - **c.** The dean of the College of Charleston School of Education and Carol Bartlett
   - **d.** The dean of the College of Charleston School of Education, Carol Bartlett, and the NAACP

5. Which reason for applying to teach at Cario will probably have the *least* impact on nonwhite College of Charleston teacher candidates?
   a. Cario's administration supports teacher professional development.
   b. This is an opportunity to further integrate the teaching faculty of a school.
   c. Cario is known for quality relationships among teachers.
   d. They will have a chance to work with a majority of white teachers.

Application Exercise 12.4: Developing Professional Competence

---

Flash Cards 12.1

Shared Writing 12.1: To teach or not to teach

Glossary

504 plan A plan developed by a school to ensure that a child who has a disability identified under the law and is attending an elementary or secondary educational institution receives accommodations that will ensure his or her academic success and access to the learning environment; a safeguard for students with disabilities that do not qualify them for special education services.

5-E lesson plan A way for teachers to guide students through a cycle of inquiry learning; most commonly used for science exploration.

A Nation at Risk: The Imperative for Educational Reform Report commissioned by President Reagan in 1983 that referred to U.S. public education as a "rising tide of mediocrity." In response, various proposals for reform and improvement surfaced.

Academic freedom A form of expression that allows teachers to use their judgment in making decisions about what to discuss, what to assign as readings, what teaching strategies to use, and so on.

Academic rigor The content of what teachers teach is meaningful, and the teachers' expectations of the learning of that content are demanding.

Academies Early secondary schools designed to teach content intended to prepare students to participate in business and trade.

Achievement gap The disparity among students, with some excelling while others languish, with respect to learning and academic success.

Action research Research conducted by teachers in their classrooms around a concept or question that captures their interest; results of research may be added to the teaching knowledge base.

Active engagement Involving students in meaningful experiences that promote learning; providing an environment for creativity and collaboration, all with increased learning as the goal.

Advocate for students Support and defend students, always putting their needs first.

Alternative assessment Generally any assessment other than traditional paper and pencil and/or forced choice assessment.

Alternative school School designed for students who are not successful in a traditional school setting.

American Association for Health Education (AAHE) Organization with a mission to promote and support health education in K–12 schools.

American Council for the Teaching of Foreign Languages (ACTFL) Organization working to help students communicate successfully in a pluralistic American society.

American Federation of Teachers (AFT) The nation's second-largest professional association for teachers.

Analytic rubric Specifies separate parts of an assessment task, product, or performance and the characteristics of various levels of success for each.

Art of teaching Knowing how and when to use particular strategies to teach the curriculum; the ability to logically, and in a variety of ways, divide content and skills into manageable components and to create experiences that lead to student learning.

ASCD Learn Teach Lead A professional organization dedicated to promote all aspects of teaching and learning.

Asperger syndrome Once a stand-alone diagnosis, is now one of several subtypes of the single diagnosis of autism. *See* **Autism spectrum disorder.**

Assimilation The process of bringing persons of all races and ethnicities into the mainstream by having them behave in ways that align with the dominant culture.

Assistive technology Devices and services that reduce the impact of disabilities by helping people communicate, increase their mobility, and aid in multiple ways that enhance their capacity to learn.

Association for Childhood Education International (ACEI) A professional organization that focuses on global education issues.

Association for Middle Level Education (AMLE) A professional organization that provides standards for the preparation of teachers for grades 5 through 9, and advocates for the needs and education of young adolescents; formerly the National Middle School Association (NMSA).

Associative play Children begin to share toys and verbally communicate.

At-large election Voters may vote for any candidate regardless of the area in the district the candidate represents.

At-risk students *See* **Students at risk.**

Attention deficit/hyperactivity disorder (AD/HD) A learning disability in which students demonstrate three defining characteristics—inattention, hyperactivity, and impulsivity—in persistent patterns that are more severe than in others of the same age.

Authentic assessment Students show what they know and can do in a real-life setting or situation.

Autism spectrum disorder (ASD) A complex developmental disorder that affects how a person behaves, interacts with others, communicates, and learns.

Backward design An approach to planning for teaching and learning that starts with deciding on the desired learning results (curriculum), then identifies how to collect the evidence necessary to know if the results have been achieved (assessment), and then proceeds to choosing how to help students acquire the desired knowledge and skills (instruction).

Benchmarks Statements of what students should know and be able to do at specific developmental stages.

Bilingual Education Act of 1968 Provided funds to assist non–English-speaking students (mostly Hispanic) who were dropping out of high school at a rate of about 70%.

Bilingual education The delivery of instruction in two languages.

Bisexual People who have romantic attractions to both males and females.

Black Codes, Black Laws Prior to the Civil War, Black Codes or Black Laws were enacted, predominantly in the South, prohibiting the education of slaves.

Block grants Grants that provide funding with few restrictions for its use, allowing states and school districts the freedom to use the money in ways that meet their specific needs.

Block schedule A schedule allowing for longer class periods; a block schedule may be comprised of a wide variety of schedule options.

Blog A social media form of communication; short for web log

Bloom's taxonomy A classification system of thinking and processing skills that range from simple to complex; used to classify various levels of learning objectives and experiences.

Boarding 'round To save lodging money, towns required teachers to live with the families of their students for 1 week at a time.

Boarding schools Schools where students stay overnight and eat all their meals.

Bond referendum Allows school districts to borrow money stipulated for specific projects. The school board asks voters in the district to approve the borrowing of the money (the bond) that will be repaid over a period of time.

Breach of contract Contracts are binding on both parties. If a person signs one and then backs out or takes another job, or if the district backs out, the person or district may be sued for damages.

Brown v. Board of Education In 1954, Chief Justice Earl Warren declared that segregating children based solely on race was wrong and illegal. Some schools integrated peacefully; others did not.

Buckley Amendment Also known as the Family Educational Rights and Privacy Act (FERPA) of 1974. Allows parents and guardians access to their children's academic records and requires written parental permission for the records to be shared with anyone else. When students turn 18, they have control over who sees their records.

Bullied The person who is the target of bullying.

Bully The person who bullies, or acts in relationally aggressive ways toward another; usually acts out of a need for power.

Bullying Relationally aggressive behavior; a type of emotional or physical violence where individuals use relationships to harm others.

Bystander Anyone who witnesses bullying. A bystander has choices to make: simply watch, walk away, join in, or intervene.

Case law Based on the doctrine of *stare decisis*, a Latin phrase meaning "let the decision stand." Once a decision is made in a court of law, the decision sets a precedent for future cases of a similar nature until challenged or overturned.

Categorical grants Money that is allocated or funds that are earmarked for specific purposes.

Charter school A public school that is freed in specific ways from typical regulations required of other public schools.

Child abuse Any act that results in death, serious harm, or exploitation of children.

Child neglect A form of abuse resulting from the failure to act in the best interest of children.

Civil Rights Act of 1964 Stipulates that if schools discriminate based on race, color, or national origin, they are not eligible for federal funding.

Civility Treating others the way we want to be treated.

Classroom assessment Encompasses every deliberate method of gathering information about the quantity and quality of learning.

Classroom climate The everyday environment of teachers and students working together.

Classroom community A classroom where students and teacher tend to be like-minded and have common beliefs, understandings, and aims.

Classroom management The establishment and enforcement of rules and disciplinary actions; teacher strategies ensure an orderly classroom environment.

Clinical internship Also known as **student teaching** or **clinical practice;** involves extended fieldwork in which teacher candidates teach lessons and, for a designated period of time, take over all classroom duties.

Coleman Report Report written in 1966 that concluded that family and community factors such as poverty and parental levels of education prevented some children from learning, that no matter what schools did, some children would not be successful in school.

Collective bargaining The act of negotiating with employers and/or states to gain additional benefits for members of the bargaining group; a right practiced in most states by teacher associations and unions. States often allow unions to negotiate with school boards concerning elements of teacher contracts and working conditions.

Collegial relationships Relationships with other teachers that promote growth through sharing of professional expertise.

Common Core State Standards Initiative Efforts to develop and promote common national standards by the National Governors Association (NGA) and the Council of Chief State School Officers (CCSSO).

Common schools Community-supported elementary schools for all children established in response to many economic, social, and political factors.

Community The neighborhood, town, city, and/or county in which a person lives.

Compulsory education law Requires children to attend school until a specified age.

Consequences A term that implies more natural ramifications for wrongdoing than the word *punishment*, which can be arbitrary.

Constructivism A way of approaching instruction that builds on progressivism as students are challenged to construct, or discover, knowledge about their environments. Process is valued in progressivism, often more than product. The theory is that students who learn through the processes of construction, discovery, and problem solving will be better able to adapt to a changing world.

Content standards Specific knowledge students should have and skills they should be able to do.

Contract An agreement between parties that includes the rights and responsibilities of each. When teachers begin jobs in schools, they sign initial contracts.

Cooperating teacher A classroom teacher who serves as the host and mentor during clinical practice.

Cooperative learning Loosely defined, any instance of students working together in small groups.

Cooperative play Children actively coordinate ways to keep interaction going.

Copyright laws Federal laws that protect the rights of a creator or author to own intellectual property and to prevent others from copying or distributing it without permission. Intellectual property includes written material, original audio and visual work, and computer programs. Copyright laws also provide guidelines for authorized use of someone else's intellectual property.

Core subjects Generally considered language arts, math, science, and social studies.

Corporal punishment Physical punishment practiced in some school settings.

Council for the Accreditation of Educator Preparation (CAEP) An agency that scrutinizes university teacher education programs; the result of the merger of the National Council for the Accreditation of Teacher Education (NCATE) and the Teacher Education Accreditation Council (TEAC).

Council for Exceptional Children (CEC) A national organization that represents the needs of students with exceptionalities and fosters appropriate education for them.

Council of Chief State School Officers (CCSSO) Organization composed of school superintendents and other school leaders.

Criterion referenced Student scores that are indicative of levels of mastery of a subject and are not dependent on how other students perform.

Critical thinking Observing, comparing and contrasting, interpreting, analyzing, seeing issues from a variety of perspectives, weighing variables, and then making decisions and solving problems based on these thinking skills.

Cultural identity Results from the interactions of many factors, including language, religion, gender, income level, age, values, beliefs, race, and ethnicity.

Cultural pluralism Involves the recognition that our nation is populated by a rich variety of people of varying races and ethnicities, and thus cultures, all with potential to positively contribute to our common goal of a productive, free society.

Culturally responsive Purposefully including contributions and viewpoints from the perspectives of different cultures, ethnicities, races, genders, socioeconomic levels, and so on.

Culture A composite of social values, cognitive codes, behavioral standards, worldviews, and beliefs that characterize a group of people. Culture is earned, shared, and adaptive.

Curriculum Educational term for what students experience in schools.

Cyberbullying Using technology to bully.

Cybercitizenship Responsibly using technology in ways that do not harm others.

Dame schools In colonial days, dames were respected women who, usually without formal schooling, had learned to read and write and who turned their homes into schools where parents paid to have their children educated.

Democratic classroom A classroom setting that promotes choice, community, authentic learning, and a relevant, creative curriculum; students participate in the establishment of behavioral expectations.

Departmentalized School organizational pattern in which teachers teach their own subjects and meet occasionally with other teachers who teach the same subject.

Depression Mental illness characterized by a deep sense of sadness and a loss of interest or pleasure in activities.

Developmental appropriateness Teaching and learning that matches students' physical, cognitive, social, emotional, and character development.

Diagnostic assessment Assesses student knowledge and skill levels before beginning a unit of study; also known as **Pretesting**.

Dialects Deviations from standard language rules used by identifiable groups of people.

Differentiation of instruction Varying instruction based on the needs of students.

Discrimination The prejudicial treatment of people based on differences such as race, age, or sex.

Dispositions Attitudes and beliefs that guide and determine behavior.

District school board Governing body composed of elected citizens responsible for setting policies that affect the operation of schools.

District superintendent Functions as the school district's chief executive officer; hired by the board and serves at its pleasure.

Dropout Students who do not complete high school in 4 years.

Due process The steps a district must take to pursue the charges when a tenured teacher is threatened with dismissal; an important principle that requires guidelines to be followed to ensure that individuals are protected from arbitrary or capricious treatment by those in authority.

Early childhood education The care and education of the youngest students in the United States, typically considered birth through age 8.

Ebonics Black English, one of the best-known and most controversial dialects in the United States.

Education The lifelong process of learning.

Education for All Handicapped Children Act (Public Law 94-142) The 1975 federal law that guaranteed a free and appropriate education to all children with disabilities in the least restrictive environment; renamed Individual with Disabilities Education Act in 1990.

Education maintenance organization (EMO) Organization contracted to take over the management of a public school for profit.

Education summit Organized meeting to advocate for school improvement.

Educational technology Any technology that assists teachers in teaching and students in learning.

Effective schools Schools that meet the learning needs of the students who attend them.

Effective Schools Movement Originated in the 1970s to develop research pertaining to the assertion that all children can learn; purpose was to find schools deemed effective for all children and identify common characteristics.

Elementary Level of school that usually includes grades K–5.

Elementary and Secondary Education Act (ESEA) Enacted during the presidency of Lyndon B. Johnson to provide extra funding, called Title 1 funding, for schools with high numbers of children from low-income homes.

Emotional intelligence quotient (EQ) A set of skills that accompany the expression, evaluation, and regulation of emotions. A high-level EQ indicates a person's ability to understand others' as well as his or her own feelings, respond appropriately to them, and, in general, get along.

Encore courses All courses other than what are considered the core courses of math, English language arts, social studies, and science. Also known as **Exploratory courses** and **Related arts courses**

English as a new language (ENL) *See* **English as a second language (ESL).**

English as a second language (ESL) Students receive individualized assistance; unlike bilingual education, ESL services are delivered only in English; little or no emphasis is placed on preserving native language or culture; and ESL teachers do not need to speak another language. Also known as *English as a new language (ENL).*

English learners (ELLs) Non-English speakers and students with limited English proficiency.

English-language learners (ELLs) *See* **English learners**

Entitlements Grants given to certain segments of the population that have specific needs; the federal government deems these individuals entitled to extra assistance.

Era of standards A time when content standards determined curricular learning goals; generally considered 1990 through the present.

Essentialism A philosophy of education based on the belief that there is a core curriculum that everyone in the United States should learn. This core can shift in response to societal changes, but should always be basic, organized, and rigorous.

Ethics Standards of conduct based on moral judgments; the determination of what's right and what's wrong.

Ethnicity Primarily an individual's country of origin and ancestry.

Eurocentric Contributions and traditions centered on European values.

Evaluation Judgments about, and the assigning of values to, the *results* of assessments.

Every Student Succeeds Act (ESSA) The 2016 reauthorization of the Elementary and Secondary Education Act.

Excise tax Tax on luxury items such as boats and travel trailers.

Exemplars Samples of work that fit various criteria for scoring so that students actually see what a product looks like that earns a particular number.

Existentialism Primary emphasis is on the individual. As a philosophy of education, existentialism contends that teachers teach the whole person, not just math, reading, science, or any other particular subject. Each student searches for personal meaning and personal understanding. If learning about a subject area increases a student's sense of self, then it's worthwhile.

Expectations A word with positive connotations that may be used in place of *rules*, a word with negative connotations.

Expenditure per pupil The average amount of money spent from federal, state, and local sources on an individual student.

Explicit curriculum What teachers are expected to teach, what students are expected to learn, and what society expects of schools; also referred to as **Formal curriculum**.

Exploratory courses Also known as *related arts courses* and *encore courses*, includes all courses other than math, English language arts, social studies, and science; may include art, music, physical education, industrial arts, languages, drama, computer education, and others.

Expulsion Semi-permanent or permanent dismissal from school for a semester or for an indefinite period.

Extrinsic incentives Incentives that are imposed, or originate outside the individual.

Fair use Specific limitations on the use of copyrighted materials.

Family Educational Rights and Privacy Act (FERPA) of 1974 Commonly called the Buckley Amendment, allows parents and guardians access to their children's academic records and requires written parental permission for the records to be shared with anyone else. When students turn 18, they have control over who sees their records.

Feeder system Configuration of schools in a district; typically in one feeder system of schools early childhood/elementary schools feed into middle schools that feed into a particular high school.

Field experience Observing and/or participating in actual classrooms; sometimes referred to as practicum experiences.

First Amendment Center Source of information and resources to assist schools in implementing the guiding principles of the First Amendment. Established by Association for Supervision and Curriculum Development (ASCD).

Flipped classroom Students watch a video of a teacher giving a lecture or demonstration after school as homework, and then come to class the next day, ready to interact with the knowledge and skills.

Formal curriculum Encompasses what is intentionally taught, what is stated as the goals of student learning.

Formative assessment A series of assessments in a variety of formats that help monitor student progress.

For-profit schools Schools that are operated by private companies for profit.

Full-service school A public school that provides a comprehensive program of education and includes student and community services such as after-school and family education programs.

Functional behavioral assessment (FBA) A management plan through a team of educators utilizing a process that looks for events and actions that may lead to misbehavior and that devises strategies to help students abide by classroom expectations.

Furloughing Teachers or assistants asked not to work for a certain number of days, losing the salary for those days.

Gay People who are homosexual. *See also* **Homosexuality.**

Gender bias The favoring of one gender over the other in specific circumstances.

Gender equity The fair and balanced treatment of males and females.

Gender nonconforming Children and adolescents who identify with a gender different from their physically evident sex at birth.

Gender stereotyping Occurs when perceived gender differences are assumed for all people.

Generalizations Characteristics or broad statements marked by the words *tend to* rather than *all are*.

Gifted and talented Exceptional learners who demonstrate high levels of intelligence, creativity, and/or achievement.

Global awareness Involves understanding environmental, societal, cultural, political, and economical concepts and issues that impact our world.

Grade Judgment of assessment quality (evaluation) with a number attached to it.

Graduation rate Includes students who successfully complete high school in four years.

Great Books The writings of those considered to be the great thinkers throughout the history of Western civilization, such as Homer, Shakespeare, Melville, Einstein, and many others.

Grievance A formal complaint filed by an individual teacher or group of teachers against a district.

Guided practice Opportunities for students to work independently on applying knowledge in a nonthreatening setting that includes teacher feedback.

Head Start The largest provider of government-funded preschool education, employing one of every five U.S. preschool teachers.

Heterosexuality The romantic or erotic attraction of a person to another of the opposite sex.

Hidden curriculum Curricula that is not explicit or openly expressed; similar to the informal curriculum, but with negative connotations.

Hierarchy of needs Maslow's (1908–1970) theory that all human beings experience the same needs.

High schools Schools that most often encompass grades 9–12.

HighScope An approach to early childhood education built on consistency and few transitions during the day.

High-stakes tests Standardized tests that have far-reaching consequences.

Holistic rubric A grading instrument that uses one scale for an entire project.

Homeschooled Students who receive most of their academic instruction in their homes.

Homework Independent practice outside the classroom.

Homosexuality The romantic or erotic attraction of a person to another of the same sex.

Idealism A philosophy based on the belief that ideas are the only reliable form of reality. Idealists believe that the physical world changes continually, and ideas are what should be taught.

Implicit curriculum Curricula that is implied and subtle; the informal curriculum.

In loco parentis Serving in place of parents.

Incentives A word that may be used in place of the overused and value-laden word *rewards*.

Inclusion Students attend their home school with their age- and grade-appropriate peers, participate in extracurricular activities, and receive special education and support services to the maximum extent possible in the general education classroom.

Individualized educational program (IEP) A plan developed for a student by educators, the family, and others (as appropriate), involving details of how to reach specific goals. A student's IEP must be revisited annually and student progress evaluated.

Individuals with Disabilities Education Act (IDEA) Also referred to as PL94-142 (and the revised version of the Education for All Handicapped Children Act of 1975), this act made special education services a right, not a privilege, because it required schools to place students in least-restrictive environments within public schools.

Individuals with Disabilities Education Improvement Act A reauthorization of IDEA in 2004 that compiled all U.S. laws that affect children with disabilities into one statute.

Informal curriculum What students learn that isn't written in a lesson plan or necessarily intentionally transmitted to students; sometimes referred to as **Wayside teaching.**

Information literacy Involves recognition of when information is needed, knowing how to access information, and judging information credibility.

Inquiry learning When students pursue answers to questions posed by others or developed on their own, they are involved in inquiry learning. Observation, questioning, hypothesizing, and predicting are all part of inquiry-based learning.

Instructional time Time available for teaching and learning.

Instrumental aggression Aggression based on attempting to meet a specific goal, such as grabbing a particular toy or establishing dominance in an activity; most common among boys.

Insubordination Defiance of authority; refusing to obey orders.

Integrated curriculum Involves making connections among subject areas through the use of a unifying topic or theme. *See also* **Interdisciplinary curriculum.**

Intelligence The capacity for knowing and learning.

Intelligence quotient (IQ) The results of a test that affixes a number to intelligence.

Intelligent design Includes a belief that certain features of the universe and of living things are best explained by an intelligent being (God), not by the process of natural selection espoused by evolution.

Interdisciplinary curriculum Term often used to describe curricular links or connections among subjects. *See also* **Integrated curriculum.**

Interdisciplinary team The preferred organizational structure for middle-level education, involving a team of two to five teachers working with a distinct group of students for an entire year.

International Association for the Evaluation of Educational Achievement (IEA) An independent, international cooperative of national research institutions and governmental research agencies, conducting large-scale studies of educational achievement.

International Society for Technology in Education (ISTE) Professional organization whose mission is to provide leadership and service in the effective use of technology in education.

Interstate Teacher Assessment and Support Consortium (InTASC) An organization that sets standards for what teachers should know and be able to do.

Intrinsic incentives Incentives that come from within and result from students' natural drives.

Kalamazoo case Established that the legislature could tax for support of both common and secondary schools, propelling public high schools into school systems in every state.

Kappa Delta Pi An international honor society for preservice and in-service teachers.

Kindergarten German for "children's garden," the school year that precedes first grade.

Knowledge Is Power Program (KIPP) Charter school system designed especially for students at risk.

Language The primary means of communication; transmits knowledge and passes on culture.

Language minority students Students whose native language is other than English, regardless of their current level of English proficiency.

Latin grammar school First established in 1635 in Boston for boys whose families could afford to send them on for more education beyond the dame school; considered the forerunner of modern high schools and specifically prepared boys to attend Harvard University, established in 1636.

Learning disabled (LD) A general category of students with disorders involving problems understanding or using language that results in significant differences between learning potential and achievement.

Learning modalities Auditory (hearing), visual (seeing), tactile (touch), and kinesthetic (movement)—all four are used in the process of learning, but individuals tend to favor one or two over the others.

Least restrictive environment (LRE) The setting within which students with disabilities can function at capacity; generally the setting with students who do not have disabilities that also meets the educational needs of the students with disabilities.

Lesbian A female who is gay.

Lesson plan Devising experiences for students as part of the formal curriculum.

LGBTQ Acronym for lesbian, gay, bisexual, transgender, questioning.

Liable To be responsible for; liability is what teaching is all about—accepting responsibility for students while they are under our supervision.

Literacy Involves ability to analyze and apply knowledge and skills necessary to solve problems within a discipline.

Long-range plans Lesson plans that may encompass a 9-week timeframe, a semester, or a year.

Looping School practice that keeps a teacher with a particular group of students for more than 1 year.

Magnet school A public school with a specific emphasis or theme and curriculum and instructional programs tailored with unique opportunities that attract certain students.

Manipulatives Hands-on objects that enhance and illustrate concepts and skills.

Massachusetts Act of 1642 First compulsory education law in the New World; required all white children to attend school.

Massachusetts Act of 1647 Follow-up act, also known as the Old Deluder Satan Act, establishing that every town of 50 or more households must provide a school.

McKinney-Vento Act of 1987 Federal government's response to homelessness; the act addresses the problems homeless children and youth face in enrolling, attending, and succeeding in school.

Methods courses Courses that emphasize specific strategies for specific subjects and will probably incorporate opportunities to actually apply what you are learning.

Micromanagement Managing to a level of detail that is inappropriate for a particular position. For instance, when school board members go beyond policy making into what is considered day-to-day operations, they may be seen as micromanaging.

Middle-level schools Schools for young adolescents with a distinct philosophy that embraces both academic rigor and developmental appropriateness; may include any combination of grades 5–9.

Mini-lecture Shortened, focused versions of the lecture.

Minorities A term used by many to indicate people in the United States who are not white.

Montessori An approach to early childhood education with mixed-age grouping and self-pacing.

Monument Academy Public Charter School Public boarding school in Washington, DC, founded in 2015.

Moodle (Modular Object-Oriented Dynamic Learning Environment) A course management system that allows teachers to share information and plans.

Moral compass Refers to a person's ability to judge what is right and wrong and act accordingly.

Morrill Act In 1862, the government granted states 30,000 acres of land for every senator and representative in Congress in 1860. The income the state generated from this land was to be used to support at least one college.

Multiage classroom Classroom where children in two, three, or more grade levels learn together.

Multicultural curriculum Curriculum that purposefully includes contributions and viewpoints from the perspectives of different cultures, ethnicities, races, genders, and socioeconomic levels.

Multicultural education An instructional approach that celebrates diversity and promotes equal educational opportunities.

Multiple intelligences (MI) theory A theory developed by Howard Gardner that intelligence is multidimensional, that individual brains work in ways that give each of us our own personal intelligences; includes eight intelligences.

National Assessment of Educational Progress (NAEP) Only standardized test systematically administered to a sampling of students across the United States. The NAEP is administered to fourth-, eighth-, and twelfth-graders in math, reading, writing, science, history, economics, geography, civics, foreign language, and a variety of the arts; often called the *nation's report card.*

National Association for Sport and Physical Education (NASPE) Organization with a mission to promote and support physical education in K–12 schools.

National Board for Professional Teaching Standards (NBPTS) Board that sets standards, establishes policies, and issues certificates designating teachers with skills to perform effectively.

National Council for the Social Studies (NCSS) Organization for social studies teachers and social studies content.

National Council of Teachers of Mathematics (NCTM) Organization for mathematics teachers and mathematics content.

National Defense Education Act of 1958 Called for strengthening of science, math, and foreign language programs; teachers were given training in the use of new methods and materials in hopes of bringing American student learning up to, and beyond, the levels of learning in other countries.

National Education Association (NEA) The largest professional education association in the United States, with a total of over 5 million members, including teachers, administrators, professors, counselors, and other educators.

National Governors Association (NGA) Organization of governors enabling them to share expertise and tackle dilemmas collectively.

National Science Teachers Association (NSTA) Organization for science teachers and science content.

National Standards for Arts Education Organization for arts teachers and arts content.

Nature The genetically inherited influences on who we are.

Neighborhood school Students in a geographical area attend school close to their home.

New England Primer First published in 1690 for children in upper elementary and secondary levels. Published for over 150 years with few substantial changes over its lifetime, the *New England Primer* included a spelling guide based on the alphabet denoted in brief rhymes and pictures, the Lord's Prayer, the Apostles' Creed, the Ten Commandments, a list of the books of the Bible, the Puritan catechism, and numbers 1–100.

No Child Left Behind Act of 2001 (NCLB) A federal law that held schools accountable for student learning, regardless of student diversity. States were required to test all students in grades 3 through 8 annually to determine progress. No longer in force as of 2016.

Norm referenced Tests used to compare students; administered to a group of students selected because they represent a cross section of U.S. students (norm group).

Normal schools Publicly funded secondary schools specifically designed to prepare teachers for the classroom.

Northwest Land Ordinance of 1787 Divided federally owned land in the wilderness into townships and required that schools be built.

Null curriculum What is not taught in school.

Nurture The influence of the environment, including everything that happens except for what can be accounted for genetically.

Obesity Extreme overweight as indicated by body mass index (BMI), a measure of how much a person weighs relative to height.

Objective Concise statement about what students are expected to learn and be able to do as a result of the lesson.

Old Deluder Satan Act Because education was considered the best way to fight the devil, the act (also known as the Massachusetts Act of 1647) established that every town of 50 or more households must provide a school.

Open enrollment A plan that allows students to choose from among virtually all the schools in a school district.

Overlapping A teacher's ability to multitask, to take care of several things at once.

Pacing guide A document that dictates the timing of content coverage; helps assure that all grade-level standards are part of the curriculum.

Parallel play Children agreeably sharing the same space, but not communicating; in teachers, not sharing knowledge and skills with other teachers.

Paraprofessional A teacher aide or assistant teacher; typically not a certified teacher.

Parent Teacher Association (PTA) National organization of parents and others interested in the welfare of students; some PTAs are called PTOs (Parent Teacher Organization).

Parochial schools Schools affiliated with religious organizations.

Partnership for 21st Century Skills (P21) A leading advocacy organization focused on infusing twenty-first–century skills into education.

Perennialism A philosophy of education based on a core curriculum with themes and questions that endure, that are everlasting; as life changes and times change, the real substance and truths of life remain the same.

Performance assessment May be a project, a demonstration, a creation, or anything that requires the application of knowledge and skills.

Performance standards (*see* **Benchmarks**)

Performance-based pay Involves paying teachers more when they produce whatever results are designated as desirable.

Philosophy *Philo* means "love," and *Sophos* means "wisdom." Philosophy, then, means "love of wisdom." This love of wisdom, or philosophy, becomes a means of answering fundamental questions.

Philosophy of education The *love of wisdom* regarding teaching that expresses itself in attitudes and actions every day in the classroom.

Portfolio Assessment tool for which either students or teachers assemble a cohesive package of representative evidence of student learning.

Postmodernism Grew out of a sense that those in power control those who don't have power. This control, postmodernists believe, is manifested through major institutions such as schools.

Practicum experiences Involve observing and/or participating in actual classrooms; sometimes referred to as field experiences.

Pragmatism Promotes student-centered perspectives that are integrated with firsthand experiences to be most effective.

Praxis Series A battery of tests published by the Educational Testing Service (ETS) that may be used to determine the qualifications of individuals to be licensed or certified to teach in a variety of disciplines and grade levels.

Preschool A semi-structured environment for 3- and 4-year-olds housed in a school setting; care is enhanced by exposure to basic educational concepts.

Pretesting Assessing student knowledge and skill levels before beginning a unit of study; also called **Diagnostic testing**.

Primary classrooms Typically grades 1–3. Kindergarten is a standalone category.

Principal Oversees every aspect of school life and answers to the district for all that occurs at the school. The principal's role involves administrative tasks such as facility maintenance, attendance, discipline, parent–community relationships and communication, transportation, and all manner of paperwork. Principals are also instructional leaders with knowledge of, and experience with, the teaching and learning process.

Private schools Schools in which there is no public funding and no public accountability (the two elements that make public schools public).

Privilege gap The gap between the haves and the have-nots.

Problem solving Process involved in finding a solution to a problem.

Processing Sending a student out of the classroom with the purpose of reflection and planning for better choices.

Process standards Processes that support content learning by explaining how the content might be best learned and how to use the content once it is acquired.

Profession An occupation that meets certain criteria, including (1) extensive training to enter, (2) inclusion of a code of ethics, and (3) service as the primary product.

Professional development Efforts to help teachers improve their knowledge and skills.

Professional learning community (PLC) School-based group of teachers and administrators who work collaboratively to share practices and data analysis of student progress to improve teaching and learning.

Professionalism A way of being that involves attitudes and actions that convey respect, uphold high standards, and demonstrate commitment to those served.

Progress In International Reading Literacy Study (PIRLS) The only international test of reading proficiency that compares students worldwide.

Progressive education In 1896, John Dewey established a method of involving students in their own learning through cooperative groups, which grew into a major movement with far-reaching implications; interests guide what is learned about traditional subjects.

Progressivism A student-centered philosophy of education that focuses on curriculum that is of interest to students. Progressivists view education as more than preparation for the future; it is life itself. The progressive philosophy of education endorses experiential learning full of opportunities for student discovery and opportunities to solve problems.

Property taxes Values of property are determined, and a small percentage of the assessed amount (usually less than 1%) is collected annually and used for local services.

Proximity The accessibility of teacher to students.

Public domain A work is in the public domain if it is more than 75 years old or is published by a government agency; work in the public domain is not protected by copyright.

Public Law 94-142 (PL 94-142) A common way of referring to the Individuals with Disabilities Education Act (IDEA), an act that made special education services a right rather than a privilege.

Public schools Public schools are funded through some form of taxation and are accountable to the community through elected or governmental officials who have policy and oversight responsibilities.

Race A term used to classify people according to their physical characteristics that are nature given. Race classifies people at birth.

Racism A form of prejudice that may be perpetuated by individuals or governments stemming from a belief that one race is superior to another.

Reading across the curriculum Infusing the curriculum with reading, regardless of content area.

Realism A philosophy based on the belief that some facts are absolutes whether recognized by all or not. Realists contend that the only way to know these absolutes is to study the material world.

Reduction in force Occurs in schools when there are fewer students, budget cuts, or the cancellation of a program. Reduction in force (RIF) may also apply to tenured teachers. The general rule of "riffing" is that the last hired are the first to go if it becomes necessary.

Reflection Thinking about what is done, how it's done, and the consequences of actions or inactions, all with the goal of being a better teacher.

Reflective practitioner A teacher who thinks critically about teaching and the consequences of actions or inactions, all with the goal of being more effective with students.

Reform To change, to make different, or to attempt to improve.

Reggio Emilia An approach to early childhood education for ages 3 months to 6 years based on relationships among children, families, and teachers.

Related arts courses Also known as *exploratory courses* and *encore courses*; all courses other than math, English language arts, social studies, and science; may include art, music, physical education, industrial arts, languages, drama, computer education, and others.

Relational aggression Subtle actions that may hurt emotionally rather than physically; may include name-calling, gossiping, or saying mean things just to be hurtful; most common among girls.

Reliability The degree to which an assessment yields a pattern of results that is repeatable and consistent over time.

Resilience The ability to bounce back and meet life's challenges.

Resource teacher A special education teacher who helps students develop strategies for school success.

Ripple effect An effect that occurs when one action directly affects another.

Romanticism A philosophy of education that contends that the needs of the individual are more important than the needs of society; also known as *naturalism*.

Rubric Assessment tool that makes explicit what is being assessed, lists characteristics of degrees of quality, and provides a rating scale to differentiate among these degrees.

Rural schools Schools in areas with fewer than 2,500 people and a minimum of retail stores and services.

Scaffolding The support given to children to help them move through progressive levels of learning.

School choice Method of letting parents decide which schools their children and adolescents attend.

School connectedness Occurs when students feel that they belong, that adults and students care about them as whole people.

School culture The prevailing atmosphere of a school that provides the context of learning experiences; places where people work together and learn together, schools function according to their cultures.

School district An organizational structure of local schools defined by geographic boundaries.

School venues The variety of ways Americans "do school" in the over 120,000 schools in the United States. The most prominent venues are public schools and private schools.

Schooling Formalized delivery system of teaching and learning.

School-to-Work Federal government program initiated to bring real-world, work-related skills and understanding to students through courses and experiences that introduce them to career possibilities.

Science of teaching Curriculum, assessment, and instruction.

Second Morrill Act of 1890 Stipulated that no grants would be given to states where college admission was denied because of race unless the state provided a separate-but-equal institution.

SEED Public Charter Schools Public boarding schools in Washington, DC, Miami, and Maryland, the first of which was founded in 1998.

Self-contained classroom An organizational structure involving one teacher and a group of students for whom the teacher is accountable much of the school day.

Self-efficacy An "I can" belief in oneself that leads to a sense of competence; the concept of self-efficacy is solidly grounded in the accomplishment of a continuum of increasingly difficult challenges.

Service dimension of teaching An attitude that approaches students as complete human beings, with cognitive, physical, emotional, social, and moral components; an approach to teaching from a service point of view is all-inclusive rather than focused only on academic and cognitive progress.

Service-learning When student experiences combine service with a purposeful learning component.

Settlement houses Established by early American reformers to confront the problem of urban poverty; community service centers that provided educational opportunities, skills training, and cultural events.

Sexual harassment Behavior with sexual implications that is neither wanted nor welcome; may include obvious looks with lewd intent, taunts with sexual innuendo, touching, kissing, groping, and any behavior that has sexual connotations.

Sexual orientation The sex to which a person is romantically or socially attracted.

Sin tax Tax on items some consider vices, such as alcohol and cigarettes.

Single gender All male or all female.

Single-member elections Only those who live in a specific area can vote for the representatives in their area.

Site-based management Public school management structure in which governance is in the hands of those closest to it, generally teachers, administrators, and parents.

Social cognition The process of relating to others and thinking about them and oneself.

Social media Communication using technology such as smartphones, instant messaging, and so on.

Social reconstructionism A philosophy of education that looks to education to change society, rather than just teach about it. Social reconstructionism as an education philosophy calls on schools to educate students in ways that will help society move beyond all forms of discrimination to the benefit of everyone worldwide.

Socialization Occurs through a variety of influences including home, family, church, print and electronic media, peers, and school.

Socioeconomic status (SES) Status based on economic level and other sources of power.

Soft bigotry Having low expectations for some students based on assumptions about abilities and intelligence, of previous experiences with students of various races, or of some other factor.

Special education services Services provided by schools to help students with disabilities function and learn in ways optimal to each.

Special interest group Group of people with a common mission who work to have an impact.

Stages of cognitive development Jean Piaget (1896–1980) recognized distinct differences in children's and adolescents' responses to questions that directly correlated to their chronological ages and categorized these differences into stages.

Stages of moral reasoning Noted developmental psychologist Lawrence Kohlberg contends that people pass through distinct stages as they develop morally.

Stakeholders Those who have legitimate involvement and stand to gain or lose from the situation

Standard English A composite of the language spoken by educated, middle-class people in the United States.

Standardized test Test given to multiple groups of students, designed for specific grade levels, and typically repeated annually. These tests are administered and scored under controlled conditions, and their exact content is unknown to everyone except the test makers before they are administered.

Standards Expectations for what individuals should know and be able to do.

Standards-based reform movement Efforts to improve teaching and learning through content standards; another way of expressing the era of standards.

Standards-based test Test written using the content of a specific set of standards.

State board of education Volunteers who are either elected or appointed by the governor; state legislatures give state boards oversight authority; boards act in regulatory and advisory capacities.

State department of education Operates under the guidance of the governor, legislature, and state board of education; also known as state office of education or perhaps department of public instruction.

State superintendent The one person given responsibility for managing the state department of education; also known as chief state education officer or commissioner of education.

Straight A common term for people who are heterosexual.

STRIVE Preparatory Schools A successful charter system in Denver, Colorado, primarily serving students who are at risk and/or disadvantaged.

Structured English immersion (SEI) Approach includes significant amounts of the school day dedicated to the explicit teaching of the English language, with other content supporting instruction, but not as the primary focus.

Structured observation Early field experiences involving looking for specific things and responding to prompts that purposefully call attention to certain aspects of the classroom.

Student centered The students have choices concerning what to learn, and instructional strategies actively involve students in their own learning.

Student self-monitoring Students assume control of their own behavior as they develop a sense of ownership for that behavior.

Student teaching Also known as **clinical internship** or **clinical practice;** involves extended fieldwork in which teacher candidates teach lessons and, for a designated period of time, take over all classroom duties.

Student voice Giving students choices, asking for their opinions, teaching them to reflect on their own learning, and giving meaningful writing assignments help to develop student voice.

Students at risk Those who are in serious danger of not completing school and/or who may be heading toward nonproductive or counterproductive lifestyles.

Suburban schools Schools in neighborhoods and in small-to-medium-sized towns that are located on the fringe of cities or are their own distinct locations.

Students with exceptionalities Learners with abilities or disabilities that set them apart from other learners.

Substance abuse A pattern of alcohol or drug use that can lead to detrimental and habitual consumption, impaired functioning at school and work, and legal difficulties.

Summative assessment A formal assessment involving judgments about the success of a process or product; most often occurs at the end of a unit of study.

Summer slide The loss of learning momentum that often occurs during the two or three months students are out of school in summer under the traditional calendar.

Suspension Time out of school that may range from 1 day to less than a semester, but is usually for 10 or fewer days.

Systemic involvement Extending teacher influence at the local and district levels.

Tax cap An upper limit to taxation.

Teach for America (TFA) The most widely known of all alternative licensing programs; TFA recruits individuals who are college seniors or recent graduates who agree to teach in high-needs rural or urban schools for at least 2 years.

Teacher centered The teacher is prominent in the classroom, determining, and being the center of, curricula and instructional strategies.

Teacher leader A teacher with additional responsibilities such as chairperson of a grade level of teachers or perhaps a subject area specialist who works with other teachers to help them improve their knowledge and/or skills; more generally, teachers who prove to be leaders in their schools, as well as in their districts and states, simply by being dynamic, well-informed classroom teachers.

Teacher preparation portfolio Cohesive package of representative products; may either document growth or display best work, depending on its purpose.

Teaching in 3D Incorporating the science, art, and service in teaching, with the whole child always in view.

Tenure Continuing contract status; a teacher with tenure is entitled to a contract each year unless the district has reason to not renew it or the teacher decides to go elsewhere. In most states, tenure doesn't guarantee a particular position in a particular school, but it does guarantee employment in the district.

Thinking skills Skills that aid in processing information.

Time-on-task Productive learning time.

Title I funding Federal compensatory funds provided through the Elementary and Secondary Education Act given to public schools where more than 50% of the students qualify for free or reduced-price meals; used to supplement regular school funding in schools with high numbers of students from low-income settings.

Title IX of the Education Amendments Act Prohibits government money from being used for anything that discriminates on the basis of gender.

Token economy A system of giving symbolic rewards for appropriate behavior and withholding or taking away rewards for inappropriate behavior.

Town schools Early American schools established for whole communities; while some schools still limited curriculum to reading, writing, and the classics, specialized schools in the form of academies became popular.

Traditional public schools Schools that have no admission criteria, other than perhaps residency in a particular attendance zone.

Transgender A person who lives as his or her self-identified gender rather than the gender that conforms to his or her anatomy at birth.

Transition When students change activities or locations, they are in transition; generally a time when most classroom disruptions happen.

Transparent Decisions are made with full disclosure of information and reasoning.

Trends in International Mathematics and Science Study (TIMSS) International tests that compare students worldwide; administered every 4 years since 1995.

Truancy Nonattendance during compulsory education, not including excused absences generally granted for health reasons.

Tyler Rationale Ralph Tyler developed four questions that should be asked throughout the stages of curriculum development.

Unconditional teaching Accepting students for who they are, not for what they do.

Unfunded mandate A legally enforceable law without monetary support provided.

Unit of study Organizes curriculum, instruction, and assessment around a major theme or distinct body of content; provides planned cohesion.

Universal design for learning (UDL) An approach to teaching that helps all students learn by incorporating variety in instruction, including visual, auditory, tactile, and kinesthetic experiences.

Unobtrusive intervention Consequences that do not disrupt instruction.

Urban schools Schools in cities with large downtowns and dense populations.

Validity The degree to which an assessment measures what it is supposed to measure.

Value-added teacher evaluation When student test scores are used to evaluate teacher effectiveness.

Vocational Education Act of 1963 Quadrupled the amount of money allocated for vocational education.

Voucher Government-issued piece of paper that represents part of a state's financial contribution for the education of a student; parents choose a school and present the voucher, and the government allocates funding to the school accordingly.

Watchdog group Community members who join forces to keep an eye on school district accountability by examining policies and practices.

Wayside teaching Teaching that occurs inside and outside the classroom through attitudes, values, habits, interests, and classroom climate; sometimes referred to as **Informal curriculum.**

Webinar A web-based seminar with give-and-take participation through online means, video cams, and/or voice.

Whole child Teaching the whole child includes attending to student developmental stages and needs, along with teaching grade-level and subject-area content.

Withitness A teacher's awareness of what's going on in the whole classroom, enabling the teacher to step in when needed to keep the environment positive; originated with Jacob Kounin.

Writing across the curriculum Infusing the curriculum with writing, regardless of content area.

Young adolescents Students between ages 10 and 15.

Zero tolerance Consequences that are nonnegotiable for certain infractions.

Zone of proximal development The level at which a child can almost, but not completely, grasp a concept or perform a task successfully; theory proposed by Lev Vygotsky.

References

Chapter 1

Council of Chief State School Officers. (2011, April). Interstate Teacher Assessment and Support Consortium (InTASC) Model Core Teaching Standards: A Resource for State Dialogue. Washington, DC: Author. Retrieved July 2, 2016, from http://www.ccsso.org/Documents/2011/InTASC_Model_Core_Teaching_Standards_2011.pdf

Dewey, J. (1933). *How we think: A restatement of the relation of reflective thinking to the educative process*. Boston: D. C. Heath.

Gardner, W. (2016). Teacher recruitment outlook is bleak. *Education Week*, July 22, 2016. Retrieved July 22, 2016, from http://blogs.edweek.org/edweek/walt_gardners_reality_check/2016/07/teacher_recruitment_outlook_is_bleak.html?cmp=eml-eb-popweek+07222016

Ginott, H. G. (1993). *Teacher and child*. New York: Collier Books/Macmillan.

Ingersoll, R., Merrill, L., & Stuckey, D. (2014). Seven trends: The transformation of the teaching force, updated April 2014. CPRE Report (#RR-80). Philadelphia: Consortium for Policy Research in Education, University of Pennsylvania.

National Center for Education Statistics. (2013). Digest of education statistics. Retrieved July 4, 2016, from http://nces.ed.gov/programs/digest/d13/tables/dt13_211.60.asp

National Center for Education Statistics. (2016). Fast facts. Retrieved July 1, 2016, from http://nces.ed.gov/fastfacts/display.asp?id=28.

National Education Association (2013). NEA Collective Bargaining/Member Advocacy's Teacher Salary Database, based on affiliate reporting as of December 2013. Retrieved July 3, 2016 from http://www.nea.org/home/2012-2013-average-starting-teacher-salary.html

Partnership for 21st Century Skills. (2016). About us. Retrieved July 1, 2016, from http://www.p21.org/about-us/p21-faq

Teach for America. (2016). Progress and persistence. Retrieved July 2, 2016, from https://www.teachforamerica.org/about-us/annual-report#progress

Teacher-Certification.com. (2016). Alternative teaching certification statistics and facts. Retrieved July 6, 2016, from http://www.teaching-certification.com/alternative-teaching-certification.html

Tomlinson, C. A. (2016). One to grow on / caring for teachers. *Educational Leadership, 73*(8), 92-93.

Webb, L. D., Metha, A., & Jordan, K. F. (2017). *Foundations of American education* (8th ed.). New York: Pearson.

Chapter 2

American Academy of Pediatrics. (2015). Gender identity in children. Retrieved July 16, 2016, from https://www.healthychildren.org/English/ages-stages/gradeschool/Pages/Gender-Identity-and-Gender-Confusion-In-Children.aspx

American Psychological Association. (2016a). ADHD. Retrieved July 19, 2016, from http://www.apa.org/topics/adhd/

American Psychological Association. (2016b). Answers to your questions about transgender people, gender identity and gender expression. Retrieved July 16, 2016, from http://www.apa.org/topics/lgbt/transgender.aspx

Autism Society. (2016). Medical diagnosis. Retrieved July 20, 2016, from http://www.autism-society.org/what-is/diagnosis/medical-diagosis/

Autism Speaks. (2016). Learn the signs of autism. Retrieved July 20, 2016, from https://www.autismspeaks.org/what-autism/learn-signs

Banks, J. A. (Ed.). (2004). *The handbook of research on multicultural education*. San Francisco: Jossey-Bass.

Barnwell, P. (2016). Students' broken moral compasses. *The Atlantic* online. Retrieved July 27, 2016, from http://www.theatlantic.com/education/archive/2016/07/students-broken-moral-compasses/492866/

Centers for Disease Control and Prevention. (2014). Lesbian, gay, bisexual, and transgender health. Retrieved July 21, 2016, from http://www.cdc.gov/lgbthealth/youth.htm

Clark, C. (2009). The case for structured English immersion. *Educational Leadership, 66*(7), 45.

Delgado-Gaitan, C., & Trueba, H. (1991). *Crossing cultural borders: Education for immigrant families in America*. New York: Falmer.

Feldman, R. S. (2014). *Development across the life span* (7th ed.). Upper Saddle River, NJ: Prentice Hall.

Gallahue, D. L., & Ozmun, J. C. (2012). *Understanding motor development: Infants, children, adolescents, adults* (7th ed.). Boston: McGraw-Hill.

Gay, G. (2000). *Culturally responsive teaching*. New York: Teachers College Press.

GLAD. (2016). Anti-LGBT discrimination. Retrieved July 18, 2016, from http://www.glad.org/rights/topics/c/anti-lgbt-discrimination

Goleman, D. (2011). *The brain and emotional intelligence: New insights*. Florence, MA: More Than Sound.

Gollnick, D. M., & Chinn, P. C. (2013). *Multicultural education in a pluralistic society* (9th ed.). Upper Saddle River, NJ: Merrill/Prentice Hall.

Grant, J.M., Mottet, J.D., & Tanis, J. (2011). Injustice at every turn: A report of the national transgender discrimination survey. Retrieved May 25, 2017, from http://www.thetaskforce.org/static_html/downloads/reports/reports/ntds_full.pdf

Henze, R. C., Mukhopadhyay, C., & Moses, Y. T. (2014). *How real is race? A sourcebook on race, culture and biology* (2nd ed.). Retrieved July 17, 2016, from http://works.bepress.com/rosemary_henze/33/

Heward, W. L. (2013). *Exceptional children: An introduction to special education* (10th ed.). Upper Saddle River, NJ: Merrill/Prentice Hall.

Kamenetz, A. (2015). Nonacademic skills are key to success. But what should we call them? Retrieved July 18, 2016, from http://www.npr.org/sections/ed/2015/05/28/404684712/non-academic-skills-are-key-to-success-but-what-should-we-call-them

Kids Count. (2016). Children in poverty by race and ethnicity. Retrieved January 14, 2017, from http://datacenter.kidscount.org/data/tables/44-children-in-poverty-by-race-and-ethnicity#detailed/1/any/false/573,869,36,868,867/10,11,9,12,1,185,13/324,323

Kohlberg, L. (1984). *The psychology of moral development: Essays on moral development* (Vol. 2). San Francisco: Harper & Row.

Maslow, A. H. (1999). *Toward a psychology of being* (3rd ed.). New York: Wiley.

McDevitt, T. M., & Ormrod, J. E. (2016). *Child development and education* (6th ed.). Upper Saddle River, NJ: Merrill/Prentice Hall/Pearson.

National Board for Professional Teaching Standards [NBPTS]. (2013). *The five core propositions*. Retrieved December 21, 2016, from http://www.nbpts.org/five-core-propositions

National Center for Education Statistics. (2011). *The condition of education 2011* (NCES 2011-045), INDICATOR 6. Retrieved January 18, 2013, from http://nces.ed.gov/pubsearch/pubsinfo.asp?pubid=2011033

National Center for Education Statistics. (2016a). Common core of data (CCD), "State Nonfiscal Survey of Public Elementary/Secondary Education," 1995–96 through 2013–14. Retrieved July 17, 2016, from http://nces.ed.gov/programs/digest/d15/tables/dt15_203.50.asp

National Center for Education Statistics. (2016b). National elementary and secondary enrollment by race/ethnicity projection model, 1972 through 2025. Retrieved July 17, 2016, from http://nces.ed.gov/programs/digest/d15/tables/dt15_203.50.asp

National Institutes of Health. (2013). Autism spectrum disorder. Retrieved July 20, 2016, from https://www.nichd.nih.gov/health/topics/autism/Pages/default.aspx

National Kids Count Program. (2015). *Children population by household type*. Retrieved July 17, 2016, from http://datacenter.kidscount.org/data/tables/105-child-population-by-household-type?loc=1&loct=1#detailed/2/2-52/false/869,36,868,867,133/4290,4291,4292/427,428

National Cyber Security Alliance. (2016). Staysafeonline.org. Retrieved May 26, 2017, from https://staysafeonline.org/about-us/news/national-cyber-security-alliance-survey-reveals-the-complex-digital-lives-of-american-teens-and-parents

Noonoo, S. (2017). Experts warn against teaching to learning styles in K-12. Retrieved March 16, 2017, from http://www.educationdive.com/news/experts-warn-against-teaching-to-learning-styles-in-k-12/438083/

Partnership for 21st Century Skills. (2014). Framework for state action on global education. Retrieved July 12, 2016, from http://www.p21.org/storage/documents/Global_Education/P21_State_Framework_on_Global_Education_New_Logo.pdf

Pew Forum. (2016). *Religious landscape survey*. Retrieved July 20, 2016, from http://www.pewforum.org/religious-landscape-study/

Powell, S. D. (2015). *Introduction to middle level education* (3rd ed.). Boston: Allyn & Bacon.

Reiner, C. R., & Willingham, D. (2010). The myth of learning styles. Retrieved March 16, 2017, from www.researchgate.net/publication/249039450_The_Myth_of_Learning_Styles

Resmovits, J. (2016). After years of complaints, Department of Education issues federal guidelines to prevent discrimination against students with ADHD. *Los Angeles Times*, July 26, 2016. Retrieved July 26, 2016, from http://www.latimes.com/local/education/la-na-adhd-disability-us-department-of-education-20160725-snap-story.html

Turnbull, R., Turnbull, A., Wehmeyer, M., & Shogren, K. A. (2016). *Exceptional lives: Special education in today's schools* (8th ed.). Upper Saddle River, NJ: Merrill/Prentice Hall.

U.S. Census Bureau. (2012). U.S. population projections. Retrieved April 8, 2013, from http://www.census.gov/population/projections/data/national/2012.html

U.S. Census Bureau. (2016). Poverty thresholds for 2015 by size of family and number of related children under 18 years. Retrieved July 19, 2016, from http://www.census.gov/data/tables/time-series/demo/income-poverty/historical-poverty-thresholds.html

U.S. Department of Agriculture. (2013). Food and Nutrition Service: Program fact sheet. Retrieved July 21, 2016, from http://www.fns.usda.gov/sites/default/files/NSLPFactSheet.pdf

U.S. Department of Education. (2015). Improving basic programs operated by local educational agencies. Retrieved July 17, 2016, from http://www2.ed.gov/programs/titleiparta/index.html

University of New Hampshire. (2015). Annual disability statistics compendium. Retrieved July 22, 2016, from http://disabilitycompendium.org/statistics/special-education

Vermeer, H. J., Boekaerts, M., & Seegers, G. (2000). Motivational and gender differences: Sixth-grade students' mathematical problem-solving behavior. *Journal of Educational Psychology, 92*, 308–315.

Weissbourd, R. (2012). Promoting moral development in schools. Retrieved July 15, 2016, from http://hepg.org/hel-home/issues/28_1/helarticle/promoting-moral-development-in-schools_522

Youth Suicide Prevention Program. (2011). Statistics about youth suicide. Retrieved July 20, 2016, from http://www.yspp.org/about_suicide/statistics.htm

Chapter 3

Barth, R. S. (2001). *Learning by heart*. San Francisco: Jossey-Bass.

Council for American Private Education (CAPE). (2016). Facts and studies. Retrieved July 22, 2016, from http://www.capenet.org/facts.html

Einhorn, E. (2015). The rise of urban public boarding schools. Retrieved July 25, 2016, from http://www.theatlantic.com/education/archive/2015/12/urban-boarding-schools/421704/

Eisner, E. W. (2004). Preparing for today and tomorrow. *Educational Leadership, 64*(6), 6.

Goodlad, J. I. (1984). *A place called school*. New York: McGraw-Hill.

Home School Legal Defense Association. (2013). U.S. Department of Education: Homeschooling continues to grow! Retrieved July 25, 2016, from https://www.hslda.org/docs/news/2013/201309030.asp

Jenlink, P.M., Stewart, L., Stewart, S. (2012). Leading For *Democracy: A Case-Based Approach to Principal Preparation*. Roman & Littlefield Publishers, Inc.

Johnson, J., Showalter, D., Klein, R., & Lester, C. (2014). Why rural matters 2013–14: The condition of rural education in the 50 states. Retrieved July 26, 2016, from http://www.ruraledu.org/user_uploads/file/2013-14-Why-Rural-Matters.pdf

Kajitani, A. (2016). The #1 factor that determines a toxic or thriving school culture. Retrieved January 3, 2017, from http://blogs.edweek.org/teachers/teacher_leader_voices/2016/04/the_1_factor_that_determines_a.html?cmp=eml-eb-popweek+12302016&M=57722296&U=961157

Knowledge Is Power Program. (2016). Frequently asked questions. Retrieved July 29, 2016, from http://www.kipp.org/about-kipp/faq/#commonquestions

Kostelnik, M. J., Soderman, A. K., & Whiren, A. P. (2015). *Developmentally appropriate curriculum: Best practices in early childhood education* (6th ed.). Upper Saddle River, NJ: Merrill/Prentice Hall.

Kozol, J. (1991). *Savage inequalities: Children in America's schools*. New York: Crown.

Merrow, J. (2004). Meeting superman. *Phi Delta Kappan, 85*(6), 455–460.

Morrison, G. S. (2014). *Fundamentals of early childhood education* (7th ed.). Upper Saddle River, NJ: Merrill.

National Alliance for Public Charter Schools. (2016). Charter school data dashboard. Retrieved July 28, 2016, from http://dashboard2.publiccharters.org/National/

National Association for Single-Sex Public Education [NASSPE]. (2013). Single-sex schools/schools with single-sex classrooms/what's the difference? Retrieved January 16, 2013, from http://www.singlesexschools.org/schools-schools.htm

National Association for the Education of Young Children. (2015). 15 states require kids to attend kindergarten and other kindergarten facts. Retrieved July 26, 2016, from http://www.naeyc.org/blogs/10-things-know-about-kindergarten-school-begins

National Center for Education Statistics (NCES). (2016). *Fast facts*. Retrieved July 24, 2016, from http://nces.ed.gov/fastfacts/display.asp?id=84

National Center for Education Statistics (NCES). (2013). *Digest of education statistics*. Retrieved July 23, 2016, from https://nces.ed.gov/programs/digest/d13/tables/dt13_216.20.asp

National Middle School Association. (2010). *This we believe: Keys to educating young adolescents*. Westerville, OH: Author.

Prothero, A. (2016). Charter schools aren't good for blacks, civil rights groups say. Retrieved September 2, 2016, from http://www.edweek.org/ew/articles/2016/08/31/charter-schools-arent-good-for-blacks-civil.html?cmp=eml-enl-eu-news2

Roberts, P. L., Kellough, R. D., & Moore, K. (2011). *A resource guide for elementary school teachers* (7th ed.). Upper Saddle River, NJ: Merrill/Prentice Hall.

Routman, R. (2012). Mapping a pathway to schoolwide highly effective teaching. *Phi Delta Kappan, 93*(5), 56–61.

Simon, S. (2013). Vouchers don't do much for students. Retrieved July 26, 2016, from http://www.politico.com/story/2013/10/vouchers-dont-do-much-for-students-097909?o=1

STRIVE Preparatory Schools. (2016). Who we serve. Retrieved July 26, 2016, from http://www.striveprep.org/about-us/

U.S. Department of Health and Human Services. (2016). Head Start. Retrieved July 27, 2016, from http://www.acf.hhs.gov/ohs/about/head-start

Chapter 4

Banks, J. A. (2003). *Teaching strategies for ethnic studies* (7th ed.). Boston: Allyn & Bacon.

Dewey, J. (1900). *The school and society*. Chicago: University of Chicago Press.

Dewey, J. (1902). *The child and the curriculum*. Chicago: University of Chicago Press.

Dewey, J. (1938). *Experience and education*. New York: Macmillan/Collier.

Eisner, E. (2002). *The educational imagination: On the design and evaluation of school programs* (3rd ed.). New York: Macmillan College.

Estes, T. H., Mintz, S. L., & Gunter, M. A. (2011). *Instruction: A models approach* (6th ed.). Boston: Allyn & Bacon.

International Association for the Evaluation of Educational Achievement. (2012c). *PIRLS 2011 Assessment*. TIMSS & PIRLS International Study Center, Lynch School of Education, Boston College, Chestnut Hill, MA and International Association for the Evaluation of Educational Achievement (IEA), IEA Secretariat, Amsterdam, the Netherlands. Retrieved January 4, 2012, from http://timssandpirls.bc.edu/pirls2011/downloads/P11_IR_AppendixE.pdf

Little, C. (2001). What matters to students. *Educational Leadership, 59*(2), 61–64.

Lounsbury, J. H. (1991). *As I see it*. Columbus, OH: National Middle School Association.

Marzano, R. J. (2000). *Transforming classroom grading*. Alexandria, VA: Association for Supervision and Curriculum Development.

National Center for Education Statistics. (2015). Trends in International Mathematics and Science Study (TIMSS), 2015. Retrieved December 28, 2016, from https://nces.ed.gov/timss/timss2015/timss2015_table01.asp; https://nces.ed.gov/timss/timss2015/timss2015_table02.asp; https://nces.ed.gov/timss/timss2015/timss2015_table23.asp; https://nces.ed.gov/timss/timss2015/timss2015_table24.asp

National Center for Education Statistics. (2016). *The nation's report card*. Retrieved December 29, 2016, from http://nces.ed.gov/nationsreportcard/

National Council for the Social Studies. (2017). College, career, and civic life (C3) framework for social studies state standards. Retrieved June 3, 2017, from https://www.socialstudies.org/c3

National Council of Teachers of Mathematics. (2000). *Principles and standards for school mathematics.* Reston, VA: Author.

National Governors Association Center for Best Practices, Council of Chief State School Officers. (2010). *Common Core State Standards*. Author. Retrieved January 1, 2013, from http://www.corestandards.org/

O'Connor, K. (2002). *How to grade for learning.* Arlington Heights, IL: Skylight Professional Development, Pearson Education.

Partnership for 21st Century Skills. (2012). 21st century assessment. Retrieved march 16, 2013, from http://www.p21.org/overview/skills-framework/27

The Atlantic. (2016). The ongoing battle over ethnic studies. Retrieved June 3, 2017, from https://www.theatlantic.com/education/archive/2016/03/the-ongoing-battle-over-ethnic-studies/472422/

Tyler, R. (1949). *Basic principles of curriculum and instruction.* Chicago: University of Chicago Press.

U.S Department of Education. (2016). Every Student Succeeds Act. Retrieved December 27, 2017, from https://www.ed.gov/essa

Chapter 5

Anderson, L. W., & Krathwohl, D. R. (Eds.). (2001). *A taxonomy for learning, teaching, and assessing.* New York: Longman.

Ball, D. L., & Forzani, F. M. (2011). Teaching skillful teaching. *Educational Leadership, 68*(4), 40–45.

Barth, R. S. (2006). Improving relationships within the schoolhouse. *Educational Leadership, 63*(6), 8–13.

Coley, R. J., & Sum, A. (2012). *Fault lines in our democracy.* Princeton, NJ: Educational Testing Service.

Damon, W. (2012). Failing liberty 101. *Educational Leadership, 69*(7), 22–26.

Goodlad, J. I. (1984). *A place called school.* New York: McGraw-Hill.

Johnson, D. W., & Johnson, R. T. (1999). *Learning together and alone: Cooperative, competitive, and individualistic learning.* Boston: Allyn & Bacon.

Johnson, L. (2005). *Teaching outside the box: How to grab your students by their brains.* San Francisco: Jossey-Bass.

Marzano, R. J. (2007). *The art and science of teaching.* Alexandria, VA: Association for Supervision and Curriculum Development.

Marzano, R. J. (2011). Art & science of teaching/ What teachers gain from deliberate practice. *Educational Leadership, 68*(4), 82–85.

McHugh, J. (2005). Synching up with the kids. *Edutopia, 1*(7), 32–35.

National Service-Learning Clearinghouse. (2012). Theory and practice. Retrieved April 23, 2013, from http://www.servicelearning.org/topic/theory-practice

National Youth Leadership Council (2008). K–12 Service-Learning Standards for Quality Practice. Retrieved from http://www.nylc.org/sites/nylc.org/files/files/Standards_Oct2009-web.pdf

Ostroff, W. (2016). *Cultivating curiosity in K–12 classrooms: How to promote and sustain deep learning.* Alexandria, VA: ASCD.

Powell, S. D. (2015). *Introduction to middle level education* (3rd ed.). Boston: Pearson.

Renard, L. (2005). Teaching the DIG generation. *Educational Leadership, 62*(7), 44–47.

Roblyer, M. D. (2013). *Integrating educational technology into teaching.* Upper Saddle River, NJ: Merrill/Prentice Hall.

Tomlinson, C. A. (2010). *Leading and managing a differentiated classroom.* Alexandria, VA: Association for Supervision and Curriculum Development.

Tomlinson, C. A. (2012). One to grow on/Watching us work. *Educational Leadership, 69*(7), 92-93.

Tomlinson, C. A. (2014). *The differentiated classroom. Responding to the needs of all learners* (2nd ed.). Alexandria, VA: Association for Supervision and Curriculum Development.

Wiggins, G. P., & McTighe, J. (2005). *Understanding by design* (2nd ed.). Alexandria, VA: Association for Supervision and Curriculum Development.

Chapter 6

Anderson, M. D. (2015). Where teachers are still allows to spank students. *The Atlantic* (December 15). Retrieved January 2, 2017, from http://www.theatlantic.com/education/archive/2015/12/corporal-punishment/420420/

Boynton, M., & Boynton, C. (2005). *The educator's guide to preventing and solving discipline problems.* Alexandria, VA: Association for Supervision and Curriculum Development.

Dewey, J. (1944). *Democracy and education.* New York: Free Press.

Glasser, W. (1998). *Choice theory.* New York: HarperCollins.

Kohn, A. (2005). Unconditional teaching. *Educational Leadership, 63*(1), 20–24.

Kounin, J. S. (1970). *Discipline and group management in classrooms.* New York: Holt, Rinehart and Winston.

Loeper, J. L. (1973). *Going to School in 1776.* New York: Macmillan.

Manning, L., & Bucher, K. T. (2013). *Classroom management: Models, applications, and cases* (3rd ed.). Boston: Pearson.

McCloud, S. (2005). From chaos to consistency. *Educational Leadership, 62*(5), 46–49.

Partnership for 21st Century Learning. (2017). Framework for 21st century learning. Retrieved May 27, 2017, from http://www.p21.org/our-work/p21-framework

Prensky, M. (2010). Shaping tech for the classroom: 21st-century schools need 21st-century technology. Retrieved April 9, 2010, from http://www.edutopia.org/adopt-and-adapt

Stevenson, C. (2002). *Teaching ten to fourteen year olds* (3rd ed.). New York: Longman.

Strauss, V. (2014). 19 states still allow corporal punishment in school. *The Washington Post* (September 18). Retrieved January 2, 2017, from https://www.washingtonpost.com/news/answer-sheet/wp/2014/09/18/19-states-still-allow-corporal-punishment-in-school/?utm_term=.66d9556ee6bf

Weinstein, C. S., Romano, M., & Mignano, A. (2011). *Elementary classroom management: Lessons from research and practice* (5th ed.). New York: McGraw-Hill.

Zephoria. (2017). The top 20 valuable Facebook statistics—updated January 2017. Retrieved January 5, 2017, from https://zephoria.com/top-15-valuable-facebook-statistics/

Chapter 7

Adler (1982). *The Paideia proposal: An educational manifesto.* New York: Simon & Schuster.

Banks, J. A., & Banks, C. A. M. (Eds.). (2016). *Multicultural education: Issues and perspectives* (9th ed.). New York: Wiley.

Bloom, B. S. (1956). *Taxonomy of educational objectives: Handbook I. Cognitive domain.* New York: Longman, Green.

Boyer, P., & Stuckey, S. (2005). *American nation in the modern era.* Austin, TX: Holt, Rinehart and Winston.

Button, W. H., & Provenzo, E. F., Jr. (1989). *History of education and culture in America.* Upper Saddle River, NJ: Prentice Hall.

Carnegie Corporation. (1989). *Turning points: Preparing American youth for the 21st century.* New York: Author.

Chartock, R. K. (2004). *Educational foundations: An anthology* (2nd ed.). Upper Saddle River, NJ: Merrill/Prentice Hall.

Cohen, S. S. (1974). *A history of colonial education, 1607–1776.* New York: Wiley.

Cubberly, E. (1934). *Public education in the United States.* Boston: Houghton Mifflin.

Dewey, J. (1991). *The school and society* and *The child and the curriculum (expanded ed.).* Chicago: University of Chicago Press.

Eisner, E. W. (2000). *Prospects: The quality review of comparative education.* Paris: UNESCO Publication, 30(3).

Franklin, B. (1931). Proposals relating to education of youth in Pennsylvania. In T. Woody (Ed.), *Educational views of Ben Franklin.* New York: McGraw-Hill.

Good, H. G. (1964). *A history of American education.* New York: Macmillan.

Gutek, G. L. (2011). *Historical and philosophical foundations of education* (5th ed.). Upper Saddle River, NJ: Merrill/Prentice Hall.

Holmes, M., & Weiss, B. J. (1995). *Lives of women public school teachers: Scenes from American educational history.* New York: Garland.

Johnson, J. A., Musial, D., Hall, G. E., Golnick, D. M., & Dupuis, V. L. (2011). *Introduction to the foundations of American education* (15th ed.). Boston: Allyn & Bacon.

Kaplan, L. S., & Owings, W. A. (2011). *American education: Building a common foundation.* Belmont, CA: Wadsworth, Cengage Learning.

Kneller, G. F. (1971). *Introduction to the philosophy of education.* New York: Wiley.

Loeper, J. L. (1973). *Going to school in 1776.* New York: Macmillan.

McNeil, J. D. (2002). *Curriculum: The teacher's initiative* (3rd ed). Upper Saddle River, NJ: Prentice Hall.

McNergney, R. F., & McNergney, J. M. (2009). *Education: The practice and profession of teaching.* Boston: Allyn & Bacon.

Montessori, M. (1967). *The discovery of the child.* Notre Dame, IN: Fides.

Orfield, G. (2009). *Reviving the goal of an integrated society: A 21st century challenge.* Los Angeles: The Civil Rights Project/Proyecto Derechos Civiles at UCLA.

Ornstein, A. C., & Levine, D. U. (2006). *Foundations of education* (9th ed.). Boston: Houghton Mifflin.

Pulliam, J., & Van Patten, J. (2013). *History of education in America* (10th ed.). Upper Saddle River, NJ: Merrill/Prentice Hall.

Rippa, S. A. (1997). *Education in a free society: An American history* (8th ed.). New York: Longman.

Stanford News Service. (1994). *Ralph Tyler, one of the century's foremost educators, dies at 91.* Retrieved March 1, 2006, from Stanford University News Service Website: http://www.stanford.edu/dept/news/pr/94/940228Arc4425.html

Tyler, R. (1949). *Basic principles of curriculum and instruction.* Chicago: University of Chicago Press.

U.S. Census Bureau. (2009). *Facts for features: Asian/Pacific American heritage month 2009.* Retrieved May 24, 2010, from http://www.census.gov/Press-Release/www/releases/archives/facts_for_features_special_editions/013385.html

U.S. Census Bureau. (2011). The Hispanic population: 2010. Retrieved August 30, 2013, from http://www.census.gov/prod/cen2010/briefs/c2010br-04.pdf

U.S. Department of Education. (2016). National Center for Education Statistics, Common Core of Data (CCD), State Nonfiscal Survey of Public Elementary and Secondary Education, 2003–04 and 2013–14; and National Elementary and Secondary Enrollment by Race/Ethnicity Projection Model, 1972 through 2025. Retrieved January 11, 2017, from https://nces.ed.gov/programs/coe/indicator_cge.asp

Webb, L. D., Metha, A., & Jordan, K. F. (2017). *Foundations of American education* (8th ed.). New York, NY: Pearson.

Chapter 8

Adler, M. (1982). *The Paideia proposal: An educational manifesto.* New York: Simon & Schuster.

Brameld, T. (1956). *Toward a reconstructed philosophy of education.* New York: Holt, Rinehart, and Winston.

Chartock, R. K. (2004). *Educational foundations: An anthology* (2nd ed.). Upper Saddle River, NJ: Merrill/Prentice Hall.

Counts, G. (1932). *Dare the school build a new social order?* New York: John Dey.

Friere, P. (1970). *Pedagogy of the oppressed.* New York: Herder and Herder.

Greene, M. (1978). *Landscape of learning.* New York: Teachers College Press.

Greene, M. (1995). What counts as philosophy of education? In W. Kohli (Ed.), *Critical conversations in philosophy of education.* New York: Routledge.

Gutek, G. L. (2005). *Historical and philosophical foundations of education* (4th ed.). Upper Saddle River, NJ: Merrill/Prentice Hall.

Hirsch, E. D. (1987). *Cultural literacy: What every American needs to know.* Boston: Houghton Mifflin.

Illich, I. (1971). *Deschooling society.* New York: Harper & Row.

Jacobsen, D. A. (2003). *Philosophy in classroom teaching: Bridging the gap* (2nd ed.). Upper Saddle River, NJ: Merrill/Prentice Hall.

Neill, A. S. (1960). *Summerhill: A radical approach to child rearing.* New York: Hart.

Ornstein, A. C. (2003). *Pushing the envelope: Critical issues in education.* Upper Saddle River, NJ: Merrill/Prentice Hall.

Ozmon, H., & Craver, S. (2008). *Philosophical foundations of education* (8th ed.). Upper Saddle River, NJ: Merrill/Prentice Hall.

Perrone, V. (1991). *A letter to teachers: Reflections on schooling and the art of teaching.* San Francisco: Jossey-Bass.

Pulliam, J., & Van Patten, J. (2013). *History of education in America* (10th ed.). Upper Saddle River, NJ: Merrill/Prentice Hall.

Ravitch, D. (2000). *Left back: A century of failed school reforms.* New York: Simon & Schuster.

Sizer, T. R. (1985). *Horace's compromise.* Boston: Houghton Mifflin.

Webb, L., Metha, A., & Jordan, K. F. (2017). *Foundations of American education* (8th ed.). New York: Pearson.

Chapter 9

Alcoholism Information and Resources. (2010). *Learn-about-alcoholism.* Retrieved June 5, 2010, from http://www.learn-about-alcoholism.com/index.html

Alliance for Excellent Education. (2009). *High school dropouts in America.* Retrieved June 7, 2010, from http://all4ed.org/files/Graduation_Rates_FactSheet.pdf

American Psychiatric Association. (2005). *Let's talk facts about depression.* Retrieved April 6, 2006, from http://www.fcphp.usf.edu/courses/content/rfast/Resources/depression.pdf

Annie E. Casey Foundation. (2016). *Kids count: A state-to-state comparison of economic wellbeing.* Retrieved March 14, 2017, from http://www.aecf.org/m/resourcedoc/aecf-the2016kidscountdatabook-2016.pdf#page=23

Ariza, E. N. (2002). Cultural considerations: Immigrant parents involvement. *Kappa Delta Pi Record, 38*(3), 134–137.

Bridgeland, J. M., DiIulio, J. J., & Morison, K. B. (2006). *The silent epidemic: Perspectives of high school dropouts.* Retrieved April 8, 2006, from http://www.ignitelearning.com/pdf/TheSilentEpidemic3-06FINAL.pdf

Centers for Disease Control and Prevention (CDC). (2009). *Fostering school connectedness: Improving student health and academic achievement.* Atlanta, GA: Author. Retrieved March 21, 2017, from https://stacks.cdc.gov/view/cdc/21066

Centers for Disease Control and Prevention (CDC). (2010). *Teen birth rates drop in 2008 following a two-year increase.* Atlanta, GA: Author.

Centers for Disease Control and Prevention (CDC). (2012). *Trends in the prevalence of sexual behaviors and HIV testing national YRBS: 1991–2011.* Atlanta, GA: Author. Retrieved March 10, 2013, from http://www.cdc.gov/healthyyouth/yrbs/pdf/us_sexual_trend_yrbs.pdf

Centers for Disease Control and Prevention (CDC). (2015). *Suicide: Facts at a glance.* Atlanta, GA: Author. Retrieved March 25, 2017, from https://www.cdc.gov/violenceprevention/pdf/suicide-datasheet-a.pdf

Centers for Disease Control and Prevention (CDC). (2016). *Youth risk behavior surveillance system.* Atlanta, GA: Author. Retrieved March 25, 2017, from https://www.cdc.gov/healthyyouth/data/yrbs/

Centers for Disease Control and Prevention (CDC). (2017). Childhood obesity facts. Retrieved April 3, 2017, from https://www.cdc.gov/healthyschools/obesity/facts.htm

Child Welfare Information Gateway. (2006). *Recognizing child abuse and neglect: Signs and symptoms.* Retrieved April 22, 2007, from http://www.bvsd.org/neo/Documents/Child%20Abuse%20Signs.pdf

Child Welfare Information Gateway. (2013). *What is child abuse and neglect? Recognizing the signs and symptoms.* Retrieved August 31, 2013, from https://www.childwelfare.gov/pubs/factsheets/whatiscan.cfm

Child Welfare Information Gateway. (2016). *Child abuse and neglect fatalities 2014: Statistics and interventions.* Washington, DC: U.S. Department of Health and Human Services, Children's Bureau. Retrieved January 22, 2017, from https://www.childwelfare.gov/pubPDFs/fatality.pdf

Childhelp. (2016). *Child abuse statistics and facts.* Retrieved January 26, 2017, from https://www.childhelp.org/child-abuse-statistics/

Coloroso, B. (2008). *The bully, the bullied, and the bystander.* New York: Harper Resources.

Craig, G. J., & Dunn, W. L. (2007). *Understanding human development* (p. 248). Upper Saddle River, NJ: Prentice Hall.

Dinkes, R., Kemp, J., & Baum, K. (2009). *Indicators of school crime and safety: 2009* (NCES 2010–012/NCJ 228478). Washington, DC: National Center for Education Statistics, Institute of Education Sciences, U.S. Department of Education, and Bureau of Justice Statistics, Office of Justice Programs, U.S. Department of Justice.

Dynarski, M., Clarke, L., Cobb, B., Finn, J., & Rumberger, R. (2008). *Dropout prevention.* Retrieved June 8, 2010, from http://ies.ed.gov/ncee/wwc/pdf/practiceguides/dp_pg_090308.pdf

Education Vital Signs. (2006). *As educators face a childhood obesity "epidemic," other indicators of well-being improve.* Retrieved March 30, 2006, from http://connection.ebscohost.com/c/articles/20553095/as-educators-face-childhood-obesity-epidemic-other-indicators-well-being-improve

Focus Adolescent Services. (2006). *Youth who drop out.* Retrieved April 20, 2006, from http://www.focusas.com/Dropouts.html

Gollnick, D. M., & Chinn, P. C. (2013). *Multicultural education in a pluralistic society* (9th ed.). Upper Saddle River, NJ: Pearson.

Hamilton, B. E., Martin, J. A., & Ventura, S. J. (2012). Births: Preliminary data for 2011. *National Vital Statistics Reports, 61*(5). Hyattsville, MD: National Center for Health Statistics. Retrieved January 27, 2013 from http://www.cdc.gov/nchs/data/nvsr/nvsr61/nvsr61_05.pdf

Hamilton, B. E., & Ventura, S. J. (2012). Birth rates for U.S. teenagers reach historic lows for all age and ethnic groups. *NCHS Data Brief, 89.* Hyattsville, MD: National Center for Health Statistics.

Haynes, C. C. (2006, March). A moral battleground, a civil discourse. *USA Today.* Retrieved March 23, 2006, from http://www.usatoday.com/news/opinion/editorials/2006-03-19-faith-edit_x.htm

Jensen, E. (2009). *Teaching with poverty in mind: What being poor does to kids' brains and what school can do about it*. Alexandria, VA: Association for Supervision and Curriculum Development.

Kids Count. (2016). Children in poverty by race and ethnicity. Retrieved January 14, 2017, from http://datacenter.kidscount.org/data/tables/44-children-in-poverty-byrace-and-ethnicity#detailed/1/any/false/573,869,36,868,867/10,11,9,12,1,185,13/324,323

Kids Health. (2015). About teen suicide. Retrieved March 14, 2017, from http://kidshealth.org/en/parents/suicide.html

Landsman, J. (2006). Bearers of hope. *Educational Leadership, 63*(5), 26–32.

Lewis-Charp, H. (2003). Breaking the silence: White students' perspectives on race in multiracial schools. *Phi Delta Kappan, 85*(4), 279–285.

MacDonald, G. J. (2004, October 19). Schools lay tender trap for truants. *Christian Science Monitor*. Retrieved April 6, 2006, from http://www.csmonitor.com/2004/1019/p11s02-legn.html

Mental Health America. (2016). Depression in teens. Retrieved March 20, 2017, from http://www.mentalhealthamerica.net/conditions/depression-teens

Mukhopadhyay, C., & Henze, R. C. (2003). How real is race? Using anthropology to make sense of human diversity. *Phi Delta Kappan, 84*(9), 669–678.

National Campaign to Prevent Teen and Unplanned Pregnancy. (2012). *Teen childbearing, education, and economic well-being*. Retrieved March 19, 2017, from https://thenationalcampaign.org/resource/why-it-matters-teen-childbearing-education-and-economic-wellbeing

National Campaign to Prevent Teen and Unplanned Pregnancy. (2016). *Teen birth rate comparison, 2015*. Retrieved March 19, 2017, from https://thenationalcampaign.org/data/compare/1701

National Center for Education Statistics. (2011). *Indicators of school crime and safety: 2011*. Washington, DC: Author. Retrieved March 12, 2013, from http://nces.ed.gov/programs/crimeindicators/crimeindicators2011/ind_13.asp

National Center for Homeless Education. (2016). *Education for homeless children and youths program*. Retrieved March 19, 2017, from https://nche.ed.gov/downloads/data-comp-1213-1415.pdf

National Crime Prevention Council. (2017). *Cyberbullying*. Retrieved April 24, 2017, from http://www.ncpc.org/topics/cyberbullying

National Institute on Drug Abuse. (2017). Opioids. Retrieved March 20, 2017, from www.drugabuse.gov/drugs-abuse/opioids

National Institute on Drug Abuse for Teens. (2017). *Tobacco, nicotine, & e-cigarettes*. Retrieved March 16, 2017, from https://teens.drugabuse.gov/drug-facts/tobacco-nicotine-e-cigarettes

Obama, M. (2010). *Learn the facts*. Retrieved March 10, 2013, from http://www.letsmove.gov/blog/2013/03/08/watch-travels-first-lady-lets-move-anniversary-tour

Office of the Federal Register. (2016). McKinney-Vento education for homeless children and youths program. Retrieved March 19, 2017, from www.federalregister.gov/documents/2016/03/17/2016-06073/mckinney-vento-education-for-homeless-children-and-youths-program

Ophelia Project. (2005). *Bullies, broken hearts . . . and the harsh reality of relational aggression*. Retrieved April 9, 2006, from www.opheliaproject.org

Polite, L., & Saenger, E. B. (2003). A pernicious silence: Confronting race in the elementary classroom. *Phi Delta Kappan, 85*(4), 274–278.

Project HOME. (2017). Facts on homelessness. Retrieved March 19, 2017, from https://projecthome.org/about/facts-homelessness

Rank, M. R., & Hirschl, T. A. (2009). Estimating the risk of food stamp use and impoverishment during childhood. *Journal of the American Medical Association: Archives of Pediatrics & Adolescent Medicine, 163*(11), 994–999. Retrieved June 1, 2010, from http://archpedi.ama-assn.org/content/vol163/issue11/index.dtl

Rothstein, R. (2008). Whose problem is poverty? *Educational Leadership, 65*(7), 8–13.

Simmons, R. (2002). *Odd girl out: The hidden culture of aggression in girls*. Orlando, FL: Harcourt.

Story, M., Kaphingst, K. M., & French, S. (2006). The role of schools in obesity prevention. *The Future of Children, 16*(1), 109–131.

Thompson, M., & Grace, C. O. (2001). *Best friends, worst enemies: Understanding the social lives of children*. New York: Ballantine.

Thornburgh, N. (2006, April 17). Dropout nation. *Time*, pp. 30–40.

U.S. Census Bureau. (2008). *National population projections, released 2008*. Retrieved June 1, 2010, from http://www.census.gov/population/www/projections/summarytables.html

U.S. Department of Education. (2016). *EDFacts/Consolidated State Performance Reports*. Retrieved April 7, 2017, from http://www.governing.com/gov-data/high-school-graduation-rates-by-state.html

U.S. Department of Health and Human Services (USDHHS). (2012). *Youth risk behavior surveillance—United States 2011, 61*(4). Retrieved January 29, 2013, from http://www.cdc.gov/mmwr/pdf/ss/ss6104.pdf

U.S. Department of Health and Human Services [USDHHS]. (2013). *Lesbian, gay, bisexual, transgender, questioning (LGBTQ) youth*. Retrieved March 11, 2013, from http://www.hhs.gov/ash/oah/resources-and-publications/info/parents/just-facts/lgbtq-youth.html

U.S. Department of Health and Human Services. (2016). *Administration for children and families, administration on children, youth and families, children's bureau. Child maltreatment 2014*. Retrieved January 22, 2017, from https://www.acf.hhs.gov/sites/default/files/cb/cm2014.pdf

U.S. Department of Justice. (2011). *School Crime Supplement (SCS) to the National Crime Victimization Survey, various years, 1995–2009*. Retrieved March 10, 2013, from http://nces.ed.gov/programs/crimeindicators/crimeindicators2011/figures/figure_03_1.asp

Ventura, S. J., Mathews, T. J., & Hamilton, B. E. (2001). Births to teenagers in the United States, 1940–2000. *National Vital Statistics Reports, 49*(10). Retrieved January 27, 2013, from http://www.thenationalcampaign.org/resources/pdf/TBR_1940-2006.pdf

White, J. L., & Cones, J. H. (1999). *Black men emerging: Facing the past and seizing a future in America*. New York: Freeman.

White-Hood, M. (2006). Targeting the school bully. *Middle Ground, 9*(4), 30–32.

Chapter 10

American Association of University Women. (2005). *Drawing the line: Sexual harassment on campus.* Retrieved May 4, 2017, from http://www.aauw.org/files/2013/02/drawing-the-line-sexual-harassment-on-campus.pdf

Howe, K. R. (1996). A conceptual basis for ethics in teacher education. *Journal of Teacher Education, 37*, 6.

LaMorte, M. W. (2012). *School law: Cases and concepts* (10th ed.). Upper Saddle River, NJ: Pearson.

Pauken, P. D. (2006). Student rights. In C. Russo (Ed.), *Key legal issues for schools: The ultimate resource for school business officials.* Lanham, MD: Rowman & Littlefield Education.

Riley, R. W. (1998). *Secretary's statement on religious expression.* Retrieved May 5, 2017, from http://christiananswers.net/q-eden/religiousexpression.html

San Antonio, D. M. (2006). Broadening the world of early adolescents. *Educational Leadership, 63*(7), 8–13.

Schimmel, D., Stellman, L., Conlon, C.K., & Fischer, L. (2015). *Teachers and the law* (9th ed.). Upper Saddle River, NJ: Pearson.

Underwood, J., & Webb, L. D. (2006). *School law for teachers: Concepts and applications.* Upper Saddle River, NJ: Merrill/Prentice Hall.

Chapter 11

Azzam, A. M. (2005). The funding gap. *Educational Leadership, 62*(5), 93.

California School Board Association. (2016). Robles-Wong *v.* State of California *Frustrating Conclusion to Years of Work.* Retrieved May 14, 2017, from https://www.csba.org/Newsroom/CSBANewsletters/2016/August/ElectronicOnly/2016_08_31_robles.aspx

Federal Education Budget Project School Finance. (2013). *Federal, State, and Local K–12 School Finance Overview.* Retrieved September 8, 2013, from http://febp.newamerica.net/background-analysis/school-finance

Hess, F. M. (2010). Weighing the case for school boards. *Phi Delta Kappan, 91*(6), 15–19.

Lambert, L. (2003). *Leadership capacity for lasting school improvement.* Alexandria, VA: Association for Supervision and Curriculum Development.

National School Boards Association. (2011). *School Boards Circa 2010: Governance in the Accountability Era.* Retrieved September 8, 2013, from http://www.nsba.org/Board-Leadership/Surveys/School-Boards-Circa-2010/SBCirca10-Tables.pdf

U.S. Census Bureau. (2016). *Public education finances: 2014.* Retrieved May 13, 2017, from https://www2.census.gov/govs/school/14f33pub.pdf

U.S. Department of Education. (2009). *Characteristics of Public, Private, and Bureau of Indian Education Elementary and Secondary School Principals in the United States.* Retrieved June 18, 2010, from http://nces.ed.gov/pubs2009/2009323/tables.asp

U.S. Department of Education. (2016). *The condition of education 2016.* Washington, DC: U.S. Department of Education, National Center for Education Statistics, Author.

U.S. Government. (2013). *Lottery results.* Retrieved April 8, 2013, from http://www.usa.gov/Topics/Lottery-Results.shtml

Chapter 12

Barth, R. S. (2006). Improving relationships within the schoolhouse. *Educational Leadership, 63*(6), 9–13.

Business Insider. (2017). 26 amazing facts about Finland's unorthodox education system. Retrieved May 31, 2017, from http://www.businessinsider.com/finland-education-school-2011-12?op=0#elementary-school-students-get-75-minutes-of-recess-a-day-in-finnish-versus-an-average-of-27-minutes-in-the-us-13

Cattanach, J. (2013). Support parents to improve student learning. *Phi Delta Kappan, 94*(6), 20–25.

Central Intelligence Agency. (2016). The world factbook. Retrieved May 31, 2017, from https://www.cia.gov/library/publications/the-world-factbook/geos/fi.html and https://www.cia.gov/library/publications/the-world-factbook/geos/us.html

Education Week. (May 28, 2017). Map: Tracking the Common Core State Standards. Retrieved May 29, 2017, from http://www.edweek.org/ew/section/multimedia/map-states-academic-standards-common-core-or.html

Finnish National Agency for Education. (2017). Education system in Finland. Retrieved May 31, 2017, from http://www.studyinfinland.fi/destination_finland/education_system

Frank, S. (2016). An American teacher's thoughts on the Finnish education system. Retrieved May 30, 2017, from http://blogs.edweek.org/edweek/global_learning/2016/03/an_american_teachers_thoughts_on_the_finnish_education_system.html

Gewertz, C. (2017). Which states are using PARCC or Smarter Balanced? Retrieved May 28, 2017, from http://www.edweek.org/ew/section/multimedia/states-using-parcc-or-smarter-balanced.html

National Board for Professional Teaching Standards (NBPTS). (2016). *The five core propositions.* Retrieved May 21, 2017, from http://www.nbpts.org/national-board-certification

National Conference of State Legislatures. (2015). Tuition benefits for immigrants. Retrieved May 30, 2017, from http://www.ncsl.org/research/immigration/tuition-benefits-for-immigrants.aspx

National Summer Learning Association. (2017). Smarter summers. Brighter futures. Retrieved May 29, 2017, from http://www.summerlearning.org/

Payne, C. (2008). *So much reform, so little change: The persistence of failure in urban schools.* Boston: Harvard Education Press.

Pew Research Center. (2016a). Statistical portrait of Hispanics in America. Retrieved June 1, 2017, from http://www.pewhispanic.org/2016/04/19/statistical-portrait-of-hispanics-in-the-united-states-key-charts/

Pew Research Center. (2016b). Key facts about how the U.S. Hispanic population is changing. Retrieved June 1, 2017, from http://www.pewresearch.org/fact-tank/2016/09/08/key-facts-about-how-the-u-s-hispanic-population-is-changing/

Ritter, G. W., & Barnett, J. H. (2016). Learning on the job: Teacher evaluation can foster real growth. *Phi Delta Kappan, 97*(7), 48–52.

School District of La Crosse. (2017). Rebuilding for learning. Retrieved May 29, 2017, from http://www.lacrossepartnersinlearning.com/

Name Index

Note: Page numbers followed by *f* refer to figures; those followed by *t* refer to tables.

K

L

M

N

O

P

R

S

T

U

V

W

Subject Index

Note: Page numbers followed by *f* refer to figures; those followed by *t* refer to tables.

D

E

R

S